THE BIRTH OF THE ROYAL AIR FORCE

A detailed study of the growth of British Air Power from the employment of balloons in warfare, through the Great War of 1914–18 to the formation of the Royal Air Force on 1 April 1918

THE BIRTH OF THE ROYAL AIR FORCE

AN ENCYCLOPEDIA OF BRITISH AIR POWER BEFORE AND DURING THE GREAT WAR – 1914 TO 1918

By Wing Commander
I.M. Philpott RAF Retd

First published in Great Britain in 2013 by
Pen & Sword Military
an imprint of
Pen & Sword Books Ltd
47 Church Street
Barnsley
South Yorkshire
S70 2AS

Copyright © I.M. Philpott 2013

ISBN 978 1 78159 333 2

A CIP catalogue record for this book is available from the British Library

Typeset in Ehrhardt by
Mac Style, Driffield, East Yorkshire
Printed and bound in India by Replika Press Pvt. Ltd.

Pen & Sword Books Ltd incorporates the imprints of Pen & Sword Archaeology, Atlas, Aviation, Battleground, Discovery, Family History, History, Maritime, Military, Naval, Politics, Railways, Select, Social History, Transport, True Crime, and Claymore Press, Frontline Books, Leo Cooper, Praetorian Press, Remember When, Seaforth Publishing and Wharncliffe.

For a complete list of Pen & Sword titles please contact
PEN & SWORD BOOKS LIMITED
47 Church Street, Barnsley, South Yorkshire, S70 2AS, England
E-mail: enquiries@pen-and-sword.co.uk
Website: www.pen-and-sword.co.uk

Contents

Foreword

The title of this work, *The Birth of the RAF*, may seem, to some, a little dramatic but there is a reason. The threat posed by German Gotha bombers in attacking targets in south-east England in 1917 increased the urgency to combine Britain's two air services, the Royal Flying Corps and the Royal Naval Air Service, into one new service. Secondly, no sooner had hostilities ceased in 1918 than the Army and the Navy saw no need for the extravagance of an Air Ministry in times of austerity and demanded the return of their aeroplanes. In that case the RAF would have been stillborn. Had it not been for the intervention of Winston Churchill what might have been the outcome?

It can therefore be said that the Gotha threat brought to a head the necessity to form a unified air service under an Air Ministry. The government was, by 1917, already well advanced in bringing about the RAF. The work of the Joint Air Board came about following the realization that there had be one air service with the ability to make decisions that would be binding on both the Admiralty and the War Office to prevent waste and duplication and to make rapid decisions regarding the output of aircraft and aero engines. It is fair to say that if the threat posed to the south-east of England in 1917 by German Gotha bombers had been eliminated, or at least severely limited at that time, the creation of the RAF might well have been deferred until after the war when the urgency would have diminished. Be that as it may there were so many civilian casualties in Folkestone in just one raid that questions were asked in the House of Commons about the perceived inability of the air defences to prevent these raids. RFC squadrons were having to be diverted from their duties on the Western Front to stiffen up the air defences of the London area. No.56 Squadron, for example, was relocated to Bekesbourne just outside Canterbury but the pilots kicked their heels for a fortnight before being returned to Flanders. As soon as they had gone the Gotha raids resumed. The C-in-C of the British Expeditionary Force, Field Marshal Haig, was losing his aeroplanes at a time not of his choosing; tension was rising between him and the Committee of Imperial Defence and the Prime Minister, Lloyd George, was obliged to call upon a member of the War Cabinet, General Jan Smuts, to find a solution to the problem. To cut a long story short, and it's to be found in this encyclopaedia, the General came up with the solution that everything that flew must belong to one service and that would have to be an air service. The Smuts Report was translated into legislation and a third service, the Royal Air Force, came into existence on 1st April 1918. This was no mean achievement in the middle of a war. There was a major Gotha raid in May 1918 but by that time the air defences were much improved and the losses of Gothas was so high that the raids on British airspace ceased. But by that time the RAF was already in existence. Had the success against the Gothas been achieved in, say late 1917, it might have been a different story.

The Royal Air Force, which came into existence on 1 April 1918, was principally a fusing of two services, the Royal Flying Corps and the Royal Naval Air Service. This is the history of the development of these two services in the period leading up to the outbreak of the Great War and their employment on operations. The new RAF was therefore very much a product of those experiences. This included the calibre and operational experience of those who would occupy the very top posts, the quality of the staff officers, aircrews and ground crews and the design and efficiency of the aeroplanes which became the property of the Air Ministry overnight. Perhaps one of the most surprising turn of events was the leading role played by the RNAS in strategic bombing, from the very outbreak of the war and well before Air Marshal Trenchard commanded the Independent Bombing Force in France in the summer of 1918. But then again the RAF V bombers, which were designed with strategic nuclear weapon capability during the Cold War, were replaced by submarine-launched Polaris missiles. In this case we may say that strategic bombing started and finished as the responsibility of the Royal Navy, but such a statement could spark a furious argument so I will leave that for others to judge.

Ian Philpott RAF Retd

Preface

The following is a War Office specification for a powered aircraft before the Great War. It speaks for itself and shows how far we have come since those very early days:

The machine must have a carrying capacity sufficient to carry an operator (pilot) and a passenger (observer), both weighing an average of 170lbs. The instruments / maps etc must have an average weight of 10lbs. There must be fuel for a journey of 4 hours. It must be capable of rising from or descending on to any ordinary open space of grass land or fairly smooth ground of an area of 10 acres, without damage to itself or occupants. It must have an average speed in the air of not less than 25mph in a calm, which speed it shall maintain for not less than an hour. It must be capable of rising with its full load to a height of 2,000ft above its starting point, and be able to carry its full load at heights of 5,000ft above Mean Sea Level. It must be reasonably steady when under flight, in order that observation with field glasses may be made from it and must be capable of remaining in the open in all ordinary weather for a period of one month without very material deterioration. It must be capable of flights of 2 hours' duration during which time it must describe several circles of varying diameters and must be capable of being kept in the air 'hovering' or 'circling' over any desired point for periods of a minute or more. It shall be so constructed that if the engine stops from any cause, or any portion of the machinery breaks down, there shall be a reasonable chance of the occupants reaching the ground in safety.

This encyclopaedia seeks to capture the spirit of the very early days of flying whether it be in a balloon, dirigible or airship or a powered flying machine with wings to take the reader through a world war where aircraft will leave their stamp on the conduct of war. Many books have been written about the war in the air between 1914 and 1918. What makes this one different is that it is essentially a reference book in which the reader can embark on specific areas of study or simply check on facts, figures and the like. This work seeks to give a detailed account of the development of air power which added a new dimension to warfare beginning with the use of balloons then airships in military operations and peacetime military manoeuvres. The chapters in Part 1 lead to the formation of the Royal Air Force on 1 April 1918 and end with a consideration of the use of aircraft in the strategic bombing role. This is important for it helps us to understand why military aviation experts in the immediate post-war period made what some would regard as extravagant claims for the pre-eminence of air power in war. Those whose names come to mind in this respect include the Italian Douhet, the American aviator Billy Mitchell and Air Marshal Trenchard of the Royal Air Force. With the benefit of hindsight one can see that victory in war has never been achieved solely through the use of air power but in the early years of the twentieth century air power was a new, and for some, a frightening new development in war, involving as it did civilians far from the battlefield.

Included in this work are the reminiscences of civilians who experienced air raids during the Great War. In order to defend his new service against absorption back into the Army and the Royal Navy from whence the RAF came, Trenchard would exaggerate the morale effect of bombing and with it his insistence that it was vital to maintain an independent air force that could embark on military operations unconnected with the war on land and at sea.

Details of the very early organization of military flying are chronicled here and the growth of establishments and the ever-changing internal organization within the Royal Navy and the Army to meet the needs of military air operations, very much on a 'suck it and see' basis for so little was known, particularly in the field of aircraft design and tactics. It is a common belief that the aircraft went to war solely as a means of reconnaissance with little thought given to the arming of aircraft or their occupants. Nothing could be further from the truth. A considerable amount of thought and effort went into the development of aircraft, airships, wireless communications, guns mounted in aircraft and the use of aircraft to bomb before the outbreak of hostilities in 1914. Free use is made of such terms as aeroplanes and aircraft and the author happily moves from one term to the other because both terms were used at the time.

What is also remarkable is that it was the Admiralty and not the War Office who pioneered strategic bombing. It may have been Trenchard who led the Independent Bombing Force in 1918 and made great play about the importance of going on the offensive in any future war by enshrining it in official strategic policy in the inter-war years. It cannot be denied, however, that the RNAS were there first with their 'bloody paralyser' aimed at targets of strategic importance not directly connected with the prosecution of the war on the ground. The author refers to the Great War, as it was then known, for one did not know then that there was to be a Second World War. The League of Nations, it was hoped, would prevent a repetition of the hostilities on the scale of that experienced from August 1914. Germany was to be denied an air force under the terms of the Treaty of Versailles and believe it or not the strength of the post-war RAF would be based upon that of the greatest air power on the continent at that time, namely France.

Warfare that had afflicted mankind over the centuries had been fought in two dimensions, on land an at sea. This all changed with the coming of the Great War of 1914 to 1918, but this war was not the first time that the air came to be used over the battlefield and at sea. The first recorded use of balloons as a means of observing the movement of enemy troops was at the Battle of Fleurey during the French revolutionary wars. This history starts with the use of balloons, followed by airships and heavier than air machines in wars abroad and manoeuvres at home. The formation of the RAF added a third service to the traditional two and was accomplished in the heat of war which makes it all the more remarkable.

Secondly the RAF came into existence as a result of the conflicting priorities claimed during late 1917, roles which involved the ownership of military aircraft by the Army and the Admiralty or the Royal Flying Corps and Royal Naval Air Service. Incidentally, this did not involve aircraft of either service stationed in the Middle East and Mediterranean. The War Office and certainly the C-in-C of the British Expeditionary Force on the Western Front, saw aircraft as vital to the prosecution of the ground war, i.e. the tactical use of aircraft in such roles as reconnaissance, artillery co operation, ground attack and scouting. On the other hand the Admiralty's first consideration had to be the protection of naval assets both ashore and afloat.

But at the same time there was a direct threat to the home base. From early 1915 the British Isles had been subjected to airship raids from bases in northern Germany and German occupied Belgium. Then in 1917 the Germans used their Gotha bombers to attack the London area and the south-east of England. Aircraft that could not, for reasons of weather for example, reach London could deliver their bombs on secondary targets and when a large number of civilians was killed in Folkestone in 1917, questions were asked in the House of Commons. Defence of the home base now moved up the ladder of priorities resulting in the formation of the RAF.

Be that as it may, no sooner had the guns fallen silent on 11 November 1918 than the two older sister services were asking for the return of their aeroplanes. They saw no need for the extra expense of an Air Ministry and a separately manned service and the new Chief of the Air Staff, Air Marshal Sir Hugh Trenchard, had to fight hard to keep the RAF as a separate service but that is another story and is recounted in Volume I of my two inter-war histories published by Pen & Sword entitled the *Trenchard Years*. This work follows the same format as those just mentioned. There are no footnotes as one might expect in a work of this nature but all material throughout the book is divided into paragraphs with headings in bold type to make finding subject matter easy and there is a great deal of cross referencing. Instead of footnotes the original sources used to support any paragraph in the book are printed below the paragraph or sub-paragraph heading. This is not a book one might read from cover to cover but is essentially a work of reference. I have always believed in lots of illustrations, maps and very detailed listings. Then there are the appendices where one can also find lots more detail. To begin with, Appendix A lists the technical details of the aircraft described in succeeding chapters. Appendix B lists the location and equipment of RAF squadrons between 1912 and 1918.

I hope that the reader derives as much pleasure looking things up as I have had in compiling the work

Ian Philpott

Part I
Operations

Chapter I
Balloons, Airships and Aircraft at War

The beginnings – recollections of early days of ballooning – Balloon Section manoeuvres 1903/4 – operational employment of balloons in the South African War – powered aircraft flight – correspondence between the Wright brothers and the British Army – notes on military ballooning November 1904 – thoughts on the employment of balloons, dirigibles and flying machines – April 1908

INTRODUCTION – THE BEGINNINGS

Source: Royal Engineers document preface to early military aeronauts

Since this work is titled '*The Birth of the RAF*' the earliest attempts to take to the air by the British military can be traced back to the balloon units of the Royal Engineers. Once ballooning became a reality it was natural that military minds should contemplate the use of balloons in war and in 1794 during the French revolutionary wars

A balloon of the Royal Engineers.

the movement of hostile troops was observed at the Battle of Fleury from balloons tethered by long ropes to the ground. The observer used coloured flags to signal enemy troop movements. During the American Civil War the signalling was improved through the use of the telegraph. Being able to observe the movement of enemy forces from aloft conferred upon battlefield commanders a distinct advantage over the enemy, provided of course that the enemy could not also deploy balloons. There were, however, severe limitations in their employment in the vicinity of a battlefield. When the wind was blowing in a direction that would take the observers over the area that needed to be reconnoitred, a 'free run' was permitted but, for the most part, they could not be cast off to float at the mercy of the wind for they might find they were moving away from the area that the observers in the balloon were meant to survey. They had therefore to be tethered to the ground or a substantial wagon from whence they could be allowed to drift upwards or be brought down once the mission was accomplished. As succeeding sections of this chapter will show the whole wagon train, with gas tubes and all the other impedimenta associated with balloon deployment, presented an ideal target for enemy ambush as the balloon sections moved from one area to another.

Just before the outbreak of the American Civil War the British military became interested in military ballooning. In 1861 an officer of the Royal Engineers, Captain Beaumont, and a member of the Ordnance Select Committee became interested in the possibilities of turning ballooning to military use. Beaumont then visited the United States, probably in company with a Lieutenant George Grover RE to attach themselves to the 'so called' Balloon Corps under the command of Colonel Thaddeus Lowe. During operations from the Potomac and later after the Battle of Manassas, the two British officers made numerous ascents, strengthening their belief in the balloon as an observation platform. On his return from the United States, Grover investigated the possibilities of the balloon as a weapon of war and went on to produce two papers, 'The uses of balloons in military operations' and 'The employment of balloons in warfare'. But nations embarking on aeronautics were loath to part with the results of research and it was therefore very difficult to arrive at the truth of the research. It was generally

A free balloon floating above the clouds.

Colonel Templer.

acknowledged that the French were the most advanced in the science of aerial navigation. The French military had a Military Balloon Corps at Meudon, Chalais, near Paris under the command of Commandant Charles Renard.

In 1863 Beaumont and Grover made experimental ascents at Aldershot with a balloon and improvised equipment hired from Henry Coxwell, the celebrated civilian balloonist. On 11 July they made a proving flight with the balloon being filled with military gas from the gasworks near Thorne Hill. This was an eventful flight and impressed upon the men the extensive views over Aldershot Common that could be obtained once the balloon was allowed to float free, a free balloon. On 14 July there was a Grand Field Day with their Royal Highnesses, the Prince and Princess of Wales being the honoured guests. The movements of the British Army divisions deployed on the ground were observed from a balloon for the first time in the Army's history. Further work continued taking into account changes in the weather and wind. If the wind was blowing in the right direction an observation balloon could be carried over positions held by an enemy. If a balloon was to remain tethered to the ground, a captive balloon, it could move with a cart in attendance and it would not be long before the Royal Engineers could put together teams of horses and wagons, with cylinders of gas and all the paraphernalia needed to deploy balloons in the field. With free floating balloons changes in altitude could be effected by releases of sand or gas. The repeated ascents at Aldershot on 14 July were observed and notes taken by Captain Heath CB, Royal Navy, Vice-President of the Ordnance Select Committee. The interest generated resulted in investigations into the most suitable material

for making balloons and the best method of generating hydrogen; the ability of the existing balloon material to hold in the hydrogen being a major stumbling block. Mr F Abel FRS, the chemist to the War Office, who carried out the research, concluded that military ballooning equipment could not be extemporized and it was decided not to proceed with experimental work with ballooning 'in times of profound peace'. Captain Grover continued his efforts but by 1873 he was succeeded by Major Scratchley RE and Captain Beaumont was succeeded by Lieutenant Watson RE. And there, for the time being, the matter rested.

In 1875 there was renewed activity and Lieutenant Watson met an experienced balloonist, Captain Templer, 2nd Middlesex Militia, the owner of a coal-gas balloon, the *Crusader*. This balloon was used for both captive and free ascents. By 1879 the first military balloon emerged at Woolwich, named the *Pioneer*, which had specially treated varnished cambric of 10,000 cu.ft and had cost only £71.

Colonel Capper (left).

After a long period of irresolution the War Office finally decided upon recognizing the science of aerostation and the War Office then held two military balloons with two more nearly ready for service. The War Office also took into consideration the experience of balloonists in Afghanistan and Zululand. It was concluded that balloons could serve valuable and important purposes in a military campaign.

There was a balloon equipment store at Woolwich Arsenal in 1878 and this was transferred to Chatham in 1882 and finally to Stanhope Lines, Aldershot, in 1890. In 1897 the Balloon Factory was officially separated from the operational and training units, although they shared the same accommodation at Aldershot. Colonel Templer was Superintendent of the Balloon Factory and in this capacity he answered to the War Office and not the local Army Command. The operational and training units known as Balloon Companies were brought together in April 1906 as the Balloon School, Royal Engineers, commanded by Colonel Capper. When Colonel Templer retired in 1906, Colonel Capper was appointed commander of both the Balloon Factory and the Balloon School. The Balloon Factory was renamed the Army Aircraft Factory in April

1911, then the Royal Aircraft Factory in 1912. Note that the term aircraft used here refers to captive and free balloons, steerable balloons or dirigibles / airships as well as aeroplanes.

The tactical limitations and problems outlined above could be overcome if a balloon could take off from a location away from the battlefield and propelled and steered in a desired direction and speed, not ones dictated by the direction and speed of the wind. This chapter will describe some of the methods by which this could be achieved. Making the balloons elongated, like a sausage, would help and placing the gas bags inside a semi-rigid frame would be even better. When it came to propulsion there would be the matter of engines, propellers, fuel and the mechanical control of the craft. And so the balloon was adapted to become the dirigible (steerable balloon) and later the airship. All were to be used in the Great War from 1914 to 1918.

Operational considerations in balloon operations

Returning to the activity at Woolwich Arsenal where all the initial experiments had taken place instructions were given to a class of NCOs and selected men of the Royal Engineers in the manufacture of balloons, hydrogen gas, network and the various appliances necessary for the operation of balloons. One example is the manufacturing of rope of great strength used for grappling irons and, although less than ½-inch in diameter it was tested to take the strain of 3 tons. Then there was the portable furnace, capable of manufacturing gas for two balloons in 24 hours. The basket and deflated balloon were devised to pack into three general-service wagons. Although the total weight was 3½ tons, each unit when taken to pieces did not exceed 3cwt. Unfortunately, when the balloon, the *Talisman* was being prepared for take-off the rope gave way. This did not deter the engineers or blunt the enthusiasm of the Balloon Committee. By this time there were five military balloons brought to Aldershot under the command of Colonel Templer. They were *Pioneer, Pegasus, Saladin, Talisman* and *Crusader,* Templer's own.

The utilization of balloons in war had been theoretically worked out by the Balloon Committee on the basis of the following conclusions. Firstly it was assumed that they would be chiefly used in wars of a larger scale and in civilized countries. Their use would be of the greatest advantage in sieges, the attack and defence of entrenched camps and watching a line of defence and it was also assumed that in most civilized places, local gasworks would be found either in operation or abandoned. Even if partially ruined or destroyed gasworks could readily be restored by trained military artificers and the necessary supply of gas soon obtained. Should all the works be destroyed some difficulty could be experienced in providing substitutes but for gas holders, good balloons could be used. The gas, once provided, could be conveyed for considerable distances and the balloons, protected from the wind in sheltered situations until required for use.

In ordinary weather balloons could operate some 30 miles from the gas supply and with two or more sources of supply in opposite directions free balloon operations could be sustained. In the case of captive balloons it would be necessary for wagons and a gang of men. There would need to be fresh gas supplies to compensate for leakage, say 1,000 cubic feet/day. The gas to compensate for this leakage could be carried in small balloons and to maintain one service balloon operationally would require only one wagon and a pair of horses, and a small detachment of sufficient men under a skilled officer would be sufficient for several balloons. An alternative was considered by the Balloon Committee and that was the principle used in the Montgolfier balloon, that is, to heat the air inside the balloon. There was always the attendant risk of fire but more seriously there was a tendency for hot air balloons to collapse if held captive owing to the rarefaction of the internal atmosphere. This made hot air balloons unsuitable for military operations. The various means of manufacturing gas, producing gas from coal, wood and peat independent of local resources, was considered, as well as the cost involved in transporting compressed gases with an army for it had been found possible to compress coal gas and hydrogen.

Carrying gas in a compressed state would involve producing cylinders that were strong enough. If 11lb of metal would be needed to hold a cubic foot of gas and 20,000 cubic feet of gas would be required to inflate one balloon there would be a considerable number of cylinders that would have to accompany a balloon detachment.

Much research was required to find the best material from which to construct balloon envelopes and eventually the Army settled on goldbeater's skin prepared from the lower intestines of an ox. It was impervious to hydrogen,

The Weidling family at St Mary's barracks, Chatham.

very tenacious and lighter, strength for strength, than any other balloon material. The name was derived from the material for making gold leaf. The skins were imported from the continent where they were salted down and packed in barrels. The treatment of the actual material was no secret but it was a family in the East End of London, the Weidlings, that knew how to prepare and join up the skin patches to form the balloon envelope. It was a secret that the family jealously guarded. The completion of the *Heron* was delayed when the foreman balloon hand was imprisoned for three months for an assault on the police and Templer had to work very hard to persuade the Weidlings to have two sappers trained for the work. This gave the British Army a monopoly on making balloon envelopes from goldbeater's skin, which lasted for thirty years. It was not until 1913 that the Germans were in a position to use this material for the internal gas bags in their Zeppelin airships.

Experience gained in various African theatres proved valuable. Balloon detachments went to South Africa, the

Hydrogen gas production at Aldershot.

Balloon being stowed behind a portable screen.

Sudan and Bechuanaland and when Templer returned to the United Kingdom he found that the work at Chatham had outgrown its quarters. A partial solution was achieved when Templer purchased, at his own expense, land near his home at Lidsing. No shed was available so sappers dug a hole in the hillside to accommodate an inflated balloon of 10,000cu.ft capacity to prevent it from swirling uncontrollably in the wind. Portable screens were erected to protect smaller balloons. By 1886 it became all too clear that experimental work would have to move to new quarters. Up to this point Templer had met the cost from his own resources and in 1887 the War Office at last gave him the recognition he deserved when he was appointed the 'Instructor of Ballooning' On 1 April he was gazetted Major with an annual salary of £600. He pressed the authorities to move the Balloon Section to Aldershot and the accuracy of the observations during the 1889 Aldershot manoeuvres convinced the GOC, Sir Evelyn Wood, that the Section should move for closer co-operation with the Army. But the annual ballooning

grant was reduced from £2,000 in 1886 to only £1,600 in 1888. To add insult to injury no attempt was made to recompense Templer for his expenditure on the Lidsing site. This was not the encouragement deserved by the early balloonists, particularly since balloon observations had proved accurate in war and during exercises.

The paraphernalia of ballooning began to arrive at Aldershot. There were the special wagons for the carriage of gas tubes in the field. They were built up on general service wagons devised by Royal Engineers. They could carry forty-four tubes 8 inches long by 5½ inches wide holding 100 cubic feet of hydrogen under a pressure of 1,800psi but the pressure could be increased to 120cu.ft in time of war. These tubes could be turned on independently, passing through a metal control box at the rear of the wagon. The gas was passed to the balloon through goldbeater's skin hose and metal junction pieces. Much modification would be required before these wagons would be fit for field service so there was much work to be done.

RECOLLECTIONS OF THE EARLY DAYS OF BALLOONING BY COLONEL B.R. WARD RE
Source: National Archive document AIR1/723/1/001

I joined at Chatham in 1882 and was on the establishment under instruction from that year until 1884. In 1883 Colonel Templer came to Chatham in order to carry out certain experiments with balloons. He lived in the Royal Marine barracks and a hut was allotted to him in St Mary's barracks for the purpose of carrying out his experiments. Colonel Templer brought with him that year a family of the name of Weidling in order to construct balloons on a new system devised by him. These balloons were constructed in gores, the fabric of the balloon being the internal membrane of the intestines of an ox. Mrs Weidling and her son Fred were the first arrivals at Chatham and were followed by two daughters, Mary Anne and Eugene. The last member of the family to arrive was Willie, who was about 18 and subject to fits.

At the end of 1883, the first spherical balloon of a size large enough to lift a man into the air, was constructed. She was named 'Fly' and had a capacity of 4,500cu.ft. She was followed by the 'Spy' of 7,000cu.ft. Both of these balloons were capable of lifting an observer. The 'Talisman' and the 'Tambour', each of 10,000cu.ft, were constructed at the close of 1883 and the beginning of 1884. A uniform system of naming the balloons followed. Those of 4,000cu.ft were given a name beginning with 'F'; those with a 7,000cu.ft capacity were given a name beginning with 'S' and those of 10,000cu.ft were given names beginning with 'T'. The 'Templer, and 'Thor' were two later balloons.

In September 1884, a balloon detachment was sent to Bechuanaland to accompany Sir Charles Warren's

Royal Engineer telegraphers at Aldershot.

expedition. Major Elsdale RE was in command, assisted by Lieutenant Trollope of the Grenadier Guards. One Corporal and 14 NCOs and men comprised the remainder of the detachment. The cables were fitted with a Siemens-Halske telephone, trumpet pattern. The expedition was carried through without any fighting. At Mafeking, which was then a native village, it was found, owing to altitude above sea-level, that neither 'Fly' nor 'Spy' could lift a man and the 10,000cu.ft balloons could only take one observer. A native chief, Montsioa by name, went up a short distance in one of the balloons. He was accompanied on the ground by his wives, none of whom ventured into the air. Hydrogen gas was taken out compressed in tubes supplied by Mannesman Coy., Llandore. Sufficient gas was taken for transporting the tubes. Native wagons were requisitioned in South Africa. The system of filling is described in the Note Book which I have already sent you.

Early in 1885, Colonel Templer took another detachment, consisting of Lieutenant McKenzie RE and some 15 other ranks to Suakin. An account of this is, I think, given in Sir Charles Watson's history of the Corps. On his return from the Sudan, Colonel Templer took a house with adjoining land at Lidsing, about 4 miles from Chatham and the same distance from Maidstone. A small training camp for ballooning work was started in one of the fields adjoining the house in 1887. Lieutenant Phillips RE and Lieutenant C.F. Close RE attended the first camp. A second one took place in the spring of 1888. I first joined the balloons having lately returned from India and with Lieutenant H.B. Jones RE, as my junior subaltern, I was in charge of the camp at Lidsing. I took my first run from this camp with Corporal Greener as my pilot and instructor. He carried out experiments with parachutes constructed of silk during this camp. These parachutes were about 24 feet in diameter.

It was now considered by the authorities that balloons had been long enough at the experimental stage and

that the time had arrived for arriving at a decision as to whether or not they should be introduced as a definite part of the Service. General Sir Evelyn Wood VC was at this time in command of the Aldershot Division and was infusing great vigour into the annual manoeuvres which were just beginning to form a regular portion of the Army routine. The Balloon Detachment consisting of Lieutenants B.R. Ward RE, H.B. Jones RE, Sergeant Major Niso RE and some 30 NCOs and men were sent down early in the summer in order to take part in the Annual Manoeuvres at Aldershot. I took part of a party down by rail, Lieutenant H.B. Jones taking the remainder by road, the tubes travelling in wagons drawn by a steam sapper. On arrival at Aldershot we were supplied with riding horses for the officers and draught horses for the wagons by the Field Companies RE, by whom we were voted a general nuisance. Sir Evelyn Wood was famous for keeping early hours and I remember lanterns and at least on one occasion we did not return to camp until 8 p.m.

The Detachment which consisted only of some 30 men was worked almost to breaking point. No gloves were issued at this time, so that the men's hands were in many cases very badly chafed by hauling on the balloon cables. I remember reporting on this on one occasion to Sir Evelyn Wood, who remarked, 'I am glad to know it. I wanted to know when you had reached breaking point so I shall recommend that the establishment is increased.' One lucky bit of observation work was, as I have always thought, the reason why Sir Evelyn Wood finally decided to report favourably on the use of balloons for military purposes. It was a fine day with hardly a breath of wind so that observation could be carried out quite comfortably, although at that time nothing was done to steady a balloon in the wind. The wire cable from the balloon wagon was simply made fast to an eye suspended by four short ropes at right angles to one another.

THE BALLOON SECTION, ROYAL ENGINEERS ON MANOEUVRES 1903/4

Sources: National Archive Documents AIR 1/728/176/3/9 and /10

The following record of the involvement of the Balloon Section RE on Army manoeuvres during 1903 and 1904 serves to show the progress made in balloon deployment, the problems encountered and recommendations for improvements.

The 1903 manoeuvres

In the 1903 manoeuvres the Balloon Section was attached to the Director of Manoeuvres and was neutral since it was only required to put up signal balloons. The problems encountered were not, therefore, of a tactical nature. Sixty-eight personnel were involved, which included four officers, the remainder comprising NCOs,

Aldershot, 1904.

other ranks and civilian drivers. One balloon wagon was accompanied by three gas tube wagons and a general-purpose wagon. The red signal balloons were 370cu.ft, made of skin and used on two days. On neither of these was it necessary to put up a large balloon. 1,000cu.ft carrying balloons could take up two air-filled balloons. If it was necessary to lift three signal balloons, except on a calm day, the third was filled with hydrogen to lighten the load.

The specially fitted tube wagons carried 90 six-foot gas tubes, each containing 300cu.ft of gas (total 2,700cu.ft of gas). On the front of the wagon was a drum of strong cord measuring 2,000ft. The skin signal balloons were found to be unsatisfactory, as they were too delicate and liable to damage leading to collapse when filled with hydrogen. It was recommended that coloured air-filled silk balloons should be used in future. Lifting balloons of between 1,300 and 1,500cu.ft could, it was estimated, lift four such signal balloons. The civilian horses worked well but had no lead harnesses. The tube wagons had no driving seat and the civilian drivers were not accustomed to driving when riding. It was further recommended that four horses be ordered for each tube wagon, not pairs of horses. Even then it was found that four horses found it hard going to get a loaded tube wagon up the steep hills negotiated during the manoeuvres when it was necessary to get the signal balloons rapidly from place to place.

It was felt that large observation balloons were not required for signalling purposes given the larger amounts of gas that needed to be carried. Six fills of gas for a 1,300cu.ft balloon was believed to be sufficient, requiring only one tube wagon in addition to the signal balloons wagon. Both wagons would require six horses plus forage carts. With regard to personnel there should be one officer and twelve NCOs and other ranks, all dismounted. They would need to be accompanied by an appropriate proportion of mounted NCOs and other ranks. Finally, it was recommended that experiments be made with hot air balloons since this would obviate the need to carry gas tubes.

The 1904 manoeuvres
The report for the 1904 manoeuvres was much fuller. On this occasion the 1st Balloon Section was to operate tactically with the Red Forces with whom the Section rendezvoused on 5 September at Colchester. The strength of the Section was three officers together with sixty-six NCOs and other ranks. Forty-three horses were required to pull the eight wagons, five technical and three baggage. The Colchester garrison also provided seven NCOs and other ranks on attachment together with one riding and sixteen draught horses. Communications with the General Officer Commanding (GOC) were to be via the military telegraph but if this was not available the nearest Postal Telegraph office to the Section position

Royal Engineers Balloon Detachment.

was to be used. The OC Balloon Section had the authority to frank messages for priority transmission. The gas was to come from a supply depot via two transport steam trains. The Signals Balloon Section was attached to the Chief Umpire's staff and also received its gas from the aforementioned gas supply depot.

The manoeuvres commenced on 7 September and the Balloon Section made ready a 11,500cu.ft balloon, which made its first ascent at Abberton at 11.15hrs. From altitudes varying between 700 and 1,500 feet the coastline could easily be observed, such as the entrances to the rivers Blackwater and Crouch. The objective was to ascertain whether enemy landings were being attempted at these points and at Clacton. The Abberton postal telegraph office was only ¾ mile distant and communication with the GOC was established. The latter was informed that no enemy units had been observed near the aforementioned rivers but that the area east of the River Colne and north of Clacton was too thickly wooded for balloon observation. The enclosed nature of the countryside made it very difficult to bring the balloon down from the operating height since this was achieved by running a pole along the wire. Getting a clear run amongst the trees proved difficult and, quite understandably, the report recommended the use of a motor-driven winding gear on the balloon wagon. There is reference to an 'aeronaut' achieving a height of 1,700ft.

Later that morning the GOC asked for information about the position of the enemy north of Clacton. If the line of advance of the invading force was near the River Colne movement would have been detected by balloon observers, especially if any attempt was made to bridge the river near Wivenhoe. Although the 'all clear' was reported by the Balloon Section at 11.45hrs, telegraphic delay resulted in the GOC not receiving this intelligence until 14.00hrs. After the Gas Supply Depot had replaced the empty gas tubes the Section was ordered back to Middlewick for the night.

On 8 September there was rain and no balloons were filled that day. The Section waited at Heckford Bridge then proceeded to Messing Park, arriving there with the baggage train at 16.45hrs. The following day, 9 September, the Section received telegraphic orders and the 11,000 cu.ft balloon was filled at Tiptree Heath, some four miles from camp, and the first ascent was made at 06.30hrs. The Red Force was retreating and the Cable Detachment was working through the Rivenham End postal telegraph office on the probable line of retreat towards Witham. The observer could see the immediate flank down to the River Blackwater, but towards Colchester the country was very enclosed and no enemy troops could be seen. At 09.50hrs the orders were to watch the retirement of the rearguard some 4–8 miles away and to report which roads were being used by the invaders. The Balloon Section was then to retire to Terling beyond Witham. At 11.00hrs enemy cavalry scouts could be seen followed by a large body of cavalry approaching from the south-east. There were some skirmishes between friendly sappers (Royal Engineers) and the enemy scouts were driven back. From the direction of Messing some twenty Red Force cyclists appeared to protect the Balloon Section whilst the balloon was rapidly brought down and deflated behind trees. Whilst the cyclists held off the enemy the Balloon Section beat a hasty retreat it having taken only seven minutes to be ready to move. The Section made off at the gallop for two miles to place as great a distance as possible between themselves and the enemy. Thereafter the Section proceeded at the trot then the walk to pass through Witham on the way to Terling. Several hours were spent at the side of the road before proceeding to camp at Black Notley. Meanwhile, the Telegraphic Detachment had left some instruments behind in the hurry of departure, and on returning to retrieve them members of the detachment were captured. The umpires declared them out of action for the rest of the day. When the Section arrived at Black Notley at 20.00hrs a fresh supply of gas awaited them. By then the men and horses were exhausted having been on the go for seventeen hours.

OPERATIONAL EMPLOYMENT OF BALLOONS IN THE SOUTH AFRICAN WAR
Source: National Archive document AIR1/728/176/3/8

Extracts from the source document illustrate the very effective use of observation from balloons where the enemy did not also possess them. The Boers were frequently outflanked and on a number of occasions had to withdraw when artillery fire was effectively brought down on their positions. The work of the 3rd Balloon Section Royal Engineers is contained in a report by Lieutenant R.B.D. Blakeney DSO, RE.

The Section disembarked at Cape Town on 30 March 1900, arriving at Warrenton on 23 April. The duties assigned to the Section included reconnoitring the position of the enemy camps, the discovery of gun emplacements or masked batteries and to ascertain the

condition of the piers of the deviation railway bridge over the Vaal, especially those near the north bank. Scouts had been unable to perform this task due to enemy fire. Finally, the Section was to report any attempt by the enemy to make counter-attacks on the British right flank or rear.

The absence of any cavalry units at Warrenton Camp meant that the Balloon Section had to undertake practically all the scouting. The balloon was in the air at 06.00hrs but due to high and gusty wind the ascents had to be frequent and the balloon's lift was bad. The position of the enemy's artillery was ascertained and no flank attack was in progress. Then telegraphic communication between Warrenton and Kimberley ceased at 10.00hrs but this was not due to enemy action.

POWERED AIRCRAFT FLIGHT

INTRODUCTION
The first powered flight by an aircraft built by the Wright brothers in the USA and flown for the first time in December 1903 was a major event in aviation, which transformed the possibilities thus open to mankind both for peaceful as well as warlike purposes. It must not be imagined, however, that the aeroplane would render the balloon and the dirigible redundant. Far from it. The aeroplane would soon prove to be must faster than its rivals but it would be some time before payload and effective operational ranges would exceed those of the airship. The balloon was still a very effective way of carrying out a reconnaissance of enemy movements and positions and the airship had the range to go far over the sea well beyond the range of aeroplanes with a payload well in excess of that which the first flimsy structures of aeroplanes could carry. Indeed, for the first two years of the Great War German Zeppelins would fly very long distances dropping incendiary and other devices on targets as far north as Derby and the Tyneside from bases in Belgium and Germany. Considerable amounts of defensive resources in the form of fighter aircraft and appropriately sited airfields would be a necessary diversion from carrying the war to the enemy. It would not be until 1917 that the bombing aeroplane could create as much damage and take many lives.

Clearly the invention of the powered aeroplane gave all countries with an eye to possessing such an asset the determination to have them both for civilian as well as military purposes. Although the War Office was interested in purchasing a Wright Flyer, it was also deemed important to build British aeroplanes and possess the 'know how' to design other types, i.e. for purposes other than simple reconnaissance. The passages that follow deal with the somewhat lengthy negotiations Between the War Office and the Wright brothers, which in the event came to nothing. Whilst the Wright brothers were undoubtedly ahead of the field there were European designers who were on the verge of designing aeroplanes and the War Office would take the view that money being asked by the Wright brothers could be better spent working on British designs.

CORRESPONDENCE BETWEEN THE WRIGHT BROTHERS AND THE BRITISH ARMY
Source: AIR1/728/176/3/33

The Wright brothers of Dayton, Ohio, owned a bicycle company but had spent four years making and flying gliders until they were confident enough to fit one with an engine to achieve the first flight of a powered aircraft. This took place near their camp at Kill Devil Hill, North Carolina, at 10.35hrs on 17 December 1903. The brothers were not alone in attempting to put a man into the air, indeed there were many both in the USA and Europe who were experimenting with steerable balloons (dirigibles) and other contraptions but the difference with the Wright brothers was that they adopted a scientific approach and backed up their efforts with a firm grasp of aerodynamic theory. They continued with test flights until they were sure that they had a thoroughly reliable machine that would perform as it was meant to do. They retained the 15/16hp engine but improved the propellers and, with their *Flyer III* they achieved a flight of 38 minutes on 5 October 1905. They then believed that they had a machine that would be of interest to the military authorities in the USA and Great Britain.

In Britain the experts in the use of lighter-than-air machines for military purposes were members of the Royal Engineers who reported to the Director of Fortification and Works at the War Office in carrying out their experimental work. Negotiations between the

First powered flight – 17 December 1903 at Kill Devil Hill.

Wright brothers and the War Office began in 1905 and were successfully completed in 1908. What the Wrights did not want was for a government representative to witness a flight but not sign a contract to purchase a machine. Having seen that manned powered flight was possible, foreign governments might be inclined to develop their own machines whereas, understandably, the brothers wished to profit from their research and labour. They wanted a contract that would include the purchase of one of their machines once the purchasing government had been satisfied that *Flyer III* could be used for reconnaissance purposes, i.e., to carry an operator over a long distance and land safely. If required, the names of witnesses could be provided and more could be found.

In a letter dated 28 November 1905, the brothers went on to say that if a contract was signed by a representative of the British Government they would be prepared to build an aircraft at their expense and fly it to meet the terms of the contract before any money was handed over. The War Office signalled their interest in the aeroplane in a letter of 8 February 1906 and the brothers replied on 8 May. The terms of their offer were spelt out. They were offering various governments the complete invention, which would include:

a. A flyer (aeroplane) capable of carrying a man and supplies sufficient for a long trip.
b. Instructions in the practical use of the machine.
c. Data and formulae for the designing of machines of other sizes and speeds.
d. The confidential disclosure of the original discoveries in aeronautical science, which for the first time made the designing of a practical flyer possible and rendered progress certain and economical.

Preliminary experiments with gliders.

Aircraft could be banked safely with lateral control achieved through wing warping.

The opinion of the Superintendent of the Balloon Factory was sought and in a letter to the Director of Fortifications and Works (DFW), dated 6 June, the former felt that the Wright brothers wished to come to terms but was not sure if the appointment of a commission to discuss the whole subject was advisable. He did believe that the brothers should be asked to quote for (a) and (b) above, which would not commit the British Government. The Colonel did not give his reasons for not including (c) and (d).

On 10 July the brothers wrote to Lieutenant Colonel Capper at Aldershot. They referred to legal questions that might arise in connection with the use of aeroplanes but had given little thought to the matter at that time since they anticipated aeroplanes being used by governments i.e., their armed forces and not irresponsible individuals. They did admit, however, that consideration of legal matters could only be postponed. Reference was made to the deal that they had with the French Government. A sharp difference of opinion had emerged regarding the length of period during which the French would have exclusive use of the discoveries made. For example, should the British Government agree to purchase the entire invention no other government, save that of the USA, would receive a delivery of the same within six months. The brothers expected to be paid expenses for the delivery of an aircraft. Although no firm delivery date could be agreed in advance of contract, the brothers felt that, in their negotiations with Britain, if all went according to plan this should be no later than 1 May 1907. They agreed that the payment of the purchase price would be conditional on a trial being witnessed by representatives of the British Government. This would be a 50-kilometre flight in less than one hour and they clarified the term 'long trip' as meaning not less than 100 miles.

Acting on behalf of the Army in the United States was the military attaché in Washington, Lieutenant Colonel Gleichen. Should the military attaché visit Dayton and stay in a hotel he should make no mention of the Wright brothers as the hotel clerks would notify newspaper reporters. On 31 July the brothers had written to Gleichen stating what would be included for the sum of $100,000:

(a) The provision of an aeroplane.
(b) The training of a pilot.
(c) The full rights to the manufacture of aeroplanes for the government's use under any patents secured on its mechanical details.

For a further $100,000 the brothers offered to impart, confidentially, their scientific knowledge and formulae and tables, which would allow Britain to design and build aeroplanes of other sizes and speeds without the risk of undertaking costly and abortive experiments. In a letter to the Superintendent of the Balloon Factory, dated 5 September, DFW felt that there was no probability of approval being given for the expenditure of just $100,000.

On 11 August 1906 Gleichen wrote to the War Office stating that he had visited the brothers in Dayton since he wanted to clarify their offer. He reported that they would not take a penny less than $100,000 for their aeroplane. With regard to (c) above it was felt that whether these rights were granted or not, their granting was of little or no value unless accompanied by the confidential scientific knowledge for which they had demanded a further $100,000, i.e. the British Government could produce as many aircraft as desired but only of the model purchased. Gleichen also reported that the brothers had got the parts required to build a number of aeroplanes but he could not find out if these were to satisfy contracts already secured. As things stood, no pilot training could be given until a definite order had been placed, the aeroplane had completed its trial flight and the purchase price paid. They were having difficulty in keeping their invention secret in the USA and, accordingly, would prefer to have the trial flights take place in Britain, Oakhampton came to mind. It would, in any event, be cheaper to have an aircraft brought to Britain rather than sending a team to the USA where they might have to travel several hundred miles to a place of secrecy. Finally, the attaché mentioned the practical instruction of pilots which would take three or four weeks but the imparting of the confidential scientific instruction could take several months as a totally new set of ideas would have to be taught.

The Superintendent of the Balloon Factory was asked by DFW to comment on Gleichen's letter and he replied on 6 September. He advised that the British Government should not proceed towards a contract for it was felt that the benefits to be gained were out of all proportion to the sums demanded. The claim to have special scientific knowledge was not based on fact and, in any case, it was felt that, in a reasonable time, the work on a flying machine being carried out by Lieutenant Dunne would bear fruit. This might be superior to the Wright's machine in several essentials and achieved at a fraction of the cost. There was, nevertheless, the problem of finding somewhere safe and far from the public gaze for experimenting in powered flight in Britain. Be that as it may the War Office wanted to come to a decision on the purchase of the Wright machine. Gleichen had furnished the British Embassy in Washington with a detailed follow-up report contained in a letter dated 17 August and, again, the Superintendent of the Balloon Factory was asked for comments. The attaché spoke of the interesting conversation he had had with the brothers when he met them on the 8th. His impression was of two young men, both intelligent and certainly not cranks, who were modest in demeanour and even shy. They had been working for ten years on flying machines but had only recently met with success. The four years spent experimenting with gliders gave them an understanding of the nature of flight even though the gliders could only slide downhill to fly a few hundred yards a few feet off the ground. They had started by studying the effects of wind and air pressure on planes at different angles. They compared their results with all published calculations and formulae on the subject and pronounced them totally wrong. They were certain that they could calculate the effect of air on their propellers more accurately than a marine engineer could on the effect that water would have on a ship's screws. The basis of their knowledge was novel and would take several months to impart to a third person. The theoretical calculations were thoroughly worked out before any experiments were made and they said that they had produced a flying machine 'of sorts' four to five years back. What they could not do at that time was to explain apparently inexplicable defects that made it quite unsafe and it took them two years to find a remedy. They had not flown since the autumn of 1905 due to the difficulty in keeping the flights secret. They said that they were so certain of their machine that they had built the last one purely from their formulae and took it south by train without a test flight beforehand. When they got to their destination it flew perfectly. They had completed approximately 40 consecutive flights, mostly between 16 and 21 miles. The longest was 24½ miles.

Detailed report on the performance of the Wright machine

Characteristics

The brothers would not let the attaché see the aeroplane, indeed they claimed that they had none put together. Nor could they be persuaded to let him see a drawing or photograph. He did, however, manage to extract from them, by dint of numerous questions, some details about performance. He learned that the machine had an all-up weight that included 160lb for a man + fuel. For military purposes they would build one of 800lb to carry 2 men + some fuel or 1 man + a full tank and supplies for a 100-mile flight. If required they could build a machine to carry 4 or 5 men and supplies at speeds up to 70mph. With regard to the machine designed to carry 1 man + supplies it would measure, in length, less than 50ft and have the height of a man when standing on the ground and could be taken to pieces for packing. The aircraft has a petrol engine designed for automobiles but adapted for an aeroplane. The aeroplane could have been lighter but the brothers preferred one that was heavier and stronger. The mechanism for steering and handling was not difficult to learn.

Performance

With regard to performance Colonel Gleichen learned that the aeroplane could fly at 40mph even into a headwind. The stronger the headwind, it seemed, the better it went. Downwind the velocity of the wind could be added. Unable to assess the actual airspeed the brothers reported the comments of two independent witnesses, a banker and a chemist, who said that the aeroplane 'went like a train' and turned very handily. The aeroplane did not heel over in a high beam wind. It could soar and hover, having remained stationary in the air for over a minute without the engine working This might be extended for longer periods. For starting off (taking off in modern parlance) a hill or perfectly smooth level area was required. Once airborne it could be steered to hover and it could descend accurately to stop within 100ft of the desired landing site.

Costs of production

The brothers said that the costs of developing their machine had been modest and they had spent very little money compared to other inventors. The $5,000 spent on motors had been their main expense. By their account they claimed that Mr Maxim had spent $100,000 on his experiments only to give up. They put the success in keeping their costs low, down to working on the design, in all its theoretical detail, on paper before beginning construction and experimentation with a prototype. Their asking price, of $100,000 for a Wright Flyer, would include practical instruction and a grant of mechanical patents. The imparting of formulae and scientific knowledge, for an extra $100,000, discussed earlier in the chapter, was justified on the grounds that other inventors had spent much more yet achieved nothing. Various syndicates had approached them but they had refused, choosing to sell only to governments for military purposes. They wished to avoid swindles with private concerns and also wished to keep their knowledge and experience away from the general public for approximately a further five years. No government at that time had taken them up on their offer. The French wanted a one-year and not a six-month option to be well ahead in the field of military aviation and the US Government and the Army had only, to use their words, had a smell of it. They explained why they had not taken out a patent on their machine believing it to be practically unpatentable since it involved the development of mathematics and physics in an unexpected direction. In any event the aeroplane did not depend on a particular mechanism.

The military aspect

The brothers expected the 'Flyer' to be used chiefly for scouting. Since it was constructed of very light materials with white wings it would not be easily visible until very close. It could fly at any height and at a speed to make it practically invulnerable; the pilot presented the only real target. It could easily be packed up for transport by wagon/train or could be flown slowly to keep pace with a column on the march. Two-man operation was recommended as the pilot would have his hands full flying leaving the observer to his business. After a few trials, they said, flying the machine would be as easy as riding a bicycle. In the preceding six months they had been busy perfecting their motors and constructing different parts ready for when the orders came in and there would be demand for complete aeroplanes.

WAR OFFICE CONTRACT TO PURCHASE THE WRIGHT FLYER

Reaction to Gleichen's report

Colonel Capper, the Superintendent of the Balloon Factory, commented on the report in a note to DFW on 11 October 1906. In it he said that he believed the brothers to be honest and possibly five years ahead in the field of aeronautical science but he questioned whether or not it would be worth the money and the effort unless Britain could manufacture and experiment with a machine far away from the public gaze. In a note to Colonel Capper, via DFW, the Army Council had asked Gleichen to inform the Wright brothers that it was not advisable to purchase their machine, due especially to the cost. The important word here is 'especially' since other counsels had prevailed which included those who felt that Britain could, in time, achieve powered flight at much less cost. The note was dated 20th November 1906 and it was not until 10 April 1908 that the Wright brothers again contacted the War Office with a new offer. By that time Britain still did not possess a powered flying machine and the brothers' new offer could not be rejected out of hand. They were still anxious to do business with Britain as they stressed the interest being taken by other countries in aeronautics and again offered a machine suitable for scouting able to carry two men, an operator (pilot) and

an observer with sufficient fuel for long flights. They referred to a contract recently entered into with the US Government for one of these aeroplanes. Again Capper was asked for advice on the offer and replied to DFW that the brothers be asked for terms that must include the training of two officers in the price. On 6 June the Director of Army Contracts wrote to the brothers.

The terms of the contract

The brothers replied to the letter from the Director of Army Contracts in a letter dated 27 June. They wanted clarification on the conduct of any trials held in the UK. Firstly they asked if their machine would be required to rise from a ten-acre field surrounded on all sides by trees and other obstructions. Secondly they wanted to know if the use of a tent would be permitted to protect the machine from the elements. Finally they wanted to know the location in England to which the machine was to be delivered and the conditions governing the flight trials. In a letter dated 12 August Capper advised DFW suggesting the requirements for a suitable location for the conduct of trials and the conditions that should be satisfied in the conduct of those trials with the Wright machine. Ideally it should be government property but, in any event, no unreasonable site was to be selected but this should not be a problem for probably three fields in ten in most parts of England were suitable. The field to be used was to have level ground and not to be surrounded on all sides by trees and obstructions. Only on one side should there be a wood, houses or telegraph wires. Low hedges and trees would be permitted on the other three sides and there should be ample space between the trees in at least two places on each boundary for an aeroplane to pass through. A regular tent should not be permitted to protect the aeroplane from the elements, just waterproof covers for the engine, the gear and the whole structure. The contractual requirements of the conduct of the trials differed slightly from the original advice given by Capper to DFW:

1. **Constructional Test** (only applicable to machines not tried over a course of 100 miles) The machine is to be delivered in the Constructor's cases to the construction shed. If the aeroplane is to be constructed by the contractor using his workmen it is to be ready for trial flights within 72 hours of the cases being opened. If the aeroplane is to be assembled by the Contractor and Government workmen, it is to be dismantled after assembly, repacked in the cases and reassembled by the Contractor and the same men within 96 hours of reopening of the cases.

2. **Flight Tests** The machine will be taken out of the shed on days and at times mutually agreed by the Contractor and representatives of the War Office. The trial ground shall be selected by the War Office which would be

ordinary grass and open land of an area of not less than 10 acres. There may be hedges such as are usual in all parts of England on all four sides of the plot, but there shall not be continuous rows of trees, houses or telegraph wires along more than two sides of the plot.

3. **The First Trial** The machine shall be brought to any point of the trial ground selected by the operator (pilot) and pointed in any direction as required and no assistance is to be given to the operator to start the engine and the machine. (i.e. assistance with the take-off). The machine must rise from the ground and fly round a captive balloon 12 ½ miles distant and back to the starting point at not less than 25mph.

4. **The Second Trial** The machine shall carry a sealed barograph and make a flight passing round a captive balloon, which will be at an appropriate altitude of 2,000 feet above the ground level of the starting point. The barograph chart will show, on the descent of the machine, that an altitude of 2,000 feet has been attained during the flight provided that the ground level at the starting point shall not be more than 3,000 feet above mean sea level. The balloon observer shall check, as nearly as he can, the height attained by the machine and in case of any doubt as to whether or not the altitude was reached, either the operator or the War Office representative may challenge the accuracy of the barograph which shall, in that case, be packed, sealed and sent to Kew Observatory so that the reading may checked. Should the check prove that the height attained was less than 1,800 feet the operator shall, if required, undertake the trial again.

5. **The Third Trial** The machine shall make a flight of two hours duration during which it shall describe three circles of 200 yards, ¼ mile and 1 mile. **Note** these three trials or any two of them may, at the written request of the operator, be made during one flight.

6. **The Fourth Trial** The machine shall carry an operator and a War Office observer (accustomed to captive balloon work), the weight not to exceed 170lb, in a flight of at least ½ hour's duration, during which time it shall rise to a height of at least 1,000 feet, shall proceed in such directions as required by the Observer, and shall 'hover' or 'circle' over a point selected by him for at least one minute It shall be possible for the Observer to look down from his position without his remaining in an unduly cramped attitude and the machine shall be steady enough for him to use 6-power field glasses whilst 'hovering' or 'circling'. **Note** In case the operator does not consider that the observer gave an impartial account of his machine, he may report the trial with the name of the observer or may select two other skilled military observers to take, one at a time, on similar flights. The report of a majority of such observers to be considered by the War Office before the machine is finally approved.

7. **The Fifth Trial** The machine shall make a short flight of about five minutes with petrol and lubricating tanks full. It shall then be brought to the ground, all petrol and oil save that required for a ten-minute flight, shall be emptied from the tanks and it shall then make another similar short flight. During the second flight it must prove itself equally stable and under control as on the first flight.

General Conditions

1. The machine will carry on all trials:
   a. Operator (weight made up if necessary to 170lb)
   b. Observer (or equivalent weight to 170lbs)
   c. Instruments, maps, etc., of equivalent in weight not exceeding 10lbs, and except where otherwise provided,
   d. Petrol calculated at a rate of ½ gallon per brake horse power of the motor.
2. On all trials the machine must rise from the ground under its own power, without any special starting devices outside its own construction.
3. In case of damage other than such as can be made good by the operator on the spot during flight or on landing, that flight shall not be counted as a trial flight, and any damage shall be made good at the cost of the Contractor.
4. The War Office shall provide contiguous to the trial ground a suitable shed in which the machine can be erected and housed.
5. All labour required during the trials, and all petrol, lubricating oil etc., will be provided by the War Office.
6. The Contractor may at his option provide his own staff for the erection of the machine. The War Department will, however, if requested in writing to do so, provide such skilled labour it may have available on the spot, but the Contractor shall have no claim as regards any damage that may be caused to the machine by or through the employment of such labour.
7. The Contractor shall take all the risks of accident to his operator during the trials, and 'all third party risks', but shall not take any risk as regards accident to the observer appointed by the War Department
8. In case of failure to fulfil the conditions of any one flight, the War Department representative present might consider that there was a reasonable chance that the operator would meet the conditions if extra attempts were made.
9. The observer or observers taking part in any flight shall volunteer to take part and shall not be ordered to do so.
10. The operator shall not be required to make ascents in rainy weather, where there seems to be an early probability of electrical disturbances, in winds

over 15mph, as measured by three flights of a pilot balloon as used in the British service to determine the velocity of the wind, in the dark or in twilight, in fog or thick mist. (The pilot balloon usually takes velocities at heights varying from 50ft to 300ft above the surface of the ground.)

In the event the War Office did not proceed with the purchase of the Wright Flyer since the machine had not been witnessed flying. An interesting footnote to the terms and conditions of the contract can be found in a circular memorandum to all officers and Mr Cody to the effect that some photographs of the Wright machine, sent from the War Office to Colonel Capper at the Balloon Factory, were left in a drawer in the photographic school but had since been removed. The addressees were instructed to return these photographs if they had taken them and not, in future, to remove them without the permission of Lieutenant Cammel, in whose charge they had been committed.

NOTES ON MILITARY BALLOONING BY COLONEL CAPPER – NOVEMBER 1904

In 1904 Colonel Capper was responding to a letter asking for facts about the effects of artillery fire on balloons. His experience covered peace-time exercises. These thoughts committed to paper in late 1904 should be compared with the narrative, written in April 1908, which follows. On the ranges when circumstances rendered it impossible to manoeuvre the balloons, one balloon was brought down by the ninth round from a single 6-inch gun at an unknown range. Some years previously a 15-pounder field gun at Lydd succeeded in bringing down a balloon at a range of 2,300 yards. Consequently, Capper came to the conclusion that no observations could be made from a balloon within 2½ miles of an enemy's field artillery, or 6 miles of his heavy artillery. An alternative was either to send up a balloon for a very short period before the enemy could set their sights upon it or to move the balloon about so that the elevation, range and direction were constantly being altered. In each case where a balloon had been brought down by artillery it descended very slowly and was capable of repair from half an hour to an hour. A considerable amount of rifle fire could undoubtedly bring down a balloon, he opined, but the bullet holes could, in most cases, be easily repaired. A balloon at a distance of 2,000 yards from rifles at an altitude of 700ft should remain out of range it being impossible to range upon it.

Altitude depended on the size of the balloon, the weight that it would have to carry and the strength of the wind. The length of the cable then being carried by balloon units was 4,000ft. This made it necessary to calculate the lifting power of the gas in the balloon which,

at that altitude, was 700lb and subtract the weight of the cable, which was 280lb, and this limited the weight of the crew and balloon to 420lb. The lifting power of the same volume of gas at 8,000ft above sea level is 590lb reducing the weight of the balloon and observer to 170lb weight, which was the weight of about 2,400ft of cable. Therefore at a height of 5,600ft above sea level a medium balloon in calm atmospheric conditions will ascend 2,400ft above the ground. If the wind speed is between 18 and 20mph the balloon will probably not ascend, at best, to more than half this height. Above 30mph and the balloon is unlikely to ascend.

With regard to experience in foreign wars Capper admitted that he had no really reliable information. He cited Manchuria and the Russo/Japanese war and the work of Kuropatkin who was so pleased with the uses made of balloons in Manchuria. For his first flights he sent for 600 men from the Balloon Corps to join him. During the confrontation between the Imperial Japanese Fleet and the Russian equivalent the Russian commander complained, not about the accuracy of the Japanese fire, directed as it was by balloon observers, but on the fact that they must have seen that that some of the fire was directed at the hospital ship.

Capper was of the opinion that the chief use to which a balloon was likely to be put in attack or defence was the observation of threatened flank movements by the enemy, which could be countered by friendly artillery fire. However, the results of observations of artillery fire as judged in peace time could be at times wonderfully accurate and at times just as inaccurate. It probably meant that a very considerable amount of practice was necessary before an observer in a balloon could be considered qualified to observe the results of artillery fire. He touched on the situation where the balloon observer could see the target but the gun crews could not. Experiments in aligning guns on to objects unseen on the ground involved the use of flags making it possible to direct fire on the 'line of fire', but the ranges could only be guessed at. His personal opinion was that it would be easier for the observer to correct ranges if the first shots fired as ranging shots by the artillery consisted of time shrapnel. The burst of a shell is difficult to pick up whereas the burst of time shrapnel readily attracts the eye.

THOUGHTS ON THE EMPLOYMENT OF BALLOONS, DIRIGIBLES AND FLYING MACHINES IN WAR – APRIL 1908
Source: AIR 1/729/176/4/3

On 11 April 1908 Colonel Capper, then Superintendent of the Balloon Factory, gave further thought to the employment of free and captive balloons, dirigibles or airships and flying machines in war. Chapter 2 records the enormous strides that were made in developing airships and flying machines, wireless telegraphy and bombing by the outbreak of war. The contents of this section should be compared with the corresponding sections of Chapter 2. By way of a general introduction he spoke of experience gained thus far. He began by explaining that any experience gained in the operation of captive balloons had been gained in peacetime only during the preceding five years. If they were to perform badly in war it would be because they would be used in isolated units instead of in their proper capacity, under the control of Intelligence Staff who thoroughly realized the capabilities of captive balloons. Improvements in construction had rendered balloons far steadier than they were before 1905. As regards the use to which dirigible balloons could be put, he again spoke from practical experience. The ease with which these vessels could maintain a course, even at night and the difficulty in seeing them amongst the clouds in misty weather or at night was considered. He claimed to have kept in touch with all developments, but when it came to flying machines Colonel Capper could claim no practical experience. He described the development thus far to be in a state of the chrysalis. He could only claim to have spoken to two men who had flown for half an hour covering a distance of 20 miles in one flight. They were serious men who had accepted a contract to supply the US Government with a machine that could carry a pilot and a passenger for 100 miles. There was every prospect that their contract would be literally fulfilled but could claim no particular weight for his opinion.

THE OBJECT AND TACTICAL USE OF THE CAPTIVE BALLOON IN WAR

Colonel Capper began by speaking of the employment of captive balloons in a 'civilized war'. They were in a position to obtain information of the enemy's positions and movements of any considerable body of troops at a time when the cavalry could not make progress in reconnaissance. They could also assist the artillery in

An observation balloon.

obtaining targets and direct artillery fire. Finally, they could be used to verify the positions of friendly troops and to ascertain the nature of the ground in front of them and to their flank. He believed that they should come directly under the orders of the Intelligence Staff except when placed at the disposal of the Artillery. The balloon must be closely connected to the cable cart and this connected to the central station by telephone, and observers must be well furnished with information and with the best procurable maps and glasses. Finally, the technical balloon officer should be given as free a hand as possible as regards time and place of ascent.

Colonel Capper believed that when a balloon was placed at the disposal of the Artillery the balloon must be in direct contact with the commander RA or the individual battery. Observation was most effective up to 7,000 yards or farther in the case of larger shells. Under normal conditions the radius of a balloon may be taken as five to six miles. In open country in good climatic conditions the distance is much increased and conversely in hazy conditions. An extended balloon reconnaissance should not be undertaken within three miles of the enemy's artillery but for short observations a balloon may ascend close even to the friendly firing line. The balloon detachment must be screened from the enemy's view and that included the balloons when close to or on the ground. The line of march was the direction in which an army was moving and balloon companies could move with the heavy artillery that was sited furthest from the enemy. When in contact with the enemy the Balloon Company should move with the Advanced Guard when the sappers would not be available for any other duty. Balloons should not be filled with gas until required for use since in the inflated state the Company would be slowed down on the line of march and they would be more conspicuous. He added a warning that too much should not be expected of one balloon observer who could not be expected to see everything and if required to observe minor details he must be so ordered. He believed that the effect of artillery fire would be greatly enhanced with the use of captive balloons.

He continues with reference to the use of captive balloons in a 'savage war', which he defines as one in which the enemy has no artillery. In these circumstances balloons could be used with great boldness and they should be in the air both on the march and in camp to afford considerable security. Furthermore, the cavalry would have less to do in scouting. Balloons could also act as beacons to parties that had lost their way. Finally, signal balloons could be used to advantage by putting up signals for definite movements, a combined attack for example. Visible signals from a balloon could be seen simultaneously by troops over a wide area thus reducing the time that would otherwise have to be taken in passing orders to unit commanders.

THE ROLE OF DIRIGIBLES/AIRSHIPS IN WAR

The roles of the dirigible balloon in war appeared to Colonel Capper to be both tactical and strategic. (Both terms as generally understood today.) The dirigible balloon could remain airborne for several days, during which time it could have a range of 3,000 miles, and could manoeuvre at altitudes up to 10,000ft above ordinary clouds and artillery fire. It could not be seen at night at a height of 1,000ft for more than a mile and with the requisite amount of fuel, crew and ballast, could carry from 8 to 10 tons of explosives. Such explosives could be dropped from heights of 1,000ft or less. This would clearly make the steerable balloon a strategic asset and Capper addresses the question of potential targets. Dirigibles could be a very serious menace to an enemy if bombs were dropped on dockyards, arsenals, storehouses, workshops, railway junctions etc. Important bridges might also be attacked and no army would dare to embark in fragile transports with the possibility of meeting a fleet of such balloons before disembarkation was effected. Tactically the dirigibles might proceed at height to the point where an attack could be made, sinking closer to the ground at night to proceed with the attack. He believed that in the future large vessels of 1,000,000cu.ft or even greater capacity could be used for strategic missions. At that time the Zeppelins were over 400,000cu.ft and the French design for a ship of nearly 350,000cu.ft was being considered. He concluded by saying that, short of developing anti-aircraft artillery, it was impractical to attempt to defend oneself against the attack of large dirigibles.

Capper does not rate highly the effectiveness of anti-aircraft artillery. His assumptions seem a trifle unrealistic since he had no experience on which to base his views. He does not believe that the gun crews could be ready at all times to fire upon these vessels. Without airborne early warning this is a reasonable assumption. The enemy could be obscured by cloud but even if they did come into view the speed at which they were travelling

Rigid dirigible airship.

would put them out of range before effective fire could be put up. He acknowledges that the flying machine could combat the threat of dirigibles but, given the existing state of development it would be some time before flying machine could be in that position. Even then, in the long run, he did not foresee the flying machine being able to meet the threat of the dirigible at altitude, although at low altitudes this would be possible i.e., at altitudes of 2,000ft or less.

THE ROLE OF FLYING MACHINES IN WAR

Capper's paper began with the words, 'the immediate use of the flying machine would appear to be limited'. Up to this time only short flights had been made and it was felt that the human frame could not stand the strain of long flights until use had made these flights second nature. Long-distance bombing missions by the US Strategic Air Command and, in the recent Libyan crisis, tornado bombers flying direct from Norfolk to Libya to mount an attack on air defence systems make such reservations amusing today. Indeed there were lurid pictures of the human frame being unable to survive speeds over 100mph and observers being so frightened in their rickety machines that they would be unable to take in what

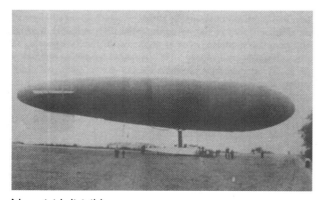

Non rigid dirigible.

Bristol Boxkite.

they could see. Another question concerned the height at which flying machines could fly. It was believed that this would be determined by the atmospheric conditions, which were little understood. Flying machines that could rise or fall at or near sea level might not be able to do this at considerable heights. A probable first use of flying machines would he for scouting with a pilot and observer, referred to in the document as 'operator' and 'passenger'. Scouting machines would probably fly at a comparatively low elevation and the radius of action would probably be not much over fifty miles.

As regards the ability of flying machines to withstand punishment the findings do appear quaint. The paper suggests that they would not easily be damaged by rifle fire or artillery since they had a good chance of escaping being hit in vital places, even when operating over an enemy's army. They would probably not be capable of carrying wireless equipment and observers would have

to make their reports on return to base. In the twilights at dawn and dusk flying machines would probably escape detection.

Speeds would be between 25 and 40mph in calm weather and they would be faster into the wind than dirigible machines of equal pace. Flying machines might be used against dirigible machines sent against Britain but these would have to descend to bomb and unless severely damaged could escape British airspace. If a dirigible flew very high to avoid an interception by a flying machine it would be practically harmless for offence.

The small flying machine, when evolved, should be no more costly to produce than a motor car so could be turned out in volume. At this point in time it was felt that larger flying machines could be developed with great speed and be able to drive offensive dirigibles entirely from the air but in April 1908 this could only be speculation.

CONCLUSION

The work carried out on balloons and the thoughts of Colonel Capper on the matter of their employment in war are of particular interest since they show the limited knowledge that these earlier flyers had of flying, although the war potential of flying machines was well recognized. The next chapter will show the enormous advances that will be made in the development of airships and flying machines. The balloon, both free and captive, will have a place, albeit diminishing, as Britain, France and Germany make great strides in the development of large airships. By the time war breaks out in 1914 the British Government, the Admiralty and the War Office will have realized that the construction, development and employment of flying machines can no longer be left

Hugh Trenchard.

Billy Mitchell.

Giulio Douhet.

to enthusiastic Royal Engineers. Flying attracted officers from other arms who came together to create, with the Engineers, a separate dedicated flying service. But from the beginning there would be those who wished to use flying machines in support of naval operations and those who wished to see them used to support the land war. This would result in a determination that two separate air services should develop in tandem, namely the Royal Naval Air Service and the Royal Flying Corps. But in 1918 these two separate air service would be merged into a third fighting service, the Royal Air Force.

In the early days of ballooning and flying there was no conception of aircraft that could be used entirely independent of the land war and the war at sea. As it happened it would be the Royal Navy that would recognize the contribution to the outcome of the war that could be made by strategic bombing. This means a belief that an enemy could be beaten not simply by sinking his ships or defeating his armies in the field but by the destruction of his factories, ports, harbours, rail networks etc. Indeed, by the end of the Great War there would be disciples of strategic bombing who would pioneer this new form of warfare. An Italian, an American and a British officer would be the three most important men in this field, the Italian Giulio Douhet, the American Colonel Billy Mitchell and the Commander of the Royal Air Force, Air Marshal Sir Hugh Trenchard.

Chapter 2
Events Leading to the Formation of the Royal Flying Corps and Royal Naval Air Service

Picardy manoeuvres – Esher Committee – proposals for the formation of a flying service – considerations of general policy – the Naval Wing of the Flying Corps – the Military Wing of the Flying Corps – employment of the RFC in the 1912 manoeuvres – First Annual Report of the Air Committee 5/8/13 – preparation for hostilities

INTRODUCTION

The five years before the outbreak of the Great War saw a flurry of activity in aviation. It was inevitable that the military use of balloons, airships and aeroplanes would increasingly occupy the thoughts of governments and military planners. In Great Britain the Committee of Imperial Defence spawned an Air Committee with a Sub-Committee to consider air matters and to plan for the future. This chapter will discuss the development of air power, which would result in the formation of the Royal Flying Corps and the Royal Naval Air Service. Chapter 1 recorded the part played by the Royal Engineers in using balloons both in military campaigns and during military exercises. It was natural that the Engineers' organization should form the basis of any new air service. Careful watch was made of other powers, particularly France and Germany, to see what advances were being made in the development of airships and aeroplanes. There was much experimentation and test flying was a very hazardous business. Great reliance had to be placed on the experience of private aviators and plans were made to impress privately owned machines in the event of hostilities and there was a gradual growth in the number of firms building aeroplanes, aero engines and trained aviators.

There would be considerable debate over the primacy of the airship, but their slow speed and large bulk made them vulnerable to attacks by aeroplanes and anti-aircraft artillery. The airship would play a considerable part in the conflict to come but would gradually become marginalized as aeroplanes became faster and more heavily armed. The airship would be used in the bombing role and for reconnaissance but it was the latter role in which the airship would prove to be the most effective.

AIR POLICY ESPOUSED BY THE FRENCH GENERAL BRUN AND THE PICARDY MANOEUVRES

General Brun was credited with being one of the most informed believers in the future of the aeroplane. A country that was compelled to defend itself against attacks by hostile airships would find that speed was of the essence. Aeroplanes had an indisputable superiority in speed. For that reason, argued the General, in the event

Dirigible at manoeuvres.

of land warfare, the bulk of a nation's air fleet must be aeroplanes. But there were other essential qualities of flying machines, namely altitude and radius of action. In this respect the airship possessed a greater radius of action and possessed the greater service ceiling making it most suitable for strategic reconnaissance. Twenty-five years had elapsed since the airship *La France* had made several journeys into the air and returned successfully to the same point with motors weighing less than 400lb per unit of horsepower. But things had moved on and the motor car industry had produced motors weighing as little as 4lb per unit of horsepower. Aeroplanes had to put down for refuelling at intervals to achieve the same radius of action. This would point to the superiority of the aeroplane for land warfare and the airship for maritime reconnaissance. For French military purposes airships should have a range of 600 kilometres but that might not suffice for Britain. When they came to land warfare lighter-than-air craft were necessarily of large bulk and therefore targets for artillery. Absolute immunity from artillery fire could not be achieved under 3,000 metres. The French army should build airships with a range of between 500 and 600 kilometres capable of carrying at least four passengers at a height of 1,500 metres for a considerable part of the journey and possessing a speed, if not superior, at least equal to those of an enemy. An airship of this quality would cost £40,000 as against £1,000 for an aeroplane. All in all the French War Department would be unlikely to countenance a large expenditure on a type (of airship) that did not seem likely to be of use for long.

The matter of comparability with Germany was raised in the French Senate and this was not favourable on the issue of airships. Germany had twelve completed and eleven being built with a further fifteen belonging to private individuals, but General Brun was of the opinion that only five or six units were capable of military use. France had only the *Ville de Paris*, the *Colonel Renard* and the *Liberté* with four others being built and due for delivery before the end of 1912. Of airship sheds or hangars, France had only two but General Brun undertook to have twenty hangars built by the year 1913, together with a complete supply of hydrogen during the same period. So far as aeroplanes were concerned he pointed out that the War Department had bought a dozen and had given every encouragement, including promotion and honorary awards to officers and under-officers engaged in the service of aerial navigation. He said that it was impracticable to offer a complete solution at the time because the developments in powered flight were taking place at such a pace that every step taken to use aeroplanes had, of necessity, to be provisional.

This led General Brun to conclude that aeroplanes and airships would be employed in strategic and tactical reconnaissance. Although the airship would be employed in the former role, aeroplanes were being developed to the point where they could be used in both roles. He returned to the point that airships were too voluminous and vulnerable but thought that they could be of service until they became obsolete. At this time aeroplanes could only be deployed from land bases but work would soon be undertaken to fly them from warships. Until aeroplanes could be flown far from the coast the airship would enjoy a measure of immunity from attack. General Brun's immediate aim was to obtain at the earliest opportunity the largest possible number of airships and aeroplanes with the commensurate number of trained personnel to operate them. As with the British

War Office he was determined that the army should profit from the resources of private industry.

The determination of the French War Department is shown in that every avenue had been used to put France in the forefront of aviation. For nine years negotiations had been in hand beginning with Monsieur Ader in 1897, followed by the work of Colonel Renard, Captains Ferber, Brianchon and Lucas-Girardville, the Wrights' contracts, the experiments at Le Mans, the work of General Roques, Colonel Hitschouer and Commandant Bouttieeaux, the report upon the Rheims week by General Vieillard, the negotiations with Blériot and the Antoinette Societies for the provision of monoplanes to carry two passengers, the Farman contracts, the instructions for the training of pilots and observers and the performance of French officers who sustained the interest in aviation at the French War Department. The success of the Picardy manoeuvres was not a matter of chance but the fruits of the work that had been put in by all concerned.

A statement was made to *Le Matin* regarding the army estimates, which showed that General Brun proposed to purchase some fifty aeroplanes of various types and to increase the number of aviation centres by adding three new establishments to those existing at Vincennes, Satory and Chalons. The existing personnel were to be distributed amongst the six centres with the mission of training pilots who would learn to cover 100 kilometres at a height of 600 metres. At the same time the War Minister was credited with ordering the design and construction of an aeroplane that could carry at least three passengers with arms and equipment over a course of 200 kilometres. This would be a two-engined aircraft that could be readily packed up and transported from point to point. It was expected that a sum of the equivalent of £80,000 would shortly be voted for these purposes with supplementary estimates if required. General Roques was placed in charge of the new air service. A report then appeared in *Le Temps* to the effect that ten Blériot aeroplanes and twenty Farman biplanes had already been ordered. Seven of the latter were being built to carry two passengers in addition to the pilot. The military aeroplane of 1911 was to carry 660lb and to cover 200 miles without landing and would travel at a minimum speed of 38½ miles per hour. There was to be a competition for a prize of £4,000 for the best design. Competitors were to receive a bonus for exceeding the minimum speed and a royalty would be paid to the designer on the understanding that the State reserved the right to construct such an aeroplane. The report ended by saying that there were already rumours of various passenger-carrying machines under construction of a large size and with engines of unprecedented power. Speculative or not the paper was simply reflecting the reality of the enormous strides that had been taken in aviation since the first powered flight from the sand dunes at Kitty Hawk in November 1903. General Brun discounted war in the air at the time. He did not see air battles between rival airships or aeroplanes. What did concern him was what an airman could do, what he could see and what he could report as a pilot on his own would have to fly the aeroplane, observe using field glasses and write down what he could for he could not radio in to base. Radios in aeroplanes were still to come.

The Picardy Manoeuvres

For the 1910 manoeuvres at Picardy, France's aerial fleet was organized into three formations. The first would be at the disposal of the Director of Manoeuvres and the remaining two were to be allocated to the commanders of the Red and Blue forces. The Director's group was to be established at Briot, west of Grandvilliers, and included four airships and six aeroplanes. Red and Blue forces each had four aeroplanes and six airships. Paulhan, Latham and several other of the best-known French airmen were present, whilst a number of French officers and under-officers also arrived at Picardy on or before 12 September. All of them were to display their competence. The airships did not play a very prominent part in the proceedings. The *Clémont-Bayard II* left Pierrefonds at 09.05 hours on 11 September and landed at Briot at 11.10 hours having carried eight passengers at a speed of 31mph and at an average altitude of 250 metres. During this journey she was in constant communication

Clémont Bayard II airship.

with the Eiffel Tower and the Director of Manoeuvres by wireless. She was given no mission of reconnaissance or at least performed none. The following day she could not get airborne due to the wind strength, although four aeroplanes were at work and this immediately disclosed a serious limitation in the use of airships in war for wars do not stop just because of high winds. On the day of the President's visit she soared over the battlefield but her great bulk and slow speed made her seem out of place in the presence of speedier aeroplanes for she presented a tempting target both for gunners in the air and on the ground. She was finally sent off on a mission to Paris on 14 September, leaving at 15.10 hours and arriving at 17.27 hours, having covered the 75 miles in 2 hours 17 minutes at a mean altitude of 400 metres with 7 passengers. The *Liberté, Colonel Renard* and a little *Zodiac* privately owned by the Count de la Vaulx, were also present and made some ascents. On the other hand no wind seemed to be too high for the aeroplanes, which were seen constantly throughout the week being flown with the utmost skill and assurance. For height and speed the Blériots and

Clémont Bayard.

Antoinettes divided the honours, whilst the Farman and Sommer biplanes proved very satisfactory.

The *Journal* of 14 and 17 September contained detailed reports of the tactical reconnaissance carried out in a Farman biplane by Lieutenant Sido, of the colonial infantry, and Adjutant Ménard, the former acting as observer. The directing staff attested to the accuracy of the press reports, which are a tribute to the work of skilled pilots and observers. The military value of these reports cannot be over estimated. Each report unveiled and exposed the dispositions of the enemy and placed the whole information at the disposal of General Picquart in a very short space of time. In the first case the report was in the Red Commander's hands by 07.34 hours. In the second case the writer was with General Picquart overnight. The Red Army had been heavily attacked and it was of the utmost importance to ascertain the enemy's intentions and dispositions at the earliest possible hour in the morning. General Picquart had ordered his outposts to keep in touch with the enemy but since the armies were already in contact he relied on his airmen to know how the battle was progressing. Were the Blue forces strengthening their attack on the Red left of the line or had the enemy transferred its forces elsewhere? Was the enemy coming on, entrenching itself or falling back? These were the sorts of questions that it was vital be answered in times of war. Lieutenant Sido's report showed that the enemy was in retreat for only cavalry and rearguards had been observed, and General Picquart could issue prompt orders for the advance. These reports resulted in Lieutenant Sido's promotion and the awarding of the Cross of the Legion of Honour to the pilot. A man who was reconnoitring for the first time found out how much he relied on his eyes, with or without glasses. He had to be able to distinguish between cavalry and infantry and when it came to the artillery he might count the number of support vehicles to determine the number of guns. The interval between artillery teams could clearly be seen. The cavalry, the *chasseurs-à-cheval*, were recognizable by the blue haze that seemed to float above the black mass of the horses. The infantry could be seen as a rose-coloured ribbon whilst the colonial infantry formed a black line and the rifles one of bluish haze. But all this took much practice and a profound knowledge of the uniforms and equipment of an enemy, hence the recognition for the performance of Lieutenant Sido and Adjutant Ménard.

One final thought emerges from the results of these manoeuvres. It confirmed the value of the aeroplane in the hands of a good pilot and an experienced observer but it was nevertheless felt that the aeroplane could not completely replace the cavalry, even for scouting, because of fighting at night or in misty conditions. In very strong winds airships would be grounded. Be that as it may aeroplanes, and to a lesser extent airships, had proved their worth in land warfare.

THE ESHER COMMITTEE – 1909
Source: National Archive documents

The preceding section of this chapter shows the extent to which the French Government was prepared to be ready should war come and the lengths that the French War Department went to prove the military value of the airship and the aeroplane. The British Government was also thinking along the same lines. In 1909 a Sub-Committee of the Committee of Imperial Defence was presided over by Lord Esher and it reported on the question of aerial navigation on 28 January. The Sub-Committee's terms of reference were to consider the dangers to which the nation could be exposed both at sea and on the land by any development of aerial navigation reasonably probable in the years that lay ahead and the naval or military advantages that might be expected from the use of airships and aeroplanes. The Sub-Committee concluded that, given the existing state of aerial navigation, Great Britain was not exposed to any serious danger by land but that the pace of development meant that an aerial threat both by land and from the sea must not be discounted. A large-scale invasion of the British Isles by airships was, however, dismissed as unlikely for many years to come. Where airships might be used effectively was to deliver raiding parties with the purpose of inflicting a damaging blow to an arsenal or a dockyard. The possibility of attacks on warships and dockyards by the dropping of explosives or incendiary bombs from dirigible balloons was considered but such attacks were at an experimental stage on the continent and it was considered sensible for Britain also to experiment

Lord Esher.

with the dropping of objects from various heights on to targets below. It was doubtful, however, whether coastal defences and men-of-war had the means to ward of aerial attacks of this nature.

The use of dirigible balloons might be used in naval warfare to ascertain the movements of fleets and to give warnings of attack but the means of preventing an enemy from using balloons for this purpose did not at that time exist. That these matters were being considered before the outbreak of hostilities in 1914 shows how the potential of air warfare was already becoming the subject of urgent consideration. Only by Britain building and flying airships and aircraft could the Committee ascertain the true nature and extent of the air threat. Indeed, this had been the case when Britain built submarines. (Note: The term dirigible balloon or steerable balloon in the texts is interchangeable with airship. Balloons used previously in military operations were mostly tethered and had to be collapsed and transported to wherever fresh reconnaissance was needed. Balloons that floated freely were at the mercy of the wind and may not go in the desired direction.)

And so the Committee considered the military advantages that Britain might expect to derive from the use of airships and aircraft. It was conceivable that they might be used for attacks on enemy warships, dockyards, canal gates and locks. The rigid type of airship was considered the best for use in experimentation. It was recommended that the War Office should be granted funds to permit further experiments and the purchase, on the open market, of either complete dirigible balloons or such component parts as may be required The Admiralty was to receive £35,000 for the building of a dirigible balloon by a firm that successfully tendered for its construction and experimentation. An Admiralty representative was to liaise with the firm at all stages of construction and experimentation and therefore be in a position to consult with expert scientific opinion. This procedure, as has already been pointed out, was used with the development of the submarine. The Royal Aircraft Factory produced the balloon envelopes that covered the balloon but balloon experiments were put out to contract for which a sum of £2000 was allotted for the firm carrying out this work.

Airships

Just at the moment when a flying service was about to be born the part that airships could or would play in war was questioned. The Sub-Committee received the expert advice of Major Sir A. Bannerman, Bart., Commandant of the Army Air Battalion, on the subject of airships, balloons and kites, that balloons could be free, i.e. could not be steered, or captive in which case they remained static and would prove to be sitting targets for enemy aircraft. Airships could be steered to desired locations

and could receive and transmit messages by wireless telegraphy. On the other hand their operations could be hampered by bad weather and in this respect the French and the Germans had a distinct advantage in that they could build sheds at intervals across the country to receive airships. Here they could be serviced, reflated or repaired, for tears in the outer canvas were a frequent occurrence. Since airships might be included in the strength of the expeditionary force the British would have to build sheds in the country of a future ally prior to the outbreak of war. As airships were slower and less manoeuvrable than aeroplanes they would enter an unequal contest in battle. This would restrict the use of the airship in reconnaissance and bombing where air opposition was unlikely to be encountered. Over the seas out of range of land-based aircraft the Naval Wing could safely carry out reconnaissance. Bombing would be part of the role of the Military Wing but this method of attack was in its infancy on the approach to the Great War. Bombing was another use but this method of attack was in its infancy before the Great War began. The Germans used them aggressively during the ensuing conflict but they were prey to fighters and eventually had to be replaced by the Gothas and in 1918 the Royal Air Force did not use airships in its Independent Bombing Force. On the other hand the Sub-Committee acknowledged that the continental nations were persisting in experiments in the use of lighter-than-air machines and that it would be wrong for Britain to abandon their use altogether particularly since it had been recommended that naval experiments should cease. No.1 Squadron of the new Military Wing would be equipped with airships for it was felt that this would suffice in permitting Britain to evaluate their use in military operations i.e., there should not be an extension of an airship building programme. The Airship Company could build two airships and together with kites they were to equip the eighth squadron of the Flying Corps.

Captive and free balloons and kites

A Sub-Committee of the CID, reporting in 1909, considering the question of aerial navigation, looked at a considerable amount of evidence with regard to balloons. Captive balloons had been in use for some time as described in Chapter 1, being used for reconnaissance and the observation of artillery fire. But being captive, troops on the ground could hide from view on reverse slopes. Only by ascending to much greater altitudes than was required for normal purposes could this deficiency be overcome. Then the observers might be unable to make out anything in detail, particularly if the ground below was obscured by low cloud. Even for artillery observation the effort needed, in terms of transport and men, to put just one balloon up in the air was considerable and the teams of horses and wagons could be ambushed or the launch site itself attacked. The Sub-

Committee therefore advised that as soon as satisfactory results could be obtained with dirigibles, expenditure on captive balloons should cease. With regard to kites, even though captive, they provided the only means of aerial observation in high winds and it was advised that two flights should be included in the Airship Squadron.

The Aircraft Factory

The advice received from the Sub-Committee was that the Army Aircraft Factory should be renamed simply the 'Aircraft Factory' (Later titled the Royal Aircraft Factory or RAF for short, the reader is asked not to confuse this establishment with the Royal Air Force.) The following functions were advocated:

1. The (advanced) higher training of mechanics of the Flying Corps.
2. Repairs and reconstruction for the Flying Corps.
3. Tests with British and foreign engines and aeroplanes.
4. Experimental work.
5. The existing work in the manufacture of hydrogen, and generally meeting the requirements of the Airship and Kite Squadron.
6. General maintenance of the factory as at present.

The chairman of the Sub-Committee was accompanied by certain members of the Technical Sub-Committee to satisfy themselves that the Factory was suitable for the performance of these functions. This would have a marked effect on the development of military aircraft in Great Britain. The Royal Navy would look to private firms for the development and provision of aircraft whereas the Royal Flying Corps favoured aircraft built in their own factory, which were stable in flight and ideal for reconnaissance purposes but not for air fighting.

British and foreign engines

Whilst the Sub-Committee believed it was vital to keep abreast of developments in aeroplane engines, foreign manufacturers attached little importance to the prospect of doing business in this country. In particular, they seemed to not want British manufacturers to learn from their experience. It was recommended that a sum of £3,500 be granted to the Aircraft Factory for the purchase of engines. They had to satisfy the Factory, following a series of tests, on the matter of horsepower, endurance, weight, fuel and oil. The makers of engines that the Government was desirous of approaching were: Anzani, Burlat, Chenu, Dansette-Gillett, Gnome, Panhard, Renault, Salmson (Canton Unné), Viale, Austro Daimler, Mercedes, NEC, ABC, Wolseley and Green.

The Aerodrome, South Farnborough

The Sub-Committee advised that improvements would need to be made to the airfield at South Farnborough

Laffan's Plain.

to cater for the requirements of the Aircraft Factory, which was experimenting with new types of aircraft. At the time of reporting there was one good flying ground at Cove Common and another at Laffan's Plain. If a passage was cleared between these two landing grounds it would increase the area in which aeroplanes could alight. If the area of Bay Hill was also cleared to become a landing ground and a passage cleared to join up with the other two, circular flights could be carried out over the combined areas. A final improvement might then be to clear a passage from Laffan's Plain to Fleet Pond.

Aeroplanes for Coastal Defence

Source: Memo of the Air Committee dated 12 April 1912

On 13 July 1912 the War Office asked the Air Committee of the Committee of Imperial Defence to make recommendations with regard to carrying out experiments in order to get the appropriate seaplane or hydro aeroplane for coastal defence. The RAFactory had been carrying out some experiments at Fleet with such an aircraft. The Superintendent of the Factory had asked the Admiralty if they wished to have this aircraft handed over to the Royal Navy. The Admiralty's response was that they did not require the existing seaplane for the time being and neither did their lordships believe it to be advisable for the Factory to continue to carry out any further experiments concurrently with the Navy's experiments at Eastchurch. They did, however, express an interest in the designs for floats and might be asking to have floats constructed at the Factory. The account of the experiments with the hydro aeroplane may be found in Chapter 7.

Whilst the Army Council did not wish to take any action contrary to the wishes of the Admiralty the matter of coastal defence, which involved the observation of fire from coastal gun batteries against hostile ships and attacks by hostile aircraft, meant that the War Office had to consider the employment of seaplanes. The Air Committee felt that both the RAFactory and the Naval Wing at Eastchurch should continue to work concurrently upon experimental work with floatplanes; indeed, the more experimentation the better, particularly on rough water. Thus there was an overlapping of responsibility for testing, producing and introducing aircraft into service. The Air Committee considered that there was a wider question i.e., the responsibility for coastal defence by aircraft and the line of delimitation between the airships and aeroplanes so employed and those working from the shore for Fleet purposes. Both the War Office and the Admiralty were asked to consider this question.

The defence of magazines, cordite factories and other vulnerable points against airship attack
Source: Memorandum of the Home Ports Defence Committee dated 19 May 1910

The Committee was asked to consider the probable nature of the attack in order to determine the best forms of defence. For these vulnerable points should they, for example, be mobile with guns mounted in airships, balloons, aeroplanes or on motor vehicles? Or should they be fixed defences consisting of earth or protective armour? They might be high-angle guns capable of being trained in a full circle close to vulnerable points. Added urgency was given to the deliberations since the Admiralty was planning to build new magazines, the design of which would depend upon the Committee's recommendations. Progress in foreign countries in the military employment of airships and aeroplanes would have to be taken into account. Advice was also sought from Colonel J.E. Capper CB, Commandant of the Balloon School, as to the possible developments in the near future.

The probable nature of attack
In 1910 aeroplanes were flimsy affairs that could carry one or two people but little else, hence attacks with bombs from aeroplanes were thought to be unlikely. Improvements would, of course, be made but for the foreseeable future effective attacks by aeroplanes on the vulnerable points could be discounted. With regard to attacks by airships the progress being made in France and Germany rendered them an immediate threat given

favourable winds and weather conditions. Colonel Capper's view was that dirigible airships could drop heavy weights from heights as great as from 4,000 to 5,000 feet; indeed, weights up to 1 ton could be dropped without the airship suffering any disability. At night and in clear weather it was easy for a balloon to be navigated and at the same time it would be very difficult for powerful searchlights to detect its presence or to follow its movement if it was in motion. Accordingly, the Home Ports Defence Committee took the view that vulnerable points should be defended against airship attack.

The nature of defence desirable
The mobile and static forms of defence of vulnerable points was considered but not thought to be sufficient in all circumstances. The answer lay in building them below ground. No form of passive defence by means of fixed armaments or overhead cover, or of mobile defence by means of guns mounted on automobiles, could be regarded as sufficient in all circumstances. In order to be effective, defence against dirigible airships should be by other airships or aeroplanes. Colonel Capper was of the opinion that aeroplanes would, in the course of the following few years, be capable of staying aloft in all weathers with a large radius of action, which would, in all probability, render attacks by dirigible airships impossible. The Committee recognized, however, that it would be impracticable to provide sufficient airships or aeroplanes to safeguard all vulnerable points by an active defence. They thought that guns mounted on automobiles would not provide an active defence against airships unless the latter were travelling at a slow speed and above or near a road. The answer lay in providing fixed armament of a special nature for vulnerable points that could not survive attack due to their construction, e.g. built below ground. This would release the nation's aerial fleet for their proper role instead of condemning them to purely local defence. It followed, therefore, that in future important magazines should be built underground but that, if this was not possible, they should be dispersed or constructed in such a manner as to be inconspicuous and difficult to identify from the air. The Admiralty wrote to the War Office drawing their attention to the hazards in storing nitro-glycerine, which could be exploded by means of a .303in bullet fired from an aeroplane or airship. No special defence was recommended for this contingency. Arrangements already existed for drowning nitro-glycerine in the process of manufacture and this means could be resorted to on the approach of hostile aircraft. Finally, the Committee recommended further experimentation at an early date with a view to obtaining information about the effect of the explosion of heavy charges on an airship. This would in turn permit the design of the most effective gun and projectile. Until then the Committee's recommendations could, at best, be

regarded as provisional. A summary of recommendations was signed by the Secretary, F. Lyon, at 2 Whitehall Gardens and dated 19 May 1910.

Vulnerability of airships of the rigid type

There were two pre-war events that demonstrated the vulnerability of rigid airships to bad weather. One happened at the airship manoeuvres held in Germany in April 1909 when a Zeppelin II was obliged to anchor on account of the force of the wind. Although the craft had been anchored to a country cart buried in the ground with a company of soldiers assisting in restraining the craft, the latter was blown away and was a complete wreck. Later a Zeppelin VII, which was constructed by a private company in order to make passenger trips, was caught in a gale. After becoming short of petrol it became unmanageable and was destroyed when it struck the ground in a forest.

In spite of these problems several European countries were spending money on airships and the amounts will serve as a guide to the importance attached to airship construction and development. In Germany the Zeppelin fund stood at £304,727 with a great deal of money coming from private subscriptions. In April 1910 the Germans had seventeen airships in service with a further seventeen under construction. The French Army Estimates for that year amounted to £126,650 with a further £60,000 to £70,000 coming from private gifts. Thus something approaching £200,000 was being spent by the French. The French War Office originally asked for £68,000 for new material but the Budget Commission of the Chamber of Deputies thought it desirable to add a further £20,000. In Italy there was a fast growing interest in aerial navigation and the amount voted for aeronautics in 1910–11 was £46,000 and in addition to this sum the Chamber voted for the expenditure of £400,000 in the form of an extraordinary grant to be spread over five years. In Britain the Army Estimates for the year 1910/11 provided for £53,631 for the balloon school and factory whilst the Royal Navy was granted the sum of £35,000.

International conference on aerial navigation

An international conference was convened in Paris in May 1910 to consider the question of aerial navigation. The proceedings of the conference dealt with such matters as the 'rule of the road', distinguishing marks, signals and certificates to aviators. International law had to take account of an entirely new phenomenon and this was the question of national airspace. Only with the coming of steerable airships and aeroplanes did nations have to consider the rights of members of one nation to fly over the territory of another and to land in it. How far up did a nation's airspace extend? In the days when aircraft, airships and balloons could only fly at low altitudes it was relatively easy to ascertain whether or not

an aircraft had entered the airspace of another country but in the future aircraft could fly at altitudes verging on space and this called into the question the ability of one nation to enforce the rules of the air as they applied to national airspace. Be that as it may the conference had, even as early as 1910, to consider the rights of aviators to navigate above foreign territory. Proposals that required careful consideration from a political and strategic point of view were already matters that had to be discussed and settled. In Britain these matters were put to the Standing Sub-Committee of the Committee of Imperial Defence and at a meeting of the Sub-Committee on 25 June 1910, with Mr Haldane in the chair, the Foreign Office gave instructions to the British delegates at the conference in Paris, which resulted in an adjournment of the conference until 29 November.

SOME CONCLUSIONS AND OBSERVATIONS ABOUT THE WORK OF THE ESHER COMMITTEE

In January 1909 Lord Esher's Sub-Committee had concluded that aerial attacks upon warships and dockyards by dirigible balloons (airships) using explosives and incendiary devices could not be dismissed as an impossible operation of war because experiments in this type of warfare were then in progress. For these reasons it was considered that Britain should have her own airships to make judgements about their use in war. Eighteen months later the Home Ports Defence Committee concluded that, given favourable wind and weather, airship attacks against vulnerable points such as magazines, were possible operations of war. Experiments in the use of aeroplanes carrying out such attacks should be discontinued by the War Office and left to private enterprise. On the other hand Colonel Capper conceived a greater role for the aeroplane particularly when it came to defending British territory against airship attack. Indeed, this was borne out during the Great War when Zeppelins were sent over southern and eastern England to bomb.

The Committee relied upon the opinion of the War Office and the Admiralty before coming to conclusions about the future course of defence policy in air matters. These involved consideration of the ability of warships to defend themselves against aerial attack, when airships and aeroplanes could replace warships in the reconnaissance role, and the best methods of attack and defence. There was also the 'thorny' question as to the division of responsibility for construction and design of aircraft and instruction in their use between the War Office and the Admiralty. The word 'thorny' in this context is important because arguments over which service should be responsible for air matters went on for years and were only to intensify when the RAF was formed on 1 April 1918. Finally, the War Office opinion was required on the role that might in future be filled by aeroplanes and airships both in civilized warfare and war against uncivilized races in countries such as the Sudan, Somaliland and the North West Frontier of India. With regard to the first question the Committee needed to know whether or not bombing civilian populations and economic targets were proper acts of war by civilized nations. With regard to the second this would become a very important role of the RAF in the inter-war years when its very existence was under threat, for its main *raison d'être* at that time lay in the policy of air control in the outposts of Empire.

In the following summary of the findings and recommendations of the Esher Committee the most interesting point is that, five years before the outbreak of the Great War, more attention was paid to airships than to aeroplanes (see sub paragraph 4):

1. The threat posed by an enemy's possession of airships could not be properly ascertained until Britain possessed them.
2. For naval use there was scouting and the destruction of naval assets, including ports, locks and lock gates.
3. There would also be a military application for which a sum of £10,000 should be added to the Army Estimates to experiment with navigable balloons of the non-rigid type, which would include the cost of all preliminary and incidental expenses and the purchase of complete airships or their component parts. Only when satisfactory results had been obtained with dirigible balloons should expenditure on captive balloons cease.
4. The experiments carried out at the military ballooning establishment with aeroplanes was to be discounted, advantage being taken of the work of private enterprise.

In the *Times* of 3 October 1910 there was a report on the French Army manoeuvres, which featured both airships and aeroplanes. Colonel Repington, the paper's military correspondent, said that the French had been impressed by earlier German airships but held the view that dirigibles of the rigid type were heavy, costly and cumbrous and should not be imitated. For tactical reconnaissance in the air and on land frontiers the aeroplane had established superiority over the airship or as the Colonel's report said, 'the superiority of aviation over the aero station'. Indeed, this was already the official policy of the French Chief of the General Staff, General Brun, as described earlier in this chapter.

Tactical reconnaissance by a Farman biplane was significant. In contrast the British Government had decided to concentrate its efforts on the airship, leaving it to private aviators and firms to carry out experiments with aeroplanes. Lord Esher was aware that the manoeuvres in Picardy had made it quite clear that the experimental stage

Farman biplane.

was over and any country that did not take advantage of the use of aeroplanes for tactical reconnaissance would be at a serious disadvantage. Aeroplanes would have to be purchased and specially selected officers trained to fly them. The Sub-Committee had between thirty and forty machines in mind for the Army at home, both regular and territorial, and overseas. But the Navy would want them too and how were the aeroplanes to be apportioned for both military and naval use?

A letter published in the press on Tuesday 4 October was from the War Office and reflected the thinking at that time for it is based on notes made by Lord Esher.

With a view to meeting army requirements it has been decided to enlarge the scope of the work hitherto carried on at the balloon school at Farnborough by affording opportunities of aeroplaning, as well as developing the training in employment of dirigibles, more fully than has hitherto been the case. The object to be kept in view will be to create a body of expert airmen, both officers and other ranks, from which units capable of acting with troops in the field can be drawn. Major Sir A Bannerman, Bart., Royal Engineers will be at the head of the new organization, having been selected to succeed Colonel J.E. Capper CB, whose tenure of appointment expires on 7th October. The officers who will form part of the reconstituted unit will not necessarily belong to the Corps of Royal Engineers. They will be selected from any branch of the Army, provided they show aptitude for aerial work. The details of establishments and organization will be published in due course in Army Orders.

It was inevitable that the Sub-Committee would come to the conclusion that officers could not simply be seconded from their normal duties on an ad hoc basis. Officers who were seconded from their primary duties could be taken back without notice so that the work of an air arm would suffer. What was needed was a corps of officers who would make flying their business and in which they would follow a career. Such officers could be trained to understand the requirements of military and naval commanders, but it was equally important that they specialized in flying both aeroplanes and airships and kept abreast of developments in aviation. As an example the work of observers was considered and, given the speed of aeroplanes, it was doubted that they could observe using field glasses satisfactorily. In the past an observer had been in a balloon and could take his time in scanning the ground below. Even if field glasses could be used in aeroplanes much practice would be needed to report on the contours of the ground and numbers and movements of the enemy. At high altitudes this would be even more difficult. These difficulties could apply equally to naval reconnaissance in reporting the movement of ships.

And so the Esher Committee concluded that a corps of aviators should be formed. Questions that needed answering included:

1. Should a school of aviation be established and if so where?
2. From what class should personnel be selected?
3. What department of state should control and organize the school?
4. Whether the officers and men of the new corps, once trained, should be handed over to the military or naval authorities for deployment and left under the control of the two services or,
5. Should these officers and men be simply loaned to the two services for manoeuvres and exercises in peacetime?
6. Under which head (financial vote) should the estimates be placed particularly with reference to the purchase of aeroplanes.

PROPOSALS FOR THE FORMATION OF A FLYING SERVICE
Source: Report of the Standing Sub-Committee of the Committee of Imperial Defence on Aerial Navigation dated 29 February 1912

Introduction
By the end of 1911 it was realized by HM Government that the use of balloons, dirigibles and aeroplanes in military campaigns and peacetime exercises had reached the point where ad hoc arrangements for further developments in the use of air power would not suffice. The Royal Engineers had done sterling work in this field but the needs of the Army and the Royal Navy called for more formal arrangements. It was necessary to have officers and men who were specialized in air matters and not ones seconded from other arms (see notes by Brook-Popham that follow). A specialized force that could concentrate on the needs of the two services was needed and the paper

actually referred to the development of aerial navigation. But this would mean reconnaissance and air warfare, which would become quickly apparent. A national corps of aviators was required and the proposals put before the Sub-Committee of the Committee of Imperial Defence were:

a. The establishment of a Naval and Military Wing of a new corps.
b. A flying school for training aviators.
c. The provision of aircraft of all types (dirigibles, balloons and aeroplanes) and
d. The provision of hangars for same.

A Technical Sub-Committee was to consider the details in conformity with the general principles by dealing with the use of dirigibles, captive balloons, free balloons and kites in war.

As compared with the progress made in the development of aerial navigation by other powers, Great Britain was relatively backward. The Sub-Committee, under the chairmanship of Lord Haldane, included such worthies as Winston Churchill who would play a pivotal role in forming an independent air force after the Great War, Lieutenant C.R. Samson who was at the cutting edge of test flying, Superintendent O' Gorman from the RAFactory and Brigadier-General D. Henderson who would command the new arm when it was formed. Short of forming a new corps the Sub-Committee could simply recommend co-ordination in the study of aviation in the Navy and the Army.

Notes by General Brooke-Popham
Source: AIR1/4/1

Brook-Popham noted the organization that preceded the formation of the Royal Flying Corps and the thinking that went behind it. He believed it was on 1 April

General Brooke-Popham.

1911 that the Air Battalion was formed consisting of a headquarters and two companies, No.1 being airships and No.2 aeroplanes. The Battalion was commanded by Major Bannerman with Brook-Smith as adjutant. Neither of these officers believed in aeroplanes and neither of them was a pilot. To the best of Brook-Popham's recollection neither of these two men had even been up in an aeroplane, at least not until March 1912. He remembered a lecture given by Bannerman at the Staff College in which he practically stated that aeroplanes would be useless for observation work in war. The pilot and observer would be so frightened and nervous that they would be unable to devote any of their attention to what was going on, on the ground. Little encouragement was therefore given from Headquarters and it was left to a bunch of enthusiasts stationed at Larkhill during the summer of 1912 to carry out work with aeroplanes with the limited means at their disposal. This was No.2 Company of the Air Battalion, which went into camp at Larkhill about the end of April. It was commanded by Major Fulton with Lieutenant (later Colonel) Connor, Lieutenant (later Colonel) Hynes, Captain Burke, who was later killed, Lieutenant Cammell, who was killed at Hendon in 1911 on a Valkyris machine, Captain Massey, Lieutenant Barrington Kennett and Lieutenant Reynolds. One of the chief difficulties to be contended with was the fact that the Air Battalion belonged to the Royal Engineers yet, with the exception of Lieutenants Barrington Kennett and Reynolds, the other officers were either gunners or infantry officers and looked upon to some extent as interlopers. This gave rise to some difficulties in matters of administration. For example, Major Fulton did not have complete command of his company. Lieutenant Cammell, being the senior RE officer, exercised a certain amount of power directly.

The machines consisted chiefly of the old box type like the Farman biplane built by the British and Colonial Aeroplane Company and fitted with a Gnome engine. Major Fulton had his own Blériot,which was an exact duplicate of the one in which Blériot flew the English Channel, and Lieutenant Cammell had a 70hp Blériot,

which was purchased in order for him to compete for the *Daily Mail* Circuit of Britain Prize. The mechanics were good but had very little knowledge either of the aeroplanes or their engines. They were allotted to individual pilots such as Burke with his Farman. Partly owing to the conditions of aviation at the time and partly due to the lack of encouragement from Headquarters there was very little effort made to co-operate with other arms except very spasmodically. The great triumph was to get into the air at all. Cammell actually started on the circuit of Britain race but one of the cylinders of his engine blew off on the second day. Reynolds also started, Brook-Popham forgot on which type, but crashed on the second day.

The requisitioning of privately owned aircraft in time of war

In these very early days of flying some enthusiasts owned their own aeroplanes and the government felt that all serviceable aircraft should be made available for operational use whether publicly or privately owned. At the fourth meeting of the Air Committee held on 3 December 1912 the Rt Hon. J.R. Seely, the Secretary of State for War, raised the matter of requisitioning privately owned aircraft in the event of war. The Air Committee had to consider the desirability of increasing the number of aircraft at the disposal of the Royal Flying Corps on a declaration of war. There was also the matter of the control of privately owned aircraft that might be used in war in ways detrimental to the interests of Great Britain. There was, however, some doubt as to whether or not private aircraft could be legally requisitioned at a time of war and the question was referred to the Treasury Solicitor. The latter replied that aircraft could not, at that time, be requisitioned under Section 115(2) of the Army Act and suggested that, following the precedent of 1909 when the Act was amended so as to make it applicable to motor cars, the difficulty might be met by the insertion of appropriate provision in the next Army (Annual) Act Appendix III. This suggestion was brought to the notice of the Sub-Committee which was considering the control of aircraft and on the recommendation of members, the Secretary of State undertook to endeavour to have the suitable provision inserted in the Army (Annual) Act for 1913. It was then necessary to consider how these powers could be applied. It was agreed that the Central Flying School (CFS) should keep a register of all privately owned aircraft that might usefully be purchased for the use of the Royal Flying Corps in the case of emergency. At the 122nd meeting of the Committee of Imperial Defence on 6 February, free balloons and airships were added to this proposed list but the Commandant of the CFS explained to the Air Committee that he did not consider himself in a favourable position to keep such a list up

Blériot monoplane 1910.

to date and it was felt that the Superintendent of the RAFactory might be in a better position. The Director of the Air Department of the Admiralty undertook to render assistance to the Superintendent to help compile the first list, which would entail visits to various aerodromes and manufacturing establishments.

CONSIDERATIONS OF GENERAL POLICY

Strategic and tactical considerations

It has been mentioned that Great Britain was lagging behind in the development of the use of aircraft in war. France at that time possessed some 250 efficient military aeroplanes and 150 military airmen, with a further 80 civilians and several airships. Germany possessed fewer military aeroplanes but a much larger number in civilian hands together with 20 airships and Italy had 22 military aeroplanes. In contrast, Great Britain possessed fewer than a dozen efficient aeroplanes and only two small airships. The Sub-Committee recognized the importance of aeroplanes in military inventories for the future. Taking off from and landing on grass had been possible from the earliest powered flight but there were problems to be overcome in taking off from and landing on both water and naval ships in various sea states. In particular, the Technical Sub-Committee had to consider both the strategic and tactical use of aircraft with reference to their use in coastal defence while operating from land bases by operating with destroyers and submarine-boats and for general reconnaissance. Over land aeroplanes were expected to co-operate directly with land forces to further the land campaign.

It was acknowledged that aeroplanes were well past the purely experimental stage and that too much reliance had been placed on the pioneering work of private enterprise. Hence there was a need for the government to be involved, making the development of air power a matter of national policy. The general principles to be complied with were:

a. That the organization adopted should provide establishments that were both adequate for present requirements and to be sufficiently elastic to permit considerable expansion in the future.
b. The organization should be capable of absorbing and utilizing the whole of the aeronautical resources of the country. This would include the work of private entrepreneurs to whom every encouragement was to be given and civilian flyers were to be induced to join the proposed corps. All combatant officers in the new corps should be practical flying men. With regard to aerodromes it was to be encouraged that existing ones be made available for military purposes.
c. It was understood that the needs of the Army and the Navy would be quite different but that the aerial resources of the nation should be available, if required, to support either a purely naval war or land war. Hence both the naval air and army air requirements should be met by a flying corps that comprised a Naval and Military Wing. This would permit the parallel technical development peculiar to sea and land warfare.
d. Experimental work in all branches of the new Corps should be co-ordinated.

General outline of policy recommended

The Sub-Committee made the following recommendations. In the first place they gave a name to the new corps, which was to be styled the Flying Corps. The Corps was to be funded and administered by the Admiralty and War Office and the Corps would supply the necessary personnel for a Naval and Military Wing and for a Central Flying School. After initial training, entrants to the Corps would proceed to the Naval Flying School at Eastchurch or one of the military aeroplane squadrons as appropriate for specialized training, or pass into the Reserve of the Flying Corps.

There was to be no attempt at that stage to fix the establishment for the Corps as a whole, only for the Naval and Military Wings. It was recognized that certain naval and military personnel were receiving a fee for maintaining flying proficiency but were still on the strengths of their ships or regiments or had joined on conditions of service resembling those of the Special Reserve of the Army. None of these officers were serving on continuous engagements in the flying role. Naval and Army officers and all civilians who were candidates for commissions in the Corps would first have to obtain their Royal Aero Club Certificates in return for which entrants would be remunerated by the payment of 75/-. The Army Aircraft Factory would be named simply the Aircraft Factory, which would be responsible for the higher training of mechanics for the

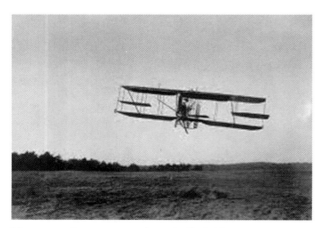

The ground is quite rough on Laffan's Plain.

Corps, the reconstruction of aeroplanes, repair work for the Flying Corps, tests with British and foreign engines and aeroplanes of the latest design, experimental work and finally there was the Central Flying School. There existed an Aeronautical Advisory Committee, which was to continue with experimental and research work and it was proposed that officers representing the Central Flying School and the Naval and Military Wings should join that Committee.

The maintenance of private enterprise in the field of aeronautics was acknowledged. The objects were to provide not only a reserve of flying men in an emergency but also to stimulate invention and public interest in flying. The private sector would also provide aerodromes, landing grounds and aircraft sheds at convenient intervals throughout the country without which cross-country flights would be impossible. Since it was known that the majority of civilian aerodromes were in financial difficulty it was proposed that the Corps pay for landing rights and the use of sheds.

Finally, it was proposed that a permanent consultative Committee should be appointed to which questions could be addressed in connection with flying affecting both the Admiralty and the War Office. It was further proposed that this committee be titled the 'Air Committee', a permanent Sub-Committee of the Committee of Imperial Defence analogous to the Navy's 'Home Ports Defence Committee' and the Army's 'Overseas Defence Committee'. The suggested composition of the Air Committee was:

The Parliamentary Under Secretary of State for War (Chairman)
The Commandant of the Central Flying School
The Officer Commanding of the Naval Wing of the Flying Corps
The Commandant of the Military Wing of the Flying Corps
The Director of the Operations Division, War Staff, Admiralty
The Director of Military Training, General Staff, War Office
The Director of Fortifications and Works, War Office
The Superintendent of the Aircraft Factory
Joint Secretaries (a member of the Secretariat of the Committee of Imperial Defence and an officer of the Naval Flying Staff)

THE CENTRAL FLYING SCHOOL

Situation
The Sub-Committee recommended that the Central Flying School should be established on Salisbury Plain, on ground south-east of Upavon, the contract for the purchase of which has been signed. This ground must be regarded essentially as a flying ground. It should only be used for the training of troops insofar as that training interferes in no way with the work of the Central Flying School.

The Technical Sub-Committee paid a visit to this site and are satisfied that it is entirely suited for the purposes of the Central Flying School in every respect. The technical members of the Sub-Committee, who visited the site twice, in order to view it under varying conditions, reported as follows:

> This area is in every way suitable for the proposed purpose. It is better than any British aviation ground with which the members of the Committee are acquainted. A certain amount of ground is at present under the plough, but there is nothing to prevent the formation of an excellent surface for rolling over very large tracts.

Apart from its excellence as a flying ground, however, the site selected presents the following advantages:

a. It is situated in a lonely spot several miles from a railway station and is therefore not liable to the inconvenience and danger of attracting large crowds of spectators.
b. The nature of the surrounding country is such that good landing places are available over a very wide area.
c. A good road runs through the centre of the aerodrome affording all necessary transport facilities.
d. The presence of large numbers of troops undergoing training on Salisbury Plain offers facilities for preliminary training in military reconnaissance.
e. It is conveniently situated with regard to the existing aerodrome; at Aldershot, &c for the commencement of cross-country flights, and is not too far distant from the sea at Portsmouth and Portland.

Number and length of courses of instruction
The Sub-Committee recommend that there should be three courses of instruction at the Central Flying School during the year, each course to last four months, which is considered to include a sufficient margin of time for leave of absence and spells of bad weather. There appears to be no reason to suppose that one season of the year is less favourable than another for training in flying. It is possible that in summer there are more days during some part of which flying is possible. In winter, on the other hand, there are apt to be less days during the whole of which it is possible to fly. The Commandant of the Central Flying School should be given discretionary power as to the standard to be obtained by individuals before graduation.

Syllabus of the course of instruction

The training to be carried out should include:

a. Progressive instruction in the art of flying.
b. Instruction in the general principles of mechanics and the construction of engines and aeroplanes.
c. Instruction in meteorology.
d. Training in observation from the air.
e. Instruction in navigation and flying by compass.
f. Training in cross-country flights.
g. Photography from aircraft.
h. Signalling by all methods.
j. Instruction in types of warships of all nations.

The naval and military flying establishments should undertake the more advanced training in observation and the transmission of intelligence. The Sub-Committee recommend that the Staff for the Flying School should be selected as soon as possible, and should be formed into a Committee to draw up the syllabus for the first course of instruction for submission to the War Office.

Numbers to be trained

It is estimated that the number of fliers required for the Navy is forty a year. To provide the war establishment for the seven Aeroplane Squadrons that are considered necessary for our Expeditionary Force, 182 office flyers and 182 non-commissioned officer flyers are required. This will entail passing through the Central Flying School one quarter of this total number annually, if it is assumed that under present conditions a flier can hardly be expected to remain at active aeroplane work for more than four years. If in excess of actual Naval and Military requirements, a margin is allowed of, say, 25 per cent, for pupils undergoing instruction who fail to obtain certificates of proficiency either through sustaining injuries or through loss of nerve, the total service requirements as regards the annual intake of pupils at the school is as follows:

One quarter military war establishment of fliers	91
Royal Navy say 40	131
Add 25%	33
Total	164
Allowing for 15 civilians per year	179

Having regard to the foregoing considerations the Sub-Committee are of the opinion that, for the immediate future, accommodation should be provided for sixty pupils at the Central Flying School each term. As these numbers are liable to be increased, when the requirements of the Army, other than those of the Expeditionary Force are decided, the school should be readily capable of expansion.

Staff

The Sub-Committee recommend that the staff of the Central Flying School should be as follows:

1 Commandant
1 Secretary (paymaster RN)
1 Meteorological expert
1 Medical Officer
1 Quartermaster (military)
1 Store keeper
1 Instructor – theory and construction
1 Engineer – for engines
3 Mechanists
20 Mechanics and labourers

Five instructional flights, each:

1 officer instructor
2 mechanics or petty officer fliers
4 riggers (or carpenters)
4 fitters (or ERA)

Purchase of aeroplanes

The Sub-Committee have obtained sanction for the purchase of the following 23 aeroplanes for the Central Flying School, and deliveries will commence as from 30th April 1912.

A Flight	3 Bristol 50 Gnome engine biplanes, to be transferred from the present Air Battalion
B Flight	2 twin F-Type Short biplanes, with Gnome engines
	2 single F-type Short biplanes, with Gnome engines
	1 Short-Tractor biplane with 70hp Gnome engine
C Flight	2 Flanders, two-seater monoplanes
	3 Roe, two-seater biplanes
D Flight	1 Deperdussin, two-seater, 70hp, Gnome engine; monoplane
	1 Deperdussin school machine, 60hp, Anzani engine, monoplane
	3 80hp Canton Unné Bréguet, biplanes
E Flight	2 Nieuport, 50 Gnome, two-seater, monoplanes
	2 Blériot, 35hp Anzani, single-seater monplanes) Substituted for 3 Bristol
	1 Blériot, 50 Gnome, single-seater monoplane) monoplanes in the list previously approved

Aeroplanes, balloons and buildings at the Central Flying School (CFS)

The Sub-Committee considered the matter of the provision of aeroplanes for the CFS and stipulated that

The first course at the CFS (note the mixture of Army and Navy uniforms).

the makers were to supply a stress diagram or skeleton drawing showing the calculated load on each strut and tie wire in various stress situations. The landing chassis had to be capable of being driven round Laffan's Plain at 15–20mph without damage and there had to be a margin of engine power beyond that for normal flight speed and the aircraft had to have duplicate controls in all cases except single-seaters. Finally, if required, one representative of the Navy or Army must be taught to have complete control for every machine built.

Major Sir A. Bannerman, Bart., Commandant of the Army Air Battalion, pointed to the value of cross-country flights in free balloons as a means of training aeroplane fliers in observation, map reading and finding their way. Those members of the Sub-Committee who were fliers pointed out that these arts are not easily taught in an aeroplane, as the attention of the flier, particularly while learning to fly, is engrossed in the management of his machine. The Sub-Committee therefore recommended that the course of instruction at the CFS should include flights in free balloons, as long as these were available, i.e., no new balloons should be constructed for this purpose at that time.

The Sub-Committee was advised that permanent buildings were more economical than temporary ones. In any case the climatic conditions encountered on Salisbury Plain called for permanent ones but the Committee pointed out that rapid expansion of the CFS could be expected and that buildings of a temporary nature could be constructed quickly to meet the growing demand for accommodation without prejudice to the construction of permanent accommodation at a later date. Early in 1912 approval was given for the construction of temporary barracks, sheds and workshops and a small hospital at an estimated cost of £21,000. Plans and specifications had been readied and tenders invited. With regard to motor transport the Sub-Committee recommended that complete War Transport for two flights of aeroplanes should be provided for the CFS.

The foregoing is an indication of the importance the Sub-Committee attached to the commencement of operations at the CFS on the earliest possible date. The buildings were to be ready for occupation by 30 June 1912 but this was not to delay the opening of the school since canvas tents and sheds could be used. Given that the instructional staff would need a few weeks to assemble, tune up and test fly the new aeroplanes it was confidently expected that the first course could be completed before the end of the year.

THE NAVAL WING OF THE FLYING CORPS

Introduction

Today the Fleet Air Arm provides the air component of a fleet at sea. Aircraft operating from aircraft carriers are clearly ones that 'should be controlled by a fleet commander in pursuance of naval operations. Since they are shipborne they are maintained and armed afloat and should be flown by naval aircrew. But there is a grey area, notably when aircraft operate from shore bases over the sea for maritime reconnaissance, anti-submarine operations, anti-shipping attacks and convoy protection. Should those aircraft belong to the Admiralty and operate on the orders of fleet commanders or to the Army, or after 1 April 1918, to the Royal Air Force/ There was to be a considerable amount of controversy between the Royal Navy and its sister services in the years that lay ahead and these questions served to sour inter-service relations. In the early 1920s the Chief of the Air Staff, Air Marshal Hugh Trenchard, managed to keep all airborne activities under the control of the Royal Air Force since it was argued that the RAF's business was flying, even to the extent that naval aircraft aboard naval vessels on the high seas were commanded and maintained by RAF officers and technical personnel. Even serving naval officers kept their naval ranks but carried the corresponding RAF rank whilst serving with the Naval Air Arm. The reader should be mindful of these questions as the Sub-Committee of the Committee of Imperial Defence proposed the organization of the Naval and Military Wings of the Flying Corps.

Provisional organization

The Sub-Committee recommended that the Naval Wing should be established at the Naval Flying School, Eastchurch. Pending the establishment of the CFS, Eastchurch could provide elementary flying training for navy fliers and continue with experimental work in the development of aeronautics. Once the Flying Corps was 'up and running' the Naval Flying School could concentrate on specialized training of naval ranks and ratings, and of selected civilians in naval air work. There was a pressing need for experiments to continue in the development of hydro aeroplanes and in flying off and alighting on ships and water in various sea states. At that point in time the Sub-Committee could not forecast what the role of aeroplanes would be in naval warfare, thus any arrangements made must be provisional.

Personnel

For administrative convenience it was proposed that the staff of the Naval Flying School should be borne on the books of HMS *Actæon* and come under the orders of the captain of that shore station. It was proposed that the Headquarters of the naval wing and the staff of the school should be as follows:

1 Commanding Officer who will also act as Chief Experimental Officer

6 Officers as instructional and experimental officers (three of these were already acting and the remainder were under training)

1 Engineer lieutenant in charge of aeroplanes, engines and stores (then under training)

1 Medical Officer

1 Carpenter warrant officer in charge of all repairs to machines, and as instructor to carpenter ratings (then under training)

1 Carpenter rating as instructor (then under training)

7 Carpenter ratings (three under training)

1 Engine room artificer as instructor – in charge of naval operations.

5 Engine room artificers (three under training)

2 Electricians (one under training)

4 Privates RMLI as officers' servants (the two already at Eastchurch were to be instructed in aviation since they already had some knowledge having spent eight months at the base.)

1 Officers' cook

1 Cook

1 Cook's mate

4 Pensioners as labourers for cleaning machines, sheds, &c and for holding aeroplanes when being started.

This list was to be subject to expansion as required.

Aeroplanes

In order to avoid delay the Prime Minister's approval had been sought and the Admiralty was able to go ahead with ordering aeroplanes. The list is interesting in showing the degree of dependence on imported machines with Short Brothers supplying all the domestically produced ones. The final list of aeroplanes, hydro-aeroplanes and floats was as follows:

Instructional and practice machines:

a. One twin-engined biplane (then in use) from Messrs Short Bros — £1400

b. One new twin-engined Short biplane from Messrs Short Bros — £2084

c One 70hp Gnome single-engined biplane from Messrs Short Bros — £1184

d. One Chenu-engined Bréguet biplane from the Bréguet Co., France — £1400

e. One Nieuport 50hp two-seater from Nieuport Co., France — £1040

f. One Short monoplane from Messrs Short Bros — £820

g. One Deperdussin monoplane two-seater 70hp from Deperdussin Co. — 1080

h. One Etrich monoplane from Austria — 1500

j. Floats for aeroplanes

k. Six sets of floats (Short Bros) (safety device for practice flying over water) — 300

Experimental and service machines:

a. Two hydro-aeroplane machines, one of the biplane and one of the monoplane type, with twin engines to be ordered from Short Bros at once — 4500

b. Six hydro aeroplanes to be tendered for at once by English firms (to fulfil the requirements as specified in Schedule I) — 20,000

c. Six further hydro-aeroplanes to be ordered from the firms making the most of satisfactory machines

Tenders had been called for all of the above aircraft except those listed at b. and c. of the experimental and service machines above. The immediate supply of these machines was not a matter of urgency. Experiments with hydro-aeroplanes were then in their infancy there having been few successful flights from water. Successful flights had mainly been from still water. The purchase of the six hydro-planes listed above would have to wait until the experiments with the two hydro-aeroplanes (above) had been successful. The imported machines listed above would have to be assembled by the respective firms and flown for one hour before acceptance. The Sub-Committee considered the desirability of testing a number of types to arrive at those most suitable for naval service and that orders should be placed accordingly.

Buildings, works and land

The Sub-Committee recommended that the sum of £7,250 be spent on lands, buildings and works and that £8,000 be spent on the general cost of maintenance of the Naval Flying School. The last item on the list of heads of authorized expenditure referred to the encouragement to be given to designers, constructors and engine makers in making improvements and in experimentation. The results of any experiments carried out were to be communicated to the Aeronautical Advisory Committee. The Sub-Committee confirmed the recommendation of a Standing Sub-Committee that six large sheds measuring 60ft × 70ft × 15ft be provided together with three large portable canvas sheds at a grand total of £,800. Fixed sheds were preferable at Eastchurch due to its exposed position, the strength of the wind rendering the use of portable ones unfit for permanent use. The three portable sheds could be used for aeroplanes employed for experimental work on the water off Bruntwick Island as well as emergency use in actual warfare. This would have the further advantage of accustoming those, under training, to the use of these sheds that they would use in actual warfare. The expenditure on land, buildings and works in connection with the Naval Flying School were estimated to be £7,250 and negotiations were already in hand for the purchase of the land required.

Eastchurch aerodrome
As the development of aeroplanes proceeded apace on the approach of war in 1914 the suitability of sites chosen for aerodromes assumed as great an importance as the suitability of aeroplanes. Eastchurch aerodrome was visited by representatives of the Sub-Committee and it was found to meet the standards required for a school of moderate dimensions. The Royal Aero Club held the land on a long lease but if the airfield was likely to serve as a permanent base then the matter of obtaining the freehold became an issue since permanent buildings would have to be erected. It was felt that securing the freehold rights for the airfield with additional land for development could be obtained at that time on favourable terms.

The development of the Admiralty Air Department
Source: AIR1/674/21/6/59 (See Appendix 'C' for the Duties assigned to Officers of the Air Department in March 1914)

The Naval Wing of the Flying Corps was the responsibility of the Admiralty and the need for a dedicated naval department was recognized by their Lordships in 1912 and a seasoned aviator, Commander Murray F. Sueter, was the obvious choice for the department's first director. The work of the department was significantly different from that of the Military Wing since the Admiralty decided that aircraft, engines and equipment should be obtained from private firms. The Army obtained its aircraft from the Aircraft Factory, which produced aeroplanes that were inherently stable and thus suitable for reconnaissance. This meant that the Air Department had to be staffed by personnel who were technically competent. The staff officers would need to deal with

questions relating to the design of aircraft and engines in drawing up air specifications before contracts could be placed, something the Aircraft Factory did for the Army. The responsibilities of the Air Department were as follows:

1. Designs, details of construction, trials and experiments and inventions relating to aeroplanes, airships and air machinery and all gear in connection therewith
2. Instructional training and practices
3. Books and instructions relating to air matters
4. Departmental correspondence with the War Office, Central Flying School and Naval and Military Wings of the Flying Corps

On 30 December 1913 the post of Inspecting Captain of Aircraft was created and filled by Captain F.R. Scarlett. With his Central Air Office at Sheerness he oversaw the administration of and discipline at air stations. The Central Air Office thus relieved the Air Department of much of its administrative work, thus reducing the latter to a purely technical department. The composition of the Department was virtually that at the outbreak of war. There were a few changes of personnel but its composition remained substantially the same until the beginning of 1915 when the post of Inspecting Captain of Aircraft and the Central Air Office was abolished and the staff absorbed into the Admiralty staff.

The use of airships for the Navy
The enormous advantage that the airship had over the aeroplane was that it could remain airborne for days if required making it ideally suited for reconnaissance but airships operating over water would have to be reliable. Any limit that might be imposed on the duration of flight of an airship might arise from gas leakage, rations, crew fatigue and adverse weather. On the other hand airships would be very vulnerable if attacked by aeroplanes, which were faster and more manoeuvrable. Clearly airships were ideally suited to maritime reconnaissance beyond the range of land-based aircraft. The rigid as opposed to the non-rigid types were more suitable since the gap between the inner and outer envelopes left a space for air, which prevented expansion and contraction of gas due to variations in temperature. When it came to mooring an airship, again the rigid rather than the non-rigid fared better. Engines would need to be powerful enough to drive the airship at the highest possible speed and to lift the number of crewmen needed to provide duty and off-duty watches. When it came to navigation the rigid airship was preferable as a position could be built in the frame on top of the airship between the gas bags from which to take astronomical readings. In a non-rigid type the readings would have to be taken from the car suspended below the balloon when the latter would

obscure the sky above. The Sub-Committee advised that where great size was required then the rigid type is best. The example of German airship development at this time showed that their rigid airships had been experimented with over water and used floating sheds to house them whereas the non-rigid types were used exclusively for military purposes over land.

Clearly then the Sub-Committee regarded the rigid airship as ideally suited to reconnaissance or 'scouting' and this should be their principal use. In clear weather the visible horizon from just 1,000ft was extended from some 12 miles (from the deck of a ship) to 40 miles and from 2,000ft to 60 miles. The cost of a dirigible suitable for naval purposes was estimated to be £35,000 compared with £80,000 for a destroyer and £400,000 for a 3rd Class cruiser. From the point of view of cost, speed and visible horizon the rigid airship scored highly. If fitted with wireless, the Sub-Committee was advised, even greater benefit would be achieved. Yet, In spite of the foregoing the prospects for the favourable employment of airships for reconnaissance were not of the magnitude that would justify the cost involved. The Sub-Committee were therefore of the opinion that naval experiments should be confined to the development of aeroplanes and hydro-aeroplanes without prejudice to revisiting the matter of airships in light of foreign developments in this field.

THE MILITARY WING OF THE FLYING CORPS

General principles of organization

This section of the Sub-Committee's report did not consider the requirements of the Army for an air element beyond the Expeditionary Force save to say that the Military Wing must be capable of considerable extension. All branches of aeronautics would be included, including aeroplanes, airships and kites. Under this scheme the Air Battalion of the Royal Engineers would cease to exist and its materiel and personnel would be absorbed as far as required in the Flying Corps. It was advised that the administration of the Military Wing should be by the War Office. The next section reveals the roles that aeroplanes would be required to fill. It shows that in 1912, even before aircraft of all descriptions were to be used in combat, they would not just be used for reconnaissance:

a. Reconnaissance
b. Prevention of an enemy's reconnaissance
c. Inter-communication
d. Observation of artillery fire
e. Infliction of damage on the enemy

These roles were not spelt out in detail but one can see that even in those early days the strategic and tactical use of air power added an entirely new dimension to the prosecution of war. Reconnaissance would lead to air fighting. It could be argued that one side in a battle could deny enemy reconnaissance using ground fire but aeroplanes would prove very effective in shooting down the enemy's reconnaissance aeroplanes. Intercommunication using aeroplanes would prove very effective with message dropping and message picking up techniques being developed. Observation of artillery fire was an obvious use of the aeroplane. From the very earliest days of flying balloons had been used for this purpose. The infliction of damage on an enemy could be achieved both tactically and strategically and in the Great War both types of air operation would feature. The following headings serve to outline the several aspects of the organization:

1. **Peace Establishment** Having provided the requisite number of trained personnel for the war establishment there was also the question of wastage in time of war, i.e., there must not simply be one flyer for each aeroplane. This meant building up a Reserve and the time required to achieve the numbers required needed to be calculated. The aim should be to maintain a peace establishment of fliers for seven squadrons equal to the war establishment. It was hoped that, eventually it would be possible to draw up a more economical peace establishment when the Reserve of the Flying Corps had been developed sufficiently to enable the Military Wing to count on an effective organized Reserve.

2. **Distribution of Aeroplane Squadrons** It was felt, by the Sub-Committee, that it would be advantageous if one squadron were situated on Salisbury Plain within reach of the Central Flying School and one at Aldershot near the Aircraft Factory.

3. **Personnel** NCOs and air mechanics would be required as engine drivers, fitters, carpenters, smiths, sailmakers, riggers etc., The term mechanic was applied to men of the flying corps below the rank of petty officer or sergeant. Selected NCOs and air mechanics should also be trained as flyers. To provide these personnel it would probably be necessary to rely largely on direct enlistment except, perhaps, flyers.

4. **Secondment and Enlistment** Although the period of enlistment recommended was four years, it was noted that the Sub-Committee were not in a position to recommend a definite period of Reserve service. On completion of the period of continuous service, re-engagement should be allowed from year to year, or transfer to the Reserve of the Flying Corps on the recommendation of the Commanding Officer of the Military Wing, or of the Commandant of the CFS. Commissioned officers joining the Flying Corps should be seconded and other ranks transferred. Men wishing to enlist in the Corps for non-flying duties

should be finally approved by the officer commanding the Military Wing, or the Commandant of the CFS.

5. **Aeroplanes** The total number of aeroplanes required for the seven squadrons of the military division would be eighty-four. The completion of these squadrons, however, and the training of flyers for them at the CFS must occupy some considerable time. The purposes for which aeroplanes would be required in land warfare were spelt out on page 38.

Having considered the organization of the aeronautical forces of France and other powers, so far as information was available, the Sub-Committee were of the opinion that the establishments laid down below would provide a suitable organization for the Expeditionary Force of six divisions and one cavalry division:

a. A headquarters
b. 7 Aeroplane squadrons, each providing twelve aeroplanes
c. 1 Airship and kite squadron, providing 2 airships and 2 flights of kites
d. Flying Corps workshop

Administration The Sub-Committee recommended that the administration of the Military Wing should be carried out by the War Office.

Flyers required for Seven Aeroplane Squadrons
Up to the present time the Sub-Committee had only attempted to train officers as flyers. It was now proposed to train non-commissioned officers and men as well. It was considered that the minimum number of of trained flyers should be two per aeroplane. Of these one should be an officer and, in the case of one-seat machines, both should be officers. For purposes of calculation, however, one officer and one non-commissioned officer were allowed. The number of flyers on this basis would be:

Commanders	7 Officers
Sergeants	7
3 Sections	84 Officers and 84 NCOs
Total	91 Officers and 91 NCOs

To allow for a reserve the number of officers and NCOs should be 100 per cent thus doubling the figures above. The organization of the aeronautical forces of France and other powers had been considered by the Sub-Committee and this helped them to advise on the equipping of the air component of the Expeditionary Force. The complete war establishment of a squadron is shown in Appendix D:

Flyers required by the Flying Corps
Up to that time only officers had been trained as flyers. The Sub-Committee believed that both NCOs and men should also be trained. The minimum number of trained flyers should be two, of whom one should be an officer but in the case of single-seat aeroplanes both should be officers. For the purposes of calculating establishments, one officer and one NCO per aeroplane would be used. On this basis the number of flyers required by the 7 aeroplane squadrons would be:

	Officers	NCOs
Commanders	7	–
Sergeants	–	7
3 Sections	84	84
	91	91

The wastage rate was then calculated using an expectation of 100% casualties over a six-month period and thus 182 Officers and the same number of NCOs would have to be recruited.

Flying Corps squadrons – war and peace establishments, personnel and deployment
The Sub-Committee advised that the peace establishment of the Flying Corps should be equal to that required in war so that the air element of the Expeditionary Force could become operational without delay. It was envisaged that there might, in the future, be commitments outside that of the Expeditionary Force but these could not be foreseen at that time. What was important was to equip the seven squadrons with aeroplanes and train the flyers. Eventually it was hoped that a more economical peace establishment could be drawn up and this could happen once a Flying Corps Reserve had been built up, providing a pool of trained personnel that could be mobilized in the event of war. The matter of officers manning had been touched on; with regard to NCOs and air mechanics there would be a requirement for personnel in the trades of engine driver (not the railway variety), fitters, carpenters, sail makers, riggers etc., recruited by direct enlistment. Of these selected NCOs and air mechanics should also be trained as fliers. The period of enlistment recommended was for four years but the Sub-Committee was not then in a position to recommend a period of Reserve service. After the initial period had been served re-engagement should be allowed from year to year in the Corps or transfer to the Reserve. Commissioned officers joining the Corps should be seconded and other ranks transferred. Men wishing to join the Corps in a non-flying capacity should have their enlistment approved by the officer commanding the Military Wing or the Commandant of the Central Flying School. With regard to the deployment of the squadrons it was advised that one should be on Salisbury Plain, close to the Central Flying School at

Upavon. Another should be at Aldershot close to the Aircraft Factory.

Aeroplanes

The total of eighty-four aeroplanes needed for the Military Wing had to be purchased and manned. This would take, in the words of the Sub-Committee, 'some considerable time'. A CID paper, AN10 had already received the approval of the Prime Minister sanctioning the expenditure by the War Office estimated to be £28,000. At that time orders had been issued for the production of these aircraft and further orders would be forthcoming during the course of 1912. The types and numbers recommended by the Sub-Committee were:

1 Nieuport monoplane 100hp, 3-seater
1 Nieuport monoplane 70hp, 2-seater
1 Deperdussin monoplane 100hp, 3-seater
1 Deperdussin monoplane 70hp, 2-seater
2 Flanders monoplane 2-seater
2 Bréguet biplanes, 100hp, 3-seater
2 Brégeut biplanes 80hp, 2-seater
2 Henry Farman biplanes 70hp (or more) 3-seater
1 'B' Type Aircraft Factory (to be made by the factory)
1 'B' Type Aircraft Factory (to be made by British and Colonial Aeroplane Co.)
1 Cody biplane, 120 hp
1 Martin-Handasyde 60hp, 2-seater
2 Blériot monoplane 50hp, single-seater

Sheds

It was advised that portable sheds should be provided for each aeroplane as it was ordered. These would be useful in the field and therefore suited to the needs of an expeditionary force. Permanent sheds should be provided at the headquarters of squadrons once those locations had been agreed.

The use of airships for military purposes

The Sub-Committee had given careful consideration to the question of whether airships should still be used for military purposes. They had the advantage of hearing the evidence of Major Sir A. Bannerman, Bart., the Commandant of the Army Air Battalion, on the subjects of airships balloons and kites. He believed that the airship possessed the great advantage over the aeroplane in military warfare in being able to receive messages by wireless telegraphy; it was also able to transmit to greater distances. It was observed that France and Germany could establish permanent sheds or shelters at convenient intervals throughout the country, where their airships could seek refuge in bad weather and they were therefore able to make better use of dirigibles than this country whose expeditionary

force was more likely to be employed overseas. It was hoped that the means would be found for overcoming Britain's difficulties and in this respect the country was experimenting in this direction and there were prospects for success. On a general view of the foregoing considerations the Sub-Committee was of the opinion that any immediate extension of the existing equipment of airships was unnecessary so far as the requirements of the Expeditionary Force was concerned. And, as stated in paragraph 89, this report does not deal with military requirements other than those of the Expeditionary Force. Having regard, however, to the persistence of all the great continental nations in experiments with this type of aircraft, they thought it would be undesirable for the Army to abandon entirely the use of airships, more especially in view of their recommendation that naval experiment should cease. They recommended, therefore, that the present Airship Company, furnishing two airships, together with kite equipment, should be retained and should become an eighth squadron of the Flying Corps.

Captive and free balloons and kites

A Sub-Committee of the Committee of Imperial Defence, which considered the whole question of aerial navigation in 1909 and took a considerable amount of evidence, reported as follows with regard to balloons.

> Captive balloons have for many years formed part of the regular equipment of all modern armies. The principal view for which they can be employed in land warfare are reconnaissance and observation of artillery fire. It has been pointed out, however, that their value for reconnaissance purposes is limited by the fact that troops on the reverse slopes of hills of moderate elevation and steepness and are entirely concealed from observers in a captive balloon, unless they rise to a great height and, in the latter case their view will frequently be obstructed by clouds. In hilly country, therefore, their value is small, though in flat country their usefulness has been proved. The advantages claimed for balloons in the observation of artillery fire are somewhat uncertain.

In this connection the evidence showed that the balloon equipment required a somewhat bulky transport, and it seems very doubtful, therefore, that it would be practicable to attach them to more than a few heavy batteries. (See photographs in Chapter 1.) The recommendation of the Sub-Committee was as follows: 'As soon as satisfactory results have been obtained with dirigible balloons the expenditure on captive balloons should cease.' With regard to kites the Sub-Committee observed that, for military purposes:

Kites are employed as a complement to captive balloons inasmuch as they could only ascend in windy weather, which captive balloons could not. Their functions were identical to those of captive balloons. The information before the Sub-Committee differs in no way from the above. Emphasis has been laid, however, on the value of free balloons as a means of training flying men in finding their way. Airships are also useful for this purpose and, apart from their possible value in war, the Sub-Committee consider that either airships or balloons, if available, would be of assistance in the training of the Flying Corps in peace. Kites form at present, the only means of aerial observation included in the Airship Squadron of the Flying Corps.

Transport The Sub-Committee recommended that transport as laid down in the War Establishments should be purchased for each flight on its establishment.

Early organization of the RFC
Source: Memoranda of Major H. Musgrove DSO, RE, RFC dated 3 February 1913

Only eighteen months after Major Musgrove turned his thoughts to the organization of the RFC the new service went to war. He had hoped that one manual would suffice but on reflection he opted for two, a war manual for the Military Wing of the RFC and a training manual for both wings. The former would cover the strategic and tactical employment of the Military Wing together with war administration. Details of piloting aircraft would appear in the training manual. The Naval Wing would compile their own war manual and Standing Orders were in the process of preparation. Standing Orders for the CFS had by then been issued. The training manuals of both wings were to include the maintenance of engines, aircraft, instruments etc. Musgrove left it to the CFS to compile most of the training manual but personally undertook to compile the sections dealing with airships and kites. So important was the proper maintenance of engines and aircraft that he believed that the most important engines and each type of aircraft warranted specialist handbooks. Indeed, instructions for the maintenance of the Gnome and Renault engines had already been translated from French.

Matters concerning the handling of aircraft, both on the ground and in the air are, today, taken for granted but Musgrove had to spell it out. Reconnaissance was going to be primary task of aircraft and observers had to know what to report upon and the forms of reporting. What, for example, would be the role of photography and wireless? At what height should the reconnaissance pilot fly and what action should be taken if fired upon from the ground? What actions should be taken on meeting a

friendly or an unfriendly aircraft in the air, which, in turn, called upon the skill of aircraft recognition and all these matters had to be considered in relation to the operation of airships and kites. Musgrove then turned his attention to the duties of officers such as those commanding squadrons, flights and detachments. To this was added the duties of pilots and observers, which included such items as procedure before and after flight, navigation by day and night and meteorology. An additional help to the officers of the RFC and the Army generally would be to circulate an annual confidential memorandum reviewing progress made in military aviation during the preceding twelve months.

Musgrove recorded detailed observations on the first and second drafts of the war manual and they are very interesting since they were not made with any experience of aerial warfare if one discounts the use of balloons in conflicts abroad, which was the substance of parts of Chapter 1. Again and again during the four years of the Great War instructions, manuals, training and the creation or reorganization of establishments reflected the experience of air warfare and the improvements made in the operational capabilities of aircraft. This was an entirely new service, which made warfare three dimensional. In these very early days much had to be conjecture and guesswork.

EMPLOYMENT OF THE ROYAL FLYING CORPS IN 1912 MANOEUVRES
Source: National Archive document CAB4/1 AC15

Naval aircraft were present at the Naval Review, which preceded the Navy Manoeuvres of 1912, and one hydro-aeroplane took part in Naval Manoeuvres.

The Army Manoeuvres featured only seven biplanes from one squadron since monoplanes had been barred following bad accidents with this aircraft type. These biplanes were joined by three from the Naval Wing. The airships *Beta* and *Gamma* were also employed, one on each side, a proportion of the naval crews under training being used. It had been hoped that the airship *Delta* would be available, but this hope was not realized. There was a lack of personnel, transport and repair facilities, which prevented the forces being used with freedom. In spite of the temporary organization of the aircraft, the information collected for the commander of each side was very complete, although one division succeeded in eluding them by concealing itself during the day. Only light damage was sustained by equipment but then the weather was generally favourable. In prolonged exercises the casualties would probably have been numerous.

Of interest are the comments of the Officer Commanding the Military Wing. He thought it probable that no aeroplanes or engines would stand the strain of more than three months' active service without relief. This comment also applied to pilots and observers. The Committee of Imperial Defence was appraised of the following points:

a. **Night work** No night work was carried out by aeroplanes. The airship *Gamma* made one night flight, with the object of gaining experience in reconnaissance and bomb-dropping. After carrying out the exercise successfully she failed to land at her field base on her return, and rather than risk a landing at an unknown spot she remained in the air until after dawn.

b. **Methods of communication** The great advantage of fitting a wireless telegraphy apparatus in aircraft was shown by the work accomplished by the airship *Gamma* which, at a height of 4,000ft, sent a continuous series of messages to headquarters, all of which were accurately received. No aeroplanes were fitted with wireless. At the time of this report no other practical means of signalling from the air had been devised. Message dropping experienced a considerable advance but much practice was required. Since it was difficult for machines to land close to headquarters with messages there was a clear need for motorcyclists.

c. **Notes on reconnaissance** One point very clearly brought out was the necessity for a high standard of the military training of observers in both strategic and tactical reconnaissance. Untrained officers were regarded as quite useless. The General Staff should ensure that observers were in possession of all information gained by reconnaissance and movement intended. Occasionally staff officers, skilled in observing, should be prepared to go up themselves. It was felt that aircraft should save the cavalry much unnecessary work but could in no way replace it.

d. **Concealment of troops** The feeling was that the introduction of aircraft into warfare would probably lead to an increased number of movements by night and concealment by day. Troops halted in open country should adopt loose formations. Given the noise of engines in aircraft it would not be possible to hear the report of guns but the smoke and flame of discharge were plainly visible.

e. **Observation from aircraft** Difficulty was experienced in discovering whether trenches were occupied or not but bivouacs were easily detected. The manoeuvres showed that it would probably be difficult to estimate the strength of troops occupying towns in billets. The Scots Greys were very recognizable by their horses. Finally, artillery was generally identified both on the march and in bivouacs.

FIRST ANNUAL REPORT OF THE AIR COMMITTEE ON THE PROGRESS OF THE ROYAL FLYING CORPS, 5 AUGUST 1913

Source : National Archive document CAB/4/1 AC15

The Committee noted that the recommended elements of the RFC had been established, namely the Central Flying School (CFS), the Naval Wing and Military Wing and a Reserve. There was a separate establishment for the RAFactory. Evidence of the progress made was ample. The CFS on Salisbury Plain had already turned out two courses of pilots. The Naval Wing had four aeroplane stations on the coast with four additional stations and two airship stations to be completed in the near future. Also a cruiser was being fitted out for aeroplane work. Four of the seven squadrons of the Military Wing had been formed in addition to the Military Airship Squadron and a Reserve had been established. A list of privately owned aeroplanes that could be commandeered in time of war had been compiled by the CFS but then passed on to the RAFactory to maintain. Arrangements had been made for landing facilities to be made available at four private aerodromes and airships and aeroplanes had taken part in army manoeuvres. Firing experiments had been carried out from guns mounted in aeroplanes and also with guns to be used against other aircraft. Finally there had been experiments in bomb dropping. The RFC was in a position to absorb and utilise the whole of the aeronautical resources of the country

The following table shows the progress in the total of flyers who had received the certificate of the Royal Aero Club.

	May 1912	May 1913
Central Flying School	Nil	9* of the total 33 officers
Naval Wing	11	57 had passed the higher
Military Wing	21	134 test for the Naval Wing
Royal Aircraft Factory	2	4 and 68 for the Military Wing.
1st Reserve	0	12
2nd Reserve	0	2
	34	218*

Similarly the number of aeroplanes available, including those under test, were compared over the twelve months:

	May 1912	May 1913
Central Flying School	0	45
Naval Wing	6	34
Military Wing	15	68
Royal Aircraft Factory	2	3
	34	150

During the year the Admiralty had formed an Air Department to administer the Naval Air Service whereas the departments of the War Office simply dealt with matters relating to the Royal Flying Corps as they would any other branch of the Army. Be that as it may an Executive Committee was formed early in 1912 under the Chief of the Imperial General Staff, to co-ordinate questions referred to or arising in the War Office in regard to the organization of the Royal Flying Corps. The work of this committee was then performed by a new branch of the Directorate of Military Training called MT4.

THE NAVAL WING OF THE ROYAL FLYING CORPS

The organization of the Naval Wing had proceeded satisfactorily. There was going to be an alteration of pay scales for some of the higher naval ratings who were not trained as pilots being less than it would have been if the men were serving in other branches of the Navy. Under consideration was the pay of ratings who were at risk when they were taken up in aeroplanes for observation, wireless telegraphy, gunnery and other duties. The Naval Flying School at Eastchurch was training most of the personnel for the Wing and served as a holding depot for trained pilots, pending posting to the various air stations that were being established around the coast. The school was in a position to take on more students if the need arose.

Naval pilots were being trained at three locations. The total of officers and men was as follows:

	Eastchurch	Farnborough*	Netheravon
Officers	24 trained	5 trained	20 trained
	1 under	3 under	nil under
	training	training	training
Men	41 trained	30 trained	64 trained
	80 under	30 under	nil**
	training	training	

* For airship work
** The last course ended on April 17th 1913

A captain had been appointed to command HMS *Hermes*, which was in the process of being fitted to carry hydro-aeroplanes for experimental purposes. The growing importance given to hydro-aeroplanes was reflected in the establishment of an experimental unit on the Isle of Grain. Station sheds were being erected at Calshot, Harwich, Yarmouth and Rosyth and negotiations were in progress for further sheds to be built at Dover, Cleethorpes, Newcastle, Peterhead, Cromarty, Scapa Flow and in other localities, including Eastbourne aerodrome where it was proposed to lease a shed. The aeroplane strengths at the time in the possession of the Naval Wing were thirty-four with sixty-eight on order, of which fifty-five were hydro-aeroplanes.

Experimental work

The Air Committee was watching the manufacture of aeroplanes and airship engines and four Naval Engineer Officers had been specially selected for this work. Inspections had been carried out on the principal continental aeroplane engines and those being manufactured in England. A 90hp Green engine had lately been purchased and was being tested by the Admiralty. Similarly experimental work was afoot in wireless telegraphy and a specialist wireless telegraphy lieutenant had been appointed for this work and twenty hydro-aeroplanes were in the process of being equipped with satisfactory apparatus. The same wireless telegraphy lieutenant had also provided apparatus for installation in aeroplanes at the Central Flying School. Lectures in wireless telegraphy were also being given at the CFS, Farnborough and the Naval Flying School Eastchurch. It was further proposed that the Parseval and Astra Torres airships be fitted with wireless apparatus. The matter of aircraft control settled on the most suitable type for naval operations, plans for which had been studied by naval pilots. Wing warping and foot steering had been adopted for practically all naval machines and several machines had been fitted with dual controls. A refinement was the mastery of one control over the other. Bomb-dropping experiments had been carried out at Shoeburyness in conjunction with Woolwich resulting in the designing of two systems and several sighting systems had been constructed and tested. Finally, there had been work on fitting guns to aeroplanes, firing practice using a Maxim gun had been conducted and several firms had received orders for hydro-aeroplane gun mountings.

AIRSHIP SECTIONS OF THE NAVAL AND MILITARY WINGS

It will be interesting to note the different approach that the two wings of the Royal Flying Corps had towards the use of airships in war. Both the German Navy and the Army were to deploy airships as bombers in a sustained bombing campaign against Britain commencing very early in 1915. For their part the Sub-Committee of the Air Committee did not feel justified in recommending any further experiments in the use of airships in naval operations but recommended the upkeep of two small airships for use with the Expeditionary Force. Airships were, in fact, more suited to operations over the sea, where their low speed and bulk comparable to aeroplanes meant that they could be very useful for maritime reconnaissance and anti-submarine work and were less likely to be involved in aerial combat, which would be encountered by airships used in land operations. But before the Committee of Imperial Defence could approve the report of the Sub-Committee the achievements of the large German airships pre-war was forthcoming. Indeed, this is something that will characterize the difference between the two countries in the inter-war years when German civil aviation used Zeppelin airships most successfully whilst the Royal Air Force put airship development at the bottom of the list of priorities in the 1920s. When at last there was a concerted attempt to build just two large airships, the *R100* and the *R101*, the whole British airship programme was terminated following the tragic loss of the *R101* over France.

What concerned the Air Committee was the failure that had been experienced with Naval Airship No.1 but the development of airships abroad persuaded a reassembled Sub-Committee to recommend the purchase of several small airships for the Royal Flying Corps. Up to this point British military airships had been in the hands of the Air Battalion of the Royal Engineers with No.1 Company of the Battalion being stationed at Farnborough leaving No.2 Company to move to Larkhill to develop aeroplanes. The purpose was intended to permit the progressive education of members of the Flying Corps in airship work and so maintain parity with progress being made on the continent. An airship training class from the Naval Wing was sent to Farnborough to gain experience in airship handling from the Military Wing.

The Air Committee took note of the airships in the possession of the Royal Flying Corps. Of interest is the cubic capacity of the various ships:

Beta	33,000cu.ft
Gamma	80,000cu.ft
Delta	160,000cu.ft
Eta	80,000cu.ft

The first three were allocated to the Military Wing. The cost of building *Eta* at the RAFactory was being shared and was also allocated to the Military Wing. *Epsilon* (180,000cu.ft) was in the process of construction. Allocated to the Naval Wing were *Willows* (20,000 cu.ft), *Astra Torres* (220,000 cu.ft) and *Parseval* (250.000 cu.ft). *Astra Torres* was undergoing trials at Farnborough and *Parseval* was then being transported there. But even the largest of these could not compare with German airships, which ranged from 600 to 800,000cu.ft capacity and some even larger. It seemed to the Air Committee that airships of this size would be those best suited for naval purposes and several of the leading ship-building firms in the United Kingdom had been approached with a view to manufacturing the largest types.

THE MILITARY WING OF THE ROYAL FLYING CORPS

Introduction
The Military Wing of the RFC was formed on 13 May 1912 and the existing Air Battalion and its Reserve were absorbed into it. The headquarters and the Flying

British airship *Eta* (80.000 cu.ft).

Depôt Line of Communication were established at Farnborough. It was originally intended that the latter should come under the Officer Commanding the Military Wing for discipline, but should form part of the Royal Aircraft Factory for technical duties in peacetime. This proposal fell through owing to objections on the part of the Factory, and as a result the peace duties of this unit remained undefined during 1912, and it was mainly employed in carrying out the repair work of the two squadrons at South Farnborough. The Air Committee noted the progress in forming the Military Wing:

Of the 182 flyers recommended by the Sub-Committee as the establishment for the Military Wing, 68 officers had qualified and 1 officer and 26 men were under training. Six officers had been killed whilst flying on duty and two had resigned their appointments. The position with regard to recruitment to the Military Wing was noted. Some 88 had been transferred from the Air Battalion, 207 from the Regular Army (exclusive of the Air Battalion) and 387 had directly enlisted. The sheds to house the aeroplanes on strength and on order seemed insufficient. No new sheds were on order and the existing 25 sheds could hold two aeroplanes. There were 68 aeroplanes on strength with 43 on order. The Air Committee also noted that, to date, the provision of transport had not kept pace with the rate

Zeppelin airship *LZ 13 Hansa*

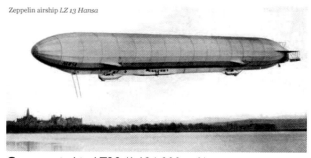

German airship *LZ38* (1,126,000cu.ft).

Wing HQ	formed	1912	Peace Station	South Farnborough
1st Squadron (airships & kites)		1912		South Farnborough
2nd Squadron (aeroplanes)		1912		Montrose
3rd Squadron (aeroplanes)		1912		Netheravon
4th Squadron (aeroplanes)		1912		South Farnborough
5th Squadron (aeroplanes)		1913		South Farnborough

of formation of squadrons when the Sub-Committee had recommended that transport in accordance with War Establishments should be purchased for each flight of aeroplanes as it was formed. Experimental work with machine guns for aeroplanes was carried out to ascertain the vulnerability of propellers to rifle fire. A wireless outfit for airships, designed by Captain Lefroy RE, was employed during the manoeuvres with success. Finally, a good time had been spent preparing for the Military Aeroplane Competitions.

PREPARATIONS FOR HOSTILITIES – MILITARY AND NAVAL WINGS

Introduction

Given the fact that Blériot had only then recently flown his flimsy aircraft across the English Channel, Britain was already making plans for aeroplanes to fly across that short stretch of water as part of an expeditionary force. This section also deals with the organizations and preparedness of the RNAS for war. It is interesting that the officers on the General Staff who dealt with these matters were Army captains at the time but would rise to the very top posts in the RAF. Captains W.G.H. Salmond and E.L. Ellington come to mind.

PREPAREDNESS OF THE RFC FOR WAR

Officers required for duty with the RFC on mobilization
Source: National Archive document AIR1/363/231/3

The letter quoted below is from the Director of Military Training to the OC Military Wing, dated 9 August 1913, on the subject of the list of officers required for duty with the Corps. Lists are in constant need of changing and the Director advises changes that needed to be made to the list. To enable the War Office to keep an up-to-date list a return was requested of the OC Military Wing on each Saturday showing any changes that had occurred during the previous week – casualties, for example. A nil return was required if there had not been any. The term 'casualty' in this context was to include any officer who had been posted, promoted, changed station, been temporarily absent from the UK exceeding three months, retired, resigned or reverted to his permanent unit or

died. Any resulting additions to the list were to come from the names of pilots on the Army List. The names of reserve pilots are listed in the original document

Composition of force required in the event of mobilization
The names of many on the lists on page 46 will reach the highest ranks of the RAF, beginning with Lt Col Sykes who will for a brief period become Chief of the Air Staff. The various regiments are well represented and any ex-artillery pilot who joined the RFC would have a thorough understanding of the needs of artillery spotting. Since the real founders of an air arm in the British armed forces were to be found in the Royal Engineers, engineer officers are to be found in the lists on the next page.

A minute No.4645 was sent by the OC Military Wing to the Director of Military Training referring to allotments of aircraft to the Field Force. Clearly the latest machines were desired but these would not be forthcoming by the time the Force had to be operational. The Director stated that four aeroplane squadrons had to be ready by 1 February 1914. It was impossible to abandon the Farman types at that time. The Henri-Farmans and the Maurice Farmans were by no means perfect and were perhaps obsolescent but nevertheless had to be retained on the War Establishment for the time being. They were, after all, fine for tactical reconnaissance. The situation would, of course, be kept under review. The letter was signed by Major W.S. Brancker, another rising star in the firmament. The allotment to Squadrons on 1 February 1914 was as follows, but the document does not include No.1 Squadron, which was equipped until 1 January 1914 with airships that were then transferred to the Naval Wing. It was not until August 1914 that No.1 Squadron was equipped with aeroplanes, namely the Longhorn and the Vickers Boxkite:

No.2 Squadron BEII
   70 Renault Qty14
   Maurice Farman Renault 70 Qty 7

No.3 Squadron BE.VIII 80 Gnome and some 70 Gnome to be made up to 80 Gnome Qty 7
   Henry Farman 80 Gnome Qty 7
   Blériot 80 Gnome Qty 7 (made up of 50 and 70hp Gnomes all to be made up to 80hp Gnome at the earliest.)

Force HQ

Officer Commanding	Lt Col F.H. Sykes	15th Hussars
Staff Officer	Major H. Musgrave	Royal Engineers
Adjutant	Lieutenant B.H. Barrington-Kennett	Grenadier Guards

No.1 Squadron

Squadron Commander	Major E.M. Maitland	Essex Regiment
Flight Commanders	Captain C.M.Waterlow	Royal Engineers
	Major The Hon. C.M.P. Brabazon	Irish Guards

No.2 Squadron

Squadron Commander	Major C.J. Burke	Royal Irish Regiment
Flight Commanders	Captain J.H.W. Becke	Notts and Derby Regiment
	Captain C.A.H. Longcroft	Welsh Regiment
	Captain G.W.P Dawes	Royal Berkshire Regiment

No.3 Squadron

Squadron Commander	Major H.R.M. Brooke-Popham	Ox and Bucks Light Infantry
Flight Commanders	Major J.F.A. Higgins DSO	Royal Field Artillery
	Captain A.G. Fox	Royal Engineers
	Captain P.L.W. Herbert	Notts and Derby Regiment
	Captain C.R.W. Allen	Welsh Regiment

No.4 Squadron

Squadron Commander	Major G.N.Raleigh	Essex Regiment
Flight Commanders	Captain B.R.W. Boer	Royal Field Artillery
	Captain D.G. Conner	Royal Field Artillery
	Captain H.R.P. Reynolds	Royal Engineers

Depot Squadron

Officer Commanding	Major A.D. Garden	Royal Engineers
Quartermaster	Lieutenant W.J.D. Pryce	Royal Flying Corps

No.4 Squadron BEII 70 Renault Qty 14
   Maurice Farman Renault 70 Qty 7

No.5 Squadron BEII 70 Renault Qty 14
   Sopwith 80 Gnome Qty 7

Depot   BEII 70 Renault Qty 8
        BE VIII 80 Gnome Qty 2
        Sopwith 80 Gnome Qty 2
        Maurice Farman 70 Renault Qty 3
        Henry Farman 80 Gnome Qty 2
        Blériot 80 Gnome Qty 2 (made up of 50 and 70
        Gnomes all to be made up to 80 Gnome at the earliest)

PREPAREDNESS OF THE RNAS FOR WAR

Principal Naval Air Stations

The preparedness of the RNAS is shown by the disposition of the units and the activities being undertaken by each unit. The disposition for the period January to August 1914 was as follows:

Eastchurch	Calshot	Farnborough
Isle of Grain	Yarmouth	Kingsnorth
Felixstowe	Fort Laing	

(Air Historical Branch reference AH.15/227/16. 0.)
The main work carried out at these locations was as follows.

Eastchurch

Since this was the principal training unit of the RNAS (see Chapter 8), it was commanded by Commander C.R. Samson RN.

Isle of Grain

This was commissioned as a seaplane station on 30 December 1912 and was commanded by Lieutenant J.M.W. Seddon RN. The station was engaged in an experimental work mainly in connection with the type and design of floats for seaplanes. It also experimented with wireless telegraphy from seaplanes and bomb dropping. At the outbreak of war this station was intended as a base for the cross channel seaplane patrol.

Felixstowe

Commissioned in 1913 and commanded by Captain C. Risk RN it was intended to be one of a chain of seaplane stations along the East Coast. Except for a few W/T experiments little took place at the station pre-war. However, when Commander Porte assumed command it became the base for large flying boats and a large number of boats were designed, built and tested.

Calshot

In March 1913 this seaplane station became a seaplane school under the command of Squadron Commander Spencer Grey RN. The principal task was to train officers to fly seaplanes but this was hampered pre-war by a shortage of training machines. Officers who had attended a flying course at either Eastchurch or CFS would be trained, not only to fly seaplanes but study technical matters as well.

Yarmouth

This was commissioned in 1913 and placed under the command of Lieutenant R. Gregory. Yarmouth was intended to be one of the chain of seaplane stations along the East Coast but very little work was carried out pre-war.

Fort Laing

Fort Laing was only a temporary base and was closed down in February 1914. The hangars and aircraft were transferred to Dundee, which was commissioned the following month as a seaplane station.

Fort George

This was a temporary base formed in 1913 and continued to function until shortly after the outbreak of war.

Farnborough

Farnborough was originally an Army Balloon Depot but was used by the Naval Wing in September 1912. When a naval airship branch was opened a small number of officers and men attended a course in airship work. When the Admiralty took over from the Army the task of airship development the sheds that housed the Army's No.1 Squadron went to the Navy and the aerodrome was temporarily allotted to the Naval Wing. Some of the Army officers and men transferred to the Naval Wing to remain with airships. Farnborough was commanded by Commander Mastiman RN. For the training carried out see Chapter 8.

Kingsnorth

This airship station was established on the Medway during 1913 and two large sheds were built. The station was not commissioned until April 1914 and it was home to the *Astra Torres* and *Parseval* airships until the outbreak of war.

Floatplane – Short 184.

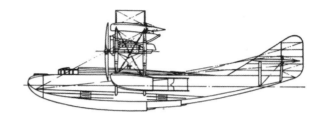

Flying boat – Felixstowe F2A.

Re-organization of the Naval Wing

On 1 July 1914 the Naval Wing of the Flying Corps was renamed the Royal Naval Air Service. It was made clear at the outset that all naval aircraft* and personnel engaged with the Naval Wing, both those on Active and Reserve service would be administered by the Admiralty. The RNAS was to consist of:

The Admiralty Air Department
The Central Air Office
The Royal Naval Flying School
The Royal Naval Air Stations

*The term aircraft included aeroplanes and seaplanes, which could be either floatplanes or flying boats and kites. A floatplane is an aircraft that sits on floats and the entire fuselage is out of the water. Flying boats have a hull like a ship and sit in the water:

For the coastal naval air stations established at places where coastguard station already existed the RNAS would take over the duties of the station, although it was appreciated that, to begin with, the coastguard service might have to loan the RNAS ratings for duty. All ranks and ratings of the RNAS were borne on the strengths of one of HM ships and would be subject to the Naval Discipline Act. The Military Wing and its Reserve together with CFS would be administered by the War Office but a portion of the staff of CFS would come from the Navy.

The Naval Review at Spithead – July 1914

The importance of the naval review in July 1914 cannot be understated. With war clouds gathering in Europe the review gave the King and the country visible evidence of the readiness of the Royal Navy, including the RNAS. Since the RNAS had been in existence for only three weeks the review gave the naval flyers an opportunity to show what they could do should war come. A large proportion of the aeroplanes and seaplanes were concentrated in the vicinity of Portsmouth, Weymouth and Calshot for the purpose and four airships were flown in to demonstrate the powers of lighter-than-air craft. Five naval air stations sent seaplanes whilst aeroplanes came from Eastchurch came under the command of Commander C.R. Samson. His pilots had been practising formation flying and it was this that was demonstrated over the Royal Yacht. Meanwhile, Commander Murray Sueter was in discussion with other officers over the merits of air aerobatics. It was felt that such manoeuvres were of little use unless performed at higher altitude but had the aircraft been flown at 6,000ft or more no details could have been seen during the King's inspection. Whilst the seaplanes and airships returned to their bases Commander Samson went on a tour with his aeroplanes visiting Dorchester before moving on to CFS at Upavon.

Samson had been at CFS for only a few hours when orders were received that, as a matter of urgency, he returned with his aircraft to Eastchurch where they arrived on 27 July 1914.

Imminence of war

With war looming there was partial mobilization and the coastal defence stations would come into play. The seaplanes were assembled at Grain Island, Felixstowe and Yarmouth with orders to patrol the coast in the event of war. The Calshot establishment of seaplanes were distributed amongst the three aforementioned places. Two aeroplanes were dispatched from Eastchurch to Felixstowe and one to Yarmouth. Two airships remained at Kingsnorth. The Admiralty issued instructions on 29 July that the duties of aircraft were to be confined to a constant protection against hostile aircraft. Scouting and patrol duties were to be considered as secondary to protection duties. All machines were to be kept in a trued up state ready for immediate action. On 30 July 1914 the Army Council agreed to send No.4 Squadron to reinforce the naval machines at Eastleigh.

Chapter 3
Military Air Operations, 1914 and 1915

Mobilization of the RFC and RNAS – German airship raids of 1915 and related Air Defence matters – RNAS operations 1914/1915 – the anti-submarine campaign 1914/1915 – operations of No.2 Kite Balloon Section RNAS – RFC Operations on the Western Front 1914/1915 – Contact air patrols – RFC/RNAS operations in overseas theatres 1914/1915 – Mesopotamia and German East Africa – Italian peninsula

INTRODUCTION

Cabinet planning on mobilization in August 1914

The War Council met at 10 Downing Street on 5 August to consider the disposition of Britain's armed forces on the outbreak of war with Germany. As the Council met Austria was at war but only with Serbia and Italy was on the sidelines. England was allied with France and the sending of an Expeditionary Force to the continent involved close co-operation with the French High Command. If the Belgians mobilized the French Army could be expected to enter that country to support the Belgian war effort. Indeed, the Foreign Secretary, Sir Edward Grey, reported that the Belgian Government had already extended the invitation. Holland was maintaining strict neutrality and this complicated any British plans for the transportation of the BEF (British Expeditionary Force) to the continent. The mouth of the Scheldt was entirely Dutch territory but in any case Winston Churchill felt that the voyage to Holland would leave the transports exposed to danger since they would be on an exposed flank. Sir Charles Douglas stated that the BEF would embark at Bristol, Southampton and Newhaven. As regarded ports of disembarkation, much would depend on the point of concentration of the BEF in France, and Amiens was suggested. On the other hand if co-operation with the Belgians and the Dutch was contemplated then landing at Antwerp should be considered or a landing in France with a land movement to Antwerp. Sir Douglas Haig, who would command the British forces on the Western Front, had several questions for the Council. He hoped that the BEF would have time to organize once on the Continent before being committed to action. He asked if the British force would have to go into action at once to prevent a French collapse? In any event would the BEF be large enough to turn the tables if the French were found to be retreating. For how long could the Belgians hold out against the Germans and for how long could an effective campaign be waged and what size of force was being contemplated; two infantry divisions and a cavalry brigade for example? Finally, he opined that the BEF should do what the French wanted. French plans were based on the assumption that the BEF should arrive on the fifteenth day of mobilization. Lord Kitchener worried that co-operation between the French and British General Staffs was not sufficiently close.

It was reported that the Royal Navy was in a state of absolute and complete readiness. This was important for four reasons. Any attempt by the German fleet to put to sea had to be prevented, the transport of men, machines, horses and other supplies to the Continent had to be protected, the threat from German submarines had to be addressed and all necessary measures taken to counter the threat of invasion of the British Isles. In the latter event land forces would need to be kept back for home defence at least until the situation on the Continent became clearer. Reinforcements from the Dominions and South Africa were also thrown into the mix. In the case of South Africa local forces could take over from British forces there to release them for service in France.

MOBILIZATION OF THE RFC AND RNAS

Introduction

The use of aeroplanes, balloons and kites in the rapidly evolving military situation described above still had to be worked out in detail, although the contents of Chapter 2 show that much thought had been given to the use of air power in war. Air warfare would prove to be of growing importance as the war progressed but at this stage the use of aeroplanes and airships/dirigibles was to give direct assistance to the forces on the ground and at sea. A serious threat from the air against the British Isles was not contemplated. The first problem to manifest itself when hostilities began was one of overall control of the air service, which had been the task of the Air Committee of the Committee of Imperial Defence. But the Air Committee had other preoccupations once hostilities commenced and so the Military Wing of the Flying Corps or RFC and the Naval Wing or RNAS went their separate ways and instead of collaboration they competed for resources and personnel. Major General David Henderson was Director of Military Aeronautics at the War Office with Major W.S. Brancker as Assistant Director. At the Admiralty the Air Committee took control of the RNAS. The duties assigned to the officers of the Air Department of the Naval Wing are to be found in Appendix E. For both services existing units were earmarked for war roles but in the light of experience and the demands of war the number of units increased rapidly. This meant new formations and changes in organization, particularly in the training of air and ground crews. The plans for training detailed in Chapter 2 were for a Central Flying School for pilots but there was soon to be a need for observers and air gunners. On the ground a large number of mechanics to work on the engines and armaments would soon be needed. The remainder of an aeroplane in those days could be repaired and maintained by carpenters and smithies.

The division of responsibility for the provision of air services for the nation would, in the fullness of time, fester and become a running sore, particularly following the formation of the Royal Air Force in April 1918. In 1916 there would an attempt to ensure the proper allocation of manpower and resources when the Prime Minister appointed a Joint War Air Committee but in August 1914 the RFC and the RNAS were preoccupied with fighting the war and constantly adapting their organizations to meet the ever-changing demands for aircraft and airships, pilots and technicians, airfields, formations etc.

The Royal Flying Corps

The mobilization scheme provided for the dispatch of four squadrons as the air component of the BEF. This left two squadrons in the UK. There was also a register of civilian pilots and privately owned aircraft that might be pressed into service in time of war. On 13 and 15 August Nos.2, 3, 4 and 5 Squadrons flew from Dover to Amiens. Just one Flight of No.4 Squadron remained behind in the UK for home defence. Personnel of RFC Headquarters, the squadrons' mechanics, transport and mechanics went by boat and train. Finally, an Aircraft Park was established at Amiens to provide replacements for damaged or lost aircraft. Sending squadrons to war was one thing, but it was another to train pilots and ground crew and to provide for the manufacture of aeroplanes and engines should the war be protracted, which proved to be the

The Shorthorn, which equipped No.2 Squadron based at Montrose in Scotland.

case. Already the Central Flying School found itself unable to cope with the depleted resources at its disposal, having lost pilots and equipment, and there was only one station in commission, i.e. the station at Farnborough. The answer was to form a Reserve squadron to train pilots. This was No.1 (Reserve) Squadron and as early as September it was necessary to send pilots home from France to expand the training organization. The policy was to form as many Reserve squadrons as possible to form the nuclei of operational service squadrons by training pilots ab initio.

Nos.1 and 6 Squadrons went to Netheravon in Wiltshire on mobilization and this became one of the best known air stations in the new service. The squadrons sent to Amiens were soon redeployed to Mauberge. These squadrons were equipped with a mixture of Shorthorns, Bristol Boxkites, Vickers Boxkites, Longhorns, Tabloids, RE1s, Shorthorns and BE8s. The airships, with which No.1 Squadron was originally equipped, were transferred to the Royal Navy. Below are pictures of some of the aircraft that went to war in 1914.

The Beta, one of the airships transferred from No.1 Squadron to the Royal Naval Air Service.

The Tabloid equipped No.3 Squadron.

The Longhorn, which equipped No.1 Squadron.

The Royal Naval Air Service

In August 1914 the Royal Navy deployed its aeroplanes on coastal airfields to cover the North Sea and English Channel and as seaplane carriers were acquired RNAS aircraft could be carried to join the Fleet. The *Engadine*, *Riviera*, and the *Empress* were commissioned for this purpose after structural alterations were carried out. These ships could serve the needs of the Grand Fleet with its base at Scapa Flow in the Orkneys where a seaplane base was established. When the Fleet went to sea it could be accompanied by the seaplane carrier *Campania*. The first RNAS unit to be deployed overseas went from Eastchurch to Ostend on 27 August to co-operate with the Naval Division at Antwerp and an aircraft and seaplane base was established at Dunkirk. The aim was to protect the United Kingdom from raids by enemy airships. A cross-channel patrol was established using seaplanes and airships between the Isle of Grain and Ostend with a temporary base at the Belgian port but the patrol was discontinued when the enemy advanced to the port. This called for an additional base at Skegness and a flight of No.4 Squadron RFC reinforced the RNAS at Eastchurch.

Like the RFC, the RNAS also underwent rapid organizational development. With the RFC committed almost entirely to the war in France the RNAS was left to provide air defence of the home base. An anti-aircraft section was established by the Admiralty and an additional station for seaplanes was opened in Dover to provide coastal air patrols.

Air defence was a matter that had been the subject of speculative study well before the Great War started. Balloons had been used as early as the late eighteenth century and again in the Boer War so military planners had to consider what might be vulnerable to attack from the air both on land and at sea. The advent of the airship then the powered aircraft only served to concentrate minds. The matter of air superiority became an issue that meant that one side in a war would have to try to deny the airspace in the war zone to the enemy. If air superiority could not be attained then vulnerable targets would have to be defended. International law had to catch up with the new situation. In the past the British home base was defended from external attack by the Royal Navy. The concept of international waters or high seas comes from the days when a nation could only enforce dominion over its coastal waters up to a range of three miles, the limit of the range of land-based cannons. Then international law did not turn on whether or not targets were vulnerable but whether or not they were defended against attack by ground forces. When ground targets remote from the battlefield could be attacked from the air then they too became vulnerable and had to be defended using anti-aircraft artillery and aeroplanes. Military objectives would then include not simply the defeat of an enemy's armies and navies but the capacity of the enemy nation to continue with the war. Thus a nation's transport networks, factories, docks, harbours and cities joined battlefield targets that might have to be defended. As aeroplanes became larger with greater endurance and range, air defence could be achieved not simply by fighters but also by bombers, which could progressively reduce the ability of a nation to continue prosecuting a war. This is the concept of offensive defence. In 1914, however, the number of aeroplanes held by the belligerents was so small that their use was unlikely to materially affect the outcome of hostilities. Nevertheless, if a nation was to achieve air superiority in the war zone then air fighting would inevitably ensue. This would affect both the RFC and RNAS.

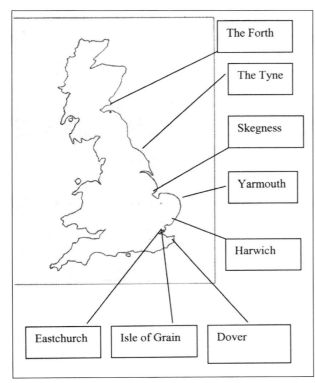

The Forth

The Tyne

Skegness

Yarmouth

Harwich

Eastchurch   Isle of Grain   Dover

Coastal Air Stations.

Guns for use against aircraft

The urgency of obtaining, as soon as possible, guns suitable for attacking aircraft was realized when it was clear the airships of the Zeppelin type could cross the North Sea to pass over the country. This would expose shipping, magazines and other vulnerable points to danger from attack with explosives. At Chattenden and Lodge Hill magazines two 6in Howitzers had been mounted at each magazine. A number of guns of various calibres were being manufactured and were on order. Plans were in place to mount 3in guns on the latest RN vessels since trials at Shoeburyness with one of these guns had been promising and steps were being taken to convert the mountings and guns of existing anti-torpedo-boat type for use as anti-aircraft weapons. It had been established that the 4in gun would reach an aircraft travelling at a height of 4,500ft at a distance of 6,200 yards measured along the line of sight. The 3in gun could engage an enemy aircraft at 5,400 yards and the 37mm pom-pom at just 3,000 yards. The steps taken to defend the home country from attacks by aircraft were soon about to be vindicated.

GERMAN AIRSHIP RAIDS OF 1915 AND RELATED AIR DEFENCE MATTERS

Sources: National Archive documents: WO158/935 and AIR1/109/15/20/2

INTRODUCTION

The military impact and effectiveness of the German airship raids over the United Kingdom during the Great War must be judged not in terms of the material damage caused but the psychological effect the raids had upon the public and the diversion of air resources from the Western Front together with the effectiveness of fighter defences. Whatever the German High Command may have believed about the airship contributing significantly to the outcome of the war, there is little doubt that airship raids alone were not going to bring the UK to the negotiating table to sue for peace. In 1917 the Gotha bomber would begin to contribute to the bombing offensive against Britain but the airship continued to be used to the end of the war, its enthusiasts believing that it remained an effective offensive weapon. The strategic bomber raids by the RAF and the USAAF over Germany and German-occupied parts of Europe during the Second World War are an example of an effective air offensive and did seriously affect Germany's ability to conduct the war on land. Goebbels was privately to concede this fact.

The early use of airships in raids over Britain showed that attacks in daylight would be very risky due to the comparative low speed of airships to aeroplanes. Airships could, of course, fly at altitudes above the operational ceilings of British fighters of the day but the higher they flew the less accurate was the bombing and there was also the possibility of targets being obscured by cloud. They also presented themselves as very large targets for defending aeroplanes and anti-aircraft fire so night raids were embarked upon but this made navigation difficult and there were instances where airship commanders bombed the wrong targets, sometimes miles from the intended ones. Bombs were dropped often in fields and non-military residential areas. For example, Derby was mistaken for Liverpool and once bombs had been dropped on the former, the commanders of following airships dropped their bombs on the same targets. However, the more daring airship commanders did fly at low altitudes and did, on occasion, inflict significant damage and casualties.

EFFECTIVENESS OF BRITISH AIR DEFENCES IN 1915

But fighting at night was equally a problem for the defence. The RFC, the RNAS and Army heavy artillery shared the task of protecting Britain's industrial areas and large conurbations. Rapid advances in aircraft design during the war would contribute to the effectiveness of fighter defences but in early 1915 the bombing of Britain was something with which the British public was still coming to terms. The major difference between the air defence situation in 1915 and the Battle of Britain was, in the latter case, use was made of radar integrated into a tried and tested air defence system. In 1940 Spitfires and Hurricanes could sit on the ground until an approaching raid was reported by the radar stations and the Royal Observer Corps. Thus fuel tanks would be near-full at the moment of interception of enemy aircraft. The fire of heavy ack-ack batteries could also be more effectively directed. In 1915, defending fighters would have to wait for visual sightings of enemy airships. They would then have to take off and reach operational altitude to intercept the raiders, by which time bombs may already have been dropped with the airship commanders making good their escape. One answer was to have fighters patrolling constantly at altitude to improve the chances of interception but this was not only very expensive in terms of fuel but the service life of aeroplanes and their engines. These were known as standing patrols. A fighter squadron would be divided into its three constituent flights to extend the coverage and the flights could use suitable fields or, in some cases, race courses. A hut for the air and ground crews and telephone communication with the Squadron headquarters would have to suffice to ensure the readiness of aircraft for action. But, as has been made clear, it was expensive in fuel and wear and tear to provide standing patrols. There was then the matter of training pilots to fly at night. It had to be possible to take off and land safely from grass fields for there were no runways with landing lights. Starting engines could be a critical factor if interception was to be achieved. It was

Air-cooled rotary-engined aircraft.

found that rotary or radial engines were preferable to ones of the water-cooled variety pictured below. This was particularly the case in cold weather. The 6th Brigade of the RFC was responsible for the defence of the United Kingdom. The Camel, pictured above would come to equip virtually all of the squadrons around the capital and the Avro 504 would equip those further north.

The War Council met at 10 Downing Street on 7 January 1915 to discuss the threat to London from aerial attack. The First Lord of the Admiralty had stated that there was no assurance that London would not be bombed in spite of the elaborate preparations that had been made. It was expected that Zeppelins flying from the Rhine would need to refuel in Belgium and RFC units in Flanders could attack the refuelling sites. On the other hand, the airship commanders might rely on the wind to carry them over Britain and on their engines for the return to base. The naval airships could attack East Coast towns and would probably wait for still, frosty weather, and come at night. Winston Churchill, First Lord of the Admiralty, reported that a special detachment of ten aircraft was stationed at Dunkirk whose primary function was to prevent the completion of airship bases in Belgium and to attack any airships that might call in that country for supplies. Should the airships penetrate British airspace he reported that there were some sixty aeroplanes stationed in a triangle London, Sheerness and Dover. Since warning of the approach of enemy airships

would come initially from lightships, coastal shipping or coastguard stations, those defending aeroplanes on the coast would probably not achieve the altitude necessary to intercept the enemy but could on their return. Those defending aeroplanes based at Hendon would be in a good position to effect an intercept as they approached the capital. These crews had incendiary bullets for their rifles and these had been effective against balloons. There were also anti-aircraft guns and pom-poms. In the event of an airship raid the police were to cycle round their beats warning the populace to stay indoors and the fire services were planning to deal with simultaneous outbreaks of a number of fires. The Prime Minister asked if warships were at risk and Mr Churchill replied that the more modern ships were equipped with anti-aircraft guns. Lord Haldane, then Lord Chancellor, told the meeting that the bombs dropped from airships would burst without penetrating the defensive armour. Finally, the question of the quality of navigation amongst airship crews was questioned. This would soon be established following the commencement of the airship bombing campaign but Lord Fisher, First Sea Lord, reminded the meeting that, to reach London, airship commanders had only to follow the Thames.

After preliminary reconnaissance over the North Sea in late 1914 the German High Command felt ready to commence airship operations against the United Kingdom. German airships were confined to night operations against targets in Britain. This followed the heavy losses in the opening months of the war during attacks by airships Z VI, *VII* and *VIII* on Liège and the Lorraine front. But raids on England had been promised to the German public and five naval airships, *L3*, *4*, *5*, *6* and *7* were readied for operations. It is therefore interesting that, as 1914 drew to a close, it would be aeroplanes that would be the first to make bombing raids. On 21 December a hostile biplane attacked Dover and two bombs were dropped in the sea 400 yards off Admiralty Pier. Three days later the raid was repeated and resulted

Aircraft with water-cooled engine.

A German Zeppelin returning to its base.

in the first bomb ever to be dropped on British soil, which landed on Dover. The first airship attack was not to take place until the night of 19/20 January. By this time the German Army had advanced into Belgium, making it possible to base airships and aircraft on Belgian soil, thus significantly shortening the distance to potential targets in south-east and eastern England. At this time the Germans introduced newer and better airships and these replaced the naval airships in the Belgian sheds, the latter moving to bases in Northern Germany. The army airships bore the prefix 'LZ' and the naval ones simply 'L'. The operational sorties of the first half of 1915 are described in the following paragraphs by way of comparison. They illustrate the shallow penetration of English airspace, the effects of the bombing and the defensive measures adopted

THE GERMAN AIRSHIP RAIDS OF 1915

(Details of bombs dropped, damage caused and casualties inflicted are contained for all raids in this section in Appendix F.)

The raids began in January 1915, barely four months into the war. It cannot be overemphasized that these violations of British airspace brought the war home to the people in a way that had never been experienced before by an island race. Yes there had been Viking raids and minor forays along our coasts over the centuries but those inland were rarely affected by them. In the seventeenth century there was 'ship tax' that would provide funds for a navy and since Aylesbury was as far from the sea as one could be in the British Isles a prominent parliamentarian, John Hampden, refused to pay the tax. His statue can be found in the town square. On the first mission there was overcast along the Norfolk coast. Overcast was a mixed blessing for airship commanders. On the one hand it made the attacking ships difficult to see from the ground but on the other it made target acquisition and navigation difficult. Naval airship commanders had a better grasp of meteorology than their army counterparts and they would not attack in bright moonlight. On these first probing attacks little was known of anti-aircraft defences or their whereabouts. Guns could be moved faster than German intelligence could keep pace, indeed the RNAAS had mobile anti-aircraft units that feature in the following accounts. But it was a sure bet that points of vital economic and military importance would be adequately protected. It was important for the German High Command that these early attacks met with some success and certainly not with the loss of airships involved.

RAID OF THE NIGHT OF 19/20 JANUARY 1915

The weather conditions were generally favourable and the barometer registered 30.4 inches on the Norfolk coast as naval airships L3 and 4 crossed the coast making a landfall at Happisburgh lightship. The time was 19.55hrs on 19 January. Both airships travelling side by side were seen by an observer in Ingham who described them as like two bright stars moving approximately 30 yards apart. The map shows that the two airships separated once they had crossed the Norfolk coast. *Kapitän Leutnant* Magnus Freiherr made only one attack and that was on Yarmouth. It was 20.25hrs after which time he crossed the coast proceeding in a north-westerly direction parallel to the Norfolk coastline before turning east at 22.00hrs to make for his home base. The commander of L4 was *Kapitän Leutnant* Joahnn Fritze and after crossing the Norfolk coast he turned in a north-westerly direction towards Cromer. As the airship passed over the town it was in total darkness. Fritze turned over the sea to cross the coast between Sheringham and Weybourne where a flare was dropped. This was followed by an incendiary bomb, which landed in a house in Wyndham Street causing considerable damaged but no casualties. After proceeding out to sea the L4 made a landfall near Hunstanton. The target here was a wireless station but the

Zeppelin *L3* raids Yarmouth on the night of 19/20 January 1915 as it appeared on the front of the *London Illustrated Weekly*.

bomb dropped into a field some 300 yards away. By the time the airship reached Snettisham it was flying so low that ground observers could see the trapdoor through which the bombs were dropped. A High Explosive (HE) bomb was dropped near a church causing much damage to the windows. At 22.50hrs the L4 arrived over King's Lynn. Unlike Cromer there were lights showing and Fritze managed to pick up the railway line at Gaywood making it possible to drop the first bomb on the town railway station. The airship was over the town for about ten minutes when eight bombs, seven HE and one incendiary, were dropped. Damage to buildings and death and injury resulted, details of which can be found in Appendix F. After the raid on King's Lynn the airship retreated eastward to pass over the coast at 00.30hrs on 20 January en route for the base in Northern Germany. Reports that the airships were receiving signals from motor cars were not substantiated. These exploits earned for both crews the award of the Iron Cross but their rewards were short lived. On the night of 8 February both airships were lost in a snowstorm off the Jutland coast.

The airship raid of 14 April 1915

The loss of *L3* and *L4* off Jutland was made good with the completion of two enlarged naval airships, L8 and L9. During the months of February and March and the first two weeks of April no raids actually took place. On 4 March the crew of the L8 attempted to raid England without success and on his return *Kapitän Leutnant* Beelitz was uncertain of the airship's position and so descended to a low altitude when a land battery spotted it off Nieuport and riddled it with gunfire causing a catastrophic loss of gas from five of the bags. The L8 was totally wrecked when it came down in trees near the town of Tirlemont. Meanwhile, *Kapitän Leutnant* Mathy, commanding airship *L9*, made several reconnaissance flights and on the night of 14 April he made the first of a succession of raids on industrial targets on the Tyne. The route taken was to proceed to Jutland, on to the Norwegian coast thence across to the east coast of Scotland before heading for the Tyne. The night was very dark and the barometer was 30.12 inches, rising slowly as England was sitting between two anti-cyclones, one centred on the Atlantic and the other on Scandinavia. Although there was no wind there was slight rain and mist over the mouth of the Tyne. Mathy reached Blyth at 19.30hrs and the airship proceeded up the River Blyth to Cambois. En route infantry soldiers fired on the L9 and Sleekburn was reached. Collieries were targeted but on the whole the raid was characterized by a succession of bombs dropped in fields, slight damage to property and fires from the incendiaries which were quickly extinguished. When the L9 crossed the coast to return to her base she was pursued by two aircraft but the pilots did not get sight of their quarry. The airship's height was estimated to be less than 2,000ft during the raid but this was probably an underestimate.

RAID OF 29/30 APRIL

The raid on the night of 29/30 April was made by a military airship, probably *LZ37* commanded by *Oberleutnant* Z. See van der Haegen but it might have been *SLII* commanded by *Hauptmann* Von Woberer. The moon was full. An attack under these circumstances

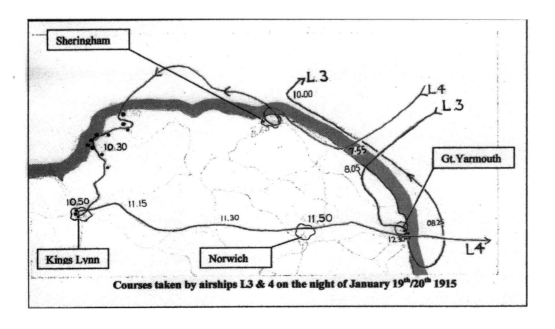

Courses taken by airships L3 & 4 on the night of January 19th/20th 1915

would almost certainly not have been undertaken by Navy pilots. The first warning of the airship's approach came from the Galloper lightship, 30 miles south-east of Harwich. The airship was heading west at about 23.00hrs indicating that it had come from Belgium and thus belonged to the Army.

Although the moon was full it was very foggy over the east coast of England and full advantage was taken of this. Anti-cyclonic weather was in evidence with the barometer standing at 30.07 inches. The wind was moderate from the ENE at 1,500ft but very light, 8mph, at 6,000ft. The coast was crossed at Old Felixstowe and Ipswich was reached at 00.10hrs on 30 April. Bombs were dropped on and around the city before the commander made for Bury St Edmunds. The town and surrounding villages were attacked but the Explosive Works at Stowmarket were probably the main objective. When the airship emerged from the fog it was over a lit town, which might or might not have been Stowmarket. Bombs were then dropped indiscriminately before the airship regained the relative safety of the fog. A great number of incendiaries were dropped on this mission, which was characteristic of Army airship operations. Defensive measures amounted to the mobile guns of the RNAAS but these did not arrive on the scene until 01.45hrs on the 20th, by which time the airship had left. No defensive aeroplanes flew due to the fog.

The map shows the relatively light penetrations into British airspace during raids by Zeppelins in mid 1915. The targets were Bury St Edmunds and installations on the Thames estuary. The airships involved were, on the 10th of the month, the *LZ38*, which attacked the Thames

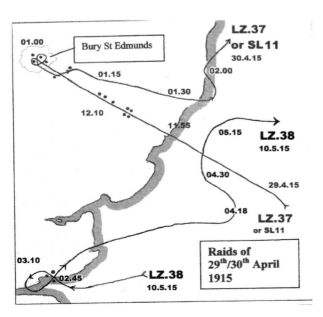

estuary. On the night of 29/30 April 1915 the airship could have been either the *LZ38* or the *SLII* when Bury St Edmunds was attacked.

THE RAID OF 16/17 MAY 1915

Three Army airships were involved in a raid on the night of 16/17 May 1915, namely *LZ37* (*Oberleutnant* Z See Von der Haegen), *LZ38* (*Hauptmann* Linnarz and *LZ39* (*Hauptmann* Masius). From their Belgian sheds the airship commanders were attempting to attack the French and British coasts of the Dover Straits. *LZ38* attacked targets in Ramsgate and Oxney near Dover, *LZ37* targets in Calais and *LZ39* did not complete a raid probably due to technical problems. When *LZ38* passed over Deal the engines were cut and it hovered for a while over the town before proceeding towards Dover dropping bombs over Oxney. As the airship approached Dover, defence was brisk and the commander put out to sea to avoid rifle fire and the AA batteries covering the port area. Finally, *LZ38* was fired on by a guardship on the Downs. On reaching the Continent the airship passed over the British lines at Armentieres at 02.40hrs. During this sortie aircraft from Westgate and Dover actively sought *LZ38* but no contact is recorded. It has already been reported that *LZ39* did not complete its mission and as it passed by Nieuport it was engaged by eight aircraft, three of which got close. The weight of Flight Sub Lieutenant Warneford's aircraft with its Lewis gun, ammunition and observer could not ascend as quickly as an airship but the observer managed to open fire from 1,000ft below the airship. Flight Commander Bigsworth, in an Avro, managed to ascend to 10,000ft and overtook the airship off Ostend. From a position 200ft above *LZ39* four 20lb bombs were dropped along her length from stern to nose and black pungent smoke was seen to issue from her. But Bigsworth was forced to break off the attack when his aircraft was subjected to accurate gunfire from Ostend. Another attack, this time by Squadron Commander Spencer-Grey, was launched on *LZ39* from a Nieuport at a height of 9,800ft. Spencer-Grey was then subjected to heavy machine-gun fire from two machine guns in each gondola. Fire was exchanged and at approximately 05.00hrs the airship was seen at 11,000ft proceeding towards Ghent in a tail-down attitude. Added to the damage caused on landing was the puncturing of five of the gas bags and the loss of the starboard aft propeller. Repairs were effected before the airship was consigned to the Eastern Front where she was destroyed by fire near her shed in November 1915.

THE RAID OF 26 MAY

This raid was carried out by *LZ38* when *Hauptmann* Linnarz paid a second visit to Southend as part of a reconnaissance of a route to London. The weather was fine and the moon was in its first quarter. At 22.30hrs the airship was over Clacton-on-Sea and three minutes later over Southminster where she was fired on by a pom-pom gun. After eight minutes a 3in AA gun fired on her as she passed over Shoeburyness. At 23.13hrs bombs began to be dropped, which included twenty-three small HE bombs or grenades and forty-seven incendiaries. Incredibly, of two women killed in this attack one died from the shell splinters of an AA shell. Five naval aircraft from Eastchurch and Grain took to the air but saw nothing. Two of these aircraft were damaged on landing.

THE RAID OF 31 MAY

There was a full moon on this fine night when two Army airships, *LZ37* and *LZ38*, set off from their base in Belgium but the former seems to have got no further than Dunkirk. Linnarz was again in command of *LZ38* and hoped to profit from his probing flight on 26 May. The airship passed over Dunkirk at 20.30hrs and Calais at 20.55hrs. The guns of RNAAS mobile AA units fired on her as she crossed the English coast at the North Foreland. The course taken was to Brentwood, Woodford and Wanstead and then the first bomb was dropped in the Metropolitan Police area. This was an incendiary that was probably intended for the railway station but descended instead on 16 Alkham Road, Stoke Newington, and penetrated two bedrooms destroying their contents by fire. Moving due south to the west of the Kingsland/Stoke Newington Road bombs were dropped in quick succession on domestic targets. Bombs were also dropped at intervals down Southgate Road but landed either in gardens or roadways. Whitechapel was next to receive the attention of *LZ38* but Linnarz made

no attempt to attack the docklands. By the time the raid ended he had expended eighty-five of his incendiaries between Stoke Newington and Commercial Road East.

The peculiar nature of the HE bombs is significant for they were really small grenades that could kill or maim many people in a crowded thoroughfare or building. Indeed, no bombs were dropped on the thinly populated areas on either side of the River Lea. The last bomb dropped was at approximately 23.35hrs leaving behind a few injuries and some fires. *LZ38* passed Brentwood at 23.55hrs and she was again fired on by an AA gun at Southminster and by the mobile guns of the RNAAS at Burnham. The final departure of the airship was at 00.40hrs from the mouth of the River Crouch. Estimates of the height of *LZ38* during the raid varied between 7,500ft and 10,000ft. The RNAAS responsible for the AA guns over London gave the latter estimate cited as the reason why the airship had not been engaged over the capital. It was flying so high that it was neither seen nor heard. It would not be until the autumn of 1916 that 12,000 feet became the normal raiding height so the raid of 31 May at a height of 10,000ft may fairly be described as unexpected. It is nonetheless remarkable that the airship steered a straight line course down the Kingsland Road from Stoke Newington to Shoreditch. *LZ37*, on the other hand, appears to have been attacked by aeroplanes off Dunkirk at approximately 21.00hrs and by a battery of the RNAAS mobile guns of the mouth of the Swale at 22.25hrs. *Oberleutnant* Van Der Haegen was not as resolute as Linnarz in pressing home his attacks and broke off without dropping any bombs.

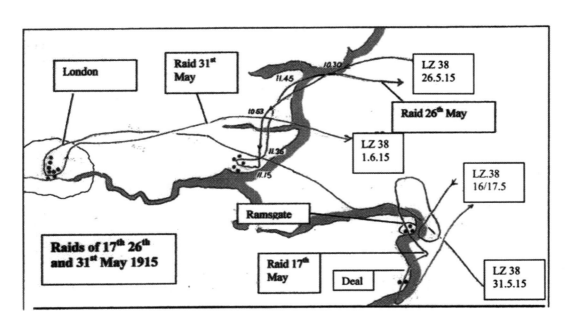

THE RAID OF 4/5 JUNE

As with all previous raids the barometer on this night stood at 30 inches and was rising as England and France stood on the edge of a high-pressure system centred over Spain and the Bay of Biscay. A light westerly wind, local mist along the east coast of England and a waning moon prevailed as two German naval airships, *L9* and *L10*, began their raid. The former headed for the coast of Yorkshire and the latter the Thames Estuary. *L9* lay off the Yorkshire coast until dark and at 22.55hrs was near Ulrome but the coast was not crossed at this point until fifty minutes later. *Kapitän Leutnant* Mathy seems to have been uncertain of his position and had moved up and down the coast to find a distinctive landmark. He steered up the coast northwards to Flamborough Head and turned south-west, dropping an incendiary between the villages of Kilham and Langtoft. The next

two HE bombs were dropped in a field and a garden and when Mathy did set a course for Hull he found that ground mist made visibility very difficult and he left passing over the coast at Flamborough Head under fire from the coastguard. Given the low altitude of the airship this was more a reconnaissance mission than a raid. *L10*, which made for the Thames Estuary, was first sighted by four armed trawlers south of the Sunk Lightship between 21.35 and 21.55hrs. One of these trawlers, the *Zephyr*, opened fire on her. The airship was then flown on changing courses around the Estuary until she was over Sittingbourne between 23.20 and 23.30hrs where three HE bombs and eight incendiaries were dropped. A house was burned out and two others damaged. Casualties amounted to a man and woman injured.

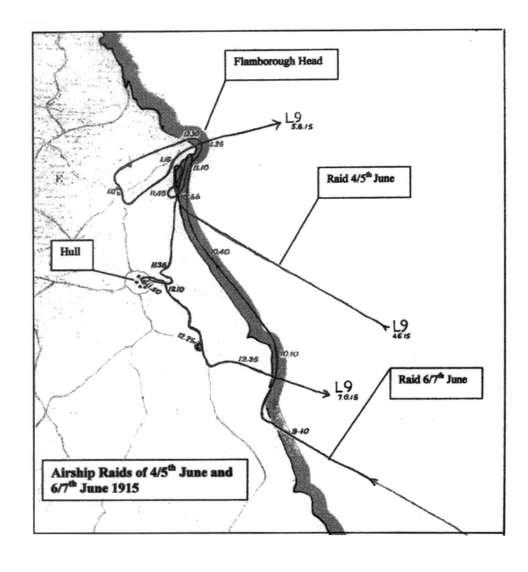

THE RAID OF 6/7 JUNE

The weather was fair with a waning moon. There was a dead calm in the Humber district and locally there was fog and mist when Army airships *LZ37* (Haegen), *LZ38* (Linnarz) and *LZ39* (Masius) left their shed together but only *LZ37* and *LZ39* came over the sea. Linnarz in *LZ38* descended almost immediately. The reason for aborting the mission is not given. Both *LZ37* and *LZ39* were unable to find the English coast probably due to the fog. *LZ39* returned safely to her shed but *LZ37* was destroyed at 03.00hrs by Flight Sub Lieutenant Warneford RNAS over Mont St Amand near Ghent. All the crew, save one who had a miraculous escape, were killed. Two nuns also died when the burning airship fell on a nunnery. To complete this bad evening for the Army airships *LZ38* was destroyed by an Allied air attack on her shed at 02.30hrs The same evening two naval airships set out to attack targets in England. *L9* and *L10* were approaching the Norfolk coast when *L10* turned back possibly due to engine trouble. *L9* continued but was spotted and indentified twelve miles north-east of Mundesley. At 20.40hrs she was in fog on the mouth of the Humber, which meant that she should not attempt to approach Hull by following the river. Reported by observers in Cromer *L9* was seen to be heading in a north-westerly direction but the commander, after reconnoitring the Norfolk coast, made for the Humber. On reaching the Lincolnshire coast the commander again began to reconnoitre. After some time Lieutenant Mathy decided to proceed to Flamborough Head and the airship reached there at 23.10hrs. A flare was dropped at Bridlington, after which Mathy proceeded due south towards Hull. Since mist enshrouded the river he spent some time trying to fix the airship's position when suddenly the mist cleared and he took immediate advantage of the situation. One HE and one incendiary were dropped on Alexandria Dock and another incendiary was dropped on the Swedish steamer *SS Igor* lying in the Victoria Dock basin doing slight damage. An incendiary that fell through the roof of a timber shed close by started a small fire, which was extinguished by North Eastern railway firemen. Then about twelve feet of railway track was destroyed when a HE bomb created a crater. More houses were either destroyed or damaged and a man, woman and child were killed. The list goes on as Mathy's airship rained down death and destruction on the city. This very successful bombing raid was carried out at low altitude when the commander realized that there was no anti-aircraft defence of the city. At a height of 5,000ft his targets could easily be identified and hit. In all, five men, thirteen women and six children were killed and a further forty injured. On making his escape Mathy was careful not to risk anti-aircraft fire and he followed the Humber on its northern bank, rising to 10,000ft where Maxims and rifle fire could not hit the airship even in good visibility.

The airship then veered eastwards reaching Grimsby at 00.25hrs. With engines stopped *L9* hovered for a while searching for suitable targets and incendiaries were then dropped on the docks causing some damage By this time the defences were fully alert and the German airmen were met with fire from rifles and pom-poms at Waltham and New Clee. The airship crossed the coast at Tetney Haven heading in a south-easterly direction at 00.35hrs. This was a finely executed mission for the airship even evaded fire from vessels of the 6th Light Cruiser Squadron anchored in the Humber due to the fog on the water and aircraft from Killinghome were prevented from taking off, again due to the fog. This was a place often shrouded in fog and therefore calls into question this choice of location for a seaplane base. So inflamed was the local population that German or supposed German shops were sacked when rioting broke out at 02.30hrs requiring the military to restore order.

THE RAID OF 15 JUNE
(See map on next page)

The last of these accounts of airship raids in the first half of 1915 concerns a naval airship, probably *L10*, commanded by *Kapitän Leutnant* Hirsch. His airship crossed the English coast between Newbiggin and Blyth in Northumberland at 23.25hrs. He cleverly avoided an approach to the industrial area of the Tyne up the river for fear of falling foul of anti-aircraft defences. The approach was therefore from the north, which caught the defences completely off guard for no attempt had been made to extinguish the urban lights. This time no bombs were wasted with some falling in open countryside. The first place to be hit was Wallsend. The North Eastern Engineering Works suffered heavily in the attack and there was a loss of houses. The Wallsend colliery was also slightly damaged as was Hebburn colliery. An ordnance factory in Jarrow and Palmer's Works was also hit with seventeen workmen being killed and seventy-two injured in the Engine Construction Plant. The Tyne was recrossed and Willington Quay, East Howden and Cookson's Antimony Works were hit followed by Pochin's Chemical Works. During all these attacks there was considerable collateral damage to civilian housing. Other locations were also attacked before the airship went out to sea on a course east by north-east flying at an estimated height of 6,000ft at 23.52hrs. Whilst the raids of 6 and 15 June were both very successful the latter achieved far greater damage to Britain's military capacity. As for the defences rifle fire was supplemented by Heavy AA artillery and fire from pom-poms. Two naval aircraft were sent up from Whitley Bay at 23.50hrs but naturally saw nothing. They had ascended whilst the raid was in progress and could not have achieved the required height to make an interception even had their pilots been able to see the airship.

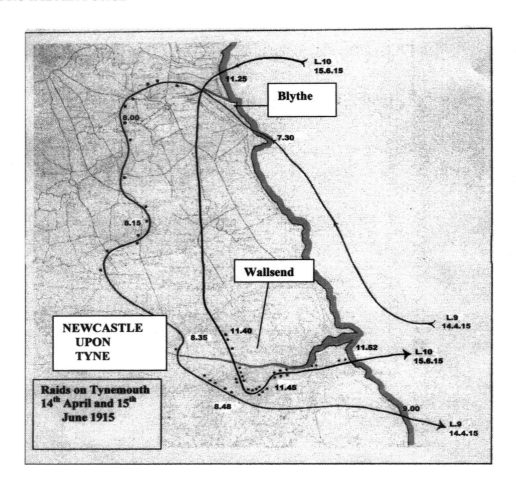

Raids on Tynemouth 14th April and 15th June 1915

AN ASSESSMENT OF THE EFFECTIVENESS OF THE AIRSHIP RAIDS AND THE DEFENCES AGAINST AIR ATTACK

It is clear that these raids in the early part of 1915 were not going to bring Britain to its knees nor substantially reduce the country's ability to wage war but what they did do was divert considerable resources in anti-aircraft gunnery and fighter defences, together with the manpower to operate them, from the war in Europe and other theatres. In all previous wars virtually all of a belligerent country's armed forces could be committed to the battlefield or war at sea. Now it was necessary to defend the home front. Indeed, it was the mixed call on aircraft over the battlefields and home defences that would eventually result in the formation of the Royal Air Force.

At the outset the airship commanders probed the English defences and reconnoitred routes to potential targets and quite a lot of these early raids were characterized by the dropping of bombs and incendiaries on open fields or villages. The early incursions were made against the coast of East Anglia and penetration was not deep. In every case raids were carried out with

a barometer reading of 30 inches and mostly rising with the country on the edge of an anti-cyclone. Reference has already been made to the fact that the naval airship commanders avoided flying in bright moonlight. Strong winds are not good for airship operations and fog and mist made navigation and the identification of targets difficult. Technical problems probably resulted in the aborting of raids but, unlike an aeroplane, an airship can hover and even if some engines are out of action it is possible to make progress. With regard to bombing, bomb sights were still in the future and the explosive and incendiary devices were dropped through a hatch in the underside of the airship. Since these raids were made in fine weather with light winds little allowance had to be made for the effects of wind on the aim taken at targets. Height was important. Low altitudes were preferable for bombing accuracy but a high altitude was essential both to reduce the chances of being hit by ground fire and for defending aircraft to be able to attain the required altitude to make an attack. Airship commanders soon learned how to use altitude to maximum advantage. Care was taken in the approach to a target area to avoid anti-

Captured Zeppelin aircrew.

Three British cruisers sunk off the Dogger Bank in the space of two hours by a German U-boat.

aircraft fire attacks on the Tyne being delivered from the North. Airships had ample defensive armament to deal with fighters but the fire came mostly from the ground.

With regard to the defences there were some serious deficiencies. The raid of 15 June is an example of the incomplete arrangements for early warning and the concomitant switching off of urban lighting. These measures were in hand but not in time to save the Tyne on that occasion. In World War II windows were taped to reduce injuries from flying glass. Too often defensive fire was directed at the attacking airships only when the raid was in progress or when they were making their escape. The siting of airfields and seaplane stations was also a factor. Aircraft were not all-weather aircraft as they are today and landing grounds sited in areas of persistent fog were going to be of limited military value. Again there was the problem of early warning. It has been shown that attacking airships were sighted crossing the coast and some were fired upon but the lack of co-ordination meant that aircraft were 'scrambled' only when a raid was taking place or where the airships were retiring from the scene. It was one thing to sight an airship, but it was another to reach the operational height to mount an attack. Thus fighter aircraft were either not scrambled, or able to get airborne or reach the operational altitude in time. On the other hand successful interceptions could be undertaken in France or Belgium when the airships were returning to their sheds and their whereabouts known.

ROYAL NAVAL AIR SERVICE OPERATIONS 1914–1915

THE ANTI-SUBMARINE CAMPAIGN 1914 AND 1915
Source: National Archive Document: AIR1/675/21/13/1385

Introduction
Even before the Great War had begun the menace of the submarine had been recognized and in April 1911 a

Submarine Committee was formed by the Admiralty. In January 1912, Lieutenant H.A. Williamson, who was both a submariner and aviator, proposed that aircraft could scout ahead of the fleet to detect the presence of enemy submarines and, if possible, to mount an attack. The latter was important since an enemy submarine commander could order a crash dive to prevent the damage or loss of his craft. It had been shown that submarines could be seen well below the surface whereas spotting the wake of a submarine's periscope could not be assured beyond a range of 1,500ft. He further suggested that the mere presence of naval scout planes patrolling above the fleet could have the desired effect of keeping an enemy submarine submerged for fear of detection and attack.

The initial reaction by some at the Admiralty was that it was the role of destroyers to mount attacks on submarines even if it was accepted that scouting aeroplanes could detect the presence of these vessels well before they could be spotted at sea level. In June 1912 experiments were carried out off Harwich and the Anti Submarine Committee Report (No.1721/12 – 01495) concluded that

Otto Weddingen's *U9*.

Otto Weddingen.

an aeroplane gave promise of providing a valuable anti-submarine weapon. Accordingly the establishment of coastal air stations around the shores of the British Isles, equipped with a mix of aeroplanes and seaplanes, was approved on 6 October 1912. To these were added airship stations as airships could remain aloft for periods greatly in excess of aeroplanes.

It did not take long for the submarine to make its mark when, in the space of two hours, three British cruisers, *The Hogue, Cressy* and *Aboukir* were sunk off the Dogger Bank by a German submarine, *U9*, on 22 September 1914 with the loss of 60 officers and 1,400 men drowned. This was followed five days later by an attack on a British cruiser in the Dover Strait. Enemy submarine operations already constituted a menace and the war had hardly begun. The map of U-boat sinkings during the Great War, which appears in Chapter 4, shows how devastating the submarine menace was to become and the vital necessity of allocating the appropriate resources to the anti-submarine campaign. When one compares the situation today with only one RAF station operating long-range anti-submarine patrols it is a reminder that the range and speed of the fragile seaplanes that patrolled the shores of the British Isles in 1914 was such that the coastline had to be ringed with seaplane stations resulting in seaside resorts such as Torquay, Poole, Skegness, Mullion and Newhaven being pressed into use.

ANTI-SUBMARINE OPERATIONS IN THE EARLY STAGES OF THE WAR

With the war only four days old the Admiralty were able to mount anti-submarine patrols right along the East Coast and into the English Channel. This was particularly important given the passage of vessels crossing over the Channel with units of the Expeditionary Force. At this time the Germans had U-boats *U5* and *U25* available for operations in the Channel, however only vessels numbered from *U19* upwards had been equipped with reliable diesel engines. Gradually the U-boats were penetrating the Dover Straits then the west coast of England, the west coast of Ireland and the north-east coast of Scotland. Eventually, U-boats would operate in the Mediterranean and off the east coast of the United States.

During the early autumn U-boats were particularly active off the east coast of Scotland. This resulted in the strengthening of anti-submarines measures, which was achieved by adding the number of seaplane units to the strength at such stations as Dundee and Killingholme. Meanwhile, the number of vessels supplying the needs of the BEF in France was exciting the attention of submarines and an Allied seaplane station was established in Dunkirk harbour on 30 October. On 21 November another seaplane station was established at Dover but with the fall of Antwerp and the occupation of Ostend and Zeebrugge by German forces any advantage was lost. The seaplanes bound for the Dunkirk base were conveyed in the seaplane carrier *Hermes*, which itself was torpedoed and sunk on its return to Dover. It was not until 7 November 1914 that an attempt was made by a seaplane to attack a submarine. Flight Lieutenant Nanson sighted a periscope and he used very lights to warn other shipping as he dropped bombs. When the periscope was sighted again it was only for a few seconds and the attack was aborted. There was some respite, however, when the German advance across Belgium was checked and the seaplanes at Dunkirk were returned to the Isle of Grain for overhaul. Dunkirk would eventually become an important naval base for the RNAS when units there were instrumental in attacking the Zeppelin bases.

The loss of the battleship *Formidable* to a torpedo from the German submarine *U24* pointed to the need to take action to close the U-boat bases in Zeebrugge and Ostend. A canal connected the former with Bruges where repair facilities had been established. When the Royal Navy could have mounted a concerted attack on these U-boat facilities the Dardanelles campaign in early 1915 called for resources that could have been used for this purpose. The U-boat campaign was already taking a toll of British shipping, The bases in Flanders rapidly extended their operations into the entire length of the English Channel and up into the Irish sea where shipping en route for Liverpool could be attacked thus interrupting the flow of goods and military equipment bound for the United Kingdom. Indeed, Commander Hersing in *U21* had passed through the Dover Straits, down into the English Channel and up into the Irish Sea. With Britain blockaded, her war effort could be seriously undermined. What the German Naval command did not bargain for was the sinking of the liner *Lusitania* in June 1915. It was counted as a Royal Naval Reserve vessel in *Jane's Book of Fighting ships* and was fair game. As it happens the Admiralty had decided, on the outbreak of war, to classify the *Lusitania* as an Armed Merchant Cruiser (AMC) but vessels of this size were deemed too expensive to operate in that capacity yet the liner remained on the Admiralty's list of AMCs. Nevertheless, a government subsidy was paid if the liner carried cargoes of a military nature so in a sense she was fair game. Be that as it may, the loss of American lives in this tragic incident would have far reaching consequences unforeseen in the conduct of unrestricted submarine warfare.

ANTI-SUBMARINE OPERATIONS IN 1915

Introduction
The voyage of *U21* led Admiral Von Pohl, Chief of the German Admiralty Staff, to issue a Press notice on 4 February 1915 to the effect that the waters around Great Britain and Ireland constituted a war zone and that from 18 February enemy merchant ships met in this zone would be destroyed. By this time Germany had twenty-three submarines suited to this purpose to which would be added coastal minelaying submarines. Using the Dover Straits was the favoured route but much depended on the state of the tide and if a passage at night was not possible U-boats could always lie on the bottom north of the Roytingen Bank until there was a favourable state of

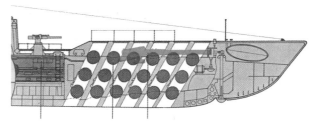
Bow section of a mine-laying U-boat.

the tide. Energetic and comprehensive countermeasures were called for. The Germans then introduced a smaller type of submarine, the UB Class. It measured some 90ft in length and was eminently suitable for making successful passages through confined channels in the Dover Straits. On 29 March 1915 the U-boat flotilla was formed and was equipped with the UB10 Class, assembled in Antwerp. To these would be added submarines of the UC Class, which were minelayers. The submarine threat had increased substantially and was located in bases much closer to the British shores. The air service would assume a major role and this included shore-based land and seaplanes and airships. This section will begin by describing the role of airships in the fight against the U-boat.

EMPLOYMENT OF BRITISH AIRSHIPS
Source: National Archive Document AIR1/723/66/5 and AIR1/675/21/13/1385

Introduction
The war began with Britain possessing seven naval airships, which were employed on reconnaissance and artillery observation in Belgium. Unlike the enemy, British airships were never used for bombing operations outside the sphere of military operations. When it came

UB Class.

Ocean-going U-boat.

Capel-le-Ferne airship station, near Dover, Kent.

to artillery observation the work of airship *Beta* produced satisfactory results but it could not observe every part of the front line and kite balloons were adopted, which speedily won the regard of both army and naval commanders. Kite balloon operations were initially an offshoot of airship operations but soon Kite Balloon Sections were operating independently on every front and on every sea with great accuracy of operation (see next section). The other airships began by escorting the British Expeditionary Force across the Channel and maintaining anti-submarine patrols in the Channel. They were also used to observe London by night to report on lighting. Given that airships were slow and lacked manoeuvrability relative to aircraft it was realized early in the war that they were best suited to naval operations, which included coastal patrols, escorting convoys of merchant ships and reconnaissance/escort for battle fleets and finally, patrol of distant minefields. An aerial photograph is shown of Capel-le-Ferne airship station situated between Dover and Folkestone. The airship stations provided all the necessary technical and supply support for airships operating from the station, which included, amongst other things, deflating and inflating the airship and carrying out the necessary repairs. Mooring-out stations provided a base for airships dispersed from their home base and had the advantage of spreading airships along the coast thus shortening the reaction time following the sighting of an enemy submarine. The major advantage of employing airships as opposed to aircraft was the endurance of the former. Thus their range of operations vastly exceeded that of aircraft. On the other hand airships were vulnerable to gunfire and to attacks by hostile aircraft. Britain but not Germany was experimenting with aircraft carriers. These extend the range of aircraft well beyond the shores of a country to hunt down submarines or attack airships. This was a deficiency that Germany was to carry into World War II, for although the keel of a German aircraft carrier was laid the ship was never completed. This may be partly explained by its being a continental power where wars could be won or lost in land campaigns alone. Ships or airships beyond the range of their shore-based aircraft were immune from air attack, except ship-borne anti-aircraft guns. Of course, British seaplanes were 'tied' to the land but the fragility of their floats rendered it impossible for them to take off anything but calm water. In any event the call for heavier-than-air machines on other duties and in other theatres meant that, during the first half of the Great War, the airship was much in demand.

Coastal Patrol work

The role of the airship was to search for enemy submarines. The term SS applied to airships means 'submarine scout'. The Admiralty decreed that the SS airships were suitable for the purpose for which they were designed i.e.,

patrolling narrow channels such as the Dover Straits and the Irish narrows. The SS Zero, for example, was a single-engined non-rigid airship of 75hp capable of a maximum of 50mph and an envelope capacity of 70,000cu.ft. After the construction of the first SS airship a large number of these crafts were ordered and by the end of 1915, twenty-nine had been built. With these craft it was decided that patrols should be established over the Straits of Dover and the northern and southern entrances to the Irish Sea. This involved the construction of accommodation and airship sheds as follows:

1. **Capel** (Folkestone) – capable of housing eight small airships in May 1915.
2. **Marquise** (France) – where a portable shed for two small airships was erected towards the end of June 1915.
3. **Polegate** (Near Eastbourne) – with a housing capacity the same as Capel, on 6 July 1915.
4. **Luce Bay** – with shed accommodation for four small ships, established about the middle of July 1915.
5. **Anglesey** – with capacity similar to the other locations established towards the end of September 1915.

In addition to the SS type of airship a larger one, known as the Coastal, had been constructed with the object of carrying out more protracted patrols of greater areas of sea. It was believed that these should patrol the sea areas off Land's End, north of Aberdeen, the precincts of the Tyne, Humber and Forth, Pembroke and Selsey. Thirty of the Coastal airships were therefore ordered. Bases for the Coastal airships were henceforth established as follows:

1. Pembroke in January 1916.
2. Pulham in February 1916.
3. Longside (West of Peterhead) in March 1916.
4. Howden (North of the Humber) in March 1916.
5. Mullion (Cornwall) in June 1916.
6. East Fortune (Firth of Forth) in August 1916.
7. Cranwell (School) in December 1916.

SS Zero.

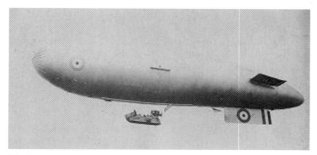

SS Coastal airship.

The rigid airships that were being constructed were to be based at Howden and some of the bases listed above. Additionally, a base for the rigid airships was established at Caldale in the Orkneys to work with the Grand Fleet at Scapa Flow. The establishment of these airship bases could not have come too soon. In the middle of March 1915 a steamship was attacked and set on fire. The penetration of *U21* into the Irish Sea was followed by *U20*, which sank *Lusitania* off the south coast of Ireland on 7 May with the loss of 1,200 lives. The importance of the Irish Command was acknowledged by the hoisting of the flag of Vice Admiral Sir Lewis Bayley at Queenstown in July. As regards actually attacking a U-boat, once sighted it was believed that the role of the airship was to transmit the position of the enemy to the destroyers, sloops and auxiliary vessels that could deal more effectively in the actual attack. An airship might drop bombs on a submarine sighted on the surface but since the airship is ponderous in movement it would be a matter of luck if the strike resulted in a sinking or disablement of a submarine. Admiral Freemantle, head of the Signals Section at the Admiralty, believed that an airship's radio was its most effective weapon and that the powers of observation should not be sacrificed by descending to a low altitude to deliver an attack. He proposed the use of a special wavelength less susceptible to interference and the establishment of direction-finding stations at intervals

along the coast. This proposal was accepted by the Board of the Admiralty in September 1915. Thus one can judge the seriousness attached to the submarine menace and the measures adopted to deal with that threat.

Change of organization and administration of the RNAS

The naval air stations were removed from the operational control of the Director of the Air Department and were placed under the command of the commanders in chief or senior naval officers in whose districts they were situated. This would have a material effect on anti-submarine operations since senior naval officers would have direct control of the naval air stations resulting in a much closer liaison between air and surface craft. But the seaplanes could only operate from calm waters and there was a lack of appropriate heavier-than-air machines to effectively deal with the U-boat threat. During this period such aeroplanes that there were, were actively engaged in anti-Zeppelin operations. Aircraft of the patrol type were needed such as Short aeroplanes with Sunbeam engines. The burden of patrolling fell, as previously described, on coastal airships. Once the senior naval officers were controlling operations they made insistent demands for sea and land planes that could not simply spot submarines but also mount an attack, probably long before surface vessels could arrive. The war could most effectively be carried to the enemy by attacking the submarine bases in Bruges, Ostend and Zeebrugge.

The effects on policy adopted by German naval high command following the sinking of *Lusitania*

Von Tirpitz and Admiral Bachmann, Chief of the Admiralty Staff, maintained that the submarine war should not to be sacrificed to the United States following the sinking of the liner *Lusitania* by *U20*. On the other hand, the Imperial Chancellor, Bethmann Hollweg, supported by the Chief of the Marine Cabinet, Admiral Müller, believed that the United States should be given an assurance that the *Lusitania* case be submitted to

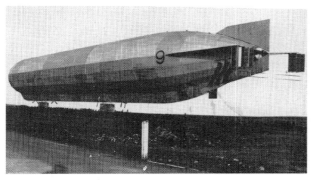

Rigid airship No.9.

The *Lusitania*.

arbitration and that U-boat commanders be ordered not to sink any passenger steamer without warning and saving the passengers. The Chancellor won the day and from 20 September 1915 onwards until the following spring no more boats were sent out in the North Sea for commerce raiding. This was shortly followed by a prohibition of attacks by submarines on merchant shipping in the Channel and along the west coast of Britain. Accordingly, there was a lull in activity in home waters from October 1915 until Christmas but not in the Mediterranean where U-boat attacks grew in intensity.

OPERATIONS OF THE NO.2 KITE BALLOON SECTION RNAS

Source: National Archive document AIR1/206/5/985

Introduction

It is remarkable that the activities of the Kite Balloon Sections of the Royal Naval Air Service should be part and parcel of land operations, as remarkable as it was that the Navy was the first service to undertake strategic bombing. It meant that the Royal Navy was involved both tactical and strategically in the three theatres of operations: land, sea and air. The following extracts are taken from the diary of No.2 Kite Balloon Section RNAS, covering the late summer of 1915, and have been chosen since they illustrate different aspects of kite balloon operations. The susceptibility of balloons to strong winds is evident and the strain on the cable and the winch becomes a problem. Mist, rain and high winds had a major impact on balloon operations during the period in question. An interesting comment is made by one observer that he should not be required to report on each individual fall of shot but on the general effects of a shoot. It is clear that kite balloon observations were of value to the artillery but that ground observers and observers in aircraft were a necessary addition.

Operations from Monday 16 August to Friday 3rd September 1915

At 14.45hrs on Monday 16 August Captains Mac Neece and Townley-Bertie ascended but it was very misty. The unit diary records that, on account of electrical disturbances the previous day, the telephone receiver bands had been insulated and no severe shock had been experienced, but the crackling of the electricity was very audible and distinctly uncomfortable. During an evening sortie that day the mist was still around and made observation absolutely impossible. The weather was little better the following day and a thunderstorm broke no sooner had the balloon come down. On the Wednesday morning the mist was still in evidence throughout the whole morning but in the afternoon the observations made by Captain Mac Neece and Flight Sub Lieutenants Gill and Bompass tallied with a ground observer and

reports coming from an aircraft. Whilst descending two shots were fired at the balloon but fell short. The day ended with reports from the balloon speaking of enemy shelling east of Ypres. On the descent the winch was pulling very badly. This necessitated a cleaning out of the boiler the following morning but the winch was not ready for use until 14.00hrs. When the weather did improve there was nothing to report.

During the afternoon of 20 August the Battery commander of Howitzers reported that he would not be firing his guns because he was being observed from an enemy kite balloon and he did not wish the flashes of his guns to be seen. When he reported that he was ready to fire the first shoot was quite successful the range and line being determined after only three rounds had been fired. A second shoot followed, which was not so successful as the first round was observed to be 1½ degrees out to the left and it was not until the sixth of the ranging shots was fired that it was even approximately effective. The observer was of the opinion at the long range of 13,500 yards from the balloon he would be likely even on the clearest of days to be of more assistance reporting general results than describing the fall of each shot. Flight Sub Lieutenants Grant and Sharpe reported the front as being very quiet except that two new German balloons had been sighted, one towards Hollebeke and the other towards Commines. Saturday 21 August was characterized by high winds and heavy rain.

On Wednesday 1 September the balloon reached a height of 2,500ft but the wind was too high so the winch began to bring it down. The strain on the cable steadily increased and several times during the last few hundred feet it seemed very doubtful that the winch would be able to continue working. When about 30ft from the ground the balloon was diving in such a way that the cable had to be clamped. It was some time before the men in the ground party could get a hold of the guy ropes. Subsequently the rigging was carefully inspected and a certain amount of it had to be renovated. From the unit diary for Monday 6 September the purpose of the artillery spotting was to knock out enemy batteries. The target was over 12,000 yards from the balloon and the light was not good. It was out of range for shrapnel and the observers were unable to observe the bursts. During the morning Captain Mac Neece and Flight Sub Lieutenant Gill were aloft, followed by Flight Sub Lieutenants Campbell and Bompass in the afternoon. A further ascent was made at 17.20hrs and the 115th Battery was seen to have registered the target after the eighth round fired with a view to knocking out the enemy battery. The weather, including haze, hampered observations for the rest of the week. When the haze did clear nothing could be seen and on the Friday the wind was too high for ballooning. On Saturday 11 September the 67th Battery attempted to range on a target but with 30mph winds and unfavourable light observations had to be suspended. The targets on the Sunday were the enemy trenches. Captain Bertie and Flight Sub Lieutenant Gill ascended in the morning and a number of shots were fired by the 12th battery but only nine rounds fired were observed as the view was bad. When the Balloon Section was up, observing for the 67th and 89th Batteries, there were frequent interruptions on the line from the winch to the batteries and it was impossible to carry out the shoots. On the Sunday afternoon whilst observing for the 103rd Battery the target was registered in eight rounds and the ascent resulted in six rounds of shrapnel being observed bursting over Neuve Eglise. Friday 3 September saw weather that was unfavourable for ballooning all day. On the following day four ascents were made. During the first the balloon would rise no further than 500ft with two observers so Captain McNeece had to go up alone. Some observations were made of shell bursts throughout the day but in the end the balloon was driven down by rain.

RFC OPERATIONS ON THE WESTERN FRONT 1914–1915

OPERATIONS – YPRES TO THE SOMME
Sources: National archive documents: AIR1/674/21/6/95–21/6/106 and 21/6/130

Introduction
By the winter of 1914 the Western Front had stabilized, characterized by a continuous line of trenches as the French and British Armies faced the Germans. In the nineteenth century Bismarck had done his best to isolate France diplomatically and create a union of three emperors, the Dreikaiserbund, consisting of Germany, Austro-Hungary and Russia and so avoid war in Europe. The last thing the German General staff wanted was to have to fight on two fronts but the impetuous Kaiser Wilhelm II succeeded in creating an alliance between France and Russia so that, on the outbreak of the Great War, Germany faced Russia in the east and the Franco British alliance in the west. The grand strategy hatched by the Germans before the war started was the Schlieffen Plan, which consisted of a right hook through Belgium curving round to isolate Paris from the rest of France. But the plan had failed and the German offensive was countered at the Marne. Thereafter, each attempt by both sides to drive an offensive forward to take ground failed as forces were brought up to counter each offensive until the line solidified. Fortress warfare had replaced field warfare. With substantial German forces having to be maintained in the east to face the Russians, reinforcements could not be sent to Flanders to begin a successful German offensive aimed at reaching the Channel ports. Not until the Bolsheviks withdrew Russia from the Great War in 1918 could the German High Command send substantial reinforcements to the Western Front. From the winter of 1914 the Germans would content themselves in holding on to their defensive line of trenches and the Allies were to make repeated unsuccessful attempts to break the stalemate but the number of guns required and the expenditure of gun ammunition required for a successful offensive was beyond the powers of either side.

The role of the RFC and RNAS in fortress warfare
In stark contrast to the way fast-moving mobile warfare characterized the battle for Poland, the Low Countries and France in 1939 and 1940, the aeroplane was going to have to be employed tactically in support of trench warfare. During the Spanish Civil War the Germans had developed the Blitzkrieg where Stuka dive bombers spearheaded fast moving columns of tanks and infantry but this was not going to be possible in 1914. Instead, the aeroplane would be used to reconnoitre enemy trenches and spot for the artillery. They would also take aerial photographs, which would inform field commanders of the situation on the ground. But these activities on both sides could not be allowed to continue unimpeded and soon aerial warfare developed with aircraft designed to shoot down other aircraft. These scouts (fighters in modern parlance) were soon to be seen on the front line. Certain difficulties faced the RFC and RNAS in the winter of 1914. One was the weather, which could disrupt aerial activities for days at a time and there was also a lack of the reliable and convenient means of signalling. Aerial photography was hampered initially by a lack of efficient cameras and when it came to bombing, aircrews were hampered by a lack of efficient bomb sights or bomb racks and there was no certainty that the bombs would explode on impact. The work of the RFC and the RNAS during the first winter of the war centred on experiment, organization and training.

THE BATTLE OF NEUVE CHAPPELLE
Great hopes were pinned on an Allied success against the German lines at Neuve Chappelle but like so many Allied attempts to launch offensives in the years 1915 to 1918 attempts to break the stalemate on the Western Front only resulted in appalling losses of life for little or no gains on the ground. This first British attempt, launched at 07.30hrs on 10 March 1915, resulted in gaining territory no larger than an average sized farm. The part played by the RFC would nevertheless be important in the coming battle and names that featured in the most senior ranks of the RAF in the 1920s would take part. These included Lieutenant Colonel Hugh Trenchard, Major John Salmond and Lieutenant Colonel Brooke-Popham. Prior to the attack the RFC operations were central to the planning of the ground offensive. The German trenches were photographed to a depth of anything between

700 and 1,500 yards along the entire front occupied by the First Army. This was particularly useful to the infantry and artillery officers who could identify various defended localities by the communication trenches that ran to them. British artillery could then be massed and registered on to the enemy strong points. Breaking up the enemy barbed wire that protected enemy positions was important prior to an attack. The aerial work was performed by squadrons of the 1st Wing RFC commanded by Lieutenant Colonel Hugh Trenchard. Nos.2, 3 and 9 Squadrons provided wireless machines and No.16 Squadron worked with the First Army and operated from Merville. The 2nd Wing RFC, with its HQ at Hazebrouck, had its squadrons, Nos.5 and 6, at Poperinghe. Lieutenant Colonel Brooke-Popham's aircraft from Nos.1 and 4 Squadrons were based at St Omer tasked to carry out strategic reconnaissance and the bombing of special objectives.

For the first eight days in March 1915 the weather was so bad as to impede essential preparatory work but this later improved. The RFC was instructed on 9 March to bomb various railway targets important for German reinforcements. To this was added, for the first day of the offensive, the Marie and Chateau la Vallée at Fournes where a hostile Divisional HQ was reportedly located. By 11.00hrs on 10 March the whole of the village of Neuve Chappelle and the roads leading northwards and south westwards were in British hands and steps were taken to consolidate the positions. At 15.00hrs the troops were being organized for a second assault. By this time the Germans had an exposed flank and they could not afford to leave a break in their lines for long. Meanwhile, the RFC were carrying out their bombing missions on railway targets to prevent the arrival of enemy reinforcements. Captain Carmichael of No.5 Squadron successfully bombed the railway line at the fork north of Menin and Captain Strange of No.6 Squadron successfully bombed the railway at Courtai. These and other missions were carried out at altitudes of approximately 100ft. Be that as it may the overall success of the bombings was doubtful.

On the final day of the offensive the RFC continued with the aerial offensive against enemy railway communications. Pilots of No.4 Squadron, Captain Ludlow-Hewitt and Lieutenants Grenfell, Barrington Kennett and Mullin, left St Omer in an attempt to destroy the railway bridge at the north-east corner of Douai and the railway junction at Don, south-west of Lille. This raid, like that of the previous day, failed to achieve its objective, There was moderate success on the following day when the centre carriages of a steam train standing in a station, were blown up.

These expeditions demonstrated the importance of thorough training and preparation of pilots, especially for bomb-dropping duties. Another factor that too often limited the effectiveness of RFC operations was the weather. On 12 March 1915 the offensive was suspended.

HILL 60

Following the termination of the British offensive at Neuve Chappelle the centre of activity shifted northwards, as far as the British Army on the Western Front (BEF), to the neighbourhood of Ypres. The front line had stabilized to produce a pronounced salient around the city and a salient can more easily be punctured by the enemy. The Messines–Passchendaele ridge to the south-east of the salient was dominated by Hill 60, which rose some 60ft above the surrounding countryside to afford the Germans an excellent artillery observation post. The enemy would have to be removed from Hill 60. The defence of the Ypres Sector was the responsibility of the Second British Army and the aerial work in support was the responsibility of the 2nd Wing RFC commanded by Lieutenant Colonel C.J. Burke DSO, with his Headquarters at Hazebrouck. No.6 Squadron at Poperinghe, commanded by Major G.S. Shepherd, was equipped with BE2a, BE2b and BE2c aircraft and was attached to the Fifth Army Corps, whilst No.1 Squadron, commanded by Major W.G.H. Salmond, was equipped with a Martinsyde Scouts, Avros, BE8s and Moranes. The Squadron was attached to the Second Army Corps and the Third Army Corps had the support of No.5 Squadron, commanded by Major A.C. Board. Finally, it was during April 1915 that the RFC in France was reinforced by two additional squadrons, Nos.7 and 8.

The taking of Hill 60 fell to the 13th Brigade and the RFC squadrons were watching the enemy closely. The aim of taking the hill was more to prevent the

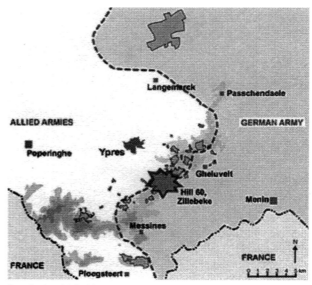

Battle for Hill 60.

enemy from using it to endanger British troop forward positions than to use the hill against the Germans. The General Staff were anxious to avoid more casualties than necessary so the intelligence that could be gained from reconnaissance flights was very important. Tunnels were dug from the forward British trenches so that they penetrated to a point below the German forward trenches and mines were placed there to be exploded at the moment the assault was launched. Major Salmond's task was to ensure that no enemy aircraft appeared over the salient and on the morning of 17 April the first RFC aircraft appeared at 04.30hrs. Signalling lamps were to be used to assist the artillery to register on certain points in the enemy defences. The assault went in during the evening and the mines were exploded at 19.00hrs. A special flash reconnaissance was carried out by Captain Ludlow-Hewitt, resulting in many hostile batteries being pinpointed, which hitherto remained immune from the attention of British gunners owing to their well camouflaged positions. The assaulting troops gained the crest of the hill with few casualties and several enemy counterattacks repulsed. On the second day the enemy forced some of the British troops back on to the reverse slope.

On the second day, the 18th, a wireless and lamp receiving station was established at Army HQ and RFC observers were ordered to report any movement of enemy troops using a special code, any flashes from enemy guns, the fall of artillery shells and to ascertain whether or not certain localities were clear or occupied. If the lamp or wireless signals were not being received by the HQ then the RFC aircrews resorted to message dropping. When fresh British troops assaulted the hill to dislodge the enemy the latter replied with a massive bombardment of British positions on the hill. This was on 19 April and during the afternoon gas shells were used but these were not recognized as such at the time. (The Germans had used gas against Russian positions in January 1915.) The following day the weather deteriorated and the pilots of No.1 Squadron did their best to pinpoint the German gun positions since British casualties were mounting. During the afternoon of 21 April the enemy ceased in their attempts to retake the hill. It was not until the evening of 1 May that a patrolling aircraft of No.1 Squadron noticed that heavy shelling of British positions had resumed. The enemy ceased firing on seeing the RFC aircraft since they did not want the gun flashes to give away their positions but when the aircraft had to retire in bad light the German artillery barrage resumed. Another German assault was mounted and great volumes of asphyxiating gas were released, which struck down the British soldiers along a 4,000 yard front. The German infantry did not attempt to occupy the hill crest due to lingering gas but on 5 May a second more severe gas attack was delivered and

the Germans regained the crest leaving British troops holding positions only at the base of the hill. Attempts to recapture the hill were made using fresh troops to replace those affected by gas and loss of sleep. The fresh assault was made to recapture the trenches east of the hill and to the north of the Zwarteleen salient but the troops lost direction, becoming involved in a network of old trenches. The recapture of the lost ground around Hill 60 and the Zwarteleen Ridge ceased to be feasible.

THE SECOND BATTLE OF YPRES

German offensive

This episode in the battle to control the Ypres Salient is interesting because it contrasts intelligence gleaned from a German POW, warning of an impending gas attack on the salient, with that of aerial reconnaissance reports. The latter gave no hint of an impending attack, which threw doubt on the words of the POW but in defence of the RFC bad weather prevented accurate reporting on a number of days before the gas attack was launched. When the British Army was about to attack it could wait for up-to-date aerial reconnaissance reports to be received but this time it was the enemy taking the initiative and the Germans could be expected to move artillery and troops at a time when RFC aerial reconnaissance was limited. The advice from No.6 Squadron was that no German gun emplacements could be found and, with the exception of 18 April, there was no significant movement of troops. Indeed, there was no sign of enemy activity to the rear of the German lines north of Lys indicating reinforcement. In the event what the POW had said proved to be correct. The Germans had been waiting for the wind direction to change so that the gas would be carried from in front of the German lines to blow over Allied positions in the salient. The right moment came on 22 April and would affect the positions held by French territorial and Colonial troops. The gas had predictable consequences, rendering the French 45th Division incapable of any action whatsoever. The casualties were either comatose or dying and within the hour the French were retiring in confusion. This left a gap between the Allied lines and on the night of 23/24 April the Germans broke through and advanced on Brielen. This advance threatened the lines of communication of the British 5th Corps and endangered the safety of all troops east of Ypres. There were also indications that the Germans were trying to drive a wedge between the French and the Belgians about Steenstraat, forcing the left of the French line into Ypres. The Second Army commander was forced to bring in the cavalry.

Work of the 2nd Wing

The tactical air work for the Second Army was split between Nos.1, 5 and 6 Squadrons forming the 2nd Wing.

The Ypres Salient on 22 April 1915 – a German gas attack.

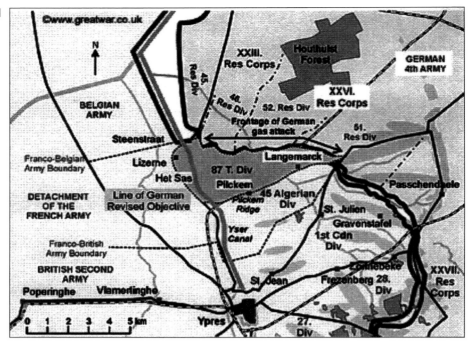

The bulk of the work, however, fell to No.6 Squadron, which co-operated with the Fifth Corps. Their work may be described as defence reconnaissance. In order for Reserves to be employed effectively previous knowledge of the enemy's intentions was vital. The latter would concentrate his forces in a particular sector. Espionage and intelligence gleaned from POWs aside, the battlefield forward artillery observing officers provided an important source of intelligence. On the other hand, Army commanders were finding that the RFC could provide positive and rapid reports but aircraft are not stationary whereas a balloon observer had a stationary platform to get a prolonged look at enemy movements, trench lines and gun positions. An air observer might spot these things but as soon as the aircraft departed the situation on the ground could change no sooner had the aircraft gone. An aircraft pilot who circled for a long period lay himself open to anti-aircraft fire. If he flew higher to avoid ground fire the quality of air reconnaissance could fall; the lower he flew the more likely it was that his aircraft might be shot down. For an offensive to be successful there would have to be a considerable amount of activity on the roads and railway lines leading to the front. Infantry and cavalry were usually conveyed in covered wagons whereas guns and stores were conveyed in open ones. Fifty railway coaches could lift a battalion of men. Movement could take place during the hours of darkness but since most of the important offensives took place in the summer months the nights were short. In

early 1915 Army commanders knew that aircraft could range further and faster than cavalry but it became clear that, in certain circumstances, railway activity on its own may not be a reliable indicator of the enemy's intentions. Prior to the German offensive of 24 April, for example, railway activity had been spotted at Menin but the aircrews did not know that the trains were there for only half an hour, an insufficient time to bring up substantial reserves. Furthermore, reports of enemy inactivity along the front might be negative when, in fact, one thousand men could be hiding in a forest safe from the prying eyes of an air observer. Such reports were of little value but the reports sent in as a result of air reconnaissance may in some cases seem of little value but when put together with reports from other sources could be of inestimable value. Such then were the advantages and limitations of air reconnaissance in early 1915.

Forms of air reconnaissance

At this time aerial reconnaissance consisted of three main and distinct forms:

1. **Reconnaissance in the immediate front of own troops** – The enemy's gun positions or reserves to a depth of eight or nine miles were reconnoitred by aircraft of squadrons allotted to or acting under the orders of Corps or Divisions.
2. **Air Reconnaissance for Armies** – In this case reconnaissance extended to some twenty miles from

the front and overlapping at the edges of the area on either side. Such intelligence would be either of a tactical or a strategic nature and made available to Army HQ.

3. **Distance reconnaissance or special mission** – The purpose was to obtain intelligence at a range beyond that achieved by the two aforementioned forms. As a rule such aerial activity was undertaken from the wing at RFC HQ under instructions from General HQ. Missions could be along a designated path or on an area basis.

The distribution of intelligence obtained by air reconnaissance was not the responsibility of the RFC. For example, after the German attack on 22 April the pilots and machines of No.6 Squadron, working with Second Corps, were pushed to the utmost to keep in touch with all the enemy movements to the rear of the enemy lines. Aircraft of No.4 Squadron had to be moved from Bailleul to Poperinghe to report to the Second Army. When Poperinghe came within the range of enemy artillery the personnel and equipment of No.6 Squadron with the exception of three aircraft and a wireless tender were moved back to an aerodrome at Abele. The original aerodrome at Poperinghe was used as an advanced landing ground until 26 April when the remaining aircraft and tender also moved back to Abele The point is, therefore, that aerial reconnaissance reports would be made by aircrews to whomever had tasked them for the mission.

Regrouping of RFC Squadrons on 25 April to meet the operational demands at Ypres
In order that the maximum aerial support be given to the British Second Army, No.4 Squadron took over all of the duties of the Third Corps from No.5 Squadron and the RFC squadrons in this sector were regrouped as follows:

1st Wing RFC – Nos.2, 3, 8 and 16 Squadrons to work with the British First Army

2nd Wing RFC – Nos.1, 5 and 6 Squadrons to work with the Fifth and Second Corps

3rd Wing RFC – No.4 Squadron to work with the Third Corps Nos.7 and 8 Squadrons of the Wing to work with GHQ

Counting the two squadrons at GHQ who at this time were working from St Omer and almost wholly employed on distance reconnaissance work, east and north east of Ypres, there were then five squadrons working over this area. On this occasion a serial reconnaissance by No.5 Squadron revealed evidence of an impending German offensive. Seven trains or rolling stock at Ledeghem was significant because it was the station that served

the needs of the German XXVII R Corps. The offensive began on 24 April against the front held by the Third Canadian Brigade. The Allied line was broken after a severe struggle and an advance was made on Fortuin. At the same time enemy reinforcements of foot soldiers and mounted troops were seen moving south from Poelcappelle. The situation for the Allies was becoming critical and Captain Hawker of No.6 Squadron could see how serious. Between 17.30 and 19.15hrs he saw two columns of infantry about 1,500 yards in length halted at the roads and considerable railway activity to and from Langemarck. Another squadron pilot observed about 1,000 infantry and 100 motor vehicles moving towards Poelcappelle. The enemy meant to profit from the original breakthrough. A heavy bombardment on the morning of the 25th involved the use of gas shells and severe hand-to-hand fighting took place along the line held by the 84th and 85th Brigades.

Strategic bombing
Days of heavy fighting with both British and French reinforcements entering the fray help to stabilize the front and the German advance was checked. The RFC attacked an armoured train that had been shelling Poperinghe and bombing attacks were also directed against railway targets of strategic importance, such as Ghent from whence German reinforcements could reach Ypres. This strategic bombing was carried out by Nos.7 and 8 Squadrons from the 3rd Wing attached to GHQ. The Wing Commander chose the actual objectives but only twenty-four of the fifty-nine bombs carried were dropped on the assigned targets. Two RE5s of No.7 Squadron and seven BE2cs were employed but only five of the nine aircraft succeeded in their missions. The other pilots lost their way, experienced forced landings or found that the bombs failed to release. The raid was therefore of very little material value. Four machines from No.1 Wing were dispatched to bomb the railway stations at Lille, Roubaix, Tourcoing and Courtrai but only two of the pilots found their objective. One flown by Lieutenant Cruikshank dropped bombs in the vicinity of Roubaix and Tourcoing stations and Lieutenant Moorhouse dropped a 100lb bomb on the railway line where it turned north just west of Courtrai Station. This mission earned Lieutenant Moorhouse a posthumous VC. This may appear a sorry tale but, having consulted Chapter 6 (the work of the Independent Bombing Force in late 1918) one may soberly reflect that a force dedicated to strategic bombing often straddled railway lines without actually interrupting railway traffic for any significant period of time and this was three years on from 1915. One may go further and say that the effectiveness of raids carried out by RAF Bomber Command in the period 1939 to 1941 were not great and the bombs used were sometimes of World War I vintage.

Effectiveness of Allied artillery co-operation

The outcome of assistance to the artillery was different. A German POW officer confirmed the effectiveness of Allied artillery assisted by aircraft reconnaissance. The task, however, was not easy. A wireless aircraft, of the squadron involved, would spot active enemy batteries and assist the gunners in hitting those targets by reporting the fall of shot, a process known as ranging. Having ranged successfully the targets were registered so that the gunners would know the elevation of the barrels and the deflection required to hit those targets. Any new targets that might be identified by air observers would be similarly ranged and registered. But the effectiveness of artillery co operation by RFC squadrons could be affected by the availability of wireless machines and in the heat of a battle the amount of work required could simply overwhelm the squadrons doing their best to keep up with targets that would present themselves. Moreover, it should be remembered that there was little if any interference from enemy scouting aircraft but this was about to change. Even for those targets previously registered the guns might still not hit their targets. Different climatic conditions, the wear of gun barrels, a process known as 'de coppering', and the fact that guns might roll backwards in mud when fired could mean that batteries often failed to shoot within 200 yards of targets previously registered. This could well mean the expenditure of a prodigious amount of ammunition to knock out an enemy battery. Added to this was the fact that enemy batteries that had been on the receiving end of Allied ranging shots could well be moved to another location, so that previously registered targets would no longer be there. The answer was for artillery co-operation aircraft to constantly update any information the Allied gunners needed for their fire to be effective. One argument in favour of registration was the targeting of enemy trench systems. These could not be vacated if the enemy was not to leave a gap in its defences. This of course excluded an ordered withdrawal to a more easily defended front line that might well be shorter and devoid of salients, which occurred in the course of offensives by one side or the other. An example would be the German Hindenburg line.

Festubert – May and June 1915

Sir Herbert Plumer had taken charge of operations to restore the Allied line at Ypres and he was ordered to retire to a new line further to the west. Close and distance observation remained the order of the day but preparations for a renewed Allied offensive had been underway even before the German offensive. This was planned for the neighbourhood of Neuve Chappelle to take place in early May. The British First Army under Sir Douglas Haig would break through the enemy lines to gain the La Bassée–Lille Road between La Bassée and Fournes and an advance would be made on Don. The aerial co-operation for this attack was the responsibility of the 1st Wing under the command of Lieutenant Colonel Trenchard comprising Nos.2, 3 and 16 Squadrons. Nos.2 and 16 Squadrons were located at Merville with No.3 at Hinges. The weather on 6 and 7 May ruled out serious air work but the 8th saw a northerly wind and clear and bright conditions. Defensive air patrols were maintained throughout daylight hours. These were patrols designed to intercept any enemy aircraft attempting to interfere with air reconnaissance and artillery co operations. No.16 Squadron was working under the direct orders of the First Army and it was moved forward to an airfield at Beaupre Ferme, 3,000 yards east of Merville on the Lys Canal. The 1st and 3rd Wings were to bomb selected targets immediately before the opening of the Allied artillery barrage, which would be followed by the infantry assault. The 1st Wing was instructed to bomb the 6th Army HQ at La Madeleine, the 7th German Corps at Loos and the railway and road bridges over the canal south-west and in Don. To attempt to interrupt a possible transfer of enemy troops from the north and east the 3rd Wing was instructed to bomb the railway junctions to the south-east and north of Lille and the railway stations at Seclin, Tournai and Roubaix. The pilots had been instructed to fly low over these targets to be sure of registering hits. At 03.00hrs on 8 May Lieutenant J.L. Jackson of No.2 Squadron left to bomb the chateau at La Madeleine but he missed his objective. Lieutenant Glanville of No.16 Squadron left in one of two Voisins to bomb Don. He was wounded on the way out and failed to hit the bridge and the second Voisin was forced to descend between the lines and so no successful results were achieved on that morning of 8 May. The bombing by aircraft of the 3rd Wing on railway targets resulted in near misses but it was deemed improbable that there was any interference with enemy rail traffic. Two Voisins of No.4 Squadron also had no perceived success, since one of them could make no headway in a strong headwind and had to return to base. The sixth bomb that was meant to be dropped that morning by an aircraft, which did get through to Seclin and Roubaix, stuck in the carrier. A bullet passed through the boot of Captain Unwin but failed to cause him any injury and this showed that aircrews could become casualties even at normal reconnaissance height. Furthermore, there had not been any enemy aerial interference with these bombing missions.

The assault went in on 9 May but little progress was made since the strength of the enemy fortifications had been underestimated. The assault failed in its immediate object of penetrating the enemy's line and occupying the Aubers Ridge. There was to be a preliminary objective, which was to gain the first line of trenches between the Neuve Chappelle–La Bassée Road and Le Quinque Rue,

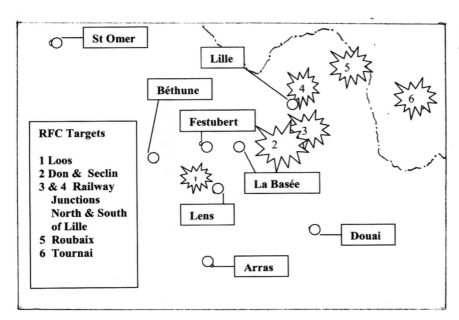

RFC Operations in support of the offensive to take Festubert.

RFC Targets

1 Loos
2 Don & Seclin
3 & 4 Railway
   Junctions
   North & South
   of Lille
5 Roubaix
6 Tournai

before gaining the La Basée to Lille road between La Basée and Fournes. A special bombing offensive was planned for dawn on 16 May but by that time the Indian Corps of the 2nd Division had made limited progress in capturing two lines of German trenches but were unable to move forward. Nos.2 and 3 Squadrons were involved using 20lb bombs but mist hampered the air operation and when the bombs were dropped on the various objectives there were no direct hits recorded. On 30 May the changes in the disposition of the ground forces brought about a change in the responsibilities of the three squadrons, 2, 3 and 16, and the movement of these units were ordered on 30 May and accomplished on 1 June without incident. Following reconnaissance of the area south of La Basée canal, Sir Douglas Haig, GOC First Army, decided that a fresh assault against the Rue D'Ouvert offered the best chance of success. Loos would have to wait until Lens and the adjoining defensive localities had first been cleared of the enemy. But this was the time of a shortage of shells for the Western Front and he was advised that there would be insufficient ammunition available to enable the assault to be launched on both sides of La Basée canal. So Haig decided to go ahead to the north of the canal. On the evening of 15 June the 1st Canadian Brigade launched their assault after a prolonged artillery bombardment and, after several postponements, succeeded in taking the German trenches north-east of Givenchy but their flanks were then exposed so were unable to hold on to their gains. Given the shortage of ammunition it was imperative to make the best use of it and the RFC would be heavily engaged ranging the shells prior to registration. There were two 15in Howitzers in the area and help was given by the RNAS from Dunkirk. The Navy provided

two aircraft and two pilots with observers to assist with this important work and June ended with the Second Army holding on to Allied positions in the Ypres Salient.

It was at this time that the Germans introduced their new Fokker monoplanes into the Western Front but they were attached to units in small numbers along the front line. These aircraft were, however, to constitute what became known as the 'Fokker Scourge' and it was some time before the German ascendancy over the Front was met with new British Scouts. The BE aircraft built by the Royal Aircraft Factory were renowned for their stability, which made them ideally suited to undertake photographic reconnaissance and artillery support but would be no match for a faster highly manoeuvrable fighter. Before ending this section the loss of a very gallant officer of the RFC is worthy of note. On 13 July 1915 Captain B.T. James was flying over the Ypres salient when his machine was hit by a shell and was observed

Martinsyde S.1.

to dive into the ground from a great height. On 29 July the Germans dropped a note from one of their aircraft saying that the pilot was dead when he fell. By a strange coincidence the other pioneer of wireless work with aircraft, Lieutenant Colonel D.S. Lewis, met his death nearly a year later in a similar manner on the same sector of the Front.

CONTACT AIR PATROLS 1915
Source: National Archive document AIR 1/674/21/6/120

It was recognized very early in the war that aeroplanes and balloons could be extremely useful in reporting the progress of a ground operation. Divisional HQ, in the heat of battle, could very quickly become out of touch with the progress of the brigades under their command. Likewise, subordinate formation commanders needed to report on the progress of a particular operation to higher formations. Even battalion commanders could very quickly lose contact with forward units which might be advancing rapidly or conversely falling back. Telephone cables laid before the commencement of a battle could so easily be cut due to explosions and with machine gun fire, smoke and mounting casualties, the chaos of battle made communications difficult in the extreme.

Observation from the air was an obvious answer. Observers could report from kite balloons, other balloons or aeroplanes. The problem with kite and other balloons was that they were tethered to the ground with cables wound round a drum that needed to be sufficiently far behind the enemy front line to reduced the threat from enemy fire. But the further back these balloons the less reliable the reconnaissance. Aeroplanes, on the other hand, could manoeuvre and could stay in close contact with forward units, thus being more likely to provide up-to-the-minute progress on the ground operations below. In this respect co-ordination of the work of the artillery was important if the latter was putting down rolling barrages that had to fall at all times slightly in front of an Allied advance so that Allied casualties would not to result from the fire of friendly guns.

The work of air observers was of critical importance if contact air patrols were to be effective. Observers would have to understand the planned ground operation that they sent aloft to observe if they could appreciate whether or not the ground commander's plan was being realized. They would also need to appreciate the nature of the ground over which a battle was to be fought. Where were the friendly force trenches and were there any obstacles that would impede the advance of friendly forces? It is one thing for an RFC observer to see elements of British forces below but were they meant to be there, were they advancing or retiring and had they reached their objectives? This called for observers who had received a military training and understood the nature

of ground operations. They also had to appreciate the strength, movement and location of enemy forces and the threat they posed to their own troops. This would lead to the establishment of a school for the training of tactical observers in kite balloons at St Riquier near Abbeville on 23 May 1916.

It was one thing to observe but another to efficiently and speedily report observations to ground commanders so that effective use could be made of the intelligence they were receiving. Ground commanders did not want to be told that enemy forces were advancing on their positions when they were already in contact with those forces. There were several means of communication: wireless telegraphy, light signals or message dropping. If wireless telegraphy was to be relied on there was a need for a properly equipped aircraft. If light signals were to be employed those on the ground had to be able to read and interpret those signals. If signals were to be transmitted from the ground there was a danger of exposing Allied positions to the enemy, which could bring down hostile artillery fire on ground troops sending light signals. Message dropping was an effective way of transmitting intelligence to a force commander provided the messages were not dropped on enemy positions by mistake. During the Battle of Neuve Chapelle in March 1915 message bags were dropped by aeroplanes at various report centres giving information concerning the progress of British troops. A lamp station was also provided by 1 Army Headquarters for communication with lamp machines. It was important that those on the ground could distinguish the lamp machines from other Allied or enemy aircraft in the vicinity. Early experiments were carried out by flights of No.16 Squadron, 1st Wing RFC, in conjunction with infantry in 1st Army training areas to determine the practicability of employing aeroplanes to watch and report their position during the advance. In the early months of 1915 No.16 Squadron possessed a variety of machines, which included the Martinsyde S1 (illustrated), the Voisin LA, BE2c, BE2a, Shorthorn and BE2b.

The results of these experiments were interesting. The infantry were quite easily seen from 6,000ft on certain kinds of ground such as ploughed fields but on wet grass or wheat the troops could not easily be made out. After the first phase of the advance it was impossible to tell whether it was the friendly forces advancing or the enemy's infantry retiring for men were seen running both backward and forward in short bursts. At the Battle of Festubert on 9 May 1915 contact patrols were put to the test. A wireless machine from No.16 Squadron was detailed to observe the progress of the 1st Army units including the 1st and 4th Corps and the Indian Corps during the attack. One machine was always in the air, the first for one and a half hours and the remainder for one hour each, and the observers were ordered to report by wireless when the infantry had reached certain predetermined points. The infantry units had received instructions to lay down white 7ft × 2ft panels on reaching these points but the observers were instructed to report what they saw whether or not panels could be seen. In the event it was impossible to distinguish between Allied and German infantry. During the attack there were casualties and one could not tell if the friendly forces had reached their positions and their diminishing numbers simply faded away. No panels were seen since the positions had not been reached. At a conference held at Gosnay by the 1st Division on 5 September 1915 prior to the Battle of Loos, it was decided that this time specified ground signals were to be placed at pre-determined points indicating whether the unit concerned was advancing or retreating. Still later it was decided that 15ft × 3ft panels forming the letter 'V' were to be displayed by the 1st Brigade on reaching Hulluck. The 2nd Brigade would use the letter 'T'. If both formations were obliged to retire then the signal panels would be reversed. Smoke signals of various colours were also used to indicate the position of ground forces. Trials were carried out by the 1st Corps on 5 May 1915 and preference was expressed for flares in blue, red and in the form of white stars. Then the Brocks firework firm produced flares emitting a cloud of yellow smoke for the purpose of signalling between aircraft and forward troops. Trials were carried out by the 2nd Corps in conjunction with No.1 Squadron RFC towards the end of August 1915. The results were good since the yellow cloud could be seen at a height of 6,000ft and issues of flares were made to the other Armies on 13 and 30 November 1915. The number of flares was, however, limited and instructions were issued for units holding them to retain them for use only on special occasions.

AN ASSESSMENT OF THE EFFECTIVENESS OF BRITISH AIR POWER TO GROUND OPERATIONS ON THE WESTERN FRONT

As the war progressed one thing that changed little until 1918 was the static nature of the front line between the Germans and the Anglo French forces. Time after time futile attempts would be made to push the line forward or break through the enemy lines so that, in open country, the war could again become fluid and provide a need for cavalry. Allied commanders really believed that they could make a breakthrough. The French General Nivelle was confident that if overwhelming force was applied in an offensive it would be bound to succeed. But it did not and the episode ended with numerous French soldiers mutinying rather than continue fruitless battles. The Germans, knowing that they had to fight on two fronts, were not going to plan any major offensives but rather build defences in such depth that they could not be penetrated. In the case of the Hindenburg Line a conscious decision was taken to withdraw to a more easily defended line, shortening the line in the process. The use of tanks and poison gas would add a new dimension to the war but this did not significantly change the overall situation on the front until the Americans came in ever larger numbers to add their weight to the Allied war effort.

So what contribution did air power make to the prosecution of the war in 1914 and 1915? Clearly the strategic bombing missions met with little success and in some case weather played its part. There were navigation errors, mechanical failures with bomb dropping equipment and the hazards which faced aircrews trying to bomb at the lowest possible height. On the other hand work with the Allied artillery did bear fruit in adding considerably to the effectiveness of British gunnery. There were occasions where the insufficiency of wireless aircraft meant that the RFC squadrons could not keep pace with the demands placed upon them at certain times in a battle. Photographic reconnaissance improved with better equipment and contact air patrols meant that ground commanders could be constantly updated on the situation on the ground both to their front and on their flanks. The deployment of the air resources was constantly changed to meet the situation on the ground as it developed. The next section will deal exclusively with the increase in the number of squadrons required to meet the growth in the BEF. What this section did not deal with was the onset of air fighting and the division between those pilots who continued to carry out the more mundane but vital tasks of artillery co operation and photographic reconnaissance and those pilots who would become the new 'Knights of the Air'. These pilots were known respectively as 'Corps Pilots' and 'Army Pilots'.

ORGANIZATION AND EXPANSION OF THE RFC FROM AUGUST 1915 INTO 1916

Source: National Archive Document AIR1/520/16/11/1

RFC Squadrons – increases and distribution – August 1915 to October 1915

The factors that persuaded Colonel Trenchard that there should be a significant increase in the number of RFC squadrons on the Western Front were an increase in enemy aircraft and an expansion of Britain's land forces, which had increased the extension of the front to be covered. He reasoned that, for reconnaissance squadrons, one should be located at GHQ and one at each Army HQ. At least one squadron should be located with each corps for artillery co-operation and aerial photography. Additionally, each Army should have a squadron for special duties such as bombing raids. Finally, an additional squadron was urgently required by the Second Army. Three squadrons should be sent as soon as available as an instalment towards the outlined complement. On 29 August the War Office indicated that No.12 Squadron would be dispatched on 5 September with three further squadrons by the middle of October. When it was learned that a fourth army was to be formed this meant a fourth wing of the RFC would be required.

Trenchard was advised by the War Office that the bombing squadrons should be concentrated in a wing under the direct control of GHQ rather than distributed to the various armies. These squadrons were to be detached on an as required basis. In addition to the squadrons already requested it was hoped to provide, at an early date, a certain number composed of fighting aeroplanes. On 27 September it was indicated that the squadrons required for a fourth wing would be forthcoming by the end of the year depending on the delivery of aeroplane engines. On 12 January 1916 GHQ in France was advised that the number of squadrons would be increased to twenty-seven by the end of March. By late February there were six squadrons with the First Army, seven squadrons with the Second and six squadrons with the Third, leaving two squadrons at GHQ.

On 14 March 1916 the War Office was advised by GHQ France of the factors that should determine future expansion of the air effort on the Western Front. One RFC brigade was allotted to each army consisting of a corps wing and an army wing. The corps units were nominally at the disposal of corps commanders for artillery, close reconnaissance and photography and it was considered essential for each corps to have the entire use of one squadron.

At this stage of the war it was necessary to provide protection patrols for machines employed on artillery work and it was no longer sufficient to employ single machines on reconnaissance. This activity had to be fought for and at least five machines should fly in formation. As a matter of interest the allocation of squadrons to armies and corps gave rise to the terms 'Army and Corps' pilots. (mentioned above).

The War Office advised that, by the end of April, there should be thirty-two RFC squadrons in France, four per army or one for each corps, three per army in army wings with the remaining four squadrons with GHQ. It was held that the raising of squadrons to the higher establishment of aircraft was to take precedence over the formation of new squadrons. At any time there were a finite number of machines available for sending to France, bearing in mind the demand for aeroplanes in the Adriatic, Mediterranean and Mesopotamia, not forgetting the equipment of squadrons for home defence. The attrition rate also contributed to a constant need for replacement machines. Furthermore, to increase the establishment of existing squadrons meant that the units remained with experienced pilots. The formation of new squadrons often meant withdrawing experienced pilots from operational units at the Front to command posts in the new squadrons. The establishment of pilots per squadron was increased from twelve to twenty. It turned out that the training of pilots was proceeding according to plan but the output of engines and aeroplanes in 1916 was uncertain (see Chapter 11 on Supply).

MILITARY AIR OPERATIONS IN OVERSEAS THEATRES

MESOPOTAMIA
Source: National Archive Document AIR 1/674/21/6/87

Introduction

By the end of September 1914 it was evident that Turkey was likely to join the Central Powers in the Great War. In that anticipation the Military Secretary at the India Office, Sir Edmund Harrow, wrote a minute entitled 'The Role of India in the Turkish War'. London was being advised that an expeditionary force should be sent from India to occupy Basra and Abadan to protect British oil interests. This would involve the protection of the oil tanks and pipelines. Additionally early British action might encourage the Arabs to throw in their lot with the Allied Powers to drive the Turks out of Arab land. An expedition was authorized and it left Bombay, under the command of General Delamain, to arrive in Bahrain on 23 October. War with Turkey was declared on 5 November and on the 22nd of the month Basra was occupied with little difficulty. A series of advances and reinforcements followed and by September the following year the British Expeditionary Force had reached Kut. Was the road to Baghdad open or would the British Army on the Tigris suffer a reverse?

In the air there were two RFC squadrons that operated in Mesopotamia, Nos.30 and 72 Squadrons, which detached flights in support of land operations. The air component began in Basra with an aviation unit and base for repairs and storage. Aerial reconnaissance was a major contribution to the land campaign but it was not without its cost to aircraft and aircrew when there were crashes due to mechanical failure and enemy ground fire. British aircrew were captured by the Turks but in spite of the difficulties the results of aerial reconnaissance played a most important part in the war. One most unusual role was the dropping of food stuffs in an unsuccessful attempt to relieve the beleaguered British force at Kut. (This chapter deals with air operations up to the end of 1915. See Chapter 4 for continuation.)

Organization of the RFC in Mesopotamia

Captain Broke-Smith, together with Captain Reilly, 82nd Punjabis (flight commander), and Lieutenant Wills (engineer) embarked for Basra on 30 April 1915. The first two weeks in May were spent selecting a site for an airfield outside Basra. This was accomplished on 15 May. The party was then strengthened following the arrival

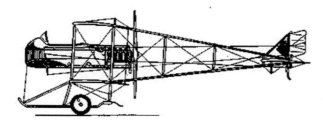

Shorthorn.

Longhorn.

from Egypt of Captain Petre. Petre had learned to fly in England in 1912 and, on returning to Australia, was invited to form a flying school, which later formed the basis of the Australian Flying Corps. New Zealand was also represented by Lieutenant Burn of the Staff Corps. With these officers there were two Maurice Farman Shorthorns, two cars and a lorry, semi-permanent aircraft hangars and other stores. New personnel included ten British mechanics, a storekeeper and five Indian mechanics, not forgetting ten camp followers.

The rest of May was spent preparing to make the flying unit operational. Progress was slow due to the excessive heat, which rendered work impossible between 10.00 and 15.00hrs. More officers and NCOs of the Australian Flying Corps arrived on 26 May, together with two more Shorthorns (without engines) and at last, on 27 May, flying could commence.

On 3 June it was possible to deploy the aircraft flight separate from the unit based at Basra. This flight consisted of two Maurice Farman biplanes, one Shorthorn and one Longhorn, one river tug with a crew of twenty-three, four officers and thirteen British mechanics. Twenty men of the 120th Infantry were attached to and accompanied the flight. In operations up the River Tigris a small river steamer and two small barges carried personnel, workshops and stores. These craft were necessary due to the very marshy conditions either side of the lower reaches of the river so stores and support services had to follow the aircraft up the river. Early in August information was received that the provision of flying units in the theatre was to be taken over by the War Office and all officers on the Aviation Unit were gazetted into the RFC on 5 August.

Operations

Initially reconnaissance was the main role of the Basra unit and the usefulness of the flight was soon evident when the telegraph system between Amara and Basra broke down. Urgent messages were conveyed by air to Amara. Great heat prevailed at this time and sickness amongst the aeroplane mechanics was exceptionally high. On 15 June it was possible to drop a message on the HMS *Espiegle*, the HQ of General Townshend for the battle with the Turks. It was reported that Bahran-Ruta-Mezebla was clear of the enemy who were in flight in every available craft. It was then possible to establish an aircraft refuelling base at Bahran. On 2 June the same method of reporting was adopted when messages in tins, to which streamers were attached, were dropped alongside naval vessels pursuing the enemy up the Tigris river.

A very notable reconnaissance flight was undertaken by Captain Reilly on 14 June 1915 from Amara to Kut-al-Amarah and back, a distance of 123 miles, and the disposition of Turkish forces below Kut could be seen. It was necessary to establish a refuelling point at Imam Ali Gharbi, sixty miles from Amara. The strength of the wind on this occasion was great but it was necessary to fly more than a few feet off the ground whenever possible to enable Turkish positions along the Tigris to be seen. A sketch map of enemy positions was made and passed to General Townshend prior to his attack on the enemy. Further assistance was given by Captain Reilly when he assisted the artillery to range on enemy trenches on 22 and 23 July. Early on 24 July an attack was mounted along both banks of the Euphrates and Turkish positions were captured. The part played by the RFC in the campaign was recognized by General Sir John Nixon, commanding the Indian Expeditionary Force, and in a dispatch he said: 'I have to place on record the excellence of the work performed by officers and men of the RFC whose valuable reconnaissances

HMS *Espiegle*.

The Tigris and Euphrates rivers.

flight, which left Amara on board a lighter. This comprised a Maurice Farman MFI, a Caudron Gn3 and two Martinsydes (MH5 and MH6). This was reduced to three aircraft when the MFI crashed on landing. On the 14th Major Reilly reconnoitred the Turkish positions at Es Sinn near Kut. On the right bank of the river the trenches and camp sites appeared to be deserted but there was enemy activity on the left bank. Thereupon the GOC ordered another reconnaissance and at the same time the naval flotilla was ordered to engage the enemy in an attempt to get them to show their guns. But uncertainty prevailed as it could still not be shown whether or not the enemy in Es Sinn was in strength. The GOC needed more information before deciding to cross over to the left bank.

By the 15th the Army had advanced as far as Abu Rummanam and the Caudron was manned by Lieutenant Trelcar with Captain B.S. Atkins as his observer. But soon these two officers were POWs when their aircraft was downed by enemy rifle fire, since they landed immediately in front of the enemy's advanced trenches. Major Reilly then carried out a more successful reconnaissance in MH6 and he was able to report that the enemy positions were more extensive and more entrenched than previously thought. These were of the most modern type and extended for some twelve miles on both banks of the river. It was later learned that the Turks had concealed their guns and placed the infantry in covered trenches on sighting an aeroplane. This was clearly an adversary that knew its business. General Townshend praised Reilly for his reports and sketch maps and he was then able to issue the appropriate orders to his brigade commanders.

The work of No.30 Squadron

On 7 November the aviation unit was reorganized into No.30 Squadron RFC consisting of a headquarters, A and B Flights and No.4 Aircraft Park. A Flight comprised the personnel and equipment at Aziziyah whilst B Flight consisted of personnel who had just arrived from England. The mule transport and MT drivers were amongst the HQ personnel. A Flight left Basra for Aziziyah on 9 November on lighters towed by tug T3. But the tug grounded twelve miles above Kut and could not be refloated so it was necessary to get the aircraft ashore and erected after which they were flown to Aziziyah except for the BE2c piloted by Captain Murray. He had to force land and his aircraft was towed to the river bank where it was embarked on a naval flight barge. A week before the intended attack on the Turkish positions Captain White

materially assisted in clearing up the situation before the battle of 24th July.'

To the initial equipment of two Maurice Farman biplanes were added two Caudrons with 80hp Gnome engines prior to the battle of Nasiriyah. Sadly the Gnome engines did not perform well in the heat and dust. When four Martinsyde Scouts arrived in August 1915 the engines gave continuous trouble, resulting in two of these aircraft being lost behind the enemy lines in November of that year.

On 20 August 1915 information was received that the aviation unit in Mesopotamia was to form part of No.30 Squadron RFC. On 8 September a RNAS seaplane Flight arrived at Basra, from East Africa, under the command of Squadron Commander R Gordon. This unit would work with the naval unit and was equipped with three Short Seaplanes powered by 150hp Sunbeam engines. In the event these engines gave constant trouble and the seaplanes could not take off with floats. To make matters worse the river above Kut was not suitable for seaplane operations. In the October two of these seaplanes were converted for land use.

On 13 September the 6th Division moved forward from Ali-al-Gharbi. The air support was provided by the

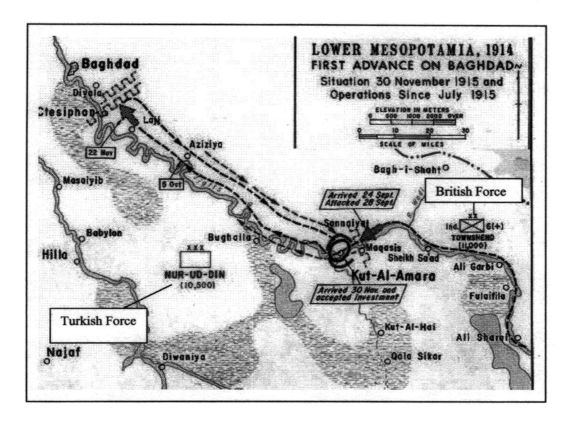

with his observer Captain Yeats Brown were instructed to land to cut the telephone lines, first to the west then to the north of Baghdad. They landed to cut the wires to the west but were apprehended in the act. Although taken prisoner they later escaped. Such were the difficulties encountered by the air units in attempting to provide air support to the land forces. During late November 1915 the work of the aircraft consisted of:

1. Watching both flanks and looking out for enveloping movements.
2. Reporting on the enemy's dispositions and changes therein.
3. Observing the enemy's rear along both banks of the Tigris to above Diyala river junction, to look out for movements of reinforcements or signs of retreat.
4. Locating enemy guns – particularly the heavy gun battery near Seleucia (this commanded the river below the bend at Bustan and prevented the naval flotilla from moving up and cooperating; it also prevented troops approaching the river to fetch water by night).
5. Bombing with 100lb bombs masses of enemy troops in the rear and boat bridge across the Diyala river etc.
6. Noting the movements of the naval flotilla during the day.

The siege of Kut

For the next six weeks preparations were made for further advances up the Tiger and by 18 November 1915 General Townshend had concentrated his entire force and shipping at Kutunie, which was occupied

Turkish commander on the Tigris 1915 – General Nureddin.

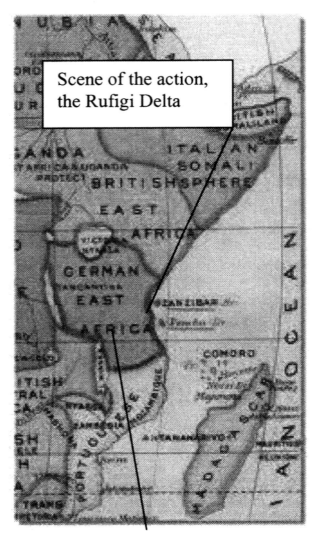

Scene of the action,
the Rufigi Delta

German East Africa.

German cruiser *Konigsberg*.

without resistance. The advance then continued on both sides of the river and Lejj, on the left bank of the river, was soon reached. Lejj was only nine miles south of Ctesiphon, which itself was only twenty-five miles south of Baghdad. Given the speed of the British advance the Turkish high command realized that insufficient forces had been deployed on this front. The battle at Ctesiphon lasted five days with an inconclusive result and both sides retired from the town. However, when the Turks realized that the British force was in full-scale retreat the Turkish Commander, General Nureddin, began to pursue the British force, which made an orderly retreat to Kut, arriving on 5 December. An encirclement of the town then began and Turkish forces proceeded downstream to prevent a British relief of Kut. The siege of Kut began on 7 December and the role of aircraft in the coming months was to prove critical for Townshend. (This is described in Chapter 4.)

DESTRUCTION OF THE GERMAN CRUISER KONIGSBERG IN THE RUFIGI DELTA, EAST AFRICA – 6 TO 11 JULY 1915
Source: National Archive document AIR1/674/21/6/86

Introduction
Reference to the destruction of the German cruiser *Konigsberg* in July 1915 is an apt reminder of the extent of the conflict, which made calls upon British military air assets at a time when there was mounting pressure on the Western Front. The episode also illustrates the flexibility of air power. This was to be a RNAS operation where aircraft were acting in direct support to naval operations in the Indian Ocean. The war had hardly begun when in September 1914 the German cruiser *Konigsberg* sank HMS *Pegasus* off Zanzibar. The German warship then took refuge in the Rufigi Delta. This was necessary to effect repairs to the cruiser's engines and parts were having to be transported across land to the delta where she lay. Since the enemy cruiser was a menace to shipping in the Indian Ocean it was necessary to blockade the delta until

HMS *Pegasus*.

such time as she could be sunk. A blockade was mounted by HMS *Chatham*. One solution to close the exit from the point where she had taken refuge was to sink two colliers in one of the many channels comprising the delta, but there were other channels that could be used for escape. This operation is significant in several respects. It was organized at the very beginning of the Great War with precious little experience upon which the Admiralty could frame its plan of action. One problem was the effect that climate would have on the structures of the flimsy aircraft that were to take part and some will be lost to accident even before the operation could get underway. This will be an example of the close collaboration between aircraft and military vessels. The *Konigsberg* could be destroyed by air bombardment or by aircraft directing the fire of surface vessels. Of course the enemy will not sit there and let their cruiser be destroyed without a fight. These were matters that engaged the C-in-C East Africa.

At first the exact position of the *Konigsberg* was not known and it could not be observed from the entrance to the delta and so the services of an exhibition flyer, Mr Cutler, were pressed into use. He had an old Curtiss boat seaplane at Durban and Mr Cutler was granted a temporary naval commission so that he could fly his aircraft over the delta to pinpoint the cruiser's mooring. On the morning of 22 November 1914 he located the *Konigsberg* some seven to eight miles from the entrance. Unfortunately, his aircraft suffered an engine failure and Sub Lieutenant Cutler was forced to descend and was taken prisoner. Since he was alone when this happened he had no way of transmitting the information to the Royal Naval ships offshore and by the middle of November 1914 the military and naval forces on both sides were marking time. The delta was being watched by two British warships with two armed tugs whilst HMS *Chatham* was at Mombasa. The C-in-C then asked for a seaplane with bombs to be sent, or better still a light armed vessel.

The Admiralty at once took action and the Air Department was instructed to form and equip a small flight of aeroplanes to proceed to East Africa to locate, and if possible, destroy the German cruiser. The officer chosen to command this expedition was a Flight Lieutenant J.T. Cull and he received orders to proceed to Calshot to inspect two Sopwith seaplanes prior to their shipment from Tilbury. Cull was joined by Flight Lieutenant Watkins and eighteen ratings. The party left Tilbury on 16 January arriving at Bombay on 5 February. The aircraft were taken ashore at the dockyard and crated and were re-embarked on the HMS *Kinfauns Castle*, an armed merchant cruiser, which proceeded to Zanzibar and thence to Niorora Island, a small island some 100 miles south of Zanzibar. This site was chosen so that trials with the aircraft could be carried out in the utmost secrecy. It was at this point that the effects on the climate

on these fragile machines was observed and one of the two seaplanes was wrecked in the first week. The Admiralty was informed of the failure of the two seaplanes to be fit for operations. The Admiralty response was to send three further Short aircraft towards the end of March. They arrived at Durban on board the HMS *Laconia*, an armed liner, in April and were taken ashore and erected by the RNAS flight sent down from Niororo Island. When these aircraft arrived back on the island a reconnaissance could, at long last, be made. Flight Lieutenant Cull, with an observer, saw the German cruiser on 25 April, which was in good condition, and photographs were taken of her position. Once the German captain knew that his ship had been spotted it was necessary to move her to avoid shelling or bombing and the map below shows the various numbered positions occupied by SMS *Konigsberg* during this period.

On 13 May HMS *Chatham* was ordered to the Dardanelles and the Admiralty decided to destroy the *Konigsberg* using monitors, the fire being directed by land or seaplanes. Two monitors, *Severn* and *Mersey*, arrived at Aden on 15 May and were ordered to proceed to Pemba Island where they arrived on 3 June. They were of shallow draft and could easily penetrate the delta. The positions of the two monitors once they had entered the delta for the attack are marked as M1 and M2 on the map. Meanwhile, four aircraft had been dispatched from the UK and further seaplanes were sent to Zanzibar. An aerodrome was prepared on Mafia Island to receive the land planes but when HMS *Laurentic arrived* from Aden with the crated aircraft the climate had again done its worst. There were two Henry Farmans and two Caudrons and as the crates

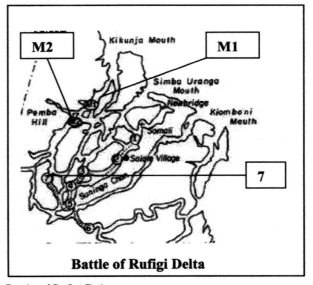

Battle of Rufigi Delta

Battle of Rufigi Delta.

HMS monitor *Mersey*.

SMS *Konigsberg* after the action.

were unloaded it was found that many of the propellers had warped and were therefore useless, leaving only one spare for one machine and two for the other. In spite of this setback, the erection of the aeroplanes proceeded and it was possible to fly a reconnaissance mission on 23 June. The *Konigsberg* was located west of Kotoni Island (position 7 on the map). Meanwhile, one Henri Farman and one Caudron had been wrecked during trial flights leaving only two serviceable aircraft for the forthcoming operation. Since the German cruiser was out of sight of the monitors it was necessary for the aircraft to direct their fire on to the *Konigsberg*. The Germans had spotting stations ashore and it was quite possible that the monitors could be disabled on attempting to enter the river.

On 6 July the two monitors entered the river at 4a.m. and were heavily fired upon and both the *Konigsberg* and the monitors opened fire at 06.30hrs. The *Mersey* was hit twice, a shell killing four men and wounding a further four. Her forward turret was put out of action and she was holed on the waterline. Spotting by the aeroplanes was very difficult but five hits on the German ship were obtained quite early. The cruiser's mast could be seen and then a salvo struck her and she was seen to be on fire. For the last hour and a half of the engagement she did not fire at the British vessels at all. Captain Fullerton was of the opinion that the German ship was not destroyed but was totally incapacitated. However, bad weather intervened to prevent aerial reconnaissance to confirm this to be the case and a further attack on the enemy ship was planned for 11 July. On that day *Hyacinth* and *Pioneer* bombarded the Simba Uranga mouth and the two monitors went in under cover of this fire and on reaching the islands east of Pemba hill the *Mersey* engaged the *Konigsberg* whilst the *Severn* was mooring. The German cruiser returned fire with four guns but the spotting from the aircraft overhead was most efficient and the

fourth salvo from the *Severn* hit. This was followed by up to nine hits and fire was observed to break out on board shortly followed by a large explosion. By 14.00hrs following several explosions the cruiser was burning fiercely. It was virtually destroyed (see picture above). The only casualty amongst the air component was one aircraft hit with the pilot and observer being rescued. The aircraft was subsequently destroyed. HM ships and personnel returned to their normal stations following a final reconnaissance flight by Flight Commander Hull and Flight Lieutenant Blackburn from Mafia Island on 5 August. (Note: the rank of flight lieutenant is not an RAF rank, since the new RAF ranks did not come into use until after the formation of the RAF in 1918. This is a rank in the RNAS at the time.)

THE ITALIAN FRONT AND THE MEDITERRANEAN
The Italian front gets only a reference since the RFC and the RNAS did not arrive in the Italian peninsula until very late in the war. The activities of British landplanes on the Italian front against Austria and seaplanes against the warships of the Central Powers operating in the Adriatic and Mediterranean appear therefore in the appropriate sections of Chapters 4 and 5. British land and air forces were rushed to Italy following the Italian defeat at Caporetto in October 1917 to bolster that front in the war, which faced imminent collapse. The Italians persisted in trying to break the Austrians on the Isonzo river and the end of the Caporetto battle also marked the virtual end of air battles over the Isonzo.

Chapter 4
Military Air Operations, 1916 and 1917

Royal Naval Air Service – operations and planning – anti-submarine warfare including operations involving airships, an assessment of night bombing – RFC operations and planning 1916–1917 – air defence of the British Isles – operations in other theatres; the Western Front, the Mediterranean and Adriatic, Mesopotamia

ROYAL NAVAL AIR SERVICE OPERATIONS AND PLANNING

THE ANTI-SUBMARINE CAMPAIGN 1916–1917
Source: National Archive Document: AIR1/675/21/13/1385

Employment of British Airships 1916–1917
Source: National Archive Document AIR1/723/66/5

There was a significant increase in the commissioning of airship stations in mid 1916 to meet the growing menace of U-boats. The range of German submarines in 1917 was limited, approximately 200 miles out and 200 miles back. This meant that they were rarely seen in Scottish and Irish waters. Their hunting grounds were chiefly in the Western Approaches and the English Channel as the accompanying map shows. Unrestricted submarine warfare meant that any Allied vessel was a potential target, including passenger ships. The sinkings lay mainly within 100 miles of Land's End and in the restricted waters of the Mediterranean. Incoming convoys or ships sailing independently were heading for Falmouth, Plymouth, Southampton, and London on the one hand and Liverpool and the Bristol Channel ports. By mid 1917 the submarine menace was increasing and this called for more airship mooring out stations. Anti-submarine forces included surface craft, destroyers, motor launches, aircraft, trawlers and Q-ships. The latter were disguised merchant ships that only disclosed their true identity when a U-boat surfaced hoping to dispatch the vessel with gunfire in place of an expensive torpedo. The hunter promptly became the hunted. This section includes the contribution of British airships to counter the U-boat menace.

U-Boat activity in 1916 and 1917
Following the sinking of the *Lusitania* in June 1915 there had been lull in U-boat attacks on unarmed merchantmen but this situation did not last long in spite of the adverse reaction that might ensue if more American lives were lost. On 24 February 1916 the order was issued to U-boat commanders that the capturing of prizes was permitted but that if vessels were recognizable as troop ships or armed merchant ships they could be sunk without warning. (It has been reported in the previous chapter

that the *Lusitania* was listed as a RN Reserve vessel and was carrying war materials.) Again, US citizens were killed when the cross-Channel steamer, the *Sussex* was torpedoed. Again the United States dispatched a strong note to the German Government about attacks without warning on passenger vessels. Be that as it may, orders henceforward issued to U-boat commanders was that passengers and crew were to be removed from such vessels before their destruction according to Prize Court rules. For the remainder of 1916 U-boat activity was practically confined to the Mediterranean.

Some U-boat activity did continue in Home Waters when submarines succeeded in penetrating the English Channel inflicting serious losses in the neighbourhood of Portland Bill and the Isle of Wight, which resulted in the expansion of seaplane patrols in the English Channel. The naval C-in-C Portsmouth recommended the setting up of a seaplane base at Portland, in addition to the one at Calshot (with a landing base at Bembridge on the Isle of Wight). The training machines at Calshot were not fit for anti-submarine work. He further recommended the establishment of two SS type airship stations on the Isle of Wight and Portland since airships were more effective scouts. The seaplanes were more suited to the mounting of attacks and this point was brought home when Flight Sub-Lieutenant Spear thwarted a U-boat attack upon the Norwegian steamer *Bourgundi*. The latter was being attacked on the surface but the pilot could not drop bombs as lifeboats containing passengers and crew were close to the U-boat and he had to wait until the submarine had submerged before dropping 16lb bombs, which failed to sink it. By September a patrol flight of Short 184s and 827 had been established for mid-Channel work.

Tactics involving seaplanes and Q ships proved effective, resulting, for example, in the sinking of the *UB19*. Seaplanes that spotted U-boats on the surface could fly towards friendly vessels and issue warnings using signal lamps. On a number of occasions seaplane pilots could not be sure that their signals had been seen and understood. If the sea state permitted a seaplane could land on the water alongside a vessel permitting pilots to talk directly with the captain. Since U-boat attacks on merchantmen were being conducted according to Prize Court rules attacks would be made on the surface. In any event it was more economical to sink a vessel using

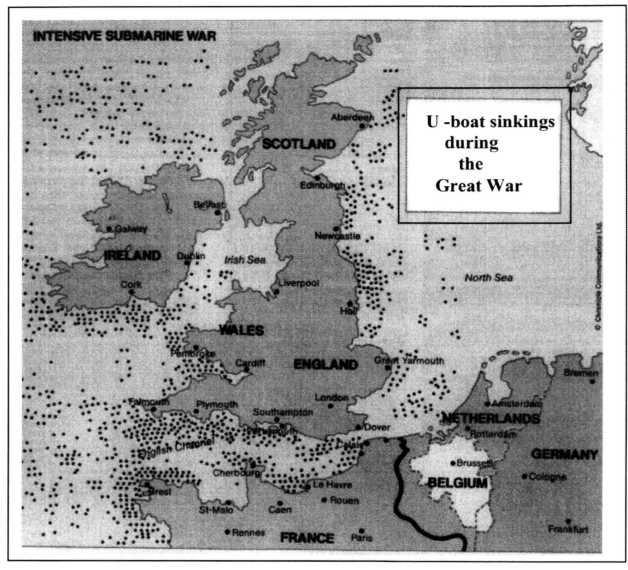

U-boat sinkings during the Great War.

gunfire than a torpedo. But some merchantmen were not what they seemed. They were the Q or decoy ships that had hidden guns on deck and the unsuspecting U-boat commander found his vessel under fire from more powerful weapons. Some of the crew made the pretence of evacuating the vessel so that the submarine commander would surface to present an ideal target for the Q ship's guns. Needless to say the usefulness of Q ships would decline once the threat was understood by most U-boat commanders (see next paragraph).

Anti-Submarine Division (ASD) of the Admiralty

On 18 December 1916 the ASD was formed to co-ordinate existing A/S measures and to advise on new measures. This would vastly improve the organization of aircraft so employed. This included co-operation between heavier and lighter than air craft. In the first two years of the war the utility of aircraft in submarine hunting had been poor. Long hours of patrolling by airship crews did not often bring forth fruit since airship operations were disjointed. The aim of the new organization was to co-ordinate the activities of airships and aircraft. The actual control of air assets was devolved to C-in-Cs or senior naval officers

A Q-ship's hidden gunnery.

Wing Commander J.C. Porte.

in the different sea areas. Each commander would be permitted to employ his air assets according to his own needs or ideas. There would be an organized system of air patrols around the coasts of Britain. In some areas the patrol activity would be concentrated where U-boats were known to be working; in others patrols would take place at dawn and dusk. The offensive would be taken by air and sea planes and kite balloons. Airships and kite balloons would serve defensive purposes. Search areas were defined to avoid overlap. For example the aircraft from the Yarmouth air station patrolled in the south, to the northern limit of Harwich Command and in the north, a line from Cromer to a point ten miles north of the position of the Swarte Bank Light Vessel and thence due east.

Meanwhile, in February 1917 the enemy declared unrestricted submarine warfare. Surface attacks using gunfire would be replaced by torpedo attacks, which were increased in their intensity reaching a peak between 17 and 27 April. The worst day for sinkings was 19 April when eleven British merchant ships (excluding eight fishing vessels) were sunk by submarines and two mines. The daily average of sinkings for the month was over

five against less than three for the year. One of the very important aircraft used in the countermeasures was the family of flying boats designed by Wing Commander J.C. Porte at the air station Felixstowe. These flying boats had good seaworthy quantities, were unequalled in their facility for observation and provided good crew comfort on flights of long duration. They were, however, slow making them vulnerable. To the Porte boats were added the 'small' and Large America flying boats.

Spider's web

The flying boats based at Felixstowe operated an octagonal search pattern known as the 'spider's web'. This was sixty miles in diameter with eight radiating arms thirty sea miles in length and three sets of circumferential lines joining the arms, 10, 20 and 30 miles from the centre. This provided eight patrol sectors and all kinds of combinations could be worked out. In this way 4,000 square miles of sea could be covered. Under ordinary operating conditions a flying boat could search two sectors or a quarter or the whole web, in five hours or less. The spider's web that operated out from the North Hinder light vessel was put into operation on 13 April 1917. Although only five flying boats could be spared, their work in the first eighteen days more than justified its inauguration. Twenty-seven patrols were carried out during which time eight U-boats were sighted with three being bombed. One patrol had an engagement with four enemy destroyers. On 20 May 1917 a Large America flying boat, No.8663, sank *UC36* and this was the first occasion when there was a confirmed sinking of a hostile submarine by aircraft during the Great War.

War channels

Another device used to prevent friendly shipping from being attacked by U-boats was the provision of 'war

A U-boat attacks on the surface.

The Large America flying boat.

HM hospital ship *Gloucester Castle* – after being torpedoed in 1917.

Felixstowe F2A used for patrols in the North Sea.

channels' around the coast of the British Isles. These were special sea lanes parallel to and about ten miles from the coast, bordered by shallow minefields and patrolled by surface craft as well as being clearly swept of mines. These channels would often be used by port shipping.

CHANGE OF POLICY IN FEBRUARY 1917
Source: *The Times History and Encyclopaedia of the Great War – The Navy's work in 1917*, published in December 1918

German military and naval opinion was strongly opposed to any restriction on U-boat activity since the country was being blockaded. The reasons given by the German government can be found in the source quoted above. The Imperial government took the view that the Allied powers intended to blockade Germany to bring about starvation of its people. Since Allied trade involved American shipping and that of other neutrals sailing to ports in France, Great Britain and Italy in the Mediterranean the American ambassador in Berlin was informed that the German Government intended to enforce the blockaded areas shown on the map, on the next page, from 1 February. It was felt that the freedom of the seas and maintaining an 'open door' for trade were

the guiding principles of German policy. The German view was that for the preceding two and a half years England had misused the power of her Navy in a criminal attempt to force Germany by hunger into subjection. Thus Germany had to fight with all the means at her disposal to preventing this from happening. Neutral nations were advised that their shipping would enter the 'barred zones' at their own risk. There were certain conditions attached to American shipping that entered the zones. Such ships were to bear alternate red and white vertical stripes with the American national flag on the stern. It will be remembered from Chapter 3 that in June 1915 the *Lusitania* had a number of American passengers on board but was carrying military stores and had been listed as a vessel of the Naval Reserve making her, in the eyes of the Commander of *U20*, a legitimate target. But, of course, the German government was anxious not to draw the USA into the war hence the warning in 1917 that US vessels were not to carry 'contraband' according to the German definition of this term. Once the enforcement was declared US and Dutch vessels were subjected to U-boat attacks and a hospital ship, *Asturias*, was sunk without warning. The same fate befell the hospital ship *Gloucester Castle*, pictured above.

THE CONVOY SYSTEM

Introduction
By 1917 the Admiralty realized that the losses of merchant ships to U-boats had become unacceptable. The end of April saw the institution of convoys in the North Sea and to Scandinavia and serious thought could be given to the institution of ocean convoys. There were problems in assembling a large number of vessels since the speed of the convoy would have to be determined by the speed of the slowest vessel if all ships were to maintain station. Loading and unloading was also a problem since those

The area of the German 'Barred Zones' in February 1917.

loaded first could not simply leave harbour. They had to wait until all the ships in the convoy were loaded, fuelled and ready for sea. Protection from U-boat attack came in the form of observation to spot submarines that posed a threat to a convoy and actually attacking a submarine to either drive it below the surface or better still to sink or seriously damage it. A combination of airships and aeroplanes together with surface vessels were needed.

Airships were well suited to the task of observation since their slow speed and long endurance meant that they matched the speed of the convoys below and stayed with them for prolonged periods. Kite balloons were also useful in this respect. Some land planes and sea planes could not only observe but, in some instances were equipped to mount an attack on a submarine. Warships, notably destroyers, were posted along the length of convoys and one or two going ahead or taking up a rear position. Their speed and manoeuvrability meant that they could be directed by, say an airship commander, to proceed to a position where a U-boat had been sighted and hopefully destroy or damage it. In many cases the sight of an airship would be enough for a U-boat commander to steer clear of a convoy but the airship was ill suited to mounting an attack. Their lack of speed and manoeuvrability meant that a U-boat could dive long before an attack could be mounted.

Coastal convoys

The coastal convoys could be protected from the land and seaplane stations together with the mooring out stations for airships that then ringed the British coastline. The larger airship stations such as Longside, East Fortune, Howden, Pulham, Mullion and Pembroke had the Coastal Class of airship. In the early part of 1917 it was decided that airships could be effectively employed for the following duties:

1. Co-operation with the Fleet or various units thereof, for scouting purposes.
2. Escort of ships or convoys
3. Anti-submarine patrol and searching for mines.
4. Co-operation with the Fleet or various units thereof, for scouting purposes.
5. Escort of ships or convoys
6. Anti-submarine patrol and searching for mines.

Each station had its own patrol areas and C-in-Cs could order their airships to sweep areas that were about to be used by convoys. The latter could be warned of the presence of submarines, which could then be engaged. The airships could also summon assistance to torpedoed vessels. In this way the convoy routes around Britain were under constant observation, the only limiting factor being the weather. The tactics employed on sighting a submarine are dealt with below. Kite balloons, towed by surface vessels also proved effective since they could be towed at the maximum speed of the towing vessel. The kite balloon observer was in direct telephonic communication with the bridge so that, on sighting a submarine, the countermeasures could be put into immediate effect. Sometimes patrolling aeroplanes could hand over to airships and vice versa. This happened on 9 August 1917 when a very important convoy was proceeding up the Channel. A Large America seaplane from the from the Scillies handed over the convoy protection duty to a Short seaplane from Newlyn and at about 09.00hrs two airships from Mullion took over, each one taking up station either side of the convoy. When a submarine was sighted sailing on a course to intercept the convoy bombs were dropped on its position which by then was submerged. Although seaplanes joined the hunt

for the submarine it was not detected but a successful attack by the enemy had been thwarted.

Protection of convoys passing through the English Channel involved the co-operation of the French. Indeed, a squadron of Wight Converted seaplanes was based at Cherbourg for the protection of cross Channel convoys supplying the needs of the British Expeditionary Force. On 11 May 1917 a conference was held at the Admiralty between British and French representatives to reach agreement on aero logical liaison, i.e. liaison between aerial patrols in the Channel and communication by visual and W/T signals. With regard to aero logical liaison it was arranged that the head of the French Meteorological Service should communicate direct with the Hydrological Officer at the Admiralty. This degree of co-operation was more than justified when, on 18 August 1917, Flight Sub Lieutenant Mossop, piloting a Wight seaplane from Cherbourg, was successful in sinking *UB32* by bombing the submarine in the act of submerging, hitting the submarine just forward of the periscope.

There was a certain inter-service rivalry and intra-service rivalry. The sailors did not trust airmen to deal effectively with U-boats. Airships and aircraft should confine their activities to spotting submarines, leaving it to surface warships to close with and destroy a submarine. Airship captains often proceeded on reconnaissance without any form of intelligence. When reports did reach airship stations their content was not passed on to surface ships and in one instance an airship commander arrived back at his station to learn that a submarine had mounted an attack within fifteen miles of his position. But then both sides in this war experienced instances where commanders refused to accept aerial reconnaissance reports. Naval airship crews had been trained by the Army without due emphasis on naval requirements and seaplanes allotted to anti-submarine duties could only take off in calm waters. The aeroplane could not hover to probe the suspected presence of a U-boat whereas the airship could. Airships could fly in fog and in darkness but could be prevented leaving their mooring out stations in high winds. Both aeroplanes and airships lacked effective defensive armament and suffered from mechanical problems. Of the airship stations only those at Mullion and Pembroke were situated to provide effective cover of the greatest concentration of the enemy submarine effort in the Western Approaches.

There were three airships that were deployed in the anti-submarine effort.

SS Zero – The SS *Zero* had a crew of three and could stay aloft for 12 hours at full speed of 48 knots. On one engine it had an extreme range of 200 miles.

Coastal – The Coastal airship had a crew of five and could stay aloft for 11 hours at a full speed of 42 knots.

The duration could be increased to 15 hours at 31.5 knots and the range to 543 miles.

North Sea – This type came in to service late in the war. It had a crew of ten and with a full speed of 57mph the duration was 21 hours. It had two engines and an extreme range of 2,000 miles.

Airship tactics

The controversy about the effectiveness of airships in countering the U-boat menace has been mentioned. The Admiralty was chiefly concerned with the safe transit of convoys and ships sailing independently. The seaplane operators would claim that seaplanes would be more effective than the slower and less manoeuvrable airships. Airship operators claimed that their craft had the endurance to stay with convoys to give permanent cover, one airship handing escort duties to another positioned on the route of the convoy. An airship could hover and with a crew of three or more there were more eyes to spot anything suspicious, whereas the seaplane pilot could not take his attention off flying the plane, leaving only the observer to give directions. But some in the Admiralty felt that the presence of an airship or kite balloon would advertise the presence of a convoy and it took sometime before the Admiralty would agree to inform airship stations of convoy movements. On the other hand, a kite balloon was instrumental in securing the destruction of *U69* on 12 July 1917. HMS *Patriot* was towing a kite balloon, which directed the warship to close with the submarine before it could deliver an attack. This incident gave impetus to those who favoured the use of kite balloons and more bases were established by the end of the year.

Regular convoy movements were to be avoided but in some cases it was necessary to move ships in convoy on a daily basis. No.243 Squadron, equipped with Wight Converted seaplanes was based at Cherbourg to cover the nightly departure of a French convoy of coal and munitions. Only when the Admiralty was confident that the presence of an airship was a positive deterrent to the submarine commander did convoys move at less irregular intervals. It is significant that during the Great War no ship was ever attacked whilst under the close escort of an airship. If a torpedo track was spotted the seaplane operator would argue that the seaplane could more quickly move to bomb or torpedo the source.

On the other hand the airship could hover in a position relative to the convoy dictated by the wind direction to enable an attack upon the submarine to take place in the minimum time. Being upwind of a convoy would mean that the airship would be carried downwind towards the vessels likely to be attacked. The means of destroying a submarine on or near the surface was by torpedo or bomb. The former would only be effective if the submarine was caught on the surface, and the latter depended on delayed-action fuses to be effective. Initially only 16lb bombs were supplied to airship stations but these were ineffective. The poundage was increased to 65, 100 and 112 with delayed-action fuses designed to explode at a given depth. But even when the poundage was increased to 150 then 250 the bomb aimer had to achieve extreme accuracy for them to have any effect. Later in the war submarine commanders did retaliate by attacking airships but if the airship was not destroyed or badly mauled the submarine commander could find himself the subject of a counter-attack before he had submerged his vessel.

Airship handling

As an airship was prepared for a patrol both the crew of the ship and the ground handling parties had well rehearsed duties. The airship would have the fuel tanks topped up and hydrogen levels checked whilst the armourers were bombing up and wireless equipment of batteries also received attention. The ground handling party then held the airship down in the shed whilst the engines were run to three quarter power. A number of watches could be assembled to assist in handling the airship. Obviously strong winds would require a greater number of men than that required in calm conditions. Station buglers cycled round the station calling the men to report to the landing officer who would detail the men to their various duties. The airship would be 'ballasted up' as ballast bags were dropped from the control car and the lines would be slackened to allow the airship to ascend. If it did not ascend then it was not 'lighter-than-air' and extra bags or even bombs might have been discarded. Once the airship was readied for flight the forward and after guys were manned to move the airship out of the shed. If the conditions were calm the airship would be unlikely to come into contact with the shed doors. If the winds were strong, particularly if they were gusty, it was vital to bring the airship into wind when the wind resistance would be at a minimum and the craft could be walked towards the landing ground. Strong sunshine would make an airship lighter and rain heavier so it might be necessary to 'ballast up' again. When the

Wight Converted seaplane.

captain was ready the engines would be opened up as the lines were let go. The ship would climb to patrol altitude, usually 800 to 1,000ft. The coxswain would steer seated behind the ship's compass on the course given him by the navigation officer. The elevators would be used to control the height at which the ship flew. It was important to check the pressure inside the envelope; too low and the airship would become flabby and lose shape, too high and there would be too much strain on the envelope. In turbulent conditions maintaining the right pressure was doubly important. If it was necessary to descend rapidly the gas valves could be opened to release gas. If it was necessary to deflate the envelope quickly a panel in the top of the envelope could be ripped out but care had to be taken to ensure that this panel, operated by a red tape, was not ripped out by accident.

The convoy being protected would be sighted, consisting of as many as forty merchant ships in three columns with destroyers and armed trawlers acting as close escort. The course would follow a zig zag pattern in an attempt to upset a submarine commander who was attempting to work ahead of the convoy or aim his torpedoes at one of the ships in the convoy. If an airship was already escorting the convoy the relieving airship would exchange messages using an Aldis lamp. The patrol of a North Sea airship could last between 12 and 48 hours. Severe weather conditions experienced, for example off the north coast of Scotland might end a patrol earlier than planned. On approach to land the airship might be too light due to the consumption of fuel, in which case gas would be released. If the ship was heavy water ballast could be dropped. The aim was to approach the landing ground head to wind and with speed so low that the handling party could catch the rope attached to the fore end known as the trail rope. This rope was then passed through a snatch block on the ground so that the ship could be pulled down and brought under control. But getting the ship back into its shed could be very difficult in strong winds and it was not unknown for as many as 500 men to be dragged along whilst attempting to line the ship up with the shed doors. Sometimes great courage was required by members of landing parties as individual members could be dragged aloft until sufficient men got a hold of the line. Deaths amongst members of the landing party occurred at both Kingsnorth and Cranwell. In spite of the above, things could go badly wrong as the experience of the crew of HMASS No.42 illustrates:

On 15th September 1915 the captain of HMASS No.42 was ordered to patrol the Bristol Channel in the vicinity of Lundy Island looking for enemy submarines reported to be working in the area. He took off at 06.00hrs when the weather conditions were fine but two hours later the wind began to freshen from the north. In squally conditions he decided to return to base arriving back at about 11.00hrs. The airship was no sooner on the ground than a violent gust caught the ship on her starboard bow, lifted her some 30ft from the ground before smashing the ship to the ground on the port side. The port suspensions of the control car were severed turning it virtually upside down and the wireless operator and the captain could remain in their seats only with great difficulty. When the trail rope broke the airship was free to ascend and with a rapid ascent the wireless operator was thrown out when some 20ft off the ground and the pilot clambered on top of the upturned car as it reached 1,000ft. The safety valves had blown, which saved the airship from bursting as she quickly gained height with all the controls gone. The pilot could see that the ship was being blown over the Bristol Channel passing over Cauldy Island at approximately 3,000ft and by the time he was over Lundy Island the ship had risen to 7,000ft. The petrol tanks were leaking thus lightening the all-up weight causing the continuous increase in altitude. Then the situation grew most grave as the forward suspensions, bearing the weight of the engine, broke and the car fell into a vertical position. The pilot managed to crawl downwards to sit on the axle of the undercarriage. By approximately 14.00hrs the airship reached its maximum altitude and it began to descend ever more rapidly and passed through heavy clouds at 6,000ft. The airship had, by then a flabby envelope and began to spin. The final descent was made at a rate of between 1,000 to 1,500ft per minute and the airship crashed into a field near the small village of Ermington in Devonshire. The pilot suffered a fractured and dislocated spine and spent a long period in hospital. When he was fit to return to duty he was posted back to his old airship base in command of HMASS No.42A.

Longside Airships: anti-submarine patrols and night flying from 7 December 1916 to 15 March 1917

Source: National Archive document AIR1/642/17/122/235

On 7 December 1916 a telegram was sent by the Senior Naval Officer Peterhead to the Admiralty to inform the latter that on moonlight nights it was proposed, weather permitting, to carry out night flying from Longside. HM ships, patrol vessels and military authorities would be given as much advance notice as possible of intended flights. These flights would not commence for several days after the telegram was dispatched. Whilst the Admiralty did not concur with this proposal on 12 March 1917 it was felt necessary to rethink the matter of anti-submarine airship patrols given the successes achieved by airships operating out of the Mullion airship station in Cornwall. A letter from the Admiralty to the C-in-C

Scotland Coast three days later spoke of the effectiveness of airship patrols from Mullion where they were working with destroyers and auxiliary vessels resulting in reports of submarines on the surface followed in some cases by attacks. To date no attempt had been made by enemy submarine commanders to repel these attacks seeking sanctuary in diving but it was probable that a submarine had been damaged by delayed action bombs. It was therefore proposed that anti-submarine patrols should be mounted to seaward from Longside making use of W/T directional stations for position fixes. Night patrols should be carried out, weather permitting. The policy was to harass enemy submarines as far as possible to prevent minelaying in the vicinity. In view of possible engine failure airships were not to fly to seaward during NW and W winds of over 15 miles an hour. (For the position of Longside see Chapter 9, Airfield location Map for Scotland and Ulster.)

CLOSURE OF THE SEAPLANE BASE AT DOVER
Source: National Archive Document AIR1/642/17/122/233

In December 1917 the usefulness of Dover as a seaplane base was questioned. The Vice Admiral Dover Patrol had expressed his opinion that aeroplanes were more suitable for patrolling the Belgian coast than seaplanes. It had been decided that aeroplanes would be employed almost exclusively in the area marked 'A' in the map. The only exception would be anti-submarine work out from the

coast with the Large Americas or Handley Pages which can be defended by fighters.

It was the intention, he added, that floatplanes based on Dover be used in the area marked 'B' in the map. Machines operating in this area were less likely to meet enemy opposition. Thus the Director of Operations wanted to know whether or not the Vice Admiral intended to use Dover and Walmer aerodromes, and if so, whether or not Dover seaplane base could be closed. Facilities for refuelling and attending to aircraft in passage could be retained at the seaplane base. In a letter from HQ RNAS to the Vice Admiral Dover Patrol the decision to use aeroplanes for patrolling Dover and Dunkirk, which comprised the Dover Patrol Area south of a line joining the North Foreland and Thornton Ridge, was discussed. Aeroplanes operating from either Dunkirk or Walmer would suffice but the HQ had decided not to close the Dover Seaplane Base completely. A flight of Short Seaplanes would be based there and the existing sheds and machinery would provide an additional repair depot. A decision was still pending on the future of the Dunkirk seaplane base.

AIRSHIP PILOTS TO PRACTISE WITH BRITISH SUBMARINES
Source: National Archive Document AIR1/642/17/122/239

In November 1917 the Director of Air Services of the RNAS wrote to the Operations Department suggesting

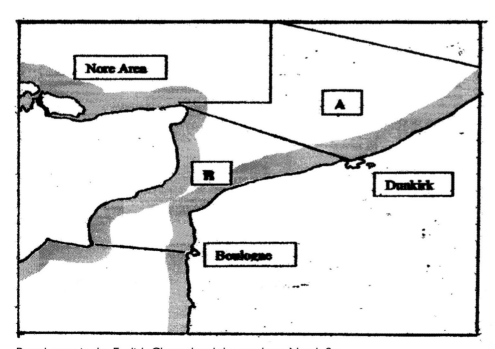

Patrol areas in the English Channel and the southern North Sea.

that the acquisition of enemy submarines and attack procedures could be improved if British airships practised using Royal Navy submarines. Four questions were posed in the letter, which would be answered after exercises had been carried out. They were:

1. At what depth can submarines be seen on an average day and under different conditions?
2. Can a submarine be tracked by an airship although not definitely recognized?
3. Is there an oil track always visible when a submarine is submerged?
4. What colour makes it most difficult to distinguish a submarine?

Senior naval officers with both airships and submarines under command could carry out the necessary experiments on any suitable flying days. The letter ends with the suggestion that submariners and airship pilots could usefully meet to discuss forms of attack etc. The commanding officer of the Mullion Airship Station had previously suggested these joint exercises but it had not been possible in the Plymouth area. The latest proposal would involve airships from Pulham and submarines from Harwich or Yarmouth. Then submariners could be taken aloft to see what their submarines looked like from altitude. If the submarine sailed to a position between Pulham and Howden, airships from Howden, Pulham and Cranwell could take part.

As a result of this and other related correspondence the Vice Admiral East Coast was to be advised when exercises could begin using the Wash as the exercise area. This prompted a letter, dated 26 November, from the Captain (Submarines) at HMS *Maidstone* in Harwich to write to the Secretary of the Admiralty with advice on what was and was not possible. He said that sea areas where experiments could safely be carried out were limited and that the Wash would be most sensible. The larger classes of submarine were temporarily short in number due to detachments and refits but a 'C' Class submarine from Immingham could be made available. If this was not satisfactory from the airship commander's point of view they could always approach the Captain of Submarines at Harwich or the Commanding Officer of HMS *Alecto*.

AN ASSESSMENT OF NIGHT BOMBING BY THE RNAS AND RFC – 1916 TO 1917
Source: AIR1/642/17/122/250

Nos.5 and 7 Squadrons of No.5 Wing RNAS were involved in bombing military targets in German-occupied Belgium during the summer of 1917. The use of the DH4 in daylight attacks and the HPO/100 in night bombing attacks permitted a comparison to be made of the effectiveness of day versus night operations.

Handley Page O/100 of No.7 Squadron RNAS.

During the months of June and July bombing operations were carried out by Nos.5 and 7 Squadrons RNAS and Allied agents' reports were compared with those furnished by the aircrew. These were largely supportive and photographic evidence was also added. At the headquarters of the Vice Admiral Dover Patrol a Staff Captain Lambe was able to write a report on 25 July 1917. He commented particularly on the night bombing by HPO/100s on the night of 3/4 May on the seaplane base at Ostend and the day bombing by No.5 Squadron on 3 June on St Denis Westrem aerodrome followed that night by bombers of No.7 Squadron on the same target. He agreed with the view of Wing Commander Spencer Gray that large machines designed for night bombing were of great value since, on moonlit nights, the objective could be more easily found than during the day and the night bomber could operate at lower altitudes than the day bomber. On dark clear night parachute flares could be used for target acquisition. Speed had to be sacrificed if large numbers of bombs were to be carried but aircraft flying at higher altitudes at greater speed could have a considerable effect on morale. Lambe believed that heavy bombers proceeding to their various targets would go unescorted at night since, unlike daylight bombing missions, they will be very unlikely to encounter enemy aircraft and anti-aircraft guns. Heavy bombers could also be used in daylight operations against objectives near the lines or where there are few anti-aircraft batteries.

Lambe was clearly in favour of using heavy bombers at night as opposed to lighter day bombers such as the DH4 pictured below. Wing Commander Spencer Gray,

DH4 of No.5 Squadron RNAS.

commanding No.5 Wing, had reinforced Lambe's views in his report. Spencer Gray added that there are more clear and calm nights than days during the year and that AA fire is more inaccurate at night. About four times the weight of bombs per unit of horse power can be carried by a night bomber. At night enemy machines would be in their sheds. Day bombers would be more likely to receive hits from AA and machine gun fire and daily serviceability would be reduced. Finally, train activity and movements of convoys were most likely to occur at night.

A comparison was made between the use of the HPO/100 and the DH4. It would take six DH4s with six pilots and observers and six engines to carry 1,200lb of bombs. Fuel consumed would be 120 gallons, not counting the fuel for the escort of three fighters or more. On the other hand one Handley Page O/100 would use one pilot, two observers and two engines to carry between 1,344 and 1,792lb of bombs. It would have an advantage on shedding, accommodation and engine technicians but be less convenient for transporting spare parts.

It was admitted that a certain amount of day bombing might be necessary in purely military land war operations, such as attacks on bodies of troops and trains. For naval purposes attacks were principally on shipping, enemy aerodromes and dockyards and these could be undertaken at night. The upshot was that an Admiralty specification for succeeding heavy naval bombers could be issued. In the meantime an order for 100 modified Handley Pages was made and the Air Board decided that the heavy bomber type should be developed and the new specification that could carry a still larger load of bombs should be issued. This can be found in Appendix M.

Light night bombing overseas
Source: National Archive Document AIR1/109/15/20/2

In late 1916 corps squadrons of the BEF were called upon to carry out a certain amount of night bombing. To secure efficiency it was decided to form night bombing squadrons for this duty alone. At this time the training of night pilots was confined to the Home Defence

Wing in England. In the event it was decided to form a squadron in England (No.100 Squadron). This squadron was formed and trained using the resources of the Home Defence Wing in terms of personnel and machines. The aircraft were FE2bs and the squadron joined the BEF in March 1917. By June 1918 there were eight night bombing squadrons in France. The 6th Brigade provided the pilots and observers to deal with wastage. All the squadrons were equipped with FE2bs, which consistently performed good work. But they could not carry more than 400lb bombs and had poor performance, which handicapped them considerably. What was needed was a night reconnaissance machine that could also attack troops and transport with machine gun fire at night and rapidly climb out of machine gun range after completing the mission.

FUTURE OF THE AIR SERVICE IN THE ORKNEYS
Source: National Archive Document AIR1/642/17/122/246

The strategic importance of the Orkneys can be seen from the map, lying as they do off the tip of the north coast of Scotland because seaplanes can reconnoitre the sea passages from the North Sea into the North Atlantic. In those days the range of seaplanes was very limited

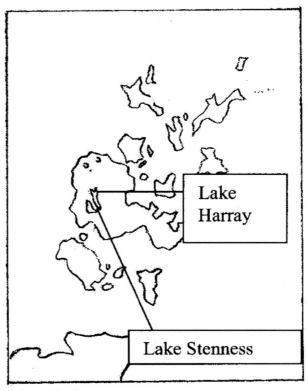

Orkney Islands.

The FE2b.

and these islands were ringed with seaplane and airship stations. Until recently one maritime reconnaissance base at Kinloss in Scotland had to cover all of the sea around the British Isles. In 1917 the threat from a very large German surface fleet and submarines was great (refer to the map of U-boat sinkings at the beginning of this chapter).

In September 1917 the Admiral Commanding the Orkneys and Shetlands had heard through unofficial channels that developments in the air service provided from the Orkneys were planned and in a letter to the Secretary of the Admiralty, dated 9 September 1917, he asked for clarification on the matter since there were considerable alterations to plans already formulated. He referred to the possible use of Lochs Stenness and Harray in the mainland of Orkney, an increase of accommodation at Houton Bay and for the addition of quarters at Scapa Seaplane Station.

For a photograph of the Large America flying boat refer to page 86. The plan was to use these flying boats, which could land on either of the two lakes shown on the map. This would occasion an increase in personnel accommodation and the Admiral wanted to restrict fresh construction, which would impose a further call on public funds. The closure of the Scapa seaplane station had already been mentioned to him and it was thought unwise to start building fresh accommodation at that location, which was destined for closure.

On 17 September the Admiralty's reply spoke of increasing the number of Large America flying boats from eighteen to thirty-six in order to provide intensive anti-submarine patrols in the summer of 1918. There was to be similar provision both at Peterhead and the Shetlands. The maintenance and repair of seaplanes could be carried out at Houton and the Stenness Loch would be required for so large a number of boats and a certain amount of new construction would be required. The necessity of meeting the U-boat threat was overriding and economy was not to hamper the operational requirement. A letter would follow about the probable increase in the kite balloon establishment. A letter to the Orkneys Command and the C-in-C Grand Fleet dated 22 September reaffirmed the need to be ready in the spring of 1918 for an intensive anti-submarine campaign.

SERVICES RENDERED TO THE REAR ADMIRAL EAST COAST BY FOUR HANDLEY PAGE MACHINES
Source: National Archive document AIR1/642/17/122/234

Little illustrates more clearly the threat posed by enemy submarines during the third year of the war than when the Senior Naval Officer River Tyne sent a letter dated 5 October 1917 to the Rear Admiral Commanding the east coast of England. In it he made a plea for the return of the four Handley Page machines, which had hitherto been allocated to him for anti-submarine work. Incidents

occurring after the writing of this letter pointed to the threat posed by submarines. From Newcastle it was reported that the steamer *Linhope*, on 7 December, narrowly missed being struck by a torpedo. Five rounds were fired, which caused the submarine to submerge. Also on the 7th an enemy submarine was sighted by an armed trawler and the steamer *Ben Lawara* had a torpedo fired at her off the coast at Whitby. At 15.03hrs that day the *Swallow* reported that a steamer had been blown up off South Cheek. At the same time at Culler Coates a report was received that a steamer had blown up off the 'I' Buoy. At 15.35hrs a report was received from Robin Hoods Bay that a steamer had blown up some 2 ½ miles east of Robin Hood's Bay with another steamer apparently sinking on the same bearing. Two motor launches and two trawlers were standing by to pick up survivors. Finally, from Newcastle a report was received that the steamer *Highgate* had blown up at about 15.00hrs. Doubtless the several reports were referring to the same vessel. But if that was not enough the following day brought no respite and Sunderland Coastguard reported that a merchant steamer steering north apparently struck a mine or torpedo about four miles ENE from Roker Lighthouse and appeared to be sinking by the stern. This was identified by the steamer *Emma Minlos* as the steamer *Devonia*, which had been torpedoed three miles SSE of Soutar.

The letter referred to the work performed by four Handley Page machines that had arrived at Redcar on 5 September 1917 and were withdrawn on 2 October. These aircraft could fly in weather unfit for seaplanes. Bombs were dropped on eleven occasions and seven enemy submarines were reported and it is highly probable that one submarine was sunk or at any rate disabled by bombs from one of the machines. This points to the opinion of many naval officers at this stage of the war that land planes were far more preferable than seaplanes for anti-submarine work, with of course certain reservations (see Chapter 7).

ROYAL FLYING CORPS OPERATIONS AND PLANNING 1916 TO 1917
Sources: National Archive Document AIR1/943/204/5/980, *The History of the Great European War*, published by Caxton Publishing Company for photographs and Chapters 49, 50 and 51 of Volume VI *Pillars of Fire* by Ian Passingham, Sutton Publishing

ORGANIZATION OF THE RFC IN THE FIELD – 10 FEBRUARY 1916
Source: National Archive Document AIR1/1/4/3

Basic organization
Each army had one RFC brigade commanded by a brigadier-general and each brigade consisted of two wings

Kite balloon.

Camera mounted in a BE2c reconnaissance aircraft.

and an aircraft park, One of the two wings was known as the corps wing and consisted of as many squadrons as there were corps in the army. These squadrons were under the orders of the corps commander and were used for observation of artillery fire and close reconnaissance work. The other wing was known as the army wing and worked directly under the corps commander. Each wing consisted of three squadrons and was used for carrying out Army reconnaissance (Corps pilots) and for fighting enemy aircraft (Army pilots). Photography was carried out by pilots of both wings with photographic work being distributed by the brigade commander.

There were four kite balloons with each army under one squadron commander. These were then attached to corps wings as required. For work directly under the command of GHQ there was one wing of six squadrons used for long-distance reconnaissance and bombing. These squadrons consisted of twelve aeroplanes of the same type with the addition of one or more small single-seat machines for attack on any hostile aeroplanes that came near the aerodrome.

The corps and army squadrons were organized into three flights that were self-contained as regards transport etc. Further back from the front were the aircraft depots, one for each line of communications. The depots, which came under the orders of the GOC, RFC, held three months' stock of spares for aeroplanes, engines and

motor transport and over-hauled the same. Repairs were effected to photographic equipment and wireless apparatus. The depots also erected aircraft that had come over from England in cases. The aircraft park carried one month's stock of spares for aeroplanes and engines and also carried out repairs.

In February 1916 there were nineteen squadrons with the Army in the field. These squadrons were equipped as follows:

12 Squadrons of BE2c machines with 90hp RAF engines

2 Squadrons of Morane Parasol machines with 110hp Le Rhône engines

2 Squadrons of Vickers biplanes with 100hp Monosoupape engines

1 Squadron of FE machines with 120hp Austro-Daimler engines

1 Squadron of DH Scouts with 100hp Monosoupape engines

1 Squadron of RE machines 120hp Austro-Daimler engines

The Vickers, FEs and DH scouts were used to attack hostile aeroplanes. To some extent the FEs were used for reconnaissance whilst the REs were used for long-range reconnaissance and bombing. Every aeroplane on a reconnaissance mission had at least one Lewis gun and a two-seater machine usually carried two. The chief work of the RFC in February 1916 was the observation of artillery fire, signalling results with wireless equipment using a low-powered accumulator. For photographic reconnaissance the cameras used had a focal length of 8½in the cameras being rigidly attached to the machine. There was a changing box with eighteen photographic plates.

There were four types of bombs in use, an incendiary weighing approximately 10lb, and high-explosive or HE bombs weighing 110lb, 112lb and 336lb respectively.

There were some bombs that were heavier but these were not regarded as being as efficient as those weighing 336lb. To train pilots to drop bombs a camera obscura was used, which proved to be a valuable method.

The RFC was by this time training its pilots to fly in company and manoeuvre in the air. The enemy were not going to let British reconnaissance and photo reconnaissance aeroplanes go about their duties unmolested. Four aeroplanes were thus sent out together and on distant reconnaissance the RFC expected to have to send out double or three times that number. As to future requirements in February 1916 a two-seater with a speed of 100mph capable of patrolling for four hours was one. A second was for a long-distance machine capable of patrolling for eight hours at a speed of at least 80mph and capable of carrying about 800lb of bombs. Two gunners on such a machine were necessary with all-round fields of fire.

EXPANSION OF THE RFC IN FRANCE – 1916 INTO 1918
Source: National Archive Document AIR1/520/16/11/1

Introduction
The GOC RFC in France, by then Major-General Hugh Trenchard, regarded the War Office letters of the early summer of 1916 as 'very satisfactory' but he continued to send his recommendations to London giving the progress of the air war. In particular he pointed out that it was impossible to train 'scout' pilots in France. When these pilots did arrive in France they should be 'really capable' flyers. In his letter dated 15 June 1916, the C-in-C spelt out his thoughts to the War Office on the future expansion of the RFC in France. These were based on the presumption that, by the spring of 1917, the British Army in France would consist of five armies each comprising four corps. He stressed the need for a larger number of fighting squadrons the value of which was increasing on a daily basis. For example, fighting squadrons were based at GHQ for protection of the home base. It was felt that it was essential that the necessary number of pilots and observers be found, even at the expense of a reduction in other directions. This would involve a corresponding increase in the capacity of aircraft parks and repair depots. There would also be a requirement for forty kite balloons. A forecast from the Director of Air Organization at the War Office, in August 1916, indicated an expansion from twenty-nine squadrons to thirty-five squadrons by the end of September 1916 and forty-nine squadrons by the end of January 1917. The Admiralty had pledged forty aeroplanes and pilots for service in France in case of an emergency such as a general retirement of the enemy. The RE type was regarded as being unsuitable for BEF operations on account of its engine being 'absolutely unreliable'. Reference was made to the French machines being used by the RFC and the only type in England suited to replace them was the Sopwith two-seater of the tractor type but this model was urgently required by the Admiralty. The GHQ protested in June 1916 saying that operations would be seriously hampered if these aircraft were not provided.

An increase in the number and efficiency of RFC squadrons in France – September 1916 to November 1917
The allies had gained a distinct advantage in fighter planes by 1916 following the initial setback with the 'Fokker Scourge'. With fighters such as the Nieuport and DH2 the Allies had the measure of the German machines by the spring. Then the Germans regained the advantage with the introduction of the Albatross D1. Up to this time the installation of two forward-firing guns added weight, which caused a significant loss of performance. This was not the case with the Albatros D1, which appeared on the Western Front in August 1916. Armed with twin 7.92mm Spandau guns and powered by a 160hp Mercedes engine, the Albatros caused the War Office to consider how this new threat would be addressed. In a letter dated 30 September 1916 the War Office was asked to give urgent consideration to a very early increase in the numbers and efficiency of RFC fighting aeroplanes.

The Germans were achieving mastery on the Somme except perhaps over the single-seat Nieuport and one of the Sopwiths. With rising RFC casualties the GOC RFC France was requested to forward his estimated requirements to remedy the situation. On 10 October the War Office replied that the provision of fast fighting machines in the spring of 1917 was receiving close attention. It was not, however, clear if the situation on the Somme was the result of the Germans concentrating resources on this particular sector at the expense of other fronts or whether there was an overall increase in the German air effort. The answer was that it was a combination of three factors. There had been a concentration of enemy air effort on the Somme but there was also an increase in the air effort being experienced by the French and other British fronts. Thirdly the performance of the German fighters

Albatros D1.

Sopwith Tractor biplane.

DH9.

threatened the air superiority held by the Allies in the spring. There was by then an urgent need to provide fighter cover for artillery spotting machines for the entire day. The Admiralty indicated that they could contribute a squadron of fighters, with naval pilots, from Dunkirk. By February 1917 four more RNAS squadrons were placed at the disposal of the C-in-C. This reinforcement was to be phased over the four months February to May 1917. The developments in wireless communication meant that more artillery spotting machines could be employed simultaneously in a given area but rather than increase the number of squadrons it was believed that greater economies could be achieved by simply increasing the establishment of squadrons from eighteen to twenty-four machines. On 27 March 1917 the War Office agreed and corps squadrons would in future comprise three flights of eight aircraft. But in November 1917 there was a shortage of machines required by the increased establishment so, for the winter, the establishment reverted to the former figure. The ability to seek out and destroy the enemy's fighting machines called for single-seat fighting machines. The direct protection of corps machines was no substitute for seeking out and destroying the enemy before the friendly machines could be threatened. It was agreed that headquarters communications squadrons should be formed consisting of machines that fell short of the standard required for active operations. No observers would be required and there would be a reduction in personnel and mechanical transport compared with active squadrons.

In July 1917 there were fifty-one squadrons: eighteen fighting, twenty corps, twelve fighter reconnaissance and one night bombing. Again in July 1917 the Air Board appeared to have sanctioned an increase in the establishment of the RFC to 200 service and 200 training squadrons. On 13 July the War Office agreed that such an increase had been sanctioned. In addition to the eighty-six squadrons demanded by GHQ an extra forty could be expected by August 1918. These additional squadrons were to be mainly bombing squadrons. But the difficulty in adhering to agreed targets for equipping army and corps squadrons is exampled in the preceding paragraph.

The War Office continually had to revise statements in light of the output of aeroplanes and engines. For example, of the delay in the programme of development was the shortage of DH9 machines pictured above. On the other hand the War Office was able, in January 1918, to announce the increase of Sopwith Camel (Clerget) squadron establishments to twenty-four machines with six squadrons forthcoming during the following month. And so throughout 1917 and into 1918 the establishments of squadrons and the forecasts for delivery of aeroplanes and engines were subject to amendment on a weekly basis and the deployment of squadrons, including those of the RNAS, were also subject to constant review in the light of the state of the war on the Western Front. Extra squadrons meant agreement by the French authorities for the siting of airfields, aircraft storage and repair depots. (See the 'Supply' section of Chapter 11 for the supply position of aircraft at this time.) Early in 1918 there was a further addition of squadrons on the Western Front as the Americans joined the fighting. Ten American squadrons, partially trained in Canada, arrived in the United Kingdom and were dispatched to France for final training with the RFC. The first four of these squadrons were attached by flights to different RFC and RNAS squadrons and the remaining six joined the American Expeditionary Force.

CONTACT AIR PATROLS
Source: National Archive document AIR 1/674/21/6/120

The French were working along the same lines as the British in organizing contact air patrols. Their observers plotted their observations of the progress of the land battle on small-scale maps and dropped them at report centres. Captain Reymond on the staff of the 2nd French Army Corps, in a paper addressed to units of the 6th Army on 10 February 1916, said:

In the event of the failure of our attack, or the enemy starting a counter-attack, it is necessary to either instantly release a 'barrage' fire or instigate an immediate counter-attack. It is therefore important to have apart from Divisional balloons, a W/T machine whose observer will report immediately any incidents of primary importance, as well as releasing barrage fire (without attempting to control it). One machine should suffice for this purpose on an Army Group front.

At the Battle of Verdun, some of the greatest lessons of the air were learned, both with regard to policy and tactics. By this time, 8 March 1916, the French Air Service had been both reinforced and reorganized. Specially qualified observers reported directly on *Missions de Combat* for the Army Command and all French squadrons were detailed to provide observation aircraft to take part in these missions. Using wireless telephone or light signals, these observers reported all the requests of the infantry made by flares or lamp signals. Before an attack they would report any part of the enemy front line that had not been bombarded and during the attack the observers would note the extent of the front being attacked, the progress of the assaulting waves, all enemy positions reached by the infantry and the accuracy of artillery fire. In the event, of all the methods of communication that could be used, coloured lights were mostly used even though their use gave away their positions to the enemy.

As a result of both British and French experiments in communicating the substance of aerial observation to commanders on the ground, the necessity of providing an efficient and close liaison between aircraft and the infantry had been demonstrated. Following these experiments provisional instructions, based upon those issued by General Joffre to French Armies, were drawn up by General Headquarters and issued to the British armies on 26 May 1916. These were very detailed and procedures were practised to be ready for the major offensive planned for July (see Appendix F). At 07.30hrs on 1 July the British and French attacks on the Somme were opened. The main British front extended from Maricourt, round the salient of Fricourt to the Ancre in front of St Pierre Division. On the first day of the offensive the attacks were clearly followed from the air, but communications from the infantry were infrequent. This was due to the fact that the field telephone system was functioning normally and therefore sufficient. Once battle was joined there was always the possibility that telephone lines could be cut. Mirrors on the soldiers' backs were clearly visible in the 13th Corps but once the attack began and movements became confused the mirrors were found to be an unsuitable method of communication since they could be confused with so many other shining objects on the ground. This method was therefore discarded for the time being but was later revived in 1918.

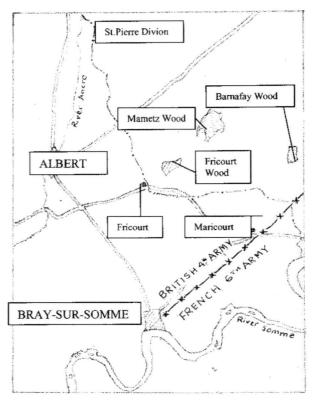

Somme Offensive, July 1916.

The attack on Fricourt Farm on 2 July was followed by contact patrol observers reporting with great accuracy a few minutes after it took place. From the results obtained during the month of July it was ascertained that flares could easily be seen and distinguished from the air and as stated above proved their worth on many occasions. From the observers' point of view, however, they were not lit in sufficient numbers; this was partly due to a shortage in the supply from England, only a proportion of the men carrying them in consequence. (See map opposite.)

The system of lighting flares in specified places and times was not found to be entirely satisfactory owing to it being impossible to guarantee that an aeroplane would be in a position to see them. During the last days in July, however, this was to a large extent overcome by the adoption of Klaxon horns fitted to the aeroplane, a prolonged hoot saying, 'Where are you?' By this means an economy in flares was also effected. The Klaxon horn was also used to announce signals from the ground. Lamps were used with success by day and by night especially by No.9 Squadron working with XIII Corps. Considerable use was made of signal panels but difficulty was experienced by the aeroplane observer in knowing when a ground station wanted to signal to it and by the ground station in knowing when its message had been received.

In order to observe troops when stationary it was necessary to descend to 300ft. This was much lower than observations during inactive periods along the front-line trenches, where observations could take place between 300 and 1,000ft. The normal height for patrolling during periods of inactivity was between 1,300 and 2,500ft. Aircraft that flew below 2,000ft attracted machine gun and rifle fire and below 1,000ft ground fire was usually very heavy. Rifle fire was experienced by pilots even when the soldiers below were actually in contact with the enemy. An RFC report dated 30 July 1916 stated that some aircraft were so riddled with bullets when they landed back at base that it was often necessary to dismantle and reconstruct them. Kite balloons were also used in the 4th Army area during the opening weeks of the battle. Their use, however, was adversely reported on by General Rawlinson, referring to 18 July and 3 August, and their use for contact work was discontinued.

Acting on the lessons learned from the Battle of the Somme the orders for contact patrols were revised. The most important of these revisions was the change in the method of indicating positions, the Clock Code being substituted for the co-ordinate system. It had proved difficult to read long messages and numerals on the panels. With regard to communication between patrolling aircraft by wireless there was a danger that the enemy could listen to the transmissions. Furthermore, there was apt to be conflict with Allied aircraft spotting for the artillery. Transmissions from the latter could drown out those from the contact patrol transmissions. The solution was to rely on message dropping from contact patrol aircraft on Formation HQ. Much use was made of skeleton maps, which reduced the work of observers who had only to mark on them the positions of troops. It was found that accurate observation could be achieved flying at altitudes between 600 and 700ft due to the difference in the colour of the uniform, although the steel helmets of both Allied and German troops appeared black. On the other hand it proved possible to see whether or not trenches were occupied at altitudes between 1,500 and 2,000ft.

Warning of impending enemy attacks and the presence or otherwise of enemy troops in the vicinity of Formation HQs was also provided for in proposals circulated to RFC brigades in March 1917. During the spring offensive of the 1st and 3rd Armies against the enemy front from Vimy Ridge to south-east of Arras, the determination and force of the enemy counter-attacks clearly demonstrated the importance of accurate observation and quick and effective reporting. An order of 1 May 1917 laid down that special machines should be detailed for this work. Care had to be taken that the work of artillery spotting aircraft did not conflict with contact air patrol aircraft. It was important for aircraft operating behind captured enemy positions to report the change of occupation to the artillery to avoid casualties from friendly fire.

The squadron deployment in the early spring of 1916 on the Western Front was:

Army	Corps Sqn	Reconnaissance Mild Fighting	Fighting Squadrons Up to date types	Out of date types
1st Army	3	1	–	2
2nd Army	4	1	2	1
3rd Army	3	–	1	2
4th Army	4	–	1	3
5th Army	4	–	1 (naval)	3
GHQ	–	1 (bomber)	2	–

THE WESTERN FRONT – OPERATIONS AND CASUALTIES FROM 9 JANUARY 1917

The following additional squadrons were expected to arrive by 1 April. At the time it was thought that estimates might not be realized or might possibly be exceeded: eight squadrons of up to date types, one reconnaissance squadron and one bombing squadron. There were five armies of the British Expeditionary Force on the Western Front and each army had an attached RFC brigade:

Deployment of RFC squadrons – January 1917

GHQ – 9th Brigade RFC
The First Army – 1st Brigade RFC
The Second Army – 2nd Brigade RFC
The Third Army – 3rd Brigade RFC
The Fourth Army – 5th Brigade ~RFC
The Fifth Army – 10th Brigade RFC

No.8 Brigade RFC would become the Independent Bomber Force for strategic bombing. All bombing carried out on the Western Front in 1916/7 was of a tactical nature and some of these bombing operations are described in the passages which follow.

The extracts from official reports furnished by HQ RFC in France to the C-in-C BEF cover the early part of 1917 and are illustrative of the part played by tactical air power in the trench warfare that characterized the land campaign. The deployment of squadrons reported upon and the aircraft with which they were equipped during the period January to August 1917 may be found in Appendix G.

Introduction to RFC operations

The following descriptions of RFC operations during the period 1 January to August 1917 show the contribution made by the squadrons to land operations along the five army fronts. The missions of the aircraft included artillery co-operation, aerial photography, photographic reconnaissance and contact air patrols. Bombing operations included attacks on railways, enemy wire defences, gun pits and associated ammunition stores and to protect the aircraft employed on all these duties there were fighter aircraft that could engage enemy aircraft. Units of the 9th Wing attached to GHQ had at their disposal a distance photo reconnaissance squadron, No.70, three fighter squadrons, Nos.19, 56 and 66, and two day bomber squadrons, Nos.27 and 55. By June No.11 Wing, in the Messines area, had two fighter reconnaissance squadrons, Nos.20 and 45, and three fighter squadrons, Nos.1, 45 and 46. By the time of the Messines battle the RFC could muster 300 aircraft of which over one third were fighter aircraft. The German Armies facing the BEF in this sector also numbered some 300 aircraft of which half were fighters.

Artillery cooperation was principally the role of corps pilots and the BEF would plan their operations with HQ RFC. Aircraft would direct the fire of British guns on enemy gun positions, wire, enemy trenches and selected strong points. There was also a need to identify and attack 'masked gun positions' and so the RFC would try to get as many aircraft as possible in the air before an assault was to be launched. At Messines the RFC had to secure air superiority and the air offensive was more concentrated than it had been during the preceding Somme and Arras offensives. Not only did RFC aircraft provide accurate information to the guns but they also had to deny the battle front to prying eyes of enemy machines. To achieve this latter purpose there were formations of fighters flying in excess of 15,000ft with a further formation of some six fighters flying at 12,000ft or below over the centre of the barrage-line. Army wireless bases or 'compass stations' would take bearings of a German aircraft and by means of intersection on a map the position of the aircraft was passed to the RFC and

forward ground stations so that code strip signals could be displayed to the fighter pilots in the area where the enemy aircraft had been located. Air combat also features prominently in the following passages and consideration is given to the quality of fighter aircraft on both sides. The army pilots were to the fore and some of the air aces of the Great War came to prominence during this period.

Operations in late January 1917

On the 21st a German aircraft landed in the Third Army area and the pilot and observer became prisoners. The circumstances are not given in the source but during the Great War many combat aircraft were forced down after contact with the enemy and if an aircraft was disabled it would be the only means for the crew to survive if serious damage had been sustained preventing a return to friendly lines. Deaths or injury could be sustained by accident and combat. 2nd Lieutenant Hodgson of No.52 Squadron was killed as a result of an accident and multiple casualties of No.10 Squadron resulted from a mid-air collision. No.42 Squadron took photographs of the condition of enemy barbed wire prior to a British assault and bombs were dropped by aircraft of the 1st Brigade RFC. Two days later there was a major aerial engagement when six German aircraft were destroyed and three were more forced to land. 2nd Lieutenant Hay of No.40 Squadron destroyed a hostile machine and later met a formation of eight German aircraft and destroyed the aircraft of the formation leader. During the unequal contest Hay was then himself brought down and killed. Pilots and observers of Nos.6, 41 and 45 Squadrons were either wounded or were recorded as missing.

The reason for retaining so many fighter squadrons on Nos.9 and 51 Wings at the disposal of GHQ was to enable these units to be directed to any part of the front that the C-in-C considered, at any given time, to be of the greatest importance to the successful outcome of ground operations. From an aerial point of view a single fighting front extends over the fronts of several armies and far beyond their outer flanks.

On 24 January Nos.6, 23 and 41 Squadron pilots were killed in action and one pilot of No.43 Squadron was killed en route to France, not at that time therefore on the strength of the BEF. Also missing were pilots of No.53 Squadron and an RNAS pilot was also recorded as missing. On 29 January there was a great deal of artillery co-operation and 485 photographs were taken. Bombing attacks were launched on Provin, Pont-a-Vendin and Meurchin and bomb bursts were observed on the objectives. Three German aircraft were destroyed and three driven down. On 25 January artillery co-operation continued as fifty-one targets were engaged by British artillery. Five enemy aircraft were brought down, three on the British side of the lines. No.18 Squadron's base at St-Leger-les-Authie was heavily shelled necessitating the move of the squadron to

Bertangles on 27 January. From the 26th to the 31st artillery co-operation and photography featured mainly in Allied air operations and eight enemy aircraft were destroyed. On 31 January the weather was unfavourable for aerial operations with snow and mist.

Operations in February 1917

Units of the 1st Brigade attacked Garvin on 1 February and the railway and sidings were damaged whilst the 5th Brigade attacked dumps at Mory and Fremicourt. No.22 Squadron was involved in the Garvin attack and Captain Jones and Lieutenant Pickthorne dived at an AA battery mounted on a lorry. The casualties from this attack amounted to one killed and two injured and four machines were missing together with 7 officers. The following day saw fifty-eight targets being attacked with forty-one aimed at gun pits. Three squadrons were involved in these raids, Nos.20, 29 and 32 Squadrons. An enemy machine was brought down by Major Gratton Belew and 2nd Lieutenant McCudden from No.29 Squadron, whilst aircraft of No.32 Squadron engaged nine enemy aircraft, driving one down out of control and forcing another to land. As a result three aircraft were reported missing and that was a loss of four officers. A German Halberstadt was destroyed near Lille by Captain Hartney and 2nd Lieutenant Wilkinson of No.20 Squadron. Artillery co-operation continued on 3 February and sixty-three hits were recorded on gun pits and trench mortar targets. There were three explosions of ammunition. Bombing continued on the night of 7/8 February when the airfields at Provin and La Pouillerie were attacked by aircraft of the 1st Brigade together with the station at Lattre. Aircraft of No.4 Squadron attacked and dispersed a party of German infantry with machine gun fire whilst on artillery patrol. A notable encounter between aircraft of No.16 Squadron and two Albatros scouts occurred on 4 February. One aircraft was artillery spotting when it was attacked by one of the Scouts but was brought down in German lines, but a second scout then attacked this aircraft when both pilot and observer were severely wounded resulting in the downing of the aircraft and the death of both men. The same Albatros then attacked another of No.16 Squadron's aircraft and the observer was killed in the air. The machine then caught fire at approximately 4,000ft and the pilot, Lieutenant Massey, side-slipped in an attempt to put out the flames. By the time that the aircraft reached 1,000ft his legs were so badly burned that he climbed out of the cockpit and miraculously managed to jump clear just before the aircraft struck the ground. He survived and responded to hospital treatment.

Operations throughout the remainder of the month were characterized by artillery co-operation, photography and bombing. Air combat was a natural corollary of these operational missions. By the middle of the month the total of German aircraft brought down was seven with

The nose of a huge bombing aeroplane showing how the gun is used and the instruments used by the pilot.

four more driven down in a damaged condition. Five RFC single-seaters and one two-seater were missing together with seven crew members. Four men had been killed in combat and five by accident with ten wounded both in combat and by accident. Nos.4, 15 and 23 Squadrons were engaged in reconnaissance missions and Lieutenants H. Fowler and F.E. Brown of No.2 Squadron destroyed a Halberstadt scout near Lens. Lieutenants Probyn and Wood of No.34 Squadron were believed to have destroyed an enemy machine near Harrieres Wood. On 26 February a patrol of No.29 Squadron engaged five hostile aircraft with indecisive results. The German aircraft involved were using explosive ammunition.

Operations in March 1917

On 4 March it was noted that the Germans were using only one gun per battery, which pointed to the removal of the remaining guns. Three single-seater and a couple of two-seater aircraft went missing. There were five combat deaths with two from accidents. Reconnaissance on 6 March disclosed a considerable number of fires behind German lines following explosions. Aircraft of the 5th Brigade reported that train movements behind the enemy's lines were above normal and 545 photographs were taken during the day. Bombing targets included Achiet-le-Grand, Maison de Fre and Bucquoy, Courcelles, Vraucourt and Ecoust stations. A sugar factory near Ervillers was also attacked. On 6 March German aircraft were particularly active opposite the First Army front. Approximately seventy German aircraft were involved and RFC pilots brought down three German aircraft and at least three were driven down damaged. At the same time four RFC aircraft were brought down with seven declared missing. An indication of the amount of aerial activity at this time is number of flying hours for one day's operations.

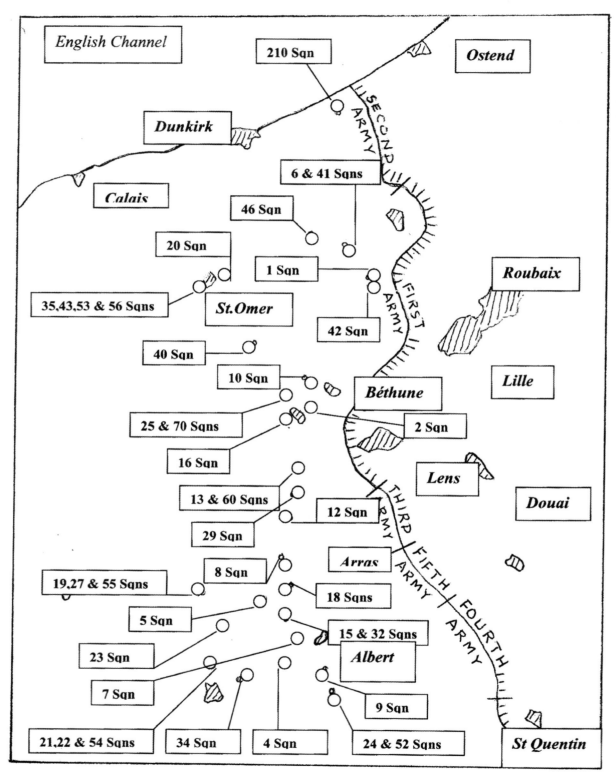

English Channel

210 Sqn

Ostend

Dunkirk

6 & 41 Sqns

46 Sqn

Calais

20 Sqn

1 Sqn

Roubaix

35,43,53 & 56 Sqns

St.Omer

42 Sqn

40 Sqn

10 Sqn

Lille

25 & 70 Sqns

Béthune

2 Sqn

16 Sqn

Lens

13 & 60 Sqns

12 Sqn

Douai

29 Sqn

19,27 & 55 Sqns

8 Sqn

Arras

18 Sqns

5 Sqn

15 & 32 Sqns

23 Sqn

Albert

7 Sqn

9 Sqn

21,22 & 54 Sqns

34 Sqn

4 Sqn

24 & 52 Sqns

St Quentin

SECOND ARMY · FIRST ARMY · THIRD ARMY · FIFTH ARMY · FOURTH ARMY

RFC squadron location map and BEF army fronts, 1 January 1917.

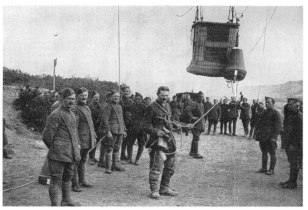

Kite balloon.

Balloons were often the subject of attack and one of No.9 Section's balloons was attacked by three German aircraft on 11 March and brought down in flames. Both observers made successful parachute descents. On the 9th nine FEs of No.40 Squadron were attacked by a German formation and a half-hour period of aerial combat ensued. At least one hostile aircraft was destroyed but three of the FEs failed to return and the remainder were badly damaged. On 17 March 1,356 hours were flown. Some of those hours were accounted for by eighteen aircraft of the 1st Brigade taking photographs of the front line at Courrières. Nineteen German aircraft then appeared and engaged in aerial combat. Three German aircraft were destroyed and three driven down in a damaged condition with one driven down under control, but three British machines did not return. The photographic missions were, however, completed successfully.

Another means of reconnoitring enemy gun positions of trenches lay in the kite balloon and on 24 March both aircraft and kite balloons were used to attack thirty-five targets. Nineteen gun pits were hit and explosions were

heard amongst ammunition. Hostile aircraft were active in the vicinity of Arras and Lens. On 23 March reconnaissance was carried out by No.18 Squadron. This unit reported no defensive German line existed east of the Hindenburg line within the areas seven miles north-east and south of Cambrai, nor was any defensive line seen east of this as far as Denain-le-Cateau. Additionally, four new enemy airfields were reported to be active. No.18 Squadron was a constituent unit of No.9 Wing, which reported direct to Army HQ. Railway targets continued to be attacked and included Don station, the sidings at St Quentin and the railway line at Pont-a-Vendin. On the 30th train movements proceeding north on the Pont-a-Vendin – Don- Haubordin line and the Douai–Lille lines were above normal. Like an increase in signals traffic, increased railway movement probably heralded an enemy offensive.

Operations in April/August 1917
On the second of the month the Izel–Drocourt line and the Drocourt–Queant lines were reconnoitred and much useful information was provided for the 7th Division. On 3 March reconnaissance was carried out by all but the 3rd Brigade RFC. Aircraft and kite balloons continued to co-operate with the artillery often resulting with successful shoots against live ammunition dumps. Captain Hudson of No.54 Squadron attacked and brought down in flames an enemy kite balloon and on his return to base he opened fire from an altitude of 200ft on a party of some 100 men unloading boxes from open trucks in Gouy railway station. Some men were seen to fall and the rest scattered. By August little had changed. The targets remained substantially the same and the opposing trench lines remained intact even though their positions had changed little. That is to say the war did not become fluid as it had been before the Battle of the Marne. Casualty reports for three consecutive days in August are illustrative and one can calculate the number of killed missing and wounded over the period of a month bearing in mind that the weather, on occasion, could prevent any flying on given days.

	9 August	10 August	11 August
Missing in action	4	16	9
Killed in action	1	1	2
Wounded in action	4	8	3
Killed – accident or duty	1	–	–
Wounded in action –	1	–	–
Killed – accident	–	2	2
Wounded – accident	–	2	1
Total	11	29	17

A comparison of British and French results on the Western Front between 1 July 1916 and 15 October 1918 discloses the following:

		British	French
1.	Enemy aircraft destroyed by the	4104	2026
2.	Enemy aircraft driven down	2257	1985
3.	Machines missing	2321	971*
4.	Weight of bombs dropped (in tons)	6072	4553

* The official document disputes the figure of 971 since it was claimed that the figures provided by the French for the preceding 3½ months were somewhat approximate.

Comparison of the adversaries
Source: *SPAD VII V Albatros DIII* by Jon Guttman, Osprey Publishing

April 1917 became known as 'Bloody April'. A section of the German line was pulled back at the end of March on the orders of Von Hindenburg (the Hindenburg Line) and it was moved eastward from a point just south of Arras to a point just west of Vailly. Since the German armies had failed to defeat the Allies in the west in 1914 (the Schlieffen Plan), the initial war aim was changed. In 1917 the Germans would fight a defensive battle in the west and aim to defeat Russia in the east. This shortened defensive line would be heavily reinforced and the German air units would try to ensure that Allied artillery and ground-attack aircraft did not weaken that line. The French C-in-C, General Nivelle, had planned a major offensive with the aim of breaking through the German trenches but little was achieved at the cost of thousands of lives. Likewise, in the north the third Somme offensive petered out and only the Canadians made an advance at Vimy Ridge. The air battles over the line became intense as a result giving rise to the term 'Bloody April'. Oswald Boelcke had brought the German fighter units up to airfields close to the line so that they could respond

Albatros DI.

SPAD SVII.

quickly and with less expenditure of fuel to the approach of Allied air units. At that time the RFC enjoyed numerical superiority and the aim was to carry the air war to the enemy. But Trenchard's aggressive tactics actually played into the hands of the defenders and Richthofen took the view that there was no point going to look for the enemy when the Allied fighters would come to them. Moreover, the prevailing westerly winds gave the Germans the advantage that Allied aircraft attempting to make it back to their lines ran into headwinds. So it came down to the quality of the opposing aircraft.

Given the numerical superiority of the Allies the Germans had to husband their resources. The SPAD on arriving over German lines could well meet the Albatros. The SPAD VII arrived on the Western Front in August 1916 and would have given the allies a distinct advantage in aerial fighting had it not been for the arrival over the German front of the Albatros DI followed by the DII and DIII. What the Albatros lacked in manoeuvrability it made up for in fire power since twin machine guns were mounted on the fuselage in front of the pilot compared with the one which armed the SPAD. When the Albatros III arrived over the battlefront the lower wing was liable to structural failure due to the increased weight of this derivative, which had to be removed from service for two months until the appropriate modifications had been made. When an even sleeker version of the Albatros fighter arrived in service, the DV, it too suffered from wing flutter. The greatest success was achieved with the DIII where the wing strengthening resulted in very few instances of structural wing failure. The SPAD also had its problems and the SPAD VIII, which was more heavily armed, suffered from a failure of the spur reduction gear whereas the SPAD VII had its most reliable direct-drive engine. The RNAS units equipped with the Sopwith Triplane caused some concern and during April the RFC added the SE5 and new Bristol F2. Initially these last two did not make a great impression on the Germans but when improvements were made to both aircraft, the SE5a and Bristol F2B, then these aircraft came into their own. As matter of interest the Bristol F2B would remain in RAF service into the early 1930s, being the workhorse of the RAF, together with the DH9A, in the air policing of the outposts of Empire.

Conclusions that may be drawn about aerial operations over the Western Front

The BE (British experimental) series of aircraft produced by the Royal Aircraft Factory had been unsuited to the hurly-burly of aerial conflict. Once the Fokker monoplane arrived at the front, with its Spandau machine gun, which fired directly through the span of the propeller, the 'plodding' BEs needed protection whilst they were carrying out the vital work of aerial reconnaissance and photography and artillery co-operation. Trenchard insisted that his men carry out these duties regardless of the risk and hoped for a British or French aircraft that could rival the Fokker III. The multipurpose FE2b and, later, the DH2 were such aircraft. As 'pusher' types a machine gun mounted in the nose could be fired without the need for an interrupter gear and the fields of fire were ideal in a chase. For a while the RFC had the ascendency and scouts could fly missions far behind enemy lines attacking every German aircraft that was sighted and the ethos of the RFC was that no odds were to be considered too great. Following the deployment of the Albatros German fighters the enemy again gained the ascendency but were countered by the SPAD and Nieuport fighters. With regard to artillery the number of German batteries that opened fire along the front meant that the artillery spotting aircraft simply could not assist in the registration of all the targets firing away. The number of British guns trying to range on enemy batteries also had a tendency to 'swamp' the squadrons involved. When it came to British bombing raids the BE2c aircraft were mostly used and these did not have the load-carrying capacity to deliver a significant number of bombs on the designated targets unless an observer was not to be carried. This required great courage since the pilot would have no means of protection in the air. The bombing was hardly devastating by modern standards but occasionally it proved effective. Bombs dropped on St Quentin station that killed or wounded 180 German soldiers of the 71st Regiment provides an example. Finally, the contact air patrols continued to provide ground commanders with vital information in fluid battle situations

The preceding extracts paint a picture of attritional conflict in the air matching that on the ground. Certainly there was very little likelihood of either side achieving air superiority for any significant length of time let alone air supremacy. The loss of aircraft and aircrew was substantial on both sides. Missions of all five RFC brigades on the Western Front comprised photography, reconnaissance, artillery co-operation and bombing. The aircraft of the 9th Brigade were available to GHQ to throw its weight to support threatened army fronts. Balloons and artillery co-operation aircraft certainly improved the effectiveness of artillery on both sides. Counter-attacks on gun pits and ammunition dumps featured prominently in Allied missions. Thousands of aerial photographs were taken and undoubtedly influenced decision making, especially by army commanders about to launch an attack. Once an attack had been launched contact air patrols were invaluable in keeping army and subordinate commanders up to date in a fluid battle situation.

One thing that the student of air power will perhaps find difficult to grasp is that fast modern jet aircraft that are engaged in combat today might see aircrews ejecting from stricken aircraft but in the Great War RFC aircrews, unlike balloon observers, did not wear parachutes, hence the frequent references to aircraft being forced down, sometimes under control. A previous extract refers to a RFC pilot who got out of his cockpit to avoid any further injury to his legs and face from burns and who leapt clear of his aircraft just before it hit the ground. Even though Everard Calthrop had completed tests on his 'Guardian Angel' parachute in 1915 and offered it to the War Office, it was declined. The reason given was that parachutes were too bulky to be worn in the confines of an aircraft cockpit. This in turn would affect the handling of an aircraft and add unacceptably to the all-up weight. A further thought was that a pilot who knows that he can abandon and aircraft rather than fight or fly a damaged aircraft back to base was not acceptable. Alternatively, a pilot could be issued with a pistol to end his life if he is trapped in an aircraft on fire. There were parachutes that had been developed and these were used by French. German and American pilots when they arrived in Europe. When the Air Ministry eventually approved the issue of parachutes to aircraft crews they were to be of American design.

AIR DEFENCE OF THE BRITISH ISLES

Introduction

One thing that the air defence of the British Isles in the Great War had in common with that in the Second World War was that enemy aircraft did not reach the western and north-western extremities of the British Isles in large numbers. This was indeed reflected in the radar coverage of UK airspace developed in the late 1930s. It meant that

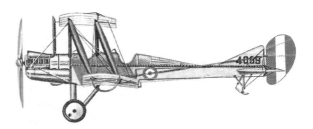

RA Factory BE2c.

in both world wars the majority of fighter squadrons were based at airfields down the North Sea coast around the capital and along the Channel coast. In terms of reaching targets in the British Isles, the Zeppelins had a far greater range but, compared with aeroplanes, airships were slow and lacked manoeuvrability and in 1917 were replaced by bombing aircraft as the main attack weapon. Britain's fighter defences therefore had to adapt to the changing threat. Although Zeppelin raids continued until August 1918 the German airships did not constitute a serious threat. As this section of Chapter 4 will make clear, however, the demands for fighter aircraft on the Western Front competed with those for home air defence. This clash of demands would lead to the formation of the RAF on April 1st 1918, events described in Chapter 5.

AIR DEFENCE ARRANGEMENTS FROM JANUARY 1916
Source: National Archive document AIR1/109/15/20

The situation up to the end of January 1916
Source: AIR1/109/15/20/2

A certain number of aeroplanes and pilots were allocated to the defence of London and other key points, but these aeroplanes were, on the whole, quite unsuitable for air defence due to their poor ceiling and armament. Moreover, no attempt had been made to standardize night flying equipment or armament, provide lighting for night operations at Home Defence airfields or arrange for co-operation between guns and searchlights. Very little had been done to vote for money for the provision of machines and it had been possible only to train pilots for day work in the event of war. Even at the end of 1916 the demands of other theatres came before home defence when it came to the allocation of scarce machines.

Situation from February 1916
At the beginning of February approximately twenty-five BE2cs were allocated to home defence but it was not numbers alone that mattered; aeroplanes for home defence had to possess the performance to reach the altitudes required to intercept the enemy. Service ceilings and rate of climb would be important. The BE2c could reach 11,000ft, which matched the service ceiling of German airships at that time. Interception however, was one thing, destruction was another. Attacks on airships at night had been the exception since the pilot could look forward either to serious or fatal injury. The aircraft were scattered in widely separated detachments of two or three machines under the command of Officers Commanding several different training squadrons. The officer commanding the Training Squadron at Hounslow had also to command the ten detachments allotted to the defence of London. Clearly the organization was

unsatisfactory. In February No.19 Training Squadron was formed from what remained of No.24 Squadron, which was posted overseas. The squadron had a dual role, namely the training of night pilots and the defence of the London area against Zeppelin attacks. To achieve this the latter pairs of BE2c aircraft were detached to Hounslow, Hendon, Chingford, Hainault Farm, Sutton's Farm, Joyce Green, Framingham, Croydon and Wimbledon Common. Systematic training of night pilots now commenced at Hounslow and fittings for night flying were standardized. Since Zeppelins attacked at night it was particularly important to master night flying techniques but night flying had been looked upon as a dangerous and expensive form of flying as crashes resulting in fatal or serious injury was the norm rather than the exception. This made it abundantly clear that one squadron could not efficiently carry out both training and operations so it was decided to form a Home Defence squadron to defend the London area. This was No.39 Home Defence Squadron with headquarters at Woodford and flights at North Weald Basset, Hainault Farm and Sutton's Farm. Work began on standardizing night flying equipment and armament and the lighting of aerodromes and landing grounds.

Method of attacking a Zeppelin
The improvement in capability of home defence forces was apparent during the night of 25/26 April 1916 when ten machines went to intercept a Zeppelin raid and all descended safely, only two machines sustaining light damage. The night airship equipment carried by the home defence machines included two 20lb HE bombs and two 16lb incendiary bombs. Later Rankin explosive darts were carried. It was very doubtful that a defending fighter would find itself above a Zeppelin, and if it did it was doubtful if a bomb could, with accuracy, be dropped on the airship and if the bomb missed there was the threat to life and property below. The best method of attacking a Zeppelin was by gunfire and the BE2c was fitted with a Lewis gun. It was believed that three drums of ammunition should be sufficient to cause gas leakage to bring the airship down in the North Sea. Since no incendiary bullets were available, gas leakage was the best hope. The Rankin (or Ranken) darts with explosive tips could accelerate the loss of gas. It was then felt that the carriage of bombs and Rankin darts slowed the aircraft down and hindered the rate of ascent to effect an interception. A significant advance in anti-Zeppelin weaponry occurred in the summer of 1916. The Brock explosive bullet was followed by the Buckingham and Pomeroy bullets. The problem with the Pomeroy bullet was that the dynamite content failed to detonate at low temperatures such as that experienced at night at altitudes of 10,000ft and above. Finally, there were Le Prieur rockets, which would certainly set an airship

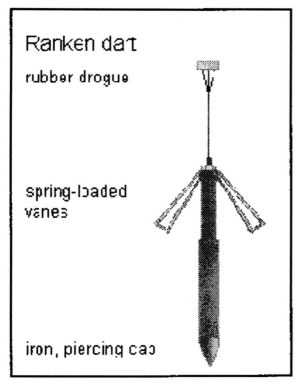

Ranken dart.

alight. But they were erratic in flight and their heads and weight added unacceptably to the all-up weight of an aircraft. There is no record of a Le Prieur rocket ever having been fired at a hostile airship and their use was discontinued in February 1917.

Le Prieur rockets attatched to the interplane struts.

Reorganization

From 16 July onwards, No.16 Wing undertook the air defence of the UK and squadrons were formed at various training stations. Following the reorganization No.16 Wing was retitled the Home Defence Wing with squadrons to cover the following defence areas.

39	London
37	Essex
50	Kent
78	Sussex and Hants
75	South Midlands
38	Midlands
51	Norfolk
33	North Midlands
76	Yorkshire
36	Tyne and Tees
77	Forth

The training of Night Pilots was carried out by No.198 Depot Squadron based at Rochford. The new organization bore fruit when No.39 Squadron bagged five Zeppelins between April and October 1916. In April, 2Lt A. de Brandon and 2Lt C.A. Ridley brought down a Zeppelin in the Thames Estuary. In September Lt W.A. Robinson, 2Lt F. Sowrey and 2Lt A. de Brandon brought down three Zeppelins at Cuffley, Billericay and Little Wigborough respectively and in October, 2Lt W.J. Tempest brought down a Zeppelin at Potters Bar. No.36 Squadron covering the Tees added a sixth Zeppelin in November when 2Lt J.V. Pyott brought down one of the airships off the Tees Estuary. During 1917 further expansion of the Home Defence Squadrons took place and the eleven squadrons listed on the previous page were increased to fourteen and the Night Training Squadrons went from one to eight with a Wireless School at Penshurst. In February 1917 Lt Col Holt DSO, who had commanded the Home Defence Wing, was posted to France his place being taken by Lt Col T.C.R. Higgins.

During the first half of 1917 the War Office felt that the aircraft with which the Home Defence squadrons were equipped were not up to intercepting Zeppelins

Sopwith Camel.

or aeroplanes in spite of the successes logged in the previous paragraph, although it was conceded that the squadrons had done a good job training night bombing pilots. When an airship was unable to rise to get it out of trouble then success was possible. This happened when Lt L.P. Watkins, a BE12 pilot from No.37 Squadron, downed a partially disabled Zeppelin that could not rise above 11,000ft. There was a clear necessity for fighters that had the speed, rate of climb and manoeuvrability to intercept the Gotha bombers that were undertaking daylight bombing of south-east England from bases in Belgium. Comparison with the BE and FE machines is instructive. The BE2c, for example, had a service ceiling of only 10,000ft and maximum speed of 72mph at 6,500ft. The Camel had a top speed of 104.5mph and a service ceiling of 18,000ft. The other fighter brought into service to meet the threat was the Sopwith Scout (known in the trade as the 'Pup' because it was a scaled-down version of the Sopwith 1½ Strutter). So what was the threat?

The Gotha threat

In late 1916 the Imperial German Air Service, the *Luftstreitkräfte*, began planning a daylight bombing offensive against England called *Türkenkreuz*. The Gotha bomber was produced during the autumn of 1916 and thirty were to be made ready for daylight operations on 1 February 1917. The urgency stemmed from the obvious limitations of the Zeppelin airship but in the event the bomber was not ready until the early summer. The unit known as Kagohl 3 was formed and commanded by *Hauptmann* Ernst Brandenburg. Equipped with the Gotha GIV, Kagohl 3 operated from St Denis Westrem and Gonterode in German-occupied Belgium. The unit was ready for operations by April 1917.

The Gotha bomber had a performance that equalled, if not exceeded, that of the fighters which Britain could put up into the air to defend the home base. With a speed of 87mph the Gotha could be outstripped by the Camel but

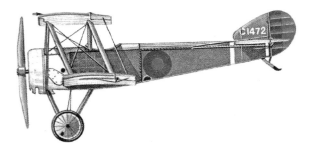

Sopwith Scout (Pup).

with a service ceiling of 21,325ft it could be out of reach. Having said that the greater the altitude of an attack force the less likely it would be for the bombers to be accurate. The Gotha that was to attack Britain was the GIV. The earlier versions had seen service on the Balkan and Western Fronts. One interesting feature of this aircraft was its defensive armament. It had a crew of three and the gunners could move between the gun positions, one of which was in the ventral position as shown in the diagram. This would prove a rude surprise, initially, if the defending fighters attacked from below.

Further developments in air defence arrangements

On the commencement of aeroplane attacks on London additional squadrons were raised and equipped with Sopwith Camels. The Camel was a very important fighter in the scheme of things but as the war drew to a close the Camel and the Bristol Fighter would man the southern squadrons, particularly around the capital, and the Avro 504K the northern units. The systematic training of night fighting pilots took place on the Pups. With the training came a growing confidence that one aeroplane could successfully attack another at night and on 18 December

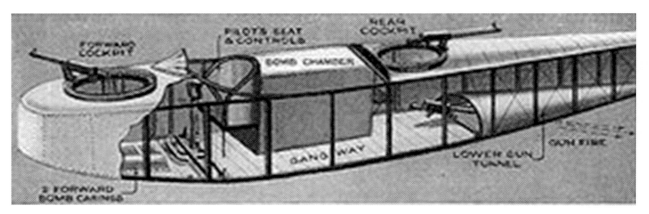

Gun positions in the Gotha bomber.

Gotha IV bomber.

1917 during a night raid by Gothas, Captain Murlis Green of No.44 Squadron brought down one of these bombers off Dover. As other Home Defence wings were formed they eventually were subsumed into the 6th Brigade. The 6th Brigade became the Great War equivalent of Fighter Command in World War II. In addition to the aerial defence of England and southern Scotland and co-operation with coastal batteries the Brigade had a training role, namely the training of night fighting pilots and night light bombing pilots and the formation of and training of night fighting units and night light bombing units for France.

It was important to co-ordinate the deployment of aircraft to intercept airships or aeroplanes with searchlights and the aeroplane and searchlight barrage was instituted. Each officer commanding a Home Defence squadron would have at his disposal a searchlight company, permitting both operational control and tactical training. There was a direct telephone line between the squadron HQ and the searchlight company known as an 'air bandit' facility. When intelligence indicated the approach of hostile airships each aeroplane flight would send up two or three machines with orders to attempt to reach the highest altitude possible. There was a difference for squadrons situated southwards from Melton Mowbray and those situated northwards. For the southern squadrons orders to patrol were received from the Officer Commanding the Home Defence Wing who acted on intelligence received from various sources at the War Office. For the squadrons situated from Lincoln northwards to the Forth Estuary, the squadron commanders ordered their squadrons aloft on intelligence received from the appropriate warning controls.

The next stage, which began in the late summer of 1916, was the preparation of a number of landing grounds along the line of the barrage. These would permit pilots who had lost their way due to adverse weather conditions or had experienced engine failure, to make a safe descent. These landing grounds were divided into three categories:

1st Class landing grounds – Landings would be possible from most directions. The landing surfaces were good and there were no obstacles in the vicinity.

2nd Class landing grounds – Landings would be possible from most directions but the ground surfaces could be irregular in places and there might be obstacles on some approaches. This could prevent flares being laid out in certain positions.

3rd Class landing grounds – These usually only permitted landings in two directions but were chosen or kept on since they constituted the only location for an emergency landing ground in the locality. Indeed, in some districts it was impossible to site both 1st and 2nd Class landing grounds. Since the landing grounds were marked by a different number of flares pilots would opt for a 3rd Class ground only in an emergency.

By the end of the war there were:

35 6th Brigade aerodromes
29 1st Class landing grounds, which included 11 at training stations
79 2nd Class landing grounds, which included 12 at training stations
31 3rd Class landing grounds, which included 1 at a training station

OPERATIONS IN MESOPOTAMIA
Source: National Archive document AIR1/674/21/6/87

'The Forgotten Air War – Airpower in the Mesopotamian Campaign' by Major Lambert USAF

Introduction
Chapter 3 described the British advance from Basra up the River Tigris making for Baghdad. When that advance reached Ctesiphon, only twenty-five miles south of Baghdad, the Turkish high command realized that insufficient force had been deployed on this front. The battle of Ctesiphon lasted for five days with an inconclusive result but when the Turkish commander realized that the British force, under General Townshend, was in full-scale retreat the Turks began a pursuit. The British force made an orderly retreat arriving at Kut on 5 December 1915. Major Lambert in his work shown above describes how Major Reilly of No.30 Squadron was tasked to survey the Baghdad area. He had noticed a significant change in the Turkish positions to the east of Ctesiphon together with large numbers of Turkish reinforcements. Rather than proceed to Baghdad, Reilly decided to survey the build up of Turkish forces near Ctesiphon and he made the appropriate sketch map, which would have

been so valuable to Townshend in his forward planning had not Reilly's machine been hit with shrapnel forcing him to land near the Turkish lines. The unfortunate pilot was then captured by Arabs who handed him over to the Turks. The sketch map meant nothing to the Arabs but it did to the Turkish high command. The latter then knew what Townshend needed to find out in planning the effective defence of his positions in Kut. Townshend admired Reilly and his capture was regarded by the General as a great loss. Not having Reilly's map meant that he did not send for the appropriate reinforcements and the town was quickly encircled by Turkish forces and troops were detached to proceed downriver to prevent a British relief force from reaching Kut.

The siege of Kut began on 7 December. Throughout the campaign the aircraft of the newly constituted No.30 Squadron RFC had provided very valuable intelligence. Reports and sketches made during reconnaissance flights made it possible for Townshend to prosecute the war with success. There were problems of aircraft serviceability and there was sickness amongst personnel due to the heat and dust, and forced landings were not uncommon. Given the very marshy conditions on either bank of the Tigris stores, repair facilities and aircraft had to be ferried up-river by lighter or barge. With the siege of Kut, the role of aircraft was to become of critical importance in the beginning of 1916.

The role of aircraft during the siege of Kut

Between January and March 1916 Townshend launched several attacks in an attempt to lift the siege but without success and at great cost. Disease was spreading rapidly and the food was running out. An attempt to get supplies through in the paddle steamer *Julna* also failed. The only other hope was that Kut could be supplied with food from the air. The most strenuous work of the air services took place during the last fortnight of April. The sands were fast running out and the garrison had reached the extremity of its endurance for disease and sickness was rife. General Townshend stated that as least 5,000lb daily would have to be dropped, consisting of flour, sugar, chocolate and ghee (a kind of rancid butter). Beyond 24 April he would be totally dependent on air supply, except for horse meat, which was expected to last until the 29th.

Orders were issued to No.30 Squadron and the RNAS squadrons that as much food as possible was to be delivered to Kut on a daily basis over a distance of 23½ miles whilst maintaining reconnaissance flights and artillery co operation. The bomb frames had to be modified and a hastily designed apparatus was the work of Captain Murray RFC. He had to devise a quick release gear that consisted of a long bar attached to the bomb frame, which had been stripped of its fittings and bomb guides. This bar was pivoted at one end and made fast

by a quick-release gear operated from the pilot's seat. By stitching two bags together at the top, they were dropped either side of the bar. When the release was operated the bags would slide off the bar.

There were problems. The first was the stability of the aircraft in flight and the distribution of weight on the otherwise stable BE2c was vital. The seaplanes were not able to carry suspended the bags in the same way as the land planes since the bags would be immersed in the water. So a broad canvas band had to be strapped under the bomb frames. The Voisins and the HF Voisins carried their entire load without difficulty but in the event the seaplanes were not successful due to heavy gales at the beginning of April and also because they were unable, on many occasions, to get off the water for various reasons. All food drops had to be made between 5,000 and 7,000ft for, as soon as the Turks realized what was happening, every effort was made to impede the drops with gunfire.

The delivery of food in bulk commenced on 15 April when 3,350lb of food was dropped and this was well below the required amount. Then enemy aircraft began to attack the food-carrying machines, but providing fighter escorts would, of course, reduce the number of aircraft available for the food drop. The escorts had to carry a Lewis gun and ammunition. One seaplane escort was brought down after an air combat and Lieutenant Davidson RFC was returning from a food drop when he was attacked from the rear by a German Fokker. His aircraft was holed in thirty-two places and the right aileron controls were shop away. Davidson was hit in the left arm and shoulder but, in spite of his injuries and damage sustained by the aircraft, he got his machine back to the airfield, actually waiting for an aircraft ahead of him to land first.

Extra aircraft were brought in to assist with the air drop. Three Maurice Farmans were flown up from Basra but a heavy storm completely wrecked all three, when one of the aircraft was lifted bodily into the air to descend on the other two. Sadly the air service had failed to sustain the British garrison and on 29 April General Townshend was obliged to negotiate surrender to Major General Khalis Pasha, who had succeeded Nurredin as commander-in-chief of the Turkish forces on the Tigris. They met on a steam launch and Townshend agreed to have his guns and ammunition destroyed. A Turkish battalion marched into the town and took over the guard. Townshend went into captivity together with 13,164 of his officers and men.

The 'Fokker Scourge' comes to Mesopotamia

The Fokker Eindecker, meaning single wing or monoplane, was unleashed on the Western Front in July 1915. These fast and manoeuvrable monoplanes immediately gave the Germans the upper hand. The Allies in Mesopotamia were still flying very early types and needed to redress the balance.

The technical personnel at the aircraft park at Basra worked hard to a render a few Bristol Scouts airworthy that had arrived from Egypt pending the arrival of SPADs from England. Two of the Bristols were flown up to the front on 5 and 17 April by Captain de Havilland and 2nd Lt Maguire.

Military operations on the Tigris in 1916

To avoid any future failure in the field like the loss of Kut and inability of relief forces to reach the beleaguered garrison, what was needed was a vast improvement in logistical infrastructure. There were long delays in loading and unloading ships at Basra, the lack of a highway north required the use of shallow draft vessels to carry not only stores and equipment but also aircraft, and there was the lack of a railway, which was at first turned down then ultimately agreed etc. Good roads were built around Basra, new hospitals were set up to care for the sick and wounded, better river steamers were introduced and vast camps and supply depots were established. Before the new commander of British forces on the Tigris made any attempt to regain the initiative he spent the remainder of 1916 training his army. Meanwhile, it was the Turks who were being pressed on a number of fronts, in Palestine and Arabia for example, and the forces at the disposal of Khalil Pasha were being depleted. It was not until 13 December that Maude launched his offensive. He simply bypassed the Turkish forces standing between him and Kut by advancing along the opposite bank of the river. Kut was retaken and the Army advanced towards Baghdad. After the occupation of Baghdad Khalil Pasha withdrew to Mosul with his weakened 6th Army. Sadly General Maude died of cholera on 18 December and his place was taken by General William Marshal who halted operations for the winter.

RFC operations in 1917

No.30 Squadron maintained one flight of six BE2cs and one Bristol Scout, later increased to two. The point has already been made that the Scouts had to be the answer, albeit temporarily, to the threat from the German Fokkers. This flight was based at Sindiyeh for counter aircraft duties and reconnaissance over the 13th and

RE8.

18th Turkish Corps' positions. The remaining two flights of the squadron remained at Baghdad. For the next few months of 1917 the heat was considerable, rising to intense temperatures at the beginning of August. During this period of Army inactivity photographic work enabled the compilation of maps urgently needed for the campaign ahead. The enemy was similarly employed and the German photographic aircraft were unusually active at this time flying at a great height escorted by a Halberstadt. On 15 June the HQ of the aerial unit in Mesopotamia was reformed into No.31 Wing, as part of the Middle East Brigade remaining under the command of Lieutenant Colonel J.E. Tennant.

The earlier mention of cholera is very important in this context. Fighting the air war alone was fraught with difficulty. The roles of the aircraft in this theatre remained as reconnaissance, artillery spotting, photography and bombardment but these roles were sometimes almost impossible for air units to carry out. Temperatures could be so high that aircraft could not gain enough lift to fly and whole units were depleted of men not through death in action but through heat stroke or disease. During July 1917 the temperatures were so high that the Martinsydes could not get into the air. Then No.63 Squadron arrived at Basra coming as it did from a bleak Northumberland coast. It was the middle of August and the squadron personnel had no time to acclimatize. The port was notorious for sand fly fever and that, together with heat stroke, put practically the whole squadron in hospital. Three men died and thirty had to be sent to India to recover. The upshot was that there were no men available to disembark the

The Fokker Eindecker.

The Bristol Scout.

aircraft and it was not until the heat abated that this was possible. September had arrived and an advance party of the squadron arrived by river craft at Baghdad on the 8th to prepare the airfield at Samarrah for the arrival of the aircraft. The first RE8 arrived on the 14th and the second, piloted by Captain T.R. Philpott MC, arrived with Major General Hoskin commanding the 3rd Division. The first operational sorties were flown on 25 September when two aircraft flew on reconnaissance.

Neither returned. It appears that the two RE8s were flying some 100 miles north of Baghdad when they were engaged by an enemy machine and the one piloted by Lieutenant Begg was forced down, crashing on landing. Captain Philpott followed him down hoping to be of some assistance but his engine would not open up and he was forced to land at the enemy airfield of Tekrit.

The remaining aircraft arrived at intervals throughout October and it was not until the end of the month that the entire squadron was concentrated at Samarrah. The aircraft had arrived at intervals from Basra and again the heat was the cause. It had caused excessive warping of the main spars of the aircraft necessitating the complete stripping of all of the wing and the fuselage. Even the propellers did not escape when the laminations of the wood split. Be that as it may much had been accomplished during the summer months prior to the autumn offensive The RFC carried out bombing operations both against hostile Arab tribes and Turkish positions. The main work was accomplished during the first three weeks of September when 742 films were taken and 200 photographic plates exposed representing an area of 400 square miles.

Success had been achieved on the Euphrates when the entire Turkish force, under Ahmed Bey, surrendered. On the Dialah, at the beginning of October 1917 it was decided to clear the Turks from the left bank of the river and to occupy the Jebel Hamrin astride the river. This operation was intended to secure control of the canal system and was entrusted to Lieutenant General W.R. Marshal commanding the 3rd Indian Army Corps. Before the attack the RFC was employed, in the main, in photographing enemy positions on the Deli Abbas and on the Jebel Hamrin and reporting movements and dispositions of the enemy force.

Enemy aircraft were more than usually active on all fronts but contact was not made with the enemy until 18 October. Two days earlier a bombing raid was carried out on Kifri aerodrome by three Martinsydes of No.30 Squadron. The bombs dropped were of 20lb and 112lb and they fell on enemy aircraft. Machine gun fire was also effective. One of the Martinsyde pilots had to make a forced landing eighteen miles west of Kifri when his petrol tank was holed with gunfire. Lieutenant Welman in the second aircraft landed nearby to rescue the downed pilot

while the pilot of the third aircraft kept the enemy at bay with machine gun fire whilst the rescue was in progress.

Organization of the RFC in Mesopotamia in October 1917

HQ No.31 Wing	at Baghdad
No.30 Squadron (less one Flight)	at Baqubah (where they had been transferred after the operation of 19 October)
B Flight No.30 Squadron	at Felujah on the Euphrates
No.63 Squadron	at Samarrah
No.23 Kite Balloon Coy.	at Baghdad (under command Samarrah)
Aircraft park	at Basra
Advanced Aircraft Park	at Baghdad

For the remainder of December 1917 there was a lull in military operations and this permitted the RFC to carry the war to the enemy by bombing his airfields. That at Kifri was moved to Tuz Kurmatli, 85 miles north of Baqubah. On the Tigris river the enemy operated from Humr. In the middle of December the weather broke and heavy rain and high winds damaged and reduced the aerodromes to marshlands. No.51 Kite Balloon Section was also busy working with the artillery but their work was also hampered by high winds and low visibility. In spite of the weather on 28 December 1917 an attack on Humr was led by Captain F.L. Robinson. Twelve RE8s, a Martinsyde and a SPAD took part and a ton of bombs were dropped. Two enemy aircraft attempted to intercept the raid but retired on seeing the SPAD.

THE ITALIAN FRONT AND THE MEDITERRANEAN

Introduction

The Italians, who came into the Great War in May 1915, had been fighting a long but inconclusive campaign against Austro-Hungarian forces both on the ground and above the battlefields whilst the seaborne threat from the Central Powers in the Mediterranean and the Adriatic had to be contained. The Italians persisted

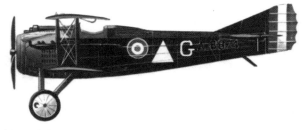

SPAD fighter.

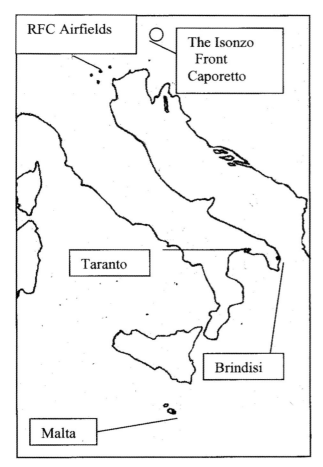

British air units in the Italian Peninsula.

Alps. An engine failure would probably result in death or serious injury. Landing strips were laid in valleys so that aircraft in trouble might make a safe landing. The weather at the beginning of 1916 was very harsh, aircraft were damaged and engine failures increased. As winter gave way to spring the front-line Italian air strength grew. There were seven Caproni bomber squadrons with two Voisin and eight Farman reconnaissance squadrons together with two artillery spotting, five fighter and one seaplane squadron. It was not until 1917 that Italian fighters were fitted with synchronizing gear. Until then the fighter pilots had to content themselves with pusher aircraft or mount the guns on the upper wing firing outside the arc of the propeller, as did British fighter pilots. Pitted against the Italians were the Austrian Aviatiks, Fokker E1 monoplane fighters and the Fokker D1 or 'Star Strutter', which symbolized the Austrian air effort over the Isonzo.

The battle that brought the RFC and RNAS into the conflict on the Italian front was the triumph of Austrian arms in what became the twelfth battle of Isonzo, the Battle of Caporetto. The map on the next page shows the extent of the ground lost by the Italians between 24 October and 12 November 1917. The Italian front was on the point of collapse and the Allies had to divert scarce resources to Italy. Four airfields housed the RFC squadrons sent to the Alpine front. (See map for the clutch of RFC airfields.)

Northern Italian Front
The clutch of airfields shown on the map of Italy comprised, from top right to bottom left, Arcade, San Luca, Sarcedo and the most southerly was San Pietro-in-Gu. British air units did not enter the Italian theatre until November 1917 just after the Battle of Caporetto. The airfields mentioned were those occupied by RFC units on the last day of the Great War. The RFC squadrons were Nos.28, 34, 66 and 139. They were a mixture to provide the best support possible at the time. It will be recalled that late 1917 was a critical time for the deployment of RFC squadrons on the Western Front, which coincided with the urgent need to protect the south-east of England against attacks by Gotha bombers. Indeed, three of these units had to be taken from France:

No.28 Squadron equipped with fighter/ground attack Camels – arrived in theatre on 28 November.

No.34 Squadron equipped with artillery observation/reconnaissance RE8s – arrived in theatre as above.

No.66 Squadron equipped with fighter/ground attack Camels – arrived in theatre on 4 December.

No.139 Squadron equipped with Bristol F2B fighters – arrived in theatre on 2 November.

in the view that the best place to break through on the land front was on the Isonzo River. The Italians compensated for their lack of field artillery pieces by building a bomber fleet at the expense of fighters. But this approach did not bode well for the future when the Austrians entered the field with well trained fighter units and air fighting was a threat to the Italian bombers. There were successive battles along the Isonzo front and on the second of these the Italians first encountered serious air opposition.

The Italian Air Force
The Italian air force or *Aeronautica del Regio Esercito* (Royal Army Air Force) was constituted by decree on 7 January 1915. Some of the Italian pilots operated from the comfort of home airfields with permanent buildings and messes on the outskirts of towns, very different from conditions on the Western Front. On the other hand they had to fly over some of the most inhospitable landscape of the

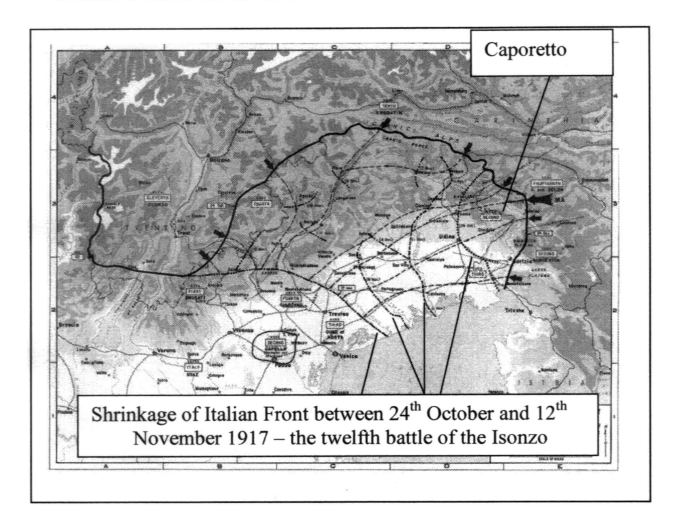

Shrinkage of Italian Front between 24th October and 12th November 1917 – the twelfth battle of the Isonzo

There had been some air contests on this front and both sides produced their air aces. The Italians had their Francesco Baracca and the Austrians had their Godwin Brumowski. It was not until the Second Battle of the Isonzo that the Italians first met real Austrian air opposition but it was on the ground that the war would be won and the Caporetto battle seemed to seal the fate of the Italians. The Allies dispatched the Italian brigade and the above mentioned squadrons of aircraft to stem the tide of defeat. The air tasks were shared by Italian, French and British squadrons. In June 1918 the Austrians mounted another offensive, this time on the River Piave. This, it was hoped, would bring about the final collapse of the Italian army but the latter drove the Austrians back across the river. The RAF squadrons carried out ground attack missions, artillery observation, reconnaissance and air fighting. No.66 Squadron based at San Pietro-in-Gu and No.28 Squadron at Sarcedo carried out the

ground attack missions. No.34 Squadron's RE8s based at San Luca were involved in artillery observation and reconnaissance and on the arrival of the Bristol F2Bs of No.139 Squadron based at Arcade provided escorts and an air fighting capability. The CO of No.139 Squadron was Major W.G. Barker VC, DSO, MC who had previously shot down fifty-three German aircraft.

Southern Italy

The RAF squadrons operating in the south of Italy were principally involved in containing the threat posed by enemy naval forces. Following the renumbering of ex-RNAS units on 1 April 1918, which started with 201 Squadron, it is not surprising that it was these squadrons that were deployed to Taranto (Pizzone) and Brindisi (Otranto.) (See Italian map.) The squadrons at Pizzone, Nos.226, 224, 225 and 271, were a mixture of Felixstowe, DH4s and Camels. At Otranto was No.263 Squadron engaged on anti-submarine duties using Short 184 and 320 seaplanes with Sopwith/Hamble Babies. The 'Otranto' barrage was designed to close the southern end of the Adriatic to enemy submarines and the Austrian ports in the Adriatic were bombed. Nos.267 and 268 Squadrons based at Kalafrana, Malta, equipped with Felixstowe flying boats and Short 184/320 floatplanes had the task of protecting convoys and harassing enemy submarines in all parts of the Mediterranean. Other functions of the units in Southern Italy were the bombing of lines of communication and places of military importance in Turkey and Albania and the defence of Allied territory from enemy aerial attack.

Greek and Palestinian Theatres and Egypt – See end of Chapter 5

Chapter 5

Military Air Operations of 1918 and the Formation of the RAF

The Western Front and imminence of a German offensive – the German Offensive of 21 March – Home Defence and the 6th Brigade – the Gotha threat – the formation of the RAF – the organization of the RAF – the expansion of the RAF June to December 1918 – night fighting overseas – the Italian, Mesopotamian, Egyptian, Palestinian and Aegean Fronts.

Introduction

The formation of the Royal Air Force on 1 April 1918 had its genesis in the divided responsibility for the air defence of the United Kingdom, prosecuting the air war on the Western Front and at sea and the procurement, design and development of aircraft. This chapter confines itself to the air war, which brought matters to a head and prompted the Prime Minister to task General Smuts to see if there was a case for forming an Air Ministry and thus creating a third armed service. This chapter should be read in conjunction with Chapter 10, which chronicles the political debate, meetings and decisions made. The activities of various air aces of the period are also described in Chapter 10 dealing with personnel matters

THE WESTERN FRONT – IMMINENCE OF A GERMAN OFFENSIVE – SPRING 1918

Source: National Archive Document: AIR1/675/21/13/1422, The employment of the RFC in defence (Appendix H to the above)

Introduction

Following the signing of the armistice between the Bolsheviks and the German Government on 3 March 1918 at Brest Litovsk the end of hostilities for the German Army on the Eastern Front had been achieved. One thing that the German military had feared was a war on two fronts. Bismarck could see that he had to isolate France militarily and the formation of the Dreikaiserbund, between Germany, Austria and Russia was an alliance that sought to achieve this end. But this was not to reckon with Kaiser Wilhelm II's impetuosity, which destroyed that alliance, and on the outbreak of the Great War, France was allied with Russia against the central powers of Germany, Austria, Bulgaria and the Ottomans. With the Bolshevik revolution in late 1917 came Lenin who wanted his country out of the war to concentrate on the building of a socialist state. The German Army on the Western Front had failed in their attempt to realize the objectives of the Schlieffen Plan by taking Paris in 1914. Following a thrust through Belgium the front line between the German Army and the Allies had solidified into a line of trenches. The German High Command then decided to play a waiting game and withdrew to a shorter more easily defensible line, the Hindenburg line,

then strengthen the defences to the point where the Allies would have to use overwhelming strength to penetrate that line at any point. Successive Allied attempts both under Field Marshal Haig and General Nivelle to mount offensives that would change the static trench war into a mobile one had failed, proving the Germans right. Now, with forces being withdrawn from the Eastern Front to face the Allies in the west, it was Germany's turn to mount an offensive, to divide the British from the French armies and make a thrust towards the English Channel.

THE EMPLOYMENT OF THE ROYAL FLYING CORPS IN DEFENCE

Source: Appendix I to AIR1/675/21/13/1422 January 1918

Introduction

The first and most important of the RFC's defence duties was to watch for the symptoms of attack. That may seem a startling glimpse of the obvious if it was not for the determination of the enemy to make sure that reconnaissance missions by Allied aircraft were impeded. Reconnaissance aircraft could be shot down and that meant countering enemy fighters. This in turn meant denying the enemy unimpeded access by both his reconnaissance aircraft and his fighters and that involved air fighting. If the reconnaissance is good and reports get to those who need them most, as quickly as possible, then the armies can prepare themselves. GHQ staff made the requests for air reconnaissance to the RFC. Every detail possible was required for what may seem unimportant to the observer could well be of vital importance to the intelligence staff. A single piece of information could be the piece that fits into the jigsaw to give a complete picture and it is seldom safe to draw conclusions from observations in one locality. It was necessary for the RFC on the Western Front in early 1918 to watch out for enemy concentrations for it was known that German forces that had been withdrawn from the Eastern Front facing Russia were being transferred to the Western Front.

Advice given to the RFC

The indications of impending attack to look for were regarded, in order of importance to be the construction of:

a. Railways and sidings
b. Roads

c. Dumps
d. Aerodromes
e. Camps
f. Gun positions

The intervals at which photographs were taken were important to show the rate of progress of works for obviously from the latter the imminence of an offensive could be determined. For long-range reconnaissance beyond the areas occupied by the Allied armies along the front, aircraft from No.9 Brigade would be used since these were at the beck and call of GHQ. If preparations for an offensive beyond the army areas were being reported then these could be interfered with by the following means:

a. Co-operation with the artillery, the activity of which had probably increased at this stage.
b. Extensive bombing attacks so as to inflict casualties on enemy troops and to destroy their rest.
c. An energetic offensive against the enemy's airborne forces to prevent interference with a and b.

At this stage of preparations for an enemy offensive the primary duty of RFC was to render British artillery fire effective. If artillery fire into the enemy's rear areas was to be effective the Germans would have to redouble their efforts to be able to reinforce their own front line. The enemy would be preparing its own artillery for the imminent offensive. In the case of a surprise attack this could take place at the same time as the infantry was advancing; indeed, a prolonged artillery barrage lasting several days was a sure sign of the imminence of an attack. Once the offensive was underway Allied artillery would have to concentrate on suppressing the fire of enemy batteries, hindering his preparations and destroying his infantry and tanks and their places of assembly. The RFC's role, in order of importance, was seen as:

a. Attacking the enemy's reinforcements a mile or two behind the assaulting line with low-flying aircraft.
b. Attacking the enemy's detraining and debussing points, transport on roads, artillery positions and reserves.
c. Sending low-flying machines, on account of their morale effect, to co-operate with the infantry in attacking the enemy's most advanced troops.

Field Marshal Haig on the imminence of a German offensive

In February 1918 it became evident from various sources that the Germans were preparing a major offensive on the Western Front. There was constant air reconnaissance over the enemy lines. The Germans were improving road

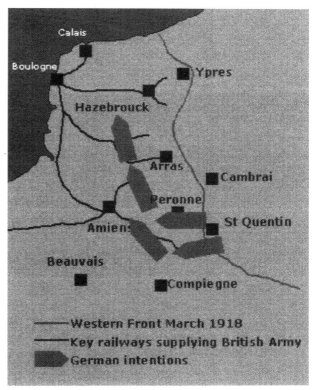

Operation *Michael* – German offensive on 21 March 1918.

and rail communications and creating ammunition and supply dumps along the whole front from Flanders to the Oise. These preparations were very marked opposite the fronts held by the British Third and Fifth Armies and it was considered probable that the enemy would mount an initial attack from the Sensée River southwards. This would be a defensive battle from the Allied point of view. Meanwhile, the 3rd Brigade RFC was involved in the Cambrai battle, which took place between 4 January to 4 February, and the targets selected for attack included hostile aerodromes, artillery batteries, infantry, machine gun posts and general targets. Four Scout squadrons took part and attacks were to be delivered at these ground targets at low level using both bombs and machine gun fire. Six aerodromes were to be attacked, each by four machines. The attacks upon the other targets were intended to help Allied tanks and infantry. On 19 February 1918 the HQ RFC laid down the principles for the concentration of fighter, fighter reconnaissance and bombing squadrons on a comparatively narrow front. If this concentration was to cover the fronts of both the Third and Fifth Armies it would almost certainly be necessary to reduce the RFC support for the remaining British fronts to one fighter reconnaissance and three fighter squadrons each. There were several possibilities for squadron redeployment and a meeting was called of RFC Brigadiers on 24 February. The deployments were agreed and detail promulgated on 2 March. (See Appendix J.) The main blow was expected along the St Quentin/Arras front and the battle opened on 21 March. From north to south No.2 Brigade RFC was to support the Second Army between Houthulst Forest and the north of Armentières. From there southwards to the north of Arras was No.1 Brigade RFC in support of the First Army. From Arras to the north of Gouzeaucourt No.3 Brigade supported the Third Army and finally No.5 Brigade supported the Fifth Army down to Barises. To a numerologist this probably seems a very neat and memorable way of allocating brigades to armies.

Instructions issued to the RFC with regard to reconnaissance and bombing

On 16 February 1918 GHQ issued instructions and gave guidance in the matters of reconnaissance and bombing. Reconnaissance machines should not, as a rule, carry bombs since this might divert the observer from his primary role. The furnishing of full and accurate reconnaissance reports outweighed the possible gains that might have been achieved by accurate bombing. With regard to bombing it was held that spasmodic bombing was wasteful. Bombing should be concentrated in time though not necessarily in area. If the aim was to lower the morale of enemy troops hutments and billets should be bombed continually, weather permitting, especially at night. In other words these attacks should not be interspersed with raids on other targets. Attempts to interrupt railway traffic should not be made until operations on the ground have commenced since the effects are then much greater. Ammunition dumps were unsatisfactory targets except when they were large and easily approached. Headquarters (except during a battle) supply and pioneer dumps were also regarded as unsuitable targets. Concentrations of railway rolling stock and repair shops made particularly suitable targets since it was known that the Germans lacked high-speed machine tools and rolling stock. The same applied to enemy aircraft repair depots and supply parks. Factories, large depot camps and training centres might be suitable targets but were, at the time, beyond the range of night bombing squadrons.

The German offensive 21 March 1918

During the period 21 March until 5 April the 5th and 3rd Brigades were chiefly engaged in air work together with the 9th Brigade, which came directly under the GHQ. The air work was predominantly in direct co-operation with the ground troops. Both the 5th and 3rd Brigades were employed on the low work but the latter also maintained normal activities. Low-level strafing was probably the most demanding of pilots since at any moment they could be struck from rounds fired from the ground. The previous chapter gave details of the deployment of the various squadrons on the Western Front and those of 9th Brigade were available to GHQ to be employed to meet the changing progress of the land battle. From the 23rd to the 31st the activities of 9th Brigade units illustrate the changing priorities. Initially they were employed on reconnaissance, bombing rail centres and fighting patrols to be followed by the air fighting squadrons attacking ground targets. On the 25th concentrations of enemy troops west of Bapaume were attacked then those south of the Somme, and on the 31st the fighting patrols returned to the upper air. Indeed there was always the need to protect corps squadrons but also the requirement to defeat the enemy fighters and experience showed that the effective support to ground forces depended on the maintenance of air superiority.

The opposing forces at the commencement of the German offensive consisted of 730 German aircraft of which 326 were single-seat fighters and 579 serviceable RFC aircraft, 261 of which were single-seat fighters. The fighters were mostly SE5s and Camels. Five squadrons were equipped with Bristol Fighters and one with the Sopwith Dolphin.

The RFC C-in-C believed that aggression would overcome the defence but the Germans were well prepared for a defensive battle. Indeed, the British casualties proved to be greater than those sustained by the Germans. On 18 March, for example, three days before the launching of the German offensive, five DH4s, escorted by twenty-four Camels and SE5as were pitted against thirty Albatros, Pfalzes and Fokker triplanes, led by the German ace, Richthofen, plus eight Staffeln flying the same variety of fighter. The British aircraft were badly outnumbered and the RFC was lucky to lose no more than five Camels, two SE5as and two DH4s for the price of one Albatros. The German advance also meant rapid evacuation of airfields and No.84 Squadron commanded by Sholto Douglas got out with only an hour or two to spare. Sholto Douglas, who would rise to one of the most senior officers by the Second World War insisted in operating his squadron in three flights of five aircraft and flying in formation. This put the leader in a position where he could decide the right moment to go into the attack and often resulted in the leaders scoring most air victories. McCudden also adopted this system but his subordinates complained that he was claiming all the victories whilst he was being protected by them. Squadron leaders who adopted these tactics defended them by saying that the junior and less experienced pilots were exposed to greater danger when the formation broke up.

It is difficult to assess the effectiveness of the work of the RAF during the German offensive, which in the event did not succeed. There is little doubt that the work of low-flying aircraft considerably harassed the advancing Germans by bombs and machine gun fire. The Germans aimed to take Amiens and it was believed that Abbeville would fall soon afterwards and this involved making a gap in the line near Roye. There seems little doubt that squadrons of the 5th Brigade helped to stabilize the line of the Fifth Army by closing the gap. Had the Germans been successful the flanks of the British and French armies could have been rolled up and there might have been a collapse of Allied morale. Preventing enemy reserves from reaching the battle area meant that it was vital to disrupt the transport system

HOME DEFENCE

The problem

From the beginning of 1915 until the end of the war Zeppelin airships bombed targets in England from bases in Belgium and northern Germany. In 1917 they were joined by Gotha bombers flying from Belgium that attacked targets in south-eastern England, principally London. This threw into sharp relief the need for effective air defence. Fighter defences were provided by squadrons of the RFC and the RNAS. The Army provided heavy ack-ack and the RNAS manned mobile anti-aircraft units. The local authorities provided air raid warnings and civil defence measures. To be really effective air

The Prime Minister David Lloyd George.

General Jan Smuts.

defence operations needed to be organized and directed by one body but this was not the case since both the War Office (RFC) and the Admiralty (RNAS) divided the responsibility. But both services had their priorities and could divert air units from air defence to other duties. For example, if the C-in-C British Armies in France, Field Marshal Sir Douglas Haig, was about to mount an offensive in Flanders he would be loath to release any RFC squadrons for air defence duties in the London area. The alternative would be to raise new squadrons but these would need to be manned by some experienced pilots who would have to come from existing squadrons. The Admiralty too had priorities as they faced the U-boat threat to convoys and coastal shipping not to mention a break-out of the German High Seas Fleet with all of its battleships and battle cruisers. During 1917 the Gotha bombers had largely replaced the threat posed by the Zeppelin airships. When there was a large loss of life in Folkestone, from Gotha bombing, questions were asked in the House of Commons. The Prime Minister, David Lloyd George, turned to a member of the War Cabinet, the South African General Jan Smuts, and tasked him to study the problem and come up with recommendations to the Cabinet. Smuts' recommendation became known as the Smuts Report. (See Chapter 12 for the legislation that brought the RAF into being.)

ORGANIZATION OF NO.6 BRIGADE – HOME DEFENCE

Introduction

The Air Defence of the British Isles was entrusted to No.6 Brigade RFC. In early 1918 the main threat was from the Gotha bombers against targets in the London area and the Home Counties. These raids were confined to the south-east given the range of the Gothas from their bases in Belgium. The Zeppelins, on the other hand, had a much longer range and could easily reach targets in the north of England. Even though the threat from the German airships in early 1918 was much reduced the northern RFC squadrons had to be ready to intercept them if they penetrated British air space. The list of formations and units with aircraft below is complete for No.6 Brigade at this time.

Unit	Aircraft	Station	Officer Commanding
HQ 6th Brigade		Horse Guards Parade	Brigadier General T.C.R. Higgins
49th Wing		Upminster	Lt Col M.G.Christie DSO, MC
39 Squadron	Bristol Fighters	North Weald Basset	Major W.T.F. Holland
44 Squadron	Camel	Hainault Farm	Major A.T. Harris AFC
78 Squadron	Camel	Sutton's Farm	Major C.J. Truran
141 Squadron	Bristol Fighter	Biggin Hill	Major B.E. Baker DSO, MC, AFC
189 NT Squadron	Camel and Avro	Sutton's Farm	Major H.S. Powell MC
AA Defence Flight	Camel	Gosport	Captain C.A.B.B. Willcock
50th Wing	Chelmsford		Lt Col P. Babington MC
37 Squadron	Camel	Stow Maries	Major F.W. Honnett
61 Squadron	Camel	Rochford	Major E.B. Mason
75 Squadron	Avro	Elmswell	Major C.S. Ross
198 NT Squadron	Camel & Avro	Rochford	Major C.O. Usbourne AFC
33 Wing	Harrietsham		Lt Col A.A.B. Thomson, MC
143 Squadron	Camel	Detling	Major F. Sowrey DSO, MC
112 Squadron	Camel	Throwley	Major Murlis Green DSO, MC
50 Squadron	Camel	Bekesbourne	Major W. Sowrey
188 Squadron	Camel & Avro	Throwley	Major C.B. Cooke
No.2 Wireless School	DH6	Penshurst	Captain W.P. Cort
47 Wing		Cambridge	Lt Col H. Wyllie
51 Squadron	Avro	Marham	Captain H.L.H. Owen
192 NT Squadron	FE2b	Newmarket	Major J. Sowrey AFC
191 NT Squadron	FE2b	Upwood	Major J.C. Griffiths
190 NT Squadron	Avro	Upwood	Major A. de B. Brandon DSO, MC
48 Wing		Gainsborough	Lt Col A.T. Watson
33 Squadron	Avro	Kirton-in-Lindsey	Captain G.M. Turnbull
186 NT Squadron	Avro	Retford	Major W.C. Mackey
187 NT Squadron	Avro	Retford	Major T.R. Irons
199 NT Squadron	FE2b	Harpswell	Major J.C.C. Orton
200 NT Squadron	FE2b	Harpswell	Major W.E. Collinson
46 Wing		York	Lt Col A.C.E. Marsh
77 Squadron	Avro	Penstone	Major A. Somervail MC
36 Squadron	Bristol Fighters	Usworth	Major W.J. Tempest DSO, MC & Sopwith Scouts
76 Squadron	Avro	Ripon	Major A.C. Wilson

The letters NT designate a night training squadron and this is because No.6 Brigade had the dual role of defending the British Isles against air attack but also to train night pilots both for home defence squadrons and night bombing units overseas. (See Chapter 8 on training.) Units were actually formed in the UK before being sent abroad. For example, Nos.100, 101 and 102 Squadrons were formed by 6th Brigade and sent overseas in February, July and August 1917. In the first half of 1918 Nos.83, 58, 149 and 148 Light Night Bombing Squadrons proceeded to join the BEF. Nos.151 and 152 Night Fighting Squadrons proceeded overseas in June and October and No.153 Squadron was ready for deployment with the BEF on the signing of the Armistice.

The air defence of London became a matter for serious concern when the first daylight raids began in 1917 carried out by Gotha bombers. Previously the Home Defence Wing was equipped with BE12 and 12a aircraft, which precluded any effective defence against air attack. To remedy this deficiency a few Bristol monoplanes were allotted to the Wing but these were soon withdrawn. To make matters worse 25 per cent of the most experienced pilots were posted for service overseas, which coincided with the poor output of aeroplanes. Until 25 May 1917 German raids were made by one or two aeroplanes on coastal towns such as Margate and Dover. The daylight raids on London on 25 May had an inevitable effect of public opinion and the War Office had to act fast to allay the public's fear Nos.46 and 56 Squadrons were brought back from the Western Front and three additional squadrons were formed, equipped with Camels and Scouts. These were then stationed at Hainault Farm, Rochford and Throwley. Then the two squadrons that had come from France had been returned to the BEF by the end of August in spite of a raid on Southend on 12 August. The enemy had made a bad landfall at Orfordness and had to face a strong wind from the south-west, which impeded the progress of the enemy formation towards London giving the defending fighters patrolling over London a chance to intercept. The bombs had to be dropped over Southend before they made off.

The Gotha bomber.

Considerable damage was caused on what was regarded as a secondary target by all enemy machines that could not, for a variety of reasons reach the capital.

The problem with the fighter defence of England during the Great War, was that, unlike the situation in the Battle of Britain in 1940 when there was radar and an integrated fighter defence system, there was little in the way of advanced warning of the enemy's approach. Both for the scrambling of fighter aircraft and the need for the civilian population to take cover from air raids, advanced warning was vital. In 1940 fighter controllers knew exactly when the enemy was coming, the direction and altitude of the enemy approach and, with the help of the Royal Observer Corps, a pretty good idea of the numbers of enemy aircraft involved. Crucially this meant that the aircraft of the fighter squadrons could sit on the ground, fully armed and with full petrol tanks until called into the air. That gave the defenders an enormous advantage. Without radar the Home Defence Wing in 1917 could put aircraft into the air in rotation in what are called 'standing patrols'. Being aloft they could spot the enemy coming but running standing patrols along the entire length of the Channel and North Sea coastlines would be prohibitively expensive in fuel and wear and tear of aircraft, engines and aircrew. And if the enemy was sighted at the moment when the aircraft on standing patrol were running out of fuel they could not join in combat. Accordingly the fighter squadrons of the Home Defence Wing would have a headquarters airfield with one of the three flights with the remaining two flights in fields some distance from the headquarters. At the dispersal fields a hut for aircrew and ground crew, with fuel and basic spares plus a telephone to squadron headquarters would mean that the fighters of the various squadrons were spread thinly but in a way that it was hoped left no gaps for the enemy to break through.

Chapter 4 described the growth in the number of air defence squadrons covering the United Kingdom and how these came to be organized into wings then groups and finally into the 6th Brigade. The BEF in France and formations in other theatres were to benefit greatly from the training effort of the 6th Brigade. In addition to the formation of service squadrons for the defence of the British Isles, the Brigade's night training squadrons produced reinforcements of night fighting pilots and light night bombing pilots and observers. Units formed by the Brigade during this period were Nos.100, 101 and 102 Squadrons before being sent overseas in February, July and August respectively. No.100 Squadron was equipped with BE2cs and went to St André aux Bois as did the aircraft of Nos101 and No.102 Squadrons. Night light bombing squadrons that went abroad were Nos.83, 58, 149 and 148 Squadrons whilst Nos.151 and 152 Night Fighting squadrons were sent abroad in June and October respectively equipped with Camels.

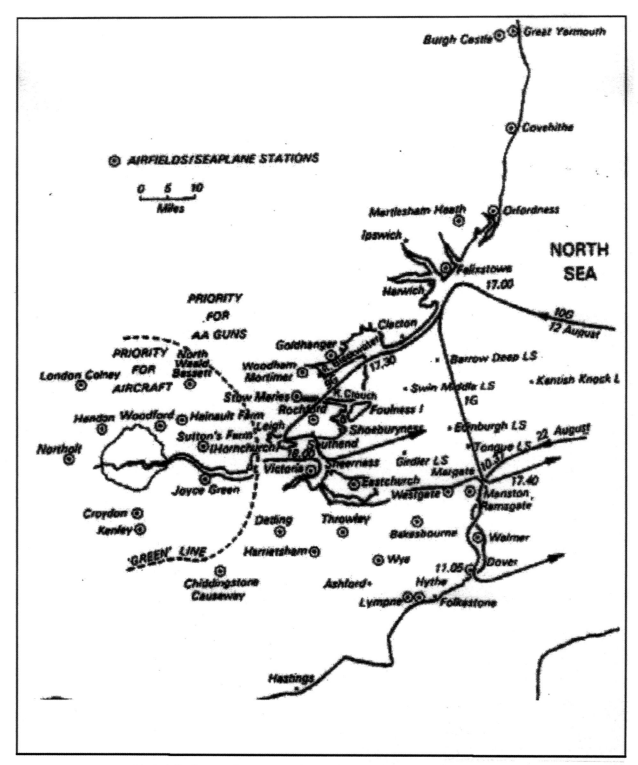

Typical Gotha attack patterns when not hitting primary target (London).

POLICY MATTERS - 1918 – FORMATION OF THE ROYAL AIR FORCE
Source: AIR1/674/21/6/94

The political debate over air policy
There were difficulties in achieving agreement between the two service departments about the future of the air services. It was recognized at the outset that there would need to be government oversight of military and naval aviation. The two services could not be allowed to go entirely separate ways in employing air power. The design of aircraft, the development of tactics, the maintenance of aircraft and the training of the men to fly them could be most economically achieved by the two services coming together. The last thing that was needed was competition for men, material and allocation of scarce resources yet the naval and military wings of the Flying Corps would, in 1914, largely go their separate ways. The Joint Air Committee formed before war began in 1914, ceased to exist as hostilities commenced. The prosecution of the war took priority; indeed, both the War Office and the Admiralty saw little point in talking if their joint deliberations could not result in executive action.

Mr Balfour, First Lord of the Admiralty.

Wartime arrangements
As the war progressed the question of the coming together of the two services again raised its head and early in 1916 the Prime Minister decided to form a Joint War Air Committee under the chairmanship of Lord Derby for there was already the need to decide priorities when it came to allocating scarce resources and determining which aircraft designs should be adopted and contracts awarded to the appropriate aircraft manufacturers etc. But after only a few months the Committee broke down over its membership. Any decisions arrived at by members of the Committee would be of little value if they were not supported by the War Office or the Admiralty. Lord Derby's reason for resigning sums up the problem. The Committee had no executive power or authority. Even a unanimous agreement of the various Committee members could not guarantee approval by the two services. Sir David Henderson was a member of the Army Council and, with the powers of plenipotentiary, could commit the Army to a course of action but the naval member of the Committee was not also a member of the Board of the Admiralty so could only refer questions back to that body.

This then begged the question as to what could, if anything replace the Joint War Air Committee. Lord Curzon, in an advisory paper, had even then considered the formation of an Air Ministry and a separate air service. This might prove very difficult and in the meantime an Air Board with greatly increased functions was considered. One function of such a Board was to consider matters of air policy that could then be put to the two services. In the case of disagreement over air policy reference could be made to the War Committee. The Army felt that the heads of the aeronautical services of both the Army and the Navy who would be on the Board could not bind either service on any matter that did not fall within the competence of one or the other of the two services. This would lead the Army Council to take the view that such a Board should keep an open mind on the creation, as they put it, of an Imperial Air Service. But to amalgamate the two air services in wartime would be administratively difficult. On the other hand there could be an amalgamation of staffs dealing with aircraft and equipment design, contracts and perhaps inspection. This should not extend to the provision of personnel. There was some agreement about joint air operations, which could well demand the appointment of one officer in overall command and the appointment of either an Army or a naval officer could well be determined by the nature of each operation.

On 8 May 1916, Mr Balfour expressed his views in a memo to the War Committee. They seemed to accord with the views of their Lordships at the Admiralty. He felt that the two service departments should have full control over the instruments they used, subject of course to Treasury and Cabinet control. The question still remained about the handling of joint air operations and it was conceivable that a third government department would be required to assume control of such operations if only to allocate resources. Would a third department acquire its own resources? Consideration of this matter could surely only lead to the formation of an Air Ministry but Mr Balfour was not, however, to be deflected by such questions and felt that a machinery of adjustment would suffice. A Joint Air Board could undertake this task on the rare occasions when it might be necessary. He believed that a separate government department, formed simply as a machinery of adjustment, was wasteful and that past experience had shown that there had always been insufficiencies of resources in war. Both service departments had, in the past, made allowances without recourse to a third party.

Formation of a Joint Air Board
The whole matter was debated at a meeting of the War Committee on Thursday 11 May and the formation of a Joint Air Board was recommended. It was proposed that the Board should be composed of a President who would also be a member of the Cabinet. One naval representative should either be a member of the Board of the Admiralty or be present at its meetings when matters connected with the work of the Air Board were under discussion. There should also be an additional naval representative who would not always be the same individual. The Army representative should be a member of the Army Council with an additional member who need not always be the same individual. An independent member with administrative experienced and a second Parliamentary member would complete the composition of the Board. The second Parliamentary member would come from the House other than that from which the President came.

Given this composition the way in which its terms of reference were discussed meant that it would be an advisory board where decisions arrived at would not be by voting:

1. The Board would be free to discuss matters of general policy in relation to the air and in particular combined operations of the naval and military air services, and to make recommendations to the Admiralty and War Office.
2. The Board would be free to discuss and make recommendations upon types of machines required for both naval and military air services.
3. If either the Admiralty or War Office declined to act upon recommendations of the Board the President would be free to refer the question to the War Committee.
4. The Board would be charged with the task of preventing competition between the two departments.

5. The Board would organize a complete system for the interchange of ideas upon air problems between the two services and such related bodies as the (Naval) Board of investigation and research, the Inventions Branch of the Ministry of Munitions, the Advisory Committee on Aeronautics, the National Physical Laboratory, etc.

The proposed Air Board had powers that were much wider than the defunct Joint War Air Committee but it still lacked executive power. Be that as it may the Prime Minister, Mr Asquith, initialled the above minutes on 15 May and appointed Lord Curzon at its first President.

The meetings of the Joint Air Board
The first meeting of the Joint Air Board took place on 22 May 1916 and the minutes show that Lord Curzon took a very wide view of the functions of the Board. He explained that, unlike the Joint War Air Committee, no question connected with the air would fall outside the purview of the new Board. Points of detail and the formulation of policy could be settled. The President was also in a position to advise the government on the necessity to form a larger body if that became necessary, including the formation of a separate air service. In the event the minutes of the succeeding meetings of the Board illustrate the difficulties confronting it since the views expressed by the President were not exactly shared by the other government departments concerned. At the seventh meeting of the Board on 5 June 1916, Mr Winston Churchill stated that the Air Service, in his opinion, had suffered of late since there was no one in the Cabinet specially concerned to look

Lord Curzon.

after its interests until the appointment of Lord Curzon. He provided the example of Lord Kitchener who, on becoming the Secretary of State for War, had handed responsibility for air defence of the British Isles to the Admiralty leaving the rest of the Air Service in the charge of General Henderson. Mr Churchill would have preferred the creation of an Air Ministry but, he added, had he remained at the Admiralty he would have retained a personal control of the RNAS. What had been achieved by the RNAS had been against the views of the Naval Lords who had remonstrated at the amount of expenditure on air matters. Both the RFC and the RNAS had benefitted from the Presidency of Lord Curzon.

Mr Churchill's recommendations illustrate the problems engendered by having two flying services. He went on to suggest that the Joint Air Board should be charged with all constructive and experimental and training work in the widest interpretation of these terms. Training might present a problem where the employment of airships and aeroplanes on warships, including aircraft carriers, was concerned since airmen and aircraft technicians would require some nautical knowledge. The answer was to hand over the necessary training establishments to the direction of the Air Board, which could then prepare squadrons for the Fleet or Army as required. This might, he suggested, be achieved without recourse to legislation. On the matter of home defence, a matter that would two years later result in the formation of the RAF, the plan of defence should be the business of the Air Board. He conceded that whilst the main plan of air defence would be a matter for the Board, the tactical arrangements would be left to Lord French.

At the twenty-second meeting on 28 August 1916 the subject for discussion was the submission by the Admiralty to the Treasury of its programme of expenditure amounting to £2,875,000. There had not been any prior communication with the Air Board, the latter being required to co-ordinate the supply of material and prevent competition between the two departments and ensure a fair distribution of aircraft. Indeed, this would prove to be one of the determining factors considered by General Smuts in his report, which resulted in the formation of the Air Ministry. One of the Board's functions was to exercise financial control of the two service departments and at least have proposed expenditures passed by them if not to veto certain votes. The Admiralty was surprised when it learned that the proposed expenditure should have been notified to the Board. Admiral Vaughan Lee, the naval representative on the Board was unable to reply to certain questions and the matter had to be dropped for the time being.

The activities of the Board were reported in the press when a leading article in *The Times* dated 24 October 1916, spoke of friction, overlapping and competition.

F.C.T. Tudor.

Under the headline 'Air Board Failures' *The Times* was directing its criticism at the Admiralty and not, as Lord Curzon thought, the President. Put on the defensive the Admiral Tudor wanted it placed on record that, if the *The Times* was right, the other members of the Board should say so. The President declined to have the charges investigated since he was in no way responsible for the article.

Other matters that came before the Board indicated the need for arbitration and in some cases decision. The following are examples that show that it was performing a valuable function. Colonel Bares of French Aviation had insisted that bombing operations against German towns was most important and that the Allies should concentrate on two types of engine, the Clerget and the Hispano Suiza. But when the Colonel appeared before the Board he said that the air fighting capability was more important. The naval members of the Board, on 26 October, were asked to consider whether or not Renault should be persuaded to make the Hispano Suiza engine under licence. Secondly, they were to consider that the Navy keep a force of at least 200 bombers in France and thirdly, that orders for 1,000 Hispanos and Clergets for the RNS should be placed in France in addition to those required by the RFC.

Sir David Henderson disagreed with Colonel Barres for he thought that the proportion of fighters to bombers was too low and he disagreed with the Admiralty that the RNAS should maintain 200 bombers in France. Finally, he believed that all available material should be allotted afresh in the coming winter irrespective of the source of previous orders made under the present competitive method. Later the Board learned, through General Brancker, that in a meeting with Bares and Trenchard, Bares had modified his previous stance of concentrating on the production of just two engines and he was then in favour of adopting also the 150hp Le Rhône or 150hp Monosoupape engines. For the present the Colonel wished to see the British Commission in Paris order 4,000 Hispanos but not Clergets. Brancker agreed with Sir David Henderson that Bares was wrong about the proportion of bombers to fighters. Command of the air on the Western Front in 1918 was vital.

These discussions led Lord Curzon to the conclusion that the Board must form an opinion on three questions:

1. Was it sensible to undertake long-range bombing operations?
2. If so, which force should carry out these bombing missions?
3. Whether or not a large order for Hispano engines should be placed and, if so, by whom the arrangement should be made.

The naval and military members of the Board were asked to express their opinions on these questions. Disagreement between the Army and the naval members would mean that it was one of those questions that would have to go before the War Committee. The Navy thought that long-range bombing missions were of great importance whereas the Army felt that the maintenance of air strength on the Western Front was vital. So the President agreed to put the question to the War Committee. The Army had prioritized their operational commitments, namely fighting for air superiority over the Army fronts, followed by reconnaissance, bombing in direct support of ground operations and, lastly, long-range bombing missions. The highest authority would have to determine whether or not resources should be tied up in long-range bombing missions or providing squadrons to fight over the Western Front. In his submission to the War Committee Lord Curzon discussed the question of who should undertake long-range bombing missions, the RNAS or the RFC. On the matter of the acquisition of the Hispano Suiza engine it was decided to send Commander Briggs to Paris to determine which firms and in what quantities such firms would produce the engine. In all, eight firms would produce a total of 8,000 engines provided Britain furnished these firms with the materials, and the French Government would retain a lien on the engines on order. General Trenchard reminded the Board that production of engine spares was just as important if half the engines were not to be wasted. Cannibalizing engines for spares was not a solution since it did not produce the proportion of spares required.

At the twenty-ninth meeting of the Air Board on 22 November 1916 the President stated his opinion that the passing of every month brought the country to the point of exhaustion. This is what is meant by a war of attrition and Lord Curzon's concern was that, unlike ships that might have a peacetime use (given Britain's imperial status), the country could be left with a large number of aeroplanes. He would prove to be right. At the end of hostilities in 1918 brand-new aircraft were going from the factory to the scrapyard and those which survived were sold on to a variety of customers, both at home and overseas, by the Aircraft Disposal Company. Moreover, since the peacetime RAF was having to survive on a very low budget World War types such as the DH9A and the Bristol Fighter continued in operational use until the early 1930s. This also had the effect of stunting the development of new designs, which affected struggling aircraft manufacturing companies in the 1920s. Be that as it may, Admiral Tudor insisted that the order for aircraft for the RNAS go ahead. So Lord Curzon proposed putting the matter before the War Committee to include the views of both the Admiralty and the War Office. To this was added the provision of engines discussed in the preceding paragraph.

This, of course, was an important function of the Joint Air Board, to allocate scarce resources between two competing services and to arbitrate where necessary or present areas of unresolved dispute to the War Committee. The outcome was not exactly what was intended for it appeared that the Admiralty and not the War Office was the less amenable to arbitration. Lord Curzon included in his report to the War Committee the contention by a 'distinguished naval airman' that the country was not getting its money's worth out of the RNAS. The Army also wanted more aircraft and Sir Douglas Haig, speaking for the army on the Western Front, was asking for twenty more fighting squadrons to be ready by 1 April 1917. In this instance Lord Curzon sent a note direct to the War Cabinet on 19 December 1916, stating that these squadrons could not be provided from the present strength. There was a commitment to overseas theatres as well as the all-important task of providing squadrons for home defence. He told the War Cabinet about the material being set aside for the production of aircraft both for the RNAS and the RFC and that a decision was required on the best use of this material. For good measure he added that there were a number of other subordinate questions that can only be decided upon when the precise relations of the different departments were determined. This was a hint for the widening of the powers of the Air Board.

Formation of a Second Air Board

At a meeting held on 22 December 1916 the War Cabinet moved to widen the powers of the Air Board. At the

Lord Cowdray.

thirty-second meeting of the Air Board on 3 January 1917 Lord Cowdrey, who had succeeded Lord Curzon as President, read out a statement that had been prepared from the War Cabinet's decisions. The Board then discussed the statement paragraph by paragraph so that a charter of the Board's new composition and functions could be drafted. The Air Board thus became known as the 'Second Air Board'. Section 7 of the Act bringing the Second Air Board into being sums up the role of this body.

Buckingham Palace, 8 February 1917

For the purpose of organizing and maintaining the supply of aircraft in the national interest in connection with the present war, it shall be lawful for His Majesty to establish an Air Board, consisting of a President appointed by His Majesty, who shall hold office during His Majesty's pleasure, and of other members who shall be appointed in such manner and subject to such provisions as His Majesty may by Order in Council direct. The President of the Board shall act with the advice of the other members of the Board. For the purpose of this Act the President of the Air Board shall be deemed to be a Minister appointed under this Act. The Air Board shall, in relation to aircraft have such powers and duties of any Government Department or Authority, whether conferred by Statute or otherwise,

as His Majesty may by Order in Council transfer to the Board, or authorize the Board to exercise or perform concurrently with or in consultation with the Government Department or authority concerned.

The new Board would have as its members, in addition to representatives of the Admiralty and Army Council, the Controller of Aeronautical Supplies and the Controller of the Petrol Engine Department of the Ministry of Munitions and other members who from time to time would be appointed to the Board. It would now be up to the Board to determine priorities in aircraft and engine production and their allocation to the two armed services. The Board would have to bear in mind what existing types of aircraft should be produced given their performance and cost and what new types should be brought into service given the need to keep up with German aircraft development. In this respect the service representatives would offer advice. This was, of course, a step closer to the formation of an Air Ministry since with the best will in the world, the service representatives on the reconstituted Air Board would be bound to defend their corners. It became increasingly clear that the only way of removing, once and for all, the competition for aeroplanes and their aircrews was to put all that flew into a new air service. As 1917 progressed the demands for aeroplanes, and with them the creation of fresh squadrons, increased for three reasons. One was to give as much air support as possible to the armies fighting on the Western Front, the second was to combat the growing menace of the U-boat and the third was to provide adequate air defence of the United Kingdom. This would lead the Prime Minister, David Lloyd George, to task one of the members of the War Cabinet, General Jan Smuts, to examine:

1. The defence arrangements for the Home Defence against air attacks.
2. The air organization generally and the direction of aerial operations.

Sir Douglas Haig would keep up the pressure for more aeroplanes for France whilst Lord French worried about the adequacy of the air defences of the British Isles. In addition to the Navy's task of combating submarines there was also the question of the involvement of the RNAS in long-range bombing operations.

Air Organization memorandum by Lord Milner on 26 October 1917

Misgivings about trying to create an independent air force in the middle of the war were expressed by Lord Milner in a memorandum dated 26 October. He began by saying that he could not help feeling that the position as regarded future air policy was very far from

Lord Milner.

A family takes cover during an air raid in the Great War.

satisfactory but also recognized that matters of air policy and the direction of the air war required decisions to be taken that could not wait for the end of the war. He referred to the correspondence between the CIGS and Haig on 24 August, the day that the Cabinet decided in principle to adopt the recommendation of the committee formed by the Prime Minister and General Smuts, to establish an Air Ministry. Public opinion demanded that a committee should be formed to work out the details to give effect to the policy and on 8 October Smuts advised that a communication should be issued to the press that the Cabinet was moving towards the creation of an Air Ministry and that a Bill embodying the Government's proposals would be introduced in the forthcoming session of Parliament. On 15 October General Smuts reported that his committee had drawn up a draft Order in Council prescribing the organization of an Air Council whose functions in the new Air Ministry would correspond with those performed by the Board of the Admiralty and the Army Council respectively. Lord Milner reflected on the major task facing the Smuts Committee in working out the details and the fact that the General had conceded that it might not be possible to form an Air Ministry during the course of the war, in which case it would be necessary to arrive at an interim arrangement for the co-ordination of air policy. The Cabinet responded by forming a committee, under the General's chairmanship, to advise the War Cabinet on all questions of air policy.

Lord Milner was still worried, believing that there should be an air staff constantly reviewing the whole field of air policy, to co-ordinate the requirements of the Army and the Navy and devising the best methods of offence and defence and giving consideration to the conduct of impendent bombing operations. He reflected that the Cabinet was making decisions in reaction to German air raids but he was not clear in his own mind whether these decisions were consistent with each other or whether or not they were being carried out. With regard to the procurement of aircraft he felt that, without an air staff the Cabinet could not know whether or not the best use was being made of the existing aircraft and what types should be built in future. For these reasons he believed that the creation of an air staff could not wait until an Air Ministry was formed and that this was by then an urgent necessity. Smuts' draft Order in Council was supposed to deal with the creation of an Air Council but Lord Milner wondered if this had to wait for the creation of an Air Ministry. He wondered if the creation of an interim committee under General Smuts' chairmanship (the Air Organization Committee) was intended simply to give advice or make executive decisions. In any case, he felt this arrangement was quite inadequate with meetings once or twice a week. He understood that setting up an Air Ministry took time but returned to his main point that the war in the air would not wait! He had every confidence in General Smuts' ability to give direction in these matters but said that he was a very busy man who needed a Department for the Air no matter how embryonic. He finished by reminding his readers that there was an Air Board but that the body dealt with construction, which itself depended on policy. We cannot continue, he concluded, with the ill-defined organization that the government appeared to possess.

FORMATION OF THE SMUTS COMMITTEE
Source: National Archive Document AIR 1/674/21/6/94

The Minister of Munitions had expressed his belief that the availability of new machines should not present a problem in 1918 but could not, of course, promise that the full programme could be realized given the requirement to replace wastage due to air action. This forecast included aircraft used for long-distance bombing raids. The Second Air Board had worked hard to ensure production targets that would meet the needs of both armed services. Lord Cowdray, the President of the Air Board had communicated his opinion to General Smuts on the matter of dealing with any surpluses of aircraft. He also felt that the Air Board should be converted into a permanent ministry with a war staff capable of dealing with the allocation of surpluses.

The Prime Minister could see the increased pressure for a Ministry to decide air matters so why not create an Air Ministry? He handed the matter over to General Jan Smuts, a member of the War Cabinet. Given the aerial threat to the British Isles from the Gotha bombing offensive General Smuts had to investigate the arrangements for home defence as well as the air organization generally for the direction of air operations. General Smuts had been given full rein to investigate the desirability of forming an Air Ministry. The first report of the Smuts Committee dealt with the defences of the London area against air raids. As a result the War Cabinet sanctioned the Army Council to place General Ashmore at the disposal of Lord French to work out schemes of defence for the capital. The second report dealt with the air organization in general terms. With regard to the Air Defence of London there was bound to be conflict with the Admiralty who provided squadrons for home defence as well as meeting the needs of anti-submarine warfare, convoy protection and containing the threat imposed by the presence of the German battle fleet in home waters. The conflict with the Army would arise because squadrons might have to be diverted from the Western Front to 'beef up' the home defence at a time when an all-out effort was being made in the land campaign. Thus the second report of the Smuts Committee assumed greater importance. Just as the Joint Air Board had wrestled with the competing claims of the two services for aircraft, there was by late 1917 a competition for squadrons. Creating new squadrons for home defence was not as simple as it sounds. Leadership would have to come from commanders with combat experience and that would mean robbing the operational RNAS and RFC squadrons of some of their best men. Also, one could not simply staff any new home defence units with inexperienced young pilots.

Accordingly, General Smuts spelt out the questions he considered must be answered for an early settlement of the air organization, of vital importance to the successful prosecution of the war. The three most important questions were:

1. A real Air Ministry responsible for all the air organization and operations should be instituted.

2. A unified air service should comprise both the RNAS and RFC and if this were approved:
3. The determination of the relations between the new service and the Royal Navy and the Army.

Point 3 was particularly important if the existing services were to be satisfied with these arrangements. Since the formation of the Flying Corps in 1912 and its division into naval and military wings air operations had been ancillary to naval and military operations. Smuts cited the fate of the Air Committee and the Joint War Air Committee, which foundered on the desire of both services to keep absolute control of the supply and design of aeroplanes and their squadrons but he believed that that had resulted in wasteful duplication. With regard to the advisability of creating an Air Ministry in the middle of a war Smuts referred to the rapid developments that had taken place in aircraft design and armament and the growth in aerial warfare. With events moving so rapidly there was no time to lose. The new air service needed to be led by aviators who specialized in the new form of warfare. There would, of course need to be a transfer to the Air Ministry a sufficient number of officers at the various command and staff level from the Army and the Royal Navy and he hoped that these would be forthcoming and that future recruitment both on temporary as well as permanent commissions would be realized. There could also be secondment of officers for those who wished to pursue their careers in the service in which they first joined. The same would apply to the transfer of warrant officers and NCOs.

The second Smuts Report – limitations of the Joint Air Board

Smuts felt that the Joint Air Board had done admirable work especially in the provision of aircraft engines and aircraft and controlling supplies to the two services. Be that as it may the Board even as reconstituted was little more than a conference where representatives of the two services and those from the Ministry of Munitions could consult with one another. The Board had no technical experts of its own and so had to rely on the service representatives to advise. It could not exercise control of training upon which the provision of pilots for any newly formed squadrons depended, nor could it control the production of lighter-than-air craft, which was very jealously guarded by the Admiralty. It had authority to discuss air policy but no power to force the services to follow any policy decision. An independent air service can pursue operations of war unconnected with the land battle or the war at sea. Here one is speaking of strategic bombing as opposed to tactical bombing. The strategic use of air power relates to operations on an enemy's homeland, his factories, ports and railways etc. Tactical air operations are those directed at targets on the battlefield or enemy vessels at sea. If there was not to be an independent air force would it be the RFC or the RNAS or a combination of both. Who would prioritize enemy targets for the two services? Would this inevitably intensify competition for resources? One could, in late 1917, envisage a situation where attacks on strategic enemy targets became the principal operations of war relegating military and naval operations to that of secondary importance. One solution that offered itself was to raise the Air Board to ministerial status. The Board had done its job in raising aircraft and engine production far in excess of expected requirements. This would mean that the production capacity of the aircraft and engine manufacturers could be used to provide for an independent bombing force. Who would be responsible for management of any surplus? Why should the two services worry about them? An air staff working within an Air Ministry would be better equipped to deal with all of these matters since air staff officers would be pilots or observers and see things from an 'air' point of view. The Air Board had already reached the stage where the settlement of future air policy was vital but, as described, the Board was little more than a conference. The need for an Air Ministry and an Air Staff had become urgent. It should be borne in mind that the land war had become almost totally static from the first winter of the war. Millions of men had sacrificed their lives only to gain hundreds of yards, a mile or two at most, in the war of the trenches.

Strategic bombing provided a way out of the impasse

A bombing force that was to take the war to the enemy's homeland had to be equipped with the right aircraft, with aircrews trained in long-distance navigation, both by day and by night, and the dropping of bombs on the target, often not in the best weather and with the threat from defending fighters. An Air Staff could consider these matters quietly without being diverted from the progress of the war at sea and on land. In Palestine the Turks depended very much on the railway for resupply and railway communications could be cut by an independent force. Success in the future would come not with men but with arms and machines and an industrial capacity to match. This had been found with the submarine, which had changed the nature of naval warfare. But any suggestion that an air force could, by using strategic bombing, push an enemy to sue for peace was one that the Admiralty and the War Office simply was not going to accept. Men on the ground win wars when they occupy an enemy's territory, said the Army Council, and navies can mount blockades and have the responsibility to escort convoys with imports that are the lifeblood of the country. Of course they had a point but the Prime Minister wanted an answer from Smuts not further argument.

Smuts pointed out that aircraft production had increased greatly since it had become the responsibility of the Air Board. Moreover, air operations unconnected directly with the war on the sea and the land called for new skills and an air doctrine; in other words, a new air organization. Aircraft were being developed at a prodigious rate and plans had already been laid to build bombers capable of reaching Berlin from airfields in the east of England. Smuts believed that the new air service should absorb all the operational and training units of both the RFC and RNAS. If the Army and the Navy were to retain their own special air services in addition to the new air service, which forces would be controlled by the Air Ministry? This would be a recipe for confusion and make the situation only worse. The maintenance of three air services was, he believed, out of the question. The intimacy between both services and their air arms was acknowledged but if a separate air service was not required for tasks in direct support of the naval forces then neither was it for those in support of the ground war. This left strategic bombing, which alone hardly made a case for an Air Ministry. One could see the way Smuts was thinking. A viable air force would be one that embraced all British aircraft. What had to be safeguarded was the efficiency and security of existing air support for the two services once an Air Ministry was formed. This would involve ensuring that training of aircrews and technicians was fitted to the operational requirements of the Army and the Navy. Air units could be seconded to army and naval formations and it would have to be made absolutely clear who would determine the use of such aircraft, i.e. who would have operational control. Of course local air commanders would have the right to advise and arrangements would have to be made with regard to discipline and subjectivity to the Army and Navy Acts. The report does not say that but it is one of the many questions that would need answers when the Draft Air Force Act was published.

The Air Organization Committee

On 24 August 1917 the Cabinet met and decided to accept the principle that an Air Ministry be established. What was needed was a committee to work out how to give effect to their decision and an Air Organization Committee was formed under General Smuts' chairmanship and consisted of representatives of the Treasury, the Air Board, the Admiralty and the War Office. On 18 September the Committee met and the chairman circulated the Cabinet's memorandum on air preparations and offensives. The amalgamation of the RNAS and the RFC was to be take place in wartime and it had not only to cover the operational aspects but deal with discipline, pay, recruitment, storage of equipment, airfield procurement and a host of other things. A subcommittee had been formed under the chairmanship of Sir David Henderson to undertake the precise organizational work. General Smuts reminded the Committee that, as the war was in progress, it was necessary to make preparations for operations in the spring and summer of 1918. This would include the proposed bombing offensive against the German homeland for which the appropriate aircraft would be needed. The supply of aircraft was under the direction of Sir William Weir. General Trenchard, who commanded the RFC in France, was of the opinion that the Germans had never been stronger in the air. Air superiority must not be lost for if it was, he added, it would be most difficult to recover it. He pressed for an increase in the supply of aircraft before the winter. The Allies had to achieve air superiority on the Western Front to ensure the success of long-range bombing missions. The Germans may be expected to do everything in their power to frustrate these missions. General Smuts said that the supply of aircraft to the Army in France had been agreed between Sir Douglas Haig and Sir David Henderson but Trenchard still pressed for an acceleration of the aircraft construction programme. Smuts agreed that the War Cabinet had to give the highest priority to Haig's request for eighty-six squadrons on the Western Front. New aircraft were going, not simply to provide for more squadrons, but as replacements for ones lost in combat. The War Cabinet had authorized an increase in production, which would permit the establishment of 200 service squadrons of the RFC to be in the air by the end of 1918. Be that as it may Smuts said that the output of aircraft was not even meeting the requirements of the more limited programme.

There was then a question of the proportion of aircraft being supplied as between fighters for home defence, aircraft for reconnaissance both over land and sea, anti-submarine aircraft, tactical aircraft to give direct support to the ground war or bombers for strategic bombing missions. This would also mean having the appropriate numbers of pilots trained and airfields prepared. He believed that there should be someone to head a programme of airfield construction under the Master General of Ordnance or the Ministry of Munitions. He had in mind Sir John Hunter, the Director of Factory Construction. In order to provide an answer Smuts had to ponder how the war could be brought to a successful conclusion by securing an honourable peace or best an unconditional surrender. The Navy might achieve final victory through blockade or the Army might secure a decisive military victory on the Western Front, although the experience of the past three years did not hold out too much hope. Would an extended air offensive prove decisive where other forms of warfare had not? Answering these questions would be the responsibility of the Air Organization Committee, and ultimately the Air Ministry.

MEETINGS OF THE WAR CABINET

15 October 1917

Parliament was due to reassemble on 16 October and the Prime Minister had been given notice of a question about the formation of an Air Ministry and he wanted to be briefed on aerial matters. So the War Cabinet invited General Smuts to make a statement reviewing the progress made to date. He reported that his Committee had already covered a good deal of ground. A draft bill had been prepared with the help of the Law Officers of the Crown including a discipline act, pay warrant and other regulations for the new service. He thought it premature to define the exact powers of the new Ministry for a great number of details remained to be worked out, which would take a considerable time. He believed that Parliament should be informed that a bill was in preparation, which would give wider powers to the Air Ministry, although those powers might not be exercised before a considerable period of time had elapsed. The Secretary of State for War was concerned that the Air Force might not offer life service to those who joined. In any event, neither the War Office nor the Board of the Admiralty had had the opportunity of studying the draft bill. The Foreign Secretary believed that there were two questions before the War Cabinet. One was whether the institution of an Air Ministry could be achieved during the present conflict since he thought that General Smuts did not believe that it was possible. Secondly, how best could the Air Services be could be co-ordinated without an Air Ministry. In the event that it was not possible to institute an Air Ministry before War's end General Smuts would head a small Cabinet committee responsible for the direction of air policy. This was particularly important given the 1,500 machines + Reserves on the Western Front, together with 1,500 naval machines + 500 seaplanes. Sir William Weir said that if the existing programme was to be fully completed, aircraft would have to be given absolute priority with regard to materials and labour.

2 November 1917

The War Cabinet began by discussing what progress had been made to set up an Air Ministry being acutely aware that public opinion was becoming restless. This would mean forming such a body with loosely defined powers, leaving the details to be filled in later. General Smuts, as Chairman of the Air Organization Committee, said that he saw no reason why the draft Bill, then in the process of completion, could not go before Parliament in the course of the coming week or so. It had been circulated to the Admiralty and the War Office, the latter promising to submit their comments and suggestions early in the following week. Speaking with his other hat as Chairman of the Air Policy Committee, Smuts stated that he was already having to work through the Naval War Staff and the Imperial General Staff and knew only too well the difficulties that he faced in trying immediately to form an Air Ministry. With regard to the output of aircraft he believed that the enlarged programme of aircraft construction could be carried out but doubted if the training of a sufficient number of pilots could keep pace with the output of aircraft. The preparations for the formation of an independent bombing force (IBF) in France were proceeding according to plan with the construction of aerodromes and depots ready for operations to begin in the summer of 1918. Sir Douglas Haig had indicated that he would like to see General Trenchard, then Commander of the RFC in France, appointed commander of this force whereas the Air Policy Committee preferred it to come under the direct orders of Haig. The feeling was that if the IBF was to come under the command of Trenchard he might subordinate the role of the force to the ordinary operations of the RFC in France. Smuts therefore agreed to discuss the matter with the CIGS and Haig the following day.

Progress with the draft bill was to be circulated to members of the War Cabinet at the earliest opportunity. The Admiralty had concurred in its provisions but the War Office was still considering the matter and hoped to discuss its content at a meeting of the Army Council. Lord Derby, for the Army, said that he was unwilling to support the draft bill until he had received the opinions of Sir William Robertson and Sir Douglas Haig. Smuts had concurred with this view since he believed that the Army was more particularly affected than the Navy but as Mr Bonar Law anticipated, being asked questions in the House the following day, the War Cabinet decided that the bill was to be deferred due to the absence of Robertson on the Continent but that as soon as the General's views could be obtained the bill could then be laid before the House.

The Draft Air Force Act 1917
(See Appendix J for the document)
Source: CAB21/21

The formation of the RAF would involve, amongst others things, the wholesale transfer of officers and men from the RNAS and RFC. Along with them would go the aircraft, stores, transport facilities and airfields previously administered by the older sister services. It made sense to leave some supply matters as they were but both servicemen and civilians would be affected. The draft act covered the whole business of the transfer of RNAS and RFC personnel from their respective services to the RAF and made clear that no person would be compelled to transfer against his will. Concomitant consideration of pensions-pay, half-pay, rank on transfer and length of engagements was also included. The Chancellor of the Exchequer was to consult on the matter to ensure that

Lord Derby, Secretary of State for War.

the pay and allowances of persons joining the Air Force should not cause individuals to suffer.

In relation to the transfer of personnel they reserved the right not to be transferred. The Draft Act dealt with the personnel aspect in some detail and added sections on the creation of an Air Council through which political control could be exercised. Finally, the matter of service discipline had to be included. In the 1920s this proved to be a tricky problem for naval officers incorporated into Fleet Air Arm units. They were given RAF ranks for incorporating into Fleet Air Arm units and had to come ashore for training on RAF training units. At what point did affected personnel become subject to the Navy Act or the Air Force Act? To say that all the aeroplanes, aircrews and ground crews belonged to the RAF sounded tidy but required care in the application of personnel matters. It would be the Army Act that would form the basis of the disciplinary section of the Air Force Act. Indeed, Section 88 of the Army Act was to form the basis of Section 88 of the Air Force Act and the Draft Act states clearly that 'the Air Force Act shall continue in force only as long as the Army Act continues in force' (Paragraph 12, sub paragraph (2)). There would be plenty of friction between the Admiralty and War Office on the one hand and the Air Ministry on the other. From the date that the RAF was formed the Great War had only months to run but no one could foresee that at the time so all concerned in the creation of an independent air force got on with the job of fighting the war. With the USA on the Allied side the weight of personnel and material would, however, begin to tell.

QUESTIONS ARISING FROM THE PUBLICATION OF THE DRAFT AIR FORCE ACT
Source: National Archive document CAB 21/21

The Army Council considers the proposal to form an Air Ministry – 22 August 1917
At their 228th meeting the Army Council considered the formation of an Air Ministry emanating from the Second Report of the Prime Minister's Committee on

Air Organization and Home Defence against Air Raids. The proposal to form a new air service was accepted in principle but concern was expressed about who would be responsible for laying down the aircraft requirements for the Army. An amendment to the Draft Act was proposed that the Air Ministry should, from time to time, attach to the Army and the Navy such air units as were deemed necessary by the two services. The members of the Council were also concerned about rank, pay, recruitment, transport, stores, quarters etc., and that a detailed scheme should be worked out with the help of the Admiralty, War Office and the Treasury. A copy of the Second Report was sent to Haig for his comments and these appear below.

Letter from Chief of the Imperial General Staff to the C-in-C British Armies in France
Source: National Archive document CAB/21/21

With the Cabinet, having agreed in principle to the formation of a separate Air Ministry, the Army Council wished to hear the views of Army commanders in the field to learn how the new arrangements would work in practice. Accordingly, the Chief of the Imperial General Staff, General Robertson wrote to Field Marshal Sir Douglas Haig on 24 August 1917. Haig, who replied on 15 September, was primarily concerned that there should be no loss of efficiency as RFC squadrons were transferred to the RAF. In his experience the usefulness of military aircraft lay in the contribution they made directly to the progress of the land battle. When he was confronted

with the possibility that air units might be employed principally on strategic bombing missions he could only speculate since it was outside his own experience. The idea that the employment of air power should be aimed at the utter devastation of an enemy's industrial and population centres could mean that the other forms of bringing a war to a successful conclusion could become secondary and subordinate to strategic bombing missions, which would become the principal operations of war. He felt that the importance of long-distance bombing missions should be considered alongside the older forms of military operations. Air units assigned exclusively to strategic bombing missions would not, therefore, be immediately available to the commanders on the ground in prosecuting a land campaign. Haig did not deny that missions designed to cripple an enemy's industrial capacity as well as attacks on population centres would help in ending the war. The latter could be justified as punishment for similar acts on the part of an enemy, but once started it would have to be actively pursued until the ends had been achieved.

Haig's main concern was over the feasibility of long-distance bombing missions. There was little experience on the Allied side upon which to base opinions. It was, in fact, the RNAS that had mounted them as far back as 1914. On the enemy side airships and aircraft were being used for attacks on Britain but they had not brought the country to its knees. Furthermore, the Germans could attack from Belgium and pass over the sea before making a landfall whereas British bombers

General Robertson CIGS.

C-in-C British armies in France, Sir Douglas Haig.

would have to fly much greater distances over hostile territory before reaching their targets. Haig said that prevailing winds assisted German bombers returning from missions over Britain, which would be the opposite for British bombers. He was further concerned that the creation of a third service, with its own priorities, would not solve the existing problem of trying to reconcile the competing claims of two services. If the Air Ministry was to be the final arbiter, might not strategic bombing take precedence over the need to maintain air supremacy over the battlefield? The problem for the Navy would be even more acute since it had to be agreed who would man aircraft on board aircraft carriers and train naval pilots and manage shore-based air stations.

Haig's use of terms in relation to air warfare do not clarify matters. In his reply he spoke about 'air ascendancy' and 'air supremacy' since the latter should not be confused with 'air superiority'. Air supremacy is intended to be used in a situation where a country has almost complete command of the air as was, for example, the case for the Allied tactical air forces that accompanied the Normandy invasion forces in 1944. Haig did not imagine that he would achieve almost complete uncontested control of the airspace above the battlefield but he did worry that, at critical moments in the land battle, he might not get the squadrons he needed to achieve limited objectives. He further worried about the tasking of squadrons allotted to him. At that time all officers in the RFC had joined the Army and as a result of their training understood the requirements for the prosecution of the land battle. Air commanders and air staff officers, initially trained by the RAF and sent to RAF staff colleges, might not in future have the understanding required by the Army staff. Indeed when Hugh Trenchard became the Chief of the Air Staff he was adamant that he was going to create an 'air force spirit' and that his pilots were not going to be mere taxi drivers at the beck and call of army commanders. Nevertheless, if the RAF was to satisfy naval and military requirements for aircraft as well as providing aircraft for purely air operations i.e., strategic bombing and air defence of the home base, his pilots risked becoming jacks of all trades and masters of none. Since the Army had hitherto maintained repair and supply bases in France and taken over landing grounds it was the army staff officers who understood the situation on the ground. They knew where their anti-aircraft units were located and the best routes for aircraft to fly in a sky already congested with aircraft, some enemy. There was also a question of who should train the operators of kite balloons. Sir David Henderson, in his observations (see below) felt that kite balloons did not differ significantly from other kinds of aircraft.

Haig's concerns about disciplinary powers extended to the selection of air commanders, many of whom were known to him at the time, and to transfer of air units within his command and out of and into his Army. He felt that the airmen who were to be assigned to him had to be competent in all the branches of air work with an army such as artillery observation, reconnaissance, and photography and air fighting. If the Army was to be responsible for handling air units assigned to Commands one should not depart from the principle that the Army should undertake the training of pilots and observers who were going beyond mere flying. Haig doubted whether an Air Ministry would be capable of training in all its branches.

Haig ended his submission by urging a thorough investigation into the questions that he raised. Whilst agreeing that the full potential of the aeroplane should be realized he said that the enemy could be expected to do the same. Haig might have added that the Germans were not going to create a unified air service requiring them to have to consider these questions whilst a war was in progress.

Sir David Henderson's observations

Observations were also made by General Sir David Henderson, Secretary to the Air Organization Committee. Henderson acknowledged the differences of opinion as to the efficiency of air bombing. He said that it was important to gain the views of officers who have actually carried out such missions. Although the Committee had not then received evidence from officers with practical experience in this field, members of the Committee had

Sir David Henderson.

individually acquired a large amount of information chiefly through the RNAS whose units had achieved some successes going back to 1914. For the Expeditionary Force air fighting, reconnaissance and artillery spotting had come before long-distance bombing raids. He agreed with Haig that the army force commander must have a sufficient number of air units to achieve objectives in the land battle. With regard to independent air operations, Henderson said that it was as important to hear the reaction of the people being bombed as it was the bomber crews. On this matter the government could form an opinion without the advice of military experts.

On the matter of the difficulties faced by British bomber crews as opposed to German airship and Gotha units, Henderson agreed with Haig but said that if Britain was not to abandon all attempts to bomb German industrial and economic targets then every effort must be made to compensate an independent air force commander for the extra difficulties faced. If independent bombing by the RAF was to be undertaken then the requisite aircraft, personnel and materials must be set aside for this purpose. A force with its own air commander would be needed but the committee had the information required to know if this was feasible.

Henderson appeared to disagree with Haig on the matter of the dispute over competing claims for aircraft by two authorities. If the Navy and the Army were fighting for a finite number of air units then Haig said that he did not believe that the creation of an Air Ministry would solve that problem, whereas Henderson believed that its creation was all the more important. Interestingly, Henderson suggested that the peculiar technical problems of air warfare were not well enough understood by either the General Staff or the Naval Staff to judge which service had a greater claim to air units in achieving their separate war objectives. Of course, the Army and Naval Staffs understood the technical problems of their own air service if not those of the other. The insinuation was that Air Staff officers would appreciate the technical problems of all three services. But that would mean that the opinions of Air Staff officers would override naval and army staff opinion. In conclusion, Henderson put the points raised by Haig under two headings. Firstly, with regard to independent bombing missions he saw no alternative to bombing from bases in France. It would only be at the very end of the war that the HP1500 bombers would reach squadron service and be based in Eastern England from where they were capable of reaching Berlin. But the Armistice had been signed before any practical experience could be gained and this is very important when it came to Air Staff doctrine after the war when the experience of bombing from French bases had to form the basis of that doctrine. The second point referred to the adjustments that would have to be made by the Navy and the Army to implement the new policy and he believed that problems

could be overcome. Indeed, he thought that the effect of the creation of an Air Ministry upon Haig's prosecution of the war in France would be slight.

Arguments against the formation of an Air Ministry

Found in a file 2218 G is an undated and unsigned memorandum thought to have been written by General Trenchard. The writer felt that the whole argument for a separate air service was based on the belief that the war could be won in the air as against on the ground. He said that these were but opinions when the facts proved otherwise. The Zeppelin and Gotha attacks on Britain had not changed the course of the war so why should Allied attacks on Germany succeed in ending the war? He referred to matters already mentioned such as the prevailing wind and the approach to British shores over the sea when Allied bombing missions would have the wind against them on the return and much of the flight would be over hostile territory. He added that the appropriate bombing aircraft and trained bomber crews would not be ready in sufficient numbers by the summer of 1918. Attacks against German munitions works might result in retaliatory attacks on French cities and was the French Government ready for that? An Air Ministry with a civilian head would be uncontrolled by naval or Military opinion and might be tempted to do something spectacular in response to public clamour and factional pressure rather than co-operate with the Navy and the Army. Those detached to work with the Army or the Navy but who relied upon the Air Ministry for promotion might try to please the latter. Would the air forces attached to the Army, for example, be controlled by the Army or the Air Ministry? Failure would result if air commanders had insufficient knowledge of the Army's requirements. The memorandum moved on to the question of supply and said there had long been problems that were at last being handled well by the Air Board, A further reorganization might only cause a check in output. Finally, it had to be borne in mind what aerial forces might be required after the war, implying that there might not then be a need for a separate air service.

There is a rich irony here if this is indeed a memo written by General Trenchard, for it is he who would command the RAF through the entire 1920s and it would be very much an air force of his making. He would, in the event have to fight off attempts by both the Army and the Navy to reabsorb their air units back into their respective services. Moreover, it is he who would write a War Book for the RAF, which would suggest that it was possible for the RAF to win a war on its own, bringing considerable opprobrium on his head as he might have expected. Moreover, he had to be reminded that an enemy can move his centres of production well out of range of

Britain's bombing aircraft and that the experience of the Great War showed the limitations of the application of air power.

Letter from the Air Organization Committee to the Secretary of the War Office, dated 7 November 1917

Smuts was dealing with the matter of the system whereby RAF contingents would be supplied to the Army or the Navy. Eventually, RAF brigades would be allotted to the various Armies in France and it was necessary to anticipate the position of RAF commanders in the field in the deployment of the squadrons on a particular front. Essentially, the RAF commanders had to direct the air effort to achieve the tactical objectives of Army commanders. Of course, the former would be permitted to advise on the best use of air resources but the latter should have the last word. Should there be an irresolvable difference of opinion, Army field commanders should have ultimate powers to enforce discipline and carry out punishments. (Note the Army terminology and the use, initially, of Army ranks in the newly formed RAF.)

The next matter was the allocation of aircraft to the various fronts because Smuts could foresee possible friction between the Army and the Air Force. Heretofore it was a matter for the War Office to determine, for example, whether or not squadrons could be diverted from the Western Front to the Home Defence Wing. This dilemma is covered on page 121 when two squadrons were returned to France at the end of August 1917 in spite of the attack on Southend on the 12th. It was agreed that if the Commander-in Chief in any theatre was short of aircraft for military purposes, the Army Council would ask the Air Council to increase its allotment. If the units were available from the reserves or from other non-military allotments, the Air Council would arrange for the requisite units to be allotted. If these units were not available then the Army Council would be asked whether or not units could be released from previously agreed allotments and transferred to the Army formation needing the extra unit or units. But the choice of units transferred must be made by the Air Council since only the Air Force would be able to judge the possibilities of the efficient supply of replacement aircraft engines and spares to the geographical localities involved.

Thirdly, Smuts agreed that the C-in-C in the field should have the right to remove the commander of the Air Force Brigade assigned to his field force since this power was essential for the proper conduct of operations. The permanent replacement of such an officer would require consultation with the Air Council. The removal of subordinate RAF commanders should, however, be the responsibility of the Air Force commander. Other matters in this letter included training, the competition between the three services for officers at the cadet stage and joint exercises and deployments. All these matters were to be the subject of ongoing discussion between the three services since it would be wrong to come to any hard and fast decisions at that time.

Reorganization of the Air as it affected the Royal Navy and the Army

Source: National Archive document CAB 21/21

On 25 September 1917 the Air Organization Committee set out their thoughts on the allocation of air forces to both the Army and the Navy. It was not proposed that Air Forces be allotted to the Navy and the Army in bulk, but in formations suitable to the Commands (either geographical or engaged in operations) for which aircraft were required. An example was given of air formations required for the Grand Fleet, Naval Commands (whether at sea or ashore), at home and abroad, for the expeditionary force in France, for Home Defence and for forces in Egypt, Salonika, Mesopotamia, East Africa and India. For convenience of administration the last five were already grouped together in one brigade. These contingents should be under the control of one commander to whom they were allotted for operations, and when in the field or with the Fleet, they must come under him for supply. Disciplinary matters should be left to the Air Commander allotted to a formation. With regard to administration the Committee could not, at that stage, anticipate the extent to which an air contingent would be dependent on the service to which they were allotted for certain matters of administration.

Where units were allocated to the Navy, the problem was complicated and was divided into three groups:

1. Air units allocated to the Fleet and serving on board regular men-of-war.
2. Air units serving on board seaplanes or aircraft carriers.
3. Air units working from land bases or floating bases which were within the district controlled by an officer of the Army or the Navy.

It was anticipated that there would be problems with aircraft used in the anti-submarine role and in a situation where a naval officer was in command and commanders of air units were subordinated to him or conversely where the Air Unit Commander was in overall command with subordinate naval forces.

Correspondence between the Ministry of National Service and the Air Board

Sir Auckland Geddes drew attention to Clause 5 of the draft bill, which dealt with the application of the Military Service Acts. In a letter dated 6 November 1917 to Sir Paul Harvey at the Air Board offices in the Strand reference was made to the Military Service Acts of 1916 and 1917 in which any man who was called up for service under the terms of both Acts would be liable for transfer to the RAF. Geddes felt that the clause was in need of some modification. As things stood it would be a matter for the Army Council to decide what proportion of the men recruited under either of the Acts should be transferred to the RAF. He felt that the number should be determined by War Cabinet leaving it to the Minister of National Service to carry out the allocation in detail. In the case of men still in civil life who voluntarily attested under Lord Derby's scheme it would not be considered desirable to make such volunteers subject to compulsory allocation to the Air Force, without, at any rate, some restriction. It was also noted that comparatively few recruits were raised under the Military Service Acts of which a very large proportion were of a low category of physical fitness.

Meeting of November 22nd 1917

Needless to say the Draft Air Force Act came under close scrutiny by those that would be affected by it from both the Royal Navy and the Army and a meeting was held in London on 22 November 1917 under the chairmanship of Sir Edward Carson to consider various amendments to the Act. The first to be considered were disciplinary matters. Sir Edward outlined the problems that might arise when Air Force personnel were part of an expeditionary force with airmen who were subject to air force law and not military law. How, for example, could airmen be tried by air officers when they were detached from Air Force units? Admiral Mark Kerr and Commodore Paine both opposed the proposed amendment as it would render Air Force personnel subject to the Navy or Army Act if detached from the Air Force as part of an expeditionary force when the purpose of the Act was to create a co-equal force entirely separate from the Royal Navy and the Army. This view was supported by General Sir David Henderson. This is to emphasize that some of those at that meeting, although still Army officers, would soon become senior members of the Air Force after its creation, Army officers such as Henderson and Major General John Salmond. Commodore Paine, a naval aviator, pointed out that members of the RNAS had throughout the war been subject to the Naval Discipline Act but he felt that members of the RNAS who were soon to be transferred to the RAF and some who would not, would rather be subject to the Air Force Act. They would have some misgivings about being placed under military law. He had in mind that the RNAS, being a flying service, would have more in common with RAF airmen. Lord Hugh Cecil added his weight to the argument that anything that made the RAF less than a co-equal service should not be permitted. He said that even though nineteen-twentieths of Air Force Law was the same as military law, the twentieth part

dealt specifically with offences committed in the conduct of flying duties of which military officers would have no experience. Lord Crawford countered on behalf of the Adjutant General. He used an example of street brawling involving members of both the Army and the Air Force whereby, unless the amendment was accepted, there would have to be separate trials resulting in punishments being awarded by Army and Air Force officers for the same offences. This could lead to unfairness if one service treated its members more leniently than the other. General Sir Neville Macready referred to Commodore Paine's reference to members of the RNAS being subject to the Navy Discipline Act throughout the war but from his experience as Deputy Adjutant General in France problems had arisen in Dunkirk and other area when similar offences were committed by members of the Army and RNAS. He feared that similar problems would arise by the establishment of Air Force law. Lord Cecil offered a way out by giving the Air Council the responsibility of bringing in regulations in the light of experience once the Air Force Act was passed. These regulations could spell out the specific circumstances where Air Force law might be suspended in favour of military law. This modification to the original amendment was adopted.

CABINET COMMITTEES UNDER THE CHAIRMANSHIP OF GENERAL JAN SMUTS

Sources National Archive Documents: CAB/24/34 and WD/246

Meeting of the Air Policy Committee on 28 November 1917

By the date of this meeting Lord Rothermere had been appointed as Air Minister and he attended with Lord Derby representing the Army and Commodore Paine for the Royal Navy. Others attending this meeting were those already prominent in aviation, namely Sir David Henderson and Hugh Trenchard and two future Chiefs of the Air Staff, John Salmond and Arthur Newell. First on the agenda was the situation on the Western Front and General Trenchard reported that it was not as good as it had been since eight miles of land had been lost. (This is significant in the static war of the trenches.) He put this down to an insufficiency of machines to mount a good aerial offensive. This was put down to a change of machines during the offensive whereas the Germans had changed their types earlier in the year. The SE5 was a good machine but there was such a variety of engines fitted to this machine that pilots could not exploit the aircraft's full potential. Four-fifths of Germany's fighting machines faced the British Army on the Western Front. The RFC had forty-nine squadrons operating in France and five squadrons in Italy. Casualties varied month by month according to the intensity of the fighting. The total number of squadrons available at the end of the autumn offensive was fifty-four. In June the preceding year he had asked for sixty-six squadrons and by November the number had increased to eighty-six. But by the end of the year the number had decreased to fifty-four squadrons.

A letter from Sir Frederick Maurice to General Trenchard – 2 September 1917

The letter from Sir Frederick Maurice, Director of Military Operations, to General Trenchard is of interest since Sir Frederick had gone public over troop levels in France, blaming the Prime Minister for misleading the House of Commons, and he was forced to resign but was refused a court martial. Clearly this was a man who would be at the centre of controversies and in this letter he is free with opinions about who should and who should not take command of the soon to be created Air Force. In writing this secret letter he was, in effect, breaking a confidence. He spoke of the rumours that were flying about on the matter of the formation of an Air Ministry and asked Trenchard what he knew about it. He had the General in mind to become the first Chief of the Air Staff, saying that he did not think Henderson was up to the job. This was because the officer who would be appointed to head the RAF would face an Army Council that was determined to use its air resources as it saw fit. In other words they might nominally belong to the RAF but would be handed over to the Army, leaving the RAF only to provide and train the air squadrons. Only those aircraft that were surplus to the requirements of the Army and the Navy would be at the disposal of the Air Ministry, for example as strategic bombers, assuming that those were the aircraft that were surplus. Maurice expressed his opinion that this was Henderson's idea. Brancker, he felt, was full of energy but lacked judgment and was too casual in

his approach to administration. He knew that Trenchard was busy in France and told him that if he could not be spared then that was an end to the matter. Trenchard was asked for his views so that he could advise the Chief of the Imperial General Staff.

There is in the archive the copy of a letter dated 6 October 1917 but it is unsigned and without an address. It may have been a reply to the secret letter sent by Maurice or a memorandum addressed to GHQ. The latter seems the more likely since, having been alerted to the fact that Trenchard could be called upon to accept the post of Chief of the Air Staff, he wanted it known that his presence in France was more important. Indeed, he had already argued against the formation of an Air Ministry. The efficiency of the RFC in France depended on his remaining there and not being sent to London. He had the added responsibility of arranging for strategic bomber bases to be set up in the Nancy area, in the French zone of operations. With the new squadrons the total of RFC units would come to eighty-six and he had the task of co-ordinating the whole RFC effort. Trenchard added that he was not an 'office' man and that there were others best suited to working with other departments of state with all the administration that that required. As regards the RFC at home he blamed Henderson for allowing the chaos that existed in the matter of design and supply of aircraft. He cited the Ministry of Munitions, which controlled supply on the basis of demands made by the Air Board but had no further control of the demands put forward. As regards design, this was left to the technical department of the Air Board. But the aircraft and engines that were supplied to military units and formations, for which Henderson as Director General of Military Aeronautics (DGMA) was responsible, could only be those that had

Name	Present appointment	Proposed appointment
Major General J.M. Salmond	Commanding Training Division in the UK	DGMA
Brigadier-General C. Longcroft	Commanding the 5th Brigade of the RFC in France	To succeed Major General Salmond
Brigadier-General L.E.C. Charlton	Director of Air Organization	To succeed Brigadier-General Longcroft
Brigadier-General W.S. Brancker	Deputy DGMA	To command Middle East Brigade
Brigadier-General W.G.H. Salmond	Commanding Middle East Brigade	To command Training Brigade in the UK
Brigadier-General E.R. Ludlow-Hewitt	Under orders to command a training brigade in the UK	To Training Division as Inspector of Training

Note: Trenchard felt that the post of Deputy Director of Military Aeronautics was unnecessary. The GOC Training Division WAS a very large organization to run so an Inspector of Training would be of great assistance. In closing, Trenchard had thought these matters over for more than a year. Aerial warfare would be even harder in 1918 than it had been. Someone who knew the difficulties in the Field was the best person to get things done. Of course, he was writing his own CV for the post of Chief of Air Staff. He hoped that the C-in C would agree with his proposed organizational changes.

already been designed and manufactured. It seemed to Trenchard that there was an obvious lack of co-ordination. Since Henderson was the senior member of the RFC at home the advice he gave to the War Cabinet might be diametrically opposed to his own or any other officer appointed as DGMA under the present arrangements. As the commander of an RFC force in the field Trenchard felt that his opinions should not be overridden by Henderson who lacked operational experience.

Trenchard did not pull his punches over the position occupied by Henderson and said that the latter should be appointed to some other position not connected with the RFC or the air. He wanted to be left to carry on his work in France, which was approaching a critically important phase including as it did the formation of an independent bombing force. He also wanted the DGMA to have sufficient control over design and supply to give the RFC what it required. Creating an Air Ministry in the middle of a war was clearly not in his list of priorities. For good measure he gave his advice on the matter of future appointments. These names would feature prominently in the future RAF and civil aviation.

On 21 October there was a further letter. The Chief of the Imperial General Staff had sent a private letter to Lieutenant General Sir L.E. Kiggell KCB about the changes being proposed for the Air Service. Trenchard had seen this letter and was replying to Kiggell. He could not see why it was necessary to change the Air Service with which there was nothing wrong save the supply of material and, in some cases, the quality. He had already made his views quite clear. On the matter of the strategic bombing organization Trenchard said that he had already appointed a commander and his staff, including intelligence. It was a detached aerial army acting on his orders. There was one possible hiccup and that is that the French may refuse to permit the force to used aerodromes in the southern part of France as it could result in retaliation against French cities. The French had, however, asked the RFC not to bomb German aerodromes in the neighbourhood of the Nancy area. There had also been concern that providing machines for the long-range bombing force might result in robbing Douglas Haig of units urgently required for the land campaign but there had been a windfall following the cancellation of fifty machines destined for Russia.

THE AIR FORCE BILL 1917
(See Appendix J)

The Air Force Bill was introduced into Parliament in November, 1917 and received Royal Assent on 29 November. On 21 December 1917 and on 2 January 1918 Orders in Council were issued defining the duties of the members of the Air Council. Lord Rothermere was appointed the Secretary State of State for the Royal Air Force. The other members of the Air Council appointed at the time were:

Lieutenant General Sir David Henderson KCB (Additional member and Vice President)

Major General Sir Hugh Trenchard KCB (Chief of the Air Staff)

Rear Admiral Mark Kerr CB (Deputy Chief of the Air Staff)

Commodore Godfrey Paine CB (Master General of Personnel)

Major General W.S. Brancker (Comptroller General of Equipment)

Sir William Weir (Director General of Aircraft: Production in the Ministry of Munitions)

Sir John Hunter KBE (Administrator of Works and Buildings)

Major J.L. Baird CMG, DSO, MP (Parliamentary Under Secretary of State)

THE AIR FORCE ACT

The Air Force Act that brought about the formation of the RAF on 1 April 1918 was memorable for a number of reasons. Only two services had, for centuries, undertaken to defend the British Isles and prosecute wars abroad in pursuit of foreign policy aims. Now a third force was to be created and there would naturally be those, particularly amongst the senior ranks, who would resist the formation of the RAF as is made clear in the preceding paragraph. Trenchard, who would become the Chief of the Air Staff throughout the 1920s, would have to fight many battles to prevent the new force being strangled almost at birth and reabsorbed back into the sister services. Equally remarkable was the fact that the formation of the RAF was to take place whilst hostilities raged on the Continent and the Middle East. This is reflected in the misgivings expressed by Lord Milner in a memorandum dated 26 October 1917. One might have expected the creation of an Air Ministry to happen in the relative quiet of peacetime when mistakes or difficulties could be ironed out without the risk of the loss of many lives. As it was the Royal Navy and the Army would have to surrender administration and ownership of men and machines of the RNAS and the RFC. Fleet commanders would, however, have operational control of naval aircraft at sea but the Army Field Force commanders, such as those on the Western Front, would have, in the middle of campaigns, to accept the allocation of air units assigned to their fronts bearing in mind priorities set by the RAF for aircraft for home defence and other theatres. That is, after all, what the Smuts Report had been about. Everything that flew belonged to the RAF.

This entire organization reflected the sometimes haphazard ways in which formations and units were

THE ORGANIZATION OF THE RAF AT HOME IN 1918

AIR COUNCIL

AIR MINISTRY

SOUTH EASTERN AREA Covent Garden Hotel WC2
All units in London, Middlesex, Kent, Sussex, Surrey, Henlow Beds, Buckingham,
Berkshire, Essex, Oxford, Hertford and Martlesham Heath and Orford in Suffolk
(see Note 1).

SOUTH WESTERN AREA Chafyn Grove, Salisbury
All units in Wiltshire, Glamorgan, Dorset, Devon, Hampshire, Somerset, Cornwall,
Scilly Isles and Gloucester (see Note 2).

MIDLAND AREA Somerset House, Clarendon Place, Leamington Spa
All units in Leicester, Stafford, Anglesey, Pembroke, Rutland, Warwick, Flint,
Merioneth, Carmarthen, Nottingham, Worcester, Montgomery, Bedford, Lincoln,
Shropshire, Cardigan, Northampton, Lancashire, Huntingdon, Cheshire, Denbigh,
Hereford, Cambridge, Brecknock, Carnarvon, Radnor, Norfolk, Suffolk and Derby
(see Note 3).

NORTH EASTERN AREA Racecourse Buildings, York
All units in Durham, York, Northumberland, Westmorland, Cumberland and those
portions of Nottinghamshire and Lincolnshire north of a line Worksop – Lincoln
(exclusive), Horncastle and Ingoldmelts which were in No.16 (Training) Group.

NORTH WESTERN AREA Adelphi Hotel, Argyle Street, Glasgow

Note 1   The Sussex units did not include the airship station at Polegate and the seaplane station at Newhaven, which
came under the command of No.10 Operations Group
Note 2   The South Western Area incorporated Polegate and Newhaven. The Gloucester units did not include
Rendcombe which came under South Eastern Area, No.2 (Training) Group.
Note 3   The Nottingham/Lincoln units did not include No.8 Balloon Base at Immingham, which was under No.18
(Operations) Group in the North Eastern Area. The Bedford units did not include Henlow, which was in the
South Eastern Area. The Norfolk and Suffolk units did not include those in No.4 (Operations) Group South
Eastern Area and Experimental Group, South Eastern Area.

formed to meet the changing operational requirements,
which in turn flowed from the changing war situation.
It must be remembered that the RAF would shrink from
185 operational squadrons on the last day of the war to
only 28 Squadrons on 1 March 1921 and this included
those overseas. And so the whole structure of the RAF
at home was changed to meet the much reduced size of
the peacetime service. This would remain substantially
unchanged until the major reorganization in 1936 to meet
the needs of a fast-growing service that had to face the
menace of a rearmed Nazi Germany.

Badge worn on the Service Dress Cap of officers up to air rank. The crown is the King's Crown. The crown on the right is a Queen's crown.

Official badge of the RAF bearing the motto 'Per ardua ad astra' – Through hardship to the stars.

THE EXPANSION OF THE ROYAL AIR FORCE – JUNE TO OCTOBER 1918
Source: GHQ France correspondence 1st Echelon 78th Report

Meeting of the Air Policy Committee – 28 November 1917
The reinforcement programme would have to be based on the situation described on page 137 (Meeting of the Air Policy Committee 28 November 1917) and Trenchard proposed 113 Squadrons for France plus 66 bombing squadrons.

Reinforcement programme for 1918/19
With regard to the reinforcement programme for 1918–1919 Trenchard proposed 113 squadrons for France, plus 66 bombing squadrons. He then turned his attention to the types of machines sent to the fighting front and declared that aircraft specifications were not being observed. Examples that were cited included French requirements for endurance, which included 2½ to 3 hours when the machines sent out had only 1¾ hours. The Sopwith Dolphins had been fitted with four guns instead of three, making them short of power given the increase weight. Requirements were being laid down at RFC HQ in France but were being ignored by the aircraft manufacturers. Commodore Paine disagreed, stating that great care was exercised in providing aircraft that would meet RFC requirements but it was not always possible

to supply machines to RFC specifications such as aircraft that would fly between 130 to 140mph. Trenchard held that losses to German aircraft had been greater for the reasons given, which meant that the RFC could not mount an aerial offensive in such large numbers as in the past. It had also to be remembered that both sides had larger numbers of aircraft.

Trenchard was then asked if Sir Douglas Haig was satisfied given the air questions that had been put to him. Trenchard replied that he was satisfied that aerodromes in the Nancy area would be ready to accommodate twenty-five squadrons when they were ready to be sent out. The independent bombing force was to be set up in the Nancy area. In all, accommodation for forty squadrons in the British zone was the target. Sir David Henderson added that the Air Board could not know where the front line would be, which could mean that squadrons could be some distance behind the British section of the line with a few jumping off points closer to the line. In some cases the French were being asked to surrender aerodromes for British use and they had recently refused to give up any more. Two of them recently surrendered would be needed by the French themselves in the spring of 1918. An alternative was for the French to give ground where new aerodromes could be built but it was not ideal country for this purpose, the land consisting of ridge and furrow. Some 2,500 labourers would be used to prepare two aerodromes for ten squadrons for occupation by April 1918. Then there was the arrival of the American squadrons that had entered the war and, together with some British squadrons, had been assigned to French airfields. This made some French commanders fearful that their airfields might be attacked if the Allies were launching bombing raids from them. (See Chapter 6 for a detailed consideration of the use of French airfields for the location of Allied air units.)

[Author's note: the airfields used by the Royal Flying Corps and Royal Naval Air Service in France were either French or Belgian. The use made of these airfields was of some concern to French Commanders since they had no direct say in the role of squadrons occupying them. In Chapter 6 all the airfields used by the Independent Bombing Force were French and around the Nancy area. The French local authorities would put obstacles in the way of RAF planners in trying to establish the bomber bases for the IBF.]

General Smuts asked General Trenchard what the French were doing to prepare for daylight and night bombing. The latter replied that by April or May the French would have two bombing groups for both day and night operations. Their programme of construction was greater but they were not so active in the air. They seemed keenest on their special mission, which was to bomb the steel-producing areas of Lorraine. Their bombers were long-range Breguet types but the French Government had asked for Handley Page machines for their night operations. Reference was made to American preparations, which Trenchard said were behind. Sir William Weir stressed the importance of impressing upon the American Government that they should assist HMG in fulfilling its programme. He felt that the completion of their own programme should not interfere with what the Americans had promised the British.

With regard to the proposed scheme for the bombing organization, there would be twenty-five squadrons in all, seventeen day and eight night. This would later rise to thirty squadrons, twenty day and ten night. The medical provision for the force would be provided by the RAMC. The bombing squadrons would be supplied from Candas and Rouen, which should not create traffic problems. In

Bristol Fighter.

any case, even if work on a new depot was commenced immediately it would not be ready until August 1918. The Candas depot was providing aircraft for the five RFC squadrons serving on the Italian front. An ample supply of bombs had been ordered. Two photographic aircraft with Rolls-Royce Eagle engines had been supplied and six of these machines would be requested for 1918, which had a service ceiling of 23,000ft.

Discussion then moved on to the DH9 machine being ordered to equip fifteen squadrons and arrangements were in hand to train the necessary personnel. Sir William Weir said that after June no DH9s would be constructed fitted with BHP engines. The latter could be fitted to the Bristol Fighter, which would give the RFC a good fighting machine with a fuel capacity to permit fairly long-distance work and extra tank capacity would be considered. Sir William said that he would be in a position to supply improved two-seater reconnaissance fighter machines by June 1918. His department would press on with work on a design to supersede the DH9. Smuts asked if these would be included in the construction programme for 1919. Sir William replied that they would not be available before July 1919 and would be only slightly better than the DH9. Trenchard

DH9.

DH10.

said that the DH9 was not designed to be a bomber even though they had been used as such. What was needed was a bombing aeroplane. Commodore Paine said that the RFC had been offered a single-seat bomber from Sopwith but that it had been turned down. The DH10 was an advance on the DH9 but was only slightly so. General Henderson added that it was not the design of bombers that was lacking; the designers had gone as far as they could with the existing engines. In June 1917 the US Government had been asked to supply 500 Liberty engines. If these engines were as good as reported a better bombing aeroplane could be designed and produced. As things stood the future bombing machine was something of a gamble after July 1918. Sir William referred to the programme for the spring of 1919 saying that the number squadrons contained therein could be supplied earlier.

The Air Ministry was planning into 1919 when the Programme for the Development of Aircraft for all purposes was prepared and it showed the number of squadrons that it hoped would be in France by 30 September 1919. The thinking was that the greater proportion of available resources should be devoted to long-distance bombing operations. Forecasts were requested of requirements for that date on the basis of the then present strength and fifteen Army corps of forty-five divisions. This would be in excess of that put forward on 20 November 1917. In the event the War Office had requested that owing to the activity of enemy night bombing aircraft two additional night fighter squadrons should be sent. But the required number of aircraft would not be immediately available. However, by the summer of 1918 the Gothas were no longer attacking targets on the British mainland but had switched to targets on the Western Front. This meant that the Air Ministry could safely reduce the number of aircraft on seven Home Defence night fighter squadrons to form at least one of the two requested squadrons. The establishment was to be reduced from twenty-four to twenty-one aircraft per squadron releasing three from each to equip a night-fighting squadron of eighteen aircraft. Should extra night-fighting squadrons be required in France as a matter of urgency, consideration could be given to reducing the home establishment of aircraft per squadron by another three, from eighteen to fifteen. The threat from the Gothas had subsided but there was no guarantee that any undue weakening of the Home Defence units could invite a resumption of the bombing. Be that as it may on 28 September 1918 the War Office asked for a third night-fighting squadron and this could be obtained by the method already used.

What was happening was precisely what was intended in forming an Air Ministry when the former and neither the War Office nor the Admiralty decided on the allocation of squadrons to meet competing needs. Indeed, when it was suggested that, for the protection of tanks from hostile fire, a complete unit of fighter aircraft should be detailed for this purpose and that that unit should have no other mission, the Air Ministry replied that the Army should wait until the active operations, then ongoing, were complete before proposals were made. On 17 October it was possible to inform the War Office that one corps squadron and one fighting squadron could be allotted to each tank corps group.

Any increase in the number of squadrons sent to France involved the French authorities inasmuch as provision had to be made to accommodate them on existing airfields or open up new ones. Approval by the French had already been agreed on 4 November 1917. As the operations in late 1918 were moving into territory previously held by the Germans then German airfields could be used, with pilots and observers accommodated locally. Some French farmers were already ploughing up flying grounds as the war entered a more mobile phase.

NIGHT FIGHTING OVERSEAS
Source: National Archive Document: AIR 1/109/15/20/2

Success had been achieved by fighter defences of the UK on the night of 19/20 May 1918, leading to the demand for a night-fighting unit in France. Accordingly, No.151 Squadron was dispatched from Hainault Farm to Marquise, France, on 19 June, equipped with Sopwith Camels and under the command of Major M. Green, shortly to be succeeded by Major Brand. The airfield location was important near the Bois de Crécy for the defence of Abbeville and the railway bridge over the Somme, which was vital to communications. A number of searchlights were sited in a semi-circle approximately seven to nine miles apart, on the enemy's side of the town. On receipt of intelligence that enemy night-bombing machines were approaching the Camels would ascend to patrol on the line of the searchlights. If two searchlights picked up an enemy machine in their concentrated beams the Camels could proceed to attack. Even if an aircraft was not illuminated the Camel pilots could pick up the enemy aircraft through the glow of its exhaust. In the event Abbeville was not subjected to night attacks after the arrival of No. 151 Squadron and similar searchlight patrols were mounted over Amiens, Arras, St Pol and Doullens. At these latter locations these tactics met with considerable success. The record of No.151 Squadron speaks for itself. Sixteen enemy night-bombing machines had been shot down on the Allied side of the line, five confirmed victories were achieved against night bombing machines on the enemy side of the line and further unconfirmed victories were achieved, again on the enemy's side of the line. RAF casualties were one flying officer killed in a night accident, one flight commander killed in a machine gun accident on the aerodrome. No RAF personnel were killed or injured as a result of enemy action.

There were, therefore, no enemy successes in night bombing in the sector covered by No.151 Squadron but this was not the case in other sectors where enemy night bombing behind Allied lines had been heavy. The response was to form No.152 Squadron from resources of No.6 Brigade at Rochford, which proceeded to Carvin on 17 October. On 11 November No.153 Squadron was ready to join the fray when the Armistice was declared. The tactics that had proved so successful may be described as follows. The RAF night-fighter pilot would approach an enemy night bombing machine from astern, throttle back and align his machine below the level of the enemy's tailplane when he could recognize details such as struts and flying wires. When he was sure that it was not a friendly aircraft he aligned his night sights to fire along the fuselage of the enemy bomber. As long as the pilot had taken his time to align his aircraft and aim his sights correctly the result was never in doubt. Overeager pilots firing at longer ranges seldom produced results.

THE ITALIAN FRONT
Sources: RAF Squadrons by Wing Commander C.G. Jefford MBE, RAF

On the front Allied bombing squadrons had attacked railway lines, both by day and night, ammunition dumps, barracks and airfields and in May 1918 an Italian airman was secretly flown behind enemy lines to observe and report back enemy dispositions. By 15 June the Austrians launched a major offensive on the Piave river. The offensive was announced by the usual artillery barrage. Facing the Austro Hungarian and German air forces were 221 fighters, 56 bombers, and 276 reconnaissance aircraft of the Italian Air Corps, 20 French reconnaissance aircraft and 54 fighters plus 26 reconnaissance types from the RAF. The Austrians supported their ground offensive with low-level bombing and strafing to which the Allies replied with fighter aircraft. The first day was bloody in the skies with 37 aircrew on both sides being killed. In all, 7 balloons and 107 enemy aircraft were brought down. On 20 June American pilots joined the fray as part of Italian bombing squadrons.

Commanding the RAF in Italy was Joubert de la Ferté and his squadrons were worked hard. On 18 March 1918 he lost No.42 Squadron with its RE8s when the unit was returned to France and he decided that the one squadron of RE8s remaining to him was insufficient to cope with all the bombing and reconnaissance that was required and he had to rely on units of the Allies to take up the slack. At this time he had:

No.34 Squadron at San Luca – RE8s employed on artillery observation and reconnaissance

No.28 Squadron at Sarcedo – Camels employed in the fighter/ground attack role

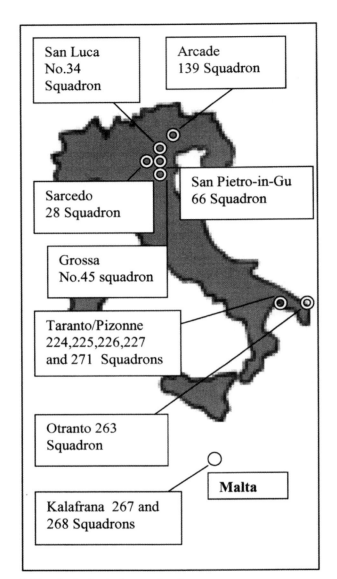

RAF units in the Italian peninsula.

No.139 Squadron at Arcade – Bristol F2B Fighters

No.66 Squadron at San Pietro-in-Giu – Camels in the fighter/ground attack role.

No.45 Squadron at Grossa – Camels in the fighter ground attack role

The roles of the RAF's aircraft on this front were very much the same as in France except that contact air patrols were not flown. The three Camel squadrons between them brought down 367 enemy aircraft and only 32 Camels were lost on the enemy side of the lines. In all, nineteen British pilots were killed with four wounded in action but who returned safely. Nineteen became prisoners of war but survived. In this way the RAF contingent in Northern Italy played their part in halting the enemy advance and forcing them to retreat back across the River Piave. The armistice between Italy and Austria was declared on 4 November, a week earlier than that on the Western Front. In Southern Italy and Malta the RAF was principally concerned with anti-submarine operations in the Mediterranean and bottling up warships of the Central Powers in the Adriatic.

MESOPOTAMIA
Sources: Thesis presented to the Faculty of the US Army Command and General Staff College by Major Peter J. Lambert USAF, National Archive document AIR 1/674/21/6/87

Introduction
The year 1917 ended with the RFC in Mesopotamia deployed as follows:

HQ No.31 Wing	at Baghdad
No.30 Squadron (less one Flight)	at Baqubah (where they had been transferred after the operation of 19th October)
B Flight No.30 Squadron	at Felujah on the Euphrates
No.63 Squadron	at Samarra
No.23 Kite Balloon Coy.	at Baghdad (under command Samarra)
Aircraft Park	at Basra
Advanced Aircraft Park	at Baghdad

There were no military operations on the ground in January 1918 but this did not prevent the RFC from carrying out photographic reconnaissance nor carrying out bombing raids. There were few encounters in the air. The RFC had bombed the enemy airfield at Humr on 28 December 1917 and it was probably a reprisal raid by the enemy on Samarra that was aimed at the camp of No.63 Squadron on the stroke of midnight on the 31st. Three days later aircraft of both Nos.30 and 63 Squadrons bombed Humr as the tit-for-tat raids continued. The two squadrons bombed Kifri airfield on 21 January with two Spads providing escort cover. Altogether, two 112lb bombs and seventy-two 20lb bombs were dropped. No direct hits were observed but bombs were exploded very close to enemy aircraft. Anti-aircraft fire claimed the lives of two crewmen from No.30 Squadron namely, 2Lt W.S. Bean and Lance sergeant R.G. Castor. On 24 January the enemy continued the tit-for-tat. There were two raids, one at 22.00hrs on Baghdad when casualties were suffered in a casualty clearing station. The second raid was at 01.15hrs on the 25th when a rest camp was targeted This tactic employed by the enemy, and emulated by the RFC, was to split the raid up over several hours. During these encounters Lieutenant Nuttal MC., a pilot of a DH4,

made a forced landing behind enemy lines following an engine fire. He and his observer, Lieutenant Siever, walked throughout the night carrying their aircraft Lewis gun and ammunition and they covered twenty-four miles before reaching Allied lines.

A tactic used by the enemy involved a pilot flying low over a concentration of British troops, which attracted ground fire. Feigning a hit the pilot would then go into a nose dive, which brought the troops out into the open to cheer what they believed was a fatal blow but the pilot would pull out of the dive at the last moment and drop bombs with great accuracy on the troop concentration below. But like all military 'spoofs' such as Q ships at sea, they had a limited life once the word got out. Another problem affecting the RFC was trouble with the interrupter gear of the machine guns. In the best environments with aircraft parks having all the facilities for repair these problems could be overcome such as the faulty cams that actuated the firing of the gun through the arc of the propeller,. But this was Mesopotamia where there was intense heat in the summer months and sickness was rife amongst ground crews. It was inevitable that at crucial moments in an air battle the forward-firing machine gun would not fire, and if it did, it would shoot away the propeller.

The map on the following page shows the progress made by British forces in their drive to the north and any interference from hostile forces entering from Persian territory would affect the right flank of the British advance. At the time Persia was neutral and it was important that a member of the intelligence staff from GHQ visit Tehran to assess the trouble involving different quasi military groupings in the country. Time was of the essence and it was decided to convey Colonel Stokes to Tehran from Baghdad by air, a distance of 700 miles. The journey would have to be made over some of the most inhospitable terrain imaginable with mountain ranges up to 12,000ft and snow covering the tracks that passed for roads that wound through the mountain passes. There were no accurate maps and nowhere to land if the aircraft got into trouble. Two RE8s were used, the first piloted by Lieutenant Browning with Colonel Stokes, and the second aircraft piloted by Lieutenant Adams carried extra fuel instead of a passenger. Both aircraft left on 25 January 1918 from Baqubah and both aircraft were replenished at Basr-I-Shirin. Lieutenant Browning's aircraft crashed on take-off and another aircraft had to be flown up to allow him to continue his journey. The flight continued on 27 January and the last 300 miles were completed the following day. There were problems on arrival for it was believed that an RE8, being a military aircraft, had violated the airspace of a neutral country. This was eventually dealt with peacefully since all the armament had been removed from the aircraft and it was shown that this was a diplomatic mission with Colonel Stokes visiting the British Legation in the capital.

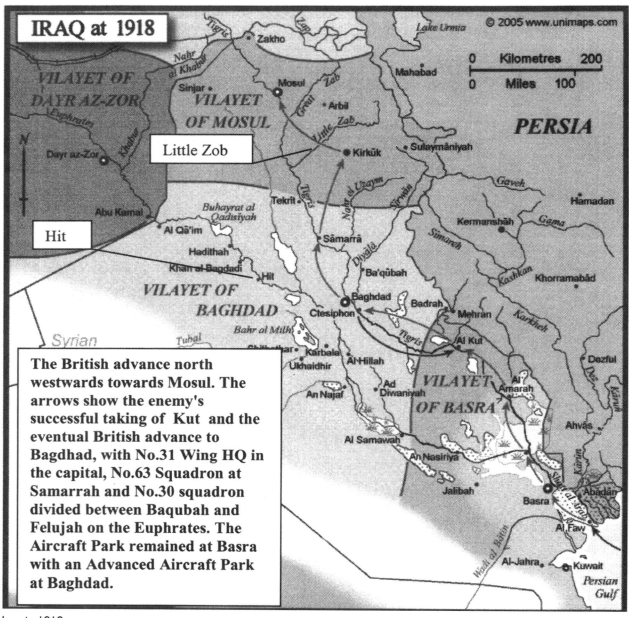

The British advance north westwards towards Mosul. The arrows show the enemy's successful taking of Kut and the eventual British advance to Bagdhad, with No.31 Wing HQ in the capital, No.63 Squadron at Samarrah and No.30 squadron divided between Baqubah and Felujah on the Euphrates. The Aircraft Park remained at Basra with an Advanced Aircraft Park at Baghdad.

Iraq in 1918.

The pilot's troubles were not, however, entirely over since his aircraft had landed in a barrack square and the heavy rain and snow made it almost impossible to take off again. The aircraft was therefore lightened as much as safely possible and Browning did succeed in getting airborne on 10 February.

At the beginning of March the RFC in Mesopotamia was reinforced by No.72 Squadron, which had flown out from England and was commanded by Major von Poellnitz, not it is stressed, a German officer. On arrival in the theatre his command was split up to the various fronts in the theatre of operations. A Flight, equipped with Spads, SE5s and DH4s, was deployed to Samarra to work with 1st British Corps. B Flight, equipped with Martinsydes, went to GHQ in Baghdad under the command of Captain Fuller, whilst C Flight, equipped with Bristol aircraft and under the command of Captain Coleman, went to work with the 3rd British Corps.

The taking of Hit on the Euphrates (See Map)

There was a lull in active military operations until the middle of February when attention was once more directed against the Euphrates front. The town of Hit can be seen on the map and it was here that the Turks were reinforcing their garrison. Enemy patrols were being pushed forward from there towards Uqbah and Nafata and so it was important for the town to be taken soonest since a British push northwards towards Kirkuk would have its left flank threatened. Major General Brooking commanding the 15th Division was ordered to take Hit as soon as his preparations were complete. As part of a feint to disguise British intentions No.30 Squadron dropped bombs and fired at hostile troops north of Kara Tepe. On 22nd February No.52 Kite Balloon Section was moved up to Uqbah and elements of Nos30 and 63 Squadrons were also brought forward to form a composite squadron under the command of Major de Havilland. This enabled the airfield at Hit to be attacked both to destroy enemy aircraft and retreating enemy columns. Enemy troop bivouacs, camel troops and cavalry units were targeted leaving a trail of destruction during the operations on 8 and 9 March. When aerial operations resumed on the 10th the effect on the enemy was such that it was possible to occupy the objective and at the same time the Turks evacuated Sahiliyah. Whilst on the offensive it was the aim to keep driving the enemy northwards so that their forces could not easily retake Hit but for a while the weather hindered British troop movements. From Sahiliyah it was intended to attack the Turkish positions in Khan Baghdadi. A special mobile cavalry unit was formed to move by night to encircle the Turkish positions. This was known as the 11th Cavalry Brigade. With the Turkish forces surrounded the RFC could attack their positions and de Havilland's composite squadron comprising A and B Flights of No.30 Squadron, C Flight, together with A and B Flights of No.63 Squadron moved up to take part in the operation. The attack by the 15th Division took place on the dawn of 26 March and the Kite Balloon Section kept observation of the ensuing operation.

The enemy air force in the theatre was then equipped with the Albatros DIII and enemy air activity was stepped up. This fighter was a major improvement on the previous Albatros marks, having improved manoeuvrability and rate of climb, and had the characteristic V struts between the top wing and the fuselage. In spite of this two pilots of No.72 Squadron were successful in downing two enemy scouts. One was shot down by Lieutenant Thomas ten miles south-east of Kirkuk on 5 May and Lieutenant Lapraik destroyed a Halberstadt on 9 May when the wings of the aircraft broke off at 3,000ft. Meanwhile, enemy camps and airfields were constantly attacked during the month by SE5s, Bristol Scouts and Spads with RE8s carrying out the bombing raids.

'Dunsterforce' in Persia

By this time the RFC units in Mesopotamia were part of the newly created Royal Air Force. At the end of May the RAF units of No.31 Wing were located at Baqubah, Kifri, Ramadi, Samarra, Baghdad, Mirjana and Hawadan. This thin spread of RAF units meant that at each location there were half squadrons or individual flights or sections of kite balloon companies. Major von Poellnitz, commanding No.72 Squadron, was sadly killed in a motoring accident and his replacement was Major Westendarp from No.30 Squadron. This was a very short-lived command with the Major being transferred to Egypt, his place being taken by Major O.T. Boyd. Hot weather brought about a cessation of operations in Mesopotamia and the RAF units were confined to aerial photography, instructional classes, practice co-operation with the Artillery and the attachment of B Flight of No.72 Squadron to the 'Dunsterforce' operating in Persia. The British operations in Persia were led by Major General Dunsterville to ensure that there was not a complete breakdown of law and order in the country. The Russian troops were retreating to the Caspian Sea and the Persians had suffered greatly at the hands of both the Russians and the Turks. They naturally resented the invasion of yet another foreign army into their country but the Dunsterforce was able to prevent any move on Tehran from north and the west from a base in Kasvin.

The final operations in Mesopotamia

General Allenby had secured both Palestine and Syria and the Turks were forced on the defensive withdrawing their troops from the Caucasus. On 5 October 1918 General Marshall was ordered to commence operations against the Turkish 6th Army covering the approach to Mosul on the Tigris (see map). Anticipating this offensive the Turks reinforced their positions south of Mosul, including the transfer of elements of the Turkish 4th Army in Persia. During the hot summer months No.63 Squadron had made extensive photographic reconnaissance of enemy positions. This was vitally important since there were no detailed or accurate maps of the country and GHQ staff were able to rely on maps compiled from aerial

Albatros DIII.

photographs. The war became very fast moving and kite balloons were of little use so No.23 Kite Balloon Company was returned to England on 1 October. Two British columns advanced on the Turkish positions at Fatha and during the night of 23/24 October the Turks abandoned them. The contribution of No.63 Squadron was to bomb enemy trenches and co-operate with the artillery. The enemy ground formations did not always scatter when attacked from the air and RAF aircraft could be continually fired on from the ground. Lieutenant Lapraik's SE5 was hit in the radiator and he had to force-land his aircraft near an advanced British cavalry unit, whilst Lieutenant Cannell received a wound in the leg. Progress was slow on the right bank of the Tigris for the tracks were bad, the supply of water and food had to be taken by pack mules and the heavy artillery had to be left behind south of Fatha. Progress was better on the left bank of the Tigris both north and south of the Little Zob and soon the area was cleared of enemy troops. Contact patrols by the RAF were essential in the fast-moving operations to keep British commanders fed with up-to-date reports of movements on the ground. The British advance turned into a rout on the part of the Turkish 6th Army and General Marshall accepted its surrender on 30 October 1918. Mosul was occupied on 14 November, thus ending operations in Mesopotamia.

EGYPT, THE PALESTINIAN AND GREEK THEATRES

Egypt

Egypt became the hub of aerial operations in the Middle Eastern theatres and remained so during the inter-war period and which Trenchard nicknamed 'Clapham Junction'. It was important because of its training role, which meant that volunteers for aircrew duties did not have to go back to the United Kingdom to attend flying courses there and having air units close to the Suez Canal was essential given the strategic importance of the water way. The organization became a brigade with a RFC major general commanding. Units could be trained up to be sent to Mesopotamia and Salonika. By October 1918 there was one training brigade of eight squadrons, three schools of special flying, one cadet wing and a School of Military Aeronautics. And so it became possible to support one brigade of seven squadrons in Palestine, one wing of three squadrons in Mesopotamia and one wing of three squadrons in Macedonia.

Palestine

The final offensive against the Turks in Palestine began on 17 September 1918. The deployment of aircraft was a telling factor in winning the war in this theatre and units of the RFC and RAAS (Royal Australian Air Force) attacked German and Turkish telephone exchanges and telegraph offices in Tulkarm, Nablus and Afula. This succeeded in cutting off all contact between General von Liman and his subordinate commanders and the main German airfield at Jenin was put out of action. For seven days roads, railways and troop concentrations were bombed and on the Nablus Beisan road the carnage was so great amongst the enemy convoys that pilots were asking to be spared any further part in what had become a massacre.

It should not be forgotten that an Arab force under the command of Major Lawrence was pushing northwards on the right flank of General Allenby's force. The politics of the promise to the Arabs that Feisal would be crowned king of an Arabian kingdom in Damascus, had been largely undermined by the Sykes/Picot Agreement of 1916 whereby the British would inherit responsibility for Palestine and Transjordan after the war and that France would do likewise for the modern day Lebanon and Syria. Thus, the British Government could not keep its promise to the Arabs. The situation was further muddied by the promise made by the British Foreign Secretary in 1917 that the Jewish Diaspora in Europe could have a national home in Palestine after the war. Although the Jewish state was not to be exclusively Jewish the promise gave rise to the protracted and ongoing Arab/Israeli conflict that persists to this day. Lawrence thus hoped that if he could reach Damascus, before Allenby's force, the installation of Feisal as king would be a *fait accompli*. He was therefore in a hurry but sadly, for Lawrence, his efforts on the battlefield and at the Peace Conference after the war did not bear fruit and he resigned his post in the Army and settled instead for a career as an airman in the RAF. Attempts by Trenchard to have him commissioned failed and Lawrence left the RAF after a short career only to be killed in May 1935 following a motorcycle accident.

The Aegean

The following will be of interest to numerologists since the numbering of squadrons in Greece did not follow the usual pattern from 1 April 1918, of adding 200 to the existing RNAS squadron number. Following the publication of Air Organization Memorandum No.800 the ex-RNAS units remote from the European theatre were numbered 220 to 227 Squadrons inclusive. Of these, the ex-RNAS squadrons in the Aegean were lettered A, B, C and D Squadrons and the best evidence points to the fact that these were renumbered 222, 223, 200 and 221 respectively. These in turn belonged to Nos.62 and 63 Wings of No.15 (Aegean) Group.

The squadrons in the Aegean theatre were equipped as follows:

No.14 Sqn – Nieuport 17, bomber and reconnaissance
No.17 Sqn – DH9, tactical reconnaissance and artillery observation.
No.47 Sqn – BE2e, bomber

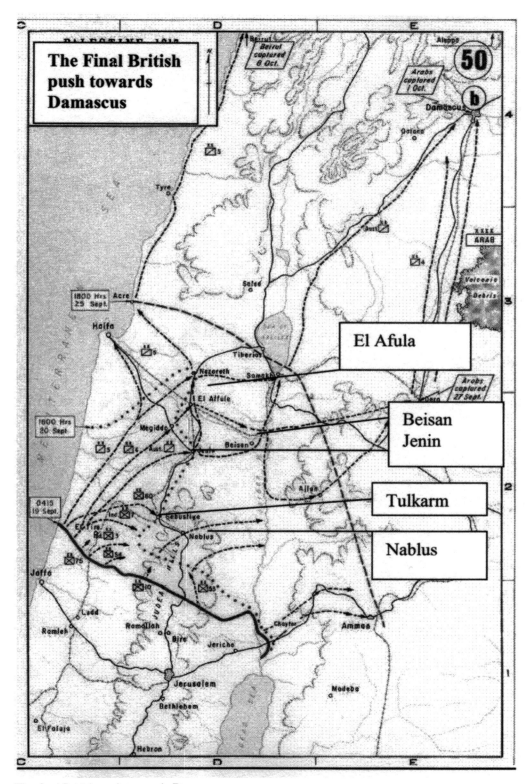

The final British push towards Damascus.

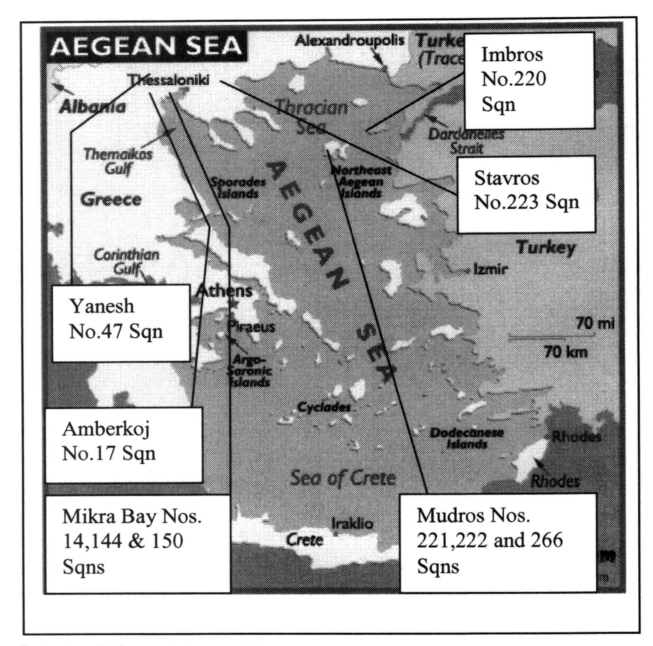

The location of RAF units in the Aegean – 1918.

No.144 Sqn – DH9, artillery Co-operation
No.150 Sqn – BE2e, fighter
No.220 Sqn – Camel, fighter reconnaissance
No.221 Sqn – Camel, anti-submarine
No.222 Sqn – DH9, bomber and escort
No.223 Sqn – DH9, bomber and reconnaissance
No.266 Sqn – Short 184 and Short 320, anti-submarine

On 14 September the Allies launched their offensive on the Salonika front with the French and the Serbian forces and it was not until the 18th that the British and Greek forces commenced their attack but suffered heavy losses at the hands of the Bulgarians at the Battle of Doiran. The Franco Serbian force maintained a vigorous attack

Allied shipping in Mudros Harbour.

and the Bulgarians began to pull back and in some cases they were surrendering their positions without a fight. The Bulgarian Command then ordered a retreat; this was not yet a rout but an ordered retreat. German forces were brought up to stiffen resistance, especially since the Skopje

had fallen to the Allies. But soon the mass of retreating and deserting Bulgarians had converged on the railway centre of Radomir just thirty miles from the capital Sofia. On 27 September the Bulgarian Agrarian National Union took control of the mutinous troops and proclaimed the overthrow of the monarchy. There were about 4–5,000 rebellious troops who then threatened Sofia and so the Bulgarian delegation arrived at Thessaloniki to ask for an armistice. On 29 September, with the armistice agreed by the French General d'Esperey, the Bulgarians left the war and the Tsar Ferdinand I abdicated and went into exile on 3 October.

The squadrons based in the Northern Aegean were employed in artillery observation, bombing, reconnaissance and Army co-operation. The roles shown against the squadrons listed above tell the story about their involvement. Only at Mudros were the units employed on maritime reconnaissance and anti-submarine duties. The concentration of Allied shipping in the harbour only serves to emphasize the importance of Allied air units in the Northern Aegean.

Chapter 6
Operations of the Independent Bomber Force in 1918

Trenchard's arguments for strategic bombing and Hankey's reply – the IBF its aircraft and operations – results of air raids on Germany and German occupied France – results of bombing on selected towns and industrial areas – an overview of the effects of the bombing.

INTRODUCTION

This last chapter of Part I is devoted to the strategic employment of air power. Since this work is titled *The Birth of the Royal Air Force*, it is nonetheless important to go beyond 1 April 1918 to consider the work of the Independent Bomber Force of the RFC/RAF. The operations of the IBF would have a profound influence on the thinking of the senior ranks of the newly formed RAF during the inter-war years and would result in a bias in favour of the bomber as opposed to the fighter. Led by Air Marshal Trenchard, the importance of carrying the war to the enemy from the outset of hostilities would become dogma. Operational exercises during the 1920s and 1930s would be slanted in favour of the offence over the defence and it was held that the bomber would always get through. Yet when the RAF went to war in 1939 its bombs and the training of bombing crews were found wanting and World War I vintage biplane bombers still equipped RAF bomber squadrons as late as 1937. The four-engined bombers that would eventually carry the war to the enemy had not, in 1939, entered squadron service.

Taken to an extreme, one could argue that the employment of air power alone could result in a successful outcome in a war. It goes without saying that the Army and Royal Navy would strongly refute such an assertion but there is an explanation for Trenchard's overstatement of his case, in the early post-war years, in favour of the strategic use of air power. Admiral Beatty, for the Admiralty, and General Wilson, for the Imperial General Staff, simply did not see the need for an independent air force and demanded the return of the aircraft taken off them on 1 April 1918. General Wilson firmly believed that aircraft should be employed tactically in direct support of the land forces fighting the war on the ground and that air squadrons should come under direct command and control of Army force commanders. Similarly, naval commanders, particularly of fleets at sea, wished to have operational control of all air units on board aircraft carriers and warships. Faced, therefore, with possibility of the RAF being still-born, Trenchard had to exhibit more than a belief in the offensive use of air power. He was driven to exaggerate the RAF's case to impress upon the government that it was only an independent air force that could take the war to the enemy. Sir Maurice Hankey, the Secretary to the Chiefs

of Staff Committee, would have occasion to question the sometimes extravagant claims made by Trenchard about the effectiveness of air operations in France and Belgium during World War I. The content of Hankey's letter is discussed and may be compared with the accounts, which follow, of IBF bombing raids and the assessment of their effectiveness in impeding the enemy's war effort during the last year of the Great War.

Hankey's argument

Trenchard had published a paper entitled 'The war object of an Air Force', and it appeared to Hankey that Trenchard regarded his document as settled doctrine. It seemed to suggest, amongst other things, that an air force alone could bring hostilities in war to a successful conclusion. Hankey felt that Trenchard would be better advised to treat his paper as a discussion document for consideration by the Chiefs of Staff Committee before settling doctrine. Hankey expressed his views in two private letters to Trenchard dated 28 April 1928. The first of these letters gave advice on how Trenchard should proceed to have his case heard before anything was set down in the RAF War Manual and that he should not attempt to settle the matter in one meeting since the Army and the Navy would wish to mull over what Trenchard was proposing.

It was in the second letter of the day that Hankey wrote to Trenchard, not in his capacity as Secretary to the Chiefs of Staff Committee, but as one man giving his personal view. Where the former found himself in disagreement was in the matter of the actual power of the air and its morale effect. He regarded the effective radius of bombing aircraft as being strictly limited. Only at the very end of the war did Handley Page produce the HP1500, which could reach Berlin from bases in eastern England. Since they entered service too late to be used operationally, their effectiveness could not be measured. Hankey could only refer to bombing operations during the war. Assuming that the figure was between 200 and 250 miles an enemy's factories, supplies and communications outside that radius would be immune to bombing attacks. Indeed, in the approach to World War II some of these facilities in the United Kingdom were moved out of range of Heinkel bombers operating from the Continent. The RAF's experimental establishments and factories producing aircraft provide examples.

Beyond the effective radius the physical and morale effect of bombing would be small. He further asserted that the morale of Londoners would not be affected by bombing attacks on Hull. To counter an argument that aircraft would in time have greater range and speed he asserted that aircraft would then become larger and more expensive. In response to the increased threat from more powerful bombers an enemy's munitions and supply works would become ever more scattered and one would not know where to mount a decisive blow. The greater the threat from bombers the greater would be the need to divert production from bombers to fighters. If Trenchard believed that the bomber would always get through then that would apply equally to an enemy's bombers. The further the penetration of bombing aircraft over an enemy's territory the greater the opportunities for fighter interceptors. Even within a country's radius of action, said Hankey, an enemy could camouflage his factories, airfields etc.

Hankey then used instances of the British use of air power during the Great War within the radius of action. Field Marshal Haig, commanding the British Army on the Western Front, was determined to continue the Battle of Flanders in spite of appalling losses of life. When asked why the RFC squadrons under his command could not move the battle in the Allies' favour by assisting in the capturing of a ridge from which British forces could bombard the Roulers/Thooroet Railway, Haig replied that the employment of air forces for this purpose was perfectly useless. Then there was the case of the canal connecting Bruges to Zeebrugge This canal was used by destroyers and submarines and a scouting aircraft could easily spot shipping movements along the canal and call up bombing aircraft, which could sink such ships and block the canal. Hankey said that, to the best of his knowledge, there was not one instance of this happening. For our part, he said, the enemy never denied our use of Dunkirk nor were there any instances of interference with shipping in the Thames and concentrations of merchant shipping on the Downs. When attacks were carried out against merchant shipping the enemy nearly always missed their targets. Hankey also referred to a bridge in the Lille region for which the Army wanted its use denied to the Germans. All attempts to destroy the bridge by bombing failed and the enemy continued to use the bridge. There were plenty of shell holes on the river banks but the bridge was never hit. This implied that RFC and German aircrews lacked shooting skills and could not bomb with any accuracy.

Turning to the morale effect, Hankey actually accused Trenchard of 'an abuse of language' when the latter said that the morale effect was overwhelming. One could not say that there was ever a widespread drop in morale. There might be localized cases of panic, which could affect disciplined members of the armed forces as much

as civilians. Bombing could actually stiffen resistance and a determination to withstand the enemy's attempts to break the national will. He cited the experience of French peasants and villagers whom he had witnessed in the war zone and who continued with their daily activities.

On 2 May Trenchard replied, stating that he was not offended by Hankey's frank opinions and although he did not agree with everything that Hankey was saying, he was nevertheless obliged to admit that he may have overstated his case. His view was changed by an admission that the RAF had more work to do to show the sister services what the junior service could do in a major European war. He then asserted that what he had been saying applied to air policing in the outposts of Empire when Hankey was talking about a major European conflict.

The content of Hankey's letter may then be compared with the official reports of the operations of No.8 Brigade RFC and the Independent Bomber Force, which was commanded by Trenchard after he had relinquished the post of Chief of the Air Staff following policy disagreements with Lord Rothermere, the Air Secretary.

THE INDEPENDENT BOMBING FORCE (IBF) – ITS AIRCRAFT AND OPERATIONS
Source: National Archive document AIR 1/109/15/17/1

INTRODUCTION
The predecessors of the IBF were No.41 Wing and No.8 Brigade RFC, both practising a degree of strategic bombing, but neither were serious attempts to form a force under one commander who could make a real difference to the outcome of the war by sustained bombing of industrial and railway targets in Germany and German-occupied France, and also to help lower the morale of the civilian population. Major General Trenchard, who had briefly been Chief of the Air Staff of the newly created RAF, had resigned this post over differences with Lord Rothermere, the Air Secretary. But Trenchard was too important in the realm of military flying to be left at a loose end, redundant so to speak. So he was appointed to command the IBF, which was formed on 6 June 1918.

The period 1 January 1918 to 11 November 1918, the day the Great War ended, covers operations by No.8 Brigade RFC and on the formation of the RAF on 1 April 1918 the operations of the Independent Force. No.8 Brigade had been under the tactical command of Field Marshal Haig, C-in-C the BEF. But it was decided to place the IBF under an independent commander. And Trenchard had been impressed with the work of the Brigade and its constituent units were absorbed into the new force with the addition of fresh bombing squadrons. Tactical command of No.8 Brigade passed from Haig to Trenchard who was then answerable to Sir William Weir, the new British Air Minister, even by-passing the Chief of the Air Staff, Frederick Sykes. The IBF was based in the Metz/Nancy area, well to the south of the British Sector of the Western Front. This was so that the force, whose aircraft had a limited range of some 350 to 400 miles could reach their intended targets The conurbations, industrial sites and railway centres targeted were cities such as Cologne, Bonn, Coblenz and Frankfort-am-Main (or Frankfurt-am-main, German spelling), the industrial sites were those producing poison gas, iron ore etc., and the important railway centres of Metz, Thionville, Treves and Saarbrücken.

AIRCRAFT OF THE INDEPENDENT BOMBING FORCE – AUGUST 1918

The quality of the Allied aircraft that attacked strategic targets in Germany and German-occupied France is considered. With the exception of the Handley Page O/400, the Independent Bombing Force (IBF) was equipped with bombers that mounted a pilot and observer/gunner and looked no different from two-seat fighters or reconnaissance machines of the day. The aircraft in question had the following characteristics:

HPO/400

The main difference between the HPO/100 and the HPO/400 was that the latter had its fuel tanks transferred from the engine nacelles to the fuselage. The HPO/400 was introduced into service in April 1917. This bomber was equipped with progressively more powerful engines. A typical O/400 had two 360hp Rolls-Royce Eagle VIII water cooled V-type engines. Its maximum speed was 97.5mph at sea level, its service ceiling was of 8,500ft and it had an endurance of 8 hours. Provided an aircraft was not diverted by weather or enemy action this would give it a range of between 350 and 400 miles. Bomb loads carried by this aircraft included the 1,650lb bomb such as the one that demolished the SAA factory at Kaiserslautern on 21/22 October 1918 (see photographs).

DH4

The DH4 was designed at the outset as a high-speed day bomber. The prototype was flown in August 1916 and was powered by a 160hp BHP engine. It was comfortable and an easy aeroplane to fly, but the main drawback was the positioning of the fuel tank between the pilot and observer. This made it vulnerable to enemy fire and inhibited communication between the two men. The maximum speed at 6,500ft was 117mph. The service ceiling was 16,000ft and it had an endurance of 3hrs 30min. The RNAS on the whole made more varied use of the ability of the DH4 to outfly and climb above enemy fighters and it could therefore operate without an escort.

DH9 and 9A

The DH9 was intended to undertake the daylight bombing of Germany. Although it had pleasant handling qualities it was beset by engine problems and its performance was inferior to the DH4 that it was intend to replace. Although the DH9 received large-scale production orders, it remained a problem aircraft even with new engines. There were engine failures and the fact that the DH9 gave as much service as it did is a tribute to the perseverance of its air and ground crews. It had a forward-firing Vickers gun and a Scarff-mounted Lewis gun for the observer. It could carry (though it seldom did) two 230lb bombs or four 112lb bombs internally but these were most often suspended from racks beneath the fuselage or lower wings. The DH9A differed substantially in that it was powered by the American 400hp Liberty 12 engine. The wings of the DH9A were larger to offset the bigger and heavier engine. The very bulky engine gave the DH9A a very large unstreamlined appearance with a huge flat radiator over which the pilots had to sight his gun and see his way forward. Although the DH9a did see service during the Great War, it was to be the mainstay of the air policing operations mounted in the outposts of Empire in the inter-war years. The armament and bomb load was the same as that of the DH9. The maximum speed was 123mph at sea level and the service ceiling was 16,750ft. The endurance of the DH9A was 5hrs 15min, which gave it an operational range of approximately 320 miles.

The Sopwith Camel

This was a highly successful British fighter of the Great War and was included in the strength of the IBF for escort purposes. Its maximum speed was 104mph at 10,000ft and it had a service ceiling of 18,000ft. The endurance was 2hrs 30min.

OPERATIONS OF THE IBF

No.41 Wing was split into two wings to form No.8 Brigade RFC. No.41 Wing comprised Nos.55, 99 and 104 Squadrons of day bombers, whilst No.83 Wing comprised Nos.100 and 216 Night Bombing squadrons. Additional squadrons were added before the Armistice and these

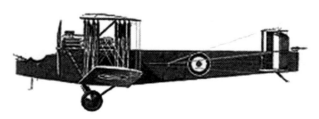

HP1500 four-engined bomber.

were Nos.97, 115 and 215 Squadrons, which went to No.83 Wing, and Nos.45 and 110 Squadrons constituted No.88 Wing.

Had the Armistice not intervened the IBF would have been a much larger force and would have included the new four-engined HP1500 bomber, which could fly from bases in eastern England to bomb Berlin (pictured on the preceding page). But this was not to be and the success of strategic bombing had to be judged on the operations carried out in six short months. This is important because the material effects of the bombing will be modest and would have been unlikely to bring the German Government to sue for peace. The morale effect was, however, very marked. The operations of the IBF began when twelve DH4s of No.55 Squadron and eleven DH4s of No.99 Squadron attacked rail targets at Thionville. By 11 November 1918 the IBF had dropped a total of 550 tons of bombs, 390 tons of which were dropped at night. Over 220 tons of bombs were dropped on German aerodromes, which Trenchard justified on the grounds that whilst the Germans were stronger in the air, their aircraft might be destroyed on the ground. He added that, during the period of IBF operations, no British aircraft were destroyed on the ground.

The nine bombing squadrons and the one fighter escort squadron of Camel fighters did not get it all their own way. The cost to the British was 109 aircraft lost. Reference has already been made to the effectiveness of the DH4 as a day bomber, which had the power to climb out of trouble if German fighters were encountered. To ward off enemy fighters the aircraft would fly in arrowhead to concentrate the fire of the formation on enemy aircraft sent to intercept them.

The official report of the operations of the IBF, like that dated 21 July 1918, was very bullish. Understandably, Trenchard and his officers wished to impress upon the

DH4s in arrowhead formation.

Service chiefs and HM Government that the activities of force would cause real damage to the enemy's capacity to carry on the fight and so hasten the end of the war. Claims made of damage inflicted on enemy targets were often backed by photographic reconnaissance. Nevertheless, these should be contrasted with reports compiled with the help of town mayors and local officials, as well as evidence gleaned from captured letters. The IBF report states that since the formation of the Force on 6 June, 474 raids had been carried out upon objectives in enemy occupation, including factories, railways, aerodromes and points of strategic importance. The report continues by saying that the enemy has been incalculably hampered in his transport arrangements and the greatest confusion has been caused to him. There is a clear mismatch on this claim since the railway authorities planned diversion routes to avoid bombed railway junctions and even a bombed bridge could be repaired in forty-eight hours. If anything, the greatest delays were caused by air raid warnings when trains might be held, sometimes for hours, outside stations, which were often the target. Yes, the enemy did have to divert resources from the front, such as anti-aircraft artillery and fighter aircraft, but that was to be expected. The force results for four days in the period that follow do say that they are 'approximate' and the dates given may be compared with the reports compiled after the war for the same dates, which appear later in this chapter.

The period 04.00hrs 31 July to 04.00hrs on 1 August 1918

By day the atmosphere was misty with a few detached low clouds. During darkness there was a little high cloud and thick mist. No.55 Squadron's DH4s attacked factories, station and barracks at Coblenz. The bombs ranged from those which weighed 230lb, 112lb, 40lb and 25lb. When No.99 Squadron attacked Vergaville aerodrome and Saarbrücken, observation was impossible due to the cloud cover but when No.104 Squadron attacked the factories and railway sidings at Saarbrücken bursts were observed on the factory. One enemy aircraft was shot down and one driven down. Seven RAF aircraft missing and 2,299 rounds had been fired.

The period 04.00hrs 21 August to 04.00 hrs on 22 August 1918

Some 8½ tons of bombs were dropped during the night by HPO/400s of Nos.97, 100 and 216 Squadrons. Nos.97 and 100 Squadrons concentrated their attacks on the airfields of Buhl, Morhange and Lorquin. Bomb bursts were observed near hangars and six on huts, causing a fire at Morhange, whereas at Buhl direct hits were observed on hangars. No.216 Squadron attacked the railway stations at Cologne and Frankfurt-am-main, the aerodrome at Boulay and the railway junction at Treves. At Cologne four direct hits were observed on the railway, and a 550lb

DH4.

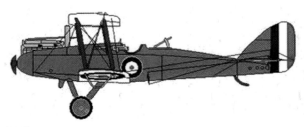

DH9.

DH9A.

Sopwith Camel.

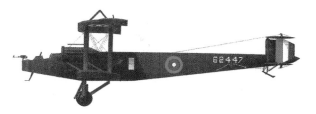

HPO/400.

bomb was seen to burst close to the station, making a very large explosion. Good bursts were observed in the vicinity of the station and on the sidings at Frankfurt. Good results were obtained at Boulay, two direct hits were observed on hangars and one on a searchlight. Some 5,544 rounds were fired and one RAF aircraft was missing. During this period enemy machines dropped eleven bombs on Baccarat and two machines dropped eight bombs in the area of Xafféville, the base of three squadrons of No.83 Wing, and some enemy machines dropped some bombs on Epinal.

The period 04.00hrs on 2 September to 04.00hrs on 3 September 1918
Some 24 tons of bombs were dropped in total, some during the day of 2 September, the remainder during the

night. During the day No.55 Squadron concentrated its bombs on Buhl aerodrome. These were 230lb, 112lb and 25lb bombs. In the morning raids, bursts were observed on and around hangars. There was one direct hit on two machines, one of which was completely destroyed. Direct hits were observed on hangars and sheds. The afternoon raids resulted in bursts on and around hangars, with fire in one hangar. The night raids were carried out by four of the HPO/400 squadrons of No.83 Wing. Nos.97 and 100 Squadrons attacked Buhl and Boulay aerodromes respectively. Good bursts were observed and two fires started at Buhl. No.215 Squadron attacked Buhl and the railway junction at Ehrange with 112lb and 25lb bombs. Three hangars were demolished at Buhl and Ehrange was bombed from 90ft, resulting in many direct hits. No.216 Squadron attacked the Burbach Works, the railway station at Saarbrücken and Boulay with a mixture of 550lb and 112lb bombs. Two hits were obtained on the Burbach Works, starting a very large fire and some smaller ones.

The period 0400 hrs on 10 November to 04.00 hrs on 11 November 1918
Some 9 tons of bombs were dropped on this last day of the Great War. The attacks were on the railway sidings at Ehrange and four enemy aerodromes. Suffice to say that one RAF aircraft did not return.

CONSTITUENT ELEMENTS OF THE FORCE – 11 NOVEMBER 1918
(Pictured on the preceding page)

Formation Squadron	Aircraft	Base
No.41 Wing		
No.55 Sqn	DH4	Azelot
No.99 Sqn DH9	DH4	
No.104 Sqn DH9	DH4	
No.83 Wing		
No.97 Sqn	HPO/400	Xaffévillers
No.100 Sqn	HPO/400	Xaffévillers
No.115 Sqn	HPO/400	St Ingelvert
No.215 Sqn	HPO/400	Xaffévillers
No.216 Sqn	HPO/400	Rovilles-aux-Chenes
No.88 Wing		
No.45 Sqn	Camel	Bettencourt
No.110 Sqn	DH9A	Bettencourt

NOTES
No.45 Squadron of Camel fighters provided escort cover for the bombers. The only one of these aircraft that looked remotely like a bomber was the HPO/400. But it was the Royal Navy that was first to use a Handley Page bomber on strategic bomber missions. They called it the 'bloody paralyser'. There were lorry parks, aircraft parks, an aircraft depot, an air ammunition column and an aeroplane supply depot that provided support to the operational squadrons and were an integral part of the force.

RESULTS OF AIR RAIDS ON GERMANY JANUARY 1 – NOVEMBER 11 1918
Source: National Archive document AIR/1/2104, Experiences of bombing of the IBF in 1918 by Wing Commander J.E.A. Baldwin

Introduction
The reports contained in this document were divided into three editions dated August and October 1918, with the third edition being compiled in January 1920. In order to assess the effectiveness of Allied bombing on strategic targets in Germany and German-occupied France the reliability of reports was important. The Allied raids were judged under two headings, i.e., the material and morale effect. The official German reports often understated both these effects for it was important that the morale of the general public did not suffer. But hiding the true effects might work for those far removed from areas being subjected to bombing. It was a different matter for those directly affected. German censorship of newspapers was very strict and references to Allied bombing were very scarce and incomplete.

First edition (August 1918)
The assessment of the material effect of Allied bombing relied heavily on photographs taken on the day or on the day following the raid and these often provided exact evidence as to the accuracy of the bombing. The morale effect was assessed in a number of ways. Letters captured on German prisoners painted a picture of an unsettled and terrified populace. Those who received these letters could well be demoralized by what they had read. It was also believed by the British commanders that the morale of the German population became lower as the range and power of Allied bombing squadrons increased. Neutral observers with a first-rate knowledge of Germany believed that the people were accustomed to being disciplined and rationed in everything but could not understand why the German Government was unable to prevent the bombing raids. The populace felt powerless in face of invasion from the air. There was a public outcry following the raids on Cologne, the huge chemical works at Ludwigshafen and the destruction of the goods station at Thionville. In spite of official German censorship there was an accumulation of evidence from all quarters of Germany, which provided indisputable evidence of the efficacy of air raids during this period.

Second edition (October 1918)
During the period August to October 1918 a large number of letters found on captured prisoners bore witness to the morale effect of Allied bombing. The fighting value of the recipients of these letters could be expected to decline. To meet the public concern about the powerlessness in the face an aerial invasion, there was the urgent need for the provision of air defence squadrons, anti-aircraft batteries, searchlights and balloons and these would be a serious drain on the German economy. Though material damage was then slight compared with the morale effect, the lowering of public morale could in turn affect output before the destruction of factories could be achieved.

Third edition (January 1920)
On the cessation of hostilities it was decided to send a small commission to investigate the results of air raids and the organization of the enemy's countermeasures. It was discovered that copies of plans, documents and photographs relative to air raids on factories, stations and industrial centres had been retained for the local archives by civilian and municipal authorities. As regards counter measures it was found rather difficult to obtain information as all the military directly concerned had left and taken all documents with them. The information is therefore, in some cases, largely hearsay, and in consequence possibly exaggerated or belittled.

THE EFFECTS OF THE BOMBING ARE NOW DEALT WITH UNDER THE FOLLOWING HEADINGS:

a. Railways
b. Blast furnaces
c. Chemical works
d. Industrial centres

RAILWAYS

The report begins by saying that the material damage to railway stations was moderate on the whole but that in specific instances very considerable damage had been inflicted. Apart from the expenditure of large sums of money, the repair work had caused an enormous amount of confusion and delay in the normal working of traffic and the enemy spared no pains to ensure the smooth circulation of traffic. The railway buildings that were damaged were, more than any other, the locomotive sheds and accompanying workshops. Railway officials stated that during the period 1917–18 the difficulties of repairing locomotives became so acute that the very seriously damaged ones had to be considered a 'write-off'. Cases where locomotives were still awaiting repair went back to September 1917. The same remarks applied to rolling stock, large quantities of which were destroyed. A railway official stated that damaged trucks were often taken to add cover to existing dugouts. Officials also stated that several cases occurred of bombs falling on vast quantities of stores piled up at or near stations. These stores were either seriously damaged or were completely burned out. This can be seen in the raid on Thionville with burned out ammunition wagons featured in the foreground.

To what extent traffic was interrupted was considered next in the report and was classed under two headings, that caused by damage and that caused by alarms.

The raid on Thionville 16 July 1918.

From conversations with railway officials, signalmen and linesmen interruption caused by bombing was not very great. To achieve maximum disruption the damage should occur at points where tracks converged or to the track itself. Diversion schemes had been worked out so that traffic could avoid sections of damaged track, but if a vital point had been hit, such as a bridge spanning a river, delay could be anything up to forty-eight hours. Interruption caused by the alarm being sounded could be serious. Sometimes trains were held up outside a station for hours. At night all lights had to be extinguished and the progress of all trains in the vicinity had to slow down, which could cause delay over the whole system. At Saarbrücken, for example, the railway authorities stated that whenever a raid took place, stoppage of traffic for two hours invariably ensued.

BLAST FURNACES

With few exceptions the directors of works stated that damage to works had not been very great. The damage, such as there was, was confined to masonry, roofs, gas pipes, windows, blowing engines, coke ovens etc. The works, on the whole, were huge, the roof consisting of massive slabs of concrete and glass, 6cm thick. Examples of the cost of repairs to four leading steelworks are taken from the archives of the respective works.

Burbach	488,100 marks
Carlshütte	66,000 marks
Dillinge	300,000 marks
Rombach	170,000 marks

Instances of the loss of production as a result of bomb damage were few in number. Yet again, as with the railways, alarms caused the greatest disturbance. Once the alarm had been sounded work had to be stopped and the furnaces would sometimes get cold so that both the quality and the quantity were adversely affected. The mental state of the workmen might also be affected but it was not possible to estimate to what extent it affected output. Obviously, the material effect could reinforce the morale effect and vice versa. From the archives of the Roechling Works at Voelklingen the number of alarms reached their peak of fifty in August 1918. The estimated cost of repairs reached its peak of 36,240 marks in May before dropping back, peaking again in September at 23,798 marks. (British factories would shut down during an air raid in the Battle of Britain in 1940 and the workmen would take to the shelters provided, but after a while they simply donned their steel helmets on hearing the alarm and continue working unless and until enemy aircraft were actually overhead.) A comparison with the same period in 1917 is revealing. In March 1917 there were three raids and six false alarms and a record amount of damage was sustained by the Roechling Works. In August 1918 there were fifty alarms but no raids took place yet the deficit in production was 2,881 tons, more than double that of March 1917. This clearly points to the effectiveness on morale. Figures for the Mannesmann works at Bous point to the same conclusion. The manager of those works was definite; there had been no noteworthy falling off in the number of employees nor had he been forced to limit production due to a lack of raw materials.

The conclusion that can be reached for 1918 is that more production was lost from alarms than from bomb damage. This situation reached its peak in 1918 since hardly a night passed without an air raid warning. It was not unusual for the alarm to be given half an hour before the arrival of Allied bombing aircraft. On receipt of the alarm everyone took to the shelters, where they remained until the 'all clear' was given. In the summertime this could mean that production had to cease from 20.30hrs until 04.30hrs the following morning. Bous, the home of the Mannesmann Works, experienced 293 alarms during the year but was bombed only seven times during the entire war. Works closer to the front would therefore lose even more production.

CHEMICAL WORKS

The Director of the Badische Anilin und Soda Fabrik, Herr Julius, stated that the material damage both from a military and destructive point of view had been small. A large proportion of the bombs having burst between the buildings, little or no damage was done except to pipes. No signs of any extensive damage or repairs were seen. The chief engineer said that, generally speaking, the damage caused had never been of such a formidable nature that repair had been impossible and such damage that was caused was annoying and entailed extra labour, but did not affect the output of the factory in any way. The director stated that the total output from a military point of view was never once diminished and only on one occasion was the work stopped due to damage done and this occurred at the Oppau Works. The Badische Anilin und Soda Fabrik was never forced to stop work owing to damage sustained during air raids. The moonlight periods appear to have affected the works on occasions, and during such time the output was certainly reduced by two or more hours, but it was always made up.

INDUSTRIAL CENTRES

Most of the factors that applied to factories applied to industrial centres. However, the mayors of most industrial towns stated that their populations were exhorted to take no notice of night alarms,   until they were told that their built-up areas were on the Allied bombing list. Even though there might be the distant sound of anti-aircraft guns, there was no provision for transmitting air raid warnings. It had been hoped to delay the drop in morale that would result from hours spent at night in

the cellar. Whether this policy had the desired effect is doubtful. The policy had to be reviewed in towns such as Neustadt, which had not been subjected to bombing. In those towns, such as Metz, that had been subjected to bombing raids the populace took to their cellars on just a rumour that an attack was imminent.

The conurbations that were most affected as long-distance raids increased in number, were those such as Düsseldorf, Frankfurt and Cologne. They became more liable to actual attacks, which made the effects of constant alarms most apparent. The mayors of these towns did admit that the morale effects of air raids was considerable. Both rich and poor were affected alike. Health suffered following nights spent either in cellars or dugouts and there was an influenza epidemic. The authorities were obliged to put up placards and posters exhorting the populace to keep calm. Unless damage was serious people did remain calm but once there were deaths then panic could become general.

Once it was realized that the government could not put a stop to the air raids those affected by bomb damage made compensation claims. This was at first ignored even though the government was bombarded with claims and this caused a great deal of dissatisfaction, particularly in Saarbrücken. The government then produced a form for those affected by bombing. If the amount of damage exceeded 15,000 marks payment was deferred until a more convenient date. For those whose claims were below that amount they were to receive immediate settlement. In the event the payments were not prompt and the government was in no doubt of the public's deep dissatisfaction. The town authorities were also outraged at having to pay out the sums claimed. Dissatisfaction was particularly high in Saarbrücken and Ludwigshafen. The sources of this information were the mayors of Saarbrücken, Kaiserslautern and Landau.

This damage to the SAA factory at Kaiserlautern on 21/22 October 1918 was caused by a 1,650lb bomb.

General view of the South Wing.

The photograph above depicts the damage sustained by a factory in Kaiserslautern producing small arms ammunition.

The town mayors of those localities that did contain military objectives, raised objections to the siting of AA guns and searchlights since it was the general opinion that these would simply invite the attention of Allied bombing squadrons, which may explain why the military authorities proposed siting air defences in those localities that contained no military objectives but were, nevertheless, likely to receive the attention of the bombers. The military prevailed over the opinions of the local populations and the installation of AA guns and searchlights went ahead.

Two cases are of interest in this context and concerned Landau and Wiesbaden. Up until May 1918 Landau had never been bombed. The Mayor appeared to forget that the barracks and station were used by the military and that the recent bombing attack had not been deliberate. The public did not want AA defences for the reasons advanced above and only wished to be left alone. In spite of these public protests AA defences were installed to be followed by two more raids. The second raid was on 30 June 1918 and the Mayor's own observations led him to believe that this raid was not intended to hit Landau. Before any bombs fell the Mayor could hear repeated machine gun fire. He deduced that this fire deterred the Allied bombers from attacking another target and they got rid of their bombs over Landau in their hasty retreat. Wiesbaden had not suffered an air attack until October 1918 but towards the end of July the military placed three AA batteries on the surrounding hills. The idea was to co-operate in the air defence of Mainz and Blebrich and

secondly to protect the town. According to the Mayor, the public was enraged at this deployment. The firing of the AA batteries on the night of 22/23 October was followed thirty minutes later by an aircraft that, it was believed, had been attracted to Wiesbaden by the sound of the AA guns. AA defences were unpopular since it was believed that the defences themselves rendered the defended areas more likely to be attacked.

Conclusions

From this evidence alone it is impossible to state the likelihood of any locality to be subjected to air attack. The public reaction to the siting of AA guns in the locality was irrational if understandable. One cannot be sure about the reaction of Allied aircrews to the siting of AA defences without asking them. The mayors can only have guessed what that reaction might have been. From this evidence it can be deduced that claims for damages were considerable and that the populace simply wanted to be left in peace. AA defences only reminded them that they were vulnerable and the fact that the initial siting of AA defences was followed by bombing confirmed their view that the defences attracted bombers. If bombers attacking one target could be made to switch targets at the last moment it would make sense if there were initial and

Damage caused by a 112lb bomb.

A 230lb bomb crater – Hagondange.

secondary targets allocated to attacking squadrons prior to take-off. What follows, is a description of bombing raids on specific targets.

Assessment

For bombing operations to be successful the attacking aircraft needed the right weather, an ability to ward off defending fighters, or the ability to outclimb them and good luck in staying out of the beam of searchlights and the reach of AA guns. The most powerful bomber, the HPO/400, had a comparatively low top speed and service ceiling, which rendered it vulnerable to fighters and AA fire. The DH4 was nimble and could climb out of trouble but carried only a light bomb load. The DH9 and 9A had a moderately heavy bomb load. The DH9A had a good maximum speed and service ceiling. Both aircraft could climb out of trouble. The operational radius of the attacking units was, by today's standards, very modest, which explains the choice of the airfields in the Metz/Nancy area close to the intended targets. With the best will in the world the total bomb load that could be dropped on selected targets in one night, even if they did hit their intended targets, was unlikely to bring the Central Powers to the point of military collapse. The details of the bombing of selected targets that follow will show that the morale effect will be more important than the material effect. The effects of both 112lb and 230lb bombs is illustrated in the photographs.

DETAILS OF BOMBING OPERATIONS AGAINST SPECIFIC TARGETS

BONN (DATE OF RAID 31 OCTOBER 1918)

The official British report on this raid stated that weather conditions were bad. In spite of this the attacking aircraft flew through low clouds and rain to reach Bonn where the railway station in the centre of town was attacked. The official German report stated that the material damage was of small importance but twenty-six people were killed, thirty-six severely wounded and twenty slightly wounded. According to the Mayor's report considerable damage was caused to a number of houses, particularly glass panes in the houses of the quarter attacked. The figures for killed and injured were very close to those contained in the official report.

COBLENZ (DATES OF RAIDS – 12 MARCH, 20/21 MAY, 6 JUNE, 2 JULY, 5 JULY AND 22 AUGUST 1918)

Raid of 12 March

The official British report stated that this was the third raid within the preceding four days. On this occasion the targets were the factories, station and barracks in the town. Over a ton of bombs was dropped and bursts were seen on all the objectives, causing two fires. A hit on a building in the south-west corner of the town created a very large explosion. The official German report stated that the town was attacked at about midday and about ten bombs were dropped in different quarters, which caused material damage, and, unfortunately, there were

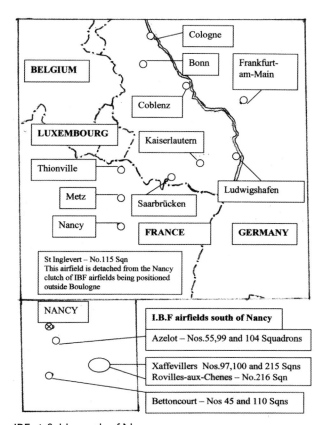

IBF airfields south of Nancy.

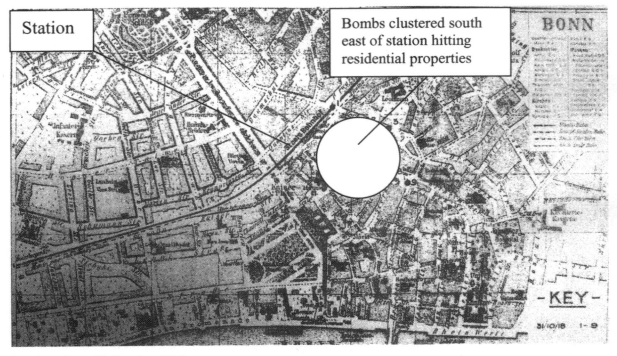

Station

Bombs clustered south east of station hitting residential properties

BONN

- KEY -

31/10/18   1 - 9

Attack on Bonn 31 October 1918.

several casualties. According to the Mayor's report one bomb fell on the Friedrich barracks amongst a company of soldiers, killing four and wounding twelve. A government automobile shed was hit and damaged. Another bomb landed in front of the post office, causing serious damage and a total of seventy people were killed or wounded. With regard to the morale effect the Mayor did admit to panic amongst the civilian population. In spite of their being advised how to behave during an air raid, this advice was not heeded and numerous casualties were caused in the ensuing panic. A reliable report from a French source confirmed the cases of panic and well-to-do-families had taken refuge in Bavaria and Saxony.

Raid of 20/21 May
The official British report stated simply that bombs were dropped on the stations in Coblenz. On the other hand, the German report published the following day stated that there had been only slight material damage and that there were no reports of casualties. The Mayor's report, however, stated that the railway between Coblenz Moselweiss station and the Guls railway bridge were seriously damaged, rendering the line useless for two hours. Four bombs fell in the Kartause barracks, causing considerable damage, another bomb burst in the street beside the courtyard of the Pioneer barracks and considerable damage was caused to private property.

Raid of 6 June
The official British report stated simply that the railway station at Coblenz was heavily bombed and good bursts were observed. The German official report stated that ten enemy planes attacked the city, dropping fifteen bombs. As a result of effective air defences no bombs fell within the town. The Mayor's report of the material effects of the raid differs somewhat from the official report. One bomb had dropped on a building material depot. The reservoir tower behind the despatching office for express goods at the main railway station was damaged. Three bombs fell in the barracks north-west of the main railway station, causing damage to masonry and the officers' mess. Private property was also damaged.

Raid of 2 July
The British report stated that bombs were dropped on the railway sidings and sheds at Coblenz with good results. The Germans replied that shortly before noon raiders dropped a few bombs on Coblenz, which did some damage. Actually, these fell in the harbour situated on the left bank of the Moselle, causing damage to tugs and barges. A building material depot and a wood depot also suffered hits, as well as tram lines and tramcars. Considerable damage was caused to private property.

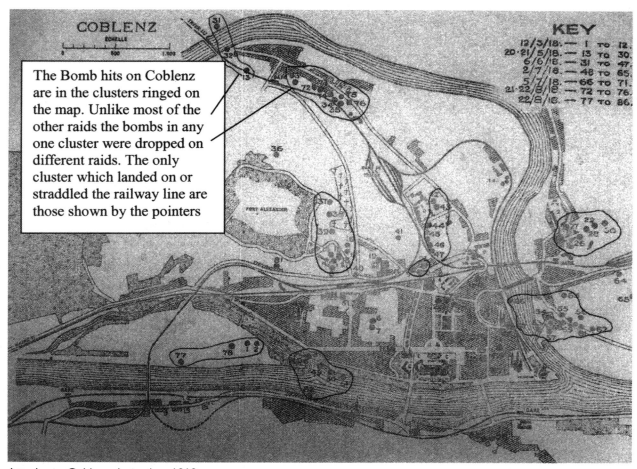

The Bomb hits on Coblenz are in the clusters ringed on the map. Unlike most of the other raids the bombs in any one cluster were dropped on different raids. The only cluster which landed on or straddled the railway line are those shown by the pointers

Attacks on Coblenz during late 1918.

Raid of 5 July

The railway station was attacked again. The British described it as heavy; the Germans stated that 'some' damage was done. In the official report it was stated that the raid caused considerable damage chiefly to public buildings such as the printing office of a local newspaper. Eight people were wounded as considerable damage was caused to the streets. A captured letter described the population as terrified. This letter, dated 6 July, reported the raid as follows: 'Thank God we are all still well. We have lived through terrible hours. Yesterday we were obliged to go into the cellar. The ground trembled so I thought our last hour had come. Thank God Nina and the child are safe. If only this miserable war was at an end.'

Raid of 22 August

The last report of raids on the city of Coblenz spoke of an Allied squadron attacking railway sidings with good

results. The Germans stated that, in spite of heavy anti-aircraft fire ten bombs were dropped, causing material damage. Two people were killed and two injured. The actual damage was to an aqueduct, which was pierced by a bomb, and considerable damage was done to private property. A captured letter said, 'that the airmen were here again. I am quite ill with worry'.

COLOGNE (DATES OF RAIDS – 24/25 MARCH, 18 MAY AND 21/22 AUGUST 1918)

Raid of 24/25 March

The British official report stated that half a ton of bombs was dropped on the railway station where a fire was started. In contrast, the German report stated that eight bombs were dropped but the airmen were warned off from the inner city by gunfire and the extinguishing of the lights. The only object hit was a pile of timber, which caught fire. Captured letters added a few more details.

One spoke of a wood store 50 metres north of the south bridge, which was set alight. Another spoke of houses that were set on fire. A reliable source spoke of the morale effect. Much more damage was done than was admitted and the population was much affected. The air raids were much dreaded and created dissatisfaction and panic with which the authorities found it increasingly difficult to cope.

Raid of 18 May

The official British report spoke of a most successful raid, which was carried out in broad daylight on the railway stations, factories and barracks. Thirty-three bombs were dropped and bursts were seen on the railway sheds. British bombers were attacked by several German scout aircraft, which were driven down out of control. The German report spoke of an attack shortly after 10.00hrs by several British aeroplanes. The anti-aircraft guns were in action and the bombs dropped caused inconsiderable damage. Unfortunately, there were some victims amongst

the inhabitants. The report in the local paper dated 22 May stated that of those injured in the last raid on Cologne a further ten had succumbed to their injuries so that the total deaths amount to thirty-five. The number of wounded was stated as definitely eighty-seven. The Mayor's report is yet more detailed and differs significantly from the official report. The latter stated that thirty-eight buildings had been hit and the serious damage amounted to 340,000 marks. Photographs showed bomb bursts on the western end of the Neumarkt, on the infantry barracks, the gymnasium, the Alte markt, the Rathaus, the town water and electric works and on other buildings in the town. A man who was in Cologne during the raid states that the authorities were taken completely by surprise for the raiders were thought to be going north or north-east. Great damage was caused to the gasworks and barracks and a direct hit was witnessed on a tramcar, killing seventeen people. He ended by saying that the officer commanding the Cologne AA defences was dismissed. A very reliable source affirmed the great deal of material damage during

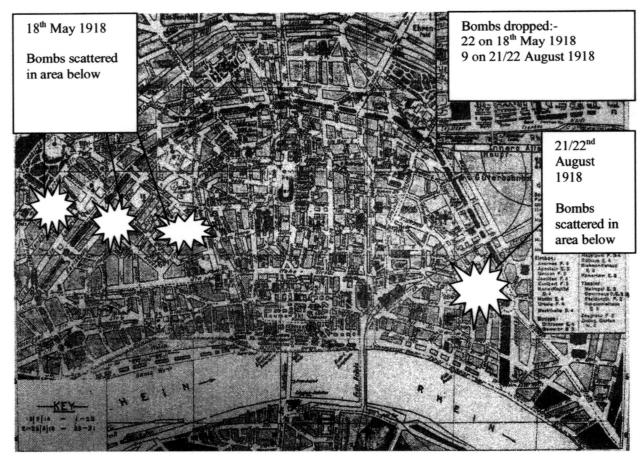

Bombs dropped on Cologne – 18 May and 21/22 August 1918.

the attack on the Neumarkt. Between 19 and 24 May industrial activity of Cologne was reduced by 50 per cent. The AA guns did not commence firing until after the raid had finished and only succeeded in bringing down one Allied machine. The women drivers on the tramcars forgot to switch off the current to their cars, which then ran away. The reliable source ended by saying that the electric power station was badly damaged. Captured letters confirmed the damage to tramcars and one spoke of the near total destruction to a building used as a clothing and rifle depot.

The morale effect is evident in the *Frankfurter Zeitung* of 8 June – General Major von Weisberg gave the following reply in answer to a question by Deputy Kuckhoff in the Reichstag on 7 June: 'The inhabitants were not given the alarm in time to enable them to take shelter as they should have done.' The enemy attack seemed at first to be intended for Treves and then for Coblenz. In the meanwhile, although no news had been received, the inhabitants should have been given the alarm. This was not done. With regard to mutual limitation of air raids the following can be stated: 'The Germans cannot make the first approaches to the enemy to stop raids on towns outside the war zone. The German Government, on the contrary must wait for the enemy to approach it. Should such an offer be made it would be conscientiously examined by Germany, and at the same time it would be considered what qualifications would have to be made to secure that German interests should not be affected.' Captured letters spoke of the raid of 18 May as scaring the people of the city and one asks for God's protection against anything as awful as the Allied air raids. A reliable source spoke of the intervention of the Pope to prevent raids upon Cologne for these prevented the movement of military trains through the city. The Court of Bavaria obtained the intervention of the Papal Nuncio at Munich, informing him that that, according to official statistics, the industrial output of the Rhine region would be reduced by more than a third if the raids continued. Another reliable source stated that the panic was terrible. Everyone in Cologne was in deadly terror of air raids. On 23 May the *Könische Volkszeitung* printed the following:

> Once already the population of Cologne has been in danger of being directly affected by the war and its horrors. The extremely painful experiences of 18th May will also have a sure and permanent effect in this direction...but Cologne has remained a fortress. That is the reason for the necessity for adapting one's nerves to unpleasant surprises from the air. It remains to be seen whether Kuckhoff's question will give the impulse to the realization of such desires which are the common property of all citizens without differences of party or creed. It is a naive notion that our enemies would stop their bombing raids the minute the Germans stopped theirs.

Raid of 21/22 August

It would be some time before Cologne was bombed. On the night of 21/22 August bombs would be scattered in the general area shown on the map. Only nine bombs would be dropped near the railway station on civilian properties.

EHRANGE (DATES OF RAIDS – 23/24 AUGUST, 2/3 SEPTEMBER, 7 SEPTEMBER, 14 SEPTEMBER, 14/15 SEPTEMBER AND 10 NOVEMBER 1918)

In general it was impossible to obtain reports of raids on Ehrange, other than that of 23/24 August. The remainder relied upon either British or German official reports hence the paucity of evidence. This was an important railway junction hence the number of raids.

Raid of 23/24 August

The British report stated simply that the junction was attacked and that a fire was caused with considerable damage done, although it does not say to what. The official German report stated that two bombs dropped on railway land but that the damage was inconsiderable. The delay in the working of the line was of no importance. No persons were injured. The report from the head stationmaster was very different and he stated that the tracks to Coblenz were hit and that only one track could be utilized for twenty-four hours. A captured letter dated 24 August reported the dropping of fifteen bombs on the station and in the neighbourhood, one exploding opposite the post office by the railway station tracks. The morale effect is borne out in a captured letter, also of 24 August, which began:

> Yesterday evening I was disturbed as the light went out. We had hardly been in bed when the airmen were here. They were never so terrible before in our town. The shooting woke us up. For a time everything was quiet. All at once there was a terrible noise as if a train was quite close. Suddenly a terrible 'crack' and we were all lying breathless on the floor of the room. We had hardly stood up again when down came the second and third bombs. We thought we should have the house down on our heads.

Raid of 2/3 September

There are only the official British and German reports for this and all succeeding raids. The RAF squadrons were credited with a descent to 90ft to drop their bombs, all of which obtained a direct hit. The Germans reported the dropping of twenty-five bombs when the material damage was inconsiderable and no one was hurt.

Raid of 7 September

Only a British report is recorded for this morning attack when good bursts were observed on and beside the railway lines.

Raid of 14 September

The British report spoke of three direct hits on the railway and the German report conceded that there was some material damage from the dropping of six bombs.

Raid of 14/15 September

Only a British report spoke of heavy attacks being kept up throughout the night on the railway at Ehrange.

The Raid of 10 November

Significantly, this will be the last raid of the war since the Armistice took effect the following day. The report said simply that the Allied bombers successfully attacked the railway junction at Ehrange.

FRANKFURT-AM-MAIN (DATES OF RAIDS – 12 AUGUST, 21/22 AUGUST, 25/26 AUGUST, 16/17 SEPTEMBER AND 25 SEPTEMBER 1918)

Raid of 12 August

The cluster of thirty-three bombs are marked 'A' on the map that follows. The British official report spoke of a successful attack on the aeroplane and chemical works whereas the German report quoted the *Cologne Gazette*. 'HM Kaiser and King deeply sympathizes in the misfortune which has befallen the open town of Frankfort as the result of the enemy air attack, which is contrary to international law. It claimed many victims and requests you to convey to the relatives of those who had fallen for the Fatherland, and to the wounded, the sympathy of the All Highest.' The material damage was learned from conversations between officials and civilians. One bomb fell on the Opera House and, although considerable damage was done, the evening performance was held as usual. The remaining bombs fell on private property doing considerable damage especially in the Bockenheimer Landstasse where two houses were completely demolished. The total damage was valued at 650,000 marks and the casualties included sixteen killed and twenty-six injured.

Given the cluster of bombs (marked A on he accompanying map) that fell on a populated area of the city, officials stated that the morale effect was prodigious. Officials stated that the morale effect was prodigious. The population marvelled at the shooting of the airmen. About thirty bombs were dropped within a circle of 1,000 metres diameter. Great indignation was expressed against the government and the military. It was the worst experience the population had ever had. Panic was rife for days. A reliable source, a prisoner of war, makes and interesting observation, during the hostilities, that he felt great satisfaction that the bombs had been dropped on the west end of the city where he thought that the morale effect was greater than it would have been had the bombs dropped on the poorer parts of the city. A captured letter

of 15 August stated that 'Twelve times this week we have had big visits from on high and this is not pleasant when there are so many warnings. You can imagine how nervous one becomes.' The local newspaper, the *Frankfurter Zeitung*, of 12 August stated that the Frankfurt market was depressed.

Raid of 21/22 August

The official British report stated simply that military objectives were heavily attacked with good results. The cluster of bombs is marked 'B' on the map and shows hits alongside and on the railway lines. The official German report quoted the local newspaper: 'Last night, about 12 o'clock an air raid was carried out on Frankfort and its environs. A number of bombs were dropped, which, as far as it known at present, only caused material damage.' From conversations with civilians, it was discovered that one bomb fell on the railway lines close to the main buildings of the east station, causing considerable damage. The remaining bombs also fell in this area but only caused slight damage to private property, the total damage valued at 25,000 marks. This is borne out by reference to the map. With reference to the morale effect a captured letter of 22 August spoke of the raid at midnight causing an hour and a half of great fear. They were dropping bombs continuously, about sixty in all, so one can imagine what the writer felt whose nerves were all upset. She and her children shivered. This account may well be an exaggeration over the duration of the raid and the number of bombs dropped.

Raid of 25/26 August

The British report stated simply that the railway station at Frankfurt was successfully bombed. The principal stations are shown on the map and show that the cluster of bombs marked 'C' fell wide of the mark. The official German report states that bombs were dropped and that material damage was caused. Inhabitants stated that one bomb fell on the Westhafen, causing considerable damage to stocks of material located there. The remaining bombs caused damage to private property, the total valued at 100,000 marks. A reliable source makes reference to the morale effect, which is somewhat surprising: 'The effect on the people was very striking. We felt so safe. The way they speak and look shows that something new has entered into their lives'. No reasons are advanced as to why this should be so.

Raid of 16/17 September

The official British report stated that the station at Frankfurt was heavily attacked with good effect. This does not tally with the cluster of bombs marked 'D' on the map. These straddled the railway line but far from the main railway stations. The local paper stated that bombs were dropped, which caused considerable material damage. Local civilians stated that the damage was mostly confined to the partial destruction of private property, which was valued at 55,000 marks. In stark contrast to the reported effect on morale, which appears in the preceding paragraph, a prisoner of war stated that the people of Frankfurt lived in constant fear; alarms were always sounding. One reliable source spoke of a woman in one of the air raid shelters protesting violently against a continuation of the war. Apparently, the police tried to interfere but the crowd took the woman's side.

Raid of 25 September
On this occasion the noonday attack was described, in the British report, as an attack on factories with good results. On the other hand the official German report stated that sixteen bombs were dropped, partly in the town and partly in open country. No material damage was suffered by any military objectives. One person was killed and five injured. The cluster of bombs dropped during this raid are marked 'E' with some in cluster 'C' on the map. According to statements of the inhabitants one bomb fell in the main thoroughfare, the Kaiserstrasse, causing considerable damage. Another bomb fell at the northern end of the Wilhelm bridge but only caused damage to a house. Several bombs fell on the south side of the river near the lock causing slight damage to the lock gates. Damage was also caused to private property valued at 320,000 marks. The clusters of bombs indicate strikes along the river and one strike at the northern end of the river bridge, which supports the evidence of the local inhabitants. The *Wolff Bureau* had stated that the hospitals and churches had been singled out for attack but this was ridiculed by the *Offenbacher Abendblatt*, which was of the opinion that any who witnessed the air raid knew only too well what the airmen were aiming at and it was far more important than the killing of a few sick people.

General conclusions about the effects of the attacks on Frankfort
An official who resided in Frankfort during the air raids stated that it was the consensus of opinion that the material damage was insignificant given the number of bombs dropped. This was seventy-six between 12 August and 25 September. It was conceded that the damage caused on the raid of 12 August was considerable but that possibly the damage appeared greater because the area being bombed was smaller. Of the seventy-six bombs dropped thirty-three alone were dropped on that occasion. There was no attempt to deny that the morale effect was enormous. In 1917 raids had been carried out by single machines and no panic had ensued. In quarters of the town unaffected by the bombing by a single aircraft some in the population did not even know a raid had taken place but this all changed in 1918. The population was terrified and believed that they were revenge bombings for German raids on London and Paris. Some consolation was felt since the ruthless attacks on Frankfort must have been matched by those mounted by German machines. Be that as it may, the population felt that the raids on their city were not justified and they blamed the military authorities for not coming to some agreement as to the cessation of raids before 1918. Again, the assertion is made that the morale effect was greater amongst the upper classes. It was then learned that German attacks on London and Paris were no longer taking place but that they were to expect an increasing number of Allied raids on German cities. The fact that the Americans were by then in the war appeared to have a morale effect. Night raids were said to be the worst and the most demoralizing, especially amongst women and children.

RAIDS ON FREIBURG AND HAGONDANGE
Both towns were subjected to Allied bombing raids. Only one recorded raid was made on Freiburg with five on Hagondange. The British targets in Freiburg were the munitions works and barracks. All machines were said to reach their objective and nearly a ton of bombs were dropped. Reports later confirmed damage to the barracks for Reserve troops, the damage valued between 1,000,000 to 2,000,000 marks. The local paper accused the Allies of attacking an open city with the intention of killing innocent civilians and destroying their homes. In the case of Hagondange there is ample evidence from the map of the importance of the railway to the town and local works. The map records raids dating from January 1918 until August of that year. Only a few bombs were dropped on the edge of the inhabited area to the north of the map. These were in June and are marked 'A'. Two bombs from a cluster of bombs dropped in June, marked 'B', did hit the railway line with some near misses. The best results for attacks on the railway line were made in August and are marked 'C' on the map when most bombs were a direct hit. No hits were made on the Central Station ('D'). The raid of 24 May was recorded as the dropping of nearly a ton of bombs on the railways and factories at Hagondange but a Director stated that only unimportant damage was caused with one man killed and one wounded. Again, on 8 June the British report stated that a ton of bombs was dropped but these are in the cluster marked 'A' on the map, only two hits being made on industrial buildings. The British official report of the raid of the night of 16/17 July states that appreciable damage was inflicted on the works at Hagondange. One or two bombs fell on industrial buildings but most were well away in the cluster of bombs marked 'B'. The official records of the raids gave details of the material damage and it was said that installations did not suffer serious damage but that the office at the cement works was destroyed with the roof of the stacking room badly damaged. An Alsatian

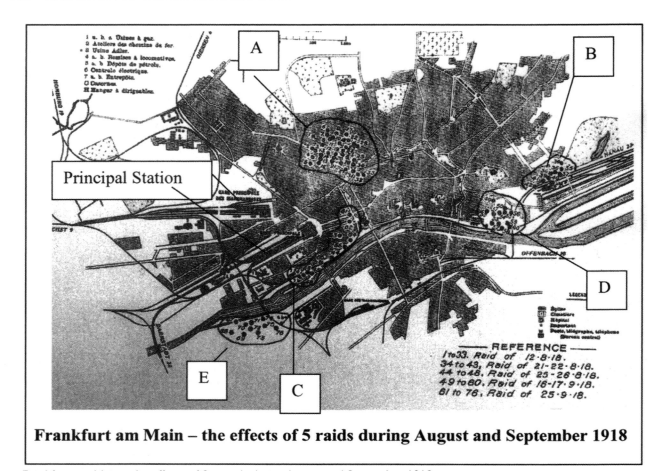

Frankfurt am Main – the effects of 5 raids during August and September 1918

Frankfurt-am-Main – the effects of five raids during August and September 1918.

who had been with the works throughout the war stated that one bomb pierced the tunnel leading from the office to the railway. This tunnel was being used as an air raid shelter and nine men were killed with fourteen wounded. As a consequence, dugouts were commenced at various localities in the works.

RAIDS ON KAISERSLAUTERN

The British official report for the raid of 17 March stated that the barracks and railway station were attacked with good results. The German report mentioned an attack upon an 'open' town where the damage to houses was quite serious with three men and three women killed and several people wounded. The material damage was, firstly, to the boiler room of a furniture works in the Kohlbruchstrasse. The beams of the roof were almost entirely blown off, a large portion of the window glass in the factory was broken and the electric circuits destroyed. The value of the damage was approximately 10,000 marks. A brewery in Pariser Strasse was also hit and

suffered not inconsiderable damage. Private properties also suffered and total damage amounted to 123,663 marks. Evidence of damage and casualties is provided by the content of letters captured during hostilities. One dated 18 March stated that enemy machines came on the previous day and bombed the town very badly. Bombs fell on the Gross Armature Works in the Park Strasse and in the Eisenbahn Strasse the debris of glass would fill a dung cart. A second letter, dated 25 March, said 'I suppose we are on the English "Black List". Last Sunday we really had a dose of it, the damage is quite sufficient. Not a pane of glass was left intact: it was terrible. One can no longer walk about as there is so much glass. One of the bombs fell on Jaeinsche's Brewery. He, of course, with his millions can replace the broken glass.' The morale effect is also to be found in captured letters. One, dated the day of the raid, spoke of passing through very sad times and the people wearing their shrouds every day. They would go to work in the morning never knowing if they would return home that day. Several times of late,

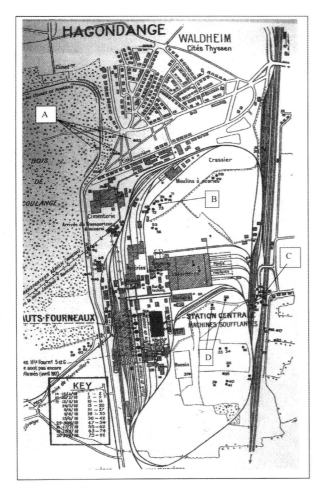

Allied bombing list with its factories and the fact that it was a major railway junction. The map that follows shows the bomb clusters but all the bombs in one cluster will not necessarily have resulted from one raid but, in some cases, several over the period. The cluster marked 'A' was from bombs dropped south of the main station and were in May and early June. The cluster marked 'B' indicates bombs dropped in June and mid July in the residential districts. The cluster marked 'C', which had little effect, indicates bombs dropped in June and October. The cluster marked 'D' were bombs dropped on the night of 23/24 October and were all hits on the railway tracks. The cluster marked 'E' were bombs dropped on the 5 July and were, again, all hits on the railway lines. The cluster marked 'F' on the map were all bombs dropped during the raid of the 6/7 of November and were all wide of the mark. As with all the previous official reports included in this chapter the British reports on the raids on Saarbrücken state simply that the raids were carried out and that they were successful. The report of 16 May gave the number of bombs dropped as twenty-four in all. Significantly, death and injuries were sustained amongst soldiers waiting on trains, which were often halted outside a station when a raid was imminent. Indeed, as a result of this raid, traffic was suspended for eight hours. There was a great deal of material damage to track and rolling stock. The raid of 21/22 May produced

the writer said, the district had been visited by 'birds of passage' and once these birds had seized their prey and this on a larger scale. A second captured letter, dated 25 March spoke of living a terrible life but that the writer was about to travel to somewhere safer, presumably a relative's home.

The British report, for the raid of 7 July, stated simply that the station and factories in the town were attacked and the German report spoke of a number of bombs being dropped on the town causing a certain amount of damage. The material damage was considerable to streets and houses and gas and water mains. This was valued at 177,231 marks. It was the raid of 21/22 October that resulted in the damage sustained by a small arms ammunition factory at Kaiserslautern featured in photographs in the early part of this chapter when 1650lb bombs were used. The damage was substantial.

RAIDS ON SAARBRÜCKEN

The records of raids on Saarbrücken start in May through to October. This town was an important target on the

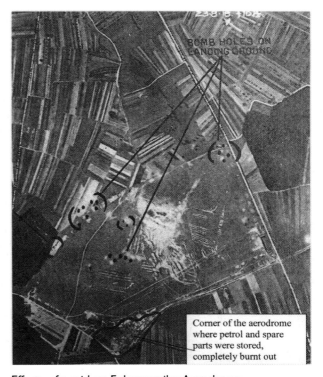

Corner of the aerodrome where petrol and spare parts were stored, completely burnt out

Effects of a raid on Folpersweiler Aerodrome.

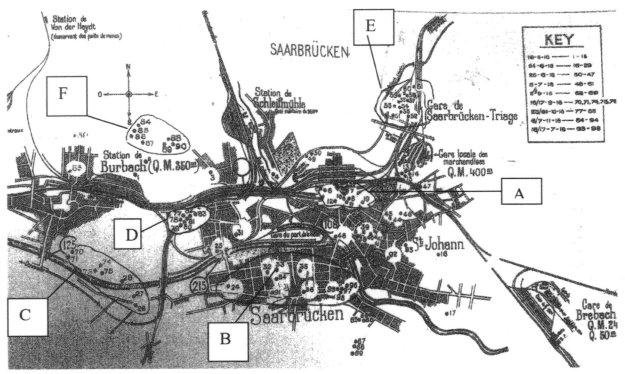

Recorded raids on Saarbrücken from 16 May to 23/24 October 1918.

traffic delay on railway lines entering the town owing to the long duration of the attack. Of the raid of 24 June the British official report spoke of a successful attack in spite of high winds and clouds. The German report did concede that material damage had been caused and this was confirmed. Malstatt station was hit by one bomb and six bombs dropped on the Burbach works. Railway workshops were damaged and an electrical tramway put out of action. The damage was estimated at 40,000 marks. The Burbach works were again bombed during the night of 16/17 July and yet again on 31 July when the works sustained considerable damage. The report of material damage for the night of 2/3 September confirmed the British report that the Burbach works were hit by bombs. These put the carpenter's shop out of action for fourteen days and caused damage to adjacent railway tracks. The damage was estimated at 400,000 marks. Throughout September, October and November the raids continued causing damage to private properties, railway tracks, engine sheds and tramways. The morale effect gets little mention in the reports but it is obvious that the populace was suffering from the air raids, both the daylight ones and the night raids.

AN OVERVIEW OF THE EFFECTS OF THE BOMBING
The official British reports overstate the effects of the bombing and German reports understate them. This chapter began by explaining that the German Government and military wished to prevent a serious drop in civilian morale. Where deaths and injury from the bombing were acknowledged it was to make the point that the attacks were being inflicted on 'open' cities, causing unnecessary suffering of the non-combatant members of the public. Mayors and local officials could be relied upon to make more frank admissions of the damage and casualties being inflicted since they would be faced with demands for compensation and this strengthened the argument that the military were doing too little to protect the public. When AA defences were deployed around cities there were mixed feelings. Some believed that the existence of AA guns and searchlights only served to attract the attention of the Allied bombers. This would suggest that the Allied bombing squadrons set out to bomb targets of opportunity rather than those that would cause real economic and military damage.

The bombing of airfields features prominently in the IBF report of raids undertaken. The attacks were on hangars, aircraft in the open and bomb/fuel dumps. The airfields of Morhange, Buhl, Boulay and Lorquin are mentioned. Photographic evidence of an attack on the airfield at Folpersweiler aerodrome shows that some bombs caught some of the hangars. Others that fell in the grassed area of the airfield would cause craters that could soon be filled in. The claim was made of the destruction of the fuel and spare parts store on the edge of the airfield furthest away from the hangars. It was normal practice on RAF airfields to site bomb and fuel dumps on the edge of an airfield furthest from the domestic and technical areas and aircraft hangars.

There is ample evidence that a lot of civilian properties were damaged and significant that if these were the properties of the well-to-do then the morale effect would be more likely to receive the attention of the authorities. The less well off social classes, from the evidence of captured letters, almost cheered at the discomfiture of the rich who could, if conditions became intolerable, leave the town to live with relatives in the country.

Throughout these reports the effects of the raids on the railway system receive the greatest attention. It is evident that the railway authorities had planned diversion routes to avoid bombed areas and thus keep the rail traffic moving. Be that as it may, there is also evidence that the warning of imminent air raids would result in trains being held up outside railway stations, sometimes for hours, causing disruption to traffic. The backlog of repairs to damaged railway locomotives was a problem, which could add to difficulties.

The morale effect was out of all proportion to the size of the bomber force or the material damage caused. The fear of death or injury to a civilian population from the air was something quite new in warfare and air defence units had to be taken from the front line to provide adequate protection of the bombed population and industrial centres. There is ample evidence of the fear of bombing and the number of alerts that drained a person's will to carry on a normal life. Since the total material damage from all operations of the IBF was small in national terms the war was not going to be brought to a conclusion as the result of raids by eight night-bombing squadrons. It is therefore significant that Trenchard would play greatly upon the morale effect in the immediate post-war years since the material effect was not great given the size of the force and the bombs used for the attacks.

Part II

Organization

Chapter 7
Aircraft Design and Development

Aircraft types – manufacture of aircraft by private firms – development aeroplanes and seaplanes for naval use – experimental work including RA Factory – specification for aeroplanes RAE Farnborough 1912 – the development of British and French aircraft prior to the outbreak of the Great War and for the war years 1914–1918 – aircraft industry including designers and test pilots of the period

Introduction

This chapter deals with the progressive development of aircraft and engines, both in the pre-war period and the war years to 1918. Reference should also be made to Chapter 11, which deals with technical developments and organization to meet the rapidly changing needs of the RFC/RNAS in light of operational experience. This chapter begins with a general view then concentrates on the pre-war years and the war years. Ready reference to all the aircraft in operational and training use during the period 1914 to 1918 is to be found in Appendix A. References will be made in this chapter and elsewhere in this encyclopaedia to tractor and pusher aircraft. A tractor aircraft is one where the propeller is mounted on the front of the aircraft and 'pulls' the aircraft behind it, whereas a pusher aircraft is one in which the propeller is mounted behind the pilot and observer or air gunner and 'pushes' the aircraft through the air. This distinction is important for two reasons. Firstly, if speed was important

the tractor type was preferable but, secondly, observation and the firing of guns could be of equal importance. If forward observation or gun mounting was important a pusher aircraft was preferable for there would not be the problem associated with firing a gun through the arc of the propeller nor with the lower wing obscuring the view of the ground to the observer. One solution was to mount the gun on top of the upper wing, as illustrated by the SE5, but this placed the gun out of the easy reach of the pilot who might have to fix a 'jam' in his gun during combat.

The following accounts of test flying are contained in the many reports that were sent to naval and army authorities and on occasion involved the Royal Aircraft Factory. These aircraft are so far removed from the modern jet aircraft of today. They were made of wood and fabric with primitive control devices and simple engines. Much of the work of construction and repair fell to carpenters. Aircraft armourers, airframe and radio fitters were to come. A great deal of experimentation was carried out both before and during the war. Experimentation on weapons, wireless telegraphy and bombs are included in Chapter 11. The tests carried out at Martlesham Heath on prototypes may be found in Appendix K.

THE PERIOD UP TO THE OUTBREAK OF THE GREAT WAR IN 1914

MANUFACTURE OF AEROPLANES BY PRIVATE FIRMS
Source: CAB 4/1 AC4

It is made clear in Chapter 11 that the Royal Aircraft Factory both developed and constructed aeroplanes but equally that the Admiralty preferred purchasing machines in the market. In a memorandum of the Government Air Committee dated 8 March 1913, the Committee worried about the release of confidential information to civilian firms. On the other hand, the government wanted to encourage private industry and felt that it would be some time before there would be a sizeable demand for aeroplanes for commercial purposes or private use. In August 1912 the government had asked the Air Committee for their opinion on the desirability

'Pusher type of aircraft'.

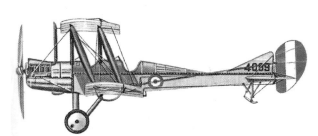

'Tractor type of aircraft'.

Army Aeroplane No.1.

of releasing details of airship construction to private firms. On the 11 October 1912 the Committee came down against the release of sensitive information. But when it came to aeroplanes selected firms could be given the specifications, leaving it to the firm to decide on the design with the firm's employees being bound by the Official Secrets Act.

Aircraft No.1 of the Army is shown, i.e., its first military aircraft, and it is clear just how fragile the early aircraft were. Also shown is the famous aviator of the day, S.F. Cody, who flew this machine. As has been stated the work in building and repairing aircraft like these was mainly the work of carpenters. The photograph below depicts Colonel S.F. Cody outside the office of the new balloon factory at Farnborough in 1900. It was here that Cody built the first powered aircraft to be flown in the UK. Chapter 1 describes the negotiations that took place between the Wright brothers and representatives of the British Government to purchase the Wright Flyer, which came to naught, so Cody's flight is important in that progress in powered flight was being made in Britain. This American born ex-showman is not to be confused with Buffalo Bill Cody.

During the period leading up to the Great War, which commenced in 1914, the aeroplane industry was

Colonel S.F. Cody.

in a very early stage of development. There were a few firms building aeroplanes and seaplanes and the advice given by the Committee of Imperial Defence was that the private sector should be left to develop aeroplanes, leaving government agencies to develop airships. When there was a call for a large number of aircraft the newly formed Royal Naval Air Service would rely on private firms for aircraft, both land and seaplanes, whereas the Royal Flying Corps would obtain their aircraft from the Royal Aircraft Factory, misleadingly referred to as the RAF. In those early days the prototypes would have simple numbers, such as Aircraft No.74. Test flying was, of its very nature, a hazardous business and at times two people would take to the air as there was a need for someone not in control of the aircraft to observe a machine's behaviour in the air.

DEVELOPMENT OF AEROPLANES AND SEAPLANES FOR NAVAL USE
Source: National Archive document: AIR1/ 642/17/122/238

(See also Chapter 11 for the armament and wireless telegraphy.)

S.F. Cody in flight 1909.

Report on the 100hp Avro Gnome biplane
Source: AIR2/164

In a letter dated 5 May 1914 from the Naval Flying School, addressed to the Commanding Officer, the reporting officer, Sub Lieutenant L.C. Parse, said that he had been flying the Avro Gnome biplane continuously since November 1913. He felt that the aircraft was nicely balanced except from a nose heaviness, which meant that the aircraft should not be dived steeply. This was particularly important since the small size of the elevator rendered recovery somewhat slow. In bad weather the aircraft remained stable but there was a risk of wing tip damage on take-off and landing and during taxiing. Two great advantages of this machine were regarded, by Parse, as slow landing speed and an exceptionally sound landing chassis.

Suggested additions in future specifications of seaplanes
Source: A letter to the Admiralty Air Committee dated 18 September 1913

It was recommended that there should be fuel and oil sufficient for a six-hour flight. More attention should be made to the comfort of aircrew such as the addition of windscreens. A non-magnetic compass should be fitted in a good position for it to be seen easily from the pilot's seat, which would not affect the steering of the aircraft and would be unaffected by control levers. The bonnet or cowl of the engine should be so designed as to prevent oil being flung back to the seats but not in a way that interfered with the efficient functioning of the engine. The motor should be capable of being started from both the passenger and pilot's positions and the supply of fuel and oil to the engine should be automatic. Magnetos should be made watertight and short circuiting made impossible. There should be dual controls, a stout fitting for mooring and aluminium, or its alloys, were not to be used.

Report on RA Factory Hydroplane No.17 – Report by Superintendant RA Factory dated 21 September 1914
The report begins by stating that the machine was tested on September 10 at Calshot Air Station by Mr Longmore. The water was fairly smooth and there was a moderate wind. At rest the main floats drew 14 inches at the stern and a third of the rear float in the water. When the machine was under way at slow speeds there was no tendency to roll or pitch more than normal and the aircraft lifted well over the wash from Solent steamers. On the other hand there was a great deal of water disturbance between the floats due to their being arranged so close together causing a very large wash at the rear. This was regarded as important since, at the usual speed that

the machine is not actually hydroplaning, the wash is in such a position that the tail float rests on it. As this wave is about 18 inches high it means that the machine's seaworthiness is spoiled in rough water. The wash only occurs at slow speeds and since the machine soon pulls through into hydroplaning speed it is not noticeable. When the machine is hydroplaning it behaves well with most of its weight on the main step with the stern floats just touching the water. There was stability both laterally and fore and aft with just the slightest sign of pitch. The steering was really good at all speeds with the wind on any quarter.

In flight the behaviour was as good as could be expected but getting off the water and climbing was a slow business. This was unexpected and was put down to the high weight of the 100 hp Renault engine. It was felt that this problem could be addressed by fitting a 'climbing' airscrew, which would involve a small sacrifice of top speed, and by adding about 50ft of surface to the top plane as advised after the 1913 trials. The balance in the air was satisfactory as were the controls. Although it was agreed that the airscrew was unsuitable the demands of war together with the instructions that no further expenditure was to be incurred meant that the aircraft would have to go to war with the existing airscrew.

The construction of the tail float was such that it filled with water at once on entering the water and was the same as the one fitted in 1913. A note had been added in pen to the effect that a better float did exist. The float suspension was strong but Mr Longmore felt that it should be sprung on an aircraft as heavy as No.17. Superintendent O'Gorman penned a note indicating that he agreed.

With regards to the engine the 100hp Renault proved to be very unsatisfactory but it had to be handed over to the Navy as it was, due to the ban on any further expenditure. On arriving at the Calshot base, however, the engine was found to have a cracked base and was leaking oil. The power output was low and this was put down to the valves not getting their proper lift resulting from loose tappets. The high-tension leads also gave trouble and broke away at the plug ends. The steelwork on the machine was not, in a good many places, sufficiently protected from the damp and a protective coating was recommended if trouble was to be avoided later. The main struts inside the streamline were unprotected and the fairing was open at the top and the bottom. Finally, the report suggested that the metal body covering was not quite satisfactory or strong enough and it rattled and vibrated in flight. It should be remodelled but again reference was made to the cap on spending.

On 12 September Arthur Longmore, commanding the Naval Air Station at Calshot, had written to the Director of the Air Department at the Admiralty about RA Factory seaplane No.17 with his own recommendations. These included larger surface mainplanes, springing for the main floats and the substitution of the 150 Sunbeam engine for the Renault 100. He found that fitting folding wings would be a problem owing to the shape of the tail. The whole business of folding wings was, however, under review and new designs could be forthcoming. When the wing tip floats hit the water there was considerable strain on the wings. Whilst the necessary alterations to the design were put in hand, Mr Longmore suggested testing an RE5 on floats which, if one could be spared, should be the one with the large-span top plane.

Bristol Tractor Biplane No.43 – Report to the Commander Naval Flying School, 7 May 1914

This aircraft had been test-flown after repair by Sub Lieutenant Sippe in company with Lieutenant R.B. Davies. It had been flown for half an hour with the specified amount of fuel and had received a pre-flight check by a competent shipwright and found to be satisfactory in structural details and conformed with the specifications, including instruments. The height-recording instrument was the aneroid barograph made by Short Bros of Eastchurch. The Bristol Company had supplied a barograph made by Messrs Short and Mason but was unsuitable for the purpose hence the substitution of the aneroid version.

EXPERIMENTAL WORK PRIOR TO THE OUTBREAK OF WAR (INCLUDING THAT AT THE ROYAL AIRCRAFT FACTORY)

Introduction

Aircraft were being taken into a major conflict for the first time and originally it was thought that their use would be restricted to reconnaissance but when it was realized that there were other roles that they could usefully perform then the carriage of guns, bombs and other equipment had to be developed but so much experimentation was 'suck it and see' and, by today's standards, crude. For example, during the war some pilots would personalize their aircraft and have guns fitted in positions that suited them. Bombs that were originally simply dropped over the side by hand were eventually dropped by other means. It was often not known what the destructive effect of a bomb would be; much depended on the state of the ground, ice, was it soft or hard and from what heights should bombs be dropped to achieve the greatest desired destructive effect? The greater the height the greater the chances of a lack of accuracy or the target being obscured by cloud. Aerial gunnery depended for its success on weapons that would not easily jam or freeze up in very cold weather. In 1914 there was so much to learn yet it is significant that wireless telegraphy and guns in aircraft were the subjects of experimentation as early as 1912, barely three years after Blériot's crossing of the English Channel.

The period 1910 to 1913

This period was characterized by the development of dirigible airships. These were destined for the Royal Navy. There was also a small amount of work on captive balloon fabrics and varnishes but the hydrogen-producing plant was dismantled and removed. The growing importance of the aeroplane could not be ignored and in 1914 the four main types, the BE, RE, FE and SE were already in existence and being developed for use in war. Up to about 1913 the letters referred to aircraft developed from designers.

BE – Blériot Experimental – tractor or propeller-first layout

SE – Santos Experimental – canard or tail-first layout

FE – Farman Experimental – pusher or propeller behind the pilot layout

SE1.

BE1.

FE2b.

RE1.

British Experimental 2.

From 1913/14 the letters referred instead to the aircraft role:

RE – Reconnaissance Experimental – two-seat machines

First Annual Report by the Air Committee on the Progress of the Royal Aircraft Factory Source: National Archive Document CAB/4/1 AC 15

Development of aeroplanes, engines, weapons and ancillary equipment was reported on in the first annual report of the Air Committee of the Committee of Imperial Defence. Some aspects of the report of the work carried out at the Royal Aircraft Factory illustrate the advances being made in the design and development of aircraft. By the time of the Committee's report aeroplanes were achieving flights of longer duration. This emphasized the importance of reliable engines and the wear and tear on airframes and control mechanisms. Six sets of control were being made for trial purposes on BE aeroplanes. Particular attention was being paid to the position of wings and wing loading.

Wing warping

Wing warping was still the method by which the pilot could maintain lateral control of his machine and it had been found that aeroplanes with a large number of wings

experienced automatic wing warping by the action of wind gusts, i.e. without the interference of the pilot. Aeroplanes were flying higher and experiencing gusty winds, 54mph being recorded at this time. The automatic movement then given to the aeroplane control lever by the gusts was found to be sufficiently large to be fatiguing to the pilot. It was surmised that this was largely due to the movement of the centre of pressure when warping occurred, thus leading to over-warping. This surmise was found to be correct with wings not allowed in other respects, but having various positions of the main spar. The extreme forward position which was expected to be found satisfactory in extremely high winds, entirely cured the deficit of excessive automatic warping. On the other hand, when this was obtained pilots found themselves, in lesser winds, deprived of that suggestive movement of the wing that they had come to like, and accordingly an intermediate position for the wing spar was successfully adopted.

Wing shapes

A number of studies of wing shapes were made at the National Physical Laboratory and the best of these were selected for a new series of full-size experiments. An increase of the section of the rear spar, which was desired by the Royal Aircraft Factory, solely for the purposes of strength, led to further alteration of the wing profile, thus the section named RAF6 was evolved, which proved, on testing in the wind tunnel, to be an improvement on any of the previous models. The best position of the wing spar on this model was again studied and found by full-scale experiment. On this improved wing shape experiments were being made simultaneously in the wind tunnel and on the full scale model by alterations to the trailing edge and shape generally, to regulate the movement of the centre of pressure.

Controls

The Royal Aircraft Factory flyers had from time to time flown machines fitted with the various types of control. These were either the universal lever with foot steering or a wheel warp with to-and-fro movement of the wheel for elevation, combined with foot steering. A small number of variants of these had been tried as well as a third type, namely foot warp and wheel steering, combined with to-and-fro wheel movement for elevation. It was understood that the standardization of a good control was much desired by the Royal Flying Corps, but in this matter so much depended on individual experience and opinion that some half dozen machines would be appropriately equipped and handed to Army flyers for prolonged tests.

Tails

A long series of research had been made by the time of the report, based upon the NPL and Eiffel wing shape

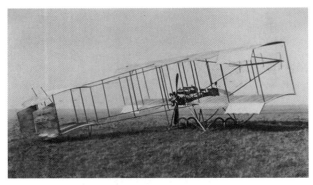

The Bristol Boxkite was developed in 1910 by Britains first private aeroplane company, the British and Colonial Aircraft Company.

results, to secure at all times an appropriate longitudinal righting couple from the tail. A larger number of different tails were made with various cambers and eventually a shape was obtained that was preferred by all those who had tried it on the BE2 type of aeroplane.

SPECIFICATION FOR AEROPLANES – RAE FARNBOROUGH, 17 NOVEMBER 1912
Source: National Archive: CAB/4/1 AP.1

On 17 November 1912 the Superintendent of the Royal Aircraft Factory, Mervyn O' Gorman, sent to the Secretary of the Air Committee the specifications for aeroplanes grouped in six classes since he found that they could not be treated broadly as a single class of mechanism.

Class F
These were machines considered to be easy to learn to fly and the Henry Farman, the Short and Maurice Farman were typical examples. They were slow with a wide speed range, mostly biplanes having a large wing area with the engine behind the pilot. The lateral control was mainly with ailerons and not wing warping. The engine was about 70hp. Guns if fitted were not suitable for firing backwards, forwards or sideways. (Which does not leave much!)

Class FE
There should be an exceptionally clear view ahead with a forward-firing gun (gun and ammunition = 200lb) plus two crew. The endurance should be in the region of 4½ hours with a landing speed of 44mph, preferably 40mph) and capable of destroying the 'Scouter Class', which would mean a top speed not less than 70mph. Due to the weight being carried this might drop to 65mph. Compared with the endurance of a Zeppelin (38 hours, perhaps even 48 hours) there would be little time to catch

an airship. There would be only 2½ hours to overtake and attack before returning to its base so this class would not be much use in the anti-airship role. The climb rate would be 400ft per minute.

Class BE
This was the two-seater 'Scouter'. It could only fire backwards but the engine was behind, which made even that difficult. The class specification meant that the aeroplanes in this class performed less well than the best aircraft at the Military Aircraft Competition 1912. A concession could be made to builders to allow the acceptance of types that were, in one way or another, interesting or promising. It was open to discussion whether the standard should be lowered with regard to slow and high speed and rate of climb. The 'Scouter', being unarmed and lighter than a 'fighter' without the weight of guns and ammunition, needed to have a rate of climb of 400ft per minute to get out of trouble. A lighter aircraft meant that the engines were not being worked too hard. Moreover, there should be a reserve of power to permit pilots to combat gusts, recovery from sideslip and get over clouds quickly in order to escape observation.

Class BS
This class sacrificed everything for speed, was single manned and had a top speed of 85mph. This may have made landing a problem where a slow speed was required but a 10 per cent tolerance could be acceptable to 48mph.

Class FET
This class was intended to provide a stand-by for engine breakdown as it was twin-engined. No efficient stand-by was provided unless horizontal flight could be achieved indefinitely with a margin of power for combating gusts and climbing at, say, 150ft per minute on one of the engines. On the other hand, such an aircraft with its long endurance would be suitable for attacking airships. To overcome the problem of crew fatigue this class should carry four men in addition to fuel and oil for six hours on one engine. Other equipment would bring the all-up-weight to 1,000lb. This equipment could be changed to fuel and oil to increase the range. Other alternatives to make the all-up weight could include a small torpedo, a gun and extra ammunition, long-range wireless, extra crew members, large timed bombs, and important packages such as tightly packed balloons or even ammunition to a besieged ally.

Class BEW
This class comprised the 'Scouter' warplane, which at that time should have fulfilled the conditions of the 'fighter' class with regard to loading tests, air endurance, speed, range and rate of climb. But the useful load would

only be 350lb. It would be best not to hamper this design by calling for the clear field of view of the 'fighter' until some progress had been made.

THE DEVELOPMENT OF BRITISH AND FRENCH AIRCRAFT PRIOR TO THE GREAT WAR

Introduction

Several aspects of aircraft development will become apparent to the reader in studying this chapter. These are airframe design, engine power, carriage of armaments and handling in the air. Several times in this history the products of the Royal Aircraft Factory have been mentioned, since they were designed primarily for their stability in the air. This is fine if the only concern is to provide a stable platform from which to observe the movements of the enemy and spotting for friendly artillery. But once air fighting became a reality, such stable aircraft had to be protected by dedicated fighter aircraft or be extremely well armed to ward off enemy fighters. This problem for Royal Aircraft Factory designed aircraft crops up time and again. But, of course, the more defensive armaments an aircraft carried the heavier it became. Developments in aircraft and engine design before the outbreak of war were not based upon combat experience but one must not imagine that experimentation did not take place. Aircraft on both sides went to war initially to reconnoitre when only personal arms were carried by pilots and observers but experimentation was carried out in a number of areas, including aircraft armament (see Chapter 11). The reliability of engines crops up time and again and, in several instances different engines were used in order to find one that combined reliability with the power that enhanced performance. Shortages of the right type of engine for an aircraft often meant switching to one of unproven performance. In those early days aero engines were developments of car engines and these did not always perform well in the air. The design of the propeller could also be of critical importance. In those early days it was often a carpenter's job to repair airframes and there were lots of cables, both internally and externally, to warp the wings, operate the elevators and rudders etc.

Making improvements to aircraft often meant bolting on extras on a very much 'suck it and see' basis that could make the handling in the air better or worse. Improvements in design were sometimes matters of constructional detail. An example is provided by the work of George Challenger, the chief engineer at Bristol's factory in Filton who had studied details of a Farman machine in the aeronautical press. He proceeded to design a machine based upon the Farman machine and Bristols were sued for infringement of patent. The law suit was dropped, however, when it was shown that Challenger's design was a substantial improvement. Extra gun positions, mechanisms for dropping bombs, firing of guns and controls operated by the pilot or members of the crew in aircraft that carried observers are examples. In some cases the carriage of bombs or torpedoes could mean dropping the observer when the pilot alone would have to fly the aircraft, navigate, observe and drop bombs or torpedoes. The number of Nieuport fighter models that came out during the Great War is testament to the development of a basic design. The time from the design of an aircraft, to its maiden flight and entry into service could take only months, something that would take years today. There are examples, during the Great War when the performance of an Allied aircraft would be overtaken by one belonging to the Central Powers and, for a while, the enemy would have the upper hand. Sometimes desperate attempts were made to bring in a British or French fighter (scout) aircraft without delay that would restore the Allied ascendancy. The 'Fokker Scourge' is a classic example.

Please note

In the passages that follow aircraft names printed in heavy type are accompanied by pictures of same.

BLÉRIOT

One of the earliest aircraft to go into service use was the **Blériot XI**. This had wing warping for lateral control, which was normal in early aircraft, the fuselage was of box-girder construction and the engine was mounted directly in front of the leading edge of the wings. The positioning of an engine in these earlier days would be determined by the type of aircraft, i.e. pusher or tractor engine. In this case the Blériot was a tractor aeroplane. It handled well but its engine was extremely unreliable. The propeller was also replaced with a Chauvière two-bladed propeller made from laminated walnut wood. This propeller design was a major advance in French aircraft technology, and was the first European propeller to rival the efficiency of the propellers used by the Wright brothers. At the time that the **Bristol Coanda** was being designed the War Office had organized a competition with a view to seeing which one or ones would be suitable for military purposes. Since a side-by-side version was

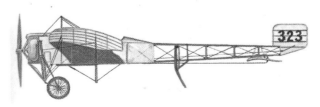

Blériot XI.

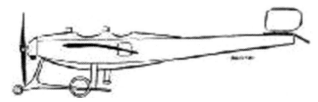

Bristol Coanda.

built it made the aircraft suitable as a trainer. The Coanda did well in the Monoplane Competition, coming fifth, and was described as 'well designed and constructed but heavy for the wing area'. The two Competition Monoplanes were purchased by the War Office after the Military Aircraft Competition, being used as trainers for the RFC. However, on 10 September 1912, one of the Competition Monoplanes crashed, killing Lieutenants E. Hotchkiss and C.A. Bettington. While this was traced to one of the bracing wires becoming detached, it resulted in a five-month ban of flying of all monoplanes by the military wing of the RFC.

The **Bristol Boxkite** was based on one of Henri Farman's successful machines and resulted in a law suit. Bristol claimed that the Boxkite was a considerable improvement on Farman's design. It first flew on 30 July 1910, piloted by Maurice Edmond. Most of the aircraft eventually produced had an extended upper wing and were known as the Military Version. There were also a few modified 'Racers'. The Boxkite went on to become Bristol's first successful production aeroplane. A total of seventy-six were built, sixty-one of which were the extended military version. Although satisfactory by the standards of the day, the Farman design was obsolescent even in 1910, and no serious development of the Boxkite was attempted.

In 1911 the War Office announced their first Military Aeroplane Competition for aircraft to meet the requirements of the newly formed Royal Flying Corps. The competition was won by S.F. Cody with his **Cody V biplane**. The aircraft's performance had to meet the following requirements:

1. Carry a live load of 350lb (160 kg), in addition to its equipment and instruments and with fuel and oil for 4½ hours.

2. Provide accommodation for a pilot and observer, and the controls should be capable of use by either occupant.
3. Fly when loaded for 3 hours during which they should climb to 1000ft (304m) in five minutes or less and reach an altitude of 4,500ft (1,400m), maintaining that altitude for an hour.
4. Attain an air speed of not less than 55 miles per hour.
5. Take off from long grass or rough ground in 100 yards (91m) or less in calm weather, and be capable of being landed without damage on cultivated land by a pilot of ordinary skill.

This gives the reader a good idea of what the War Office wanted in an aircraft before the outbreak of war. The trials were very different to modern military aircraft trials. Although the public were excluded from the aircraft hangars and flying field, free access was otherwise allowed. Aviation was then a subject of great popular interest, and many people came to watch. The **Farman III** was also a pusher biplane with

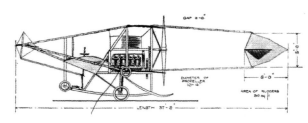

Cody V.

Farman III.

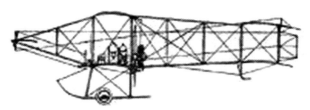

Bristol Boxkite.

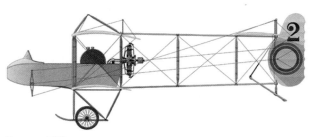

Farman F20.

Longhorn.

Avro 504.

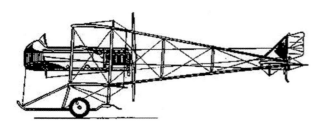

Shorthorn.

a single forward elevator and originally a cellular tailplane and ailerons on all four wings. It first flew in April 1909 powered by a 50hp (37kW) Chauvière four-cylinder inline engine. Farman soon introduced an open tailplane with trailing rudders and an extended-span upper wing and a lightweight four-wheel landing gear. Farman also replaced the engine with the new and more reliable 50hp (37kW) Gnome rotary engine. The elevator was positioned in front of the pilot. This aircraft established what became known as the Farman type and was imitated by other designers to produce such aircraft as the Howard Wright 1910 biplane and Short S27. The **Farman F20** was a refined version of the Farman MF11 'Shorthorn' that did away with the type's distinctive landing skids. The HF20 was seriously underpowered, and a variety of engines were trialled in the hope of correcting this, none with much success. The problem was eventually solved only when an engine of twice the power of the original powerplant was fitted to the HF27 variant, by which time the aircraft was already obsolete. Nevertheless, the performance of this machine made it adequate for use on secondary fronts. One can see that the **Shorthorn** illustrated has dispensed with the elevator position in front of the pilot. The **Longhorn** only saw service from 1913 to 1915 before being relegated to training duties. The pilot or observer would not wish to have an elevator in front, which would prohibit the fitting of a forward-firing machine gun, and neither could the pilot or observer fire to the rear for fear of shooting through the propeller. The Shorthorn, on the other hand, did have a machine gun that could be fired

forward. This would be a feature of succeeding pusher-type aircraft in the Great War, such as the Vickers FB5 (Gunbus). One thing is evident from the preceding passages and that is the Farmans were a pre-war aircraft design but it would soon become apparent that aircraft with the elevator to the front of the pilot restricted the pilot's ability to fire forwards if the aircraft was to be armed with machine guns. There was also a need to have skids protruding out in front to prevent the aircraft pitching forward on landing. This practice did continue, however, for some time to prevent damage to propellers should aircraft pitch forward on landing such as the Avro 504.

The **Avro 504** was a truly remarkable aircraft of the Great War and inter-war years. It was a bomber, fighter and a training aircraft first flown on 18 September 1913, powered by an 80hp (60kW) Gnome Lambda seven-cylinder rotary engine. Small numbers of early aircraft were purchased both by the (RFC) and the (RNAS) prior to the start of World War I, and were taken to France when the war started. One of the RFC aircraft was the first British aircraft to be shot down by the Germans, on 22 August 1914. The pilot was 2nd Lieutenant Vincent Waterfall and his navigator, Lieutenant Charles George Gordon Bayly (both of 5 Squadron RFC) The RNAS used four Avro 504s to form a special flight in order to bomb the Zeppelin works at Friedrichshafen on the shores of Lake Constance. Three set out from Belfort in north-eastern France on 21 November 1914, carrying four 20lb

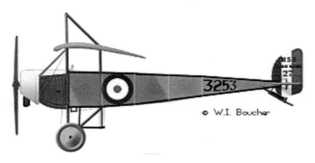

Morane – Saulnier LA.

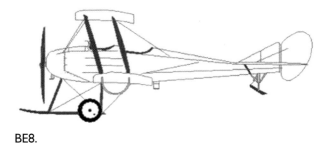

BE8.

(9kg) bombs each. While one aircraft was shot down, the raid was successful, with several direct hits on the airship sheds and destroying the hydrogen plant. Another reason for saying that the Avro 504 was truly remarkable is that the 504N was finally replaced in 1933 by the Avro Tutor in RAF service, with small numbers continuing in civilian use until 1940, when seven were impressed into RAF service, where they were used for target- and glider-towing. The Avro 504 was the first aeroplane to strafe troops on the ground as well as the first to make a bombing raid over Germany. It was also the first Allied aeroplane to be downed by enemy anti-aircraft fire and was Billy Bishop's first army aircraft. The Avro 504 is easily recognizable because of the single skid between the wheels.

Another pre-1914 aircraft that departed from the Farman open fuselage type was the **Morane Saulnier Type L**. It was the LA that equipped the RFC and RNAS. Although wing warping was used on the Type L, the LA version had ailerons. The Type L became the first successful fighter aircraft of the Great War. The machine gun fired through the propeller but was not equipped with an interrupter for the propeller was fitted with deflector plates. The Type L soon sparked off an arms race and once the war started it was soon rendered obsolete. The British Experimental **BE2b** entered service in 1913 and the **BE8** made its maiden flight on 20 August that year. Not far behind was the Reconnaissance Experimental **RE1**. The ability of aircraft to fight in the air came about almost as soon as hostilities began but in early 1913 reconnaissance was the main role, which is why the Royal Aircraft Factory

turned out many aircraft that were inherently stable in the air. This will explain the acceptance into service of the early experimental types. The Aircraft Repair Depots could produce BE2b and BE2c aircraft from spare parts and partly salvaged from damaged aircraft. Technicians in these depots and on the active service units became thoroughly familiar with these aircraft, many of which used the Royal Aircraft Factory engines. The RE1s were intended as experimental machines. Exposure to the elements was considered as new types were introduced and on the BE2 a section of decking had been added between the pilot and the observer. On the BE2a some decking had been added between the observer and the engine and the decking was greatly increased on the BE2bs to protect the crew. The Royal Aircraft Factory BE2b was a slightly improved version of the BE2a two-seat reconnaissance aircraft, developed early in 1914 to increase crew comfort. On the original BE1 the crew had sat in a single open-sided cockpit. On the BE2 a section of fuselage decking had been added between the observer and the pilot, and on the BE2a some decking had been added between the engine and the observer, giving the appearance of two large open-sided cockpits. On the BE2b the amount of decking around the two cockpits was dramatically increased, reducing the crew's exposure to the elements.

The last of the British Experimental aircraft is considered here. The BE8 was the last BE type to be powered by a rotary engine and the BE9 was probably the most bizarre of the attempts to combine the tractor aircraft type with a forward-firing gun. A small wooden box was placed immediately in front of the propeller to accommodate the observer so that he not only had an unobstructed view forward in reconnaissance but would be able to fire his gun without any chance of hitting the propeller. This wooden box was nicknamed the 'pulpit' and was not very popular with the observer who was placed immediately in front of a lethal propeller and cut off from the pilot with whom he may have wished to communicate. This type was soon overtaken by events with the introduction of the interrupter gear, which allowed rounds to be fired through the arc of the propeller. This would permit the pilot to fire a machine gun from the cockpit where he could reach the gun to reload it or to attempt to rectify a gun that had jammed. (See Chapter 11 under the heading Aircraft weapons.) This still left the problem of where best to site the observer with his trainable Lewis gun and succeeding sections of this chapter will show what strides were made in this direction.

Before leaving the pre-war period there remains two other aircraft to consider, both from the Sopwith stable. These were the **Sopwith 3-seater** and the **Sopwith Tabloid**. The Sopwith 3-seater is another aircraft that relied on wing warping for lateral stability. The celluloid

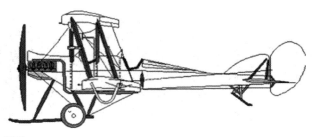

RE1.

windows were a novelty since it permitted an observer to view downwards on both sides of the aircraft. No.5 Squadron was the first to receive this aircraft but the aircraft suffered from structural weakness and two were involved in a mid-air collision and others were involved in accidents. The squadron did not take its remaining aircraft to France. The Tabloids, in common with the Schneider, were designed as sports aircraft but were later adapted for military use. When sent to France they had little value as fighting machines. RNAS Tabloids carried a Lewis gun on the top wing and there is evidence of one that had a Lewis gun firing through the propeller with deflector wedges. Earlier in this chapter reference was made to a 'suck it and see' approach when developing aircraft at this time. The aircraft's speed made it an obvious candidate for entry in the Schneider Trophy competition, and accordingly a floatplane adaptation was prepared, to be powered by a 100hp Gnome Monosoupape which T.O.M. Sopwith personally collected from Paris. This was initially fitted with a single central float, but on its first taxying trials with Howard Pixton at the controls the aircraft turned over as soon as the engine was run up, and remained in the water for some hours before it could be retrieved. A heroic effort was made to make the waterlogged machine airworthy, and, lacking the time to prepare a new set of floats, the existing float was simply sawn in half down the middle and thus converted into a pair of floats. A photograph of the floatplane version can be found in Appendix A, Annex 7.

THE DEVELOPMENT OF AIRCRAFT IN 1914

Introduction

The specifications for aircraft for the services were spelled out by the RAE Farnborough (see page 180) in November 1912, two years before the outbreak of war, and it shows that a great deal of thought had gone into classifying aircraft by type (fighter or reconnaissance etc.). It also asked the War Office and the Admiralty to consider such elements in aircraft design as weight versus speed, endurance, fuel, bomb load and so on. The rate of climb would be important for those aircraft that were not armed since they might need to escape the unfriendly fire of enemy aircraft. Such aircraft would not be weighed down by guns and ammunition and their role would be reconnaissance. This principle was adopted in World War II when reconnaissance Spitfires were not weighed down by guns but camera equipment and it was one of these that spotted the German battleship *Bismarck* before the latter broke out into the Atlantic. One of the most important issues faced by designers was the siting of machine guns on aircraft. Machine gun fire from a pilot's gun or that of an observer, must not pass through the arc of the propeller unless the blades were fitted with deflector plates or an interrupter gear was fitted. This brought in the argument that 'pusher' designs were more

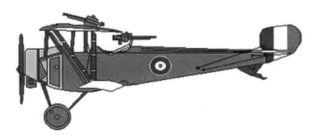

Nieuport 12.

Sopwith 3-seater.

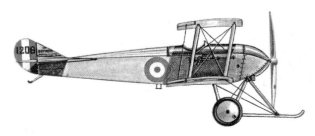

Sopwith Tabloid.

Nieuport 12.

favoured than 'tractor' types. What would change from August 1914 was that preconceived ideas of how the war in the air might develop would be tested in battle.

The **Nieuport 12** was a French biplane fighter aircraft used by both Great Britain and France during World War I. To improve the performance of the Nieuport 10 a larger and re-engined version was developed as the Nieuport 12. A Lewis gun was fitted to the rear cockpit for use of the observer and the pilot sometimes had a Lewis gun fixed to the upper wing firing over the propeller. Late examples of the type, used by the Royal Flying Corps, were sometimes fitted with a Nieuport or Scarff ring mounting for the observer's gun, and a synchronized Vickers gun for the pilot. The armament of this aircraft is typical in having the ability to meet a threat from both the front and behind. As the Nieuport was fitted with a synchronized Vickers gun, which is not a trainable gun, this meant that the use of the Vickers by the pilot could conflict with the use of the Lewis gun by the observer for the former would be attempting to line his aircraft up with the target. The BE2c (which is pictured earlier in this chapter) was a developed version of the BE2b, which was effectively obsolete when war broke out since manoeuvrability had been sacrificed for stability. What the BE2c did have was ailerons on the upper and lower wings in place of wing warping. It also had a rounded upper stabilizer and staggered wings. Where stability did count in action was against Zeppelins and that did not occur with a BE2c until 1916 when Captain Leefe Robinson downed a Zeppelin on 3 August.

The **RE5** saw service into 1915. The RE5 was designed in 1913, first flown in 1914 and was to be the Royal Flying Corps' first real production aircraft. The RE5 was a large two-seat tracker aircraft powered by a Beardmore 120hp Astro-Daimler inline engine that was enclosed in a bull nose cowling. As with most early aircraft the observer occupied the forward cockpit with the pilot seated at the rear. Twenty-four RE5s being built with the money received by the war office from the Admiralty. A sum of £25,000 pounds was allocated to the RFC for the purchase of all the aircraft. In spite of the fact that a small number of aircraft were being manufactured,

the RE5 played an important role in the RFC's early operations in France. These served with No.2 Squadron RFC from September 1914 and No.7 Squadron from April 1015. The aircraft was used in some of the early bombing operations of the war. One aircraft was used in a raid when its pilot won the Victoria Cross. The reliability and straightforward handling qualities that were inherited from its predecessor designs was offset by a lack of agility and absence of protective armament. This affected seriously its operational value, hence its short-lived career, and it was removed from front-line service by autumn 1915 to make way for newer designs. The aircraft did have other practical uses. Six of the production models were converted into single seaters and were given wings with a greater span to add to the lift for use in high altitude trials. In June 1914 one of these converted RE5s reached a height of 17,000ft. Another aircraft was used to trial bomb dropping with 336lb bombs. A final use for this aircraft was in training. This often happened to aircraft in the Great War when they had been overtaken by later friendly or enemy designs or were, in any case, unsuitable for operational use.

The **SE2** came to be designed and built by a rather circuitous route. In 1912 Geoffrey de Havilland, head of a design team at the Royal Aircraft Factory, set out to build a single seat fast reconnaissance aircraft, the first aircraft in the world specifically designed for this role. This would hopefully mean that such an aircraft could fulfil its reconnaissance role and could stay out of trouble if set upon by enemy aircraft. So no thought was given to armament. Wing warping was used for lateral control and it had a small rudder and fixed fin. Initially named the BS1 (Blériot Scout), it was test flown by Geoffrey de Havilland early in 1913. It performed well with a maximum speed of 92mph, a stalling speed of 51mph and a rate of climb of 900fpm (feet per minute) and this in spite of being underpowered. The intended engine was to have been 100hp but the prototype's engine was only 82hp. For its day the speed and rate of climb was very good and would certainly have kept it out of trouble. De Havilland was injured when this

RE5.

SE2.

Voisin LA.

prototype crashed and the subsequent rebuild still had only an 80hp engine. This was designated the BS2 and was flown by de Havilland in October 1913 and the name was again changed to Scout Experimental or SE2. By the time it had come into service with the RFC it was designated the SE2a and apart from the pilot's side arm it had two rifles mounted on the side of the fuselage turned outward to avoid the arc of the propeller. The SE2a also had a larger fin and rudder. Just one aircraft served with No.3 Squadron and it did stay out of trouble as expected but when it was damaged by an exploding bomb the aircraft was returned to the Royal Aircraft Factory. This was the last aircraft that de Havilland would play a part in designing for the Royal Aircraft Factory and he would move to Airco.

The **Voisin LA** or Voisin Type III was the version that entered service with the RFC. Having performed successfully in French Army trials in 1912 some seventy were ordered but once hostilities commenced it became evident that the French aircraft industry could not cope with orders for military aircraft. Michelin, Breguet and Voisin-Lafresnaye acted as licence builders or subcontractors. Even Russian firms became licensees. The Voisin LA was multi-purpose being both a bomber and ground attack aircraft but, like so many other aircraft developed during the Great War, it was overtaken by other designs by 1916.

THE DEVELOPMENT OF AIRCRAFT IN 1915

Introduction

The aircraft that entered service during the first full year of the war were essentially the products of pre-war designers and refinements were having to be made to types such as the BEs, FEs and the Moranes to keep them ahead of the enemy. New firms were emerging such as Armstrong Whitworth, Blackburn and Vickers, firms that would grow and become important in producing aircraft right up to, during and after World War II. French firms would contribute significantly to British air power, notably with the SPADs and the Nieuport range of fighters. Geoffrey de Havilland, it has

already been noted, had moved to Airco and a number of de Havilland types emerged, from the DH1 to DH6. Martinsyde, which went on to produce motorcycles after the Great War, came into the conflict with several important designs such as the G102 Elephant and Buzzard (see Appendix A, Annexes 34 to 36). Unlike other firms mentioned above Martinsyde did not survive the post-war years following the dearth of orders from the RAF for military aircraft. Nevertheless, the entry into the aircraft industry is of interest. In 1908 The company was formed as a partnership between H. P. Martin and George Handasyde and known as Martin and Handasyde. During its existence the company produced aircraft under subcontract as well as its own designs. In 1912 they renamed the company Martinsyde Ltd. But the company went into liquidation in 1923 even though it had produced a post-war design known as the 'Semi Quaver', which set a British record with a speed of 161.4mph. The 'Fokker Scourge' of 1915 would demonstrate the vulnerability of British and French aircraft to highly manoeuvrable fighters and pressure would mount to find a 'fighting' scout that could take on the German fighters in aerial combat as well as affording protection to the aircraft in the BE range.

The **Blackburn or Sopwith Baby** was a single-seat tractor seaplane built for naval use and it entered service in 1915 with the RNAS. The floatplane was also designated Admiralty 8200 type and was a development of the Sopwith Schneider that had won the Schneider Trophy race of 1914, a race for seaplanes which, as a matter of interest, was won in perpetuity by the British in 1931, the British team having won the race on three consecutive occasions. The Sopwith built a production version of the Baby, which differed little from the Schneider winner. The Blackburn Company stepped in at their Leeds factory by producing the Baby and altogether 286 Babies were built for the RNAS, 100 of these being built by Sopwith. It was used as a ship borne scout and bombing aircraft. A further modified Baby was the Hamble Baby. By this time engine power

Blackburn or Sopwith Baby.

Wight Converted.

FB 5 /9 Gunbus.

and top speeds were creeping up. This floatplane had a top speed of 100mph at sea level and was powered by a 130hp rotary engine. It could be armed with Rankin Darts (see Chapter 11) for use against Zeppelins, the aim being to intercept these airships before they could reach the East Coast of the British Isles. Another seaplane that proved its worth in the battle against the U-boats was the **Wight Converted** but it had a disappointing performance. This was built by J Samuel Wight & Company Ltd. Known also as the Admiralty Type 840 and equipped with a 322hp Rolls-Royce engine, it could only reach a maximum speed of 84mph. But it would not encounter enemy fighter aircraft in the Western end of the English Channel and it was employed on anti-submarine duties from Cherbourg from whence one of these floatplanes sank *UB-32*.

Three other performance criteria mattered in comparing aircraft designs, namely service ceiling, range and endurance. If bombers were to undertake strategic bombing missions, which is something the RNAS did rather than the RFC, then range would be an important factor but there would have to be a trade-off between the weight of fuel and bombs, not to mention defensive armament. These were the days of grass airfields and take-off weight (13,360lb) and landing speed would be critical factors. Handley Page was the company to come up with such a bomber, which was to be nicknamed the 'bloody paralyser', the **HPO/100**. This bomber had a maximum top speed of 97mph and a modest service ceiling of 8,500ft, which would not keep it out of trouble

if it met enemy fighters but it did have an endurance of eight hours, which meant that, weather, enemy fighters and ack-ack permitting, a HP1/100 could reach targets deep in enemy territory. The prototype flew on 18 December of 1915 and went into service with the RNAS in November the following year. The aircraft's targets were to include enemy U-boat bases, railway stations and industrial targets.

Vickers provides the example of a firm that sought to produce a fighting machine before the Great War began. With the Vickers FB5 (Fighting Biplane) a pusher arrangement was chosen since the observer positioned in the front of the aircraft with the pilot behind him meant that the gun could be fired through a very wide arc. The concept of a warplane that was designed to destroy other aircraft was embraced by Vickers as early as 1912 and this made the Gunbus the first operational fighter in the RFC. When these aircraft were issued to No.11 Squadron they became the first fighter squadron on the Western Front. To defeat the 'Fokker Scourge' No.11 Squadron experimented with twin Lewis guns, which made them FB.9s. Yet the top speed and service ceiling were both modest. From the autumn of the following year the Gunbus was relegated to training. In fact, the Gunbus did not match up to the Fokker Eindecker. No.18 Squadron was also equipped exclusively with the Gunbus but pilots of this squadron found that the Monosoupape engine was simply not up to the job as the aircraft did not have the speed or rate of climb to pursue its quarry. This is not a good attribute for a fighter. A further development of the FB5, the **Vickers FB9**, had a more streamlined nacelle and an improved ring mounting (either Vickers or Scarff) for the Lewis gun. Fifty were delivered to Royal Flying Corps training units. A few served in some FE2b squadrons while they were waiting for their new aircraft in late 1915 to very early 1916. The Vickers company persisted with an active experimental program during the Great War period, including a line of single-seat pusher fighters, but the FB5 remained their only significant production aircraft until the Vickers Vimy bomber, which entered service too late to have an impact on the war.

The FEs were also pushers based on the French Farman designs but did not have front elevators, which

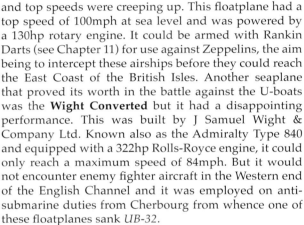

HP1/100.

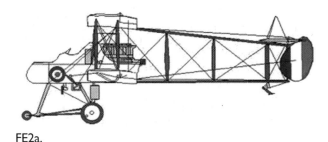

FE2a.

would have lost the advantage of having a front gunner with an unrestricted field of fire. The FE2 was an aircraft designed by Geoffrey de Havilland before he left for Airco. The crew were seated in a wood and canvas nacelle but the engine was but a 50p Gnome rotary. This was soon increased to a 70hp engine. The 1913 version was, however, heavier with a streamlined nacelle and a greater wingspan. Thus when the FE2a took to the sky in 1915 it was classed as an armed reconnaissance aircraft with wings identical to those of the BE2c. Here was the recognition that the aircraft must be able to look after itself in a fight, but the gunner was seated in the nacelle in the very front of the aircraft. The diagram shows that the pilot is seated immediately behind but above the gunner/observer. If the aircraft was 'bounced' from behind and above even, the wing was in the way. The FE2d was an attempt to overcome this problem but it was not a solution favoured by observers. As one pointed out:

When you stood up to shoot, all of you from the knees up was exposed to the elements. There was no belt to hold you. Only your grip on the gun and the sides of the nacelle stood between you and eternity. Toward the front of the nacelle was a hollow steel rod with a swivel mount to which the gun was anchored. This gun covered a huge field of fire forward. Between the observer and the pilot a second gun was mounted, for firing over the FE2d's upper wing to protect the aircraft from rear attack... Adjusting and shooting this gun required that you stand right up out of the nacelle with your feet on the nacelle coaming. You had nothing to worry about except being blown out of the aircraft by the blast of air or tossed out bodily if the pilot made a wrong move. There were no parachutes and no belts. No wonder they needed observers!

A new design development was in the upper wing of the FE2a. The whole of the upper wing centre section trailing-edge aft of the rear spar was hinged for use as a flap-cum-airbrake.

To meet the rapidly growing needs of the RFC and RNAS in war many other inexperienced producers were pressed into service. The first FE2a flew on 26 January 1915 with a 100hp Green six-cylinder inline water-cooled engine but proved underpowered and the 120hp Austro-Daimler built under licence by Beardmore became the standard for eleven more FE2as and early production examples of the FE2b. The latter was the 'productionized' version with the Beardmore engine, trailing-edge flap deleted, simplified fuel system and other changes to facilitate large-scale production by inexperienced companies. These comprised, apart from the Royal Aircraft Factory itself (which built only forty-seven of the FE2b): Boulton & Paul (250); Barclay Curie (100); Garrett & Sons (60); Ransome, Sims & Jefferies (350); Alex Stephen and Sons (150) and G & J Weir (600). A 160hp Beardmore engine was adopted later, and the oleo undercarriage with nose wheel gave way to a simplified form without the nosewheel or, later, a non-oleo V-strut arrangement. All twelve FE2a aircraft and almost a thousand of the FE2b went to RFC squadrons in France, where they engaged in offensive patrols over the enemy lines in the role of fighter escort for unarmed reconnaissance aircraft. Over 200 were issued to Home Defence units, some of these flying as single-seaters, and service use of the FE2b continued until the Armistice in November 1918. One thing can be said in favour of the FEs, they were instrumental in ending the 'Fokker Scourge' that had seen the German Air Service establish a measure of air superiority on the Western Front from the late summer of 1915 to the following spring. In combat with single-seater fighters, the pilots of FE2b and FE2d fighters would form what is probably the first use of what later became known as a Lufbery circle (defensive circle). In the case of the FE2 the intention was that the gunner of each aircraft could cover the blind spot under the tail of his neighbour, and several gunners could fire on any enemy attacking the group. On occasion formations of FE2s fought their way back from far over the lines, while under heavy attack from German fighters, using this tactic.

Other aircraft that entered service at this time were the **Caudron GIII** and the Breguet 4 and 5. Yet again we find aircraft that, in their intended original role, were well suited but they proved inadequate in light of operational experience. The Caudron was tough and reliable and

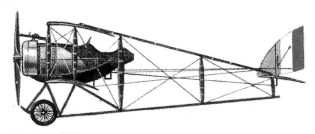

Caudron GIII.

These two photographs illustrate the lengths that the aircraft designers went to combine speed and manoeuvrability with the ability of the observer to have maximum fields of fire. Both these examples were, quite understandably, not favoured by observers. In the aircraft pictured above the observer has two guns, one that can fire over the head of the pilot and the top wing to ensure that the aircraft could be protected if attacked from behind and one that can be fire forward. The only problem was that the observer was not strapped in and the only thing preventing him from being thrown overboard if, for example, the pilot made a sudden evasive manoeuvre was his grip on the weapon. God knows what he did when changing guns! In the example of the BE9 above right there is the attempt to have a tractor aeroplane but one in which the observer's field of fire is not limited to the front. But this meant putting a forward extension on the aircraft to house the observer and his Lewis gun. There were two problems with this layout. Contact between the pilot and observer was impossible and secondly a lethal propeller was situated immediately behind the observer's left or right ear depending on which way he turned round.

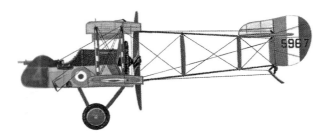

DH2.

Martinsyde S1.

a good reconnaissance machine but was too slow and unarmed. The French, realizing their vulnerability, withdrew them from front-line service in 1916. The GIII model shown in Annex 14 to Appendix A was used by the RFC into 1917 in the light bombing/ground attack role with a small calibre machine gun and some hand-released bombs. But with an 80hp engine and a maximum speed of only 68mph too much was being asked of this aircraft. It was more fitted to the training role. With the Breguet models what the French Government wanted and what they got were not always the same. It was insisted that the 4 and 5 models have a forward-firing gun with pusher engines good for armed reconnaissance. The engines were powerful enough. The Rolls-Royce 250hp Eagle powered those used by the RFC but the French

Government then wanted a bomber and these were produced in the Breguet and Michelin factories. Armed with a Hotchkiss cannon, which proved too heavy, this version had to be armed with a lighter machine gun. It was also too slow for use as a day bomber and had to be relegated to night operations in 1916.

The 'pusher' engined aircraft continued in production as long as there was not a reliable interrupter gear available to permit the firing of machine guns through the arc of the propeller. This was the case with the **DH2** but not later de Havilland designed aircraft such as the DH4 and 6. The gun of the DH2 could be fired from the cockpit but since it was a single-seat machine the pilot had both to fly the aircraft and aim the gun. This was fine perhaps in the hands of experienced pilots but many found it more expedient to lock the gun in a fixed position and aim the aircraft instead. Be that as it may this aircraft gave the RFC air superiority until the autumn of 1916 when the Germans brought in their Albatros machines. By the middle of 1917 the DH2s with the RFC had been transferred to the training role. The **Martinsyde S1** contributed little to the ascendency of British fighters in the conflict. It was underpowered and contributed little on the Western Front or in Home Defence for which it was originally intended. In Mesopotamia the vulnerability of the S1, several of which were shot down, led to Major General Townshend not receiving vital intelligence before an attack, which subsequently failed.

THE DEVELOPMENT OF AIRCRAFT IN 1916

Introduction

Thus far the development of British and French aircraft during the first full year of the Great War saw a continuation of 'pusher' aircraft, but these were to be made redundant with the move over to synchronized machine guns Ailerons replaced wing warping and there was a gradual increase in engine capacity. But during the year the Germans would steal back the ascendency that they enjoyed in 1915 with the Fokker Eindecker. This illustrates graphically how important it was for the Allies constantly to update their aircraft and match, if not better, those of the enemy. This matter is dealt with below.

The **AWFK8** was a significant addition to the RFC inventory. Orders were placed by the War Office in late 1915 for the **AWFK8**, which was a replacement for the BE2c. There was a Scarff ring for the observer's Lewis gun but initially no gun was provided for the pilot. However, the production aircraft were equipped with Vickers guns to the port and slightly behind the engine. The Armstrong Whitworth gun synchronizing mechanism was incomplete at the time the first example, A2636, had arrived in France and some early production FK8s may have used the Arsiad

AWFK8.

interrupter gear instead. The Armstrong Whitworth mechanism, like other early mechanical synchronizing systems, proved unreliable and was later replaced by the Constantinescu gear. A further improvement was the dual control facility, which permitted the observer to fly the aircraft in the event that the pilot might be incapacitated. Other problems followed. Oleo shock absorbers were regarded as an improvement but the oleo undercarriage was unable to withstand rough use on the frontline airfields, tailskids frequently broke and the original radiators blocked up quickly. This cast doubt on the thoroughness of test-flying programmes since the condition of airfields at the front were well known at this time. Following instructions issued on 30 April 1917, some FK8s were refitted with simplified vee-undercarriages from Bristol F2 Fighters. This soon led to a temporary shortage of these undercarriages and the practice had to be discontinued until May 1918, after which several FK8s were fitted with revised undercarriages. Late production FK8s had modified undercarriages, cowling, and radiators, as well as the final long exhausts.

The **Bristol F2B**, or 'Brisfit' as it was affectionately known, was, like the Avro 504K, an aircraft with a long life that extended into the 1930s. It was a two-seat biplane fighter and reconnaissance aircraft that first flew on 25 October 1916. Several engines were considered such as the 160hp Beardmore and the 150hp Hispano-Suiza, which went into the R2A and R2B, but at the right moment along came the Rolls-Royce Falcon I inline engine, which enabled Frank Barnwell to design the F2A. around this engine. Only fifty-two of these aircraft were built before it was decided to settle on the F2B. By this time it was standard practice to arm two-seaters with the synchronized Vickers gun for the pilot and a Lewis gun mounted on a Scarff ring for the air gunner/observer. The latter models had the Falcon III engine and this enabled the F2B to reach a maximum speed of 123mph and climb to 10,000ft three minutes faster than the F2A. To give the Brisfit extra firepower some were fitted with a second Lewis gun in the cockpit but the twin mounting was difficult to handle. Furthermore, in the last year of the war combat was taking place at ever higher altitudes where the air is thinner and it can be exceedingly cold.

The Lewis gun on the Foster mounting pointing vertically skywards.

To overcome this and retain the firepower in combat a Lewis gun could be fitted to the upper wing on a Foster mounting as it was in the night-fighting Avro 504s used in Home Defence. This could be fitted either instead of, or in addition to, the Vickers gun, although this caused interference with the pilot's compass, which was mounted on the trailing edge of the upper wing. Some F2Bs were fitted with a Lewis gun offset top starboard to minimize this effect. The Bristol Fighter's basic design stemmed from design studies by Frank Barnwell in March 1916 for an aircraft intended, like the RE8 and the FK8, as possible replacements for the BE2c.

Yet again, we find an instance of the right engine not being available in sufficient numbers. There was a chronic shortage of Rolls-Royce engines and there was competition for other engines that might have been suitable for the Brisfit. Plans to make the Bristol Fighter the standard British two-seater, replacing the RE8 and FK8, stalled against this barrier; there simply would not have been enough Falcons available. Efforts to find an available engine that was sufficiently powerful and reliable ultimately failed. The Sunbeam Arab was a 200hp engine but suffered badly from vibration. The 200hp Hispano-Suiza was better than the Arab but was wanted for the Sopwith Dolphin and the SE5a. This meant that most reconnaissance squadrons had to make do with the RE8 and FK8 until the end of the war.

Two Short aircraft merit a mention for the year 1916, the **Short Bomber** and the **Short 184**. There are two points of significance with the bomber, which was a land-based development of the Short 184, a discussion of which follows. Up to this time only the Handley Page Company was producing a twin-engined strategic heavy bomber that had a higher maximum speed than the Short Bomber. The latter could only manage 67mph at 6,500ft. Secondly, it had only one engine, whereas Handley Page would end the war with a four-engined bomber that could reach Berlin from an airfield in East Anglia with a significant payload. Having said that, the HP V/1500 entered the war too late to assess its true value and was discarded in the peacetime Air Force. In fact, the first post-war bomber, the Aldershot, built by Avro would also have a single engine and it only equipped one squadron. So we have to consider the roles for which the Air Department at the Admiralty had in mind in writing the specifications for this long-range reconnaissance bomber. It was armed with a rear-facing Lewis gun and could carry a 14-inch torpedo. It equipped No.7 Squadron RNAS and it has already been made clear that the Royal Navy led the way in strategic bombing. After the war Air Marshal Trenchard was to build his entire philosophy on the offensive role of air power but during the Great War he was more concerned with the tactical role of his aircraft, particularly on the Western Front. It would not be until late 1918 that he would command an independent bombing force. The Short Bomber entered service in later 1916 and the first raid was on targets in Ostend, but with only one engine it was going to be underpowered. The problems arose at the test flying stage when the bomber could not lift its top bomb load of 920lb. Attempts to rectify this shortcoming appear in detail in Annex 65 to Appendix A, but the upshot was that the bomber had a very short life of some six months being taken out of service in April 1917. It had been intended for long-range missions and over eighty were built by four manufacturers and this proved to be a waste of resources in war time. On the other hand, a lot can be learned even from a failed aircraft. The Short brothers went on to produce some very successful aircraft that were operational during World War II, notably the four-engined heavy bomber, the Stirling and the Sunderland

Short Bomber.

Short 184.

flying boat, whereas Saro failed miserably with their Lerwick flying boat.

The Short 184 was first flown in 1915 and served beyond the end of the war, unlike the Short Bomber. The Admiralty Air Department published its specifications for a two-seat reconnaissance bomber and torpedo-carrying aircraft to Sopwith, J. Samuel White and Short Brothers. Horace Short's response to Murray Sueter, the departmental director, was, 'Well, if you particularly want this done I will produce a seaplane that will satisfy you.' On the strength of this assurance two prototypes were ordered, for which serial Nos.184 and 185 were reserved, the resultant type becoming the Type 184. The floatplane had to have folding wings for stowage on board a ship or seaplane carrier. The wings could be swung out from the pilot's position, by means of a hand-winch in the cockpit, locking being accomplished by means of a splined and threaded spigot in the forward spar, locked and unlocked by a quarter-turn in a similar manner to the breech of a field-gun. In the folded position the wings were supported by a transverse shaft mounted in front of the tailplane: this was rotated by a lever in the cockpit so that its upturned ends engaged with slots on the interplane struts in order to lock the wings in the folded position. The twin unstepped main floats were carried by two struts attached to the front cross-tube and two pairs of struts attached to the rear cross-tube, both cross-tubes being arched in the middle to accommodate the torpedo crutches. The wooden tail float incorporated a small water-rudder actuated by torque tubes connected to the main rudder, and cylindrical air-bags were fitted beneath the lower wingtips. The floatplane was fitted with a radio transmitter and receiver, which was powered by a wind-driven generator mounted on a hinged arm so that it could be folded back when not being used. Other equipment carried included a basket of carrier pigeons, intended to be used as a back-up for the radio in the event of forced landings. Initial trials revealed a lack of longitudinal control, and the single-acting ailerons caused problems when taxiing downwind, so the two prototypes were fitted with lengths of bungee cord attached to control

Sopwith 1½ Strutter.

horns on the upper aileron surface to return the aileron to the neutral position. This only produced a marginal improvement, so ailerons were then added to the lower wings, these being fitted to all the aircraft built apart from the two prototypes. These were linked by cables to the upper ailerons, and the bungee cord to return the ailerons was rigged between the top of the rear interplane struts and the lower ailerons. Operational details of this floatplane can be found in Annex 66 of Appendix A.

Juxtaposed in this way one can see that the **Sopwith Pup** was a scaled-down version of the **1½ Strutter**, so named because one and a half struts joined the upper to the lower wing. The Strutter was the first British-designed two-seater tractor fighter, and the first British aircraft to enter service with a synchronized machine gun. As well as serving with both British air services, it also saw widespread but rather undistinguished service with the French Aéronautique Militaire. Two new developments were the variable incidence tailplane that could be adjusted by the pilot in flight and airbrakes under the lower wings to reduce the landing distance. The tandem cockpits were widely separated to give the gunner a good field of fire for his Lewis gun. The first prototype was flown in mid December 1915 and was officially tested in the January.

The 1½ Strutter was then plagued by a succession of new models of interrupter gear and Scarff ring. The Vickers-Challenger interrupter gear was put into production for the Royal Flying Corps in December 1915, and in a few weeks a similar order for the Scarff-Dibovski gear was placed for the RNAS. Early production 1½ Strutters were fitted with one or the other of these gears for the pilot's fixed .303-inch Vickers machine gun; due to a shortage of the new gears some early aircraft were built with only the observer's gun. Later aircraft standardized on the improved Ross gear, although the Sopwith-Kauper gear was also fitted. None of these early mechanical synchronization gears were very reliable and it was not uncommon for propellers to be damaged, or even entirely shot away.

The Scarff ring mounting was also new and production was at first slower than that of the aircraft requiring them. Various makeshift Lewis mountings as well as the

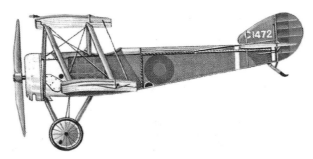

Sopwith Pup.

older Nieuport ring mounting were fitted to some early 1½ Strutters as an interim measure. When it did go into service in 1916 the Somme offensive had been planned for the end of June but the entire productive output of the Sopwith factory had been pre-contracted to the RNAS so it had to be agreed to transfer a number of aircraft from the Navy to support the planned offensive. These went to No.70 Squadron and all went well in providing long range penetrations into enemy held territory until the arrival of the German Albatros fighters. By January 1917 the 1½ Strutter had been outclassed as a fighter and No.43 Squadron alone suffered a large number of casualties. The situation in combat was slightly improved with the fitment of the 130hp Le Clerget 9b engine but this did not alter the balance of advantage in the air. The 1½ Strutter was relegated to long-range reconnaissance provided it had adequate fighter escort. Like other early Sopwith types, the 1½ Strutter was very lightly built and its structure did not stand up very well to arduous war service. It was also far too stable to make a good dogfighter. The last front-line 1½ Strutters in the RFC were replaced by Camels in late October 1917. The aircraft did, however, have a role in Home Defence.

The Sopwith Pup, a single-seat fighter aircraft, was a manoeuvrable aircraft that entered service in the autumn of 1916 but was eventually outclassed by the latest German fighters. It was then relegated to Home Defence training duties. The Pup's light weight and generous wing area gave it a good rate of climb. Agility was enhanced by installing ailerons on both wings. But the prototype and most production Pups were powered by the 80hp (60kW) Le Rhône rotary engine. Armament was a single 0.303-inch (7.7mm) Vickers machine gun synchronized with the Sopwith-Kauper synchronizer. So the Pup had half the horsepower and armament of the German Albatros DIII, but was much more manoeuvrable, especially over 15,000ft (4,500m) due to its low wing loading. Fighter ace James McCudden stated that 'When it came to manoeuvring, the Sopwith Pup could turn twice in the time that it took an Albatros to turn once.' It was a remarkably fine machine for general all-round flying. It was so extremely light and well surfaced that after a little practice one could almost land it on a tennis court. The Pup's docile flying characteristics also made it ideal for use in aircraft carrier deck landing and take-off experiments. On the other hand, the Pup was also longitudinally unstable. In Home Defence the Pup was of value in combating the threat from the Gotha bomber raids over south-east England and two Squadrons, Nos.61 and 112, were formed specifically to meet this threat.

Air superiority on the Western Front
Sources: National Archive Document AIR1/520/16/12/1

The failure of the latest Sopwith fighters did not mean that they were ill designed or armed, but was more a result of the see-saw war of advantages gained and lost in the air. As the year drew towards its conclusion the Commander-in-Chief, British Expeditionary Force, Field Marshal Haig, made an urgent plea to the War Office for fighting aircraft that could restore Allied aerial ascendency on the Western Front. In a letter dated 30 September 1916, Haig speaks of the urgent necessity to increase the number and efficiency of Allied fighting aeroplanes. He describes how it is not just the number of fighters that the enemy had introduced into the German front but the fact that they were faster, handier and capable of attaining a greater height than any at his disposal. The Albatros D1 had arrived on the Western Front in the summer of 1916. He singled out one squadron of Nieuports and one equipped with Sopwiths that could hold their own in battle. Even then he says that the Sopwiths are inferior in some respects though superior in others. All his other aircraft were decidedly inferior and this had resulted in a rising casualty rate suffered by RFC units. He finishes by stating that he does not anticipate losing Allied predominance in the air during the following three to four months but that the situation could become very serious unless adequate steps were taken to deal with the situation. General Trenchard was required to forward a statement of the RFC's estimated requirements to the War Office.

On 10 October a letter of reassurance was sent from the War Office to the effect that close attention was being paid to restoring the position of the RFC on the Western Front in the Spring of 1917. The supply of engines of the later types was improving and the necessary allotment of labour and materials to increase output was in hand. Indeed, it was the supply of engines that was the critical factor for aircraft of the types were already on order that would give performance superior to those currently in use. Engine production in the USA had been considered and the orders placed. Finally, the War Office referred to the increase in the number of hostile aircraft on the Somme front. The Army Council wanted the opinion of the GOC-in-C whether or not more aircraft might be concentrated on the Somme at the expense of other parts of the line or whether there appeared to be a material increase in the total enemy air force on the Western Front as a whole. As a temporary measure the RNAS detached a squadron from Dunkirk to the Fifth Army and were prepared to replace that unit in the new year.

THE DEVELOPMENT OF AIRCRAFT IN 1917

The list of military aircraft that were tested at the Experimental Aircraft Flight Martlesham Heath, both during 1917 and 1918 may be found at Appendix K.

Before returning to the pressing matter of restoring

Felixstowe F2A.

Fairey Campania.

aerial ascendency on the Western Front some maritime aircraft came into service during the year. Their addition to the RFC inventory was extremely important in the fight against the U-boat. One such maritime aircraft was the flying boat, the **Felixstowe F2A**. A flying boat differs from a floatplane in that the flying boat has a hull and the aircraft sits on the water like a boat. Hence the quality of the hull is very important in that it must be waterproof. The man responsible for the design of the F2A and the development of the hulls was Commander Porte. Before the war Porte had worked with American aircraft designer Glenn Curtiss on a flying boat, the *America*. Following the outbreak of war in Europe, Porte returned to England and rejoined the Royal Navy, becoming commander of the naval air base at Felixstowe where he recommended the purchase from Curtiss of an improved version of the *America*, the Curtiss H4 but, this flying boat was found to have a number of problems, being underpowered with its hull too weak for sustained operations and having poor handling characteristics when afloat or taking off. Experiments centred on designing an improved hull. Rather than the lightweight boat-type structure of the Curtiss boats, the F1s hull was based

around a sturdy wooden box-girder similar to that used in contemporary landplanes, to which were attached a single-step planing bottom and side sponsons. Once modified by the fitting of a further two steps, the new hull proved to have much better take-off and landing characteristics and was much more seaworthy. Porte worked on the Curtiss H4 and H12 boats. Rolls-Royce Eagle engines were added and the result was the Porte F2, which first flew in July 1916 and entered production as the F2A. This flying boat then gave rise to the F3 and F5, the last named joining the service too late for the Great War. The Felixstowe F2A was widely used as a patrol aircraft over the North Sea until the end of the war. Its excellent performance and manoeuvrability made it an effective and popular type, often fighting enemy patrol and fighter aircraft, as well as hunting U-boats and Zeppelins. The larger F3, which was less popular with its crews than the more manoeuvrable F2a, served in the Mediterranean as well as the North Sea. The Felixstowe F2A pictured below left, is in the dazzle paint scheme during an anti-submarine patrol. The dazzle camouflage adopted aided identification during air combat and on the water in the event of being forced down.

The **Campania** was the first aircraft ever designed specifically for aircraft carrier operations. The Royal Navy was the leader in building and developing aircraft carriers and in the autumn of 1914 purchased a liner, the *Campania*, for conversion to a seaplane carrier. Because the carrier would have to stop to lower the Campania into the water it was vulnerable to U-boat attacks and when a flight deck was constructed it became possible

Felixstowe F2A with zigzag pattern. The reason for this dazzle camouflage is explained in the text.

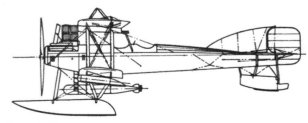

Short 320.

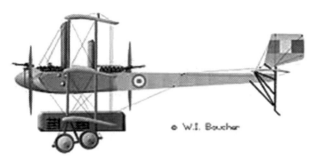

Caproni Ca 42.

to launch aircraft while the carrier was moving. If it was moving into wind this would assist the aircraft becoming airborne but because the Campania was built with floats, wheeled bogies had to be fitted to the floats, which could be jettisoned after take-off. This floatplane had an undistinguished career and although 100 were ordered only 62 were completed. Its use was a as a spotter plane.

The third seaplane to be considered is the **Short 320**. This was a scaled-up version of the Short 184. To the numerologist the figure 320 for this type was determined by the horsepower of the Cossack engine. The Admiralty requirement was for a floatplane to carry a Mark IX torpedo. By the end of April 1917 the Type 320 was in service with the RNAS in Italy. The first prototype proved to be little better than the Short 184 already in use and its operational career was delayed when there were two accidents. The fuselage collapsed as the torpedo was released, which was caused by the method of securing the fuselage bracing wires. Considering the Admiralty specification for this floatplane, it never dropped a torpedo in action. Lack of operational use did, however, mean that four of these aircraft could be used for torpedo-dropping trials carried out at Calshot. The torpedoes were dropped at different heights and speeds on separate occasions and proved a valuable source of information.

Two bombers will now be considered, one Italian and one British, the **Caproni Ca42** and the **HPO/400**. A more ungainly looking aircraft would be hard to find. The coffin-

like container immediately above the undercarriage was for the carriage of bombs. The endurance may have been seven hours but its maximum speed was only 87mph, which meant that it could not escape the attention of fighters. Their lack of speed made it unsuitable for day light operations and they were not used by the RNAS for combat and were returned to Italy after the war; indeed, the Ca4s were withdrawn from RAF service in the same month that they entered service. The significance of the entry into service of the O/400 is not simply that it is a powered-up version of the O/100 but that it was an important aircraft in the inventory of the Independent Bombing Force (IBF), which began operations in the second half of 1918. Indeed, all five squadrons of the 83rd Wing were equipped with the O/400. On the drawing board at Handley Page at this time was the HP V1500, a four-engined bomber that appears in the next section. Vickers were also working on a heavy bomber and orders for these are shown in Chapter 11. Deliveries of the Vickers Bomber were too late for operations with the IBF. (The specifications for a heavy bomber may be found at Appendix L.)

As regards fighters the call for a British aircraft to restore aerial ascendency on the Western Front was met by the SE5a, the Sopwith Triplane and the Sopwith Camel. The SE5a and the Camel were both extremely successful in combat. There was a succession of Nieuport variants but there was a limit to what could be done with a basic design, if one excepts the Spitfire. In RAF service the variant went up to the **Nieuport 28** but by that time the SPAD SVIII was already in most respects superior. Be that as it may, the Nieuport 28 was the first fighter to equip the American air units. Changes were often refinements to the aircraft. The rounded tail, for example, was modified to the point where the tail design could be standardized and, in later models, tailskids were sprung. Armament and engine capacity were always a matter of balance of advantage. The engine capacity was fairly uniform, any thing from 110 to 130hp but in a fighter armament could be as important as performance. The fitting of two guns to some of the Nieuport 27s was found to have a severe effect on performance. The Nieuport 27 illustrated in Annex 49 to Appendix 'A' shows a top-wing Foster Mounted Lewis gun. (A photograph of a top-wing mount on an Avro 504 appears in the next section.) The French preferred to have a Vickers synchronized machine gun in their machines. By the end of the war many Nieuports were relegated to training duties, their place being taken by SPADs. The Americans would have liked to equip their pursuit (fighter) squadrons with SPADs but there being a shortage of these fighters when the United States entered the war; the Nieuport 28 had to do.

Earlier reference was made to the urgent plea for the Allies that could restore air superiority, following

HPO/400.

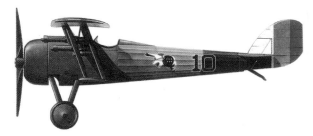

Nieuport 28.

Sopwith Camel.

SE5a.

'bloody' April 1917 on the Western Front. There is no doubt that the **SE5a**, the **Sopwith Camel** and the **Sopwith Triplane** went a long way to give the British fighters an advantage in combat. The SE5a had a 200hp engine but not before troubles were encountered with earlier attempts to find the best engine. With the Hispano Suiza 8b engine there were serious problems with gear reduction, which resulted in cases of the propeller separating from the engine and airframe in flight. In a few cases the entire gearbox parted company with both the airframe and the engine. It took a direct drive engine made by Wolsey Motors, under licence, to solve the problem. The Camel also made an extremely good fighter aircraft and was variously engined with Clerget, Bentley and Le Rhône power plants. The RFC specified which of these it wanted in those production models it purchased. The Le Rhône Camels had the superior Constantinescu gear and was faster in the climb and were employed in the Home Defence role. On the Western Front the Camels were used in the ground attack role but when used as a trench fighter extra armour was required. Those employed aboard ships had a shorter wing span. The last of the trio of fighters to come into service in the last full year of the war is the triplane. This is perhaps surprising because there were no triplanes in service after the end of the Great War. It was successful to the degree that the Germans copied the triplane design with thirty-four prototypes.

The Sopwith triplane ailerons fitted to all three wings, which would have made the aircraft exceptionally manoeuvrable. It had a service ceiling of 20,000ft and an exceptional rate of climb, which exceeded that of the German Albatros DIII. It was not always the power of the engine that could make an aircraft a superior fighter for power: weight ratio was a most important factor. The only drawback was the difficulty in effecting repairs. To access something as important as the fuel tank entailed disassembly of the aircraft, which meant that repairs could not be effected by ground crews on the squadron but had to be carried out at a repair depot.

From the de Havilland stable in 1917 came the DH4, 6 and 9/A. The DH4 was supposed to be a high-speed day bomber but ended up in a variety of duties. The fuel tank separated the pilot from the observer, which not only made it vulnerable to enemy fire but rendered communication between the two men all but impossible. It could, on the other hand be got out of trouble if the pilot encountered enemy fighters when it could out climb them. The DH6 was first flown in 1916 and was designed as a training aircraft and this at a time when most training aircraft were those that had become obsolete in their operational wartime role. The DH6 could use the same engine as the BE2, the 90hp RAF 1a engine, which

Sopwith Triplane.

DH9.

was readily available. It was very easy to fly and with a low landing speed it was almost impossible to stall. It was also very easy to repair following mishaps in the hands of trainee pilots. If any criticism could be levelled at the design of a training aircraft it was that it was too safe and this in spite of it possessing a degree of inherent instability in all three axis. Data for the DH4 and 6 can be found at Annexes 21 and 22 of Appendix A.

The **DH9** and **DH9A** differed in that the former had a very short service life, the latter a life which, in RAF use, continued into the early 1930s. The prototype DH9 was, in reality, a converted DH4 and flew in July1917 but this time the pilot and observer's cockpits were moved closer together. This provides a classic example of where a new engine was becoming available at the same time as the design was on the drawing board. This was the BHP/Galloway engine expected to deliver 300hp. Moving production from the DH4 to the DH9 was facilitated and much was expected of this aircraft being able to outperform enemy fighters. Such optimism was evident in the placing of orders for over 4,500 DH9s. In the event, the engine was unreliable since it could not deliver its expected power output and the engine had to be de-rated. At high altitude the DH9 could not out fly enemy fighters as could the DH4. On the Western Front this resulted in heavy losses in action or loss due to engine failure. Only in the Middle East, where they did not encounter stiff opposition, could the DH9s be effective operationally and there they were used in coastal patrols designed to deter U-boat operations. The DH9A was, in contrast, a successful light bomber. Certainly it was

intended that this aircraft should have the right engine. The illustration above discloses a very square front end, which housed the American Liberty engine, but the DH9A did not arrive on the squadrons until June 1918. By the time of the armistice over 1,700 DH9s had been built and one of Trenchard's strengths in building the new peacetime RAF was his ability to 'make do with a little'. By using the huge inventory of Bristol Fighters and DH9A aircraft he could equip the RAF with aircraft without the necessity of purchasing new aircraft designs. In the event, both these aircraft would be very valuable in the air policing role in the outposts of Empire, such as the North West Frontier of India. Since no aerial combat was experienced all that was required was aircraft that were workhorses, reliable and sturdy in inhospitable climates.

THE DEVELOPMENT OF AIRCRAFT IN 1918

Introduction
A consideration of aircraft development during the last year of the Great War begins with the government still looking for a fighter to replace the existing aircraft such as the Camel and Dolphin. The qualities and development of other aircraft will be considered before an overview of the war years is undertaken. The entry of the United States into the war will tip the balance of forces against the Central Powers. The Brest Litovsk treaty signed in March 1918 resulted in the Bolsheviks taking the Soviet forces out of the Great War. The Germans could then move their armies from the Russian front to the Western Front and the German High Command had to attempt to end the war with victory for the Central Powers before the build up of US forces could become critical – hence the April offensive by Germany on the Western Front. The growth of the intensity of the war in the air would be a corollary of the ground offensive. Finally, the formation of a RAF independent bombing force in June 1918 to mount strategic warfare on targets in Germany and German-occupied France would mean that the Air Ministry would be extremely busy in developing existing and new types such as the HPV1500 four-engined bomber.

Requirements for a single-seater fighter – March 1918
Source: National Archive document AIR1/6A/4/44

Aircraft equipped with the BR2 engine, the Snipe, Austin Triplane and the Boulton Paul machines, had provided the War Office with enough information regarding speed, rate of climb and ceiling to determine the design of a fighter that would incorporate the best features of these machines and be an improvement where possible. At the time of writing there was no information on the latest

DH9A.

Nieuport machine but it was held not to be important. Propellers were changed between machines and this did not materially affect performance thus it was fairly representative of engine performance. It was found that the single-seater fighters with the BR2 engine carrying the specified gun and ammunition, endurance and a given fuel capacity performed slightly better than the Camel but worse than the SR2 Dolphin Class. Having said that, it was felt that extra gun power and patrol radius as against performance could be justified. The BR2-engined fighters should not replace the Dolphin Class but could replace the Camel without loss of fighting efficiency.

However, the ABC 170 and 340hp engines may be considered in this connection but insufficient reliable data was available. It was possible to make informed predictions that could form the basis of action. The proposed design with the 170hp (Wasp) engine could have the manoeuvrability superior to the machines already mentioned and the ability to outclimb other current enemy designs. This might render a top gun unnecessary. Indeed, a Wasp engined machine could have a performance far superior than aircraft with the BR2 engines. The 340hp (Dragonfly) engine in a single-seater fighter would also have a materially better performance than the BR2 engine fighters. On the other hand, there was a body of opinion that put the superior performance of a lighter machine ahead of one that had greater gun power and combat radius. The ability to overtake or avoid combat was more important.

The policy recommended was therefore:

a. Introduce either Wasp or Dragonfly engine single-seater fighter as rapidly as possible
b. Carry on with the SE5 and Dolphin Class to the extent that may be necessary.
c. Replace Camels with the BR2 type machines as the engine output changes from the 130 Clerget to the BR2 but arrange for a minimum number to be produced.

With regard to the alternative mentioned in a. above sufficient engines of each type to equip a (test) squadron were now approaching completion. Owing to the concentration of effort necessary, either engine would be produced more quickly.

The Avro 504s cropped up again in 1918. These aircraft could be used in the Home Defence role in northern Britain. The Gothas that had posed such a threat to south east England did not have the range to reach northern targets and the Avro 504 would be adequate against the threat from Zeppelin raids. Avro 504J and K aircraft were modified as single-seaters and a Lewis gun was placed on a Foster mounting on the top wing (see photograph). Notice the cable that activated the trigger. These night fighters were powered by 100hp (75kW) Gnome or 110hp (80kW) Le Rhône engines. Some 274 converted Avro 504Js

A 504K with a Foster mount.

and Ks were issued to eight Home Defence squadrons in 1918, with 226 still being used as fighters at the end of World War I.

Sopwith came up with three aircraft in 1918, the Cuckoo, Salamander and Snipe, and Vickers produced the Vimy. All four played little part in the war since their arrival in squadron service was too late to have a significant impact on the conduct of the war. The Cuckoo was important since the Admiralty wanted a land-based torpedo-carrying aircraft. Previously, seaplanes carrying torpedoes required calm water to become airborne.

HPV1500.

With a range of 291 miles the Cuckoo could have been extremely useful in the North Sea and in the Aegean but the Armistice intervened. The Salamander was important since it was a trench fighter that had armour plating to protect the pilot and fuel tanks that added 650lb to the gross weight. Again, their arrival in France amounted to two aircraft by the time of the Armistice. Trench fighters were an important addition to the RFC inventory in France since trenches could be attacked without the need for an artillery barrage. The Snipes equipped the Independent Bombing Force as fighter escorts and units of the Home Defence force. They also served with the Royal Navy. This aircraft was chosen to be the standard night fighter of the RAF after the war. Finally, the Vickers Vimy would have been an effective addition to the inventory of the Independent Bombing Force but by 31 October 1918 only three had been delivered. Nevertheless, this bomber was an important part of the strategic bomber force in the 1920s. Its late arrival in France can be put down to engine supply difficulties.

Yet another aircraft that 'missed the boat' was the **HPV1500**. Three of these bombers, based at Bircham Newton with No.166 Squadron, were about to take off for a mission to bomb Berlin when the Armistice intervened. What made this aircraft so interesting was that its four engines were mounted in two nacelles. Each nacelle housed one tractor and one pusher propeller. Given Trenchard's conversion to strategic bombing one might have expected the HPV1500 to remain in RAF service after the war, but this was not to be. Offensive defence was the watchword in the 1920s but the League of Nations had been designed to ensure that the Great War was to be the 'war to end all wars'. Such a potent offensive symbol would not sit easily in an air force committed to defence not offence. The first peacetime bomber, the single-engined Aldershot, was not in the same league and there would not be RAF four-engined bombers until World War II. The Lancaster, Stirling and Halifax come to mind.

The **Martinsyde Buzzard** deserves a mention even though the prototype Buzzard F4 did not test fly until June 1918 and so it was too late for the Great War. The Buzzard was a private venture since it was not built to

BAT Bantam.

an official order. It was very manoeuvrable and fast. An early prototype reached 142mph and could have been a thorn in the side of the Central Powers. In spite of its excellent performance it was not used in the post-war service, the Air Ministry preferring the Snipe, which was cheaper if of lower performance. When one considers that the peacetime RAF was being run on £15 million pounds per annum it is perhaps not surprising. The British Aerial Transport **Bantam** falls into the same class as the Buzzard, it too achieved high speeds, 146mph with a Wasp II radial engine, but the engine was very noisy and continued to give trouble. It was abandoned and the designer, Frederick Koolhoven, returned to Holland to work on a Bantam powered by a Lynx engine to achieve a speed of 152mph. The aircraft did not, however, appear in the post-war inventory of the RAF. What is certain is that the quest for speed was creeping up, which could well shorten the time taken to effect an interception but was not the only criterion for a successful fighter. Speeds of aircraft did continue to climb in the inter-war period for most types of aircraft and the standard fighter in the 1920s, the Siskin, had a top speed of 134mph. Rate of climb, armament and manoeuvrability were also important.

THE LEGACY OF THE DEVELOPMENT OF AIR POWER IN THE GREAT WAR AS PEACE COMES

What then was the legacy of all the pre-war and war-time development of air power to a peacetime air force? What would the RAF do with the aircraft that it had inherited from the RFC and RNAS as it moved from war to peace? This would be a peace where the League of Nations had been created to prevent any possible resumption of violent conflict in the future, a conflict that took the lives of millions of European citizens. The cost alone was staggering and there would follow a period of austerity where expenditure on arms in Britain would be kept to a minimum. The cost of running an Air Ministry with bases both at home and overseas and the squadrons with all their personnel would cost only £15 million a year in the first year of peace. The India Office would, however, fund the maintenance of air forces on the North West Frontier.

Martinsyde Buzzard.

Clearly there would not be a need for all the airfields and landing grounds nor the aircraft that equipped the squadrons. The attraction of appointing Trenchard to the post of Chief of the Air Staff was that 'he would make do with a little and would not have to be carried'. It did not help his cause when the Admiralty and the War Office no longer saw the need for an Air Ministry and a separate air service in a time of austerity. They wanted their aeroplanes back! Churchill believed otherwise and the RAF survived, which is another story told in the author's history of the inter-war years (*The Trenchard Years 1920 to 1919*, published by Pen & Sword). What gave the RAF a real purpose in peacetime was helping to keep the peace in remote regions of the Empire. When Churchill moved to the post of colonial secretary, the policy of air policing was initiated.

Now we return to the question, of what the RAF would do with the aircraft that it had inherited from the RFC and the RNAS. The number of squadrons was cut from 185 to a mere 29 by 1 March 1920. With them went the aircraft, personnel and real estate. Those aircraft that had done so much in aerial combat towards the war effort went too, such as the SE5a and the Sopwith Camel, which survived only on one squadron. Two years later the DH9, the Short 184, RE8 and Handley Page O/400 had gone. Only the Vimy survived amongst the heavy bombers and it was used for training. Thus as far as land planes were concerned the only fighters were the Snipe and the Bristol Fighter (the Camel was designated a maritime aircraft). The only bombers were the DH9A and the DH10 and in the maritime role were the Felixstowe F2a and F5 flying boats, the Camel SF1 and the Sopwith Cuckoo. New aircraft coming into service included the Vickers Ambulance and the Vernon, the Fairey IIIs, the Westland Walrus and the Parnall Panther. The aircraft industry would suffer since the orders for production aircraft would dry up but Trenchard had the foresight to fund the production of prototypes that would permit companies to maintain a core of design and production staff. Competitions would be held amongst these prototypes, which could lead to production orders. As regards air policing it would be the DH9A, the Bristol Fighter, the Vickers Ambulance and the Vernon that would feature. Air policing demanded only aircraft of rugged construction that could be maintained in flying condition in inhospitable climates. There would be no aerial combat and so the Snipe would be phased out.

What was the legacy be in terms of aircraft design? Pilots clung to the idea of open cockpits from whence they could escape most easily in an emergency and biplanes also survived because of the low wing loading and stress. With regards armaments the synchronized Vickers gun and trainable Lewis gun featured in fighter and reconnaissance types and trainable Lewis guns were mounted in open cockpits in bomber aircraft. Not until the early 1930s would defensive armament be mounted in rotating enclosed turrets. A heated debate ensued as to whether or not the fuselage of an aircraft should be constructed of metal or fabric covering wooden frames. Abroad, the termites would love those constructed principally of wood. This debate would continue throughout the 1930s as Hawkers produced a variety of aircraft such as the Audax, Hind, Fury, Hardy and Demon and even the Hurricane, so vital in defence of Britain in 1940, which would represent the last of the old with wooden stringers covered in fabric. The Spitfire would be the first of the new in terms of all-metal construction.

There has been no mention of the need for airships in the peacetime air force. All that Trenchard could afford, from his small budget, was a unit at Howden to carry out research into their possible use in a future conflict. At the end of the 1920s only the *R100* and *R101* would represent a serious attempt to consider the usefulness of large airships, the *R100* being built by private enterprise and the *R101* being developed from public funds. The Secretary of State for Air, Lord Thomson, was enthusiastic about the role of airships. Certainly, Germany had made good use of them commercially. But the only military justification that could be advanced for any expenditure on airships was that they could be requisitioned in a national emergency to be used on long-range reconnaissance missions or troop transports. If this was over the sea then land-based fighter aircraft could not reach them. In the event, the *R100* would make a successful return flight to Canada even though there was serious damage to the outer fabric from wind turbulence in attempting to land and one engine was out of action for the return journey. It was, however, the tragic loss of the *R101* over Beauvais in northern France in 1930 on a flight to India with Lord Thomson on board that spelt the end of the military airship as far as Britain is concerned.

THE BRITISH AIRCRAFT INDUSTRY INCLUDING AIRCRAFT DESIGNERS AND TEST PILOTS OF THE PERIOD

The aircraft companies are listed in alphabetical order. This list is not exhaustive.

The Aircraft Manufacturing Company (Airco)

Airco operated as a British aircraft manufacturer from 1912 to 1920. Most of the aircraft produced during the war were designed by their chief designer, Geoffrey de Havilland, who was initially with a design team at the Royal Aircraft Factory. Some 30 per cent of all training, bombing and fighting aircraft used by the Britain and the USA were produced by Airco. In December 1918 it was claimed that Airco was the largest aircraft company in the world. Besides aircraft products, including propellers and

Geoffrey de Havilland.

engines, there was a variety of land-based aircraft as well as flying boats and airships. Engines built under licence included the Le Rhône and Gnome rotary engines. At Hendon there were between 7,000 and 8,000 employees. The company had a wind tunnel and material testing laboratory. Some of the aircraft, all of which can be found in Appendix A, included the DH2, 4, 6, 9 and 9A.

In spite of the tremendous contribution the company made to the war effort the lack of government interest in military aircraft made the company unprofitable and it was sold to the British Small Arms Company. But this did not prevent Airco establishing the fist airline in the United Kingdom.

A.V. Roe and Company Ltd

A.V. Roe and Company, better known simply as Avro, was one of the most famous of all British aircraft manufacturers and was originally founded in 1910 by the aircraft pioneer Alliot Verdon Roe. His interest in aircraft developed before the Great War, his first design being the Roe I Biplane of 1907, which lacked a powerful enough engine to take off without assistance. When an engine was loaned in 1908 it did take to the air but only with a series of short hops.

The fledgling aircraft company was given engineering space at Brownsfield Mills Manchester where A.V. Roe's brother H.V. Roe owned Everard and Company. The first aircraft produced by the new company was the Roe II Triplane, one of a series of early designs that culminated in the Avro 500 biplane of 1912, considered by Roe to be his first truly successful design. His early aircraft were produced in small numbers but his fortunes would change with the Avro 504 with 8,340 being built over two decades. Although only a small number of Avro 504s saw active service with both the RFC and the RNAS, it was as a training aircraft that it was most valuable.

In 1928 Roe sold the company to J. D. Siddeley, and Avro became part of the Armstrong Siddeley

Alliot Verdon Roe.

Development Company and a sister-firm of Armstrong Whitworth. Roe himself moved on to form Saunders-Roe Ltd. His legacy would be long-lasting with such aircraft as the Manchester and Lancaster bombers, the Anson and a training aircraft aptly named the Tutor, which contributed in no small way to this country winning World War II.

The Bristol and Colonial Aeroplane Company Ltd

The Bristol and Colonial Aeroplane Company Ltd was founded in February 1910 by Sir George White, who was also Chairman of the Bristol Tramway and Carriage Company. Seeing a future in aviation, the access to technically trained personnel and the use of tram sheds to store and build aircraft proved a good start, although the Aeroplane Company was a risky venture at the time. Accordingly, it was constituted as a separate company from the Tramway business with Sir George subscribing all of the aero company's working capital of £25,000 and George Challenger transferred from the Tramway business to become the chief engineer and works manager. Test flying was carried out at Brooklands where a flying school was established with another at Larkhill where land was leased from the War Office. By 1914, 308 of the 664 Royal Aero Club certificates issued to date had been gained at the company's schools.

One of the earliest projects was to build the Bristol Boxkite. Although satisfactory by the standards of

Sir George White.

Sir Richard Fairey.

the day, the Boxkite was not capable of much further development and work was started on new designs. At this time both Challenger and Low left the company to join the newly established aircraft division of the armament firm Vickers. Their place was taken by the former chief instructor at the Blériot flying school, Pierre Prier, together with Gordon England. In January 1912 the Romanian engineer Henri Coandă was appointed as chief designer. Frank Barnwell was taken on as the design engineer and took over as Bristol's chief designer when Coandă left the company in October 1914. Barnwell was to become one of the world's foremost aeronautical engineers. The company expanded rapidly, employing 200 people by the outbreak of the Great War. Probably two of the most successful products of the company in the war years was the Bristol Scout and the Bristol Fighter, the latter surviving in front-line service to 1931.

The Fairey Aviation Company Ltd

Charles Fairey left Short to form his own company and built other company designs under licence or as a subcontractor. The Fairey Campania, first flown in February 1917, was the first aircraft to be designed and built by his company, which had three sites, Hayes in Greater London, RAF Ringway in Greater Manchester and Heaton Chapel, Stockport. The primary location for aircraft production was at North Hyde Road, Hayes (Middlesex), with test flying at nearby Northolt aerodrome. This was during the period 1917 to 1929. In the third report of the Royal Commission on Awards to

Inventors, reported in the *Flight* magazine of 15 January 1925, aviation figures prominently. C. R. Fairey and the Fairey Aviation Co. Ltd were awarded £4,000 for work on the Hamble Baby seaplane, which was a floatplane of the RNAS during the Great War. Another Fairey design that came into service at the end of the war was the Fairey III. Although the Fairey Swordfish does not belong to the Great War period it was probably one of the most successful in combat. Swordfish aircraft sealed the fate of the German battleship *Bismarck* in May 1941 and sank Italian capital ships in Taranto harbour in November 1940.

Martinsyde Aircraft

The company began as a partnership between H.P. Martin and George Handasyde beginning in 1908. The company was renamed Martinsyde Ltd in 1915 and by then had become the third largest manufacturer of aircraft with factories in Woking and Brooklands. From 1919 the company also built motorcycles, but in 1922 they were forced into liquidation allegedly by a factory fire. At the end of the war the demand for military aircraft dried up but Martinsyde were not alone in trying to cope without any orders.

Their No.1 monoplane was built in 1908–1909 and succeeded in lifting off the ground before being wrecked in a gale. They went on to build a succession of largely monoplane designs, although it was a biplane, the S1 of 1914, which turned Martin Handasyde into Martinsyde, a most successful aircraft manufacturer. In addition to

No.4b Dragonfly of 1911.

the aircraft listed below the company also manufactured the BE2c and SE5a under subcontract.

Martinsyde-designed aircraft included:

1. Martinsyde S1 single-seat scout, 1914
2. G100 and G102 'Elephant' – scout aircraft, 1915 onwards
3. Martinsyde RG
4. Martinsyde F1
5. Martinsyde F2
6. Martinsyde F3 – private venture design with the Rolls-Royce Falcon engine
7. Martinsyde F4 Buzzard – fighter, the F3 with a Hispano-Suiza engine

The Royal Aircraft Factory

No description of the British aircraft industry would be complete without describing the products of the Royal Aircraft Factory. In 1912 the Army Balloon Factory was renamed the Royal Aircraft Factory. Between 1911 and 1918 the Royal Aircraft Factory generated a number of

Royal Aircraft Factory 1912.

aircraft designs. Most of these were essentially research aircraft, but a few actually went into mass production, especially during the war period. Some orders were met by the factory itself, but the bulk of production was by private British companies, some of which had not previously built aircraft. Among its designers was Geoffrey de Havilland who later founded his own company, and John Kenworthy who became chief engineer and designer at the Austin Motor Company in 1918. Henry Folland was a Royal Aircraft Factory designer who was later chief designer at Gloster Aircraft Company. But he was a pre Great War designer who stuck doggedly to the biplane design and his very last RAF biplane fighter was the Gloster Gladiator, which had a closed cockpit but was soon overtaken by the monoplane eight-gun fighters. Folland then went on to found his own company, Folland Aircraft.

On pages 178 and 179 the various designations for aircraft such as BE, SE, RE and FE were applied to the Royal Aircraft Factory types. These are not easy to follow for FE2 referred to three distinct types of aircraft. It was only the FE2 of 1914 that went into production. It was a two-seat fighter and general purpose aircraft. There were one-off conversions such as the FE2c where the seating positions of the pilot and observer in the FE2b were reversed. Thus the FE2c was not a sub-type. The BE1 was basically the prototype for the early BE2, but the BE2c was really a completely new aeroplane, with very little commonality with the earlier BE2 types. On the other hand, the BE3 to the BE7 were all effectively working prototypes for the BE8 and were all very similar in design, with progressive minor modifications of the kind that many aircraft undergo during a production run. The SE4a had nothing in common at all with the SE4, while the SE5a was simply a late production SE5 with a more powerful engine. Several early RAF designs were officially 'reconstructions' of wrecked aircraft, because the Royal Aircraft Factory did not initially have official authority to build aircraft to their own design. In most cases the type in question used no parts whatever from the wreck; in some cases not even the engine. Included in this list are the Dunne and Cody designs built and/or tested at Farnborough, although these were not strictly Royal Aircraft Factory types. The Royal Aircraft Factory also built aero engines, including the RAF 1, 2, 3, 4, 5 and 8.

Short Brothers

Eustace and Oswald Short started their career in aeronautics by producing balloons. They persisted with balloon manufacture, moving to a site beneath the railway arches situated conveniently close to the Battersea gasworks for their coal gas-filled balloons. The brothers won a contract for three balloons for the British Indian Army and other contracts followed.

Lankester Parker.

But everything changed when they heard about the demonstrations of the Wright Flyer at Le Mans in France. They decided that the future lay in aircraft production and design and they called upon the third brother Horace, who was then working on steam turbine development, to join them. He would design the early aircraft. Frank McClean, who was a member of the Aero Club, bought several of Short's aircraft and became an unpaid test pilot. One of these aircraft purchased by McClean was the Short No.1 biplane. Meanwhile, the brothers had obtained British rights to build copies of the Wright design.

In February 1909 the brothers acquired marshland near Leysdown on the Isle of Sheppey and a workshop was constructed. When aircraft production began at this site Short Brothers became the first aircraft manufacturing company to undertake volume production of aircraft. Soon it was necessary to move to a larger site at Eastchurch. When McClean agreed to become an instructor for the RNAS a close association was established between Short Brothers and the Admiralty, resulting in the company producing naval aircraft such as the Short 184 and 320. In 1913 Gordon Bell became the company's first paid test pilot who was then followed by Ronald Kemp. Kemp could not cope with the amount of test flying involved and a freelance pilot, named Lankester Parker helped. In

1918 Lankester Parker succeeded Kemp as the company's chief test pilot, a post that he was to hold for the next twenty-seven years. Probably the most famous aircraft produced by the company was the Sunderland flying boat.

Siddeley/Deasy

The Deasy Motor Car Company Ltd was founded by Henry Deasy and when J.D. Siddeley took up the appointment of managing director in 1910 the company was renamed Siddeley-Deasy Motor Car Company. It grew rapidly and during the Great War the company had 5,000 workers producing ambulances and aircraft engines, which included the Puma. The company was one of six to produce the RE8 from 1916. The company then turned its attention to fixed-wing aircraft. In 1917 three designers moved there from the Royal Aircraft Factory. They were S.D. Heron, an engine designer, F.M. Green, who became the chief engineer, and John Lloyd, who became chief aircraft designer. The Siskin fighter, which was produced in the 1920s, was designed by a team led by Lloyd.

Sopwith Aviation Company

Thomas Sopwith was only twenty-four when his company's first factory premises opened near Kingston railway station in December 1912. An early collaboration was with the S.E. Saunders boatyard of East Cowes the following year.

Thomas Sopwith circa 1910.

Float- equipped Tabloid.

This resulted in the production of the 'Bat Boat', an early flying boat with a laminated hull, which meant that it could operate over both land and water.

A small factory subsequently opened in Woolston, Hampshire, in 1914. During World War I, the company made more than 16,000 aircraft and employed 5,000 people. Many more of the company's aircraft were made by subcontractors rather than by Sopwith themselves, including Ruston Proctor, Fairey, Clayton and Shuttleworth, Fairey and William Beardmore and Company. Initially, Tom Sopwith himself, assisted by his former personal mechanic Fred Sigrist, led the design of the company's types. Following a number of pre-war designs for the Royal Naval Air Service, such as the 3-seater and the Bat Boat, Sopwith's first major success was the fast and compact (hence the name) Tabloid, a design which first showed the influence of the company's test pilot, the Australian Harry Hawker. A float-equipped version of this aircraft won the Schneider Trophy in 1914. The landplane version was used by both the RNAS and RFC at the start of the war. With higher power and floats, the type evolved into the Sopwith Baby, which was a workhorse of the RNAS for much of World War I.

In 1916, Herbert Smith became chief engineer of Sopwith, and under his design leadership the company went on to produce its other successful Great War aircraft, details of which can be found in Appendix A and include the 1½ Strutter, the single-seat scout, the Pup, the Triplane, Camel, Snipe, Cuckoo, Salamander and Dolphin. The Pup and 1½ Strutter were the first successful British tractor fighters equipped with a synchronizing gear to allow a machine gun to fire through the rotating propeller. This gear was known as the Sopwith-Kauper gear from its designers. The Pup was widely used on the Western Front by the RFC and from ships by the RNAS from the autumn of 1916 to the early summer of 1917, and was considered a delight to fly by its pilots. It continued in use as an advanced trainer for the remainder of the war. The Pup began the famous series of *animal*-named Sopwith aircraft during the war, giving the company's

aircraft the collective nickname 'The Flying Zoo'. The twin-gun Camel fighter was highly maneuverable and well-armed, and over 5,000 were produced up until the end of the war. It destroyed more enemy aircraft than any other British type, but its difficult flying qualities also killed very many novice pilots in accidents.

Upon the liquidation of Sopwith, Tom Sopwith himself, together with Harry Hawker, Fred Sigrist and Bill Eyre, immediately formed H.G. Hawker Engineering, forerunner of the Hawker Aircraft and Hawker Siddeley lineage. Sopwith was chairman of Hawker Siddeley until his retirement.

Vickers Armstrong Ltd

Vickers Armstrong Ltd was a British engineering conglomerate formed by the merger of the assets of Vickers Limited and Sir W.G. Armstrong Whitworth & Company in 1927. The advertisement shows the wide variety of services and military products that came from the Vickers stable. Before that Vickers Ltd formed an aviation department in 1911. Vickers became renowned as a manufacturer of large aircraft at its main factory at Brooklands in Surrey and by the end of the Great War Vickers had produced the Vimy heavy bomber.

In 1913, a Vickers machine gun was mounted on the experimental Vickers EFB1 biplane, which was probably the world's first purpose-built combat aeroplane. However, by the time the production version, the Vickers FB5, had entered service the following year, the armament had been changed to a Lewis gun. During World War I, the Vickers gun became a standard weapon on British and French military aircraft, especially after 1916. Although heavier than the Lewis, and using a belt feed that proved problematic in the air, its closed bolt firing cycle made it much easier to synchronize to allow it to fire through aircraft propellers. The famous Sopwith Camel and the SPAD XIII types used twin synchronized Vickers, as did most British and French fighters between 1918 and the mid-1930s.

Products of Vickers Limited.

Westland aircraft – Yeovil

In 1915 the Westland Aircraft Works was founded as a division of Petters Limited The name 'Westland' was chosen by Mrs Petter as new land purchased as part of an expansion in 1913 at West Hendford, which had been earmarked for a new foundry, but ended up becoming the centre for aircraft production. In response to government orders for the construction under licence of initially twelve Short Type 184 seaplanes Westland began production. This was followed by a host of Sopwith, Airco and de Havilland designs when the parent companies could not meet deadlines for various aircraft. The 1½ Strutter, DH4, DH9 and DH 9A come to mind. As a result of the experience gained in manufacturing aircraft under licence, Westland began to design and build its own aircraft, starting with the Westland N1B in 1917, which was followed in 1918 by the Wagtail and the Weasel.

J. Samuel White & Co. Ltd

J. Samuel White was a British shipbuilding firm based in Cowes, taking its name from John Samuel White (1838–1915), building ships for the Royal Navy. In 1912 the company started building aircraft at Cowes. Their first aircraft, the Samuel White Navy plane, was a 'high-powered hydro-biplane' built to a design by Mr Howard T. Wright who was in charge of the newly formed Aviation department at J.S. Whites. The aircraft, which was built in the 'Gridiron Shed' on the banks of the Medina at East Cowes, was shown in partly assembled form at the Aviation Show at Olympia in February 1913. Test flying was carried out during the summer of 1913 by Mr Gordon England.

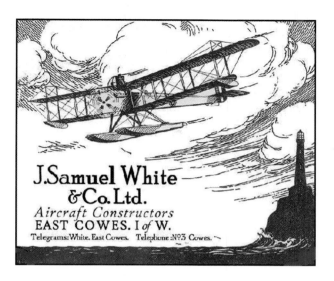

J. Samuel White
&Co. Ltd.
Aircraft Constructors
EAST COWES. I *of* W.
Telegrams: White. East Cowes.   Telephone: Nº 3 Cowes.

Between 1912 and 1916 the company had an aviation department that built a number of seaplanes using the name Wight Aircraft, namely the Wight Pusher, Twin, Seaplane, Baby, Bomber, Seaplane Type 1000 and the Wight Converted. It was the last named that equipped Nos.241 and 243 Squadrons and the latter was based at Cherbourg. It was a Wight Converted floatplane from this squadron that sank German U-boat *UB 32* on 18 August 1917. The company had ceased producing its own designs by the end of the Great War, although some maritime aircraft were built for the RNAS under licence.

Chapter 8
The Development of Training

Training in military and naval wings of the Flying Corps – the work of the Central Flying School in 1913 – RNAS training prior to the outbreak of war – an overview of aircrew training during the Great War – general method of teaching scout (fighter) pilots – training of night pilots – RAF training in 1918 – training of US flying personnel – training matters affected by the proposal to form an Air service – RAF training courses in October 1918.

Maxims for pilots in 1912
Source: AIR1/ 6A/4/30

This introduction to training is a very good pointer to what makes a good pilot. In 1912 Major C.J. Burke RFC gave some advice to new pilots, particularly those under training. This is important for young pilots, whom like newly qualified car drivers often drive beyond their capabilities by taking unnecessary risks and or not accepting the advice of their seniors. He begins by saying that, on the ground, one overrates capacity for air work and that time in the air alone will make a pilot. It isn't wind that is the problem for an aircraft but it is for a pilot. A good pilot must feel comfortable in the air for rigid muscles are no help. If he cannot relax he should give up flying. The passenger must have confidence in the pilot for if the pilot lacks confidence trouble is a certainty. At the same time the pilot must have confidence in the rigger.

A Handbook for Training in the Military and Naval Wings of the Flying Corps
Source: National Archive document

Consideration was given at a very early stage to the publication of a handbook for pilots of the Military and Naval Wings of the Flying Corps and, in 1913, suggestions were forwarded by the staff at South Farnborough to the War Office. Initially, it was felt that one book might suffice for training. There were, of course, Standing Orders for routine purposes, but in the light of experience it was felt that the following publications be drawn up.

a. **A Training Manual RFC** – For instructions in the art of piloting an aircraft, which would include the care of machines, engines, instruments etc.,

b. **A War Manual for the RFC (Military Wing)** – To include instructions as to strategic and tactical employment and War administration of the Military Wing (other than the details of piloting aircraft (see above)

c. **A War Manual for the RFC (Naval Wing)** – To be compiled by the Naval Wing

d. **Standing Orders for the Central Flying School** – Already issued

e. **Standing Orders for the RFC (Military Wing)** – In the process of preparation. Ditto the Naval Wing

Additionally, it was felt that there should be special handbooks for each type of aeroplane and engine in service. Instructions for the maintenance of Gnome and Renault engines had already been translated. The remainder could be prepared by both wings of the Flying Corps. Finally, there should be an annual confidential memorandum for circulation amongst officers of the RFC and Army generally. This would review the progress of military aeronautics at home and abroad during the preceding twelve months. This should be compiled by the Admiralty and War Office.

THE WORK OF THE CENTRAL FLYING SCHOOL IN 1913
Source: National Archive Document CAB/4/1 AC 15

Introduction
The members of the Air Committee of the Cabinet were pleased with the site chosen for the Central Flying School and consideration was being given to the establishment of a site on the coast within easy flying distance so that pilots undertaking the sea portion of the elementary training did so in machines capable of alighting on and rising from the land or water. There had been progress with training. The programme of three courses per year was maintained but the length of each course had been reduced to thirteen weeks so that, in the intervals between courses, the aircraft could be overhauled and leave could be granted to officers and men on the staff. These intervals also permitted the extension of particular courses where, for example, it had not been possible to complete training in the scheduled time due to adverse weather conditions. The list of military officers chosen to attend the course of instruction at the CFS commencing on 17 September 1913 is to be found at Appendix N.

First and Second Class Flyers
On graduating from the school pilots were required to obtain the Pilot's Certificate of the Royal Aero Club to which was added a requirement to possess the technical knowledge in the care and maintenance of aeroplanes and engines for the Second Class Flyer's certificate and the test to be passed for the award of the First Class certificate had been agreed. But it was recognized that Second Class pilots would not be suitable for naval work

where navigation played such an important part. It was believed that such pilots employed on naval work should be regarded as on probation, and liable to the forfeiture of rating and pay, until they qualified as First Class pilots within a reasonable time. The Air Committee held the view that the CFS should maintain a universal standard of merit throughout all branches of the Royal Flying Corps, with the examination of all candidates being held at the school.

Syllabus of the course of instruction
The Air Committee noted that all the subjects proposed by the original, subcommittee with the exception of photography, had been included in the syllabus, namely flying, general principles of mechanics and construction of engines and aeroplanes, meteorology, observation from the air, navigation and steering when flying by compass, cross-country flights, signalling by all methods and types of warship. The construction of aeroplanes and the stripping and assembling and tuning up of internal combustion engines were also studied. The aim was to turn out pilots who could not simply fly an aeroplane but keep an aeroplane in thoroughly good order. It was likely, concluded the Air Committee, that only a small proportion of students would pass out as First Class flyers. A large number of men would therefore require extra training in the care and maintenance of aeroplanes. The numbers of pilots who could be trained annually was most likely to be determined by the ability of the technical personnel to maintain the training machines in flying condition for experience had shown that the number of personnel required was largely in excess of the numbers originally estimated. The original estimate of 179 flyers per annum had to be revised downwards to ninety-six officers and thirty men. The conclusion of the Air Committee was that the total staff of ninety-six people, a figure already in excess of the original estimate, was insufficient to cope with the work expected of it. The aeroplane totals at the CFS were: thirty-six biplanes with three on order and nine monoplanes. There followed a prohibition on the use of monoplanes for training and those intended for the CFS were retained at Farnborough.

Training in balloons
Cross-country flights had been recommended as part of the training in aerial observation but these had not been carried out at the CFS as the present stock of free balloons had been in constant use by officers and men undergoing training in airship work at Farnborough. The Air Committee felt that training in air observation was best carried out in balloons since explanations and instructions could be given in the air, something not feasible in an aeroplane.

Buildings, transport and wireless
The replacement of temporary buildings by permanent ones was proceeding according to plan and this included a power station. Permanent buildings were of particular importance at Netheravon for the school occupied one of the bleakest and most isolated parts of Salisbury Plain and was seven miles from the nearest railway station. It was of particular importance that the officers and men of the staff who had to spend the entire year at CFS should have the personal quarters and messes. The motor transport consisted of a collection of lorries, second-hand Daimler cars and motorcycles. Only one driver was from the Army Service Corps, the remaining being air mechanics trained at the school. The wireless consisted of two Rouzet sets borrowed from the Navy. One of them was mounted in a Maurice Farman machine and reception was very good up to a distance of 36 miles with a 150ft aerial, which could be extended to 50 miles with a 200ft aerial.

RNAS TRAINING PRIOR TO THE OUTBREAK OF WAR
Source: National Archive Document AIR1/363/231/3

Training of men entering the service
Men could enter the RNAS from Fleet service with the Navy or from the Army, typically the Military Wing of the Flying Corps or from civilian life. The men selected for training were liable to be detailed for any branch of the RNAS, namely work on seaplanes, aeroplanes, airships, seaplane ships or on kites. On entry they had to show that they had experience in one of more of the following trades:

1. General upkeep, construction or repair of aircraft, erecting, truing up etc.
2. Carpenter's work, joinery, cabinet making etc,
3. Boat building
4. Fabric work (airship or aeroplanes)
5. Fitting, turning
6. Care and maintenance and repair of petrol engines
7. Coppersmith's work
8. Electrician's work
9. Cycle mechanic
10. Motor driver

If none of these skills were possessed a man could be accepted into the service if he had above average intelligence. They were required to pass an examination in education up to Standard 4 Elementary Education Code and also an examination in their trade qualifications before selection. Men entering from civilian life as opposed to existing servicemen received preliminary training at the Naval Depot, Sheerness. Men selected for airship training were formed into separate classes from those who would work on seaplanes etc. Ratings who qualified as pilots were eligible from the date of qualification for additional pay at the rate of 4s per diem for First Class flying certificates. Men were allowed to hold Second Class flying certificates for only twelve months. It they had not then qualified for a first class certificate, it was considered whether or not their Second Class certificate was to be retained. The first six weeks of training was conducted entirely at the Naval Depot for civilians. After the initial training men selected for seaplane training went daily to the Naval Flying School, Eastchurch, or to the Isle of Grain Air Station for practical instruction. The classes for airship training went to the Airship Training School.

AN OVERVIEW OF AIRCREW TRAINING DURING THE GREAT WAR

Introduction
In the Great War there were principally two aircrew categories, pilot and observer. The observer was regarded as the one who would have to assess the situation on the ground and report his findings to ground commanders. This would imply that the captain of the aircraft should be the observer since he should direct where the aircraft was flown and at what height the aircraft was flown so that the best results could be obtained in a reconnaissance. This would relegate the pilot to one of chauffer carrying out the bidding of the observer. This was reversed at an early stage since the safety of the aircraft and the necessity to take evasive action could well call for a split-second response. During the author's time in the RAF it was recognized that it was a pilot's air force when 'drivers airframe' (RAF slang for pilots) were in the driving seat. At the same time it could well be the navigator who would command a multi-engined, multi-crewed aircraft. On the other hand, instances are recorded in this history of pilots having to drop an observer when the weight of an aircraft carrying bombs or torpedoes would be unacceptably high and to carry an observer would severely limit the range of an aircraft. The pilot would then have to drop a bomb or release a torpedo as well as fly the aircraft; an observer was not expected nor trained to fly an aircraft.

Observer training
Few aircraft had dual controls like the AW FK8, which would permit the observer to fly the aircraft should the pilot become incapacitated. Nonetheless, many observers gained at least rudimentary piloting skills, and it was very common for experienced observers to be selected for pilot training. Indeed, many pilots were initially seconded to the RFC from their original regiments by becoming an observer. One could tell those who had entered the

RFC from other army regiments since they continued to wear their regimental uniforms whereas an entrant from civilian life had to wear the 'maternity jacket'. There was no formal training for observers until 1917. Until then the observer would receive a brief introduction to the aircraft from the pilot before being sent out on a first mission. A qualified observer wore a half-wing brevet, which could not be forfeited once awarded

Aircrew entry and training
Applicants for aircrew generally entered the RFC as a cadet via the depot pool for basic training. Next was a posting to the School of Military Aeronautics either in Oxford or Reading where theoretical training was given. From there they attended a flying training squadron course, which could be at home or overseas. Indeed, applicants for aircrew training who were serving in overseas theatres, such as the Middle East, might well be trained in Egypt, thus shortening greatly the time before an applicant could be ready for posting to an operational squadron.

With the outbreak of World War I in August 1914, it was clear that the RFC would have to expand if it were to serve the Army in France and replace its own casualties. The CFS did not have the capacity to support this growth, so new training units were opened and civilian flying schools commandeered. The quality of the instructors engaged varied, however, and many of the aircraft used were unsuitable. Accidents were common and for most of the war casualties at training units were greater than losses in action. In early 1916, the RFC began regulating training standards, with pupils expected to fly at least fifteen hours' solo. Unfortunately, the ever-increasing demand for pilots at the front, and a lack of resources at the flying schools, meant some students received insufficient training and arrived at operational squadrons unprepared for combat. Partly because of this, casualties rose sharply and by the spring of 1917 the life expectancy of a new pilot could be measured in weeks. This led Colonel Robert Smith-Barry to complain about the poor standard of newly trained pilots arriving at the Front and a high fatality rate during training. With the agreement of Trenchard, Smith-Barry returned to the United Kingdom in 1917 to implement a comprehensive training programme for pilots. The curriculum was based on a combination of dual flight instruction and classroom theory. Fatalities in training were halved but this did not mean that student pilots were not allowed to undertake dangerous manoeuvres. The aim was to expose the students to potentially dangerous situations in the air in a controlled environment so that errors of judgment could be corrected.

During the dual flying training period approximately 45 per cent of a class intake would be deemed unsuitable. There was a lack of trained instructors, however, and initially a 'tour-expired' pilot was sent for a rest from an operational squadron in France, without any specific training on how to instruct, so this problem had too to be rectified. After the dual training period of between ten to twenty hours the remaining pupils would be ready to 'go solo'.

Growth of the aircrew training organization

Gradually the situation improved and, as the RFC continued to grow, its training organization became more sophisticated. A Training Brigade was formed and specialist schools, staffed by veterans, were established to teach air fighting, bomb dropping, night flying and a variety of other skills. The Sopwith Pup saw extensive use as a trainer. Student pilots completing basic flight training in the Avro 504k often graduated to the Pup as an intermediate trainer. The Pup was also used in fighting school units for instruction in combat techniques. Many training Pups were, in fact, reserved by senior officers and instructors as their personal runabouts. Schools were also set up overseas in Egypt, Canada and the USA. Specialist schools were established in May 1916 to teach air fighting at East Fortune, Marske, Sedgeford, Feiston, Ayr and Turnberry. In this case veteran pilots supervised simulated combat flying. In 1917, the American, British, and Canadian Governments agreed to join forces for training. Between April 1917 and January 1919, Camp Borden in Ontario hosted instruction on flying, wireless, air gunnery and photography, training 1,812 RFC Canada pilots and 72 for the United States. Training also took place at several other Ontario locations. Training could be hazardous and at Camp Taliaferro near Fort Worth, Texas 39 RFC officers and cadets died under training. Training carried out in Egypt was mentioned earlier. Seven training squadrons were located here and five Training Depot stations to accommodate them. When the Royal Air Force (RAF) was formed in April 1918, it inherited over 100 training squadrons and 30 specialist schools; units that would later boast more than 7,000 aircraft. By the Armistice in November, pilots were receiving instruction in all aspects of air fighting on an eleven-month course, which included an average of 50 hours' solo flying.

From a single flying school in 1914, the RAF's training organization had, in four years, grown to become the largest and most effective in the world. Be that as it may a total of 8,000 had been killed under training by the end of war. The experience of flying accidents on just one airfield illustrates these hazards. The table below gives details of accidents at RFC Lilbourne, located in Leicestershire.

Date	Incident
25 July 1916	BE2d, serial 5838, of 55 Squadron crashed
9 June 1917	Avro 504, serial 2923, of 73 Squadron crashed in a spin at Lilbourne
10 August 1917	Pup A7326, of 84 Squadron spun into the ground at Lilbourne after a wing collapsed
7 December 1917	Camel B5577, of 73 Squadron stalled on a turn at Lilbourne after the engine was choked
22 January 1918	Bristol F2 Fighter, serial B1236, of 59 Training Squadron crashed near Lilbourne after its pilot was thrown out during aerobatic practice
24 March 1918	Pup B7530, of 55 Training Squadron spun into the ground near Lilbourne.

The RFC or RAF wing was the coveted badge of a qualified pilot. The original RFC Pilot's brevet or Pilot's Wings was designed by senior officers General Sir Frederick Sykes and General Sir David Henderson. It consisted of the wings of a swift in white silk embroidery with the monogram of the RFC encircled by a laurel wreath of brown silk. The monogram was surmounted by a crown. The Wings were given royal approval by King George V in February 1913 under Army Order 40/13. The Wings became the symbol of qualification worn by trained pilots. When the RAF was formed in 1918 the design was changed slightly. The wing shape took the form of an eagle and the monogram became RAF. The design of the flying badge was the first of its kind in the world. It has been used as the basis of pilot's badges for the air forces of many countries.

Today it continues to be worn by pilots of the RAF. The brevet below displays the Queen's crown to reflect the reign of Queen Elizabeth II.

Pilot's Wing RFC.

Pilot's Wing RAF.

GENERAL METHOD OF TEACHING SCOUT (FIGHTER) PILOTS
Source: National Archive Document: AIR1/728/163/6

Originally, the term scouts was applied to fast reconnaissance aircraft but with the fitting of synchronized machine guns fast aircraft became fighters. Well into the 1920s the term 'scout' was applied to single-seat fighters. The chief method of teaching scout pilots was through dual control. Every possible manoeuvre had to be taught, including flying in the wind, landing and taking off across the wind, spinning etc. The instructor always sat in passenger seat, which meant that he could not see the aircraft instruments. The next and most important thing was that about half of the dual control flying was administered after the pupil had gone solo. This was because of the necessity to repeatedly practise a given manoeuvre under supervision. In this way the pupil would appreciate the details of each manoeuvre shown to him. Conversely, advanced pupils had to be permitted to fly as they chose, the only limiting factor being the nerve of the pupil. Experience demonstrated that the number of casualties was not increased as a result.

The object of training was not to prevent pupils from getting into difficulties but rather to show them how to get out of them satisfactorily and then to do it solo. The view was that if the pupils found the risks too great then they should not be on the course for the risks would be far greater in combat.

The establishment of the unit at the school comprised nine Avros, three dual control Sopwiths and six Bristol Scouts. Originally there had been six Avros and six Sopwiths but with the number of pupil pilots coming from elementary squadrons the number of Avros was increased by three. The greater part of the flying was carried out on the Avros. With the exception of cross-country flying, which was better performed on the Sopwiths, all manoeuvres could be carried out on the Avros. The dual controlled Sopwiths were particularly

Sopwith.

Bristol.

valuable as an intermediate machine. Like a Scout they had a tendency to slew on the ground, they were fast and could climb steeply. On landing the Sopwiths had a flat glide so they had to be held off when landing. This made it difficult to get them down in a small airfield. Finally, the Clerget engine was not easy to control so if pupils could manage the Clergets in the Sopwiths they could manage most other engines. Then there were the Bristols. They were flown by experienced pilots, not those who were learning to fly. If there were accidents they were mostly due to secondary causes such as forced landings.

With regard to the acceptability of pupil pilots for training it was generally possible to decide whether or not to keep an officer on the course after 1½ hours of dual control and less if they came from higher training squadrons. The French would accept only pilots of exceptional ability and a 50 per cent rate of removal from training was usual.

TRAINING OF NIGHT PILOTS
Source: AIR1/109/15/20/2

Introduction
Since the Zeppelin airships of the Imperial German Army and Navy attacked Britain during the hours of darkness the Home Defence squadrons of the RFC and units of the

Avro.

German Zeppelin getting ready for flight.

RNAS had to have pilots who were trained in night flying but it took until February 1916 before night training was put on a systematic basis. This was a year after the night attacks began. The training organization, once in place, was extended and developed to include night observers and to train units in night flying techniques prior to embarkation or emplaning overseas.

Wireless telephony and aerial navigation were also included in training courses. With the splitting of the Home Defence areas into Northern and Southern Defence areas the training organization had to be adapted to take account of the different needs. To this was added the requirement for pilots not simply to be capable of flying and observing but also night fighting. In addition to observing and fighting, night-flying aeroplanes could carry out reconnaissance, bombing, 'low strafing', offensive and defensive patrols and artillery co-operation. By the end of the war the official opinion was that, in a future war, the night pilot would play a part equal to, if not more important than, that of the day pilot. To carry out any form of duty at night a pilot must be proficient in that duty by day. Before a pilot could become a really efficient night pilot he should have completed about a hundred hours solo flying by day and at least twenty hours day flying on the aircraft that he would fly at night. The selection of pilots for night-flying training should be from those who were expert at day flying. The sections that follow deal with the specific changes made to the flying training organization in the light of the developing needs of war.

Initial moves

To improve the competence of Home Defence pilots in night flying an officer was appointed to command the Training Squadron at Hounslow and the ten detachments allotted to the defence of London. The pilots selected for night training were those who had obtained their wings with a Day Training Squadron. On arrival at Hounslow these pilots were put through a short course in night flying consisting of five flights at night and instructions were then issued in November 1916 that Home Defence pilots must pass a course during which they were required to fire Le Prieur rockets at a target of a Zeppelin marked out on the ground and to fire at toy balloons from an aeroplane using a Lewis gun. In February 1917 No.11 (Reserve) Squadron was transferred from Northolt to Rochford, its number being changed to No.98 Depot Squadron. The Training Squadron at Hounslow with its ten HD Detachments then became No.39 HD Squadron.

No.98 Depot Squadron

To begin with, pupils were taken into the squadron after passing through an elementary Day Training Squadron. They had to complete one hour's night flying with five night landings in addition to the anti-Zeppelin tactics mentioned above. The intake of pilots proved to be unsatisfactory and trainees came direct from Schools of Aeronautics. The course content was changed to a requirement that pupils passed six tests in day flying. Those selected for night-flying training were required to make six landings in the dark, attain a height of 6,000ft and remain for not less than one hour in the air after dark. When the Home Defence Group was subject to rapid expansion No.98 Depot Squadron was unable to cope with the demand for pilots and, in April 1917, it was decided to have many pupils trained on the Home Defence squadrons but this was unsatisfactory in practice.

Light night bombing squadrons

A further demand for night pilots was created following the formation of No.100 Squadron on the flight stations of No.51 Home Defence Squadron. The squadron pilots not only had to receive night training but be capable of flying the FE2b bombing aircraft before the squadron embarked for overseas as a night bombing squadron. The FEs were originally designed as fighters but by the spring of 1917 they were outclassed in this role and they were relegated to night bombing duties equipped with either one 230lb bomb or three of 112lb. The experience gained by pilots of No.100 Squadron led to an instruction being issued to the effect that night pilots should be practised in reconnaissance, flying in searchlight beams and bomb dropping. When No.101 Squadron began to form, it was quite clear that No.51 HD Squadron could not cope simultaneously with the training of night pilots for home defence duties and bombing overseas. Eventually, No.99 Depot Squadron undertook the training of night bombing pilots for overseas but when that number also increased No.192 Depot Squadron had to take over this task in September of 1917. The training of night observers in the night bombing squadrons had to proceed hand in hand with that of the pilots and both were tested conjointly. The pilots had to manoeuvre their aircraft in such a manner as to permit the observers to be able to drop their bombs within the prescribed limits. On completion of the test the observers were sent either to the HD (later called Service Squadrons) on FEs or to light night bombing squadrons overseas.

Reorganization of late 1917

In the early part of the Great War the Zeppelins posed the only air threat to the British Isles and Tyneside, the Humber and Norfolk were commonly targeted but once the threat came from the Gotha bombers it was the south-east that took the brunt of attacks in 1917 and 1918. Of course, the Zeppelins had a greater range than the Gothas but the latter packed a harder punch and became a serious threat to the capital. Training had to be provided in night flying, light bombing overseas and home defence duties and the organization of training was constantly updated to provide the pilots in these various specialities. At the end of 1917 Depot Squadrons ceased to be described as such and were termed Night Training Squadrons whilst the Home Defence squadrons were termed 'service squadrons' in the three southern wings with the exception of No.75 Squadron, which was being equipped with scouts (fighter planes) piloted by officers trained at No.188 and 198 (N) Training Squadrons formed at Throwley in December. Before a pilot could gain his wings the number of aerial navigation tests was raised from one to two in addition to flying in Sopwith Scouts for five hours in daylight. These two training squadrons were equipped with Avros, Sopwith Scouts and Camels. Graduation from the school involved twenty-five hours of solo flying. The aerial navigation tests involved proficiency in wireless and the ability to fly a two-seater, with an instructor, cross-country wearing darkened goggles. This was introduced in May 1918 to give the impression of flying at night. The alternative was for the pupils to actually fly at night but to have done so in an operational zone the trainees could well have been mistaken for a hostile raid. They were then posted to service squadrons where they were given their wings.

No sooner had the newly qualified pilots obtained their wings than they were sent off to the School of Wireless Telegraphy at Penshurst. After instruction in night flying and night fighting on service machines they would, if successful, be declared fit to counter hostile air raids. But there was a shortage of suitably qualified pilots for both the Home Defence Southern Service squadrons and night fighting squadrons overseas. It had become necessary to find a fresh source of supply of scout pilots. These could be transferred from Northern Service Squadrons where the FEs, with their low service ceiling, had been replaced with Avros powered by 100hp Le Rhône engines and equipped with Lewis guns. The night fighting squadrons overseas could then be provided with pilots from the Northern Squadrons who could then more easily convert

from the Avro to Camels after a short course.

Night-flying observers were also under training in the FE squadrons and similar tests to those administered to night pilots were laid down before they could qualify. As far as possible the training of night-flying pilots and observers was combined. On completion of their tests the observers would either be retained in the service squadrons or posted to light night bombing squadrons overseas. When it was known that No.6 Brigade would have to undertake the training of light night bombing pilots for overseas the importance of aerial navigation training was realized. Officers appointed to give this training were first described as 'compass officers', their title being changed to aerial navigation officers in January 1918. Most of them had been electrical engineers in civilian life and before taking on their duties they were put on a course at the Royal Naval Compass Observatory at Slough. Then aerial navigation training was given to night fighting squadrons to pilots of scouts.

Royal Air Force training in 1918

The pilots in No.6 Brigade could be classified as:

1. Class 1 – Day and night fighting pilots, i.e., pilots available for defence purposes in the three Southern Wings or for posting to night fighting squadrons overseas.
2. Class 2 – Northern defence pilots and ultimate conversion to day and night pilots and
3. Class 3 – Light night bombing pilots for training in the FE night training squadrons and dispatch to light night bombing squadrons overseas.

In order to deal with these three classes of pilots it was necessary to issue a revised scheme of training and this took place on 3 August 1918. In order to bring the training of the pilots of No.6 Brigade into line with training in the rest of the RAF it was decided to split the training into three stages, called tests for Categories A, B and C. Tests for Categories A and B were made almost identical for the three classes of pilots listed above in order to facilitate the exchange of pilots who showed no aptitude for one branch to another for which they might

Bristol Fighter.

Sopwith Camel.

Avro 504.

be more suited. Owing to the specialized nature of their work it was necessary to make the tests for Category C different for the three classes. All pilots who passed Tests for Categories A and B were deemed to have graduated. Light night bombing pilots were given their wings and were available for posting to an overseas squadron after passing all three Category tests. Northern Defence pilots obtained their wings and were known as operations pilots after passing all Category tests. Finally, day and night fighting pilots obtained their wings and were known as 2nd Class operations pilots after passing all three Category tests. To become a 2nd Class operations pilot a day and night fighting pilot had to have done four hours' night flying and be thoroughly efficient on a Sopwith Camel or Bristol Fighter by day. Since these aircraft were difficult to fly at night it would put the night fighting pilots at an unfair disadvantage with day pilots until the former were thoroughly efficient on both

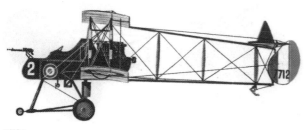

FE2b.

these aircraft by day and night they were not given their wings. When they had reached the last stage of their training they were known as 1st Class operations pilots. Light night bombing and Northern Defence pilots had to be expert both by day and night on FEs and Avros respectively on completion of Category C tests.

The training of pupils for light night bombing and Northern and Southern Defence duties

The procedure as regards the training of pupils for light night bombing and Northern Defence duties was then as follows. There were three elementary night training squadrons in the north of the UK equipped with Avros, although one of the schools still had DH6 and BE2e aircraft. These schools were engaged in passing out pupils with the Category A tests. The best trainees were selected for posting to Northern Service squadrons with whom they passed tests for Categories B and C. Those who were found to be heavy handed on the Avros but who were likely to be all right on heavier machines could go to FE Night Training Squadrons. On the other hand, those who were heavy handed and did not appear to have the qualities and determination to become a light night bombing pilot were turned down altogether. No.198 (N) Training Squadron was turned into an 'all through' scout training squadron (fighter pilot in modern parlance). The training was on Avros and Camels and put the squadron on a par with Nos. 188 and 189 (N) Training Squadrons. One of these two training squadrons was allotted each of the three Southern Wings and so kept them supplied with pilots. Remembering that we are talking about the training throughout the entire RAF, each of the service squadrons could also be fed directly with pupils from the Schools of Aeronautics. This promoted a spirit of healthy rivalry and the number of pilots increased. The training squadrons were brought under the control of the Service Wing Commander to whom it was supplying pilots. In September the dual control Camel (see page 212) was introduced, which did much to increase the number of pilots being turned out and did a lot to reduce the number of flying accidents.

The contribution made by Area Flying Schools

The Area Flying Instructors' Schools provided valuable assistance to No.6 Brigade since a large number of the Brigade's flying instructors passed through these schools during 1916. By 1918 it was believed that the future training of night bombing and night reconnaissance pilots would be entirely separated from any night-flying home defence organization that might then exist. On the other hand, there would be an obvious advantage to combine the training of pilots for Home Defence and night fighting because of the similarity of their work and the probability that the same type of aircraft would be used for both purposes. In 1918 it was expected that in future wars aircraft raiding Britain would be fast and flying at great altitude, requiring defensive forces of equal performance. Night-fighting squadrons would be required to destroy night bombing enemy aircraft. In time of peace sufficient night fighting units should be maintained not simply for Home Defence but to be part of an expeditionary force. It was noted that, during the Great War, the night-flying aircraft could be put to a variety of uses, including reconnaissance, bombing, low strafing, offensive and defensive patrols and artillery co-operation. In any future war the night pilot was expected to play a part, equal to, if not more important than, the day pilot.

TRAINING OF UNITED STATES FLYING PERSONNEL

Six American squadrons were partially trained in Canada finishing on Curtiss JNA machines with a further four squadrons being trained entirely in England. The six from Canada, without any further training, went to France, to the American authorities there. Those trained in England were attached to the RAF in the field for experience under service conditions. An agreement was entered into with the United States that a pool of 15,000 US mechanics would be maintained by Britain. This arrangement was to the mutual advantage of both countries since there was a shortage of manpower in the United Kingdom and the American squadrons could more readily become operational. These men came untrained and were attached to training units of the RAF throughout Great Britain and Northern Ireland for periods varying from three to eight months. An additional agreement was entered into whereby 200 American pilots would attend flying training in England having been partially trained in the USA on Curtiss JN4 machines. On completion of flying training they were sent to France for experience under service conditions. These pilots were subject to withdrawal by the Chief of the Air Staff of the American Expeditionary Force on his giving a few months' notice.

There was also an agreement with the USA to form thirty Handley Page squadrons for service in France but these were to be formed and trained as far as possible in the USA. The components of the machines too were to be manufactured in America and sent to England to be assembled under arrangements made by the Ministry of Munitions. There were to be five grounds set aside for this purpose, one for erection and testing, two grounds for mobilizing Handley Page service squadrons and finally two grounds for Training Depot Stations to train the pilots and maintain wastage. All five grounds were to be manned by American personnel. Additionally, the Americans were to send to Britain Constructional and Labour Companies to do the necessary building for the aerodromes required but owing to the fact that these men did not arrive during the period of hostilities the majority

of the American air stations were completed by British workers. To assist the US authorities in building their air arm approximately seventy-five officers were sent to the USA in an advisory capacity in the specializations of flying, technical, wireless, photography, gunnery, bombing and administration. The US naval aviation also received help when approximately twenty officers with specializations that included such items as seaplanes and kite balloons. Altogether, a large number of American officers visited the UK and underwent courses at most of the Training Stations of the RAF. From May 1917 an enormous amount of material, samples, drawings and technical information was supplied to both the US Army and Naval Aviation.

TRAINING MATTERS AFFECTED BY THE PROPOSAL TO FORM AN AIR SERVICE
Source: CAB/21/21

The responsibility for the training of personnel in the proposed air service was considered by the Air Organization Committee on 25 September 1917. These proposals were considered under four categories, which were pilots, observers, equipment officers and mechanics.

1. Pilots – It was proposed that the training of pilots in duties and discipline, in technical subjects and in flying up to graduation as pilots was to be carried out in cadet wings, training schools and training squadrons of the Air Force. Having qualified as pilots, they were to receive training appropriate to their intended duties to qualify as service pilots. Specializations would include pilots for fighter aircraft, bombers, artillery spotters, seaplanes and reconnaissance aircraft. Instructors at the various training schools should have experience with the Army and the Navy, particularly those whose experience had been in the various theatres of war.
2. Observers – Observers would be trained as at present in gunnery, bomb dropping, wireless and artillery observation.
3. Equipment officers – These officers should be trained in cadet wings and technical schools, as at present, thereafter specializing according to requirements of the service and to their particular talents.
4. Mechanics – They would continue to be trained as at present and be interchangeable between home and overseas establishments and forces.

Naval and military training establishments would not be duplicated but run and worked as one organization. This was so that training would proceed along uniform lines and officers could be allotted to their various duties according to aptitude. The system to be adopted was a 'war system' but could continue in peacetime on similar lines. The responsibility for air training would pass from the Fifth Sea Lord and the Director General of Military Aeronautics to the General Officer Commanding the Training Division of the RAF.

TRAINING COURSES IN THE RAF – OCTOBER 1918
Source: RAF Museum document published in October 1918.

This section deals with the RAF courses on offer when the war had only one month to go before the Armistice. But, of course, the Air Ministry was not to know that. What is important is that the course requirements represent the distilled wisdom of four years of aerial combat and the support services required given the growing sophistication of aircraft, weapons, wireless and photography. This is shown in the different aircrew categories for which courses were being run, the length and content of courses, pay and allowances and requirements for a pass. The courses were for both commissioned and non-commissioned ranks. The document also lists the various trades of the RAF in late 1918. The following pages also disclose the whereabouts of training units that had served the needs of both the RFC and RNAS and the courses with their duration.

TRAINING ESTABLISHMENTS

Schools of Aeronautics
Reading – For all types of officer pilots and observers
Oxford, Denham, Bristol and Cheltenham – for all types of pilots, except officers
Bath – for all types of observers

Aerial Fighting Schools
Marske, Turnberry and Sedgeford – Fighting scouts (officers and NCOs), two-seater reconnaissance (officers and NCOs), two-seater fighter reconnaissance observers (officers and NCOs) and day bombers (officers and NCOs)
Freiston – Fighting scouts (officers and NCOs)
East Fortune – Torpedo plane pilots, fleet reconnaissance and fighting scouts for fleet work.

Schools of Navigation and Bomb Dropping
Stonehenge, Andover and Thetford – Day bomber pilots (officers and NCOs), day bomber observers (officers and NCOs), night bomber pilots and night bomber observers

Observers' Schools
Hythe and New Romney – Corps observers (officers and NCOs), day bomber observers (officers and NCOs), two-seater reconnaissance observers (officers and NCOs) and night bomber observers
Manston – Army observers
Eastchurch – Fleet reconnaissance and submarine patrol observers (W/T observers (NCOs))

School for Marine Operations
Dover – pilots

Ground Armament School
Uxbridge – All types of pilot

Wireless/ Telephony School
Chattis Hill – Two-seater fighter reconnaissance pilots (officers and NCOs), two-seater reconnaissance observers (officers and NCOs), day bomber pilots and observers (officers and NCOs).

School of RAF and Army Co-operation
Winchester (Worthy Down) – Corps pilots and observers (officers)

School of Photography Map Reading and Reconnaissance
Farnborough – Two-seater fighter reconnaissance observers (officers)

Schools for training Marine Observers
Eastchurch – Fleet reconnaissance and submarine patrol observers
Aldeburgh – Anti-submarine patrol observers

Flying Instructors Schools
Gosport – South-west area
Shoreham – South-east area
Lilbourne – Midlands area
Redcar – North-east area
Ayr – North-western area
The Curragh – Ireland

Balloon Training Depots
Roehampton – Personnel working with the Royal Navy
Richmond Park – Personnel working with the Army

Balloon Training Base and Schools
Sheerness – Personnel working with the Royal Navy
Lydd – Personnel working with the Army
Salisbury – Personnel working with the Army

TRADE TRAINING ESTABLISHMENTS
The following tradesmen entered the service already skilled in their respective trades and were posted directly to depots where their ability could be utilized:

Draughtsman	Motor body, builder
Driver (steam-propelled vehicles)	Moulder
Jig and tool maker	Pattern Maker
Instrument repairer	Propeller maker
Millwright	Upholsterer
	Vulcaniser

	Trade	Period of course (weeks)
Halton, Buckinghamshire	Fitter, engine	16
	Fitters, general	12
(Workshops shown below)	Turner	8
	Machinist	8
	Blacksmith	12
	Coppersmith	12
	Tinsmith	12
	Acetylene, welder	8
	Electrician	8
	Magneto, repairer	12
	Rigger (aeroplane)	8
	Carpenter	8
	Sailmaker	8
	Boatbuilder	8
Grain and Calshot	Motor boat driver	Not specified
	Motor boat coxswain	Not specified
Hurst Park	Drivers, petrol vehicles	Not specified
	Fitters, MT (Motor transport)	Not specified

AIRCREW PERSONNEL

The details that appear below include entry, course content, disposal at the end of each course, pay rates and course length.

Flying Instructors on all types of machines

Class 1 comprised pilots who had returned from active service and had been recommended for a period of duty on home establishment whilst **Class 2** comprised pupils on a flying training course who had received the attention of the Squadron Commander and the Wing Examining Officer to become instructors after Graduation B. Both classes of pilots were sent to the Instructors' School of Special Flying for a course lasting a fortnight. Under the supervision of specially selected instructors the pupils were taught the latest methods of instructing, which included dual and solo flying, use of telephones and telephone patter. They would also be taught the full capabilities and handling of the various service types of machine on which they would be instructing. On conclusion of the course the pupils were categorized according to their relative efficiency and were then sent to the Training Stations from whence they went for employment as instructors. In the case of Class 2 pupils they were awarded their Wings and commenced to receive full pay of 10s per day and 8s per day flying pay.

Progression during training to full qualifications as a pilot

To save unnecessary repetition of the graduation procedure common to most of the flying specialities, the following would apply in all cases unless otherwise stated:

Entry A student joined as a cadet in the Cadet Brigade and were paid 1s 0d a day plus 1s 0d a day messing allowance on a course lasting eight to ten weeks from whence he proceeded to a School of Aeronautics for a course lasting six to seven weeks. He was then selected for training in a particular specialization. (See the selection criteria shown for the fighting scout pilot, which follows.)

Armament School The cadet spent four weeks at Armament School at the end of which he was classified as a flight cadet and paid 7s 6d a day plus 4s 0d flying pay. For NCO aircrew the rate was 3s 3d plus 1s a day.

RAF Halton Workshops.

Graduation 'A' As a flight cadet he attended the appropriate training squadron for his speciality and was trained for up to five months. After the third month he graduated with an 'A' classification.

Graduation 'B' During months four and five the flight cadet was given further training leading to his appointment to a commission as a 2nd lieutenant. His daily pay rose to 10s 0d plus 4s 0d a day flying pay. For NCO aircrew the appointment was to sergeant mechanic pilot with a pay rate of 6s 0d a day plus 1s 0d a day flying pay.

Graduation 'C' As a 2nd lieutenant / NCO Flying Branch he proceeded on a course of study/practice leading to Graduation 'C' and was awarded his wings, officers receiving 10s 0d a day pay plus 8s 0d a day flying pay. For NCO aircrew the rate was 6s 0d a day plus 4s a day flying pay.

Disposal This differed for many of the flying branch aircrew and the details are outlined below.

Fighting scout pilot (officer)

During the eight to ten weeks entry training the cadet was taught physical drill, signalling, discipline, map reading,

RFC pilot.

law and organization. During the six to seven weeks at the School of Aeronautics he recapitalized on the subjects learned at the Cadet Brigade and continued with these subjects while he was introduced to instruction on the ground in engines and engine running, rigging, aerial navigation, instruments, photography, artillery and infantry co-operation. At the conclusion of the course the cadet was selected for training as a scout pilot, either because he had shown a pronounced disposition for that type of work, or because the demand exceeded the supply of those selected on account of their pronounced disposition. In the latter case he was to be chosen to meet demands from those who show no disposition for any particular type of training. Assuming the cadet continued with his training to become a fighting scout pilot he attended the ground Armament School, which was at Uxbridge, where the course lasted four weeks to cover machine guns, ground firing, bombs and bomb gear. At the successful conclusion of this course the cadet was reclassified as a flight cadet. He progressed to a scout training squadron where he stayed for four to five months, the precise time depending on weather, aptitude and equipment facilities. He was taught flying, flying in formation, flying in cloud, forced landings and aerial gunnery. After about three months he graduated with an 'A' classification on an advanced flying standard on a 'leading up' machine with a minimum of twenty-five hours' flying instruction. During the last two months of the course he progressed with cross-country flights and cloud flying, reconnaissance and aerial fighting, compass course flying and firing down from the air on to ground targets.

During the five months spent at a scout training school he was also taught on the ground and had to pass tests in machine gunnery, signalling, map reading and navigation. With a minimum of thirty-five hours' flying instruction, of which five hours must have been on a service type machine, and if he reached an advanced standard on the service type he graduated with classification 'B'. He was then sent to a fighting school, such as Freiston, where he spent three weeks undertaking advanced ground firing, aerial firing, aerial fighting tactics and advanced formation flying. On successful completion of this stage of his training he graduated with a 'C' classification. As a service pilot he was then fit to go to a scout squadron in the field. The total (approximate) time in training would have been from ten to eleven months.

Two-seater fighter reconnaissance pilot (officer)

Following entry via the Cadet Brigade the course content was the same as above before passing on to a School of Aeronautics where again the course content was the same. At the conclusion of the course at the School of Aeronautics the cadet was selected for training to become a fighter reconnaissance pilot. On conclusion of his training at Ground Armament School he was classified as a flight cadet.

He progressed to a two-seater fighter reconnaissance training squadron or station for a course lasting four to five months, depending on aptitude and equipment facilities. He was taught flying, flying in formation, flying in cloud, forced landings and aerial gunnery. After about three months he graduated with an 'A' classification on an advanced flying standard on a 'leading up' machine with a minimum of twenty-five hours' flying instruction. During the last two months of the course he progressed with cross-country flights and cloud flying, reconnaissance and aerial fighting, compass course flying and firing down from the air on to ground targets, photography and bombing.

During the five months spent at a Two-Seater Fighter Reconnaissance Training Squadron or station he was also taught on the ground and had to pass tests in machine gunnery, signalling, map reading and navigation, bombs and bomb gear. With a minimum of thirty-five hours' flying instruction, of which five hours must have been on his service type machine, if he reached an advanced standard on the service type, which involved carrying a passenger, he graduated with a 'B' classification. He was then sent to a fighting school where he received the same training as the fighting scout pilot. On successful completion of this stage of his training he graduated with a 'C' classification. As a qualified service pilot he was then available for posting to a squadron in the field. The total (approximate) time in training would have been from ten to eleven months.

Day bombing pilot (officer)

Following entry via the Cadet Brigade the course content was the same as above before passing on to a School of Aeronautics, where again the course content was the same. At the conclusion of the course at the School of Aeronautics the cadet was selected for training to become a day bombing pilot. On conclusion of his training at Ground Armament School he was classified as a flight cadet. He then progressed to a day bombing training squadron or station for a course lasting four to five months, depending on aptitude and equipment facilities. He was taught flying, flying in formation, flying in cloud, forced landings and aerial gunnery. After about three months he graduated with a 'A' classification on an advanced flying standard on a 'leading up' machine with a minimum of twenty-five hours' flying instruction. During the last two months of the course he progressed with cross-country flights and cloud flying, reconnaissance and aerial fighting, compass course flying and firing down from the air on to ground targets, photography and bombing.

During the whole of his four to five months spent at a day bombing training squadron he was also taught on the ground and had to pass tests in machine gunnery, photography, signalling, map reading and navigation, bombs and bomb gear. With a minimum of thirty-

five hours of flying instruction, of which five hours must have been on his service type machine, and if he reached an advanced standard on the service type, which involved carrying a passenger, he graduated with a 'B' classification. He was then sent to a Fighting School where he received the same training as the fighting scout pilot. On successful completion of this stage of his training he graduated with a 'C' classification. He then attended a course at a School of Navigation and Bomb-Dropping where he spent four to five weeks. The course included bombs and bomb gear, bomb dropping, aerial fighting in formation, practical map flying, day aerial navigation and cloud flying. He was then fit for posting to a Day Bombing Squadron in the field. The total (approximate) time in training would have been from ten to eleven months.

Corps pilot (officer)

Following entry via the Cadet Brigade the training received before passing on to a School of Aeronautics would be the same as that for the fighting scout pilot. The period of training and subjects taught would also be the same. At the conclusion of the course at the School of Aeronautics the cadet was selected for training as a corps pilot. On conclusion of his training at Ground Armament School, where he was taught machine guns, ground firing, bombs and bomb gear, he would be reclassified as a flight cadet.

As a flight cadet he proceeded to a Corps Training Squadron or station for a course lasting four to five months depending on aptitude and equipment facilities. He was taught flying, flying in formation, flying in cloud, forced landings and aerial gunnery. After about three months he was graduated with an 'A' classification with an advanced flying standard on a 'leading up' machine with a minimum of twenty-five hours of flying instruction. During the last two months of the course he progressed with cross-country flights and cloud flying, reconnaissance and aerial fighting, compass course flying and firing down from the air on to ground targets photography, bombing and artillery procedure.

During the whole of his four to five months spent at a Corps Training Squadron he was also taught on the ground and had to pass tests in machine gunnery, photography, signalling, map reading and navigation, bombs and bomb gear, artillery picture targets and, having carried a passenger he then must then receive a minimum of 25 hours flying instruction, of which 5 hours must have been spent on his service type machine. If he reached an advanced standard on the service type he was graduated 'B'. He was then sent to the RAF and Army Co-operation School at Winchester for a course lasting two to three weeks. This included artillery and infantry co-operation, map reading and fighting in the air. On successful completion of this stage of his training he graduated with a 'C' rating. As a qualified service pilot he was then fit to join a corps squadron in the field. The total (approximate) time in training would have been from ten to eleven months.

Night-bombing pilot (officer – Handley Page)

Entry was via the Cadet Brigade, with pay and special messing allowance and the training received before passing on to a School of Aeronautics would be the same as that for the fighting scout pilot. The period of training and the subjects taught would also be the same. At the conclusion of the course at the School of Aeronautics the cadet was selected for training to become a day bombing pilot and again the criteria used for that selection would be the same as for the fighting scout pilot. He was then sent to the ground Armament School where he stayed for three weeks learning to use the Lewis gun, ground firing as an observer, bombs and bomb gear. On conclusion of his training at Ground Armament School he was reclassified as a flight cadet.

Students then attended a course that lasted four to five months at the Handley Page Training Squadron or Station. The precise time depended on weather and equipment facilities. He was taught flying, forced landings, flying in clouds and bombing. After about three months he graduated with an 'A' rating with an advanced flying standard on a 'leading up' machine and with a minimum of twenty-five hours' flying instruction. During his fourth and fifth months he was required to pass practical tests in any suitable type of aircraft in cross-country flights and by compass alone, reconnaissance, firing from the air at ground targets (as observer), night flying and night reconnaissance, day and night reconnaissance and day and night bombing (as an observer).

During the whole of his four to five months spent at a Handley Page Training Squadron he was also taught on the ground and had to pass tests in machine gunnery, photography, signalling, map reading and navigation, bombs and bomb gear and aerodrome control. A

FE2b – light night bomber.

minimum of thirty-five hours' flying instruction was required, of which five hours must have been by day and five hours by night, which must have been on a service type machine and of an advanced standard of flying by day and by night on a Handley Page. Having also carried a passenger the student graduated with a 'B' classification. He was then sent to a School of Navigation and Bomb Dropping where he spent four to five weeks learning practical night navigation, map flying day and night, compass flying, the use of vertical searchlights, bombs and bomb gear, night aerodrome procedure. On successful completion of this course the student graduated with a 'C' rating and was ready for posting to a Handley Page squadron in the field. The total (approximate) time in training would have been from 10½ to 11½ months.

Light night bombing pilot

Entry was via the Cadet Brigade, with pay and special messing allowance and the training received before passing on to a School of Aeronautics was the same as that for the fighting scout pilot. The period of training and the subjects taught were also the same. At the conclusion of the course at the School of Aeronautics the cadet was selected for training to become a light night bombing pilot and again the criteria used for that selection were the same as for the fighting scout pilot. On conclusion of his training at Ground Armament School he was reclassified as a flight cadet.

He progressed to a DH6 or Avro Training Squadron for a course lasting three weeks covering day and night gunnery tests, elementary aerial navigation tests and fifteen hours' solo instruction as laid down in Chapter 3. During this period the student, based upon his flying capabilities and qualities as an officer, went for further training either as a North Defence pilot or as a light night bombing pilot. If chosen for the latter the student was then passed to a FE training squadron for a course lasting between four and six weeks after passing all tests for graduation 'B'. The tests for graduation 'B' and 'C' included wireless, advanced aerial navigation, day and night cross-country reconnaissance flights of up to 100 miles, dummy bomb dropping by day and night, flying

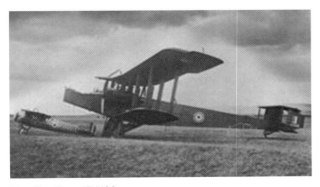

Handley Page O/400.

and bomb dropping in searchlight beams and landing at night with restricted lighting as used in France. The total time in training was from seven to eight months.

Northern Defence pilot

Chapter 4 details the arrangements for defending British airspace during the Great War. This was the task of the squadrons of No.6 Brigade. Avro 504s equipped the squadrons in the north of England and into Scotland where the threat was from Zeppelins, whereas those that equipped the southern squadrons had to combat the Gothas, hence the term 'Northern Defence Pilot'. See Chapter 7 (page 199) for a photograph of a Avro 504 with a Lewis gun mounted on the top wing with a Foster mounting. Entrants to the service were cadets of the Cadet Brigade. During the eight to ten weeks' entry training a cadet was taught physical drill, signalling, discipline, map reading, law and organization. During the six to seven weeks at the School of Aeronautics he recapitalized or revised on the subjects learned at the Cadet Brigade and continued with these subjects while he was introduced to instruction on the ground in engines and engine running, rigging, aerial navigation, instruments, photography, artillery and infantry co-operation. At the conclusion of the course the cadet was selected for training as a Northern Defence Pilot. At the conclusion of the course the cadet attended the ground Armament School for a four-week course to study machine guns, ground firing, gun gears bombs and bomb gears. He then became a flight cadet.

The flight cadet then passed to the Avro Training Squadron on No.6 Brigade where he had to complete all the tests for graduations 'B' and 'C'. These included advanced gunnery, advanced aerial navigation, day aerial fighting, day cross-country flying, 60- and 100-mile reconnaissance flights, bomb dropping by day and by night, and service ceiling tests of 17,000ft. On graduating with a 'B' and 'C' rating he was classified as an operations pilot. The newly qualified pilot then spent eight months on a Northern Defence Service Squadron before being posted to a FE Training Squadron where he received training to qualify as a light night bombing pilot. He was then either sent to a squadron overseas or trained on Camels to become a day and night fighting pilot. The total time in training was between seven and eight months.

Day and night fighting pilot

The Northern Defence pilots of No.6 Brigade flew Avros, whereas their brothers in the south flew a mixture of Camels, Bristol Fighters and SE5as. On entry to the service the cadet followed the same progression of courses as the Northern Defence Pilot to the point where he became a flight cadet. He was then posted for a period between six to eight weeks to a night-flying Camel training squadron equipped with 110 Le Rhône Avros, Camels and dual-controlled Camels. Here, the student pilot had to pass all the tests for graduation 'A' and 'B', including day and night ground gunnery, wireless telegraphy, aerial navigation and cross-country flying by day and by night. After passing all tests the student pilot was granted a commission as a 2nd lieutenant (flying) with the same pay as the Northern Defence Pilot.

The officer was then posted to a 6th Brigade Service Squadron, equipped with Camels. He had to pass all tests for graduation 'C', which included advanced gunnery, day aerial fighting, formation flying, advanced aerial navigation and a ceiling test (19,000ft). He was required to be a skilled pilot on the service aircraft and qualified to ascend by day on hostile air raids. Once qualified he was permitted to wear his Wings, was classified as a 2nd Class operations pilot and his flying pay was doubled from 4 to 8s 0d a day. He was then sent on a week's course to the Wireless Telephony School at Penshurst followed by practice in night landings with reduced lighting, night fighting and searchlight co-operation and firing at a towed target whilst wearing dark goggles. Once the squadron commander was satisfied that the officer was efficient in all these respects the latter was then qualified to ascend on hostile raids at night and was classified a 1st Class operations pilot. This took about one month taking the total time in training to between 9 and 9½ months.

Seaplane pilot (officer)

An entrants followed the usual entry training courses up to the point of selection as a seaplane pilot when he became a flight cadet. As a flight cadet he was sent to a Land Training Squadron for seaplanes. The course lasted about three months, the precise time depending on aptitude, weather and equipment facilities. In the air he was taught flying, forced landings, flying in clouds and bomb dropping (as an observer). On the ground he received instruction on types of vessels and submarines, engines and engine running, rigging, navigation, machine guns and ground firing, bombs and bomb gear and signalling, Submarine recognition was particularly important since the U-boats were a major threat (see Chapter 4, page 84). Even when travelling on the surface they presented a difficult low profile target to see, particularly in poor visibility, and it was vital to distinguish between British and German submarines. On completion of this phase of training the cadet would be tested on a leading up machine after twenty hours' flying instruction to graduate with an 'A' classification.

The student pilot was then posted to a seaplane school for a course of approximately six weeks. The course included flying float-type machines, mirror practice and compass flying. On the water he was taught handling machines, moving from a shed to the water, resuscitation of an apparently drowned man,

A large flying boat, the Felixstowe F2a.

seamanship, types of vessels etc., engines and engine running, rigging, navigation, ground armament, signalling and photography. With a minimum of sixteen hours' instruction on seaplanes the student graduated with a 'B' rating. He then passed to an aerial gunnery school for a four-week course of firing and bombing from the air (as an observer), patrol work and signalling to patrol vessels. He then graduated with a 'C' rating followed by drafting to service or trained on a large flying boat before leaving the finishing school. The total time in training was between nine and ten months.

Fleet reconnaissance pilot (officer)

The training follows the same path as the seaplane pilot except that a student is selected for training as a fleet reconnaissance pilot. He then followed the same course at the seaplane pilot at the Armament School and passed out as a flight cadet. He then went on a four to five-month course at a two-seater training squadron, the precise time depending on aptitude, weather and equipment facilities. There he was taught flying, flying in formation, forced landings, flying in clouds and aerial gunnery. After three months the student pilot was graduated 'A' on an advanced flying standard on a 'leading up' aircraft with a minimum of twenty-five hours' flying instruction. During the fourth and fifth month he was given practical tests in the air in cross-country flying, cloud flying, firing from the air at a ground target and photography on any suitable aircraft. During the whole of the three months at the Fleet Reconnaissance Training Squadron or station he was taught on the ground ready to pass tests in signalling, map reading, navigation, bombs and bomb gear and machine gunnery. When the student had received a minimum of thirty-five hours' flying instruction, of which five hours must have been spent on a service type aircraft, and having carried a passenger, he graduated with a 'B' rating.

The officer was chosen for his ability as a pilot. Those not chosen went to finishing schools to become two-seater fighter reconnaissance or day bomber pilots. The successful students then went to an aerial gunnery school or for a three-week course on advanced ground firing and aerial fighting tactics, signalling and ship recognition. At the conclusion of this course the student pilot graduated with a 'C' classification. He then went to the Fleet pool where he was taught flying off a ship's deck after which he was posted for service with the Fleet. The total time in training was approximately 9½ to 10½ months.

Fighting scout pilot (officer) for Fleet work

The training followed the same path as the seaplane pilot, except that the student was selected for training as a fighting scout pilot. As a cadet at the Ground Armament School he spent four weeks being taught how to use machine guns, ground firing, bombs and bomb gear. At the conclusion of the course the student pilot was classified as a flight cadet. As a flight cadet the student proceeded to a scout training squadron for a course lasting between four and five months when he received the same training as the flight cadet training to be a fleet reconnaissance pilot. Again, the cadet proceeded in the way described in the previous text to his commissioning. The officer was then chosen for his ability to become a fighting scout pilot from volunteers. As a 2nd Lieutenant he went to a School for Fighting for the Fleet where he spent three weeks receiving instruction on advanced ground firing, aerial fighting and aerial fighting tactics and ship recognition leading to graduation with a 'C' rating. He was then sent to the Fleet pool where he was taught to fly off a ship's deck after which he was posted for service. The total time in training was approximately 10½ to 11½ months.

Torpedo plane pilot (officer)

Entry via the Cadet Brigade followed the course of training to the point of selection to train as a torpedo plane pilot and after attendance at the Ground Armament School a student would be classified as a flight cadet. He was then posted to a two-seater training squadron for a course lasting four to five months where he was taught flying, flying in formation, forced landings, flying in clouds and aerial gunnery and after three months he graduated with an 'A' rating. During the fourth and fifth months he passed practical tests in the air, which included cross-country flying, cloud flying, reconnaissance, aerial fighting, compass course flying, firing from the air at a ground target, photography and bombing on any suitable machine. The ground work during this period led to tests in signalling, map reading, navigation, bombs and bomb gear and machine gunnery. Then, with a minimum of thirty-five hours' flying instruction, of which five hours must have been spent on a service type machine

Sopwith Cuckoo.

reconnaissance training squadron. Again, the student pilot followed the same programme as the fighting scout pilot officer and graduated with an 'A' rating after three months. During the fourth and fifth months the student was taught on the ground and passed tests in signalling, map reading, navigation, bombs and bomb gear and machine gunnery. Then, with a minimum of thirty-five hours' instruction of which five hours must have been on a service type machine, and having carried a passenger, the student pilot graduated with a 'B' classification. He then went to a Fighting School and during a period of three weeks was taught ground firing, aerial firing, aerial fighting tactics and advanced formation flying. He then graduated with a 'C' rating and was fit for posting to a Fighter Reconnaissance Squadron in the field. The total training time was approximately ten to eleven months.

Day bombing pilot (NCO)
The cadet followed the same course as above except that the selection for training was for a day bombing pilot (NCO). The same rates of pay also applied, but after completion of the course at the Armament School the student pilot was classified as a sergeant (non technical) and passed on to a day bombing squadron or station for a course lasting four to five months depending on aptitude and equipment facilities. He was taught flying, flying in formation, flying in cloud, forced landings and aerial gunnery. After about three months he graduated with an 'A' rating on an advanced flying standard on a 'leading up' machine with a minimum of twenty-five hours' flying instruction. During the last two months of the course he progressed with cross-country flights and cloud flying, reconnaissance and aerial fighting, compass course flying and firing down from the air on to ground targets photography and bombing. During the whole of his four to five months spent at a day bombing training squadron he was also taught on the ground and had to pass tests in signalling, map reading, navigation, bombs and bomb gear and machine gunnery. Then with a minimum of thirty-five hours' instruction, of which five hours must have been on a service type machine, and having carried a passenger, the student pilot graduated with a 'B' rating.

As a sergeant mechanic pilot he then spent three weeks at a Fighting School for training in ground firing, aerial fighting tactics and advanced formation flying resulting in graduation with a 'C' rating. He progressed to a school of navigation and bomb dropping for a course of four to five weeks to qualify in aerial navigation, cloud flying, bombs, bomb gear and bomb dropping, aerial fighting in formation, practical map flying and was then deemed fit to proceed to a day bombing squadron in the field. The total time in training was approximately 10½ to 11½ months.

to an advanced flying standard, the student graduated with a 'B' classification. The successful candidate was chosen for his ability. Those not chosen went to finishing schools to become two-seater fighter reconnaissance or day bomber pilots. The successful ones then spent six to eight weeks at a Special School for Torpedo Training and were graduated with a 'C' rating at the end of the course. The total time in training was approximately 9½ to 10½ months.

Fighting scout pilot (NCO)
The fighting scout pilot (NCO) followed precisely the same course as the cadet who was proceeding to a commission. On completion of the course at the School of Aeronautics the student was selected to train as a fighting scout pilot. The same rates of pay also applied, but after completion of the course at the Armament School the student pilot was classified as a sergeant (non technical) and passed on to a scout training squadron. Again, he followed the same course as the fighting scout pilot officer, graduating with an 'A' rating after three months. During the fourth and fifth months the student passed tests in the air on any suitable machine in cross-country flying, reconnaissance, aerial fighting, compass course flying, firing from the air at a ground target. The student graduated with a 'B' rating when he became a sergeant mechanic (pilot). On the course at the Fighting School he progressed towards graduation 'C', like the officer equivalent, and became eligible for posting to a scout squadron.

Two-seater fighter reconnaissance pilot (NCO)
The cadet followed the same course as above except that the selection for training was for a two-seater fighter reconnaissance pilot. At the end of the training at the Armament School the cadet was reclassified as a sergeant (non technical) and passed on to a two-seater fighter

Progression during training to full qualifications as an observer

To save unnecessary repetition of the graduation procedure common to most of the flying specialities, the following will apply in all cases unless otherwise stated. The schools attended would vary for observers who operated primarily over land and those who worked with the Fleet.

Entry: Men joined as a cadet at the Observers' School of Aeronautics in the Cadet Brigade and were paid 1s 0d a day plus 1s 0d a day messing allowance on a course lasting eight weeks where they were taught drill, discipline, map reading, law, organization, deportment, physical drill, signalling and photography, navigation, instruments and elementary rigging. They were then selected for training in a particular specialization. (See the selection criteria that are shown for the fighting scout pilot (officer).)

School of Aeronautics, Reading The cadet spent two weeks at Reading, at the end of which he was classified as an observer flight cadet and paid 7s 6d a day plus 4s 0d flying pay. For NCO aircrew the rate was 3s 3d plus 1s a day

Observers' School of Ground and Aerial Gunnery The course lasts six weeks for observer flight cadets and NCO cadets (sergeants (non- technical)).

RAF and Army Co-operation School, Winchester The course lasted two weeks.

School of Navigation and Bomb Dropping The course lasted four to five weeks for observer flight cadets or sergeants (non technical).

School of Wireless Telephony The course lasted one to two weeks at the conclusion of which the student was gazetted 2nd lieutenant and granted his Observer Wing with the pay of 10s a day plus 8s 0d a day flying pay. For NCOs the student received his Observer Wing with the appointment to sergeant (mechanic) and a daily rate of pay of 6s 0d plus 2s 0d a day flying pay.

Fleet Observers' School, Eastchurch This was a sixteen to eighteen week course leading to the observer receiving his Wing.

Anti-submarine Patrol Observers' School, Aldeburgh This was a eight to ten-week course leading directly to the observer receiving his Wing.

Disposal This differed for many of the flying branch aircrew and the details, if applicable, are included below.

Corps observer (officer)

Following entry and selection to be trained as a corps observer (officer) the student passed to the School of Aeronautics at Reading where he received instruction in map reading, artillery and infantry co-operation and signalling. At the School of Ground and Aerial Gunnery the student was given training with the Lewis gun, ground firing, bombs and bomb gear, aerial firing, reconnaissance, photography and map reading from the air. At the RAF and Army Co-operation School he learned to work with ground formations before being granted the Observer's Wing and passing out as a 2nd lieutenant. The total time in training was approximately four to five months.

Two-seater fighter reconnaissance observer (officer)

Following entry and selection to be trained as a two-seater fighter reconnaissance observer (officer) the

Observer's badge.

student passed to the School of Aeronautics at Reading where he received instruction in map reading, artillery and infantry co-operation and signalling. At the School of Ground and Aerial Gunnery the student was given training in the Lewis gun, ground firing, bombs and bomb gear, aerial firing, reconnaissance, photography and map reading from the air. The student then progressed to a School of Photography for a course lasting three weeks where he was taught photography, reconnaissance and map reading. As an observer flight cadet he was then sent on a two-week course at the Pilot's Fighting School for tuition in aerial fighting and gun camera in conjunction with two-seater fighter reconnaissance pilots under training. Finally, the student moved to the School of Wireless Telephony for a one to two-week course on W/T in the air. He was then awarded his Observer's Wing as illustrated in the accompanying photograph. The total time in training was approximately six months.

Day bomber observer – officer

Following entry and selection to be trained as a day bomber observer (officer) the student passed to the

2/Lt J. Stephen-Blanford DFC.

School of Aeronautics at Reading for the two-week course described above. As an observer flight cadet he progressed to the School of Ground and Aerial Gunnery where, again the student was taught the same subjects as described for the corps observer. Thence to the School of Navigation and Bomb Dropping for a course lasting four to five weeks where he was taught practical navigation, gunnery, bombs and bomb gear, bomb dropping and map reading. Finally, he went to the School of Wireless Telephony for a one to two week course on W/T in the air. He was then awarded his Observer's Wing. The total time in training was approximately six months.

Night bomber observer (officer) (Handley Page)
Following entry and selection to be trained as a night bomber observer (officer) (Handley Page) the student, who was classified as an observer flight cadet, passed to the Observers' School of Ground and Aerial Gunnery for the six-week course where he was taught the same subjects as described for the corps observer. After passing on to the School of Wireless Telephony for the two-week course on the use of W/T in the air the student was then granted his Observer's Wing. The total time in training was approximately six months.

Fleet reconnaissance observer (officer)
Following entry and selection to be trained as a fleet reconnaissance observer (officer) the student was sent to the course at the School of Aeronautics. There was an additional subject that was not applicable to the observers already mentioned and that is an explanation of the W/T transmitter. Classified as an observer flight cadet,

the student progressed to the Fleet Observers' School at Eastchurch for a course lasting between sixteen and eighteen weeks. During that time the cadets were taught a high rate of visual and W/T signalling, elementary W/T theory, spark and CW (Carrier Wave) wireless sets, navigation, chart reading, seamanship, recognition of ships, simple fleet tactics, naval codes and procedure, naval spotting and gunnery control, sea reconnaissance, the Lewis gun, ground and aerial firing, bombs and bomb carriers, bomb components, bomb dropping and photography. On conclusion of this course the student was awarded his Observer's Wing. The total time in training was approximately seven to eight months.

Anti-submarine patrol observer (officer)

The photograph shows what a low silhouette the U-boat had during the Great War and this one is depicted in a calm sea. In bad weather the enemy could be very difficult to see and so the work of the anti-submarine patrol officer could be doubly difficult. The entrant to the service followed the same entry course as the fleet reconnaissance observer officer described above and this was followed by the selection of the student to be trained as an anti-submarine patrol observer (officer). As an observer flight cadet the student attended the course at Aldeburgh but a few AS patrol observers were trained at Eastchurch. The Aldeburgh course lasted eight to ten weeks; that at Eastchurch was sixteen weeks. The course content was the same as that listed for the Eastchurch course above. On conclusion the observer was awarded his Wing. The time in training was approximately 4½ to 5½ months.

Light night bombing observer (FE) (officer)
Following entry and selection to be trained as a light night bombing (FE) (officer), the student was classified as an observer flight cadet. He then progressed to an Observers' School of Ground and Aerial Gunnery where his course was the same as that for the corps observer. He then passed on to the 6th Brigade RAF where he spent eight weeks being taught cross-country flying by day and by night, location of dumps, unlit aerodromes, trains, railway stations, camps and other targets, bomb dropping by day and by night, aerial navigation, gunnery, W/T, use of night flying, armament and

equipment and method of making out reconnaissance reports. There was a minimum of five hours' night flying. At the conclusion of this course the student was awarded his Observer's Wing. The total time in training was five to six months.

Night flying Bristol Fighter observer (Home Defence officer)
Following entry and selection to be trained as a night flying Bristol Fighter observer (Home Defence officer) the student was classified as an observer flight cadet. He passed to the two-week course at the School of Aeronautics at Reading where he received instruction in map reading, artillery and infantry co-operation and signalling. He then progressed to the School of Ground and Aerial Gunnery for the same six-week course as the corps observer (officer). At the 6th Brigade on the eight-week course he was then taught day and night cross-country flying, day and night fighting, aerial navigation, gunnery, reports on action taken during hostile air raids and W/T. The minimum time spent in the air at night was twenty hours. On conclusion of the course the student was awarded his Observer's Wing. The total time in training was five to six months.

Corps observer (NCO)
Following entry and selection to be trained as a corps observer (NCO), the student passed to the School of Aeronautics at Reading where he received instruction in map reading, artillery and infantry co-operation and signalling. At the School of Ground and Aerial Gunnery the student, a sergeant (non-technical) was tutored on the Lewis gun, ground firing, bombs and bomb gear, aerial firing, reconnaissance, photography and map reading from the air. At the RAF and Army Co-operation School he learned to work with ground formations as he was taught further photography and map reading, artillery and infantry co-operation in the air before being granted the Observer's Wing and passing out as a sergeant (technical). The total time in training was approximately four to five months.

Two-seater fighter reconnaissance observer (NCO)
Following entry and selection to be trained as a two-seater fighter reconnaissance observer (NCO) the student passed to the School of Aeronautics at Reading, thence to an Observers' School of Ground and Aerial Gunnery. As a sergeant (non-technical) he followed the same course as the corps observer described above. The student then passed to a four-week course at a Pilots' Fighting School where he was taught aerial firing, photography and map reading from the air. Following a two-week course at the School of Telephony learning W/T in the air the student was granted his Observer's Wing, passing out

as a sergeant mechanic. The total time in training was approximately five months.

Day bomber observer (NCO)
Following entry and selection to be trained as a day bomber observer (NCO) the student passed to the School of Aeronautics at Reading thence to an Observers' School of Ground and Aerial Gunnery as a Sergeant (non-technical) where he followed the same course as the corps observer above. The student then went on a four-week course at the School of Navigation and Bomb Dropping where he was taught navigation, bomb dropping and the use of bomb gears and sights, advanced gunnery, formation flying and aerial navigation. Finally, he attended the two-week course at the School of W/T Telephony, learning to use W/T in the air. At the conclusion of this course he was granted his Observer's Wing as a sergeant mechanic. The total time spent in training was approximately seven months.

W/T NCO observer
The entrants were selected from civilian life or from RAF personnel. They joined at No.1 (T) Wireless School, Flower Down, as a private 2nd class and were paid 1s 0d a day unless they already held a paid rank in the service. The course lasted five months and they were taught signalling, use and care of wireless instruments, spark and CW telegraphy, wireless telephony, directional wireless in the air and on the ground. At the conclusion of the course they were classified as sergeants (non-technical) and paid 3s 0d a day plus 1s flying pay. A student was selected either for large flying boat or Handley Page work, the usual criteria for selection being applied. The student then attended No.3 Observers' School for a four-week course where he was taught to use the Lewis gun and ground firing and taught aerial gunnery. On conclusion of the course the student was awarded his Observer's Wing and given the rank of sergeant mechanic. The total training time was six months.

Engineer NCO observer
He was selected as a capable engine mechanic from a RAF unit and joined a one-week course at No.3 Observers' School in his existing rank where he was taught to use the Lewis gun and ground firing. On conclusion of the course he was classified as a sergeant (non-technical), was paid 1s 3d a day and 1s flying pay. After a one-month course he qualified for his Observer's Wing and was graded as a sergeant mechanic with a pay of 6s a day and 2s a day flying pay. If his original pay was higher he retained it while under training, but on conclusion (on qualifying after 1 April 1918) he was paid as above, whether it was an increase or a decrease.

Kite balloon officers for work as sea

Recruits were drawn from officers and cadets and attended a course at No.1 Balloon Training Depot, the latter as flight cadets, receiving 7s 6d a day plus 4s flying pay. The course lasted twelve weeks and they had, on completion, to be able to pass an air test in a kite balloon. To qualify as a free balloon pilot seven flights had to be made, four as a passenger and the fifth flight as i/c (in charge) balloon with the instructor in the basket. The sixth flight was solo and the seventh was a night flight as a passenger but this last flight was only carried out when time permitted.

The subjects that had to be mastered on the course were the theory of ballooning, compass and chart, winches, inspecting and checking the balloon and rigging from drawing, rigging a model from memory, knotting and splicing, fabric, packing a balloon, setting the valve inside the balloon, packing a parachute, notes on kite balloon drill and kite balloon drill in the field, spotting from the balloon, transferring (elementary), telephone, signalling (semaphore), arm and flag, Morse, lamp, buzzer and flag, ship recognition. The student was then marked in each subject and the pass mark in each subject was 70 per cent.

After passing in all subjects, the student passed to No.1 Balloon Training Base. The course lasted four weeks and included advanced practical work. Subjects taught were organization of balloons on battleships, light cruisers and destroyers, transferring the balloon from shore to ship and ship to ship by means of (a) hemp downhauls and no winch and (b) by means of winches and (c) by ship's winch cable, sandbags, grass line and snatch block. The list continued with the use of snatch blocks, wire pennants, permanent flying leads (choosing the best position), installation of winches on different types of craft, best position to select, changing observers while altering course from flying balloon most high (method to adopt), topping up at sea, telephone system on board, general hints on temporary repairs at sea, elementary meteorology and law of storms, guns used; spotting, navigation (elementary), bearings and inclinations, organization of British and German fleets, how to recognize various units, each class of ship and squadrons

to which she belongs, composition of battle squadrons, cruiser squadrons, scouting groups etc., fleet formation, cruising formation, Aldis lamp signalling from a balloon, signal hoists, ships' routine, watch keeping by day and by night, practical chart work, reading and checking signals whilst on patrol, internal economy of a ship and naval discipline.

On completion of this course a flight cadet was ready for active service, was gazetted 2nd lieutenant flying branch for kite balloon work and was awarded his Observer's Wing.

Kite balloon officer for work on land

Recruits were drawn from artillery officers and infantry officers and appointed to No.2 Balloon Training Depot. If an army officer he drew his pay plus 4s flying pay; if a cadet he drew 7s 6d a day plus 4s flying pay. The six-week course comprised the ability to pass an air test in a kite balloon. To qualify as a free balloon pilot seven flights had to be made, four as a passenger, and the fifth flight as i/c balloon with the instructor in the basket. The sixth flight was solo and the seventh was a night flight as a passenger but this last flight was only carried out when time permitted.

Subjects taught were:

1. Maps (theory of map reading), perspective, aerial photography and magnetic compass
2. Artillery observation (organization of RA and RAF elements of guns and gunnery, balloon observation, co-operation between RA and RAF and chart room work)
3. The balloon (theory of ballooning, construction, adjustment and maintenance of kite balloons)
4. Telephone and winch

An examination paper for each of the four groups had to be sat with a 70 per cent pass mark for each. Subjects covered included flash spotting from a balloon, model targets, dummy shoots from a balloon, model target shoots, dummy shoots from high country, work in balloons, the chart room, rigging and repairs, including rigging model, packing, inflation, adjustments on balloon, balloon drill, packing parachutes, telephone line construction, fault finding, and buzzer and lamp signalling. Opportunity and encouragement to practise parachute descents were given throughout the course The student then passed to No.1 or No.2 School for a four-week course, which included work with gunners, advanced map reading, general advanced observation work and elementary instruction on the Lewis gun.

When considered efficient for posting overseas the student was gazetted as a 2nd lieutenant flying branch for kite balloon work and was awarded his Observer's Wing.

Kite balloon over a cargo ship.

GROUND TRADES

The details that appear below include, entry, course content, disposal at the end of each course, pay rates and course length.

Introduction

When circumstances permitted all men entering the RAF had to pass a preliminary course of instruction irrespective of their trades to give them a general knowledge of aircraft and engines. When at training establishments men were taught the details of the trade to which they had been allocated in addition to general knowledge of aircraft and engines and their maintenance to keep them in flying condition. They were given practice in squadron routine and handling of aircraft in the field. They were also given instruction and practice in drill and discipline. At the end of his course a man was given a certificate of his ability and then drafted to a unit as a fully qualified air mechanic. At the time the Training Manual was published (October 1918) there had been the most urgent demands for mechanics and skilled men were frequently being drafted to stations before completion of the disciplinary course. In this case they received no service technical instruction at all. They were graded as ordinary mechanics of the station to which they were appointed, receiving a daily rate of pay of 2s 0d.

Balloon riggers

A balloon rigger attended a five-week course at a Balloon Training Depot. He was taught the details of all rigging and rigging fittings in kite balloons, including hemp and wire splices, the nature and care of winch cables, fabric work and repairs and dope and its application and removal. On completion of the course and having passed the examination the student was graded air mechanic 3rd class with a pay of 2s a day and was then available for active service.

Winch drivers and fitters

Candidates for this course would be expected to have had some engineering knowledge. The course of between three and four weeks at a Balloon Training Depot covered engine faults and their remedies, care and maintenance, the construction of different types of winch units, the winding gear unit and power control unit. The construction and operation of various winch mechanisms was covered, which included surge drums, storage drums, snatch brakes, paying out brakes and oil brake. There was also study of Cliquett gear, serving gear, general construction of the gear box, power and brake controls, dismantling various mechanisms, reeving and unreeving cables on winches; operating and driving various winches, Scammel, Jenkins, steam, electric and high speed. Only the students who were to be employed at sea proceeded to Sheerness for one to two weeks to carry out practical transfers. If intended for land employment only the course was complete. On completion of the course the student was graded air mechanic 3rd class with a daily pay of 2s and was available for posting to an active service unit.

Hydrogen workers

Candidates for this course would be expected to have had some engineering knowledge. The course lasted four weeks at a Balloon Training Depot. Subjects came under three headings. Firstly silicol plants – types, capacities, quantities of materials, temperatures, pressures, purity meter, storage of caustic soda and silicol, and care of valves, etc. Compressor studies included the working and construction, the care of electric motors, and dismantling etc. If, however, compressors were left out, the course could be completed in between ten to fourteen days. Thirdly, manipulation and maintenance of tubes covered care in handling, stacking, valves, the general properties of hydrogen and precautions against fire. On completion of the course and after passing examinations, both practical and theoretical, the student was graded air mechanic 3rd class with a pay of 2s a day and was available for posting to an active service unit.

NCO gunnery instructors

Candidates could come from several sources:

1. NCO machine gun instructors
2. Instructors of the Corps: Schools of Musketry (through the War Office)
3. Promoted armourers
4. NCO pilots or observers unfit for flying.

The twelve-week course was held at the RAF Armament School, Uxbridge. Eight weeks were spent on guns and

St Andrews Gate, Uxbridge.

gun gears with four weeks on bombs and bomb gears. Those NCOs who failed to qualify could become NCO armourers provided they passed the necessary special workshop test. NCO instructors on probation from units other than the RAF could be transferred to the RAF on qualifying. This would be in their own rank provided that it was not higher than that of sergeant. On conclusion of the course, qualified instructors were posted either to schools at home or abroad or to a station at home.

NCO armourers
Candidates could come from one of two sources:

1. Suitable NCOs who have failed to qualify as instructors but who had passed the workshop test
2. Armourers who passed the necessary technical test

The seven-week course at the RAF Armament School Uxbridge was divided with four weeks on guns and gun gears and three weeks on bombs, bomb gears and sights. Those who qualified were posted to squadrons overseas, squadrons that were mobilizing or to gunnery schools.

Armourers (technical)
Candidates could come from one of three sources:

1. Personnel enlisted as armourers. (This applied practically only to civilians with special qualifications, if not Grade A.)
2. Suitable RAF personnel who were remustered in either of the above categories, on qualifying in their course.
3. Boy armourers.

The six-week course at the RAF Armament School Uxbridge was divided into four weeks on guns and gun-gears with two weeks spent on bombs, bomb gears and sights. Those who qualified as assistant armourers were posted to gunnery schools and squadrons at home and abroad.

Air mechanics (photographers)
Candidates could come from one of two sources:

1. Civilian employees of photographic businesses
2. Transfers from the Army with experience as above

Candidates were sent to the School of Photography, South Farnborough, from OC Records, Blandford Camp, for a course of training that lasted, on average, about ten weeks. During this time they were trained in photographic subjects such as identification, titling of negatives and indexing, elementary camera mechanism, attachment of camera equipment to aircraft etc., copying, loading of magazines, printing, developing of plates and prints, washing and drying, lantern slides, stereoscopic photography, recovering silver residues, mixing solutions and, last but not least, the value of photography in warfare. The student had to pass a test in all these subjects before leaving the school.

All the time a student was at the school he was paid 1s 6d a day as a private 2 class until remustered as a photographer, which was done when all tests were passed. He then became an air mechanic 3rd class with the pay of 2s a day. He was then posted, as required, to wings where he was trained for work in the field on exactly the same lines as at the School of Photography until he reached the required standard of speed and efficiency. This usually took about three months in the case of first class men; 5½ to 6 months for men of ordinary ability. He was then fit for posting overseas as required.

Camera repairers (photographers)
There were two sources of supply of men to this trade, namely instrument and watch makers. Like the air mechanic (photographers) above candidates went to the School of Photography, as a private 2nd class from the Record Office. The pay was 1s 6d a day and the course included the adjustment and repair of camera mechanisms such as the ½ plate camera and the Mark III, Hythe Gun Camera. On completion of the course of approximately five weeks a student was graded a 3rd class air mechanic with the pay of 2s 0d per day. He was then sent to a wing where his training continued on the same lines as that of photographers.

Wireless operators
Candidates for the wireless operators' course, if suitable, were found at the Reception Depot. Most of these had some post office experience or had been to a wireless school. The wireless operator (learner) was paid 1s 6d a day, given the rank of private 2nd class and for two weeks was instructed in drill and routine at Blandford from whence he was sent to No.1 (T) Wireless School at Flowerdown for a preparatory course of ten weeks. The practical side of the course was devoted to Morse and the use of tuners on the ground with lectures on magnetism and electricity, the use of instruments and air service procedure. At this point in the course the students were selected to prepare them for the different branches of their trade to equip them for their future role on squadrons.

Those intended for corps squadrons were to be ready having completed the course above, except for an additional two weeks for leave and equipment. Men who had shown the greatest promise were chosen for training in continuous wave and direction finding. Thus at the end of the ten-week preparatory course there were three classes of operators, men earmarked for:

1. Corps squadrons
2. Continuous wave work
3. Directional finding work

Those earmarked to join corps squadrons were ready for posting twelve weeks after the commencement of training. They were graded air mechanic 3rd class with a pay of 2s 0d a day. Those earmarked for continuous wave training started a special course of ten weeks on the principles of continuous wave work, continuous wave reception and transmission, adding up to twenty weeks in all when the student was then graded air mechanic 3rd class with a pay of 2s 0d a day. The direction finding (DF) operators followed their preparatory course with a twelve-week course, two weeks being spent with the continuous wave students and eight weeks of work of every description ending with two weeks for leave and equipment.

The DF operators posted to a DF squadron then had to qualify as W/T observer NCOs. Those DF operators intended for work with airships and airship ground stations attended a special course of twelve days' airship work at Cranwell and then went on to Eastchurch for gunnery and bomb-dropping practice.

Wireless mechanic
A volunteer for service as a wireless mechanic was verbally examined at the RAF Reception Depot then sent on to the nearest Trade Testing Distribution Centre for assessing suitability. If positive he would then be sent to Blandford, paid 1s 6d a day and given the rank of private 2nd class. The first two weeks at Blandford led to a trade test, which if he passed, made him a wireless mechanic. Having received drill whilst at Blandford he passed on to No.1 (T) Wireless School, Flowerdown.

The preparatory course at Flowerdown lasted ten weeks. With lectures and practice the students learnt fitting, turning, elementary electricity and magnetism and the care of aircraft tuners. From this point the students were divided, by selection, into the different branches of their trade for which they received special training before finally being sent to squadrons, rated air mechanics, on a daily rate of pay of 2s 0d. Those students who had shown the greatest promise were then chosen for training in telephony, Handley Page and CW mechanics. The remainder then received further final training for their work as wireless mechanics with a corps squadron. To sum up, the students had, at the end of their training, been earmarked for:

1. Corps squadrons
2. Continuous wave work
3. Handley Pages and large flying boats
4. Wireless telephony (W/T)

The corps squadron mechanics then continued with a six-week course, four given over to theoretical and practical instruction in the use of aircraft tuners, transmitters and care and fitting of wireless fittings in aircraft, with two weeks for leave and final equipment. A wireless mechanic intended for an artillery squadron was then ready for employment as an air mechanic 3rd class with a pay of 2s 0d a day.

The mechanics earmarked for special instruction in Handley Pages, large flying boats, continuous wave work and wireless telephony all did a course lasting two weeks on generators, High Tension (HT) and Low Tension (LT) before splitting up. Those who were selected for wireless telephony training were sent on a special course at the School of Wireless Telephony in conjunction with W/T officers also under instruction.

Mechanic (man)
These men entered the RAF at one of nine RAF Reception Depots, enlisting for the duration of the war. If accepted they were graded private 2nd class with a daily rate of pay of 1s 6d. They were then sent to RAF Depot Blandford to be medically examined, given a service number and kitted before being passed through the Trade Testing Sheds and classified according to trade:

Acetylene welder	Instrument repairer
Armourer	Machinist
Blacksmith	Magneto repairer
Boat builder	Millwright
Camera repairer	Motor body builder
Carpenter	Moulder
Coppersmith	Pattern maker
Draughtsman	Pilot
Photographer	Propeller maker
Driver: Motor boat	Rigger (aeroplane)
Petrol	Rigger (airship)
Steam	Tinsmith and sheet metal
Electrician	worker
Fitter: Aero engine	Turner
General	Upholsterer
Mechanical transport	Vulcaniser
(MT)	Winch driver and fitter
Jig and tool maker	Wireless operator
Hydrogen worker	Wireless mechanic

Each entrant then commenced a course of drill and disciplinary training lasting three weeks. This was followed by a course of musketry instruction lasting six days before being drafted to the appropriate training establishment listed on page 218. On completion of his training he was graded air mechanic 3rd class and paid 2s 0d a day.

Mechanic (boy)

Finally, it is stated in the Training Manual that no boys were being entered, in October 1918, as mechanics. Before the formation of the RAF, boys had either been enlisted:

1. For the duration of the war
2. Four years with the colours (active service) and four years in the Reserve
3. Or twelve years on active service

Boys who had entered through the RNAS went to Crystal Palace and those who entered through the RFC went to Farnborough. There they were medically examined, kitted and classified according to trade on a daily pay rate of 1s 0d. All boys were sent to Halton Park to learn drill and discipline. This was nominally for a period of eight weeks but owing to infection and consequent quarantine this was much prolonged. At the end of this course the boys enlisted for the duration of the war were sent direct to units where they were put to work as assistants to men skilled in the various trades. Boys who enlisted ordinarily as 2 or 3 above, were drafted to one of the following training establishments for training:

Establishment	Trade
Cranwell	Fitters, engine
	Machinists
	Riggers
Eastchurch	Fitters, engine
	Blacksmiths
	Tinsmiths
	Coppersmiths
Letchworth	Machinists

At the end of the training period a boy was turned out as a skilled mechanic of the trade for which he had been taught. He was then given a certificate stating his ability and progress and was then drafted to a unit.

INTER-WAR TRAINING

Volume 1 of the inter-war history titled the *Trenchard Years*, written by this author and published by Pen and Sword describes RAF training in the 1920s and this subject can therefore be followed in that publication.

Chapter 9
Airfields, Landing Grounds and Seaplane Bases

*Location of airfields – choice of aerodrome sites – the retreat and advance to the Aisne – the provision of aerodromes in 1916/7
– airfield/seaplane bases and landing grounds in the United Kingdom – followed by the Western Front and the Middle East*

LOCATION OF AND ROLE OF AIRFIELDS, SEAPLANE BASES AND LANDING GROUNDS

The airfields in each geographical area of the United Kingdom are listed in alphabetical order. Each geographical area is headed with a map of the area and this shows all the airfields listed. Many of the airfields and seaplane bases at home were opened for the first time as the need arose and were not part of a preplanned national siting, except for those opened before the commencement of hostilities in August 1914. It must be remembered that military aviation by powered aircraft was entirely new to warfare. No one could know how it would develop and there had to be a great deal of improvisation. Names of schools and the roles of operational units in particular changed constantly in response to the tactics involved. At Hythe, for example, on 3 September 1916 the Machine Gun School became the School of Aerial Gunnery, which changed again in March 1918 to become the No.1 (Observers') School of Aerial Gunnery. Other examples abound as the art of air warfare developed at a pace unforeseen at the commencement of hostilities. It must be remembered that the RFC went to war with only four squadrons but this number grew rapidly and at many of the airfields units were formed and, no sooner were they formed, than they went off to war. As the tactics in the air developed there was a growing need for training stations to teach air fighting, observation, ground attack, reconnaissance, anti-submarine tactics and bombing. Stations/airfields often changed roles. In many cases airfields coped with increasing numbers of

aircraft, technical buildings and personnel by adding canvas Bessoneaux hangars and wooden buildings or ones made of corrugated iron. If the role assigned to an airfield was believed to be permanent then permanent accommodation replaced temporary constructions. All airfields in the Great War were grassed and racecourses provided ready-made landing grounds. Many were pressed into use.

British military aviation soon developed as two separate organizations, the RFC, which came under the War Office, and the RNAS, which came under the Admiralty. This had the advantage that the two air services could use existing works and supply services. Formation of the RAF in 1918 as an independent air arm would have been virtually impossible if it had to start everything from scratch once hostilities had commenced. The location of airfields in the United Kingdom was dictated largely by the direction of the expected threat. As in World War II the north-west was furthest from any expected attack by enemy aircraft and storage, aircraft construction and flying training were concentrated in the Midlands and north-west (see the section dealing with Wales and the north-west). Once the Zeppelin threat developed, followed by the threat from Gotha bombers, then a string of fighter airfields down the east coast had to be established. This meant positioning a squadron's headquarters at a base airfield with detached flights situated at landing grounds (these abound in the listings that follow for the various areas of eastern England). No.6 Brigade RFC would be responsible for Home Defence and the squadrons were titled HD or Home Defence squadrons. The short range and endurance of fighter aircraft at this time meant that they had to be spread thinly in a continuous line up the east coast. There was no early warning radar and to have fighter aircraft mounting standing patrols to counter any possible air attack would have been prohibitively costly in fuel and wear and tear on engines. The threat in the English Channel came principally from U-boats and this dictated the siting of seaplane bases and airship mooring out stations along the south coast of England and in the Western Approaches. (See the sections on airfields in the south-west and central south and south-east.)

On the Western Front the war was mostly fought from a line of trenches that stretched from the Channel coast between Dunkirk and Ostend right down to the frontier with Switzerland. This largely dictated the situation of

Sopwith Camels of No.76 (HD) Sqn with a Bristol fighter coming in to land.

SE5as in Palestine.

airfields close to the front line. The RFC brigades were committed to giving direct support to the five British armies that comprised the BEF. There was one RFC brigade assigned to each army with the greatest concentration of airfields in the area of Cambrai, where major offensives were most likely. (See the airfield location map in Chapter 4.) One should not forget the valuable strategic bombing work carried out by RNAS units and the support given by the RNAS in supporting Allied ground operations (see Chapter 3). In the Mediterranean the threat came from enemy warships and submarines and seaplane bases in Malta were important. In the north of Italy where the Italians were fighting the Austro-Hungarians the siting of airfields was dictated by movements of the friendly and enemy forces on the ground. In Mesopotamia where, again, a more fluid situation developed, the enemy were the Turkish forces equipped with German fighting aircraft.

Choice of aerodrome sites in 1914
Source: National Archive document AIR1/6A/4/55

Writing from his headquarters of RAF Fighting Area in Uxbridge in 1926, Robert Baden-Powell recalls how he set about choosing sites for aerodromes and setting them up for air operations. In the first few months of the war there was rapid movement of the ground forces for it was not until the end of the year that the line solidified into the endless lines of opposing trenches that characterized the Great War. Initially, therefore, it was necessary to have a checklist of site requirements, which included matters such as the siting of parked aircraft, ammunition dumps, a technical area for the repair and servicing of aircraft, parking of motor transport, tent lines, cookhouses, bathhouses and latrines. The list is not exhaustive and unit commanders made up their own lists quickly learning by experience. Once the war had settled down into one of attrition, however, there was a much reduced need to change the sites of airfields. There was then a security problem both on the ground and from attacks by enemy aircraft. Of course, the French military authorities

were involved since the siting of airfields most often affected local farmers and landowners.

The retreat and advance to the Aisne
Initially, four squadrons went to France and Sir David Henderson arranged for one day's supply of food, petrol and oil to be sent to the railhead serving the 1st and 2nd Corps so two days' supply was always available to the RFC at any time. This was in the event wasteful but with the fluid battle situation one had to play it safe, the more so since the rail heads were constantly changing and it was the job of the Army Service Corps officer with his lorries to get to the appropriate railhead for the RFC supplies. Baden-Powell was armed with a float of 300 gold sovereigns at the start of the retreat so if anything, such as canvas to cover the vehicles, was not available through service sources he could locally purchase items. This even stretched to include maps and he had to forage ahead to purchase these as required. He was responsible for the selection of most of the airfield sites during the retreat. It was fortunate that the crops had been harvested so there was an ample number of suitable sites available. He never had to cut a crop but did, at some locations, have to remove corn stoops. Some French grass airfields were available like those at Compiègne, Senlis and Melun, otherwise it was fields of stubble.

Transport movements were the most difficult. With over 100 lorries allocated to the RFC, Baden-Powell had to determine the most appropriate routes to be taken particularly when moving across the front of Army Corps. A convoy speed of 8mph was adopted and he had to be prepared for the removal of blockages along the chosen route. In the event, most stores were successfully moved, surplus food and lubricating oil being an exception. Replacement aircraft came either from Paris or England and arrived by air. Some of the pilots returned to the UK, others remained with the Corps.

It was important for aircraft not to fall into the hands of the enemy and the RFC in France at this time had only to burn four aeroplanes. No aeroplanes were moved by road, the rest being successfully flown out of their airfields or burned. Six spare rotary engines were carried and a 80hp Gnome could be replaced in a day. Aircraft and engine spares were not a problem, at least up to the Aisne, but transport spares were. Some light vehicles were exchanged through the offices of the Director of Transport.

THE PROVISION OF AERODROMES IN THE UK – 1916/1917
Source: National Archive Document AIR1/109/15/20/2

Introduction
There was to be a Home Defence line stretching from Dover to Edinburgh with aerodromes sited at distances varying between ten to thirty miles. Squadrons consisted

Short Seaplane A 320.

Airships like this SSZ37 provided valuable maritime reconnaissance and convoy protection.

of a headquarters and three flights. The HQ would be located at some central point with the three flights, which were detached from the HQ. Given the speed and range of aircraft at this time an effective defence line relied upon defending fighters being able to respond to an approach of enemy airships or bombers attempting to penetrate the defences to attack industrial or military targets. One only has to look at the number of seaplane and airship mooring-out stations that ringed the eastern and southern coasts of the UK during the Great War, which were needed to provide adequate convoy protection and maritime reconnaissance. Today just one maritime reconnaissance station suffices for the UK as a whole. In the Great War there was no radar to warn of an enemy's approach and it would have been terribly costly to keep some fighters aloft for given periods of time to better ensure interception of the enemy. These are known as standing patrols. Apart from the expenditure on fuel there would be the wear and tear on airframes and engines.

The Home Defence squadrons were placed under active service conditions and flight accommodation at the detached landing grounds was simple and inexpensive. Thirty small aerodromes sufficed to provide an adequate defence line. The flights were provided with a double aerodrome shed to accommodate eight aircraft with hutting for ten officers and seventy other ranks. Telephonic communication with squadron HQ was also provided. At the squadron headquarters there were outbuildings to accommodate stores and simple workshops. One reason for siting the HQ away from all the three flights was so that the squadron commander could not favour one flight over another. But the policy of having the HQ on a non-airfield site resulted in extravagant use of transport and the prevention of the efficient direction of training

by the squadron commander. The obvious answer was to site the HQ with the central of the three flights and this was the policy in 1917. There was an exception and that was No.76 Squadron whose HQ was at the racecourse outside Ripon. There was the facility to store one aircraft for the squadron commander with plenty of grass to effect a take-off and landing.

In the spring of 1917 there was a further change of policy. The Gotha bomber threat meant that additional squadrons were needed to cover the south-east. Squadrons in this region were concentrated on one airfield, releasing the airfields of the detached flights for other squadrons. Airfields that had previously housed just one flight of a squadron had to be upgraded in terms of accommodation for personnel, stores, and workshops. Five aerodromes were selected for training, three housing two training squadrons and two housing a single squadron. One of the latter was sited at the Newmarket racecourse where the Jockey Club placed the racecourse land and buildings at the disposal of the Home Defence squadron force free of all expense. Later it was found expedient to co-locate a training squadron with a Home Defence squadron and the total number of airfields used for training rose to seven when co-location was adopted at Sutton's Farm and Throwley.

General rules of the air as applied to aerodrome use

In August 1917 Major General J.H. Salmond, commanding the Training Division of the RFC, issued orders relating to rules in the air. These were reflected in the orders issued to trainee pilots by the Commandant of the Central Flying School. These special regulations applied only to aerodromes and covered avoidance of collisions, aircraft overtaking and the determination of which side to pass an aircraft. Before taxiing out for take-off, the mechanic holding the port wing was to salute when it was safe, i.e. there was no risk of collision with another aircraft. If two aircraft were effecting a landing the one that was closest to the ground should have priority in completing the landing. If there was a danger of collision the pilot who saw another aircraft in his path, was to open up his engine and make a fresh approach. Whether or not a pilot was in the process of landing or taking off, if he was on the ground he was to look round to make sure the airfield was clear before either taking off or proceeding towards the tarmac. On approaching the tarmac the pilot was to slow down to 'dead slow'.

Pilots approaching an airfield to land had to observe the colour of the flag, red for a right-hand circuits or blue for left-hand. Short circuits were not to be flown that may conflict with pilots flying normal circuits. No simulated fights were to be carried out over an aerodrome nor were practices involving flying under 2,000ft. Although stunting was encouraged such flying was prohibited under 2,000ft. Unnecessary low flying over towns, villages and wireless stations was prohibited. Apart from the danger from low flying, Major General Salmond wanted to emphasize the fact that such practices gave the Corps a bad name.

The rules laid out in this letter were echoed in orders issued to trainee pilots at the Central Flying School. This was to cater for aeroplanes using the south and east tarmacs. If a pilot made a bad attempt at landing he was to fly another circuit and try again. All undergraduate pilots under instruction were required to wear helmets and goggles at all times. No pilot was permitted to fly over Netheravon under 2,000ft. Only graduate pilots were permitted to loop, 'zoom' or indulge in aerobatics but then not under 2,000ft and not in the vicinity of the aerodrome.

AIRFIELDS AND MISCELLANEOUS UNITS IN THE BRITISH ISLES DURING THE GREAT WAR

Introduction
The country was divided into regions and the airfields, seaplane bases and landing grounds to the following sequence:

1. Greater London
2. Central south and south-east of England
3. South-west England
4. East Anglia
5. Cotswolds and Central Midlands
6. Lincolnshire and East Midlands
7. North-west England
8. Yorkshire
9. Scotland, Ulster and the North East

AIRFIELDS IN THE GREATER LONDON AREA

AIRFIELDS AND LANDING GROUNDS IN ALPHABETICAL ORDER

ACTON – LONDON W OF LONDON
Acton was opened as an aerodrome in 1910 and known as London Aviation Ground. It was used by a variety of aircraft until taken over by the National Guard on the outbreak of the Great War. It was used initially as a civilian flying school to train service personnel, but it was not up to standard in either machines or instructors, and the temporary hangars were taken down and the other buildings were taken over by the newly formed Alliance Aeroplane Company. Flying did not take place after the war, for when the Alliance Aeroplane Company was wound up Acton was closed early in 1920.

ALL HALLOWS – NE OF CHATHAM
All Hallows was a third-class landing ground used by No.143 Squadron as a relief landing ground during the Great War and was closed at the end of the war.

BENTLEY PRIORY
This airfield was purchased by the Air Ministry in 1926 for approximately £25,000. It was the HQ of Inland Area RAF from 26 May 1926 before becoming HQ Fighter Command.

BIGGIN HILL – N OF BIGGIN HILL AND WESTERHAM
Biggin was opened on 14 February 1917 as a RFC radio signals unit and used for wireless experiments. In February the following year No.141 Squadron arrived and remained there until the end of the war. It was one of Biggin's Bristol Fighters that shot down a Gotha bomber over Harrietsham aerodrome, Kent. When No.141 Squadron moved out on 1 March 1919 it was replaced by No.37 Squadron, then No.39 Squadron as a cadre unit, which then went to Kenley in 1922. The following year No.56 Squadron and the Night Flying Flight moved in but when these units left, No.56 Squadron to North Weald in October 1927 and the Night Flying Flight in 1929, the empty station underwent an extensive building programme.

BROOKLANDS – SW OF WEYBRIDGE
Brooklands was used by A.V. Roe in 1908 and Short's joined A.V. Roe to build aircraft from 1910 as also did Martinsyde (Martin and Handasyde). The airfield was taken over by the Royal Flying Club as a training station for ab initio pilots. In 1915 the station was also home to Nos.1, 8 and 10 Squadrons. Firms such as Sopwith also began to build aircraft at Brooklands, the total built by

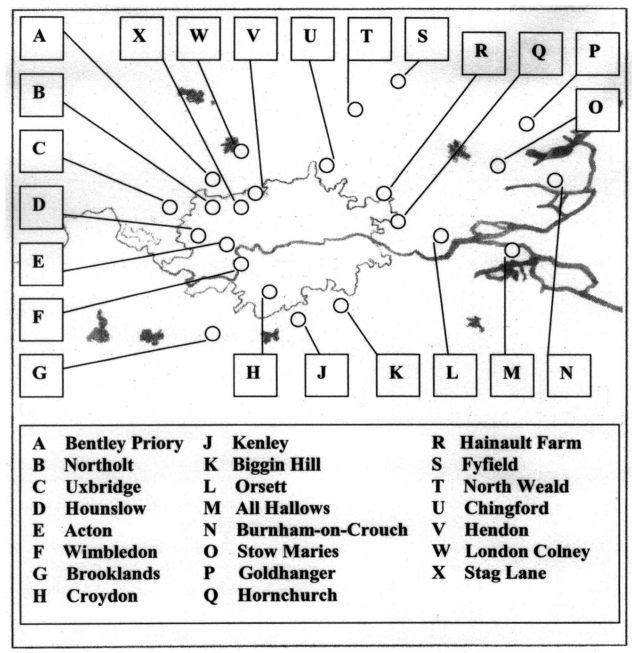

Airfields in Greater London.

A	Bentley Priory	J	Kenley	R	Hainault Farm
B	Northolt	K	Biggin Hill	S	Fyfield
C	Uxbridge	L	Orsett	T	North Weald
D	Hounslow	M	All Hallows	U	Chingford
E	Acton	N	Burnham-on-Crouch	V	Hendon
F	Wimbledon	O	Stow Maries	W	London Colney
G	Brooklands	P	Goldhanger	X	Stag Lane
H	Croydon	Q	Hornchurch		

all firms exceeding 4,600 including SE5s and the Vickers Gunbus. No.10 Aircraft Acceptance Park at Brooklands stored SE5s and Snipes. On 31 January 1917, No.2 Reserve School left for Northolt. The airfield itself was situated inside the motor racing circuit and was bounded on three sides by high tension cables. In spite of this the airfield continued to be used after the war but it did not remain in RAF use.

BURNHAM-ON-CROUCH – E OF BURNHAM-ON-CROUCH

This was a 1st class landing ground sited on the north bank of River Crouch and came under the control of No.50 Wing throughout the Great War. It was used briefly in the war by No.37 Squadron but it was too low lying and marshy so was abandoned.

CHINGFORD – JUST N OF LONDON BETWEEN ENFIELD AND CHINGFORD

Chingford was opened in 1915 as a 2nd class landing ground. It came under the jurisdiction of No.49 Wing and was used by No.44 Squadron on HD duties. Chingford was also a depot and main training station for the RNAS. Eventually, No.207 TDS was housed there and the station remained in the training role for the remainder of the war. It closed in 1919.

CROYDON – SW OF CROYDON

Throughout 1916 and 1917 No.17 Reserve (Training) Squadron was based at Croydon to be replaced during 1917 by No.40 TS, which then moved to Tangmere in 1918. Croydon was used by No.141 Squadron, as a landing ground, and No.29 Squadron, with whom Prince Albert (the later King George VI) gained his 'Wings' in 1919. In July of that year the airfield was used by an Air Council Inspection Squadron as No.1 Group Headquarters. In October Nos.207, 32 and 41 Squadrons came to the station but all without aircraft. No.207 Squadron moved out on 16 January 1920 and the other two squadrons were disbanded. When the RAF left in February 1920 the airfield returned to civil flying.

FYFIELD – CLOSE TO CHIPPING ONGAR

Sited 1½ miles from Chipping Ongar station, this landing ground came under the jurisdiction of No.49 Wing and No.39 Squadron used it for HD duties. It closed immediately after the Great War.

HAINAULT FARM (FAIRLOP) – W OF ROMFORD

Hainault Farm was taken over for service use in 1915 and soon housed a flight of No.39 (HD) Squadron giving air defence cover to the east of London. Hainault aircraft were successful in tackling the Zeppelins when *L32* was shot down by Lieutenant Sowrey and *L33* was hit by Lieutenant Brandon. On 24 July 1917 No.44 Squadron was formed at Hainault, remaining there to the end of the war. In May 1918 No.207 TDS began to use Hainault as a substation and No.151 Squadron formed there on 12 June, moving to France within the week. There then followed No.153 Squadron, which was not formed until November, by which time the Armistice had been signed. When Nos.44 and 153 Squadrons had disbanded the airfield was returned to agriculture.

Hendon Airfield.

HENDON – BETWEEN EDGWARE AND HENDON

This airfield had the very earliest connections with flying well before the Great War but the military use of Hendon did not arise until 4 August when the aerodrome was requisitioned under the Defence of the Realm Act. There were, at the time, five flying schools at Hendon, including the famous Grahame-White's school, contracted to train pilots for the RFC including such famous names as Mannock, Ball and Warneford. The RNAS established a delivery centre for aircraft at Hendon, which became No.2 Aircraft Acceptance Park. Hendon was becoming a centre for aircraft production being responsible for some 7,800 aircraft produced during the war years, including DH2s, 4s, 5s, 6s, 9 and 9As, BE2cs and Avro 504Ks. When the war ended the newly formed No.1 (Communications) Squadron began ferrying officials and documents to Paris for the Peace Conference. When this unit moved to Kenley in May 1919 only civilian concerns operated from the airfield, though it was still in service hands.

HOUNSLOW – SE OF THE SITE OF THE PRESENT LONDON AIRPORT

Hounslow was taken over in August 1914 for RFC training. Operational squadrons also came and went, including Nos.10, 15, 24, 27, 39, 52, 85 and 87, some of which had formed at Hounslow. When No.18 Wing Aeroplane Repair Section came it remained until August 1919. When Nos.85 and 87 Squadrons moved to France in mid 1918, No. 42 TDS moved in and in March 1919 No.107 Squadron came home to disband, and once No.42 TDS disbanded the site returned to civil use.

KENLEY – S OF CROYDON OF THE A22

Kenley was opened in summer of 1917 as No.7 Aircraft Acceptance Park. From the summer of 1918 several squadrons were in residence but by November 1918 all but No.91 Squadron had moved out. When this unit moved out on 3 July 1919 it left only No.1 (Communications) Squadron, which had come from Hendon in April. On 1 April 1920 No.24 (Communications) Squadron formed at Kenley. The station was eventually selected for retention as a permanent RAF station in early 1920s

LONDON (COLNEY) – 5 MILES SW OF HATFIELD
London (Colney) was established as a 2nd class landing ground during the Great War and came under the SE Area. It was used by No.44 Squadron during the early part of the war and in the spring of 1916 a training aerodrome was established and the first resident squadron was No. 56, which came from Gosport on 4 July, the first squadron to receive SE5 fighters. The fighter ace Captain Albert Ball was one of the squadron pilots when it flew off to France on 7 April 1917. No.56 Squadron was replaced at the station by No.56 TS. On 10 July No.74 Squadron came to the airfield with 504Ks and SE5as but it moved to Goldhanger in March 1918. Under RAF administration No.56 TS became No.41 TDS flying 504Ks and Snipes. When the training role of the station came to an end after the Armistice Nos.1 and 24 Squadrons arrived but only in cadre form and it was decided not to retain the airfield in the peacetime RAF and it closed in December 1919.

No.74 Squadron SE5as at London Colney 1917.

NORTHOLT – W OF LONDON ON THE A40
Construction began in early 1915 and the aerodrome officially opened on 1 March with the arrival of No.4 Reserve Aeroplane Squadron. It was also a night landing ground having primitive airfield lighting. From No.4 Reserve Squadron No.18 Squadron was formed, which later went to France. A number of units passed through. Meanwhile, the airfield was used for flight-testing aircraft constructed by the nearby Fairey works. Only one contact was made with the enemy during the Great War by

Northolt-based aircraft when Gothas were intercepted over Ilford, Essex. Both Americans and Russians came to Northolt for flying training. Indeed, Northolt as a training aerodrome witnessed many accidents, some fatal. In 1917 there were three fatal crashes killing sixteen people in all. In February 1918 the three training squadrons, Nos.2 and 4 TS and 86 Squadron, became No.30 TDS. After the Armistice and following the disbandment of its units Northolt ceased to be a fighter training station and in June 1919 it was home to South Eastern Communications Flight, which provided refresher courses for officers. By then, Northolt had become a joint RAF/civil airfield and the Central Aircraft Company moved in to operate a flying school.

NORTH WEALD – W OF CHIPPING ONGAR
The aerodrome was constructed in 1916 and in the August No.39 Squadron had a detached flight there. It was from North Weald that 2 Lieutenant W.J. Tempest shot down Zeppelin *L31* over Potter's Bar on 1 October 1916. When the Gotha threat replaced that of the Zeppelins No.39 Squadron put two more detached flights into the airfield so that the squadron was complete at that airfield. On 22 May 1918 No.75 Squadron joined No.39 and in October the latter left for France. After the Armistice No.75 Squadron was disbanded and although No.44 Squadron moved in for a short time, when it too was disbanded, North Weald had no resident squadron and it lay dormant for a few years.

ORSETT (ESSEX) – NE OF GRAYS
From 1917 until 1919 Orsett was used by No.49 Wing being a 1st class landing ground. The airfield had only tented accommodation and was closed after the war

PENSHURST (KENT) – 4 MILES NW OF TUNBRIDGE WELLS
During the Great War Penshurst housed No.2 Wireless School, formed on 8 November 1917. Equipped with DH6s the school provided a one week's course for scout pilots and one week for wireless personnel. Penshurst was also a depot for wireless stores and repair and testing of wireless apparatus. When the school closed on 23 March 1919 the airfield closed and the buildings were dismantled.

STAG LANE – EDGWARE TO THE N OF LONDON
This was a 2nd class landing ground in the south-eastern area under No.49 Wing. It was used during the Great War by No.44 Squadron and was closed after the Armistice. It later became famous for de Havilland aircraft production.

STOW MARIES – 9 MILES SE OF CHELMSFORD
Stow Maries started life in 1916 as home to a No.37 Squadron detachment. It was the policy in the Great War to spread a HD squadron over three landing grounds with up

to eight aircraft at each. The squadron headquarters could well be at another location, in this case Woodham Mortimer with two other detachments at Goldhanger and Southend (Rochford). In June 1918 the squadron headquarters moved to Stow Maries and No.37 Squadron became a night-fighter squadron with Camels. When the detached flight at Goldhanger withdrew to Stow Maries on 20 February 1919 the unit was at last all together at one airfield but when it moved to Biggin Hill on 17 March that year the airfield was abandoned and returned to agriculture.

UXBRIDGE – SE OF UXBRIDGE

Acquired by the government in early 1915 it was intended originally as a POW camp but became a convalescent hospital for Canadian soldiers then the RAF Armament School in 1918. One of the first tasks undertaken by the school was to give armament training to cadets prior to flying training but this was threatened with closure after the Armistice. In August a detachment of the RAF Depot moved from Halton which, together with the Recruits' Training Depot, was to train recruits and to be called the Uxbridge Depot. In September 1919 the Armament School left and the same month the School of Music arrived from Hampstead. Other units included HQ No.2 Group, HQ Southern Area, Southern Area Medical HQ and Southern Area Barrack Stores. There then followed Southern Area HQ of the Air Construction Service and the South Eastern Group HQ of the same service and, just to fill the place up, the cadres of Nos.4 and 39 Squadrons arrived followed by those of 3 and 207 Squadrons but it was not long before these squadrons were on the move again on reformation. Uxbridge remained very active after the Armistice.

WIMBLEDON

Wimbledon was a 3 class landing ground, which came under 49 Wing during the Great War and was used mainly by No.141 Squadron. It was dismantled soon after the Armistice.

Wimbledon Airfield.

AIRFIELDS, SEAPLANE BASES, MOORING OUT STATIONS AND MISCELLANEOUS UNITS IN CENTRAL SOUTH AND SOUTH-EAST ENGLAND

ANDOVER – 2½ MILES W OF ANDOVER ON THE A303

The station was built on 400 acres of flat pasture land and was opened in August 1917 even though much of the accommodation was incomplete. Personnel had to live under canvas and the aircraft had to be housed in a row of canvas Bessoneaux hangars along the station's northern boundary. The first task of the new station was to work up bomber squadrons that would use nearby bombing ranges on Salisbury Plain. These units were Nos.104,105 and 106 Squadrons to be joined by No.148 Squadron in February 1918. The latter was, in fact, first to leave for the Continent in April and the remainder went to Ireland. These units were replaced by Nos.207 and 215 Squadrons, which returned from operations to convert from the HPO/100 to the O/400. On 1 May 1918 No.2 School of Navigation and Bomb Dropping was formed. The school had a night training squadron using HPO/400s where trainees were being prepared for a projected assault on Berlin. This was, however, cancelled when the Armistice intervened. In 1919 the Air Pilotage School, which had replaced the previous training units, was subject to the post-war axe but the station did survive to become part of the post-war RAF.

BEKESBOURNE – KENT 4 MILES SE OF CANTERBURY

Bekesbourne was requisitioned in 1916 as an emergency landing ground. It was large sloping field just south-east of the village and was first used by B Flight of No.50 Home Defence Squadron. Although the airfield was small it was large enough to operate the BE2 and BE12 variants and the AW FK 3 and 8s. Not very much happened at Bekesbourne until the German Gotha bombers began their raids on targets in the south-east of England. The public outcry against these attacks resulted in some scout (fighter) squadrons being recalled from the Continent to protect the capital and No.56 Squadron arrived at the airfield on 21 June but during the squadron's brief stay the only daylight raid by the German bombers of Kagohl 3 was on East Anglia. Two days after No.56 Squadron's return to the Continent on July 5 twenty-two Gothas bombed London. This is not to suggest that there is any necessary link between the two events. In 1918 the airfield was upgraded with the construction of two large Belfast truss hangars and with other buildings that were constructed in the north-west corner a hutted domestic site was erected close to Chalkpit Farm. No.50 Squadron moved in on 8 February and additional training tasks

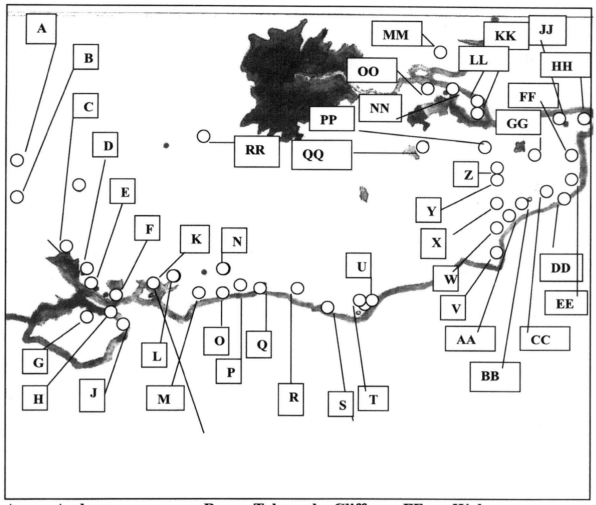

A	Andover	R	Telscombe Cliffs	FF	Walmer
B	Chattis Hill	S	Newhaven	GG	Bekesbourne
C	Eastleigh	T	Polegate	HH	Westgate
D	Hamble	U	Eastbourne	JJ	Manston
E	Lee-on-Solent	V	Lydd	KK	Leysdown
F	Gosport	W	New Romney	LL	Eastchurch
G	Somerton	X	Lympne	MM	Rochford
H	Bembridge	Y	Wye	NN	Sheerness
J	Foreland	Z	Godmersham Park	OO	Grain
K	Tipnor	AA	Hythe/Dymchurch	PP	Throwley
L	Southbourne	BB	Hawkinge	QQ	Detling
M	Tangmere	CC	Capel	RR	Farnborough
N	Slinden	DD	Dover Guston Road & Marine Parade		
O	Ford	EE	Dover St Margarets		

Central south and south-east England.

were taken on. By September 1918 the work on the hangars was complete and then, in November, the squadron's Camels were replaced by SE5as. Then, with the Armistice, came the run down following the disbandment of the squadron in 1919 and the airfield was relinquished in 1920.

BEMBRIDGE – ISLE OF WIGHT (MARINE) 3½ MILES SE OF RYDE

The Solent Defence Scheme had its HQ at Calshot and the role was to combat the U-boat menace in the English Channel and there was a requirement for a substation at Bembridge so that Calshot-based seaplanes could move forward to Bembridge Point. The facilities were Spartan when the slipway came into use in 1915, the seaplanes being moored in the harbour. In November 1916 four Short 184 floatplanes were stationed at Bembridge so that they could reach sixty miles out into the English Channel from the island and these seaplanes became part of the reorganized Portsmouth Group on 1 January 1917, operating on the orders of the Naval C-in-C. Accommodation was provided for the officers in the Spithead Hotel with the ratings in an adapted coastguard station. On the hardstanding were two seaplane sheds and a number of huts. From the harbour the floatplanes had to taxi out into open water to the north-west of St Helen's Fort to take off. Hunting U-boats often involved hours of fruitless searching of the sea below for any tell-tale sign of a submarines such as one executing a crash-dive on seeing the approach of the 184, but patience paid off on 18 October 1917 when there was an unconfirmed kill of a U-boat by Flight Commander McLaurin and his observer. On 1 April 1918 the RAF was formed and the Portsmouth Command became No.10 Group at Warsash. The personnel all became RAF officers and men, although outwardly there was little to show any change. The Bembridge unit therefore became No.253 Squadron composed of Nos.412 and 413 Flights. The squadron was disbanded in May 1919 and the site disposed of in 1920.

Short 184.

CAPEL (FOLKSTONE) KENT – 2 MILES NE OF FOLKESTONE

When the Germans declared unrestricted submarine warfare the Admiralty responded by bombing their bases in Belgium, forming convoys to negotiate the Straits of Dover and formed airship units at bases with detached craft at mooring out stations. Capel was the ideal location for siting an airship station to cover the Dover Strait and the site at Capel-le-Ferne was cleared. By April 1915 airship sheds were erected. When the base was commissioned on 8 May 1915 the work was far from finished but such was the urgency that this had to be overlooked.

Airships *Beta*, *Delta* and *Gamma*, which had once belonged to the Army, were stationed at Capel to be joined by the first of the SSI Type airship flown down from Kingsnorth in the Thames estuary. This cross-country flight was entrusted to Flight Sub Lieutenant R.S. Booth (who later became famous for his captaincy of the *R100* airship in 1930). The landing party had laid out an illuminated arrow to indicate the direction of the wind but Booth took it to mean the direction in which he was required to land. He therefore did so downwind and overshot the landing party, colliding with the telephone wires on the side of the main road. This caused a fire and the crew had to jump clear on the very edge of a 450ft drop over the cliff. After this initial hiccup there were soon four airships employed on convoy patrol. The next problem was the inability of the airship sheds to accommodate the SS type so a trench was dug in the concrete base into which the gondola car could be lowered.

Later Capel became the main base for the assembly of airships of the SS type and this attracted the attention of the enemy when a German seaplane appeared over Capel on 23 January 1916. The five bombs that were dropped missed the airship sheds but this was an audacious attack in broad daylight. When another enemy aircraft was sighted on 24 January the Royal Navy had to look to its defences. The SS airships could stay aloft throughout the entire daylight hours but the gondola car was very uncomfortable due to draughts and it was cramped so the Capel staff set about building a car that proved much more comfortable and the converted airships became the SS Zero, which had then gone into production.

Kite balloons were also held at Capel and were used for convoy protection. The crew of an SSZ1 airship launched an attack on a U-boat in the act of surfacing at a range of two miles. Two bombs were dropped on the point where the boat had submerged giving rise to a large patch of oil mixed with air bubbles. Even though the airship returned to Capel for more bombs to drop on the oil patch it could be claimed, at best, that the U-boat had been seriously damaged.

During 1917 the Capel airships provided escorts for the transports on the cross-channel convoy runs from

Folkestone to Boulogne. Organizational change came in 1918 when Capel became part of No.5 Group RAF, which embraced the whole of the Dover area. By this time personnel were accommodated in large wooden huts close to the Royal Oak Inn and there were three large airship sheds fitted with windbreaks at either end. At the end of the war there were seven SSZ airships and two SSTs (a twin-engined version). There were substations at Godmersham Park and Wittersham. Capel was closed in 1919 and the land and buildings passed to the Disposal Board in 1920. A caravan park occupies the site today and the concrete hangar bases are used, including the one with the lowered floor section.

CHATTIS HILL, HAMPSHIRE – 2½ MILES W OF STOCKBRIDGE

A windy hill above the River Test does not sound like the ideal spot for an airfield. Be that as it may the site on Houghton Downs was prepared during the summer of 1917 ready for the arrival of Nos.91 and 93 Squadrons, which had been formed during September at Spittlegate and Croydon respectively. These squadrons were then joined by No.92 Squadron, which came with its Sopwith Pups from London (Colney). No.91 Squadron was equipped with BE2cs, FK8s and RE8s. Nos.92 and 93 Squadrons were to be fighter training units, the former equipped with Avro 540Ks, Pups and SPADs and No.93 with SE5as. The aircraft were housed in Bessoneaux hangars erected near Chattis Hill House and alongside the main road a tented camp was established for personnel, although many of them were billeted in Stockbridge whilst the officers used the Grosvenor Arms as their mess. This 120-acre airfield sloping down towards Chattis Hill House was not satisfactory and the area around the hangars became a sea of mud and badly rutted. In spite of this only No.92 Squadron was extricated going to Tangmere in March 1918. Then No.43 Training Squadron (TS) came from Tern Hill and No.34 TS came from Castle Bromwich, both units being equipped with Avro 504Ks and Camels to undertake flying training. The School of Wireless Telegraphy arrived from Biggin Hill and absorbed No.91 Squadron ready to start courses for pilots and observers and longer courses for W/T officers and mechanics. On 5 July 1918 the two training squadrons were merged into No.43 Training Depot Squadron (TDS) coming under No.34 Wing of No.8 Group RAF. An American construction unit was brought in to build a more permanent station but there was a clash between the units using the airfield. Avros and Camels of the TDS were buzzing round the circuit conflicting with the more staid machines of the Wireless School, which trailed yards of wire behind them. Fortunately there were no incidents. Personnel moved into hutted accommodation just prior to the Armistice but work on the technical site and the hangars was not complete. After the war the

hangars were dismantled and the hits auctioned the site being abandoned probably early in 1920.

DETLING, KENT – 4 MILES NE OF MAIDSTONE

Early in 1915 the Directorate of Works surveyed an area of the North Downs for an air defence landing ground. Initially, the site was levelled to remove rough turf for the arrival of a detachment of four Curtiss aeroplanes in June, which were proved unsuitable as fighters and instead formed the nucleus of the RNAS Strategic Bombing Wing late in 1915. Sopwith 1½ Strutters arrived at Detling in late February 1916 but not as part of the air defence organization but as No.3 Wing RNAS, which was then relocated to Manston two months later leaving Detling under C & M (Care and Maintenance). Not until 3 April 1917 did the RFC take responsibility for the airfield and No.50 HD Squadron moved in with BE2cs and BE12s, which were then tasked to fly day and night patrols over Kent. By this time accommodation for the aircraft was provided by canvas Bessoneaux hangars with tented accommodation for personnel. Two extra hangars were constructed for the arrival of the AWFK8s of No.143 Squadron, which arrived from Throwley on 14 February 1918. On 18 March No.143 Squadron was re-equipped with SE5as. Action came at last on the night of 18 May when forty-three Gothas mounted a major night raid on London. The CO of No.143 Squadron, Major Sowrey, damaged a Gotha near Maidstone, which was finally brought down by another fighter unit. The Germans lost ten aircraft that night and never flew again over Britain. The water-cooled engines of the SE5as of the squadron took too long to warm up when called into action, not a good quality in an air defence fighter and in August the squadron was re-equipped with Camels then Snipes in June 1919 but since the war was over No.143 Squadron was disbanded on 31 October and the airfield was abandoned.

DOVER – (ST MARGARETS/SWINGATE DOWN) KENT – 2 MILES NE OF DOVER

This airfield was closest to the continent, an ideal jumping-off point for RFC squadrons proceeding to France to join the BEF. The War Office had already planned to use the site in the event of war. On the outbreak of war the aircraft of No.6 Squadron were donated to other units to free the squadron personnel and to prepare the Dover site for the reception of aircraft proceeding to France. A landing ground was cleared, fuel supplies organized and a workshop built. When aircraft of Nos.2, 3 and 4 Squadrons arrived they were promptly ordered to France, leaving just one flight of No.4 Squadron to mount patrols. The first to arrive in France was Lieutenant H.D. Harvey-Kelly in a BE2a of No.2 Squadron, reaching Amiens two hours after leaving Dover. When the motley collection of aircraft that constituted No.5 Squadron left for France a few days later with the detached flight of No.4 Squadron the Swingate Down airfield was left deserted for the RFC had no more aircraft to send to France. No.6 Squadron staged through in October then there was nothing so then there was an opportunity to convert the landing ground into an established airfield.

By the time No.15 Squadron arrived in May 1915 it was well established with a long row of wooden sheds along the southern edge of the aerodrome. No.15 Squadron became an unofficial training unit when the unit kept losing its pilots to front-line squadrons. An additional task was to maintain one BE2c plus pilot on standby to mount anti-Zeppelin patrols.

In July 1915 No.9 Squadron arrived at Dover positioned for anti-Zeppelin operations. An unusual arrival was the Machine Gun School, which stayed for a month before moving on to Hythe during November. Meanwhile, work was in hand to provide accommodation for a flying school and No.12 Reserve Squadron was formed at Dover but left immediately for Thetford and No.13 RS became Dover's training unit and also took over the role of Home Defence. Flying from Dover was not without its hazards. With the landing ground situated close to the top of the White Cliffs, aircraft that overran their landing run could topple over on to the beach below. No.20 RS formed on 1 February 1916 and No.49 Squadron acted as an advanced training school from the April. This was a very important role given the high casualty rate amongst aircrew in France. Up to this time the Zeppelins had an almost free run over England. The problem was one of early warning and the inability of defending aircraft to ascend with a sufficient rate of climb to ensure an interception. In an attempt meet the threat on more equal terms No.50 Squadron was formed at Dover on 15 May as part of No.18 HD Wing, but with only BE2c variants available the poor rate of climb was evident when Captain T.W. Woodhouse strove to intercept Zeppelin L32 on 24 August. The airship was held in the Dover searchlight beams so its commander took refuge in cloud. When Woodhouse again caught sight of the huge shape of the enemy ship he was still 2000ft below. He emptied an entire drum into the L32 but the tracer showed that his rounds were passing beneath the enemy airship. Whilst he attempted to load another drum he lost the airship and he had to return to Dover disappointed, with the searchlights leading him in to the airfield. When No.50 Squadron HQ moved to a mansion in Harrietsham and its constituent flights dispersed, Dover Swingate was left with just a training unit. There followed a great deal of shuffling of units until Dover settled down becoming the host station to two training squadrons and work commenced to enlarge the site. Following the formation of the RAF in April 1918 Training Depot Stations were introduced and the Dover TDS was equipped with twenty-four Avro 504Ks and twenty-four Camels with

personnel strength rising to 570 and by the summer of the final year of the war the station covered 219 acres and more work was in hand to increase accommodation. This was intended for another TDS but in the event the Marine Pilots' School was formed at Dover instead. This school gave specialized instruction in anti-submarine and convoy work using DH6 and DH9 aircraft. The intended establishment was for DH10s and Vimys but this was cancelled following the Armistice. Both No.53 TDS and the Marine Pilots' School closed in 1919 and the aerodrome was closed to all but aircraft in distress. When the station was derequisitioned in 1920 the sheds were retained for storage until auctioned and removed.

DOVER (GUSTON ROAD) KENT – 1¼ MILES NE OF DOVER

As early as November 1912 the Admiralty had, in their plans, a naval air station in Dover to protect the Dover naval base and, as with the RFC at Dover Swingate Down, to provide a jumping-off point for the Continent. When it came to spending priorities four other air stations were in the process of construction (see Chapter 3). By June 1913 the authorities had gone so far as to select a site between Fort Burgoyne and the Duke of York's Military School to provide an area of 55 acres. The site was on military land so requisition was not necessary On the outbreak of war in 1914 work on the aerodrome was not complete but there was a RNAS base established at Dunkirk and the need to provide air defence of the British Isles hastened the completion of the site. In early December 1914 a detachment of No.2 Squadron RNAS arrived. However, in January 1915 this detachment returned to Eastchurch and was replaced by No.1 Squadron RNAS, which completed its training and provided an element of air defence. The word element is used since the description of the role of Dover Swingate Down was also air defence. This duplication of roles and co-ordination of air defence operations was to be the kernel of the case for forming a unified air service (the RAF). The naval threat came from Zeebrugge-based U-boats and on 10 February a collection of some thirty machines was assembled to attack dock installations at Zeebrugge and Ostend. Not all of this motley collection of aircraft was serviceable on the 11th and only one reached the target due to bad weather but on the 17th seven float planes and seventeen aircraft attacked the dock installations at both locations but since the largest bombs were 100lb this was only a token effort. At the end of February 1915 No.1 Squadron moved to Dunkirk leaving behind the Dover Defence Flight; this in turn formed the nucleus of No.4 Squadron RNAS on 25 March, which moved to Eastchurch leaving Guston Road to develop as a training base. Improvements were made to the accommodation and the airfield was then home to a variety of aircraft. No.5 Wing RNAS was formed at Dover in March 1916 and was soon deployed to Coudekerque for operations.

A major operation was undertaken in July in an attempt to put the *Tirpitz* battery out of action. This was to be achieved by mounting fighting patrols from Dunkirk and Dover that would provide protection to the artillery observation aircraft spotting for a 12-inch Dominion Gun. Unfortunately, the operation was not successful.

Another squadron, this time No.6, was formed at Dover on 1 November 1916 then took its Nieuport Scouts to Petite Synthe. Meanwhile, the Dover Defence Flight was using black BE2cs for night work. On 24 April 1917 a RNAS pilot waiting for a passage to France volunteered to take up an aircraft during a raid alert. The heavily laden BE crashed on the roof of the Duke of York's Military School killing the observer. On 24 April 1918 No.218 Squadron was formed but in May moved to Petite Synthe and Guston Road aircraft mounted inshore anti-submarine patrols and coastal convoy patrols. In August 1918 the former aircrews and aircraft at Dover and Walmer were reorganized as No.233 Squadron, the DH9 element at Guston Road becoming No.491 Flight. The Dover Straits were virtually closed to U-boats, the six DH9s flying intensively right up to the Armistice. When No.491 Flight moved to Walmer in 1919 Dover Guston Road was virtually abandoned and was closed in 1920.

DOVER (MARINE PARADE) KENT – ½ MILE FROM DOVER TOWN CENTRE

This seaplane base barely covered two acres and was selected as a site for hydro/aircraft during 1913. Only when the gunboat *Niger* was sunk off Deal Pier by U-boat *U12* on 11 November 1914 was action taken to open a base. Although desperately short of floatplanes, Squadron Commander Bromet was ordered to take two Wight navy seaplanes to open a base at Dover. He was accompanied by Flight Commander Bigsworth on 18 November. A skating rink on the Marine Parade was requisitioned just one week after the sinking. A slipway was then constructed to enable the floatplanes to be manhandled up the beach and across the road to the base. Dover Harbour at this time was small and overcrowded and

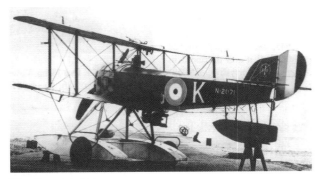

The Sopwith Baby.

The Dover type 184 floatplane.

taking off and landing had to be accomplished outside the breakwater. Nothing could be achieved, however, at night or during the day if the U-boats remained submerged. The next order that Bromet received was to keep two seaplanes in readiness in case German seaplanes attacked coastal towns near Dover. With only two seaplanes at his disposal Bromet's men would be on permanent watch and even if these two machines got airborne in time to make an interception the two Wight machines were hardly suitable for air combat! A number of Short seaplanes then arrived and after a spate of U-boat sinkings in May 1915 the much-improved Short 184 arrived. In August 1915 Dover concentrated on training and seaplane repair and two extra sheds were erected for this purpose. A second slipway was constructed alongside the skating rink building. Meanwhile, operational flying was carried out from Dunkirk. In October there were four Short floatplanes, one FBA flying boat, seven Sopwith Babies, two Schneiders and one White and Thompson floatplane. The scout planes were introduced to prevent enemy interference with the Dover Patrol. Further improvements were called for to the Short 184 to combat the rough seas and swell both at Dover and Dunkirk. The main floats were enlarged and the wingtip floats were streamlined and this was known as the Dover Type 184. In April 1918 the Dover-based seaplanes joined No.5 Group RAF and on the night of 22/23 April assisted in the Zeebrugge raid by diverting enemy attention from the approaching British naval vessels. The number of U-boats passing down the Channel after May 1918 was greatly reduced due to the combined work of the air and sea patrols. In August 1918 the operational Short 184s at Dover became No.407 Flight of No.233 Squadron RAF. The HQ of the squadron was on the Marine Parade with detached flights at Dover (Guston Road) and Walmer. On 15 May 1919 No.233 Squadron was officially disbanded, by which time the Marine Parade base had been vacated. The site was de-requisitioned in 1920.

DYMCHURCH (HYTHE/PALMARSH) KENT – 2½ MILES SW OF HYTHE

The RFC Machine Gun School moved from Dover to Hythe on 27 November 1915 to take advantage of the gunnery ranges near the town The HQ was in the Imperial Hotel, Hythe, whilst the BE2c, RE7 and Vickers FB5 were stationed at Lympne. On 3 September 1916 the Machine Gun School became the School of Aerial Gunnery. As activity increased it was found necessary to move the Kite Balloon Section away from the ranges and in November 1916 a rate of £1 per acre was agreed with the farmer of a site near Dymchurch Redoubt to position two balloon sheds and a winch. The ancient redoubt was given over to accommodation but before the War Office could finalize the lease the farmer upped his demand to 30 shillings per acre plus rates. The finance branch paid in full without argument! The Aerial Gunnery School was supposed to move to Loch Doon in Scotland but the site was found unsuitable. Fighter pilot training went to Turnbury so Hythe then became the home of No.1 (Auxiliary) School of Arial Gunnery, which concentrated on two-week courses for observers. Lympne was then required for other purposes, which meant repositioning the aircraft. This was achieved by using the new aerodrome known as Hythe and Palmarsh but its official title was Dymchurch to distinguish it from other units at Hythe. The proximity to the ranges was one thing but the airfield quickly flooded in the winter and experienced sudden sea mists. Aircraft were frequently subject to forced landings and ended up in the drainage ditches. In March 1918 the Hythe unit was renamed No.1 (Observer) School of Aerial Gunnery and just before the Armistice the school moved to a better airfield at New Romney and the Dymchurch field simply became an emergency landing ground for any aircraft using the ranges. When the school moved to Manston, Dymchurch was closed, the site being cleared in 1920. Now the Romney, Hythe and Dymchurch railway cuts in two what was the Dymchurch airfield.

EASTBOURNE, EAST SUSSEX – 2 MILES N OF EASTBOURNE

A site just to the west of St Anthony Hill was chosen for a 50-acre aerodrome, home to a flying club. Although the field was flat it was criss-crossed by a large number of drainage ditches, which had to be covered by wooden boards, and with a second-hand corrugated shed and two Blériots, the Eastbourne Flying Club opened on 1 December 1911. The Admiralty became interested in Eastbourne when a seaplane factory was established on the Crumbles. A shed was leased at the aerodrome and the construction of two more hangars were subsidized and positioned by the Crumbles factory. Many famous aviators of the day flew into the airfield, including Commander Samson RN. On the outbreak of the Great War private flying was suspended and the Admiralty established a training school at the airfield and the Crumbles factory was put on full production beginning with BE2cs for the RNAS and later Avro 504A and K aircraft for the RFC. But the main work centred on repair work for the Admiralty. Training was ab initio for the RNAS and a wide variety of aircraft was used but by mid 1916 only Maurice Farmans and Curtiss JN4A (Jennys) were employed. The drainage ditches remained a problem but flying continued throughout the War. When Eastbourne was taken over by the RAF the Aeroplane School continued and No.54 TS was transferred from Castle Bromwich on 6 July 1918 to provide the nucleus of No.50 TDS and aircraft types were then standardized as Avro 504K, DH9 and DH9A, the trainees being intended for day bomber squadrons on the Western Front. No.50 TDS remained active until November 1919 when the airfield was then empty.

EASTCHURCH, KENT – 1½ MILES S OF EASTCHURCH VILLAGE.

Flying at Eastchurch started at the end of July 1909 and the new aerodrome was an immediate success even though it was low-lying and close to marshlands. The 400-acre site was well drained and free of all ditches and dykes, which abound on the Isle of Sheppey. Persuaded by two naval airmen, Lieutenants Samson and Longmore, the Admiralty agreed, in October 1911, to set up a school and two Short biplanes were purchased. A benefactor loaned other machines and with the help of four naval flyers, Samson and Longmore could start a flying course. In February 1912 the Admiralty expanded the facilities and ten acres close to the RAOC sheds were leased and work started on six large sheds and three portable canvas hangars for the Naval Flying School formed in the previous December, which was commanded by Captain Godfrey Paine. Following the formation of the RFC in April 1912 with its Military and Naval Wings, Eastchurch became the HQ of the Naval Wing. It is the sign of the times that, when Paine was nominated for the post of Commandant of the CFS he was given two weeks to get his 'Wings'. Indeed, many of the future heads of the RAF and Fleet Air Arm, such as Edward Ellington, gained their wings at this time. Samson was left commanding the Naval Flying School, which trained not only future aircrews but acted as a depot for pilots awaiting posting. Experimental work with wireless, bomb dropping and night flying was also carried out. As war approached the Admiralty worked to reduce the reliance on the Military Wing and by mid July their Lordships were ready to form the Royal Naval Air Service and this occurred on 1 July. In preparation for mobilization the Navy's landplanes went to Eastchurch. The Eastchurch War Flight was formed and stood ready to defend the Sheerness and Chatham bases. Samson went to great lengths to provide weapons for the ground defence of the bases whilst the aircrews went aloft with nothing more than a revolver but some pilots might enjoy the protection of a marine armed with a rifle.

Following the outbreak of war Eastchurch was formally requisitioned on 22 December 1914 under the Defence of the Realm Act. In 1915 the Germans stepped up attacks on shipping around the British Isles and No.2 Squadron RNAS moved to Eastchurch to defend the Thames bases. The first enemy attack on Eastchurch was by the German naval airship *L10* whose commander believed he was bombing London.

Flying at night might reduce the chances of being intercepted by British fighters or falling prey to anti-aircraft guns, but accurate navigation was often lacking. On this occasion a stick of twelve bombs fell across the aerodrome and only windows were broken. But then the two Eastchurch pilots who were on patrol saw nothing in the darkness. It was not the only time that Zeppelin commanders bombed what they thought was the target by trusting the judgement of the commander in front (see Chapter 3).

By October 1915 Eastchurch hosted such a wide variety of aircraft that it was a problem finding sufficient trained mechanics. The flight trials of the Handley Page O/100 were carried out at Eastchurch. This bomber would be nicknamed the 'Bloody Paralyser' and would be used as part of the RNAS strategic bombing campaign. An enlargement of the site was approved early in 1916 permitting the opening of a station headquarters and a gunnery school and a War Flight was opened operating Bristol Scouts and BE2cs. Although air defence of the British Isles was the responsibility of the War Office it did not prevent the Admiralty from contributing units to this end. On the night of 23/24 September 1916 eleven German naval Zeppelins set out to bomb targets in East Anglia and London. Two of them were shot down but not by Eastchurch pilots. In February 1917 the War Flight was disbanded and the naval air station concentrated on training for pilots and observers and a growing number of mechanics. When the German Gotha bombers began to target London and the south-east, RNAS Camels were sent from France during June 1917. On 7 July twenty-two Gothas of Kaghol 3 approached London and again RNAS pilots engaged the enemy over Chingford but the guns of the two aircraft involved jammed so once again the Navy was unlucky. The aerodrome underwent further expansion ready for the amalgamation of the RFC and the RNAS into the RAF, formed on 1 April 1918, and No.58 Wing RAF was formed at Eastchurch. The ground instructors' school of the old Gunners' and Observers' School remained whilst the Aerial Flying and Gunnery School reformed at Leysdown. The Naval Flying School, Eastchurch, became No.204 TDS equipped with Shorthorns, DH5s and Avro 504s for ab initio training and Camels, Snipes and DH9As for advanced instruction. Eastchurch remained in service with the peacetime RAF

EASTLEIGH, SOUTHAMPTON, HAMPSHIRE – 1½ MILES S OF EASTLEIGH TOWN

The airfield was used by early aviators but was not requisitioned by the War Office when it was decided to expand the RFC Depot in Leigh Road into an AAP. The farm on the site was taken over and four large storage hangars and five storage sheds were constructed alongside the Eastleigh to Southampton railway line. Following the entry of the USA into the war the US Secretary of the Navy planned a special unit to operate against German U-boat bases in the Zeebrugge area of Belgium. This unit, known as the Northern Bombing Group, needed an assembly base for American-made bombers expected to arrive during the summer of 1918. Several sites were surveyed but were rejected and the Americans accepted the half-completed AAP at Eastleigh. The Naval Air Station was commissioned on 23 July but the US-built DH4s did not arrive and a deal was struck allowing the Naval Aviation Force to obtain fifty-four DH9As in exchange for Liberty engines. Indeed, Liberty-engined DH9As were used by the RAF on air control operations well into the 1920s. By late 1918 Eastleigh had become most successful in carrying out assembly and repairs of aircraft that were distributed to the 10 Bombing Group on the Western Front. Assembly work ceased four days after the Armistice and the US Navy finally withdrew on 10 April 1919 when Eastleigh was handed back to the RAF.

FARNBOROUGH – 2 MILES NW OF ALDERSHOT

The use of Farnborough for air-related activities dates back to 1905 and the Royal Engineers (RE), when a balloon-erecting shed was built in May of that year. On 28 February 1911 the Air Battalion of the RE was formed with No.1 (Airship) Company at the site. With the coming of the RFC on 13 May 1912 that unit became No.1 Squadron. The Royal Aircraft Factory was also established at Farnborough and whilst a variety of RFC units came and went the station settled down to build aircraft and undertake research and development. It was War Office policy at the time for its aircraft to be designed and built at Farnborough, whereas the Admiralty were disposed to try aircraft built by private companies, notably Short Brothers, A.V. Roe and Sopwith. Since the War Office requirement was at that time to build aircraft for reconnaissance it wanted aircraft that were stable in flight, not ones that were highly manoeuvrable as fighters needed to be. In July 1918 the Royal Aircraft Factory was renamed the Royal Aircraft Establishment. At the end of the war aircraft design and construction were discontinued and the Wireless School moved to Flowerdown. Farnborough was part of the South Western

Area in November 1918 but became a 7 Group station in Southern Area on 20 September 1919. On the research side experiments had concentrated on armaments and aerodynamics and two wind tunnels were built during 1916/17 when trials were conducted on aircraft spinning.

FORD – 2¾ MILES W OF LITTLEHAMPTON

Officially known as Ford Junction, this airfield was one of a large number of training stations authorized in 1917. Work started in 1918 with German POWs building most of the camp and it was earmarked for the US Air Service as a training aerodrome to train crews for the US-built HPO/400 bombers expected to arrive in large numbers during the summer of 1918. But the RAF was in first with No.148 Squadron on 1 March 1918 and No.149 Squadron on 3 March. When these units left for France on 2 June 1918 the airfield was free for the Americans to move in, which they did on 15 August. A Night Bombardment Training School, intended to teach night navigators by radio interception, opened on 15 September. As for the Americans, there were snags in receiving the O/400s and the Armistice was signed before one machine was assembled or one training course completed. On 17 November 1918 the Americans moved out and Ford was then used to demobilize RAF squadrons. Reference to Annex B will show which squadrons came to Ford for this purpose. Only one squadron, No.97, was turned round at Ford and this one left for India in July 1919 equipped with DH10 bombers. The station closed in January 1920.

FORELAND (ISLE OF WIGHT) – 5 MILES S OF BEMBRIDGE

Foreland was used by aircraft on anti-submarine duties. When the RAF took over in April 1918 No.253 Squadron operated DH6s from the station, which contributed to the significant reduction in shipping losses to U-boats. Nos.511 and 512 Flights of the squadron were disbanded on 21 January 1919 and the airfield site was relinquished early in 1920.

GODMERSHAM PARK – 2½ MILES N OF WYE

This was a mooring-out-station for Capel Le Ferne, protected from the prevailing wind by Kingswood and it was usual to moor-out one SSZ airship at Godmersham Park from the late spring of 1918. The base was abandoned after the Armistice.

GOSPORT 4 MILES – W OF PORTSMOUTH

Work on the airfield began early in 1914 and No.5 Squadron moved in from Netheravon on 6 July. When that unit left for France the RFC had neither the aircraft nor personnel to man the airfield. When these later became available a succession of units came and went and in December 1916 Major R.R. Smith-Barry was given command of No.1 Reserve Squadron at the station. He had been appalled at the quality of pilots arriving for operational duties on the Western Front and was determined to bring in proper instructor courses. One of his ideas was for a speaking tube between instructor and pupil and this became the 'Gosport Tube', which came into use all over the world. In May 1917 he wrote a set of training notes and General Salmond then sanctioned the formation of a Special School of Flying at Gosport, Nos.1, 25 and 55 Training Squadrons being amalgamated for this purpose in August 1917. By early 1918 all training schools were instructed to adopt Gosport training methods. On 31 January 1918 Gosport became home to the School of Aerial Co-operation with Coast Defence Batteries. With the formation of the RAF, Gosport was placed in No.2 Area, No.8 Group still housing No.1 Special School of Flying, but in July each RAF area was given its own training organization and the former was renamed South West Area Flying Instructors' School. HQ Gosport was formed on 28 October 1918 to deal with an unwieldy collection of units but with the Armistice, Gosport's future was uncertain. However, in June 1919 it was confirmed that the RAF's torpedo school was to be sited there and in September it was formally listed as a permanent No.10 Group Station in Coastal Area. During the 1920s Gosport fulfilled a variety of roles, including observer training, coastal battery co-operation and night landing on aircraft carriers.

GRAIN – 1½ MILES S OF GRAIN VILLAGE

Grain was commissioned by the Admiralty on 30 December 1912 to carry out development work on seaplanes. Following further development of the air station, Grain succeeded Eastchurch as the HQ Sheerness Naval District. During 1914 all available seaplanes were concentrated on Felixstowe, Yarmouth and Grain to control the approaches to the Thames Estuary. Early in 1915 the emphasis moved from operations to repair. Adjoining rough grazing fields were levelled and Grain became a land plane and seaplane base to be commissioned as the Royal Naval Aeroplane Repair Depot and, at the end of the year, the Experimental Armament Section was established alongside the repair depot. When an experimental construction section was proposed the Admiralty agreed to the combined unit, which became the Marine Experimental Aircraft Depot and simulated aircraft landing trials were conducted at Grain, indeed the construction section produced several naval aircraft types. Equally the Experimental Armament and Test Depot was busy evaluating such weapons as the anti-Zeppelin Rankin darts and the Davis recoilless gun. After the war work on the station proceeded at a more relaxed pace but when Orfordness closed in 1921 the Armament Experimental Squadron moved in, testing such aircraft as the Short Cromarty and the Fairey Atlanta.

But on March 17 1924 the Marine Aircraft Experimental Unit moved to Felixstowe and Grain/Port Victoria was closed.

HAMBLE – 4 MILES SE OF SOUTHAMPTON

Although used for seaplane construction during the Great War, the construction sheds at Hamble were demolished in 1919. Hamble is best known for its association with Fairey Aviation and A.V. Roe Co. Ltd during the decade after the Great War.

HAWKINGE – 2 MILES N OF FOLKESTONE

The War Office acquired the land for an airfield in 1915 and it was initially used by squadrons transiting to France. By the autumn of 1915 Folkestone (Hawkinge) had Bessoneaux hangars and tents. Since compasses were so inaccurate at the time pilots were literally pointed at St Omer in northern France by having two circles cut in the turf so that, when lined up, the aircraft was pointed in the right direction. In January 1917 HQ 21 Wing RFC changed the name from Folkestone (Hawkinge) to simply Hawkinge to avoid confusion with Folkestone (Capel) the airship station. The unit then became the Aeroplane Dispatch Centre, later developed into No.12 Aircraft Acceptance Park (South East Area). Work on the park was almost complete by the time of the Armistice and squadrons awaiting demobilization were held there. Early in 1919 with chronic shortages of food and clothing in Belgium, Hawkinge was used by the Air Travel and Transport Ltd to ferry these items across the Channel using DH9As with service pilots. Mail was also flown from the station to the occupation forces. HPV1500 bombers were stored at Hawkinge along with other smaller types awaiting scrapping. Hawkinge survived the post-war rundown and eventually became a fighter station.

KINGSNORTH – 5 MILES NE OF ROCHESTER

Kingsnorth started as an Admiralty establishment providing airship cover close to the Chatham naval base. In October 1913 it was agreed that the Admiralty should have the sole responsibility for powered lighter-than-air craft so that the Navy took over the airship facilities at Farnborough also. Kingsnorth was commissioned in January 1914 and on 1 July the Naval Airship Branch was absorbed into the RNAS. In March 1915 the remaining design staff and equipment was transferred from Farnborough and a training school was opened to train air and ground crews to operate the new non-rigid airships. Experimentation with new types and the building of established types was undertaken but with the end of the Great War the programme was rapidly cut. When it was decided that aircraft were more effective than airships, airship stations were closed down during 1919. Kingsnorth was dismantled early in 1920.

LEE-ON-SOLENT – 2½ MILES NW OF GOSPORT

With the heavy shipping losses of the spring of 1917, the seaplane training unit at Calshot could not cope with increased training requirement for aircrews. A brand-new school was planned on Holy Island off the Northumbrian coast and in the mean time a temporary substation was established at Lee-on-Solent. Work started in July 1917 and the Naval Seaplane Training Unit was opened on 30 July. In the November the plan to move to Holy Island was scrapped so Lee-on-Solent became permanent. On 1 April 1918 the station was transferred to the Air Ministry and the Training Unit became No. 109 TDS, No.10 Group. Personnel numbers peaked in December 1918 but all training ceased in January 1919. It was then decided that the station was to be retained in the much reduced peacetime air force and on 16 June 1919 the RAF Seaplane School was established. Although there was a brief training commitment for crews going to Russia, budgetary cuts forced Lee-on-Solent on to a C & M (Care and Maintenance) basis in December 1919. It did survive and featured in the post-war RAF.

LEYSDOWN (SHELLBEACH) – 1½ MILES SE OF LEYSDOWN-ON-SEA

Leysdown is recognized as the first flying field in Kent and was associated with J.T.C. Moore Brabazon and the Short Brothers. With the expansion of the naval flying school at Eastchurch the Leysdown landing ground was used for emergency forced landings until 1917 when bombing and gunnery ranges were established offshore. The airfield became the Pilots' and Observers' Aerial Gunnery and Aerial Fighting School (South East Area) on 1 April 1918. After the Armistice the school was closed in 1919 but the station remained open to administer the ranges used by aircraft from Eastchurch and this situation continued throughout the inter-war years and World War II.

LYDD – 2½ MILES NW OF LYDD

In 1916 sixty acres of Dering Farm were requisitioned as a landing ground, which was then used by aircraft of an artillery co-operation flight working with guns on a local range and was in full operation by January 1917. It was then graded as a 3rd class landing ground to be used by No.112 (HD) Squadron. No.2 Balloon School was also situated just north of Lydd and this was closed in September 1918 followed shortly by the Artillery Co-operation Flight and No.53 (HD) Wing. Lydd was relinquished as a landing ground and returned to farmland.

LYMPNE – 2½ MILES W OF HYTHE

The aerodrome originated as a flying field for the Machine Gun School, Hythe. The original site was found to suffer from water-logging and a new site was chosen nearby in March 1916. Lympne was then an emergency landing ground for Home Defence and by October 1916 the aerodrome was well advanced. In 1917 work on storage accommodation began for No.8 Aircraft Acceptance Park but on 25 May 1917 Lympne received the attention of Gothas of Kagohl 3 whose crews were prevented from attacking London due to the weather and chose Lympne as a secondary target. No.8 AAP was involved in ferrying aircraft to France and since the airfield was designated as a 1st class landing ground in 1918 it was used by Home Defence squadrons. After the Armistice the presence of the AAP prevented an immediate closure and extensions to the airfield were being negotiated in April 1919. Lympne was used for military aircraft engaged in ferrying mail to the Continent as well as disbanding squadrons but as the mail commitment dwindled the Air Ministry did not need both Hawkinge and Lympne and the latter was turned over to civil aviation.

MANSTON – 2 MILES W OF RAMSGATE
It was the RNAS that looked for a safe night-landing ground and selected a large field near Ramsgate. The field known as Manston LG was improved in 1916. A variety of operational units used the airfield during 1916/17, notably No.3 Wing and in the spring of 1917 part of the Pilot Training School at Eastchurch was transferred to Manston and formed the nucleus of the War School to provide advanced instruction on aircraft that pilots would be flying operationally. Again in 1917 the Admiralty selected Manston and Cranwell for the training of air mechanics, of whom there was an acute shortage. With the training came the necessity to construct buildings so that Manston could become a permanent station. With the formation of the RAF in April 1918 came the establishment of a three-squadron day bomber unit. No.203 TDS and the War School became a pilots' pool. The former was then renumbered No.55 TDS and the War School was absorbed by the newly formed No.219 Squadron, which operated land planes at Manston and seaplanes at nearby Westgate. Next was the formation of No.2 School of Observers and No.55 TDS moved to Narborough (Marham). At the end of September 1918 the station was virtually complete. With the Armistice came the usual rundown in activity but Manston was one of the few stations that was to avoid closure. Indeed, it remained an active station until its closure in March 1999.

NEWHAVEN – ½ MILE SE OF NEWHAVEN TOWN
Selected as a seaplane base in 1917, following the upsurge of U-boat activity, RNAS Newhaven opened in May 1917 as an offshoot of the main base at Calshot housing four Short 184 floatplanes. Due to the unprotected nature of the base, there being no sea wall, the improved Dover type 184s with strengthened floats were later used that could cope with the swell. By the end of 1917 there were six aircraft in all, numbered 408 Flight. When the RAF took over in 1918 No.408 Flight was joined by No.409 Flight becoming No.242 Squadron RAF in the August. Campanias and Fairey IIIBs joined the 184s as the resident aircraft. During 1919 activity wound down and, when No.242 Squadron was disbanded on 15 May, the station closed and the buildings were auctioned early in 1920.

NEW ROMNEY – 2 MILES N OF NEW ROMNEY
The aerodrome was opened on 1 August 1917 when No.3 (Auxiliary) School of Aerial Gunnery was formed at Littleton/New Romney to increase training facilities for observer pupils. Amazingly, three public roads crossed the aerodrome thus it was not a convenient place from which aircraft could operate. On 9 March 1918 the unit became No.1 (Observers) School of Aerial Gunnery and aerial activity was conducted at Dymchurch/Palmarsh. After the Armistice it was decided to close New Romney and in September 1919 the School of Aerial Gunnery moved to RAF Manston. In November pilots flying in the vicinity were ordered to avoid landing except in an emergency. Shortly afterwards the airfield passed into the hands of the Government Surplus Property Disposal Board.

POLEGATE – 3½ MILES NW OF EASTBOURNE
Polegate was officially opened as an airship station on 6 July 1915. It was sheltered and had good access by road, which was ideal for airship operation but in spite of all the efforts the sheds remained water-logged for most of the year. An SS40 airship operated from Polegate over enemy territory and was supposed to be used for clandestine operations, e.g. dropping agents hence the black colour. Instead, it was used on night reconnaissance duties. Parachute trials were also conducted at Polegate and these were successful leading to the introduction of parachutes for airship crews and, later, aircraft. In 1917 Polegate was transferred to Portsmouth Command and the SS Zero airship came to the station. When the RAF took over Polegate in 1918 the airships remained on Admiralty charge. In October 1918 No.10 Group at Warsash took control of the station and its substations at Slindon and Upton. Polegate was closed in 1919.

ROCHFORD – 2 MILES N OF SOUTHEND
Following the Zeppelin raids on London in the spring of 1915, there was recognition that landing grounds were a necessity for aircraft employed on HD duties and the Admiralty established eight forward landing grounds to counter the Zeppelins that were attempting a landfall in East Anglia. But naval priority was given to the defence of the Fleet and aircrews with little or no night-flying experience were allotted to HD duties. In February 1916 Home Defence became a War Office responsibility. Rochford was transferred to the RFC on 4 June 1916.

No.37 then No. 11 (Reserve) Squadron took up residence, the latter becoming the Home Defence training unit, being renamed No.98 (Depot) Squadron. Soon pupils from the School of Military Aeronautics came to Rochford and undertook night defence training in Avro 504s and Sopwith Pups. When No.99 Depot Squadron moved in to take care of the increasing numbers of trainees No.98 Squadron was retitled No.198 (Depot) Squadron. No.99 Squadron then moved to East Retford and No.37 Squadron to Stow Maries. In its place No.61 (HD) Squadron was formed on 2 August 1917. Rochford aircraft were soon in action against the Gothas mounting daylight attacks and the station was bombed. When No.190 (Depot) Squadron was formed at Rochford in October 1917 the new unit concentrated on primary training allowing No. 198 (Depot) Squadron to concentrate on the advanced phases of the course. Both squadrons were designated night training squadrons on 21 December 1917 and in March the following year No.190 Squadron moved to Newmarket. By September 1918 the station was virtually complete but once the Armistice was signed it began to run down. No.61 Squadron was disbanded on 13 June 1919 followed by No.198 Squadron in September. Apart from some joy-riding immediately post war no other flying was taking place and the station closed in 1920, the land being released for agriculture.

RUSTINGTON – 2 MILES E OF LITTLEHAMPTON

In 1918 Rustington was accepted as one of a string of training depot stations built along the south coast for the US Air Service capable of operating HPO/400s. The Armistice intervened whilst construction was still in progress and in October 1919 instructions were issued for the buildings to be disposed of and the land relinquished.

SHEERNESS – THE PORT OF SHEERNESS

It was not until 1917 that the town was again directly involved with flying. One site was developed to the south of the dockyard for kite balloon training under Admiralty control. There was a RFC establishment one mile to the east of the town. The balloon training base trained observers for sea reconnaissance and was titled No.1 Balloon Training Base (SE Area). The RFC at their establishment provided an emergency landing ground for Home Defence aircraft, notably No.37 Squadron at Rochford. During 1918 Sheerness was also used as a landing ground for artillery co-operation aircraft. Both units closed down after the Armistice, though the balloon base was not transferred to the Admiralty for naval use until September 1919.

SHOREHAM – 1 MILE NW OF SHOREHAM-BY-SEA

This established aerodrome was acquired by the War Office in August 1914 and immediately became a training base but at the beginning there was a lack of instructors and aircraft, which left Shoreham practically deserted. On 21 January 1915 the nucleus of No.3 Reserve Aeroplane Squadron moved in but no sooner set on the business of training when No.14 Squadron was formed using No.3 RAS personnel. At the beginning of the war there was always the problem of competing operational and training requirements. With the decentralization of the Training Brigade on 10 January 1917 No.3 Reserve Squadron, as it now was, came under Eastern Group Command, the Reserve squadrons now becoming training squadrons. No.3 TS was employed training pilots from scratch on a six-week course, including a minimum of three hours' dual and three hours' solo. In July 1918 the South Eastern Area Flying Instructors' School replaced No.3 TS and the former was disbanded early in 1919. In April 1919 No.1 Wing Canadian Air Force moved into Shoreham but in 1920, when the Canadians returned home it left only a packing section. When this unit had completed its work in December 1921 the aerodrome was closed and the airfield returned to grazing.

SLINDON – 6½ MILES NE OF CHICHESTER

Slindon was activated as a mooring-out station for Polegate on 28 April 1918 where two SSZ airships operated. Mooring-out stations proliferated during the Great War so that, with the dispersal of airships, fog or high winds would be less likely to impede airship operations and Slindon had the reputation of being the best mooring-out station in the group. The site was abandoned soon after the Armistice.

SOMERTON – 1 MILE S OF COWES

Somerton was opened initially by J. Samuel White and Co. Ltd for development flight trials of their products. In 1918 the School of Aerial Co-operation with Coastal Artillery started to use Somerton as a day landing ground. The Armistice brought an end to Samuel White production on 21 January 1919 but the Coastal Battery Co-operation unit, as it was now called, was still operating there in the August when it was decided to close and dispose of the air station.

SOUTHBOURNE – 6 MILES W OF CHICHESTER

Southbourne was intended as a training depot station for a O/400 unit of the US Air Service and construction was well under way in August 1918 but following the Armistice the buildings were auctioned off and the land returned to agriculture.

SWINGFIELD – 6 MILES N OF FOLKESTONE

Swingfield was used as a 2nd class landing ground for HD squadrons but was promptly returned to agriculture in 1919.

TANGMERE – 3 MILES E OF CHICHESTER

Tangmere was not requisitioned under the Defence of the Realm Act until 25 September 1917 and German Prisoners of War (POWs) assisted in clearing the site so that the aerodrome was well advanced in February 1918. The War Office offered the station to the US Air Service and the Americans decided to have it as a Handley Page training depot station, which meant modifying the hangars to take the larger aircraft. This delayed the planned June take-over. Between March and July No.92 Squadron RFC used Tangmere for training on their SE5as and No.61 TDS was formed here with 504s and F2Bs. It was further used by the aircraft from Somerton (see above), until the Americans finally took over in September. No sooner had they done so than they were leaving following the Armistice and Tangmere was left in the hands of No.61 TDS. Training continued at a reduced rate into 1919 with the unit re-designated No.61 Training School. Squadrons returning from France were held at Tangmere awaiting disbandment and in December 1919, with demobilization largely complete, Tangmere was declared surplus to requirement and the airfield closed in 1920. The Air Ministry retained the land and buildings and on 1 June 1925 Tangmere re-opened.

TELSCOMBE CLIFFS – 2½ MILES W OF NEWHAVEN

This airfield was first used by detached flights of No.78 Squadron in the war against the U-boats. With the formation of the RAF in 1918 'A' Flight of No.253 Squadron came to the airfield, then 514 Flight of No.242 Squadron, which had its headquarters at Newhaven. With the disbandment of 514 Flight on 20 January 1919 the landing ground was relinquished and the site reverted to farmland.

THROWLEY – 5 MILES S OF FAVERSHAM

Throwley was opened as a HD aerodrome in October 1916 to house No.50 Squadron, which had its HQ at nearby Harrietsham. No.112 Squadron was formed at the airfield on 30 July 1917 from 'B' Flight of No.50 Squadron. On December 20, No.188 Training Squadron equipped with Avro 504s came to the station and when No.143 Squadron formed there in February 1918 the place was really crowded. Accommodation was at a premium until 143 Squadron went off to Detling. Throwley squadrons were active in defending London against the Gothas in May 1918. The German attack of 19 May was so soundly rebuffed that the raids were not repeated. At least No.112 Squadron scored its first if only success of the war. No.188 TS, now a night training unit, received some Camels in July to provide advanced training. With the Armistice came the usual rundown as Throwley's resident units were disbanded, No.112 Squadron being the last to go on 13 June 1919. The airfield site was subsequently cleared and the land returned to agriculture

TIPNOR – 2½ MILES N OF PORTSMOUTH CITY

Tipnor was opened in 1917 as an operational kite balloon station and provided balloons for the ships of Portsmouth Command. With the formation of the RAF this unit became No.15 Kite Balloon Base in No.10 Group. In August 1919 the RAF handed the base over to the Admiralty and it was later developed as a range.

WALMER – 2 MILES S OF DEAL

Walmer was established in May 1917 as a satellite of RNAS Dover to provide cover for merchant ships anchored in the Downs off Deal the unit being known as the Walmer Defence Flight. But the title belies the fact that Home Defence operations were also carried out. In August 1918, the resident 471 Flight became part of No.233 Squadron Dover under the operational control of No.5 Group. In January 1919 No.491 Flight moved to Walmer followed by 233 Squadron headquarters in March. On 15 May 1919 No.233 Squadron was disbanded and the aerodrome was abandoned soon afterwards.

WESTGATE – 1½ MILES W OF MARGATE

Westgate opened on 1 August 1914 when the Admiralty became increasingly concerned about the vulnerability of the naval bases in the Thames Estuary. Once the British Expeditionary Force was safely in France there was no longer any need to provide anti-submarine cover and Westgate was then simply a stand-by base. By 1915 Zeppelin commanders were becoming more confident and visits were paid to Margate and Ramsgate. But Westgate-based aircraft did not score their first victory until 20 March 1916 when five German seaplanes were intercepted over the Goodwin Sands and one was shot down. The use of Westgate aerodrome ceased when accidents occurred in high winds or when aircraft made take-offs or landings into the cliff, but the seaplane base continued in operation with the Short 184s. When Westgate became a RAF station in August 1918, No.219 Squadron took over the squadron's aircraft, both at Westgate and Manston. Even after the Armistice there was a need to maintain anti-submarine patrols until the whereabouts of all enemy submarines had been established. When these operations ceased in the late summer of 1919 the station was closed on 7 February 1920 the installations and hangars being dismantled and sold by auction.

WORTHY DOWN – 3 MILES N OF WINCHESTER

The Wireless and Observers' School had been obliged to leave Brooklands due to the expansion of aircraft construction and in August 1917 the racecourse was acquired for use by the school. The construction of hangars and accommodation continued and the station was opened in 1918. In August the school was retitled the RAF and Army Co-operation School, acting as a finishing school for Corps reconnaissance pilots. This was joined by a detached flight of the Artillery Co-operation School, Lydd. After the Armistice the station was retained and was an active airfield,

WYE – 4 MILES NNE OF ASHFORD

During the Great War, Wye was used for pilot training and housed a variety of RFC units to be joined by the Americans in mid 1918. At its height there were Avro 504Ks, Sopwith Camels, 1½ Strutters and Bristol M1Cs on the airfield. After the Armistice the Americans departed and No.42 TS was disbanded on 1 February 1919. For a while No.3 Squadron personnel from the Continent, came to Wye, sans aircraft, but when they departed for Dover in June, Wye was surplus to requirements and, following disposal, the site was returned to agriculture.

AIRFIELDS, SEAPLANE BASES AND MISCELLANEOUS UNITS IN SOUTH-WEST ENGLAND

BEAULIEU – WILTSHIRE

Beaulieu was used by the RFC/RAF during the Great War but was put up for sale by the Aerodrome Disposal Board in July 1919. The site was sold by auction in 1920.

BOSCOMBE DOWN – WILTSHIRE

The building of the aerodrome was about half-complete by the end of 1918. Despite the ending of the Great War, construction of GS sheds and a similar-sized repair shed (180ft × 100 ft) was continued, which when completed in 1919, was used for storage. The station closed in 1920.

BROCKWORTH – NR HUCCLECOTE, GLOUCESTERSHIRE

At least one operational squadron, No.90, briefly dwelt at Brockworth, leaving Shotwick on 15 July 1918 newly equipped with Sopwith Dolphins. But the squadron was disbanded on the 29th of that month. Brockworth was also an Aircraft Acceptance Park (AAP) for Gloster aircraft during the Great War. In 1919 the AAP was disbanded and the RAF withdrew, though the Air Board retained ownership of the assembly sheds and used them for storage. Glosters purchased the airfield, hangars and offices in November 1926. Before that Glosters had rented the hangar space.

BUDE, CORNWALL

Bude was a mooring-out site for coastal type airships for RNAS Mullion. Operational patrols of St George's Channel and the Bristol Channel areas were the day-to-day task of the Bude detachment and it had become part of No.9 Group RAF by October 1918. When a decision was made in early 1919 to cease non-rigid airship operations the Bude substation was soon abandoned.

CALSHOT – SE OF FAWLEY

Calshot was used by the RNAS during World War I for Channel patrols using float planes then flying boats. When the RAF was formed in April 1918, Calshot became HQ No.10 Group and was the base for No.240 Squadron. Post war it became the School of Naval Co-operation and Aerial Navigation.

CHICKERELL – NW OF WEYMOUTH

Chickerell was originally established in 1918 as one of a series of small aerodromes strategically positioned around the coastline of Britain for use by short-range anti submarine aircraft. 'D' Flight, No.253 Squadron, equipped with DH6s was detached from Bembridge in June 1918 and aircraft of No.241 Squadron came from Portland in August. But post war it was planned to be part of a chain of civil aerodromes and civil aviation came under the Air Ministry at that time. And so Chickerell was retained during the 1920s. From 1927 to 1930 the airfield was used as a temporary base for Fleet Air Arm units exercising with ships off Portland.

FALMOUTH, CORNWALL – N OF TOWN IN OUTER HARBOUR

Falmouth was used occasionally by small detachments of seaplanes during the Great War and moorings between Trefusis Point and the village of Flushing were used by squadron cruises during the inter-war years.

FILTON – 4 MILES N OF BRISTOL

This was the base of the British and Colonial Aeroplane Co. Ltd from February 1910. Expansion took place on the outbreak of the Great War and at the Armistice 3,000 people were on the payroll. From December 1915 the RFC made use of the airfield to work up new squadrons before they left for France. The South West Aircraft Acceptance Park was formed at Filton to process aircraft completed by the factories in the area. Post war the company was awarded a contract to run a reserve school for the RAF, which opened on 15 May 1923.

LAIRA, DEVON – OLD PLYMOUTH

Laira was a mooring-out station for RNAS Mullion. Commissioned in May 1918 for two 'SS' or coastal type airships Laira came under No.9 Group RAF but was closed in 1919 along with Bude.

LAKE DOWN, WILTSHIRE – 7 MILES NNW OF SALISBURY

Otherwise known as Druid's Lodge, Lake Down was requisitioned early in 1917 as a flying training station. No.2 TDS formed here on 15 August 1917 with BE2cs, RE8s and DH4s but moved to Stonehenge in December. This unit was replaced by Nos.107 and 108 Squadrons, which were day bomber units 'working up' for operations. No.136

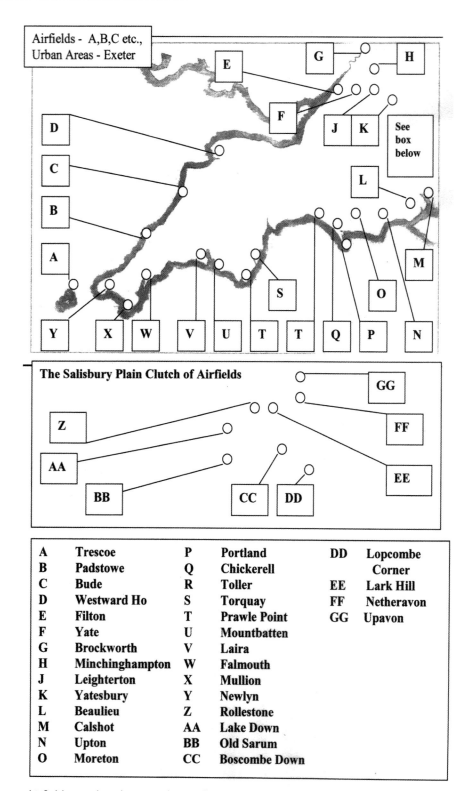

A	Trescoe	P	Portland	DD	Lopcombe
B	Padstowe	Q	Chickerell		Corner
C	Bude	R	Toller	EE	Lark Hill
D	Westward Ho	S	Torquay	FF	Netheravon
E	Filton	T	Prawle Point	GG	Upavon
F	Yate	U	Mountbatten		
G	Brockworth	V	Laira		
H	Minchinghampton	W	Falmouth		
J	Leighterton	X	Mullion		
K	Yatesbury	Y	Newlyn		
L	Beaulieu	Z	Rollestone		
M	Calshot	AA	Lake Down		
N	Upton	BB	Old Sarum		
O	Moreton	CC	Boscombe Down		

Airfields, seaplane bases and miscellaneous units in south-west England.

Squadron also formed here on 1 April 1917 then No.14 TDS formed on 6 June 1917. To make way for the TDS No.107 Squadron went to France and No.108 Squadron to Kenley. Then No.136 Squadron was disbanded. Construction of the station was almost complete by early August 1918 but No.14 TDS was reduced to a cadre by the end of the year. No.201 Squadron moved in briefly before it too was disbanded at Eastleigh. Accordingly, the buildings were removed and the site auctioned. Lake Down was completely abandoned by 1920.

LARKHILL – 4 MILES NW OF AMESBURY

Old Larkhill is one of the oldest military airfields in British aviation history preceding even the formation of the RFC. In the spring of 1911 No.2 (Aeroplane) Company was formed here, becoming No.3 Squadron on formation of the RFC in April 1912 but with the coming of war in 1914 the airfield site became covered with corrugated iron huts as the barracks expanded. Aircraft were by then operating from such nearby airfields as Old Sarum, Upavon and Netheravon. The site was maintained for use by aircraft taking part in the annual Army Exercises on Salisbury Plain during the inter-war years with the participating aircraft usually taking off from Sarum.

LEIGHTERTON, GLOUCESTERSHIRE

Leighterton was built in 1917 for the Australians and was opened in February 1918 as No.2 Station of the 1st Wing, Australian Flying Corps, housing No.8 (Training) Squadron equipped with Sopwith Pups and Camels to provide embryo fighter pilots. This unit was followed by No.7 (Training) Squadron to train pilots and observers on Avro 504s, BE2es and RE8s for reconnaissance duties over France. By October 1918 an aircraft repair section had been formed at Leighterton capable of dealing with all types except the Snipe, which had to go to Yate for crash repairs. There was a rapid rundown post World War I and, although building work continued until early 1919, Australian personnel started to leave from the February. Nos.28 and 66 Squadrons came to the airfield awaiting disbandment and the government auctioned the assets in 1919.

LOPCOMBE CORNER, WILTSHIRE – 8½ MILES NE OF SALISBURY

Lopcombe Corner was opened in September 1917 as No. 3 TDS, a single-seat fighter pilot training school. The tail skids cut the thin turf to stir up the chalk forming dust clouds in fine weather. Following the formation of the RAF the unit operated as part of No.34 Wing, No.8 Group, using Avro 504ks and Camels. With the Armistice Lopcombe gradually wound down during 1919. Nos.74 and 85 Squadrons were housed there on their return from the continent in February but the remnants of these units were dispersed in July. In November 1919 the aerodrome

officially closed to aircraft except in an emergency. A series of auctions was completed in 1920 and the disposal of the airfield was completed.

MERIFIELD, CORNWALL – 2½ MILES WNW OF DEVONPORT

Merifield commenced operations in 1918 with No.16 Balloon Base, No.72 Wing, No.9 Group. From here kite balloons were deployed for convoy protection duties. Merifield was closed after the Armistice.

MINCHINHAMPTON, GLOUCESTERSHIRE – 1½ MILES SE OF CHALFORD

Minchinhampton was opened for the 1st Wing Australian Flying Corps, No.6 (Training) Squadron, which arrived from Tern hill on 25 February 1918 and was joined by No.5 (Training) Squadron on 2 April. By August 1918 the establishment comprised twelve Camels, twelve SE5as and twenty-four Avro 504s, though many more machines including Pups were actually on strength. Flying ceased at the Armistice and the two training squadrons were disbanded. When the Australians went home the station was all but deserted. The buildings were auctioned in 1920 and the site was cleared for agriculture.

MORETON, DORSET – 4½ MILES E OF DORCHESTER

Moreton was intended to plug the gap in the chain of airship stations providing convoy coverage off the south coast of England. The land was requisitioned early in 1918 but the Armistice intervened before work on the airship sheds and a gas plant was completed. The work was terminated and the site cleared.

MOUNTBATTEN (CATTEWATER) – 1 MILE S OF PLYMOUTH ACROSS THE SOUND

Cattewater was recognized as a natural seaplane base early in the 1914–18 war and it became RNAS Cattewater in February 1917. After the formation of the RAF in April 1918 two large hangars were built alongside the Cattewater. During August 1918 No.237 Squadron with Short 184s and No.238 Squadron with Felixstowe F2As formed here. Most of the building work was completed as the war ended but patrols continued up to the end of 1918 (in case any U-boat commanders had not heard that the war had ended). No.237 Squadron disbanded in May 1919 and No.238 Squadron remained in cadre strength as a storage unit for spare flying boats until it was closed down in March 1922. RAF Cattewater was put into reserve until 1925 when an Act of Parliament secured the land for the Crown to become a permanent base.

MULLION, CORNWALL – 2 MILES NW OF MULLION VILLAGE

The RNAS Mullion was commissioned in June 1916. This airship station on the Lizard peninsula was intended to cover the Western Approaches. On 3 April 1917 Mullion became part of South Western Group. Early in 1918 DH4s joined the airships at Mullion to provide inshore patrols. In August 1918 ex naval squadrons became part of the RAF with No.236 Squadron at Mullion with DH6s and DH9s. At the Armistice the airships were deflated and the land planes were flown occasionally until No.236 Squadron was disbanded on 15 May 1919. Mullion was soon cleared and abandoned.

NETHERAVON – 6 MILES N OF AMESBURY
On 16 June 1913 No.3 Squadron RFC moved from Larkhill and, two days later, No.4 Squadron moved from Farnborough to take up residence. In 1914 the whole military wing of the RFC assembled here to test the use of aircraft in war. Nos.3 and 4 Squadrons then left for France as part of the Expeditionary Force to be replaced by No.1 Squadron in November and this unit acted as a training school until March 1915. Since Netheravon was thus being used to build up new squadrons it soon began operating reserve and school squadrons, which became No.4 Reserve Wing in 1917. During 1918 Netheravon housed both Nos.8 and 12 Training Depot Stations flying types as diverse as Avro 504 Ks and HPO/400s. Post World War I, Netheravon was used to disband operational units e.g., 35, 42, 52 and 208 Squadrons. No.12 TDS was disbanded in April 1919 but was replaced by Netheravon Flying Training School in July 1919, to be renamed No.1 Flying Training School (No.1 FTS) in the December.

NEWLYN, CORNWALL – 2 MILES S OF PENZANCE
Newlyn was a seaplane base with Short 184s. These aircraft co-operated with the airships out of Mullion and the flying boats at Trescoe in the Scilly Isles to provide continuous cover for the convoys. In August 1918 No.235 Squadron was formed at Newlyn and a number of Short 320s arrived to supplement the Short 184s. Following the Armistice No.235 Squadron was disbanded on 22 February 1919. Although the station was closed it remained on the Air Ministry's emergency base list and was visited by the Seaplane Development Flight in August 1922. But the site was not favoured and finally went out of use in the late 1920s.

OLD SARUM (FORD FARM) – 2 MILES N OF SALISBURY
The site was acquired by the War Department in 1917 and huts and hangars were built in the August to house Nos.98, 99 and 103 Squadrons. They were day-bomber squadrons and trained there before moving to France in the spring of 1918. By the time Ford Farm had been renamed Old Sarum No.11 TDS moved in, remaining there until the end of the war with Avros, DH4s and DH6s. Old Sarum was retained after the war and the School of Army Co-operation was formed there in 1920

Old Sarum Airfield, Wiltshire – a typical grass airfield layout.

running courses for Army officers and the RAF pilots and observers of the Army co-operation squadrons to learn artillery observation and tactical reconnaissance.

PADSTOW, CORNWALL – 1½ MILES NW OF PADSTOW
To increase inshore patrol capability in the south-west peninsula Padstow airfield was chosen more for its position than its suitability as an airfield. By removing the Cornish dry stone walls a 1,500ft landing run for lightly loaded biplanes was provided. The RNAS airfield became operational by March 1918. The DH4 and DH9 aircraft became No.250 Squadron RAF and this airfield was the most difficult one from which to operate. It remained open until March 1919 but when No.250 Squadron was disbanded the site was returned to agriculture.

PORTLAND – 3 MILES S OF WEYMOUTH
The harbour at Portland was a natural choice for a seaplane base given the number of U-boat attacks in the English Channel and Short floatplanes were based there

from 28 September 1916. With the formation of the RAF in 1918 the base was taken over by the Air Ministry and in the August No.241 Squadron was formed as part of No.10 (Operations) Group until disbanded in June 1919. Portland then reverted to naval use and was the main anti-submarine base for the Royal Navy after the war.

PRAWLE POINT, DEVON – 3 MILES SE OF SALCOMBE

Prawle Point landing ground was opened in April 1917 with nominal facilities to support four aircraft with personnel under canvas, but demands made by the forces on the Western Front resulted in the withdrawal of these aircraft in August that year. However, following the resurrection of the Coastal Patrol Scheme in 1918, Prawle Point was re-activated with DH6 and DH9 aircraft and the RNAS flights became No.254 Squadron RAF. More substantial accommodation was being built at the time of the Armistice but all flying then ceased and No. 254 Squadron disbanded on 22 February 1919. The airfield remained open a little longer for use by an Artillery Co-operation squadron but when that was withdrawn in August, Prawle Point was closed the following year.

ROLLESTONE – 1 MILE E OF SHREWTON VILLAGE

The War Office site had been in existence since No.1 Balloon School was formed in July 1916 to train personnel in the use of observation balloons. The unit survived the wholesale cuts in the services during the period 1919 to 1922 and the unit at Rollestone was renamed the RAF School of Balloon Training and continued in operation throughout the 1920s and much of the 1930s.

TOLLER, SOMERSET – 6 MILES NE OF BRIDPORT

This airship station was constructed in the spring of 1918 and commissioned in No.9 Group later that year from which Zero non-rigid airships were operated. Toller was de-activated in December 1918 and abandoned early in 1919.

TORQUAY, DEVON – CLOSE TO TOWN CENTRE

Torquay was opened early in 1918 with Short 184 floatplanes. Although a slipway was constructed it remained the usual practice to hoist the aircraft into the water using a crane. Space was at a premium and in the event only six 184s could be accommodated. No.239 Squadron was formed in August, taking over No.418 Flight. The Squadron was disbanded on 15 May 1919 and the site handed over to the Government Surplus Property Board in August when the buildings were auctioned.

TRESCOE, SCILLY ISLES – ½ MILE S OF NEW GRIMSBY

Nearby Port Mellen had been considered as a base for the Curtiss H12 Flying Boats but the stretch of water needed for taking off was considered too 'open'. So Flight Commander R.B. Maycock RN surveyed the islands and recommended a site on the almost landlocked New Grimsby Harbour, Trescoe, which provided an excellent take-off and landing area for the six-boat detachment. Felixstowe F2As and F3s followed but on 1 July 1918 only one F3 and a Short 184 were available to mount attacks on U-boats. In August the detached flight became No.234 Squadron and by the end of September eleven boats were on strength. Following the Armistice No.234 Squadron was disbanded in May 1919 and the air station was closed soon afterwards.

UPAVON, WILTSHIRE – 1½ MILES SE OF UPAVON VILLAGE

Upavon is one of the earliest known military airfields in Britain and began life as an aerodrome in 1912. When buildings were completed in June it became the Central Flying School (CFS) of the newly formed RFC. When the country went to war it differed little in its role from other advanced training units apart from the Experimental Flight, which formed in November 1914 to evaluate new equipment. This became the Aircraft and Armament Experimental Flight, which moved to Martlesham Heath in January 1917. From then until the end of World War I Upavon turned out a steady stream of pilots for the squadrons in France. There was confusion about Upavon's future come the Armistice but the station regained its role as CFS for the RAF starting operations in March 1920 turning out flying instructors.

UPTON, DORSET – 2 MILES NW OF POOLE

Upton was commissioned in 1918 as a mooring-out base for SS Zero non-rigid airships detached from Mullion. The site was quickly abandoned after the Armistice.

WESTWARD HO, DEVON – 2½ MILES N OF BIDEFORD

Westward Ho was established early in 1918 to operate ex-trainer DH6s on coastal patrol work and Nos.502 and 503 (Special Duty) Flights became operational in June 1918, both flights being absorbed by No.260 Squadron, which was disbanded on 22 February 1919. The golf links were restored to their former glory.

YATE, GLOUCESTERSHIRE – 10 MILES NE OF BRISTOL

The airfield was built during 1916/1917 to provide test and delivery facilities for No.3 (Western) Aircraft Repair Depot. After the Great War Yate was abandoned by the Air Ministry and the buildings remained empty until taken over by George Parnell & Co. in 1925.

A Bristol Scout at Yatesbury.

YATESBURY, WILTSHIRE – 4 MILES E OF CALNE

Yatesbury was opened in 1916 as a training station and was home to several units, including Nos.36 and 37 Training Depot Stations using a variety of aircraft such as the ubiquitous Avro 504K. After the Armistice the TDSs ceased to operate and the airfield closed in 1919.

AIRFIELDS, SEAPLANE BASES AND MISCELLANEOUS UNITS IN EAST ANGLIA DURING THE GREAT WAR

BIRCHAM NEWTON, NORFOLK – S OF DOCKING NORFOLK

Bircham Newton was built in 1916 and used as a training station housing No.3 Fighter School. But Bircham came into its own as a bomber base not a training station since it was chosen to host the first HP V/1500 four-engined bomber squadron capable of bombing Berlin from this Norfolk base. As part of No.27 Group, No.166 Squadron, commanded by Colonel R.H. Mulock, was formed at the station on 13 June 1918. Unfortunately, only two aircraft had arrived when the Armistice was signed. So no knowledge was gleaned of such long-range bomber operations and the peacetime RAF had no place for this four-engined bombers. Bircham Newton was not closed after the Great War and remained a bomber base in the 1920s.

BURGH CASTLE, NORFOLK – 3½ MILES SW OF GREAT YARMOUTH

No.273 Squadron was formed at Burgh Castle in August 1918 from Nos.470, 485,486 and 534 Flights RNAS with DH4s, DH9s and Camels. This unit was to disband at nearby Great Yarmouth in July 1919. The airfield also received detachments from the Westgate-based No.219 Squadron in mid to late 1918. The airfield did not remain open after the Great War.

ELMSWELL, SUFFOLK – 5 MILES NW OF STOWMARKET

Elmswell was home to No. 75 Squadron from 8 September 1917 until 22 August 1919 with detached flights at Harling Road and Hadleigh. During this period the squadron operated BE12s, BE12Bs and Avro 504 night fighters. Elmswell was not retained after the Armistice.

FELIXSTOWE, SUFFOLK – FELIXSTOWE DOCK

Felixstowe had been home to eleven RNAS flights when the RAF took control of naval aircraft in April 1918. It was in August that year that naval flights around the country were formed into RAF squadrons in the 200 Series. In common with nearby Great Yarmouth, this occurred on 20 August. Between then and the end of the war a great variety of aircraft types had to be maintained by technical personnel on the base. These were the F2A, F3 and F5, the Curtiss H16, the Camel, Short 184 and Fairey IIIB/C. After the Armistice it was decided to retain the base in service and Felixstowe became the Marine Aircraft Experimental Establishment, which complemented a similar establishment at nearby Martlesham Heath that tested landplanes, both civil and military.

FOWLMERE – CAMBRIDGESHIRE BY A1368

Fowlmere first opened as a training establishment in 1918 but ended its days as a storage unit for the HPO/400s in hangars on the airfield. The hangars were demolished in 1923.

GOLDHANGER, ESSEX – 4 MILES ENE OF MALDON

Goldhanger was used by only two squadrons during the Great War. No.37 Squadron had detached flights on the airfield from September 1916 until the Armistice whilst No.74 Squadron was there for only five days in March 1918 when it was equipped with the SE5a before proceeding to St Omer on the 30th.

GREAT YARMOUTH, NORFOLK

Great Yarmouth came into use as an airfield and seaplane base in the war against U-boats and had been the home of RNAS flights until these were combined into RAF squadrons in August 1918. The flights at Great Yarmouth became Nos.212, 228 and 229 Squadrons on the 20th of that month. Between them the squadrons had DH4s, DH9s DH9As, Felixstowe F2As, Curtiss H12/16s, Sopwith and Hamble Babies, Short 184s and Short 320s. Great Yarmouth was not selected for retention in the post-war RAF.

HADLEIGH, SUFFOLK – 8 MILES W OF IPSWICH

This was a landing ground used by No.75 Squadron between September 1917 and the Armistice.

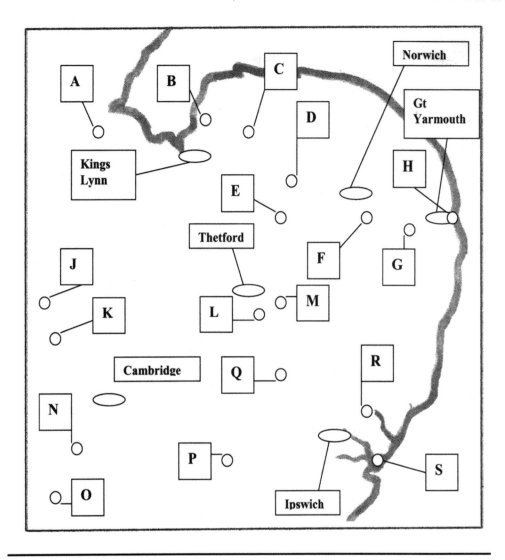

Airfields, Seaplane Bases and Landing Grounds

A	Tydd St Mary	K	Yelling
B	Sedgeford	L	Thetford
C	Bircham Newton	M	Harling Road
D	Mattishal	N	Fowlmere
E	Hingham	O	Therfield
F	Mousehold Heath	P	Hadleigh
G	Burgh Castle	Q	Elmswell
H	Great Yarmouth	R	Martlesham Heath
J	Wyton	S	Felixstowe

Airfields, seaplane bases and miscellaneous units in East Anglia during the Great War.

HARLING ROAD – 8 MILES ENE OF THETFORD

Harling Road housed Nos.88, 89 and 94 Squadrons during August 1917 and received detachments from Nos.51 and 75 Squadrons.

HINGHAM – 5 MILES W OF WYMONDHAM

No.100 Squadron was formed from the nucleus of No.51 Squadron on 11 February 1917 with BE2cs, only to move to Farnborough on the 22nd of that month. No.102 Squadron formed on 9 August 1917 with FE2bs and moved to André-aux-Bois on 24 September. No.51 Squadron was a Home Defence squadron with detachments to Harling Road, Narborough and Mattishall between 23 September 1916 and 7 August 1917, when the squadron left Hingham for Marham. Originally equipped with BE12s, No.51 Squadron was later equipped with FE2bs and BE2es.

MARHAM, NORFOLK – 10 MILES E OF DOWNHAM MARKET

The station was opened as Narborough in August 1915 as an Admiralty landing ground for night operations against Zeppelin raids. In April 1916 the RFC assumed responsibility for Marham when it became a training station for Vickers fighters with the FE2bs arriving from Thetford. In August 1916 No.59 Squadron formed with RE7s and BEs. Thereafter, the station became a TDS preparing squadrons for service in France. When the Great War ended Marham closed and did not re-open until 1 April 1937. The station remains an active flying station to this day.

MARTLESHAM HEATH, SUFFOLK – STRADDLING THE A1093

The RFC required an aeroplane experimental unit and this had been formed at Upavon. Work commenced at the Martlesham site in 1916 and the unit then moved from Upavon to Martlesham and was established in January 1917. The work included not simply the testing of aircraft but also new ideas and the RFC was responsible for the unit until the end of the hostilities. As an RAF station the unit was renamed the Aeroplane and Armament Experimental Establishment (A&AEE.) For the next twenty-two years it not only tested service types but also civilian prototypes before a Certificate of Airworthiness could be issued. The A&AEE eventually had to move to Boscombe Down on the outbreak of World War II because it was too close to the air war being fought in the skies over south-east England.

MATTISHALL, NORFOLK – 4 MILES E OF EAST DEREHAM

The landing ground received detachments of No.51 Squadron from 7 August 1917 until the Armistice. There is no recorded post-war use.

NORWICH (MOUSEHOLD HEATH) NORFOLK – ON THE EASTERN OUTSKIRTS OF NORWICH

Mousehold Heath was used during the Great War. For example, No.18 Squadron came from Northolt on 16 August 1915 and was equipped with Vickers FB5s before heading off for St Omer on 18 November. No.37 Squadron formed at the airfield from a nucleus of No. 9 RS and left the following day for Orfordness. No.85 Squadron moved from Upavon on 10 August, only nine days after its formation, and on 27 November moved on to Hounslow. Finally, No.117 Squadron moved from Hucknall on 15 July 1918 and left for Wyton in November. There is no recorded post-war use of this airfield.

SEDGEFORD, NORFOLK – 4 MILES SE OF HUNSTANTON

Sedgeford was a busy airfield during the Great War used as it was by six squadrons between 1916 and 1919. No.45 Squadron came from Thetford with Henry Farman F20s on 21 May 1916. Sopwith 1½ Strutters were also added to the squadron inventory before it moved on to St Omer, the reception airfield in France for squadrons leaving England, on 12 October. No.64 Squadron was next and formed at the airfield on 1 August 1916 from a nucleus of No.45 Squadron and was equipped with Henry Farman F20s to be followed by BE2cs, Pups and Avro 504s, before moving on to St Omer on 14 October. No.72 Squadron came from Netheravon on 1 November 1917 with Pups and Avro 504s, but a little over a month later was en route for the Persian Gulf. No. 87 Squadron, which flew in from Upavon on 15 September 1917 with various aircraft, moved on to Hounslow on 19 December. From Dover (Swingate) on 26 November 1917 came No.110 Squadron with various aircraft, which moved on to Kenley on 15 June 1918, but was disbanded before the Armistice. There is no recorded use of the post-war use of this airfield.

THERFIELD, ESSEX – 2 MILES SSE OF ROYSTON

The only recorded use of this landing ground during the Great War was for detachments of No. 75 Squadron, Goldhanger, between 12 October 1916 and 8 September 1917. The field was abandoned after the war.

THETFORD, SUFFOLK – 3 MILES SE OF THETFORD

Thetford was a busy airfield during the Great War Nos.35, 38 and 77 Squadrons were formed at the airfield in 1916, No.80 Squadron in 1917 and No.128 Squadron in 1918. Nos.25, 51 and 119 Squadrons were based here between1915 and 1918.

TYDD ST MARY, NORFOLK – 6 MILES NNE OF WISBECH

No.51 Squadron detached its aircraft from Marham between 7 August 1917 and the Armistice. There is no recorded post-war use.

WYTON, CAMBRIDGESHIRE – NE OF HUNTINGDON

Flying came to Wyton when RFC pilots learned to fly a variety of aircraft from this site that opened in 1916. Both reserve and training squadrons passed through and aerodrome buildings were built on the west side of the airfield. Between the wars Alan Cobham's flying circus made use of the airfield. Construction of a new aerodrome began in 1935.

YELLING – 6 MILES ENE OF ST NEOTS

No.75 Squadron detached its BE2cs to Yelling between 12 October 1916 and 8 September 1917. There is no recorded post-war use.

Aircraft of No.31 Training Squadron – Wyton 1916.

AIRFIELDS AND MISCELLANEOUS UNITS IN THE COTSWOLDS AND CENTRAL MIDLANDS

BICESTER – 1½ MILES NE OF BICESTER TOWN

The airfield came into use in late 1917 and from January the following year No.118 Squadron mobilized here remaining until November. In October 1918 No.44 Training Depot Station arrived to be followed by No.2 Squadron, the latter remaining until 19 September 1919 to be replaced by No.5 Squadron with Bristol Fighters. This unit was disbanded on 20 January 1920 and Bicester closed in the March. But it was not to remain unused for long and in 1925 the station was reactivated.

CARDINGTON – 3 MILES SE OF BEDFORD

Cardington first came into use when Short Brothers became involved in airship construction in 1915. The site was chosen for its scope for development and communication links and the firm built a housing estate for the workers naming it 'Shortstown'. When the Admiralty planned to take over Cardington, Short's was meant to run the station and build airships there but the firm did not agree to the terms for the take-over and the site was nationalized. With the departure of Short's in April 1919 the Royal Airship Works came into being and the *R31*, *R37* and *R38* were all associated with Cardington during this period.

CASTLE BROMWICH – 4 MILES ENE OF BIRMINGHAM

The War Office requisitioned the site in 1914 for flying schools, which included No.5 Training Squadron. Nos.19 and 55 Squadrons also formed here. Others units came and went and an aircraft acceptance park was established in April 1918 to test locally built HPO/400s and SE5as. Castle Bromwich was acquired by the Air Board in August 1919 but it was initially used for civil aviation. On 15 October 1926 No.605 Auxiliary Air Force Squadron (County of Warwick) formed here equipped with DH9As.

HENLOW – 5 MILES NNW OF HITCHIN

Construction on the site began in April 1918 and the first unit to be established was No.5 Eastern Aircraft Depot. Although the Americans came to Henlow they soon left after the Armistice and aircraft repair stopped. Aircraft held in store were auctioned at prices even lower than those that could be purchased at the Cambridge flying school. A small aircraft cost the princely sum of 10 shillings (50p) whilst a bomber cost just twice that. On April 1 1919 Henlow hit the headlines when airmen awaiting demobilization mutinied over increased working hours and fifty-six were tried by court martial. The Air Ministry planned to keep Henlow as a post-war station and an airfield for flight testing was added.

RENDCOMBE – 1½ MILES NE OF NORTH CERNEY

It was at Rendcombe that No.48 Squadron was first to equip with the Bristol Fighter. The airfield opened in 1916 and by mid 1918 housed No.45 Training Depot Station with elementary, advanced and operational squadrons. This meant a variety of aircraft including BE2cs, F2Bs and RE8s and when the Armistice came squadrons that were disbanding came to Rendcombe. When this had taken place the station closed in late 1919 and was abandoned in early 1920.

UPPER HEYFORD – 5 MILES NW OF BICESTER

Upper Heyford was first home to the Canadians who formed there on 20 January 1918 as No.123 Squadron, later renamed No. 2 Squadron Canadian Air Force and equipped with Sopwith Dolphins. When this squadron left it was replaced by No.1 Squadron Canadian Air Force, the latter moving to Shoreham in March 1919.

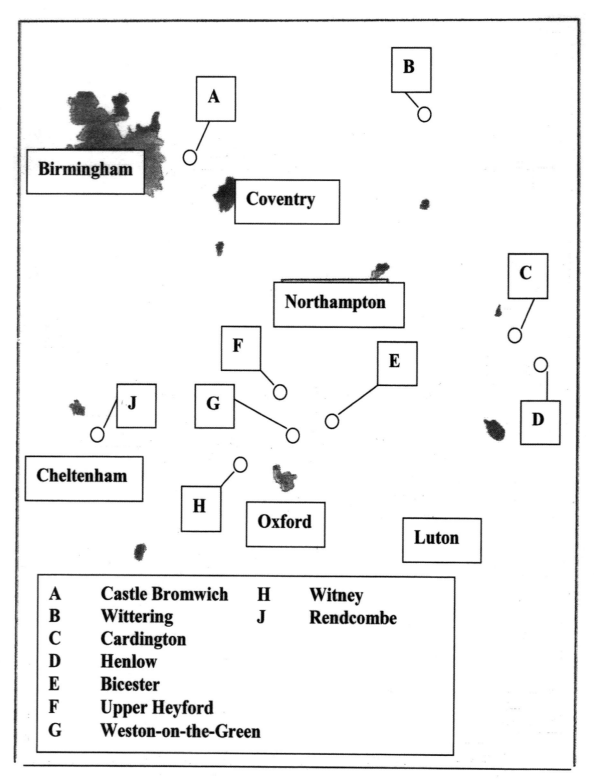

Airfields and miscellaneous units in the Cotswolds and Central Midlands.

Upper Heyford was closed in 1920 but with the modest expansion scheme of the 1920s Upper Heyford was selected as a bomber station and re-opened on 12 October 1927.

WESTON-ON-THE-GREEN – 3½ MILES SW OF BICESTER

The site was acquired for military use in 1916. By July 1918 No.28 Training Depot Station had taken up residence using Sopwith Camels and Avro 504s. By the time the TDS had closed in 1919 the Camels had been replaced by the ground attack Sopwith Salamanders. Nos.2 and 18 Squadrons came to Weston prior to disbandment and by 1921 all activity had ceased and the site returned to grazing land.

WITNEY – 1 MILE W OF WITNEY

During the Great War the airfield was used for training in fighter tactics. In 1918 Nos.7 and 8 Training Squadrons arrived with their 504Ks, F2Bs and DH5s. These units combined on 5 August 1918 to become No.33 Training Depot Station, which was disbanded in 1919 whereupon Witney closed.

WITTERING – 3 MILES S OF STAMFORD

During the Great War the site was simply known as Stamford. Between 1916 and 1917 the airfield was home to the FE2bs of No.38 HD Squadron. Between August 1917 and May 1919 No.1 Training Depot Station was at Stamford, together with 'C' Flight of No.90 Squadron. At the cessation of hostilities it became a storage depot and was eventually placed on C & M. in January 1920.

AIRFIELDS AND MISCELLANEOUS UNITS OF LINCOLNSHIRE AND THE EAST MIDLANDS

BRACEBRIDGE HEATH – S OF LINCOLN E OF A15

Bracebridge Heath was opened in late 1917 and became home of No.4 Acceptance Park. The airfield was closed in 1920 following the run-down of the RAF.

BUCKMINSTER – 1 MILE E OF BUCKMINSTER

Buckminster was opened in 1916 and housed 'C' Flight of No.38 (HD) Squadron, which had its headquarters at Melton Mowbray. Equipped with FE2bs 'C' Flight was employed on anti-Zeppelin patrols. In May 1918 this unit left to be replaced in August 1918 No.90 (HD) Squadron with Camels and Avro 504s used as night fighters. A further use of the airfield was as an aircraft acceptance park. No.90 Squadron was disbanded in June 1919 and when the acceptance park closed the airfield was returned to agriculture.

CRANWELL – 12 MILES S OF GRANTHAM

Work began on the RNAS shore station 'Daedalus' on 28 December 1915. There were two airfields, one south of the B1429 with wooden hangars and two flight sheds and a second to the north of the road with several balloon sheds on its northern edge. The station was opened on 1 April 1916 as the RNAS Training Establishment tasked to train officers and Royal Navy ratings on aeroplanes, kite balloons and dirigibles. In July 1916 the station received a visit from the King. In April 1919 HMS Daedalus became RAF Cranwell. Originally the station was home to Nos.201, 202 and 213 TDS, later renamed 56, 57 and 58 TDS respectively. Constituent units included the Airship Training Wing, Boys' Training Wing, Aeroplane Repair Section, PT School and Wireless Operators' School. When the Great War ended the future of Cranwell was in doubt but Trenchard, backed by Winston Churchill, wanted the station for his Cadet College, far enough away from the 'fleshpots' of London. And so it became, the first course for officer cadets commencing on 5 February 1920.

DIGBY (SCOPWICK) – W OF B1191 FROM SCOPWICK VILLAGE

Work began on the site in 1917 and hangars and accommodation were to be provided to take the overflow from HMS Daedalus. When further buildings such as messes and barrack blocks were built in 1918 it was possible for Scopwick, as it was then called, to operate as a separate station. In March 1918 it was ready to receive Handley Page bombers and the airfield was administered by No.12 Group. In November 1918 No.59 TDS was formed but the Armistice came before it was fully established. It seems that early in 1919 this unit became No.59 TS tasked with the training of bomber and fighter pilots. During the Irish troubles Shotwick airfield near Chester became the jumping off point for aircraft crossing the Irish Sea to Dublin and confusion arose in correspondence and signals. So Scopwick became RAF Digby and Shotwick became RAF Sealand.

DONCASTER – SW OF RACECOURSE ON A638

This racecourse turned Great War airfield housed No.15 RAS from January 1916 followed by No. 47 Squadron from June of that year. No.46 RS then formed there in the October but moved out shortly afterwards. In 1917 it was the turn of the Canadians when No.80 TS formed but it moved to Canada shortly thereafter. On 15 March No.90 TS formed at Doncaster and moved on in the April. So the airfield saw many comings and goings. From February to November 1917 No. 82 Squadron with AWFK8s was the resident unit until it moved to France. No.49 RS also left to be followed by No.47 TDS comprising Nos.41 and 49 TS with Avro 504s and SE5s. The depot station and the airfield closed in 1919.

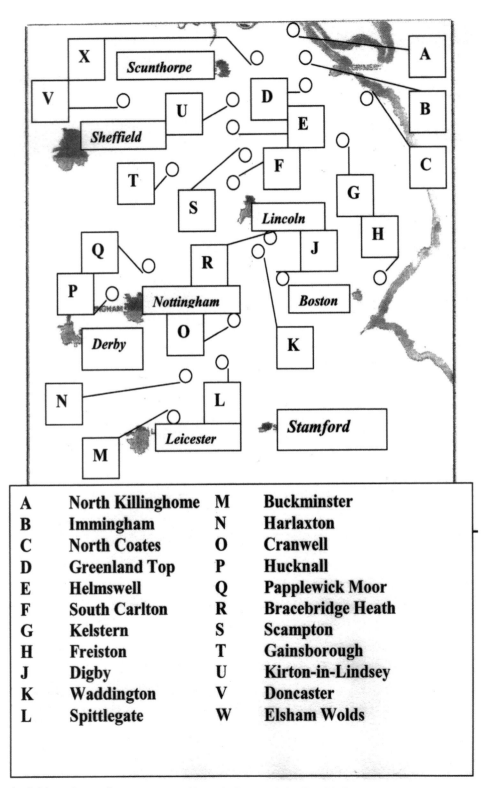

A	North Killinghome	**M**	Buckminster
B	Immingham	**N**	Harlaxton
C	North Coates	**O**	Cranwell
D	Greenland Top	**P**	Hucknall
E	Helmswell	**Q**	Papplewick Moor
F	South Carlton	**R**	Bracebridge Heath
G	Kelstern	**S**	Scampton
H	Freiston	**T**	Gainsborough
J	Digby	**U**	Kirton-in-Lindsey
K	Waddington	**V**	Doncaster
L	Spittlegate	**W**	Elsham Wolds

Airfields and miscellaneous units of Lincolnshire and the East Midlands

ELSHAM WOLDS – APPROX. 7 MILES NE OF A15
Elsham Wolds became a landing ground for HD duties and a detached flight of No.33 Squadron used this field from December 1916 until after the Armistice when the field was abandoned. This was 'C' Flight equipped with FE2bs.

FREISTON – E OF BOSTON ON WASH MUD FLATS
Freiston was opened in September 1917 as an RNAS station under the control of HMS Daedalus, sited on the mud flats and marshes of the Wash because it was ideal for live firing and bombing. Freiston thus became an armament training school. With the coming of the RAF in April 1918 No.4 Aerial School of Fighting was formed at the airfield with DH5s and SE5as, only to be renamed No.4 Fighting School training scout pilots in gunnery. When this unit was disbanded in March 1920, Freiston closed.

GAINSBOROUGH, LINCOLNSHIRE
It has already been explained that HD squadrons during the Great War usually had a squadron headquarters in one location with three detached flights at airfields close by, although one of the flights might be co-located with squadron HQ. The German Zeppelin *L13* had dropped bombs on Gainsborough and, even though little damage was caused, the War Office deemed dispersal of squadron flights necessary. (On World War II airfields squadrons were based on one airfield but with paved runways and perimeter tracks it was possible to site aircraft well away from the main station buildings on dispersal pans yet get them to the runway quickly for take-off. Refer to the airfield diagram at the beginning of the chapter). No.33 Squadron had its headquarters at Gainsborough and a small landing ground was opened in December1916. The squadron's detached FE2bs and FE2ds were elsewhere but could be flown in to the HQ airfield for maintenance or repair. In June 1918 the Squadron HQ moved to Kirton-in-Lindsey and after the Armistice Gainsborough was abandoned.

GREENLAND TOP – W OF GRIMSBY AND NE OF KEELBY
This airfield opened in 1918 and housed No.251 Squadron, No.505 Flight, with DH6s on A/S duties. The airfield closed in 1919.

GRIMSTHORPE – 4 MILES NW OF BOURNE
This was an Emergency Landing Ground only during World War I but was not retained post war.

HARLAXTON – 2 MILES S OF GRANTHAM
Harlaxton was built by the RFC in 1916 as a training aerodrome. In November that year No.44 RS moved in, equipped with Avro 504s, BE2s and RE7s. Renamed No.44 TS, the unit remained there until November 1917. A succession of training units used Harlaxton and following the reorganization of flying training establishments in 1918 the airfield was home to No.40 TDS in the summer of 1918. When this unit disbanded the airfield closed in 1919.

HEMSWELL (FORMERLY HARPSWELL) – APPROX. 13 MILES N OF LINCOLN
This airfield bore the name of Harpswell during the Great War. In common with other sites selected along the Lincoln Cliff, it was an ideal site for a training station. The airfield was a late starter, not being opened until June 1918 to house No.199 TS, tasked with training pilots and observers for night operations but when the unit disbanded in June 1919 the airfield became redundant and closed.

HUCKNALL – ON THE OUTSKIRTS OF HUCKNALL
The site was purchased from the Duke of Portland. And the airfield opened as a training ground. It remained in this role throughout the war, training the Americans as well as RFC/RAF personnel. It went out of use after the Armistice and the buildings were sold off.

IMMINGHAM – ON THE S BANK OF THE HUMBER
From April 1918 it was home to No.8 Balloon Station RAF but closed with the disbandment of the unit in 1919.

KELSTERN NW OF LOUTH
Kelstern was used as an emergency landing ground by Home Defence squadrons during World War I and the site was discarded on cessation of hostilities.

KIRTON-IN-LINDSEY – N OF LINCOLN
This airfield was opened when B Flight No.33 Squadron moved in during December 1916 using Avro 504 night fighters. The airfield was abandoned in June 1919.

NORTH COATES – S OF GRIMSBY
Opened in 1918 to house No.404 Flight of No.248 Squadron employed on coastal patrols. The unit disbanded in March 1919 and the airfield closed.

NORTH KILLINGHOLME – NW OF GRIMSBY
North Killingholme was opened as a seaplane base in August 1914 at the northern end of the Killingholme Marshes on the Lincolnshire side of the Humber. There was also an airfield so that coastal patrols could be carried out by both seaplanes and landplanes. During the latter part of 1917 Redcar and other Yorkshire-based squadrons used the airfield. In July 1918 North Killingholme was taken over by the US Navy to be returned to the RAF in January 1919. In October of that year the base closed completely.

PAPPLEWICK MOOR – APPROX. 7 MILES N OF NOTTINGHAM
In 1918 Papplewick Moor served as a Relief Landing Ground for No. 15 Training Depot Station but when

this unit was disbanded in 1919 the landing ground was abandoned.

SCAMPTON (BRATTLEBURY) – N OF LINCOLN

Brattlebury opened in November 1916 and initially housed No.49 RS, which then moved to Grantham to be replaced by No.37 RS the same month. In the December No.33 (HD) Squadron detached one of its flights to the airfield with FE2/FE2bs. A typical anti-Zeppelin patrol would be from Spurn Head to just south of Lincoln but since the Zeppelins came over at 18,000ft and the FE2bs had a service ceiling of 12,000ft there was no hope of catching them. The Avro 504s and RE8s of No.60 RS arrived in April 1917 to be renamed No.60 TS. This was followed in July by the formation of No.81 Squadron, a fighter unit strangely also classified as a training squadron. On 15 September 1917 No.11 TS moved in from Grantham and in July the following year all three of the aforementioned units were merged into No.34 TDS flying, amongst other types, Dolphins and Camels. After the Armistice the remaining machines and personnel were transferred to No.46 TDS at South Carlton and the station closed. By 1920 no trace was left of what was to become one of the most famous stations of the RAF in World War II and after.

SOUTH CARLTON – JUST N OF LINCOLN

South Carlton opened in November 1916 and housed a variety of training units. The airfield also acted as a demobilization base. When the last unit left in April 1920 the airfield closed.

SPITTLEGATE – E OF GRANTHAM

First constructed in 1916, Spittlegate started as and remained a training airfield throughout the Great War.

Waddington in 1918 home to Nos.47 and 48 Training Squadrons.

Used immediately post-war by a variety of operational units and during 1920, No.6 FTS was formed here. In April 1922 No.3 FTS moved in. In June 1928, when 39 and 100 Squadrons left it was solely a training station.

WADDINGTON – S OF LINCOLN

The station opened in November 1916 as a flying training station. The station was closed in 1919 but it was one of the few Great War stations to retain its buildings and airfield during the run-down immediately after the war. The station re-opened in October 1926 as the base for the newly formed No.503 Special Reserve Squadron. This was a bombing unit initially equipped with Fairey Fawns. In February 1929 these were replaced by Hyderabads.

AIRFIELDS AND SEAPLANE BASES IN WALES AND NORTH-WEST ENGLAND

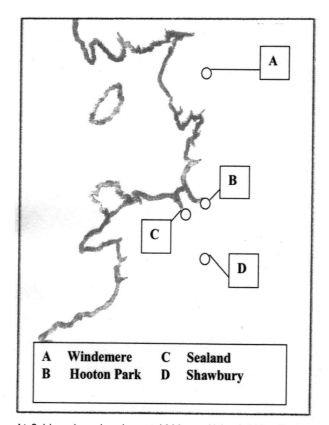

| A | Windemere | C | Sealand |
| B | Hooton Park | D | Shawbury |

Airfields and seaplane bases in Wales and North-West England.

HOOTON PARK, CHESHIRE – 1 MILE SE OF EASTHAM

During the Great War Hooton Park was a racecourse that was requisitioned by the Army for training purposes.

Belfast hangars were built in 1917 on the area once occupied by the horse paddock to house American-built aircraft shipped to Liverpool. But instead of these aircraft arriving No.4 TDS moved from Tern Hill in September 1917, and there was also an aircraft repair section. In 1919 the TDS was disbanded and the site was left unused until 1927 when it was used for civil aviation.

SEALAND (SHOTWICK) – I MILE NE OF QUEENSFERRY

In 1917 the station, then known as Shotwick, housed a variety of aircraft where aircrews worked up to operational standards. When squadrons moved to France it was intended that training squadrons should move in, but changes in policy resulted in further operational units being posted in. On 15 July 1918 No.51 TDS was absorbed into No.5 Flying Training School using Avro 504s, the station surviving into the peacetime RAF.

SHAWBURY, SALOP – ADJACENT TO SHAWBURY VILLAGE

To improve the chances of survival of RFC pilots, Shawbury was used in 1917 for pre-operational training. No.29 (Training) Wing was formed on 1 September but, having too many different types of aircraft, was not conducive to good training. Two of the squadrons involved became No.9 TDS on 1 March 1918 and training became more organized. When the war ended the airfield closed in May 1920. The hangars and buildings were demolished and the site fell into disrepair.

WINDERMERE – 2 MILES S OF AMBLESIDE

During the Great War, Windermere was used by the RNAS to fly mails to the Isle of Man and so avoid loss caused by U-boat activity in the Irish Sea. The use of the lake for this purpose ended in 1918.

AIRFIELDS AND SEAPLANE BASES OF YORKSHIRE

APPLETON WISKE, YORKSHIRE – SE OF DARLINGTON

This 38-acre grass airfield, situated just north-east of the village of Appleton Wiske, was classed as a second class landing ground. The site had heavy loam and clay soil and was by surrounded agricultural fields with many trees in the line of the landing approach. No.76 Squadron used it for Home Defence duties and it was abandoned soon after the Armistice.

ATWICK, YORKSHIRE – N OF HORNSEA

This was a 2nd class landing ground and covered an area of 50 acres and was another of those landing grounds used by No.76 Squadron for Home Defence duties. It was only rarely used for this purpose until May 1918 when No.504

Flight of No.251 Squadron used the landing ground. (The RAF squadrons that had previously been units of the RNAS were renumbered starting at 200.) The DH6s of this squadron maintained anti-submarine patrols. The landing ground was abandoned immediately after the Armistice.

BARLOW, YORKSHIRE – S OF SELBY BETWEEN THE A1041 AND THE RIVER OUSE

In 1917 this airfield was leased to Armstrong Whitworth for the construction of airships and a large airship shed and other buildings were erected. That year the airship *R25* was completed and in 1918 so was the *R29*. The German airship *LZ5* force-landed in England in 1916 and this provided data that could be incorporated in the airship *R33* but by the time this airship was completed the Great War had ended and so had the military need for Barlow. The *R33* was eventually scrapped and its control car can now be seen at the RAF Museum Hendon. Today a large airship shed can still be seen on the site of the airfield.

BELLASIZE, YORKSHIRE – E OF HOWDEN

This airfield was opened in April 1916 and used by No.33 Squadron RFC from April to October of that year flying BE2c aircraft. During the autumn of 1916 Avro 504s of No.76 Squadron RFC also used the airfield but the proximity of the site to the River Ouse meant it was subject to flooding during the Great War, even though it was listed as a 1st class landing ground.

BEVERLEY – N OF KINGSTON-UPON-HULL

The airfield was situated on the present-day racecourse and the hangars and other buildings were situated on the south-east corner of the site with easy access to the main road. From March to October 1916 both the HQ and 'C' Flight of No.33 Squadron, with its BE2cs and Ds was tasked with the protection of the Humber Ports. Also in 1916 the Curtiss JN3s and 4s of No.6 Reserve Squadron operated from the racecourse. A third squadron, formed that year at Beverley, was No.47 Squadron, which worked alongside No.33 Squadron on Home Defence duties but went to Macedonia the following September. Further movements were of No.90 TS, which arrived from Doncaster on 1 April 1917, and of No.80 Squadron, which was equipped with Sopwith Camels, but the latter moved out on 27 January 1918. Flying ceased after the war but the site was retained by the RAF during the inter-war years for work on radios.

BINSOE, YORKSHIRE – NW OF RIPON

This Great War grass airfield was classified as a 3rd class landing ground covering 35 acres. It was used by No.76 Squadron with their Avro 504s from 1916 to 1918. Very little use was made of this field, which had no

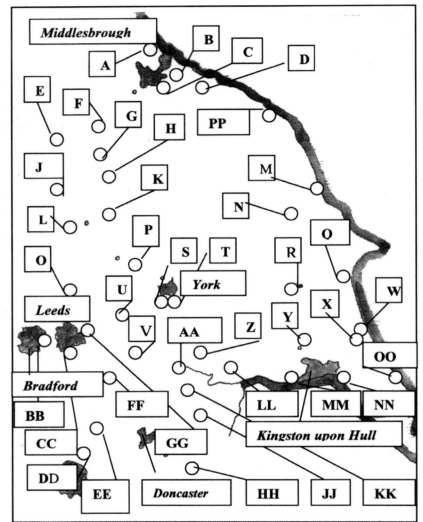

Urban Areas – eg *Bradford*
Airfields, landing grounds, seaplane Bases   eg A, B

LEGEND

A   Seaton Carew
B   Redcar
C   Kirkleatham
D   Marske
E   Catterick
F   Appleton- Wiske
G   South Otterington
H   Thirsk
J   Binsoe
K   Helperby
L   Ripon
M   Scalby Mills
N   West Ayton
O   Dunkeswicke
P   Shipton
Q   Lowthorpe
R   Driffield (Eastbourne)
S   Copmanthorpe
T   Knavesmire
U   Tadcaster
V   Sherburn-in-Elmet
W   Atwick
X   Hornsea Mere
Y   Beverley
Z   Menthorpe Gate
AA Barlow
BB Farsley
CC Middleton

DD Ecclesfield
EE Wombwell (Broomhill)
FF Pontefract
GG Seacroft
HH Brancroft
JJ Thorne

KK Carlton
LL Howden
MM Brough
NN Hull (Hedon)
OO Owthorne
PP Kettleness

Airfields and seaplane bases of Yorkshire.

permanent buildings, and it was abandoned soon after the Armistice.

BRANCROFT, YORKSHIRE – SE OF DONCASTER
This landing ground was not requisitioned by the military since the farmer agreed to its use by 'A' Flight of No.33 Squadron RFC for Home Defence duties. Avro 504 fighters operating from the field had the duty to provide air defence of Leeds and Bradford, both munitions-producing areas. The site was not developed but just to the north of Brancroft would be the site of a World War II bomber station, RAF Finningley.

BROUGH, YORKSHIRE – W OF KINGSTON-UPON-HULL
Brough became the site for land and seaplane production and a slipway was built on the west side of the landing area. In 1916 Blackburn carried out the flight trials on their second general-purpose seaplane, which did not go into large-scale production. But the land version, the Kangaroo, was a military success, After completion of the second general-purpose seaplane the Admiralty commandeered both the production hangar and the slipway. Further buildings were erected and Brough became No.2 (Northern) Marine Acceptance Depot handling most of the RNAS floatplanes until the end of the war. With the Armistice there was an almost complete end to orders for military aircraft and Blackburn's directors were determined not to follow many of the aircraft production firms that were going out of business and converted their Kangaroo seaplanes into freight and passenger services for Continental destinations. This venture did not meet with success but Blackburn remained in business. (See Volume I of this author's work on the 1920s entitled *The Royal Air Force the Trenchard Years*.)

CARLTON, CARLTON – W OF GOOLE
Carlton was a landing ground used by 'B' Flight of No.33 Squadron from March to October 1916 whilst employed on Home Defence duties. The whole area was characterized by marshland and the site was never developed for military aviation.

CATTERICK, YORKSHIRE – S OF CATTERICK
The airfield was opened in 1914 for the RFC to train pilots to assist in the defence of north-eastern England. On 27 November 1915 No.6 RS arrived from Montrose and now units began to form. Captain A Claude Wright formed 'A' Flight of No.53 Squadron on 15 May 1916 and by the October the squadron was fully formed and equipped with BE2s. By the end of the year No.53 Squadron had moved to Farnborough en route for France. On 2 November No.37 RS formed at Catterick but moved only eleven days later to Scampton in Lincolnshire. A flight of

No.76 Squadron arrived in late 1916 and remained for the duration of the war and was responsible for the defence of Leeds and Sheffield. During January 1917 No.83 RS was formed. This was a Canadian unit and moved to Beverley. Another Canadian RS was formed in April 1917 and moved to Canada shortly afterwards. When No.68 RS was formed on 7 April it was soon moved to Bramham Moor on the 14th. On 23 July 1917 No.46 RS came to Catterick equipped with BE2 and Avro 504 aircraft from Bramham Moor and on 1 October No.69 RS was formed with DH4 and DH6 aircraft but on the 10th it moved to Bramham Moor. Catterick then opened as a fully fledged aerodrome on 1 December 1917 with No.115 Squadron RFC becoming the training squadron. On 1 April 1918 Catterick became an RAF station and the Sopwith Pups of No.115 Squadron moved to Netheravon. On 15 July No.49 TDS was formed equipped with DH4 and DH9 aircraft and a few Avro 504s. The station remained in the training role for the duration of the war and was retained in the peacetime RAF.

COPMANTHORPE, YORKSHIRES – 3 MILES S OF YORK
Copmanthorpe was developed as a replacement site for Knavesmire where hangars and other buildings were constructed. This made possible the move of 33 Squadron's 'B' Flight from Knavesmire in May 1916 with its BE2c aircraft until the September but it was then replaced by 'A' Flight. No.33 Squadron then provided the nucleus of No.57 Squadron which, having formed at Copmanthorpe on 8 June 1916, then moved to France in December as a fighter reconnaissance unit. 'A' Flight of No.76 Squadron operated from the airfield equipped with Avro 504 and 504K aircraft until 1919 when the airfield was closed.

CULLINGWORTH – W OF BRADFORD (NOT SHOWN ON MAP)
This grass landing strip was used by Nos.33 and 76 HD Squadrons between 1916 and 1919. It was abandoned after the Great War.

DRIFFIELD, YORKSHIRE
Driffield was not developed as a permanent airfield until 1918 when it opened as Eastburn aerodrome and on 15 July No.21 TDS was formed here. In February 1919 construction work was finally completed but when No.21 TDS was disbanded the station was put under care and maintenance not to be reactivated until the late 1930s.

DUNKESWICKE
This World War I airfield was situated to the north of Leeds on the west side of the A6. It was grassed and covered an area of 40 acres, and was used as a landing ground for B Flight of No.33 Squadron between March

and October 1916. No.76 Squadron also used the landing ground during their patrols but it was not developed and had no further connection with aviation.

HELPERBY – S OF THIRSK
This airfield was used by 'B' Flight of No.76 Squadron's Avro 504s until March 1919. When the 504s moved to Tadcaster the airfield closed.

World War I hangar, Helperby, Yorkshire.

HORNSEA MERE – ON W SIDE OF HORNSEA
Hornsea Mere was used by the Short 184s of 404 and 405 Flights RNAS. Then Nos.504, 505, 506 and 510 Flights with DH6s became No.251 Squadron RAF. When this unit was disbanded the site was closed.

HOWDEN – N OF GOOLE
Howden opened in March 1916 and became one of the most important operational airship stations housing the newest non-rigid SSZ class in early 1918. In April 1918 Howden became part RN part RAF and, at the Armistice, the airship fleet was run down but the airfield was saved from closure as it was Trenchard's plan to maintain a nucleus of craft and personnel for airship development but with the tragic loss of the *R38* in 1921 the programme was halted and the last flight from Howden was on 20 September 1921. The station was closed and fell into disrepair but in 1924 the Airship Guarantee was formed and leased Howden from the Air Ministry. Work on the *R100* took place until November 1929, then the loss of the *R101* at Beauvais in France brought an end to the airship programme and the dispersal of Howden's staff. Howden's huge hangar was dismantled and sold for scrap.

HULL – E OF KINGSTON-UPON-HULL
During the Great War Hull was listed as a 2nd class landing ground and used by BE2cs of 'C' Flight, No.33 Squadron, and aircraft of No.76 Squadron. The field was closed after the Armistice.

KETTLENESS – NW OF WHITBY
Kettleness was used as a RNAS landing ground during the Great War and an inshore reconnaissance station. It was of no further use after the war but was retained as a coastguard station.

KIRKLEATHAM – W OF REDCAR
This mooring-out station was opened in May 1918 for airships from Howden and used during August, September and October. It was closed immediately after the Armistice.

LOWTHORPE – SW OF BRIDLINGTON
This was also a mooring-out station for Howden, which opened in April 1918. Between then and the end of the war an adjoining field was used by 'A' Flight of No.251 Squadron carrying out anti-submarine patrols. It was not selected for retention after the war and Lowthorpe mooring-out station and the airfield closed.

MARSKE – SE OF REDCAR
Marske opened on 1 November 1917 for No.4 Auxiliary School of Aerial Gunnery using DH9s and Dolphins. On 6 May 1918, No.2 School replaced No.4 School as No.2 School of Aerial Fighting and Gunnery. On 29 May 1918 this was redesignated No.2 Fighting School and equipped with Bristol 1Cs, Camels, DH4s and 9s. With the Armistice there was a run-down and closure as No.2 Fighting School was closed in 1919.

MIDDLETON – S OF LEEDS
This night landing ground was used from March to October 1916 by 'B' Flight of No.33 Squadron employed on Home Defence duties. After that period there was little activity and the field was abandoned after the war.

MURTON – E OF YORK (NOT SHOWN ON MAP)
This was a grassed landing area used by the Avro 504s of No. 76 Squadron. The site was abandoned after the Great War.

OWTHORNE –IMMEDIATELY E OF WITHERNSEA
This was an open grass field that came into use as a landing ground in 1917. During 1918 it was used by 506 Flight's DH6s on anti-submarine patrols. The site was abandoned after the Armistice.

PONTEFRACT – BETWEEN CASTLEFORD AND PONTEFRACT
This was a racecourse that became a ready-made airfield. The BE2cs of 'B' Flight, No.33 Squadron, operated from here during 1916 to be followed by No.76 Squadron. The airfield was abandoned after the Armistice.

REDCAR – ON THE OUTSKIRTS OF REDCAR
This was another racecourse turned airfield and used by the RNAS for training. The DH4s, BE2cs and Bristol Scouts of No.273 Squadron operated from Redcar on anti-submarine patrols. No.7 (Naval) Squadron and HPO/100s also operated on anti-submarine patrols. During 1918 'C' Flight of 252 Squadron with DH6s was employed on convoy escort duties. In 1918 the North Eastern Flying Instructors' School formed at Redcar and on 5 October No.63 Training Squadron came from Joyce Green. Both these units disbanded after the war and the airfield closed.

RIPON – SE OF RIPON
Ripon Racecourse was pressed into service and No.76 Squadron was formed there on 15 September 1916 using many of the local landing grounds already listed in this section. On 20 December 1917 No.189 Training Squadron formed here as a Night Training Unit, which moved to Sutton's Farm on 1 April 1918. In March 1919 No.76 Squadron moved to Tadcaster and the land was returned to the racing fraternity.

SEATON CAREW – S OF HARTLEPOOL
Seaton Carew was, in fact, two separate stations. In the Great War this was Seaton Carew Flight Station, 6 Brigade, and Seaton Carew (II) Marine Operations (Seaplane) Station. It was occupied by 'C' Flight, No.36 Squadron, on Home Defence duties flying BE2cs from the spring of 1916. The Seaton Carew area was attacked by the German airships *L30* and *L34*. The only Blackburn Kangaroos in RAF service were based here on No.246 Squadron. The seaplane station occupied seven acres on the northern foreshore of the Tees estuary. No.246 Squadron and 402/3 Flights were employed on anti-submarine patrols. Work to complete the station was scheduled to be completed by 31 December 1918 but all work stopped at the Armistice and both sites were quickly abandoned.

SHERBURN-IN-ELMET – 12 MILES E OF LEEDS
Sherburn-in-Elmet was used during the Great War as an RFC/RAF aircraft acceptance park. By 1918 there were eight hangars and storage sheds. The production of the Sopwith Cuckoo was centred here. The airfield was not retained after the war, although it was the home of the Yorkshire Aeroplane Club, which opened in January 1926.

TADCASTER – SW OF YORK
The airfield opened in the spring of 1916 with the arrival of 'B' Flight, No.33 Squadron, using BE2cs for the defence of Leeds and Sheffield. In December 1916 No.46 (Reserve) Squadron arrived from Doncaster and in April 1917 was joined by No.68 (Reserve) Squadron, to be followed by No.69 in October. No.46 RS moved to Catterick and on

15 July 1918 No.38 Training Depot Station was formed. In November 1918 No.94 Squadron arrived from Senlis, France, to be followed by No.76 Squadron in March 1919. When both these squadrons and the TDS were disbanded the airfield closed.

THIRSK, YORKSHIRE – ON THE W SIDE OF THIRSK
This was yet another racecourse used since they were ready-made airfields with little need for adaption. During 1916 No.76 Squadron RFC flew Avro 504s from the racecourse but there is no record of any further flying and it was returned to its original use.

THORNABY – W OF MIDDLESBROUGH
Thornaby was used as a 2nd class landing ground by No.36 Squadron during the Great War and abandoned thereafter.

THORNE, YORKSHIRE – SW OF GOOLE
Thorne was a grass field used during 1916 by 'A' Flight, No.33 Squadron, as a night-landing ground but was never developed

WEST AYTON, YORKSHIRE – W OF SCARBOROUGH
The site was the racecourse at Scarborough and was only one of two airfields in the area during the Great War. It was first used as a landing ground by the RNAS for BE2cs flying anti-Zeppelin patrols in 1916. Apart from this use the racecourse was little used until the end of the war. Towards the end of October 1918 DH6 aircraft of 510 Flight of No.251 Squadron RAF flew convoy and inshore reconnaissance duties at heights of only 1,000ft (according to the log book of one of the pilots). No.510 Flight departed in January 1919 and the site was not retained in the peacetime RAF.

WOMBWELL (BROOMHILL) YORKSHIRE
This was another site that was only a grass strip used as a night-landing ground by 'A' Flight, No.33 Squadron RFC, from March to October 1916 while on Home Defence duties.

AIRFIELDS AND SEAPLANE BASES OF SCOTLAND, NORTH EASTERN BRITAIN AND NORTHERN IRELAND

ALDERGROVE, ANTRIM – 4 MILES S OF ANTRIM
Aldergrove is the oldest military airfield in the Province and was opened in early 1918 as an aircraft acceptance park. The four-engined HP1500 bombers that were being produced at that time at Harland and Wolff were to be test flown from the airfield but there were teething troubles, which meant that no sooner had they been delivered for

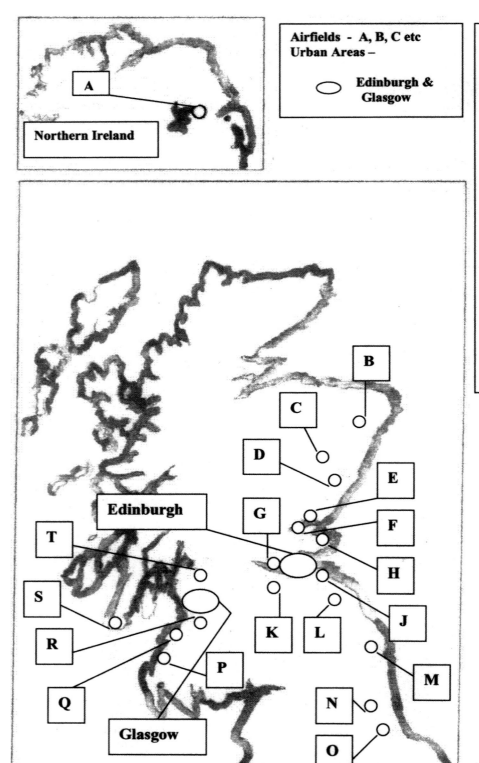

Airfields - A, B, C etc
Urban Areas –

Edinburgh & Glasgow

A   Aldergrove
B   Longside
C   Edzell
D   Montrose
E   Dundee
F   Leuchars
G   Donibristle
H   Crail
J   East Fortune
K   Turnhouse
L   Drem
M   Acklington
N   Cramlington
O   Usworth
P   Turnberry
Q   Loch Doon
R   Ayr
S   Macrihanish
T   Renfrew

Northern Ireland

Edinburgh

Glasgow

Airfields and seaplane bases of Scotland, North Eastern Britain and Northern Ireland.

squadron service than the Armistice had been signed. This bomber was designed to carry its bomb load from the UK to Berlin. The site of the airfield had been selected for military use in 1917 by Shalto Douglas (later Air Marshal). Although the airfield was closed in 1919 it was soon reopened when the RAF became involved in the Irish troubles and remained open thereafter.

ACKLINGTON, NORTHUMBERLAND – 3 MILES NE OF FELTON ON B6345
Known also as Southshields, the site was used as a landing ground by aircraft of No.77 Squadron during the Great War.

AYR (RACECOURSE) – JUST E OF STRATHCLYDE
Ayr (Racecourse) housed No.1 School of Aerial Fighting in 1917 but on 10 May 1918 it became No. 1 School of Aerial Fighting and Gunnery and it moved in July 1918 to be replaced by the NW Area Flying Instructors' School, which moved to Redcar in 1919. No further service use was recorded.

CRAIL, FIFE – 1 MILE NNE OF CRAIL
The aerodrome opened in July 1918 to house No.27 Training Depot Station. In August 1918 the Americans had a detachment of the 120 Aero Squadron. The only other use before closure in 1919 was to house No.104 Squadron from 3 March 1919 until its disbandment on 30 June.

CRAMLINGTON, NORTHUMBERLAND – 1 MILE W OF CRAMLINGTON
Cramlington airfield opened in 1916. Most units that used the airfield during the Great War were transient and its main use was as a night landing ground for Home Defence squadrons until the end of the war. Close to the aerodrome there was also an airship station. The airfield closed in 1919.

DONIBRISTLE, FIFE – 2 MILES E OF ROSYTHE
Donibristle survived the Great War and remained open until 1959. Its first use in 1917 was, like Acklington, as a landing ground for No.77 Squadron but it was later handed over to the RNAS as a naval air station accepting carrier-borne aircraft when the parent ship was in harbour and carrying out aircraft repairs. When the RNAS was absorbed into the RAF the station became a fleet repair depot.

DREM, LOTHIAN – 2 MILES S OF DIRLETON
Drem began life as a Home Defence landing ground for No.77 Squadron in 1916/1917, then known as West Fenton. No.2 TDS was formed on the airfield on 15 April 1918 flying Pups, Camels and SE5as. The American 41st Aero Squadron was also based at Drem from April to August 1918. When No.2 TDS was disbanded in 1919 the

airfield, renamed Gullane, remained unused until 1933.

DUNDEE (STANNERGATE) – 2 MILES E OF DUNDEE
Opened originally as a RNAS seaplane station in 1914 by 1918 it had developed into a multi-squadron RAF seaplane base housing Nos.249 and 257 Squadrons equipped with Short 184s, Felixstowe F2As, Curtiss H.16s and Fairey Babies. The base also acted as an aircraft acceptance park for seaplanes in 1918. When the squadrons were disbanded the base closed down probably in October 1919.

EAST FORTUNE LOTHIAN – 3 MILES NE OF HADDINGTON
Originally commissioned as a RNAS site on 23 August 1916, East Fortune's Avro 504s carried out coastal patrols. It then became an airship station housing Coastal Class and North Sea Class blimps. East Fortune is perhaps best remembered as the departure point for the first E-W transatlantic crossing by the R34 in July 1919 to a point near New York returning in August. The airfield was put up for disposal and closed on 5 February 1920.

EDZELL TAYSIDE AT BRIDGEND – 2 MILES NW OF A94
Edzell opened in 1918 and housed No. 26 TDS, which formed on July 15 for single-seat fighter training mainly using SE5as. In 1919 the unit disbanded and the station closed.

LEUCHARS, FIFE – 5 MILES NW OF ST ANDREWS
This airfield has a very long history dating back to balloon experimentation by the Royal Engineers in 1911. It was established as an RAF airfield and remained in use after the Great War. No.203 Squadron reformed on 1 March 1920, with Nightjars, together with No.205 Squadron equipped with Parnall Panthers. It will be recalled that RAF squadrons numbered in the 200 series were ex-RNAS flights combined to make up squadron strength.

LOCH DOON – ON THE SHORE OF LOCH DOON
In January 1917 the School of Aerial Gunnery was formed here to be joined by the School of Aerial Fighting. On disbandment of both these units Loch Doon closed immediately after the war.

LONGSIDE – 2 MILES S OF LONGSIDE
Longside was an airship patrol station from 1916 to 1918.

MACHRIHANISH – 3 MILES W OF CAMPBELTOWN
Machrihanish started life as a substation of the airship station at Luce Bay in August 1918 and was also the home station of No.272 Squadron equipped with DH6s, which flew coastal patrols over the River Clyde and over the Hebrides. The station closed when the squadron disbanded in 1918.

MONTROSE – 1 MILE N OF MONTROSE

This is Scotland's oldest military airfield, its connections with aviation dating back to 26 February 1913 when Montrose housed No.2 Squadron RFC's Longhorns and BE2as. During the Great War it was a training station and Nos.25, 80 and 83 Squadrons formed here. The American 41st Aero Squadron was on the station from March 1918 before moving to Gullane (Drem renamed). At the Armistice the airfield was abandoned, not to be reactivated until 1936 during the major RAF expansion.

RENFREW – STRATHCLYDE

Renfrew was used from 1915 for testing aircraft such as the FE2b and DH9. It was also home to the Beardmore Flying School between 1915 and 1918. From 1918 Renfrew was home to No.6 Aircraft Acceptance Park and No.6 (Scottish) Aircraft Repair Depot. The airfield remained dormant after the Great War until 15 September 1925 when No.602 Auxiliary Air Force Squadron was formed and DH9s, Fairey Fawns and Westland Wapitis flew from Renfrew for the rest of the decade.

TURNBERRY, STRATHCLYDE – 6 MILES N OF GIRVAN

Turnberry was first used in 1917 as the home of No.2 (Auxiliary) School of Aerial Gunnery renamed the No.1 School of Aerial Fighting and Gunnery in May 1918. It was quite commonplace in the Great War for units to undergo frequent changes of title following reorganizations to meet operational needs and the school was renamed No.1 Fighting School later that month. The airfield closed after the war.

TURNHOUSE, LOTHIAN – 5 MILES W OF EDINBURGH

Opened in 1916 as the home of No.26 Reserve Squadron, Turnhouse later housed 'A' Flight of No.77 HD Squadron. In July 1917 it was reduced to the status of a landing ground until No.73 TS moved in from Thetford in September. It then became a fleet practice station and fleet aircraft repair depot. After the war Turnhouse came alive again as home to the newly formed No.603 Auxiliary Squadron dating from 14 October 1925 equipped with DH9As.

USWORTH, NORTHUMBERLAND – 2 MILES SW OF BOLDON

During the Great War the airfield was known as Hylton and opened in October 1916 to house 'B' Flight of No.36 Squadron, then 'A' Flight of the same unit up to the Armistice when it also came to be called Usworth. Hylton/Usworth did not remain in service after the Great War but in 1930 the airfield was selected to house No.607 Auxiliary Air Force Squadron.

LIST OF AIRFIELDS, SEAPLANE BASES AND LANDING GROUNDS ON THE WESTERN FRONT (see page 275)

PERMANENT RAF AIRFIELDS ABROAD

ABU SUEIR EGYPT

Built on a site close to the Sweetwater Canal and the main Port Said railway it was first chosen in 1917 and used as a training base in the Great War. It was selected for retention after the Armistice and became No.4 FTS in April 1921 using Avro 504Ks for initial training and Bristol Fighters and DH9As for advanced courses.

CALAFRANA (KALAFRANA) MALTA

With German submarines threatening British shipping in the Mediterranean during the Great War it was deemed necessary to protect shipping routes between Gibraltar and the Aegean and the Admiralty authorized work on a seaplane base to commence at the end of January 1916. By July that year it was possible to station five Curtiss H4 flying boats at Calafrana to begin patrolling the approaches to Malta. They were effective in reporting enemy submarines to the convoys even if they did not sink the U-boats. In March 1917 three Short 184s arrived from Dundee to replace the existing boats. More 184s were added and two-seat FBA flying boats were flown in. With the formation of the RAF in 1918 No.268 Squadron was formed in the August and equipped with Short 184 and 320 float planes. After the Armistice No.268 Squadron was disbanded but No.267 Squadron, which had formed in October 1918, had, as its post-war role, aerial support for the Mediterranean Fleet.

Voisin bombers taking off from an airfield in France early in the war.

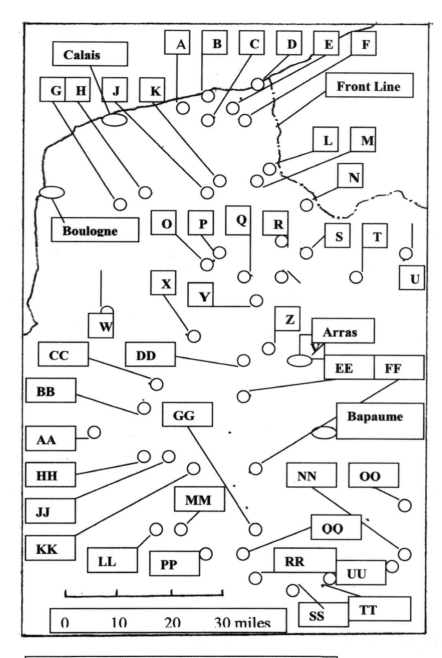

Western Front

A   Petite Synthe
B   St Pol, Dunkirk
C   Capelle
D   Bray Dunes
E   Teteghem
F   Bierne
G   Alquines
H   Boisdinghem
J   St Omer
K   Clairmarais
L   Droglandt
M   Ste Marie
N   Baileul
O   Serny
P   Liettres
Q   Lozighem
R   Merville
S   La Gorgue
T   Gondecourt
U   Ascq
V   Chocques
W   St André-aux-Bois
X   Beauvois/Humières
Y   Bruay
Z   Savy
AA Abbeville
BB Conteville
CC Auxi-le-Chateau
DD Izel le Hameau
EE La Bellevue
FF Marieux
GG Baizieux
HH Fienvillers
JJ Candas
KK Vert Galand
LL Bertangles
MM Poulainville
NN Estrées-en-Chausée
OO Longavesnes

The location of RFC Squadrons in early 1917 is shown in Chapter 4 page 102

Airfields, seaplane bases and landing grounds on the Western Front.

DRIGH ROAD, INDIA

An aircraft depot had been established in India in 1920 to undertake the assembly of aircraft shipped out from the United Kingdom and to undertake overhauls and engine repairs of aircraft on the inventory of squadrons. Moving from Lahore to Karachi (Drigh Road) in early 1921 the depot worked on DH9As, Bristol Fighters and later the Wapiti.

GIBRALTAR

The earliest military flying from Gibraltar was in 1915 when the Admiralty realized the importance of maintaining an aerial watch over the Straits, after all the German submarine *U21* was to sink two British battleships so seaplane reconnaissance was vital. A mix of 184s, Curtiss H4s and some landplanes came to Gibraltar and these early operations were hazardous given the notorious wind turbulence round the Rock. When the RAF took over the existing RNAS Nos.265, 266 and 364 Flights it formed them into No.265 Squadron, which flew 184s and Felixstowe F3s on anti-submarine patrols until the unit's disbandment in 1919. During the inter-war years the only service aircraft to visit the Rock were those disembarking from ships.

HELIOPOLIS, EGYPT

Heliopolis began life as an airfield in December 1915 with the arrival of No.17 Squadron's BE2cs. In 1916 the Australian Flying Corps arrived and their unit was numbered 67 Squadron RFC. No.14 Squadron also detached its BE2cs to Heliopolis during 1916 from its base at Ismailia. By the end of 1916 these squadrons and detachments had left. What was to become No.70 Squadron was then No.58 Squadron. The squadron came to Heliopolis on 2 May 1919 with HPO/400s, which were replaced with Vickers Vimys.

KOHAT, NORTH WEST FRONTIER OF INDIA

The use of Kohat as an airfield goes back to 1918 when BE2cs of No.31 Squadron called through with the mail. Between December 1921 and April 1923 the Bristol F2Bs of No.28 Squadron took up residence and were employed on air control operations. In 1925 the resident squadron was No.60 equipped with DH9As. Although an isolated North West Frontier base the squadron personnel enjoyed the facilities of an indoor swimming pool, bungalows for married personnel, tennis courts and a golf course.

KHORMAKSAR, ADEN

Khormaksar's career began in 1917 with the formation of the Aden Flight, tasked with reconnaissance since Turkish forces were threatening Aden and surrounding states. This involved aircraft of No.31 Squadron detached from India and these were later joined by aircraft from Quetta-based No.114 Squadron.

LAHORE, INDIA

In September 1917, No.114 Squadron was formed at Lahore to join No.31 Squadron on frontier patrols. In March 1916 the aircraft park, which had accompanied No.31 Squadron to India in 1915, had located at Risalpur. The aircraft park comprised an MT repair section, small stores, aircraft and engine repair facilities and a test and dispatch section. When No.97 Squadron arrived at Lahore in August 1919 it was tasked to support Army operations on the frontier. The considerable resources available in the park were used to form an aircraft depot at Karachi in February 1921.

Chapter 10
Personnel and Administration

Personnel matters – pre 1914 – Enrolment in the RNAS – Senior Commanders of the RFC and RNAS – Women's services – Great War air aces – personnel matters emanating from the Draft Air Force Act – personnel and administrative support for the IBF

INTRODUCTION

The entries concerning personnel matters before the commencement of the Great War provide an interesting insight into the changes in organization, particularly of training, for which there were no precedents. The air service in the form of the Flying Corps was a new service and that had come into existence in May 1912. It was divided into Military and Naval Wings. Later sections of this chapter will reveal the early schism in the new Corps when the Admiralty wanted to administer and man their own air service to meet purely naval needs. This became the Royal Naval Air Service (RNAS). Thus the Army Council came to administer and man the Military Wing of the Flying Corps only and hence it was known simply as the Royal Flying Corps. One of the first examples, which follows, shows the pre-war period when the Naval and Military Wings existed side by side. It is also significant that those who were to assume the top posts in the new air service had to come from the Army and the Navy and in 1912 very few of them had flown an aeroplane. There was also the question of to which service the pilots and ground crew should belong. Clearly those coming from civilian life into the RFC had no previous service in, say, Army regiments. But those who volunteered for flying duties by transfer from a regiment or corps, wore their regimental uniforms throughout the Great War. Be that as it may those who sought to remain in the flying service would wish to follow a flying career and be promoted from amongst those in the new service. This matter is the subject of the paragraph that follows.

Considerations concerning the personnel of the Royal Flying Corps
Source: National Archive document WO18/RFC/3 (FC)

It must be understood that on the formation of the RFC the legislation bringing the new air service into being spoke of the Royal Flying Corps (divided into two wings) and a Central Flying School to provide pilots. Hence all personnel questions concerned just these two organizations. On 15 November 1912 the War Office asked the Air Committee to consider certain questions in relation to the personnel of the Royal Flying Corps. The first concerned periodical exchanges between petty officers and non-commissioned officers, and the men of the CFS and those serving with the Naval and Military Wings. If these exchanges were thought to be desirable the Air Committee was invited by the Army Council to give their opinion as to how this might be carried out. The former believed that such exchanges should be made in giving a wider experience amongst personnel of the Corps. Personnel should not remain on the staff of the CFS for a period longer than two consecutive years except the original staff, of whom one-fourth should be relieved at the end of two years and another fourth at the end of each succeeding quarter. It was considered that all subsequent reliefs should be made quarterly. The second question from the Army Council concerned the promotion up to and inclusive of the rank of petty officer or sergeant to fill vacancies at the CFS. Should they be made by the Commandant from the men serving at the schools (of flying) or should all vacancies in the military establishment of the RFC, whether at the CFS or the wing, be made from a common roll of those recommended for promotion? The Air Committee favoured the common roll approach since it had the advantages of requiring the closest collaboration between the Commandant CFS and the Officer Commanding the Military Wing and it also meant that there was less likelihood of stagnation in promotion in either establishment, which might arise due to a lack of vacancies. The Air Committee believed that this system should be effected immediately and as soon as the organization of naval personnel allowed the scheme should be applied to the Naval Wing. The Army Council finally requested that the 'common roll' approach should be applied to promotions above the above the rank of petty officer and sergeant. The Committee agreed that it should.

Aircrew joining the Flying Corps in the period immediately before the Great War
Source: AIR1/363/231/3

Introduction

Correspondence between the Director of Military Training from the formation of the Flying Corps to the outbreak of the Great War makes interesting reading, highlighting the qualifications required, standards reached by aspirant pilots, pay and period of service for which the recruit wished to be engaged. At this very early stage in the development of aviation, even before aircraft were used in a major war, Britain wished to ensure that it had identified and prepared a sufficient number of pilots should there be mobilization given similar preparations for war by a potential enemy. A list of officers selected to attend for pilot training at CFS Upavon on 17 September 1913 is shown at Appendix N and may be of interest to descendents of these officers. It shows the variety of regiments, Corps and staff appointments from which the pupil pilots were selected. One of them was a 2nd Lieutenant Corbett-Wilson of Kilkenny in Ireland who was asked to explain reports of his flying over prohibited areas. No doubt his attendance on the course would put this officer straight about where he could and could not fly an aeroplane (see letter referred to below). Many of the letters from the Director of Military Training in 1913 were signed by a staff officer named Captain E.L. Ellington, who would, in the 1930s, rise in rank to become Chief of the Air Staff of the RAF.

Letters from Director of Military Training

A letter written by Ellington dated 16 July 1913 is to a recruit who wants to know if an aviator's certificate awarded in the United States was acceptable for service in the Flying Corps. He was advised that it would be acceptable for a recruit on probation with the Special Reserve of Officers of the Royal Flying Corps. The same would apply whether it would be for reserve or continuous service. This would equate to what would later be called permanent commissions and reserve or auxiliary commissions. Should the applicant wish to obtain a pilot's certificate with the Royal Aero Club this would be at a cost of £75. If a pilot's certificate was obtained in this manner and the applicant had been accepted on probation the applicant could receive a grant to cover the cost of the course from public funds. But the grant would have to be repaid if the applicant did not complete a thirteen-week course at the Central Flying School, proved unsuitable for service as a pilot or failed to complete four years' service with the RFC or the Reserve. Since the applicant was then residing in Canada he was advised that if he was posted to continuous service to the Military Wing of the Flying Corps or for service with the 1st Reserve it would be necessary for him to reside in the United Kingdom. If he wished to return to Canada he would be placed on the 2nd Reserve and required to repay the £75 grant for his aviation certificate. Finally, he was advised that even if his performance at the Central Flying School merited a recommendation for acceptance on a continuous basis he could be guaranteed only four years' service after training.

A letter, dated 14 July 1913, contained the general conditions of service and rates of pay in the Royal Flying Corps together with a short guide to obtaining a commission in the Special Reserve for which residence in the United Kingdom was required. If and when an officer was appointed to the Reserve of the Flying Corps

he must perform a quarterly test every three months. One applicant, an officer employed in West Africa under the Colonial Office, was not in a position to undertake the conditions of service in the Reserve of the Flying Corps. Another interesting letter was written by Captain G.M. Paine, Commandant of the Central Flying School, Upavon, on 15 July 1913. The letter 43/F.S./72 was addressed to Department MT4. In the letter he explains why he had requested that three under instruction at CFS should be withdrawn from the flying course, doubting that they would ever become 1st class pilots. They were Lieutenant G.H.V. Hathorne RMLI, Sub Lieutenant R.A. King RNR and 2nd Lieutenant H.D. Cutler RFC (SR). He had granted the three officers leave pending a decision. Their conduct, zeal and keenness were not in question, simply their flying ability. Paine added that these officers may be of use in time of war as 2nd Reserve pilots.

On 3 July 1917 Ellington wrote a letter to the Commandant of the Central Flying School on the subject of quarterly tests for pilots on the Reserve of the Royal Flying Corps. Officers serving as both Regular and Reserve officers had to be in regular flying practice; Reserve officers could well not be. It was essential in the event of an emergency call up that such pilots could man service flying units in the shortest possible time. Captain Ellington said that the provisional regulation provided for a quarterly test consisting of nine hours' flying including a cross-country flight had not, for various reasons proved feasible. It placed unnecessarily high demands on officers who were already flyers of some experience. He wished for the Commandant's views on his proposal for a shorter test but one involving greater skill. Every Reserve pilot in the military wing of the Flying Corps would face a flying test once a quarter. The test would be a triangular cross-country course covering a distance of not less than 60 miles with a landing from 1,500ft by means of a spiral volplane (with the engine shut off). To prepare pilots for this test they should be permitted to fly for any period of up to eight hours during each quarter. Practice flying and tests could be conducted at the CFS, a station of the Military Wing or civil aerodrome on a private or hired aeroplane. A pilot would enter all practice flying and tests in his log book using the system popular with officers of the Military Wing. Entries in the log book would be certified by an officer of the Regular Army, the Reserve or a member of the Royal Aero Club. These arrangements were clearly intended to cater for pilots in locations far removed from CFS and who were employed in other trades or professions. The Army would do its best to make arrangements for tests and practice flying to be carried out at a location of the individual pilot's choice but if that was not possible reserved the right to insist that the individual go to CFS or a station of the Military Wing. The type of aeroplane it was proposed to use for practice flying and tests had to be stated.

A letter from Ellington to Lieutenant A.A.B. Thomson in the Special Reserve and residing at No.4 the Marine Parade, Eastbourne, is dated 26 July 1913. The letter spelt out the grants payable and allowable expenses. For an officer who had paid £75 for an aviator's certificate from the Royal Aero Club a grant was payable. He was reminded of the requirement in Special Army Order dated 15 April 1912 that the grant would be repayable if the officer chose to leave the RFC before the completion of four years' service. A form 0.1670 was enclosed in regard to the grant of outfit allowance, which once completed, had to be sent to the Command Paymaster, Southern Command, Salisbury. The Lieutenant was to provide himself with the overcoat and undress uniform of the RFC (Military Wing) patterns of which could be seen at the Pattern Room of the War Office. On the same day Ellington wrote to an officer of the Military Wing of the Flying Corps who wished to transfer to the Naval Wing as an officer in the Royal Naval Reserve. Since he had already received his uniform allowance of £40 from Army funds he would be required to kit himself out in naval uniform at his own expense.

Lieutenant D. Corbett-Wilson of the Royal Flying Corps Special Reserve received a letter, dated 3 July 1913, at his address in Kilkenny Ireland asking for an explanation in writing, without delay, for flying offences contrary to the Aerial Navigation Act. He was apparently seen flying east to west at 05.40hrs on Saturday 14 June over Chatham dockyard, and again over the villages of St Helens and Bembridge, at 07.45hrs on Thursday 26 June 1913, both in the prohibited areas. On the same day at Bembridge, he was also seen landing opposite the Coast Guard station within the prohibited area of Spithead and Culver Cliff Signal Station. He was commanded to inform the Army Council if he was indeed guilty of these prohibited flying practices.

Another letter of interest is from Ellington to the Officer Commanding the Military Wing at South Farnborough who was being granted authority to spend a sum of money not exceeding £250 to cover travelling expenses and allowances for both officers and men in connection with visits to the works of aeroplane manufacturers. If the works were on the Continent, travel was to be by the cheapest route. This arrangement covered one financial year and was to come from Vote 6.e.2 for visits at home and from 6.e.5 for visits abroad.

Division of Military and Naval Flying

The Commandant of the Central Flying School Upavon was a naval officer, Captain Godfrey Paine, responsible for flying courses for aviators from both the Army and the Navy and Trenchard was appointed his adjutant. It was soon apparent that what the Army required of its 133 pilots from the Military Wing was the provision of reconnaissance when the Naval Wing of the Royal Flying

Corps was still experimenting with the use of aircraft in naval tactics. The Navy initially required only between thirty and forty officers to be pilot trained. The war establishment of the Military Wing was to be 364 pilots, approximately half officers and half NCOs. When the Admiralty decided that naval flying should develop along lines that diverged from military flying the term 'Naval Wing' was dropped and the title Royal Naval Air Service was substituted. The term 'Military Wing' was no longer required and the term Royal Flying Corps was applied only to Army flying. The division of the two flying services, one which came under the War Office and the other the Admiralty meant that personnel matters were separated including recruitment and training. In August 1913 Brigadier General Sir David Henderson, already Director of Military Training, was appointed Director General of the Military Aeronautics Directorate. He was substantially the Chief of the Royal Flying Corps.

ENROLMENT IN THE RNAS
Source: National Archive document AIR1/363/231/3,
Regulations for the Special Entry of Officers into the RNAS
(revised August 1916)

Officers' enrolment
Entry to the RNAS was open to officers serving afloat and officers of the marines, RN Reserve, RN Volunteer Reserve as well as officers on the retired, emergency or half pay lists. Civilians were eligible to enter the RNAS as officers under the terms of special regulations and would be gazetted as flight sub lieutenants Royal Navy on entry but were on probation until they had qualified in all respects. Existing RN officers were not eligible for selection until they had completed one year's service as commissioned officers, or in the case of warrant officers, until they had received confirmation in their rank. Similarly, officers of the Royal Marines were not selected until they had completed their courses. There was, of course, the matter of those who had already paid for pilot training and obtained a Royal Aero Club certificate and the matter of lodging allowance for officers who were receiving flying training at their own expense. One can see that the Admiralty was keen to acquire, on the personnel strength of the Navy, those who were qualified aviators although at this stage they had not been tested in battle. They were aviators who specialized in airships, seaplanes, kites and aeroplanes. They could be required to serve both at home and abroad not simply as pilots but also in an administrative capacity and on constructional work.

Having qualified for work in the RNAS officers needed to know the terms of service for which they had engaged. Some saw a career in flying whilst others wished to return at some point to seamen's service, particularly if they wished to be promoted to the higher ranks of the

Navy. Those who did so would have the added bonus that they understood the needs of the air service and how best to commit it to battle. The period of service for officers drawn from the active list of the Royal Navy had to be limited by their flying efficiency. In any event it would not exceed four years. There were those who would be needed for promotion to the higher ranks of the RNAS; the others were to return to Fleet duties after four years but could, at some future date, return to the RNAS at the discretion of the Admiralty. Unless their term of service exceeded four years officers in this category were to pass into the Reserve. There were various schemes whereby officers could extend the time on the active list. A lot would depend on military requirements since any service manning policy had to be flexible. It had also become necessary to create rank titles which reflected the responsibilities of officers in the RNAS and to declare their relativity with ranks in the RN. This was important also for career and promotion prospects:

RNAS Rank	Relative RN Rank
Wing captain	Captain
Wing commander	Commander
Squadron commander (when in command)	Lieutenant commander
Squadron commander (when not in command)	Lieutenant over four years seniority but senior to all flight commanders
	On attaining eight years seniority in the relative rank of lieutenant, these officers will rank with lieutenant commanders RN
Flight commander	Lieutenant over four year's seniority
Flight lieutenant	Lieutenant
Flight sub lieutenant	Sub lieutenant
Warrant officer 1st grade	Commissioned warrant officer
Warrant officer 2nd grade	Warrant officer

Officers employed on specialist duties, such as gunnery, torpedo or engineering, were graded in the above ranks with an added suffix, (G),(T), (N) or (E), as appropriate.

Candidates on appointment as Probationary Flight Officers RN were appointed to undergo a four-month course at one of the RNAS instructional establishments, which consisted of practical and theoretical instruction in various branches of air work. Graduation depended upon qualification in the following subjects:

a. Flying ability (including cross-country and long-distance flying)
b. Aerial engines and construction of aircraft
c. Navigation (including charts and compasses, map reading and meteorology)
d. Gunnery (including bomb sights, aerial guns, rifle and squad drill)
e. Wireless telegraph signals and aerial photography

Officers were required to obtain 85 per cent of marks in any one group of subjects to qualify for a 1st Class Certificate for thagGroup with 60 per cent being the minimum to qualify in that group and seniority in the rank would be determined by the number of 1st Class Certificates obtained in any one group, e.g. navigation. Failure to obtain at least the minimum standard would mean further training and re-examination after one month. On completion of the school course a pilot would be attached to an air station or cruiser and would be required to undertake an advanced course in seaplane, aeroplane or airship work, during which time he would be taught such naval matters as machine gun drill, seamanship and boat work.

Enrolment of ratings

All classes of ratings on the active list were eligible for selection for the RNAS. A character assessment of 'very good' was required and commanding officers had to satisfy themselves, when forwarding the names of volunteers, that applicants were likely to prove suitable with regard to education, general intelligence and quickness. Applications went to the office of the Director of the Air Department of the Admiralty. Men on the active list were required to remain for four years in the RNAS, after which they could return to their duties in the Fleet but were eligible for re-selection at the discretion of the Admiralty. Civilians were also invited to apply as mechanics etc., and were required to enlist for four years followed by four years in the RN Air Service Reserve. The selection of a man for service with the RNAS did not mean that he could rely on being trained as a pilot. Those selected for flying training would be from those who had already joined the Air Service. Candidates had to be of pure European descent and the sons either of natural born or naturalized British subjects. In doubtful cases the burden of proof laid with the candidate.

Senior Commanders of the RFC and RNAS
Sources: Various

The senior commanders of both the RFC and the RNAS had to come from the established services and they came to the air service with their military and naval training The army officers might be artillerymen, cavalrymen, infanteers or engineers. Since the Royal Engineers were given the task of forming the first aerial units using balloons and later airships it is natural that officers from that branch of the Army should feature amongst the senior ranks of the new flying services. If naval they could be officers of any branch. The earliest commanders may have diverse military backgrounds but they all shared an enthusiasm for aeronautics and aerial warfare. What is remarkable is that they learned to fly either on the eve of the Great War, or after the war had actually started. It was difficult for any of these men to have qualified as pilots any earlier given the fact that powered aircraft were still a very recent invention. So the reader must not be surprised to learn that no sooner had an officer qualified as a pilot than he might be appointed as an instructor. The officer who was appointed to command the Central Flying School, for example, was instructed to go away and qualify as a pilot before taking up his post. In those early days a service officer would have to acquire the Royal Aero Club's certificate learning to fly at a school such as that of Tom Sopwith at Brooklands. They then went to the Central Flying School.

The examples that follow illustrate the claim that these men had on the positions that they held. Sir David Henderson, who was the first commander of the RFC, did not qualify as a pilot until 1911. He joined the Army as an infanteer with the Argyle and Sutherland Highlanders and gained experience in intelligence. He was taught to fly by Captain Howard Pixton who described him as a born flyer. When the government decided that plans should be made for the development of British air power David Henderson was appointed as a military representative to the subcommittee chaired by Colonel Seely. Lieutenant Colonel F.H. Sykes who became, for a brief period, the Chief of the Air Staff of the RAF and was also a member of Seely's subcommittee, was a cavalryman who served in India and South Africa, attended staff college and was appointed, as a lieutenant colonel, to the post of Officer Commanding the Military Wing of the Flying Corps in May 1912 having qualified as a pilot. Hugh Trenchard, who was to become the Chief of the Air Staff of the RAF from 1920 until 1929, was commissioned into the Royal Scots Fusiliers with combat experience in South Africa where injury left him with a damaged lung. This was hardly the physical attribute required of a pilot, yet he qualified to fly in August 1912 at the Central Flying School. Two months later he was a flying instructor and, in less than a year was appointed Assistant Commandant of the CFS. During the war he was appointed as Commander of the RFC in France and then Commander of the Independent Bombing Force in the dying months of the war. He completed his service career as Chief of the Air Staff of the RAF from 1920 until 1929. The career of Edward Ellington was remarkable. He was commissioned into the Royal Artillery in 1897, and attended the War College, Portsmouth as a captain in 1908. In 1913 he was appointed as a staff officer in the Directorate of Military Aeronautics in the War Office having qualified as a pilot in 1912 together with

Trenchard. But he left aeronautics to serve in a variety of staff appointments during the early part of the Great War before returning to aviation as the Deputy Director General of Military Aeronautics. By the time of the War's end he had not commanded a single flying unit nor fought in the air. He had spent his entire service thus far in staff appointments. His value to the air service was in helping Trenchard, who had been appointed Chief of the Air Staff (CAS), to establish the structure of the RAF. On reaching air rank he commanded RAF formations overseas and was appointed CAS on 1 January 1933 having spent virtually his entire career behind a desk. John Salmond, Cyril Newall and Charles Portal would have distinguished flying careers during the Great War and would bring their experience and expertise to the senior command positions of the RAF. Naval officers who were amongst the earliest aviators were Lieutenants C.R. Samson, R. Gregory and A/M Longmore together with Captain E.L. Gerrard, Royal Marines. They learned to fly at Eastchurch, which was to become the centre of naval aviation.

RFC AND RNAS UNIFORMS

RFC officers' uniforms

Officers of the RFC would have been commissioned into an infantry, artillery or cavalry regiment or perhaps the Royal Engineers. Others will have entered the service direct from civilian life; the former therefore already had a service jacket, whereas the latter would have none other than an RFC uniform, which was nicknamed the 'maternity jacket'. This was worn with breeches, ankle boots and puttees. The result on RFC squadrons could be a profusion of different uniforms. Some officers preferred to wear out their regimental uniforms but had the choice to wear the official rig. So one might have seen officers

The 'maternity' jacket.

Fur flying boots.

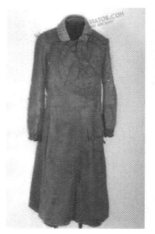

Flying coat.

RFC helmet and goggles.

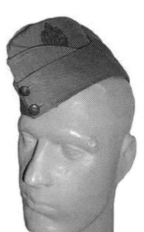

RFC forage cap.

RFC Wings.

RFC wrist compass.

wearing trews. The headdress could be the RFC forage cap, service dress cap or Glengarry. The RFC wings would be worn on the RFC tunic as shown in the photograph or might be worn on the regimental service dress. In the air, particularly in cold weather, fur boots could be worn as well as the RFC coat. Again, it was very much a matter of personal preference. With open cockpits, which remained the norm almost to the outbreak of World War II, keeping warm was important.

This may be contrasted with the dress of French pilots. Their uniforms showed flair, one might say flamboyance. They wore a black pea-jacket, khaki tunic or light blue dolman, red breeches with sky-blue stripes, black with scarlet stripes and complete uniforms of iron grey, hard or soft caps, red tarbushes, with plumage worn by some colonial regiments, berets and silk ties.

RNAS pilots

RNAS pilots wore brass (gilt) eagles of the standard pattern. They were worn in a variety of ways depending upon the uniform. The wings worn on the navy blue jacket were above the loop of the rank braid as shown in the photograph on the right with the eagle facing backwards as seen from the front or on shoulder boards attached to the white uniform. Until 1917 the wings were worn only on the left sleeve but were then worn on both sleeves with the eagles facing to the rear. With KD (khaki drill) uniform worn overseas the flying badge was pinned to the tunic above the left breast pocket and medal ribbons if worn and local jewellers devised a pin to the back of the eagle with the eagle facing to the right as viewed from the front. Removal of the eagle and medal ribbons was necessary when garments went for cleaning. In 1918 the RNAS was merged with the RFC

January 1916.

Note pilot's wings on left sleeve.

AMII Carter (driver).

RNAS ratings uniform.

RNAS officers' cap badge.

to form the RAF when the standard pattern consisted of a small gilt crown worn on both sleeves and a third eagle embedded in the crown in the centre of the cap as shown in the photograph.

WOMEN'S SERVICES
Source: History of the enrolled Women's Services

Introduction
Prior to the Great War the only involvement of women in warfare was in providing nursing services. This dated from 1854 and the work of Florence Nightingale and her nurses in the Crimea but in 1915 it was recognized that women could play a greater part in the deployment of armed forces and the Women's Legion initiated the next phase of women's service. The supply of men trained in Army schools in cookery was far too small and recruits with experience of cookery were insufficient to meet the demand. There was food waste, bad management and unattractive meals and Lady Londonderry inaugurated a cookery section of the Women's Legion and undertook to provide the necessary personnel. With the agreement of the Army Council work began in a large kitchen in the Convalescent Camp at Dartford. This proved successful and was followed by sixty cooks serving in the kitchens of the Eastbourne Convalescent Camp with twenty more going to Epsom. By July 1916 there were women working as cooks and waitresses in all officers' messes where men who were physically fit could be released for other duties. (As a matter of interest the wives of men who could then be released for active service called the female volunteers 'murderers'.) This was followed by the Army Council's agreement that the Legion could have motor transport sections.

Queen Mary's Army Auxiliary Corps (QMAAC)
As the war progressed the supplies of manpower were becoming acute. Since conscription had yet to be introduced the requirement for fighting men at the Front meant that having women working behind the lines in France released men for military deployment and in February 1917 the Army Council decided to constitute a body of women for service with the BEF. Behind the lines there were depots, stores, offices, ammunition dumps and lorry parks that could be manned in part by women. Additionally, there were airfields and aircraft depots that were subdivided into administrative areas based on convenient towns, which were generally ports. It was here that members of the Queen Mary's Army Auxiliary Corps were employed. There were two Controllers; the senior was Mrs M. Chalmers-Watson MD who was responsible for recruiting and organization and the junior was Mrs H.C.I. Gwynne-Vaughan DSc, responsible for service with the armies in France.

On 17 March 1917 the first draft of the Women's Army Auxiliary Corps arrived for service in France. Many were old members of the Women's Legion. They worked as cooks and waitresses and on 7 April a draft of female clerks arrived reporting for duty working under the Directorate of Forestry. They worked hard and wanted to show that they could suffer, if necessary, the same discomforts of the men and later that year some were subjected to an air raid when they remained on duty but higher authority felt that they should not be singled out for their devotion to duty since the men did not receive the same distinction. In the July the women in the Corps were assigned to duties in the United Kingdom. In February 1918 Mrs Chalmers-Watson retired and her place was taken by Mrs (later Dame) Leach who was appointed Chief Controller at home. She then became

Women ambulance drivers, WWI.

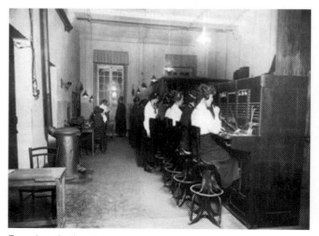
Female telephonists.

Controller-in-Chief of the newly named QMAAC, a contingent of which was working with the American Army. By this time women were working as telephonists, telegraphists, bakers and gardeners.

When the war became much more fluid in the spring of 1918 the women became used to working under the stress of retreat, then advance and learned the value of drill, being prepared to march when mechanical transport was not available and were prepared to carry their own kit on the march. The cooks were able to switch from cooking in army schools to preparing food for reinforcements at base. Some of the women who did not desert their posts when subjected to bombing, were awarded the Military Medal.

The Women's Royal Naval Air Service (WRNS)

The WRNS was formed in November 1917 under the direction of Dame Katherine Furze GBE, RRC to facilitate the substitution of women for the naval ranks and ratings in certain branches administered by the Admiralty, including the Royal Navy, the Royal Marines and the RNAS. The service was organized on a territorial basis, the most important of which were Portsmouth, Chatham, Devonport, London, Scotland, Ireland and the Mediterranean. The female ratings were classified as 'immobiles', which meant that they could not be posted away from their homes, and 'mobiles' who were accommodated in hostels or other approved accommodation in the care of WRNS officers. WRNS administrative officers were trained for a period of

WRAF riggers.

four weeks at Crystal Palace in drill, lectures on naval tradition and organization and much practical work. Non-administrative officers were trained in decoding and deciphering at the School of Signals, Portsmouth, whilst technical training of a confidential nature was given to those required to replace naval officers in special ports. The ratings undertook clerical work at naval depots and marine establishments. They acted as signallers, doing watches, and in one case a woman was entirely responsible for giving routes to ships, all cables being in code. Many were wireless telegraphists. Few worked afloat, though occasions arose where they performed clerical duties on ships in harbour. Technical work included sail making, cleaning torpedoes, making gas masks and depth charges and making mine nets.

The Women's Royal Air Force (WRAF)

During the Great War women had been employed with units of the RFC and the RNAS so that when the Royal Air Force was formed on 1 April 1918 these two services were combined into the new service. This meant that there was a nucleus of female personnel to form the WRAF. The first Chief Superintendent was Lady Gertrude Crawford who was succeeded in May 1918 by the Hon. Violet Douglas-Pennant as Commandant who was in turn succeeded by Mrs H.C.I. Gwynne-Vaughan CBE. All ranks of the WRAF undertook to serve for a year or the duration of the war, whichever was the longer period. A considerable number of the other ranks were 'immobiles', which meant that they served in the neighbourhood of their homes. Their direct value to the service was obviously less than for the 'mobiles' but they nevertheless released men for active service with the RAF. The range of trades in which women were occupied was wide, from cooks and orderlies to dispatch riders, painters and dopers, fabric workers, acetylene welders, carpenters, photographers

Navy Department Office, 1918.

WRAF uniform.

and drivers. At the most westerly air station in Britain a 'pigeon woman' looked after the carrier pigeons and helped in their war training.

In October 1918 it was decided to detail a contingent for service with the Independent Bombing Force but the Armistice in November 1918 prevented their dispatch and it was not until 25 March 1919 that the first overseas draft of women embarked for service with the RAF in the field. In September 1918 an order was issued by the Air Council that all communications in respect of the WRAF should be through the usual RAF channels, which meant women officers being able to deal correctly with official RAF correspondence and to work as nearly as possible on RAF lines. The WRAF did not possess a separate HQ but was administered by a staff of WRAF officers at the Air Ministry.

GREAT WAR AIR ACES

Sources: *The First Great Air War* by Richard Townshend Bickers, Purnell's history of the world wars

Introduction

We cannot say that the service was led by outstanding flyers. Air Marshal Trenchard was the commander of the RFC in France in the Great War, i.e., the commander of the squadrons from which the aces came, and commander of the Independent Bombing Force in 1918. He had only one effective lung following a bullet wound sustained whilst fighting the Boers in South Africa. When he qualified to fly at the Central Flying School he was an indifferent pilot and an even poorer instructor. He was an academic failure and inarticulate but his strength was administration and organization. His subordinates regarded him as a 'Pole Star' in seeing the way ahead. Air Marshal Ellington, like Trenchard, became holder of the post of Chief of the Air Staff. Once Ellington qualified as a pilot he became deskbound. Such men led the RAF in those early years and into the 1920s.

One must not believe that all the senior commanders were not successful in leading men in aerial combat and John Salmond, Cyril Newall and Charles Portal come into mind in this respect. But the war in the air was fought by young men, some of whom were outstanding pilots. There was a conflict of opinion about heralding the achievements of the fighter pilots during the Great War. Elsewhere in this work mention has been made of Corps and Army pilots. The former were those who flew reconnaissance and artillery co-operation missions so important to the success of land operations. It was the job of those called 'Army pilots' to keep the sky clear of enemy aircraft so that the Corps pilots could get on with their work unhindered. Some individual commanders were loathe to heap rewards on the aces with high scores since they believed that successful air operations depended critically on team work. Corps pilots were in danger of becoming the unsung heroes. On the other hand, tales of bravery in the air and enemy aircraft destroyed were very important for public morale. People at home needed heroes.

Inevitably, the Army pilots would seek out their prey even when there were no friendly aircraft to protect and clocking up a tally of enemy aircraft destroyed became an end in itself. Some pilots were permitted to personalize their own aircraft, which might be armed to suit themselves, and they were permitted to fly off on their own in pursuit of the enemy. The French and Germans had their medals for the number of 'kills', e.g. the Blue Max or Pour le Mérite. Some years ago a film starring George Peppard, *The Blue Max*, featured a German fighter pilot who came from humble origins and who did not care what it took to win the Blue Max even if it meant putting his own war before the needs of his unit, his friends or his country. Be that as it may overall the commanders on both sides were not inclined to limit the honours that could be conferred upon these 'knights of the air'. In Britain the Distinguished Flying Cross replaced the Military Cross for airmen who had acted with bravery and daring in the air.

There are others whose names are equally worthy of inclusion in this section but space forbids. One is Major Raymond Collishaw who survived the war and went on to fight alongside Russian White forces until the victory of the Bolsheviks resulted in the withdrawal of the British contingent. (His exploits in Russia appear in Volume I of this author's inter-war history of the RAF.) Andrew Beauchamp Proctor and William Barker also belong to a list of aces. The achievements of these men, particularly those described below eventually spread and influenced training and tactics adopted by other units. By 1918, however, the air aces had had their day and during the Allied offensives of the last year of the war, the air war had become a total effort of professional pilots. There was less time for individuals to go 'swanning off' on their own.

What follows is a short description of four aces to discover what sort of men they were and the tactics they adopted.

Edward 'Mick' Mannock

Major Edward Mannock served with three squadrons, Nos.40, 74 and 85, and scored 73 victories. Like Trenchard he was not devoid of medical problems. Having been repatriated from Turkey in 1915 where he had been very

Edward 'Mick' Mannock.

ill, he joined the Royal Army Medical Corps then the Royal Engineers. A congenital defect left him virtually blind in his left eye. This would hardly contribute to success in aerial combat. In spite of this he was accepted for training in the RFC in 1917 and his progress was scrutinized by James McCudden, who also features in this section.

He got off to a slow start with his peers on No.40 Squadron and he seemed over cautious in the air. His first victory was against a balloon on 7 May. But whilst aces Bishop and Collishaw were inflicting considerable damage on the enemy, Mannock was still striving to establish himself in the regard of his peers. Emulating the aces he would load his own ammunition drums and spent hours making repeated dives at ground targets but when he boasted that he could open fire from twenty yards he only added to the dislike. On the other hand he did appear to have a conscience and disliked pilots who used incendiary rounds since it would most probably cause the pilot of a machine hit in the petrol tank to be incinerated. These were the days when British pilots had no option but to shoot themselves if their aircraft caught fire since parachutes were not issued during the Great War. Mannock's determination to succeed in aerial combat eventually bore fruit and as a flight commander on No.74 Squadron he scored thirty-five victories in SE5as and replaced Bishop as squadron commander of No.85 Squadron on 3 July 1918. He did not achieve the public notoriety of a lower-scoring ace, Albert Ball, but he did become a respected leader of his men in the air.

Mannock spent some time in England on instructional duties and he was awarded an MC and bar. He met General Henderson whilst in London and having complained about boredom got himself posted to No.74 Squadron, which was working up for France. The squadron arrived in France on the day that the RAF was formed, 1 April 1918.

He may have been boring in conversation but he was analytical in his approach to air fighting and would help the new pilots by going through aerial engagements and he was very concerned about the effects of British losses on them. This was particularly the case when pilots had been lost through incineration and Mannock became obsessed by the sight and stench of burning aircraft and he is best described as a manic depressive. He would be the life and soul of a party and gave stirring speeches, particularly in honour of the British dead but could become depressed and full of foreboding. This happened when he heard of the death of McCudden. Often physically ill before going on patrol, Mannock was known to share victories with other pilots or didn't bother submitting claims for enemy aircraft he'd shot down in combat. For example, he shared a kill with a New Zealander who was a newcomer to the unit and had not scored any victories to date. Mannock was later shot down by machine gun fire from the ground and his aircraft was in flames. He had a score of seventy-three victories and was awarded a posthumous VC on 11 July 1919.

Lieutenant Colonel William Bishop

Unlike Mannock, Bishop had extraordinary eyesight and he became a crack shot. He was trained as a Canadian Army officer and transferred to the RFC in December 1915. Initially he served as an observer but didn't like being tossed around in the back of an RE7, preferring to be in control. When he was returned to England following a knee injury he managed to get on to a flying course and, as a pilot, joined No.37 (Home Defence) Squadron where he did a lot of night flying. He nevertheless wanted a taste of action on the Western Front and after volunteering he was posted to No.60 Squadron, equipped with Nieuport 17 fighters. It was not uncommon for newcomers to be given a machine with less performance and on his first patrol he became separated from the others. When he did rejoin the others they were bating a German reconnaissance machine known as the Flying Pig. This bumbling machine was too easy a target and it became a point of honour not to shoot these aircraft down but merriment could be had in watching the hapless observer loosing off rounds at a ridiculously long range.

Having scored his first kill he next led a patrol but was duped. On seeing a lone enemy aircraft below Bishop led the attack but as soon as the RFC aircraft began the dive they were suddenly pounced on from above. After a largely fruitless battle between two groups of aircraft the

Lt Col William 'Billy' Bishop.

patrol returned without two of its Nieuports. Bishop had learned an important lesson the hard way. On 7 April he was ordered to attack a balloon but was not to descend below 1,000ft. He began firing at 500ft and had descended to only 50ft when a 37mm cannon opened up on him. He was lucky to escape with his life and after his engine cut he managed to restart it and flew home through machine gun fire. For this exploit he was congratulated both by his Wing and Brigade Commander and received a letter of commendation from Trenchard. By the end of 'Bloody April' Bishop had shot down at least twelve enemy aircraft and he was promoted to the rank of captain.

Bishop's attitude towards the killing of the enemy was compared by Townshend Bickers to that of the German ace, Richthofen. The former hated Germans for deliberately starting the war whereas the latter enjoyed killing for its own sake. And so Bishop continued to enjoy killing Germans during 'Bloody April' and in the following months. When he was promoted to captain he was permitted to go off on his own. In this way he could score more victories without having the lives of pilots under his command on his conscience. He remembered the death of one of the two Nieuport pilots who flew under his command. This pilot was hit with an explosive bullet in the back, which exploded in his stomach. He continued fighting for ten minutes before passing out and died in hospital from his wounds. On one occasion he intervened in the ground battle when he saw that two Spandaus were pinning down British troops. He dived on the German gun positions and put them out of action thus permitting a resumption of the British advance. Other instances of Bishop's hatred of the Germans is evident in his aggressive tactics, which also added to the tally of victories.

On the other hand, Trenchard did not approve of his fighter pilots chalking up victories in the air. He felt that it was far better to ensure that the German fighters did not get airborne in the first place. On 2 June Bishop was instrumental in destroying a number of aircraft on the ground very early in the morning at the base of Jasta 5 and shot down two Albatros aircraft in the act of taking off. He was awarded a VC for this attack. He was also awarded the Military Cross and the Distinguished Service Order.

Captain Albert Ball

Albert Ball's background is important since he came from a private school where he was taught discipline and was imbued with religious belief, a sense of duty and patriotism. Above all, he left school with a sense of responsibility and obedience to the orders of his superiors. He was aware of his privileged upbringing, which imposed upon him obligations of leadership. Initially he served with the Sherwood Foresters and did not transfer to the RFC until 1915. He went on to serve

Captain Albert Ball.

on Nos.8, 11, 13, 56 and 60 Squadrons. He became the first British air ace to receive the adulation of the British public.

His first squadron posting, on 18 February 1916, was to No.13 equipped at the time with BE2cs engaged in artillery spotting. He was, therefore, a Corps pilot and in this role he was very unlikely to achieve victories in air combat. Nevertheless, he succeeded in bringing down an Albatros when returning from patrol. When the squadron lost four aircraft in a week in July Ball survived and he became known as 'John the Lonely One'. On No.11 Squadron he was an Army pilot and

Captain Ball in the cockpit of his SE5a in 1917.

Ball was keen to get his hands on the Nieuport 17. He distinguished himself on this machine and by September he had a DSO to add to his Military Cross and was eventually promoted to the rank of captain. When Ball was sent home to instruct he was selected to join No.56 Squadron. The RFC were emulating the French and the Germans in concentrating their best pilots in one squadron. The squadron pilots under the command of Major R.G. Blomfield were sent to London (Colney) to take delivery of their SE5as. With a top speed of 120mph at 6,500ft it was a strong and light aircraft and with 2½ hours endurance a Vickers gun firing through the propeller and a Lewis gun mounted on the top wing, the SE5a could fly high and wait for the opportunity to pounce on enemy aircraft. On the other hand, there were those who disliked the fact that the windscreen could become scratched and covered with oil. Also, it was very difficult to reload the Lewis gun in the slipstream. Ball took an immediate dislike to a machine, which he regarded as poor in comparison with the Nieuport. Ball had the Lewis gun removed on his aircraft and the windscreen lowered to reduce wind resistance. In his letters home he said that he was making the best of a bad job. In the event, the SE5a proved to be a valuable addition to the RFC inventory and Ball's criticisms sounded like adolescent petulance. On the other hand, the SE5a did have an unreliable Hispano Suiza engine and an erratic interrupter gear.

Having scored thirty victories over the Somme he was flying an SE5 as described in the last paragraph and it was on 7 May 1917 that his flight encountered Jasta 11. Ball entered a dark cloud and there was some confusion as to what happened. Richthofen claimed to have shot Ball down even though he, too, crashed. Such a victory has never been confirmed, particularly since a German officer on the ground claimed to have seen Ball's aircraft come out of the cloud 200ft above the ground in an inverted position with a dead propeller. It was later discovered that he had been buried in a German cemetery at Annoeullin. During his short life he was awarded the Victoria Cross, and three bars to a DSO.

Major James McCudden

James McCudden was an aircraft mechanic in the Royal Flying Corps when war was declared. One of three brothers to serve with the RFC, he saw combat in France as an observer and gunner before returning to England for flight training in 1916. His talents as a pilot were so extraordinary that he became an instructor within days of receiving his aviator's certificate. His time as an aircraft mechanic in late 1914 had not been easy. For weeks the ground crews slept under the wings of the aircraft and McCudden went for eleven weeks without a change of underwear. He managed to get a bath by using water trapped in the folds of a canvas aircraft hangar. He did

Major James McCudden.

not come from the privileged background of Ball but he acquitted himself with equal valour and tenacity.

McCudden's ability as a pilot was evident in his appointment as a flying instructor within days of receiving his Wings and he later instructed Mannock. He began flying as a sergeant observer and flew with Major Ludlow-Hewitt who later rose to the highest ranks of the RAF and was AOC–in-C India during the catastrophic earthquake of 1935. McCudden had the greatest respect for Ludlow-Hewitt, both as a pilot and his commanding officer. McCudden, as a flight sergeant observer was posted home for pilot training. He served initially as a flight sergeant pilot on No.20 Squadron on FE2ds and after only one month was transferred to No.29 Squadron in August flying the DH2 making his first kill in the September. He was commissioned in January 1917 and by the time he returned to England as an instructor in February he had downed three more enemy aircraft. When he later flew the SE5a he downed an Albatros on 18 August 1917 and two days later had claimed a further three. By late 1917 the RFC could have as many as eight formations of fighters aloft at any one time and as McCudden commented, 'The fun would begin at about 19.00hrs and go on until dusk.' These aerial combats had little connection with the land battle below. This was the job of the Corps pilots.

For the RFC aces it provided them with opportunities to add to individual tallies. And McCudden was not alone in gaining notoriety. If he did not meet the enemy in dogfights he would cross the enemy lines to seek out targets. He was awarded the Victoria Cross for most conspicuous bravery, exceptional perseverance, and a very high devotion to duty. Captain McCudden had

accounted for fifty-four enemy aeroplanes. Of these, forty-two were been destroyed, nineteen of them on the British side of the lines. Only twelve out of the fifty-four had been driven down out of control. On two occasions, he had totally destroyed four two-seater enemy aeroplanes on the same day, and on the last occasion all four machines were destroyed in the space of one hour and thirty minutes. He had participated in seventy-eight offensive patrols, and in nearly every case was the leader. On at least thirty occasions, whilst with the same squadron, he had crossed the lines alone, either in pursuit or in quest of enemy aeroplanes. By April 1918, James McCudden was the most decorated pilot in the Royal Air Force. He was killed three months later when his aircraft stalled after take-off and crashed to the ground. He was buried in the Wavens Cemetery.

Conclusions about the character of fighter pilots from the experience of the aces

So what may be deduced about the contribution these pilots made to the war effort? There was a need, if only for morale purposes alone to publicize their victories. There were periods when one side or the other had ascendency in the air due to the introduction of new aircraft but this ascendency did not affect the conduct of these men who were prepared to take on the enemy with aggressive tactics using the aircraft at their disposal. The threat from the Fokker Eindecker monoplane fighters may have been overdone, argues D.B. Tubbs in Purnell's history of the World Wars. After a year when German aircraft over the Western Front practised unarmed docility, in the Fokker they had an aircraft with a gun that could fire through the arc of the propeller. 'The Germans had simply decided to fight back,' says Tubbs. Success in aerial combat was increasingly determined by the adoption of fighter tactics such as the one that surprised Bishop on his first patrol as leader. Failure in aerial combat could result in the tendency of some pilots to open fire on an enemy aircraft when a considerable distance from the adversary. Resisting this temptation was important for it was better to close with the enemy to be more certain of delivering a mortal blow. The agreement not to shoot down certain enemy aircraft because they were very easy targets may be a very good example of chivalry in the air but is difficult to comprehend since the successful return of the German crew with, one expects, intelligence about Allied troop movement and positions would be detrimental to the Allied cause.

The reference to 'Bloody April, is important since it shows how the balance of advantage could so easily pass from one side to the other. Like the 'Fokker Scourge', when the advantage was with the Germans, so 'Bloody April' put the Allied air forces again at a disadvantage. At the beginning of that catastrophic month the RFC had 754 aircraft, of which 385 were single-seat fighters. The

Germans had 114 aircraft to oppose the British. By the end of the month 151 RFC aircraft had been lost (that is, shot down or forced down) compared with the loss of 119 German. The RFC lost 316 aircrew, dead and missing, against 119 for the Germans. The life expectancy for a RFC pilot on the Western Front was a little over three weeks.

What is clear is that some individual commanders may have been loath to heap rewards on certain pilots, believing in team work, but there were equally those commanders who permitted their good pilots to personalize their aircraft and to ensure that they received the best attention by the ground crews. Loading their own magazines was also important to some of the aces. Giving them every opportunity to clock up victories by allowing them to hunt for prey on their own, often over enemy territory, simply gave these men the opportunities they craved. Instances of boredom until they were posted to a fighter unit in France are also evident.

A determination to kill the 'hated' enemy was evident in Bishop's case but for Ball it was a matter of honour and patriotism. Concentrating the nation's best pilots in one squadron was an emulation of French and German practice and had the advantage of ensuring that a particular fighter unit had superiority in aerial combat. In Richthofen's case Chapter 4 describes how the Germans had the advantage in simply waiting for the RFC units to fly east to attack them. The German High Command had decided that their trench positions were to be heavily fortified so that most of the ground offensives were made by the British and French Armies with, as it turns out, huge losses of life. The Germans had a war to fight against the Russians on the Eastern Front so stalemate on the Western Front until victory in the East could be achieved suited them. Thus the RFC units would meet the likes of Richthofen when fuel tanks had been partially emptied and, since the prevailing winds were from the West the British pilots would have the added disadvantage in flying into headwinds on their return. This could well have to be done when aircraft were damaged.

Physical attributes differed, with Mannock being almost half blind but Bishop being a crack shot with 22:20 vision. There is no doubt about the valour of these men who risked their lives daily. On the other hand, dogfighting was something the aces obviously enjoyed, which is not to undervalue their bravery. During World War II, Fighter Command did have its aces amongst the fighter pilots but their notoriety was greatest during the Battle of Britain when, again, the maintenance of public morale was of the utmost importance.

PERSONNEL MATTERS EMANATING FROM THE DRAFT AIR FORCE ACT AS THEY AFFECTED THE ROYAL NAVY AND THE ARMY

Comparative rates of pay of the armed services consequent upon the formation of the Air Ministry

In attempting to determine the pay and allowances of the officers and men of the imminent formation of the RAF there was obviously going to be affordability and comparability with the Army and the Royal Navy. Rates that were too favourable compared with the sister services could distort recruitment and there was the matter of flying pay. Flying was hazardous but so were many military activities. Should flying be regarded as particularly hazardous when improvements in aircraft design and reliability meant that it was not as dangerous as it was when the original RFC rates were fixed? During the Great War there was no evidence of discontent amongst members of the other services arising from the existing scale of pay of flying officers.

As long as the Royal Flying Corps was administered by the War Office the latter could control recruitment into the flying service both from civilian life and transfers from other Arms. That would not be possible once the Air Ministry was formed when Army officers would have to transfer between services. Not only pay but also career development might well determine the numbers of officers who would wish to transfer. On the other hand, by late 1917 many of the officers of the RFC had been direct entrants who presumably had joined because they chose it over the alternatives. If the existing rates of remuneration for Flying Corps officers was maintained on the formation of the RAF then recruitment to the non-flying branches of the Army should not be affected once the Flying Corps was removed from the control of the War Office. In the first few years of the RAF's existence it was to be expected that Army officers would continue to apply to transfer but Trenchard's plan for the RAF included a college at Cranwell, which would henceforth train career RAF officers. Be that as it may, as long as the RAF relied upon volunteer transferees from the Army then pay had to be attractive enough to ensure a ready supply of officers.

With reference to transfers from the Royal Navy, General Smuts directed that consideration be given to the remuneration of equipment officers. Some 700 technical officers of the RNVR had been transferred from the Royal Navy since their functions corresponded to those of RAF equipment officers. It was desirable, however, that all officers of the RAF should be primarily officers of that force rather than officers of a pilot corps, an observation corps or an equipment corps. Trenchard would go further, believing that all officers of a flying service should be taught to fly. The problem of integrating these RNVR officers was the wide discrepancy of pay between the rates of pay of technical officers of the RNVR and RAF equipment officers. The former were paid 11/- a day if of the rank of lieutenant commander and lieutenant and 7/- 6d a day for sub lieutenants. This compared with 24/-6d, 18/- and 12/- respectively. The Admiralty already had in mind the regrading of RNVR technical officers to make their pay correspond to RAF equipment officer ranks. Certainly, an intermediate rate was called for since only some RNVR officers were affected. Officers transferring between the two services should not be paid rates that were very different from RAF equipment officers since it was believed that the RAF officers, of the same qualifications and performing the same functions should be paid the same rate.

Proposed new commissioned rank structure

In a letter dated 22 October 1917 from the Air Organization Committee to the Admiralty, General Smuts was transmitting his ideas on a proposed new rank structure for the RAF. He felt that it was preferable to adopt known rank titles known to both services rather than concoct strange new ones. Using the old rank titles helped members of the existing services to link them to the corresponding ranks in their services. They are an interesting mix of the rank titles of both existing services. He was asking their lordships at the Admiralty and the War Office for their comments and suggestions:

Air marshal
Admiral
Vice-admiral
Rear-admiral
Commodore (temporary rank)
Colonel
Commander
Major
Captain
Lieutenant
Ensign

Note: It would eventually be Winston Churchill who, as post-war Minister of War and the Air, would introduce a new rank structure for the RAF, which has survived almost intact to this day.

DISCIPLINARY AND ADMINISTRATIVE MATTERS

Minutes of the Air Organization Committee meeting of 25 September 1917 disclose the problems in the application of discipline as it affected air units operating with the older services. For example, should the commander of an air unit on board a man-of-war and his men be subject to the Naval Discipline Act? One can imagine any

activity that directly affects the safety of the vessel at sea. In these circumstances the Committee believed that the Senior Naval Officer's (SNO's) orders must be obeyed by all on board. If the air commander on board believed that such orders were incapable of being carried out or were excessively dangerous he was to point this out to the SNO. If the latter insisted on the order being carried out, the Air Commander was entitled to have the order put in writing with his protest and the document signed by both men. The same rule would apply to aircraft carriers. Interestingly, the Committee was of the opinion that aircraft carriers working from land or floating bases should be regarded as Air Force vessels, in which case the captain of the carrier would have the right of protest against orders already described.

One can see how complex matters were and the Committee considered questions involving administration and discipline in situations where members of two or even all three services were co-located and where members of all three services might be performing the same tasks. Examples were provided firstly by anti-submarine operations in the Straits of Dover where air units of the Air Force would come under the operational control of the Senior Naval Officer but the Air Force personnel would be subject to the Air Force Act for disciplinary purposes and subject to Air Force administration. Conversely in Otranto, Italy, naval units were attached to the Air Force and the naval personnel were subject to their operational control but for disciplinary purposes were subject to the Naval Discipline Act. Where whole commands were co-located as in Dunkirk, Harwich, Gibraltar or Fortress Malta, the question of command would have to be considered very carefully. In these places one could find detachments from the two services living and working side by side. Sailors might socialize together with soldiers and get into trouble. Would it be fair if members of one service were punished far more severely than members of the other for being found guilty of being involved in the same fight together? There had already been problems of this nature between soldiers and sailors in Dunkirk. To add a third service to the mix would not make life any easier. Determination of which services were subordinate in a given situation would have to be made at combined conferences. In the event that agreement could not be reached there might have to be recourse to the War Cabinet.

Memorandum from the Air Organization Committee 15 November 1917
Source: National Archive document CAB/21/21

The Air Organization Committee met again on 15 November 1917 to consider a proposal from the Army Council that provision should be made in the Air Force

Bill for the Air Council to place contingents of the Air Force allotted to the Army under Military Law. This proposal was rejected. Firstly, it was argued that the special conditions of air work meant that new offences were created for which there was no provision under Military Law. An example would be RAF personnel being tried by a court when the composition of the court should be officers with air experience. Officers who had not been members of the RFC would not have a proper understanding of technical matters that might arise. The Air Organization Committee felt that, given the similarity of the Air Force Act and the Army Act, it was difficult to see what advantage the Army Council expected from this proposal.

With the formation of the RAF, all flying units, including those that had previously belonged to the RNAS, would normally be subject to Air Force Law but in the future there would be air units on board aircraft carriers and warships with aircraft catapults. The conditions of service on board HM vessels afloat could be very different from those on land so that certain offences that might be trivial on shore could be very serious afloat. In the past it had always been recognized that when Army personnel served on board HM vessels they became subject to the Naval Discipline Act, without any reciprocal measures by which officers and men of the Royal Navy who were serving with the Army were automatically subject to Military Law.

A further 'grey area' revealed by the Air Organization Committee related to personnel employed as anti-aircraft gunners. In a letter dated 9 November 1917 the members of the Army Council re-affirmed their opinion that the anti-aircraft defence by guns mounted on land or on board ships was a branch of Army or Navy gunnery, i.e. the Act should not create new units of the RAF for such a purpose. In the Air Force Bill, however, the Air Council would not be limited as to the exact nature of the forces that may be raised under the general terns of the RAF, but it would seem undesirable to make special provision in the Bill to forbid the Air Council to raise anti-aircraft units in the future since a provision of this kind could hamper future decisions of the War Cabinet. There were two dissenting voices in the Air Organization Committee on this matter, namely the Director General of Military Aeronautics and a Mr Corcoran. (It may be of interest to note that the author served on a light anti-aircraft squadron of the RAF Regiment in the 1950s but before the formation of the RAF Regiment in 1942 anti-aircraft defence of airfields was performed by Army gunners.)

Views expressed by members of the Army Council on the application of Military Law

The members of the Army Council took the view that the whole of the Army, which included the Royal Flying Corps, were subject to Military Law and that it would be inadvisable to disturb a system in the middle of a war with which all were familiar and which worked well. If members of the new Air Force were serving in France, for example, it would pose no extra burden on any single person if RAF personnel were to remain subject to Military Law. As far as the Army was concerned the relationship of the RAF to other arms of the Army would be no different to that of the RFC. Members of the RAF would have to familiarize themselves with forthcoming Air Force Law but would already be familiar with Military Law. On the other hand, if the Air Force adopted Air Force Law every military authority would have to familiarize itself with that law. It was no sufficient answer to say that Air Force Law closely resembled Military Law. For example, a military officer convening or confirming an Air Force Court Martial under Section 122 (6), a military officer lent to sit on an Air Force Court Martial under Section 48(10), any officer or non-commissioned officer giving an order to an airman under Section 184A and any military policeman called in to arrest an airman, ought all to know in what respects Air Force Law differed from Military Law.

It had been shown that the Air Organization Committee objected, that the Air Force Bill would create certain offences that were not known in Military Law and that if the Air Force were placed under Military Law this valuable part of the Bill would in practice be sacrificed. This was thought not to be a problem and the case of Air Force personnel being subject to the Naval Discipline Act was cited. But Section 179 (c) of the Air Force Act provides that they may be tried and punished under that Act for an offence for which they were not amenable to a naval court martial but for which they could be punished under the Air Force Act. A similar proviso could and certainly should, it was argued, be inserted into the proposed section subjecting the force to Military Law.

The Army Council then moved on to the Air Organization Committee's objection that it would be undesirable for Air Force personnel to be tried normally by Army officers. This was recognized but this would not be the effect of placing Air Force personnel under Military Law. Air Force personnel would normally be tried by Air Force officers. In late 1917 it was not usual for members of the RFC to be tried by RFC officers on account of the exacting nature of these officers' other duties and Section 48 (10) of the Air Force Bill showed that the Air Force intended to perpetuate this system. From the Army's point of view there was no intention to impose Army officers on airmen's courts martial. During joint operations in the Great War there were instances where the powers of the Naval Discipline Act, which catered for naval personnel operating on shore, had not been sufficient as between the Army and the Navy. The Army Council pointed out that Air Force would be in close and continuous co-operation every day of the war and if the scheme could not cater for naval personnel serving ashore when working with the Army then it would be unlikely that a similar scheme could be made to work for the RAF. It was therefore concluded that the RAF would sacrifice nothing of its individuality by being subjected at times to Army Law, indeed this matter had already been addressed. (See two paragraphs above.) Above all, the Army Council wished to remove any uncertainties, particularly in the middle of a war, with regard to discipline. The advantage, as the Army saw it, was in subjecting RAF personnel subject to Military Law plus the new element in Air Force Law, namely that the Army in applying Military Law was cognisant of the technicalities of air force operations and that Army officers could sit as members of RAF courts martial.

Promotion and reward

The members of the Air Organization Committee expressed their view on this matter in these words:

Although the advancement or reward of officers and men must finally be a matter for the Air Council, yet it is evident that in war, and to a lesser degree in peace, the reputation of members of the Air Force serving with the Navy or the Army, must be judged by the reports of the naval and military commanders under whom they are serving. In the case of junior ranks, recommendations for promotion or reward will no doubt be brought forward, as at present, by their immediate superiors in the Air Force. In the case of senior officers, promotion depends now, and will under the proposed organization, on the opinion of the naval and military commanders on the efficiency of these officers in carrying out the duties with which they are charged. The recommendations of naval and military commanders with regard to Air Force oOfficers and men serving under them will receive the same consideration as the reports of Air Force commanders whose forces are not attached to the Navy or Army.

PERSONNEL AND ADMINISTRATIVE SUPPORT FOR THE INDEPENDENT BOMBING FORCE IN FRANCE

Source: National Archive document AIR1-912/204/5/847

Introduction

This section is significant in that the document details the administrative arrangements necessary to get the Independent Bombing Force (IBF) in France operational to begin strategic bombing missions against military and economic targets in Germany and German-occupied France. The details of these missions are described in

Chapter 6. This was the first time that a bombing force entirely separate from the RAF air forces in the field would have been formed. The staff planning was done entirely by the Air Ministry and dealt directly with General Trenchard who had been appointed to command this force of heavy and light bombers.

It has to be understood that the Nancy area in which the RAF squadrons of the IBF were to be situated, was some distance from the RAF forces in the field, which covered the most northern part of the Allied line. Furthermore, the support services on which the IBF squadrons would have to rely would be those previously supplied by the War Office, e.g. medical, supply and postal services. At this time the RAF was relying on Army support as it did when the RFC came under the War Office. Some of the administration and planning was to be done with the French authorities who would have to agree the situation of the bases in the Nancy area and provide for road and rail access. These are detailed in the section that follows.

The map below illustrates the distances involved and the situation of the RAF in the field and the IBF. The RAF in the field was separated from the IBF by approximately 250 miles.

Correspondence of 13 May 1918

Air Ministry letter, 11555/1918 dated 13 May to the Secretary of the War Cabinet concerned the decision of the Air Council that the time had arrived for the constitution of an Independent Bombing Force for the purpose of carrying out bombing raids on Germany on a large scale. This would be a separate command of the RAF to be commanded by Major General Sir H.M. Trenchard. It was deemed necessary that Trenchard be able to deal directly with the French military authorities. This involved bringing in the French Government so that the necessary facilities could be afforded Trenchard. Finally, it was a stated as a fact that these long-distance bombing operations would, in the near future, would be more of an international character and it was therefore proposed that the broad lines of action should be laid down by the Supreme War Council on the advice of the military representatives at Versailles. This then laid basis of the administrative arrangements that had to be made in the following weeks. The RAF was, in mid 1918, reliant on many services that continued to be provided by the Army and it would be some time before the RAF could develop its own support services. This is reflected in the texts which follow.

Further correspondence of the same date made it clear that at the outset the IBF be separated from the command of the Army but the C-in-C BEF was requested in the meantime to continue to supply labour until the Air Ministry could supply its own. Anti-aircraft guns were also requested, again until the RAF could provide its own AA defences. The Army was requested to continued

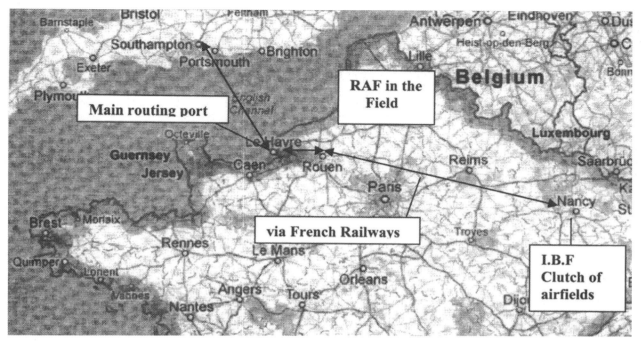

Routeing of personnel and equipment to IBF units in the Nancy area.

to supply petrol, oil, food and clothing. (The RAF was still dressed in Army uniform and this continued until after the war at the same time as the new ranks were introduced.) Thus with the exception of the supplies just listed the IBF could become independent of the Army. It was also advised that a Director of Works be appointed.

In the matter of RE (Royal Engineers) and Ordnance stores, the RE were requested to supply hutting timber, cement and general RE stores direct to the Air Ministry amounting to 700 to 1,000 tons per week. Ordnance stores, such as camp equipment, soap, nails, lamps, blankets would be supplied direct to the Air Ministry. Bombs and ammunition, on the other hand, would be a separated supply from the UK and not from the Ordnance. But the RAF Port Depots were inadequate to handle the quantities involved. Then there was the problem of train transport to the Nancy area. At the big service depots this was done by the Director of Works hence the need to have one appointed for the IBF. The supply of labour at the ports for loading and unloading ships was on a pool basis and an independent labour force for the IBF would be wasteful when ships were not arriving with stores for the Force. A suitable staff at the ports would be essential.

A labour force of approximately 10,000 was required for work on the aerodromes; indeed, the replacement of labour was a big problem. A system of dealing with the French made signals communication important and RAF signal lines would have to be provided. Two companies

of skilled labour had been allocated to road building with a further 250 to be found, together with 2,000 unskilled labourers for the new grounds. The French were unwilling to maintain local roads that could be used to travel to the airfields and this matter had been referred to GHQ. Courban was the local railhead and telephonic communication was required for this and other stations that would be involved in RAF traffic. Petrol and other supplies travelling by rail were dealt with by the Director General of Transport as were the trains necessary to convey personnel. The question was asked as to whom would do this in future. Again the requisition of land and buildings was handled by the Director of Hirings and Requisitions and the same question was asked. When it came to construction work the Director of Works normally undertook this responsibility. The skilled personnel and transport involved would have to be considered. Forestry was important and the quantities of wood required would be large.

Finally in this document of 13 May was the consideration of Postal and Medical Services. The Forces Post Office, which came under the Director of Postal Services, had provided mail for the 8th Brigade (now the IBF). Who would make the arrangements for postal deliveries to the IBF in the future? With regard to the medical services the Deputy Director of Medical Services ensured the supply of medical stores and the hospital was provided by the No.8 Canadian Stationary Hospital at Charmes. Who would provide medical supplies in the future? Since it had been decided that the IBF should be as independent as possible the Air Ministry would have to set up the necessary organization to deal the supplies involved at the ports on arrival, for their transit and distribution.

Letter to Major General Trenchard dated 13 May 1918

A second Air Ministry letter 11555/dated 13 May contained instructions to Trenchard and was also his letter of appointment. He was advised that the commanding officer of No.8 Brigade would be placed under his orders from the date of his arrival in France. There were already three Handley Page squadrons of aircraft in existence. Trenchard was required to submit weekly progress and operational reports to the Secretary of the Air Ministry. These reports would be forwarded to the French General HQ as well as the Secretary, British Section of the Supreme War Council, Versailles. He was also to inform the Air Ministry of fighter reinforcement for bomber escort which, in his judgement, was necessary in light of experience. He was also advised about the arrangements that needed to be put in hand as described in the preceding paragraphs. Hospital arrangements were to be provided on a temporary basis by the French and the Americans and Trenchard was required to send his recommendations to the Air Ministry, for a hospital to be set up once he had arrived. Aircraft engines were to be sent for repair to the Pont de L'Arche and finally a programme was attached for the flying in of the aircraft for the IBF.

Air Ministry letter to the War Office dated 14 May

Most of what had been communicated to Trenchard was repeated in this letter. The operation of the IBF meant that squadrons previously committed to support land operations on the Western Front were to be separated and the War Office was asked to convey to Field Marshal Haig the need to agree with Trenchard the date for the separation of these units. The War Office was also advised that the GOC Independent Force was empowered to work directly with the General HQ France on all questions of transport by road and rail and that was to be communicated to Haig.

Matters arising from Trenchard's brief

The airfields that had to be taken over were Azelot, housing the DH4s of No.55 Squadron and the DH9s of Nos.99 and 104 Squadrons, and Bettencourt, which housed the Camels of No.45 Squadron and the DH9As of No.110 Squadron. The Handley Page O/400 bombers of Nos. 97, 100 and 215 Squadrons were based at Xaffévillers, of No.216 Squadron at Rovilles-aux-Chenes

and of No.115 Squadron at St Inglevert, which was not in the Nancy clutch but just outside Boulogne. The layout of these airfields were to conform to the standard layout if for no other reason than squadrons were used to it. Indian labour and POWs were to be used in the work of preparing the airfields. The hangars for the HP squadrons were in sight. They had reached Rouen and were being sent on by HQ RAF. The Bessoneaux hangars for Azelot had been sent and had been erected with an additional eight on their way to Bettencourt. Bessoneaux hangars were also earmarked for additional airfields, which did not, in the event, materialize. There was also hangarage earmarked for Courban. Arrangements even covered fire appliances, stationary and typewriters.

Next was the matter of train arrangements and road transport for personnel and the Quartermaster General (QMG) had issued orders in conjunction with HQ RAF and it was suggested that the HQ RAF deal with the IBF in turn. The existing arrangement was that the Air Ministry notified the HQ RAF of the date of the arrival of units. The QMG was then requested to arrange to provide the necessary train accommodation or a Marche table if by road. In future the Air Ministry would inform the IBF of the arrival of units leaving the latter to deal with the QMG in order to move personnel from the port of disembarkation to the IBF.

Road access to the airfields has already been mentioned in the context of the French authorities being unwilling to maintain local roads in the areas affected. The Director of Roads at GHQ was to make all the required new roads and lorry standings and had both skilled and unskilled labour. The repair of other roads was under consideration at GHQ.

Matters contained in a letter from HQ RAF in the field dated 29 May 1918

The letter opens with a reference to conversations with Generals Ford and Maybury and ranges over the matters dealt with earlier in detail. This letter brings the recipient up to date. No difficulty was expected in the continued supply of food, Petrol Oils and Lubricants (POL), ammunition and Ordnance stores. The supply of tentage was being handled through the QMG and the provision of postal services presented no difficulty. General May was taking up the matter of road repair and was in contact with the Adjutant General about the supply of typewriters and stationary. The hiring of land, claims and compensation was being dealt with by the Claims Commission and it was expected that a Claims Officer be sent to the IBF. General Ford stated that he did not wish the IBF to deal direct with the Director of Works in the first instance, but only with regard to details in the same manner as was done at the time. A private letter had been sent to General Lawrence for circulation in the departments of the QMG and did not mention the repair of roads or supply of stationary. The Director of Supplies brought up the supply of lorries for moving food etc., from the railway station to Army Service Corps (ASC) Supply Depots. The existing situation was that the ASC supplied the lorries but General May was concerned that the lorries were having to operate so far from their base. In the past the distribution of food etc., to units from ASC Supply Depots had always been done by the RAF and so Trenchard would see May about this matter.

A conference in General Ford's office GHQ at 09.45hrs on 2 June 1918

Present at this meeting were Trenchard, Major Generals Ford and Maybury, Brigadier-General Brooke-Popham and Lieutenant Colonel Hudson. Communication remained a problem seeking a solution. Should there be a Regulating Station in the neighbourhood of Neufchateau to run special trains there from Rouen? The matter was referred to the Director General of Transport (DGT). Secondly, should Nantes be used as a port for the American lines of communication? But this would necessitate the RAF having to make complete arrangements for handling materials and the installation of a petrol installation? Finally, it was doubtful that the requisite amount of shipping would be available. The supply of bombs should remain under the existing organization with three weeks' stock held in the Lorraine area under RAF arrangements with a back-up of six weeks stock in bases controlled by the QMG. The IBF was to furnish a revised estimate of bomb requirements up until the end of October. A staff officer of Ordnance should be attached to Trenchard's staff to look after clothing, and other stores, including bombs, although the supply of the latter would probably present less difficulty than other ordnance stores.

Roads were still presenting a problem and it was minuted that there was still a large amount of road work to be done in the area. Not only was it necessary to make roads to the airfields, the provision of hard standing in front of the hangars was important. The Handley Page O/400 was no lightweight and, when bombed-up, could sink into the mud. The reluctance on the part of the French to maintain local roads was noted and Maybury agreed to provide a good man to supervise the work, an Assistant Director of Roads if you like. Other matters arising from the letter of 29 May received further discussion.

Letters from the HQ RAF in the field to Trenchard dated 6 and 7 June 1918

It was reported that the Controller of Labour had received a circular, which was sent to all Departments at GHQ relative to the creation of the IBF. The Controller was to transfer all his labour to the IBF through a newly appointed Assistant Controller of Labour (ACL) who

would be a staff captain. It was desirous that one of the three groups of labour allotted to the IBF should be removed. This should be the Indians who were moving but it was felt that two groups of workers should suffice, although it was agreed that the distances involved were very great. Trenchard was asked which group he was prepared to surrender and it was promised to give him a good ACL. The services of General MacDougall was proposed and it was added that any labour sent to work with the IBF should come under Trenchard's orders, which could reduce part of the work being carried out by Royal Engineers who would continue to supply the stores.

On the 7th of the month HQ RAF in the field sent Trenchard a letter. Maybury reported that fifty skilled men, a blasting plant and machinery etc., had been sent to Courban for the construction of roads and the working of quarries there. At the same time Maybury had heard that General MacDougall was on his way to Trenchard's HQ with a proposal from the Air Ministry that he take over all aerodrome work, including roads. Since Maybury was in negotiation with the French about the repair of side roads, to change any agreed arrangements would disrupt the work. Arrangements were already in hand for the supply of RE stores and their use would be under the direction of the Director of Works who was to be appointed to Trenchard's staff. If the Air Ministry were to appoint General MacDougall to supervise all the work on roads and airfields, using materials provided by the RAF, he would experience all the attendant difficulties with regard to ports, labour supply, railways, and quays which were not encountered in England

Two months previously MacDougall had offered two labour companies of Canadian foresters for work on the IBF airfields and it had been agreed that these men should be given definite jobs by the Royal Engineers who would provide the stores and men left to work under their own officers. This was to avoid an accusation by the Canadian Government that Canadians were being employed on work properly the business of the Director of Works. It was thought that there should be no difficulty in arranging for the work to be carried out under the direction of the Deputy Director of Works (South).

This was followed by a letter from the RAF in the field dated 11 June. The letter confirmed that the Air Ministry was not taking over aerodrome work for the IBF. Trenchard's thanks for all that the Air Ministry had done was mentioned and it was hoped that negotiations with the French regarding the repair of local roads was proceeding satisfactorily. A final letter on the matter of roads was sent by the Director of Roads to Colonel Hudson, RAF, in the field, dated 13 June 1918 in which he expressed his thanks that the Roads Directorate was not to be divorced from the IBF, which would have been the case had the Air Ministry scheme involving General MacDougall been implemented. He reported that he had succeeded in getting the French authorities to accept the responsibility for the repair of local roads and he had been informed that the work was in hand. A Major Steele had been instructed to maintain close supervision of the work so that he could let him know, in good time, if the road works were not keeping up with the needs of the IBF.

Supply of pilots and observers – a letter from Trenchard to the HQ RAF in the field

Trenchard wanted his own supply of pilots and observers to be sent direct from the UK to Rouen. He asked that instructions be issued to the OC Port Depot that personnel intended for him to report to Rouen for onward posting to the IBF. From Rouen they were to be routed to Charmes station (some 40km SSE of Nancy). The names of all the aircrew members were to be wired to him on arrival in France and the date of dispatch to Charmes. They were to be instructed to report to Lieutenant Regnard, the acting Rail Transport Officer, on arrival at Charmes. Trenchard expected his first draft from England on Thursday 27 June provided the Secretary of the Ministry agreed. Up to that point he expected the addressee to continue to supply him with pilot and observer reinforcements.

Trenchard followed this up with a letter dated 8 June to the Secretary the Air Ministry emphasizing the distinction between pilots and observers who were being sent as reinforcements for the RAF in the field and those destined for the IBF. He stated that he would be ready to receive his own reinforcements from 22 June, suggesting that they be routed via Rouen (Southampton to Le Havre route). His requirements would be met at that time if only one draft per week was sent and he proposed sending a wire every Monday giving the numbers required. These men should be dispatched every Thursday. If this procedure was agreed he said that he would send his first wire on 24 June.

Notes of a meeting held in the QMGs office on 12 June to discuss questions of supply to the IBF

The general policy regarding dispatch of stores to the IBF included the following points. Firstly, the extra trucks required had been estimated at 20 per week for supplies but this was felt to be excessive and that 15 should suffice taking the total to 165 per week not 200. Rouen would be the dispatching station. Representatives of directors with the IBF were to inform the base what stores were needed, giving the railheads. The stores were then to be loaded up into trucks at Rouen each truck containing, as far as possible, supplies for one railhead only, labelled at Rouen and then made up into a special train and sent to Is-sur-Thil, where they were to be attached to the different French trains and sent on to their destination.

Where a complete truck could not be made up for a single railhead, such trucks were to be sent to Courban and the stores issued from there. This was expected to apply only to Ordnance stores. Supply Depots were to be established as necessary in the Lorraine area where stocks sufficient for approximately ten days were to be kept. Bombs were to be held in twenty to twenty-five trucks, which were to be loaded at Quevilly Wharf direct from ammunition ships and sent off as required. An Ordnance Stores Depot was to be formed at Courban and issues were to be made from there with RAF stores through Aircraft Parks to units. This method was to apply to Ordnance stores for units other than RAF squadrons. It was expected that the majority of stores would go to Courban and be sorted and re-dispatched from there. Personnel also were to proceed to Courban and dispatched to units from there.

Summary of planning necessary to institute and maintain the IBF

The foregoing paragraphs emphasize the not inconsiderable amount of planning required to institute and maintain the IBF in the Nancy area. This RAF force was detached a considerable distance from the RAF brigades fighting in support of the BEF on the Western Front, a force that Trenchard had previously commanded. The normal and accepted supply routes that served the RAF in the field did not suffice and new ones had to be devised. The passages also show the various staff officers involved from the Quartermaster General to Works Officers and Directors of Roads and Postal services to Rail Transport Officers and Directors of Ordnance. The co-operation of the French Government, military and local authorities was vital. It may be confusing to the reader since much of the supply side of the new RAF was still provided from Army sources. Given also that RAF personnel continued, until after the Great War, to carry Army ranks and uniforms can result in confusion with personnel of the Army.

The reason for the siting of the airfields in the Nancy area was to place the bombing squadrons within easy reach of industrial targets in Germany and German-occupied France. The choice of Trenchard to command the IBF is interesting. He had already been appointed as Chief of the Air Staff in April 1918 but had resigned over differences of policy with Lord Rothernere and such a senior officer in the RAF could hardly have been allowed to kick his heels when a war still had to be won. Trenchard had originally believed that the task of an air force was to support land operations but he became a convert to the idea of strategic bombing. When the war ended he was re-appointed to the post of Chief of the Air Staff and he would carry his policy through into the peacetime air force.

Chapter 11
Technical and Supply Matters

The Royal Aircraft Factory – bombs and wireless telegraphy – rifle/grenade experiments – aircraft weapons – work of the Aeronautical Inspection Dept – Army and Navy supply to the RAF – supply of aircraft and engines – aircraft and engine requirements to the summer of 1919 – growth in the use of motor vehicles

INTRODUCTION

The purpose of this chapter is to plot the development of technical and supply services to the RFC and RNAS over the years 1912 to 1918 when they had to be adapted to serve the needs of the newly created RAF. The development of other technical devices that contributed to the successful operation of military aeroplanes such as wireless and bombing devices are included in this chapter. The development of aeroplanes can be found in Chapter 7; engine development is considered here. Probably the greatest contribution to the development and construction of aircraft came from the Royal Aircraft Factory, misleadingly titled the RAF. Indeed, the chapter begins with a consideration of the work carried out there. Progress made in the development of wireless in particular was remarkable since it started in balloons and not until 1912 did experimentation move on to aeroplanes. Much of the work was carried out by dedicated officers who were at the cutting edge of technology, so to speak. Bomb dropping was equally important because it was through bombing that damage could be inflicted on an enemy's ground forces, ships and submarines and reconnaissance was made much more effective with the ability to communicate with ground stations. Reference is made to machine guns in aircraft but for the most part this was confined to the Vickers and Lewis guns and this situation continued right through much of the inter-war period.

THE ROYAL AIRCRAFT FACTORY
Source: National Archive document AIR1/729/176/5/59

Introduction

The work carried out by the Royal Aircraft Factory (hereafter simply called the 'Factory') was to design and build aeroplanes to War Office specifications and here there is an interesting departure between the Naval and Military Wings of the Royal Flying Corps. Their Lordships at the Admiralty preferred to procure their aeroplanes from private sources, whereas the War Office, on behalf of the Military Wing, which was to become the RFC, preferred to have their aircraft designed and built by the Factory. The reason for this is clear with the prevailing state of aeroplane development and the roles that these aeroplanes would have to fulfil in war. Reconnaissance and artillery spotting were seen as the

task of the aeroplane over the battlefield acting in direct support of the Army commanders on the ground. This called for aeroplanes that were inherently stable, other qualities such as speed and manoeuvrability being much less important. The following will chart the contribution made to military aviation at this time.

At the outset the design and production of aeroplanes was not a paying proposition. The resources had to come largely from the state and the Factory, inadequately resourced as it was, had to struggle to prepare for war. The building and organizing of a factory had to be carried out simultaneously with the conduct of research. It did not help that the government made demands on the Factory that were perpetual and unavoidable. At the beginning of 1910 their site was occupied by the Balloon Factory on what was virtually forest land. There was little accommodation for workmen and the Superintendant had to oversee the erection of cottages with the necessary drainage, electricity etc. The Superintendant had also to provide for inspection, stores, repairs and investigation of inventions. Indeed, the RFC in its early days had to rely directly and indirectly upon Farnborough. There were few if any engineering firms, in those early days of flying, that had the machinery and know-how to produce aeroplanes or aeroplane spares. Would-be producers had to have their premises inspected by Factory inspectors. One such firm was the future Handley Page, the inspection being reported on 2 October 1912.

A factor that determined, to an extent, the aircraft types that were to be built was the progress being made in other European countries. Their governments were, understandably, loath to release details of their latest designs and it fell to the British secret service to unearth what scraps of intelligence it could. At the same time British engineering firms, capable of producing aeroplanes, were loath to invest large sums of money in projects that might be changed in the light of intelligence reports, which could bring about frequent changes of policy and priorities. The trade journals of the day contained expressions of hostility to the Factory, which was attempting to set and maintain standards of workmanship in firms engaged in aircraft production. This had the unfortunate effect of reducing its usefulness by creating suspicion and opposition to its work where there should have been confidence and helpfulness. This, in turn, led to a judicial inquiry in 1916, which brought about a reorganization of the Factory. Eventually, those officials who felt that they had been abused were permitted to resign their posts only to obtain posts in those firms from which criticism had come, often at increased salaries.

The matter of engine production had been addressed and problems solved for the time being. This had involved and enormous amount of technical work and laid the foundations of further development in the event of war. Praise is due to the Superintendent who oversaw the considerable growth in the size of the Factory and it was he who advocated the development of airships, scouting planes, large bombers and powerful engines long before official action was taken for their production. As a result Great Britain found itself better prepared for war in 1914. So great was the pace of development that departmental heads and their clerks might find that their office consisted of packing cases and in winter they might walk to their rudimentary accommodation through seas of mud where they would endure the damp and the cold. Their mess halls included rooms constructed of corrugated iron and if no other accommodation was available they might sleep in tents.

1910 was the first complete year in which Mr Mervyn O'Gorman was Superintendant. Appointed by the Secretary of State for War, Mr Haldane, in the summer of 1909, his mission was to separate construction from instruction in military aeronautics. The total number of Factory employees was 100 males and females. The

Mervyn O'Gorman.

buildings consisted of two balloon sheds, a machine shop and a small gas-producing plant. The Superintendant's programme was the construction of buildings and equipping a factory and repair dock for the construction and maintenance of airships and aircraft. At this time the Balloon Factory came directly under the Master General of Ordnance where the four dirigibles, *Beta*, *Gamma*, *Delta* and the Clément-Bayard airships were to be handled, altered, repaired and improved.

The Superintendant was to put in hand the design of one new airship, and designs for propellers and airframes. It could not be agreed at the time what types of airship were to be produced in quantity hence the decision to build not more than one airship at a time.

As a matter of policy engines were to be purchased in the open market and not designed from scratch. Four commercial engines were to be improved and redesigned to make them reliable enough to place in any chassis, which in turn might be redesigned. Should engines fail in service the workshops were to be capable of the redesign and reconstruction of the parts that had failed. Four test benches on which engines could be run in conditions that imitated those in the air were constructed. The resulting engines that entered service were designated RAF 1, 2, 3 etc. By the middle of January 1910 preparatory work was well in hand for the construction of a chassis shop, foundry, storage of hydrogen, construction of wooden items such as propellers, chassis etc. and finally office accommodation. Details of the work of the Factory by the beginning of March will show how quickly progress was being made. On 12 December 1910 Geoffrey de Havilland became a member of the Factory staff, remaining up to the end of 1913 when he was appointed to the Aeronautical Inspection Department. The work of de Havilland was of the greatest value and his name is associated with most of the early Factory productions. He gained his Pilot's Certificate on 19 December on a biplane of his own design.

Next was the drawing up of specifications for the 'B ', 'F' and 'S' types, which were in the process of evolution. This was not simply for products of the Factory but for private constructors of aeroplanes. For example, it was laid down that the mean speed was not to be less than 38mph and was not to exceed 55mph to meet military requirements. The Factory was not required to solve the problems of flight in a general sense but serving military purposes only. Experimental work was also carried out on kite and balloon instruments, gyroscopic stabilizers, compasses for correcting wind direction, kite brake trolleys and telephone drums for kite winches. For example, experimental work carried out showed that the gyroscopic stabilizer would not work but a lot was learned from that work. In September experiments were carried using an FE2 aeroplane to plot velocity resistance curves and the rate of rising possible at various velocities with various loadings. In the October the specifications were laid down for the Bristol two-seater with the mean speed of 60mph. The aircraft had to be capable of rising from reasonably level ground in a calm in not more than 100 yards and to land on similar ground and pull up within 120 yards. It had to be capable of road transport on its own wheels and was to be fitted with dual controls.

On 25 January 1912 the Superintendent suggested that the following should be ordered:

5 Nieuport monoplanes
5 Breguet biplanes
3 Deperdussin monoplanes
2 Bristol monoplanes
5 Army Aircraft aeroplanes

The suggestions were well made for the first three named aircraft above had taken first places at the French Military Trials. The Air Battalion, which became the Royal Flying Corps on 13 May, had examples of these types that had proved reasonably satisfactory. The Army Aircraft biplanes were to be of a type similar to BE1 being constructed in 1912 at the Factory powered by a 60hp ENV engine. But the new builds would have a more modern engine and capable of complying entirely with military specifications, including the desirable as well as the necessary features. They were also to be 5 to 10 miles per hour faster. The BE type of Factory machine described above took part in the War Office eroplane Competition held on Salisbury Plain in the summer of 1912. It was not a competitor but was put through identical trials and, in performance, beat all comers.

By the end of January 1912 proposals for future development included an aeroplane with adjustable wings to achieve automatic stability, an aeroplane with an unobstructed line of fire in front of the machine, and another with two independent engines, either of which could support the machine in the air with gunners' cockpits both in front and behind. Finally, suggestions also included a high-speed aeroplane and a hydroplane capable of landing on both land and water. These suggestions led to the development of Factory types, including the BE2c, FE2b, FE4 and SE5, which played a decisive part in the conduct of the war. The hydroplane was not produced.

FIRST ANNUAL REPORT BY THE AIR COMMITTEE ON THE PROGRESS OF THE ROYAL AIRCRAFT FACTORY
Source: National Archive Document CAB/4/1 AC 15

The Sub-Committee had recommended that the Factory should carry out the following duties:

a. Higher training of mechanics
b. Repairs and construction
c. Tests of British and foreign engines and aeroplanes
d. Experimental work
e. Manufacture of hydrogen and upkeep of airships and kites

As far as repairs were concerned the Factory was unable to cope with the demands made on it. When demands were exceptionally great it was the constructional and experimental work that suffered. One of the greatest demands was for propellers and 240 had been supplied to various units during a period of four months. The Subcommittee felt that the formation of the Flying Depot at Farnborough would relieve the Factory of much of this work.

British and foreign engines
The Sub-Committee believed in the necessity of obtaining a perfectly satisfactory engine for aeroplanes and recommended that the sum of £3,500 be granted to the Factory for the purchase of engines that fulfilled certain tests laid down by the Superintendant. A list of manufacturers both at home and abroad was suggested. Since then several firms had been approached and some promising types included those manufactured by Chenu, Dansette-Gillett, Salmson and Austro-Daimler. Regret was expressed that the Mercedes engine mounted, with success, in the Zeppelin airships could not be obtained. When it came to British engines the Factory was busy developing its own engine. Other domestic suppliers included Messrs White and Poppe of Coventry with a water-cooled engine, Messrs Clayton and Shuttleworth with a Salmson (Canton Unné) engine, the Birmingham Small Arms Company with cylinders similar to those of the Gnome engines, and Messrs Armstrong, Whitworth and Co. with ABC engines. The Sunbeam Vauxhall Motor Company and Green Companies were also engaged in engine production for aircraft. The Factory Superintendent believed that it would be possible to obtain good British-made engines from several of these firms in the near future.

Experimental work at the Royal Aircraft Factory
The part of the work at Farnborough that was essentially experimental was carried out by testing models at the National Physical Laboratory and the Air Committee believed that an account of this work should be brought to the attention of the Committee of Imperial Defence. The technical work of the Factory was classified under the following headings:

a. Design, relating to airships, aeroplanes and propellers
b. Physical investigations, instrument design, stability, gun measurements and aeroplane gun trials.
c. Research on fibres, dopes, fuel and oil
d. Research on metals
e. Experiments on engines and design of engines

f. Inspection of the Factory's and private firms' construction
g. Testing all aircraft except those bought under aeroplane competition
h. Flying, bomb dropping, photography, and trials with machineguns
i. Keeping the register of, and inspecting, privately owned aircraft.
j. Keeping the main aeronautical and engineering store
k. The measurements of gliding angle, speed etc. at the military aeroplane trials

PRE WAR EXPERIMENTATION – ARMAMENTS (INCLUDING BOMBS AND WIRELESS TELEGRAPHY)

The armament of naval aircraft

The Admiralty had not decided on definite roles for naval aircraft in war except to say that they would be used either offensively, in a scouting role, or what later became known as maritime reconnaissance and a bombing role. Given the frailty of aircraft the size and weight of guns would be severely limited if hostile aircraft were to be engaged. Giving the pilots or observers the best chances of a successful engagement lay in the attacking aircraft being the faster. Such a machine would only be handicapped in carrying the weight of floats. The destruction of an enemy dirigible would best be achieved using bombs since it was concluded that this could not easily be achieved by small arms fire. Bombs could be used against hostile dockyards, airship sheds, submarines when on the surface, and oil tanks etc. Again, the problem of weight had to be considered, which meant either limiting the weight of bombs or the number of occupants of the bombing aircraft. A large radius of action was called for and high speed. It was thought at the time that a pilot alone could deliver a bomb. Such an attack would have to be carried out at such an elevation that little or no sighting would be necessary. The aircraft required to operate in the scouting role should carry an observer and be equipped with receiving and transmitting wireless equipment. Again, speed and radius of action would matter and there would need to be a good view for the observer. In order that scouting aircraft could operate abroad they should have folding wings for stowage on ships. This would involve winching such aircraft aboard using the ship's davits and would be considerable assets to warships.

Bombs and bomb gear experiments

Source: AIR1/674/21/6/77

Bomb sights

As soon as the potential of bombing was realized officers of both services and some civilians began work on the invention of bomb sights. The problem was in determining the speed of the aircraft in relation to the ground. This involved the concepts of airspeed and ground speed. In a flat calm with an aircraft travelling with an airspeed of 100mph, the aircraft's ground speed would also be 100mph, but if there was a 50mph head wind it would reduce the ground speed by a half. Thus if a bomb is dropped from an aircraft it will travel forward and downwards striking the ground at a point determined by the strength and direction of the wind. The attitude of the War Office gave no encouragement to those working on bomb sights. A Mr C.J. Kennedy had a design that was resuscitated in the autumn of 1914 but was rejected for being too complicated. This was a pity since the unique features in his design did eventually see the light of day in 1916. These early designs would work only if the aircraft attitude was absolutely horizontal. The density of the air also affected the flight of a bomb once it left the aircraft. If the aircraft was flying directly into the wind the bomb dropper would find the calculation of the bomb release point relatively simple but if this was not the case the bomb would drift off, either to the port or starboard of the aircraft's heading. So in the early experiments the pilot either had to fly directly into or away from the wind. Two Royal Naval officers, Squadron Commander R.H. Clark-Hall and Flight Lieutenant Travers, were joined by Lieutenant Reilly to work on these early designs. In 1915 the CFS 'Trombone' sight was produced and this was particularly useful in seaplanes, enabling the pilot to time on the target itself. This was then superseded by a 'drift' sight designed by Lieutenant Commander Wimperis, which worked at both low and high altitudes. The greater the altitude the greater the probability of the bomb drifting from the path or heading being flown by the pilot. With the 'drift' sight the target could be attacked from any direction regardless of wind direction.

But pilots attacking a target might well have their operation of the bomb sight hindered by having to pay attention to things happening outside the aircraft, such as enemy ground fire The whole development of bomb sights was centred on the need to achieve greater theoretical accuracy and at the same time to relieve the pilot of having to use complicated sights when near the target when he might be inclined to simply use his own estimation. When large bombing aeroplanes came into service most pilots were supplied with a sight known as the 'negative lens sight' which, though not as accurate as the low height sights, was of considerable use and could also be used as a navigational aid. The larger machines had more than just the pilot and one of the crew members could be made responsible for operating the bomb sights and for dropping the bombs. By 1918 the leader of a formation would do the sighting for dropping bombs and on his releasing them it would be a signal to the other pilots to do likewise. This resulted in a salvo of explosions on or around the targets.

The problem with the accurate sighting of bombs arises when the wind is at an angle to the line of flight. In the diagram on the right the aircraft is flying directly into wind and there is no need to take account of deflection, only the strength of the wind. In the diagram on the far right the wind is blowing directly across the heading of the aircraft, which itself is pursuing a course that is a deflection from the heading. When the bomb is released it, too, will be deflected from the course being flown by the pilot and will impact, in this case, to the starboard of the course.

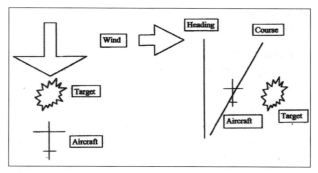

Allowance for drift in bomb aiming.

Bomb dropping

Clark-Hall began both bomb-dropping and aerial gunnery experiments as early as 1912. Using dummy bombs he wished to plot the flight of bombs dropped at various heights and to design efficient bomb-dropping equipment. The bombs used were of similar weight to those being manufactured at the time by Woolwich Arsenal, namely 10lb and 100lb bombs. The targets were constructed of old torpedo netting spread over a wooden framework about five feet from the ground. As a result of these experiments carried out in 1913 an apparatus for dropping 100lb bombs was developed. But these were only dummy bombs. One bomb was used in Aeroplane No.34 at Eastchurch and was fitted with a tail fuse apparatus for dropping on to a net at Grain. In one case a bomb apparatus received from Woolwich was too heavy to be carried in a RNAS machine but it was suggested that 'it would be suitable for mounting in a seaplane specially designed to carry the weight and the appropriate specifications were formulated at the Admiralty'. An alternative was to loan bomb-carrying apparatus to the Military Wing for periods of three or four months. At this time both the War Office and the Admiralty were working together to develop bomb-dropping installations in aircraft and aerial gunnery.

Rifle/grenade experiments

During 1913 Clark-Hall had been carrying out a considerable number of experiments with Hales rifle grenades. He wanted to test their effectiveness against airships bearing in mind that the fuse might not be delicate enough to function against fabric. In October experiments were carried out at the Cotton Powder Company's works. In the first instance a 2¼oz Military type 12-inch rod grenade was tested against two-ply rubbered balloon fabric 3ft × 2ft stretched across a frame. A large hole of about 6in diameter was blown in it with jagged edges and fabric blackened on the front side. The experiment was repeated, this time at 15 instead of 7 yards. The jagged hole was increased by 2in diameter. A third experiment was carried out using a 4oz naval type charge. Two sheets of fabric were stretched on frames 18in apart to represent the two skins of a rigid airship.

The test, conducted at a range of 15 yards, resulted in the front sheet being blown to shreds with the rear sheet exhibiting a 6in hole. The grenade appeared to explode between the two sheets of fabric.

This was followed by further experiments at Eastchurch in December 1913. Grenades were fired at ground targets from aeroplanes, both tractor and pusher types. The grenades flew correctly and the grouping was good at heights from 200 to 300ft but there was an insufficiency of grenades at this time, particularly live ones, and thus the usefulness of these weapons was not conclusively proved. Another experiment was carried out on 12 December to assess the effect of bomb explosions on the stability of aircraft that have dropped them. Floating explosive devices were detonated at sea as seaplanes flew over the charges. The weight of explosives and the height flown by the 70hp Maurice Farman seaplanes was varied. There were no discernible effects on the stability of these seaplanes and the general conclusion was that an aeroplane dropping 40lb of explosives, typically contained in a 100lb bomb, was not likely to be affected at heights of 350ft and above. These experiments did not, however, assess the possible damaging effects of bomb fragments.

Other trials with bombs were carried out at Eastchurch during the spring and early summer of 1914. These included the Hales 20lb aeroplane bomb manufactured by the Cotton Powder Company. During May five of these bombs were tested and these were largely satisfactory. An added bonus was that they could be attached to any aeroplane. The bombs fell steadily and stuck nose first from heights of 200ft and above and the fuse safety gear always worked properly. Finally, the fuse was less likely to detonate if struck by a rifle bullet than the 10lb bomb manufactured by Woolwich Arsenal at the time. The Woolwich design of fuse made it so sensitive that a drop of a few feet was sufficient to cause detonation. For the first six months of the war at least the RNAS had only the Hales 20lb bomb and it is significant that a bomb of this type was used against a Zeppelin shot down by Lieutenant Warneford on 7 June 1915.

WIRELESS TELEGRAPHY
Source: AIR1/674/21/6/78

Introduction

Experiments with wireless telegraphy (W/T) in balloons began in 1907. These began with trials using a receiving set only but by 1911 advances had been made that permitted an airship to carry W/T. Further work before the commencement of war in 1914 included the fitting of transmitters to aircraft. At the end of 1907 Lieutenant C.J. Aston RE commenced experiments with W/T in balloons. The experiments began with receiving, for transmission required considerably more electrical current. On 1 May a run was made with Pegasus and very good signals were received from a station twenty miles distant when the balloon was over Petersfield. This was followed by experiments in transmitting from dirigibles before Captain Lefrey DSO, MC, RE, commanding the 1st Wireless Company, Royal Engineers, at Aldershot, took up the experiments with aeroplanes. The airships *Delta* and *Beta* were used and on 17 January 1911 *Beta* was equipped with W/T. The engine malfunctioned and reception was affected when the engine was not running. On the other hand it was impossible to hear the signals when the engine was running close to the receiver. By the summer of that year Lefroy was working on a transmitter for installation in an aeroplane. He worked in conjunction with a Mr Wilson who estimated the cost to be £25, which was covered by an RFC allocation of £35 for the product. Using a BE aircraft piloted by Geoffrey de Havilland, Lefroy sent up an observer in the aircraft to test its suitability for fitting W/T. But it was not until May 1912 that a BE aircraft flown by Major Burke was fitted with a wireless installation deriving its power from a drive fitted to the crankshaft.

On 22 May 1912 Colonel Seely inspected the RFC and Lefroy used the opportunity to show the capability of his W/T equipment. Using the airship *Gamma* Lefroy sent a W/T message to Seely repeating the message to GOC Aldershot, which was delivered by bicycle. The Royal Navy was also busy with W/T development and when Naval Airship No.1, *Mayfly*, was laid in 1909 the specifications included the installation of powerful equipment. In 1912 the Royal Navy began experiments with W/T in aircraft but the main problem was that the equipment was too heavy for those available at the time not to mention the noise from vibration and the risk of fire. In spite of these difficulties some success was achieved in May when an aeroplane successfully transmitted over a distance of thirty-three miles during a flight from Chartres to Etampe and back. The following month Commander Samson reported success with a 100hp Gnome-powered seaplane, achieving a wireless range of between three and four miles, occasionally improving to ten miles. He expressed the opinion that the observer could, with training, both observe and signal.

The appointment of Fitzmaurice

It was then that the Admiralty appointed Lieutenant R. Fitzmaurice to lead experiments with W/T in aircraft and he deserves credit for the valuable pioneer work in the Naval Air Service. In the spring of 1912 the aim was to construct a light wireless set capable of being carried by the flimsy (by today's standards) aircraft and seaplanes. Initially there was no aircraft available for the fitment of a wireless set so an installation was constructed on Burntwick Island imitating as nearly as possible a set in an aeroplane. The power used was small since it would have been in an airborne unit but the results were encouraging with a range of five to six miles being achieved. In June an aeroplane was made available and the trial using an Exercise Set Type 4, normally used in naval destroyers, was conducted at Harwich. Signals were received clearly at three to nine miles. No attempt was made to receive signals in the aeroplane. This was followed by the construction of a temporary W/T station

Airship *Delta*.

Airship *Beta*.

at Eastchurch in August 1912, which became operational during the first week in September. The mast was 48ft high and the station was in contact with HMS *Actaeon*. In the December W/T call signs for aircraft were instituted, enabling aeroplanes to call up any particular station. The first sign to be allocated for a Triple tractor biplane No.4 at Eastchurch was AI, later NOO.

The Rouzet system

The system adopted was named Rouzet and was fitted to Machine No.4. The specification for improved Rouzet systems fitted to all aeroplanes in 1913 and 1914 was as follows. The weight of the transmitter was 31 kilos with a power of 400 watts. The generator was an alternator operated by the engine of 4,000 to 4,100rpm. It was connected to the engine by means of a clutch and could be thrown out of gear when not being used. A transformer was employed, which sustained a normal pressure of 30,000 volts in the seconding or secondary coils. The park-gap was formed of a movable disc hinged on an adjustable support. It produced eight sparks in series and twelve discharges per revolution, making 800 discharges per second. The antenna winch was formed of a wooden drum driven by a crank. A little sliding drum brake enabled the antenna to unroll by simply easing the spring holding the brake strap. As the brake only worked in one direction the raising of the antenna was effected by simply working the crank. An antenna clip to cut the aerial was operated by a cutting cord placed within reach of the operator. A key was of the ordinary type with a bayonet to allow rapid dismantling. The apparatus measure 315 × 389 × 429mm. In April 1913 four Rouzet transmitting sets were purchased by the Military Wing of the Flying Corps, followed in May by two Rouzet receiving sets. Two transmitting sets and one receiving set were handed over to the Central Flying School in June. The provision of W/T equipment led to the War Office being asked if the Factory could produce a BE type biplane of high power with a large radius of action suitable for carrying two people and W/T equipment. The OC Military Wing proposed that it be powered by a 120hp Austro-Daimler. In May 1913 a Rouzet set was installed in a BE biplane and a trial was conducted with Captain Derbyshire at the controls and Lieutenant James RE acted a wireless operator. The results were hopeful. On 4 June, following further experiments, Lieutenant James claimed that an officer by himself could both operate the aircraft and the W/T equipment.

Work on airships

Work on airships also continued. New sets had been constructed for installation in both the airships *Delta* and *Gamma*. The airship *Eta* was not ready to be fitted at this time but work went ahead for a set to be constructed for use on the ground as the headquarters set. It was planned to use the latter for work with aeroplanes as well and was capable of being installed in a motor car. £100 was granted to the Flying Corps to enable the experimental work to continue. The cost of the Delta sets was around £20 each, which included both sending and receiving apparatus. Being sending and receiving sets they could be used in co-operation with the Rouzet sets. Then the airships of No.1 Squadron were transferred to the Royal Navy and the Military Wing of the Flying Corps ceased to pursue any further work on W/T on airships.

Work on seaplanes

Experimental work continued and on 17 and 20 May 1913 Seaplane No.20 was fitted with W/T for a trial that was carried out along the coast between the Isle of Grain and the North Foreland, a total distance of sixty sea miles (nautical miles). Signals were received at Grain with great distinctiveness throughout the first trial and during the second signals were received up to fifty miles away. This was very successful since it confirmed the range of the wireless installation and ascertained the value of seaplanes for scouting purposes. The greatest distance for signals to be read was between forty-five to fifty miles and this earned Fitzmaurice promotion to the rank of Commander RN in recognition of his work with W/T in aircraft. In October 1913 he was assisted by Lieutenant de C. Ireland who would eventually relieve him.

Naval manoeuvres of July 1913

The state of readiness of W/T in the RNAS may be gauged from the report of the Captain of the *Hermes* during the naval manoeuvres of 1913. The *Hermes* weighed anchor at 14.00hrs on 24 July and Seaplane No.81 was hoisted out and sent to scout north of the vessel. There was a heavy swell but the seaplane did get airborne without difficulty. Scouting was not possible due to dense fog at a low altitude but the aircraft was in contact with the mother ship throughout. On 1 August No.81 was scouting due east of the mother vessel but was later forced to descend. There was some difficulty in deciphering the aircraft's last message but its position could be worked out approximately and HMS *Mermaid* was sent to search for her. In the event the seaplane's crew had been rescued by a German merchant steamer.

Formation of a headquarters flight

In September 1913 the Officer Commanding the Flying Corps sent a report to the War Office showing the considerable advances that had been made in the use of W/T in airships and aircraft. Tribute was paid to the aforementioned officers who had contributed so much and on 4 April 1914 a Headquarters Flight of the Military Wing was formed. The names that appear below will be recognized:

Major the Hon. C.M.P. Brabazon

Captain C. Darbayshire
Lieutenant D.S. Lewis
Lieutenant G.T. Porter
Lieutenant G. Adams
Lieutenant B.T. James
Sub Lieutenant T. O.'B. Hubbard

A Major Musgrove was placed in charge of technical work in kiting, ballooning, wireless, photography, meteorology. Major Brabazon and Lieutenant Hubbard worked on kiting and ballooning; Captain Darbayshire and Lieutenant James with W/T operating and training; Lieutenants Lewis and Adams with W/T design of apparatus, leaving Lieutenant Porter with photography. In a report dated 30 April 1914 Major Musgrove visualized the importance of W/T communication in three areas:

1. Long-range communication between aircraft and the ground for distant reconnaissance
2. Short-range communication between aircraft and the ground for tactical reconnaissance and observation of fire
3. Short-range communication between one aircraft and another for tactical purposes

Captain Lefroys's design for a receiving apparatus had proved satisfactory but there was a considerable way to go for difficulty had been experienced in sending clear signals to a ground station at much over twenty miles. However, the Factory were producing two RE5 reconnaissance aircraft with special modifications to permit the fitment of Lefrey's apparatus. The aim was to start wireless work in all squadrons of the Military Wing, beginning with two squadrons. It was a great fillip to those working on W/T that HM King George, during an inspection of the Flying Corps, was able to able to send and receive signals from BE aircraft in flight. By May 1914 Lefrey was able to receive signals in his wireless aeroplane over ranges of ninety-seven miles and on 18 June 1914 two aircraft equipped with sending and receiving apparatus communicated with each other in a flight from Netheravon to Bournemouth when the aircraft were ten miles apart. Up to the outbreak of war Lefrey continued to improve his design of apparatus with his transmitter and receiver of 1914 but there was insufficient time for evaluation of this apparatus before the outbreak of war.

Wireless and the Expeditionary Force

When the RFC went to war in 1914 the aforementioned experimental set had to be abandoned due to the difficulty in obtaining spares in France. Lefrey did, however, amplify signals received in an aircraft using Brown's relays. On the outbreak of war the Heaquarters Flight of the Military Wing was disbanded so that the equipment and pilots could be made available to the expeditionary force squadrons. Lieutenants Lewis and James, for example, went to No.4 Squadron. Signals officers were also attached to the General Henderson's staff of the HQ RFC in France.

AIRCRAFT WEAPONS (EXCLUDING BOMBS)

Introduction

On the outbreak of the Great War reconnaissance aircraft flew with the pilot armed with a pistol or sidearm. In some naval aircraft there might be a Royal Marine armed with a rifle. Soon aircraft were being fitted with a variety of machine guns. These might be fitted on top of the fuselage immediately in front of the pilot with the gun firing through the arc of the propeller, fitted on top of the upper wing of a biplane so that the rounds passed above the arc of the propeller or, thirdly they would be Lewis guns mounted on a Scaarf ring operated by an observer or air gunner.

The problem with the machine guns that fired through the arc of the propeller is obvious; the rounds might hit the propeller. An angled metal protector was affixed to the propellers to cause a round to be deflected in the manner shown in the diagram below but this proved a very clumsy way of dealing with the problem and led to the invention of the interrupter gear pictured on the following page.

The Constantinescu interrupter gear

This was a major improvement on the system pictured below and simply meant that the gun could not fire as long as the propeller blade was in the path of the rounds being fired. Problems did, however, arise, as with any mechanical contrivance, such as tappet wear on the engine, which actuated the gun-firing mechanism. This was reported by a Commander Groves when he carried out an inspection of units on the Western Front (Source: National Archive document AIR1/943/201/11). There was trouble with the Sopwith 1½ Strutters when propellers had been shot through owing to wear on the tappet of the interrupter gear and this matter was

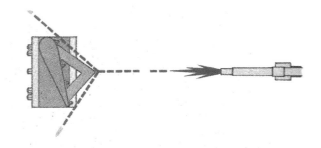

Gun firing through the arc of the propeller.

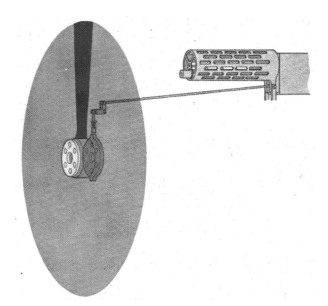

Constantinescu inerrupter gear.

The RFC SE5a.

becoming serious. The same problem was afflicting the Armstrong Whitworth 160hp Beardmores of No.35 Squadron. The interrupter gear failed to work and the propeller was being constantly hit. A replacement gear was being hastened. Information was required to ascertain the circumstances in which the Constantinescu gear might freeze. It appeared that the best way of tackling this problem, which was intimately connected with the interrupter gear, was to get the engineers to thoroughly understand it and to then design the necessary fittings and interrupter gears as part of the engine.

Machine guns mounted in aircraft

The SE5a aircraft carried two different machine guns, a Vickers mounted above the engine, and a Lewis gun mounted above the top wing. The Lewis gun had a tighter pattern than the Vickers, but suffered from being above the line of sight that the pilot had down the nose of the aircraft. The Lewis gun also needed to be reloaded when a drum was exhausted. Considering that most combat reports generally stated that the pilot put between fifty and two hundred rounds into a downed aircraft, this was not so big a disadvantage. But reloading the Lewis gun above the top wing was an impossible task while in a dogfight. The SE5a carried between 550 and 735 rounds of ammunition for the two machine guns. Normally the ammunition used was a mixture of the Mark VII Ordinary, Tracer, Buckingham and Armour piercing .303 bullets. In the Vickers belts these bullets were normally arranged in the form, three ordinary, one tracer, and one armour piercing. For Lewis guns the

mixture was commonly two ordinary, one tracer, one armour piercing and one Buckingham (for Buckingham ammunition see below). The SE5a was outstanding when the pilot used the aircraft's superior speed and strength to engage and disengage enemy aircraft at will. Captain C.H. Copp of the Australian Flying Corps describes the training he received for the SE5a that takes advantage of this strength. Copp describes fellow Australian, Arthur Conningham, instructing him with the following:

> Now, I want you to do some fast diving with your engine full on, and diving vertically. You can get up to nearly 300mph, but I must tell you how to do it without losing your wings. The airspeed indicator only registers up to 180mph, so after that has been passed, you simply look at the fabric on the lower wing. When you see one buckle appear in it, you are probably doing something like 200mph; when there are two buckles, you are probably doing about 250mph; but you want to be careful not to get three, because then the wings will undoubtedly fall off.

This amusing anecdote tells us that it was not simply the quality of the armament or the sufficiency of ammunition that might determine the outcome of an aerial engagement but the full use of the performance of the aircraft. Without an observer who can fire a trainable gun, a pilot on his own had to put his aircraft in the best position, not only to surprise an enemy but to outmanoeuvre him.

Buckingham ammunition

The first time incendiary ammunition was widely used was in World War I. At the time, phosphorus was the primary ingredient in the incendiary charge and ignited upon firing, leaving a trail of blue smoke. These early forms were also known as 'smoke tracers' because of this. Though deadly, the effective range of these bullets was only 350 yards (320m), as the phosphorus charge

An early machine gun mounting.

The concern of pilots not being able to reach their gun in flight persisted throughout much of the inter-war period as did the preference for open cockpits from which a pilot could easily escape in an emergency. By the time the Spitfire and Hurricane fighters came to be produced, with guns mounted in the wings and the rounds being fired outside the arc of the propeller, Messrs Dunlop had come up with a reliable means of firing the gun from the cockpit.

Guns fired by members of the crew other than the pilot

The picture on the left is a very early design. These were pusher type as opposed to tractor types. In two-seater aircraft carrying an observer the latter would be required to fire his gun as a defensive measure since the prime function of the aircraft could well be photographic reconnaissance and the pilot of the aircraft would flying straight and level particularly while pictures were being taken. But the enemy had a habit of pouncing on such machines that were gathering intelligence useful in a coming battle. Reporting on the situation on the Western Front, Commander Groves was required to make a number of visits.

In a second visit to the Western Front Commander Groves also touched on the problems involved in aircraft being used for reconnaissance but suddenly being subject to attack. He commented on the naval DH4s at Dunkirk, which appeared not to have synchronizer gears fitted. The dual control in the observer's cockpit had been removed to allow the carriage of a large camera and W/T equipment. It was not suggested that this be a standard modification since only twelve to twenty machines were required in this form and the necessary modifications could be carried out at the depot taking four days per aeroplane to complete. Further light was shed on the role of the observer in aircraft fitted with cameras. In a machine being used offensively the pilot did not want to position his machine so that his observer could use his camera. In these circumstances the observer was not worth carrying for it was quite impossible for him to cling on to a camera at the same time as training a gun. The observer only got a look in during purely defensive fighting. But things were changing continually and the Commander observed that it had not been long since the single-seat fighter was regarded as of less value than a good two-seater. What was urgently required was the carrying out of dummy fighting patrols with cameras fitted. Firstly, trials could involve an observer carrying only a camera gun with the pilot positioning his machine in the interests of the observer pitted against a two-seater fitted with two camera guns fighting a defensive action, e.g. a reconnaissance machine returning and being chased by enemy aircraft. Secondly, a single-seat fighter could be fitted with a camera gun. Thirdly, a two-seat

burned quickly. Incendiary rounds called 'Buckingham' ammunition were supplied to early British night fighters for use against military Zeppelins threatening the British Isles. The flammable hydrogen gas of the Zeppelins was susceptible to fire, making incendiary rounds much more deadly than standard ones, which would pass through the outer skin without igniting the gas. Similarly, incendiary ammunition was used against non-rigid observation balloons. The RFC forbade the use of incendiary rounds for air-to-air combat with another aircraft, as their use against personnel was at first considered to be a violation of the St Petersburg Declaration. Pilots were only permitted to deploy them against Zeppelins and balloons, and they were additionally restricted to shooting the gas chamber itself rather than the crew. Furthermore, they were required to carry written orders on their person when engaging these targets.

Problems with guns mounted on top of the wing

With the gun mounted on the wing firing above the arc of the propeller the use of all the complicated machinery involved with the interrupter gear was avoided. On the other hand, a gun that could not be reached by the pilot could not be cleared should there be a stoppage. A Bowden cable connected to the trigger of the gun was actuated by the pilot from his sitting position in the cockpit. A sight was mounted on top of the fuselage immediately in front of the pilot. The aircraft had to be steered so that the sight could be lined up on the target.

pusher machine could have both the pilot and observer using camera guns and fighting the same adversaries mentioned in the two aforementioned examples. There appeared to have been some slight misunderstanding on the question of altering the stagger on the wings of the Sopwith Pup but the matter had been settled. The report went on to mention oblique photography with the large camera. The RFC was then using FE2s for this work but the fitment of these cameras to smaller tractor machines was necessary.

THE ORGANIZATION AND WORK OF THE AERONAUTICAL INSPECTION DEPARTMENT

Sources: National Archive document AIR1/674/21/6/27, Ministry of Munitions of War. Department of Aircraft Production procedure book

Introduction

The work of the Aeronautical Inspection Department (AID) was divided into an Aeroplane and an Engine Branch. At the outset the duties of the Aeroplane Branch was to inspect aeroplanes and spare parts during manufacture and to receive complete machines into the AID sheds at Farnborough, to carry out final inspections and flight tests. The Aeroplane Branch started work in February 1914 and in charge of the work was the Inspector of Aeroplanes with his HQ at Farnborough. The Assistant Inspector was responsible for inspection during manufacture and his subordinate inspectors were Resident Examiners at the various works manufacturing aeroplanes. When war broke out, however, there was a vast increase in the output of aircraft and the nucleus of a Scottish division had to be formed in February 1915.

THE AEROPLANE BRANCH OF THE AID

In addition to the manufacture of aeroplanes there was a requirement for spares that would be common to all or the majority of aeroplanes, such as turnbuckles, nuts, bolts and washers. These were known as AGS (aeroplane general spares) parts and the Singer Manufacturing Company of Clydebank had the contract for their manufacture. In addition there was Messrs W.N. Branton & Sons Musselburgh producing tie rods used to brace aircraft and oval section bracing wires known as 'rafwires'. Soon the increase in manufacture of aeroplanes resulted in local inspection control centres in Coventry, Manchester and London and by November 1916 the whole of Great Britain was divided into various local centres, which were later extended into Ireland. These inspection centres operated independently of their opposite numbers in the Engine Branch of AID.

The Ordnance Aircraft Department's Store at Farnborough was the scene of the first Inspection Bond from the beginning of the Great War but the stores then moved to Milton in Berkshire and the inspection bond moved with them. The RFC stores established in 1915 at Greenwich dealt with accessories and instruments and a second inspection bond was formed to cover these stores, which were later moved to Kidbrooke. But this arrangement was not satisfactory since it meant forwarding goods for inspection to the bonds at the stores when the former needed to be near the principal production areas and independent of the Stores Depots. Accordingly, General Inspection Bonds were established, one in London in the autumn of 1917 and the other in Birmingham at the end of that year. More bonds followed to cover AGS spares and the production of cotton fabric as a substitute for linen in the production of aircraft. Inspection involved the testing of various materials used in the production of aircraft and associated equipment and it was decided that the Directorate should have its own Test Houses. These increased in number to test linen fabric and aircraft propellers, although the testing of propellers had been carried out at the Royal Aircraft Factory before the commencement of the war. But as the production of propellers outgrew the facilities at Farnborough a Propeller Test House was established in conjunction with the inspection bond at Milton. The Aeroplane Branch of the AID was responsible for the following categories of inspection:

1. Aircraft and aircraft spares, including propellers
2. Installation of power plant, armament and instruments in an aircraft
3. Kite balloons and winches
4. Electrical equipment
5. Portable oxygen apparatus
6. Hydrogen plant
7. Machine tools for the RAF (Royal Aircraft Factory)
8. Instruments for aircraft
9. All non-metallic materials
10. Hangars and tents for aircraft
11. Packing cases for aircraft.
12. Miscellaneous equipment such as hand tools
13. Parachutes

THE ENGINE BRANCH OF AID

Introduction

Engine inspection got off to a slow start in the United Kingdom and the government took the initiative by carrying out an Aero-Engine Competition at the Factory in the early summer of 1914 to encourage British designers and members of an embryo Engine Inspection Branch were appointed to attend the competition. On the Continent car makers such as Mercedes, Renault and Daimler could adapt in-line car engines for use in aircraft but in Paris the Gnome Engine Co. was producing rotary engines. At the Factory the RAF engines were being produced for aircraft such as the BE2c. This work consisted of many references to the practice of the Factory to produce aircraft that were stable in the air for reconnaissance and artillery support roles and these were the engines to put in them and other Great War aircraft. At the same time Gnome engines were also used for the British Experimental types. Other British manufacturers would eventually join the aero-engine industry such as Rolls-Royce and Beardmore, whilst British firms made foreign engines under licence.

Early inspection work

At the British aero-engine manufacturers inspectors began by observing bench tests and records were kept of horsepower, fuel consumption, wear on parts etc., and card indexes were maintained for each engine up to the point where the engines were delivered to the services. The quality of the steel used was very important and an examiner was appointed to supervise the inspection of manufactures of steel in Sheffield. The standard bench test of the Factory engines comprised a test on full power for four hours followed by a complete dismantling and inspection of all parts so that those that were in any way defective could be replaced and this was then followed by a one-hour test. It was essential for the AID headquarters to have the closest liaison with the Factory to avoid any delay in the delivery of engines to the service. It was then found that the work of the engine repair shops in France could provide valuable information of aero-engines in service use. This could then be great use in improving the design of engines and engine components. Indeed, in November 1915, Captain R.H. Verney was transferred from the engine repair shops in France to the AID as Inspector of Engines.

The purely technical and advisory work grew and many new designs of engines, accessories and components were submitted to the AID. This in turn led to the AID assuming responsibility for initiating modifications and suggesting the names of contractors capable of producing aero engines. These would eventually include British car producers such as Wolsey, Austin and Sunbeam. A particular example will illustrate the importance of the involvement of AID in improving the performance of an aero-engine. This was the 120hp Beardmore, which was based on the original six-cylinder Austro-Daimler engine. During the spring of 1916 the engine was found to be of insufficient power to be installed in the aircraft for which the engine was intended. The whole design was subjected to the scrutiny of AID inspectors and as a result a new 160hp engine was adopted and proved to be one of the most reliable engines of the Great War. The essential point is that the usual 'teething troubles' were eliminated in the redesign.

Changes in organization

The removal of AID HQ to Adastral House meant that there was much more accommodation available for staff. The Engine HQ staff, which previously had been shared amongst four members for all administrative and technical work, could be reorganized. It was possible to set up separate sections, each of which dealt with a particular phase of the work leaving the Head of Branch to organize for the future. As the war progressed the volume of engines being produced grew and with it the need to inspect to ensure that quality was not sacrificed in the name of quantity. Five sections were formed as follows:

1. **The Design Section** Apart from ongoing inspection queries there was a need to deal with all technical questions referred to the AID from the Military Aeronautics Department and Contractors, the redesign of the 120hp Beardmore engine just described above being an example. In order that English contractors developed engines that met service requirements with regard to engine power, controllability, altitude control etc., and to ensure that the appropriate spares were produced the Design Section could be enormously helpful. The section would also consider designs submitted by inventors when experimental orders might be in order.

2. **The Construction Section** The outstation staff of inspectors were working with firms producing aero-engines and technical direction could be given to them when asked. There might also be a need to arbitrate between outstation staff and the contractors. An example might be the need for a modification in the design as advised by the inspectors. This might involve assessing the suitability of materials for the manufacture of certain parts of an engine and collaboration with the Materials Branch would be essential. The section also indicated the proper distribution of the limited stock of inspection apparatus.

3. **Engine repair and Magneto Section** This section oversaw the inspection of engines returned from Service use to contractors for repair. The inspection of engines under repair was generally more difficult than the manufacture of new engines. This was often because the repair contractors were deficient in technical experience whereas the firms producing new engines had had the pick of automobile engineers. Contracts for repair specified a fixed price for the repair of every engine of a particular type and firms were unwilling to undertake a repair that took longer than average even though the fixed price normally allowed an adequate margin of profit. Then these firms believed at the outset that they were required to replace defective components but this did not

allow for the rebalancing of the engine given that some parts would be new amongst parts that were used in the original manufacture. Accordingly, this Section was headed by an officer transferred to the AID from the RFC Engine Repair Section (ERS), Pont de l'Arche, so that liaison between the ERS and home contractors engaged on similar work of engine repair was maintained. Since the officer in question had had exceptional experience in the testing of magnetos, this new AID section was given responsibility for the inspection of magneto manufacture. It is of interest to note that for the first two years of the war the RFC relied on a staple source of supply of German-built magnetos but by the summer of 1916 this supply could not be relied upon, neither could the reliability of American built magnetos designed primarily for automobiles. British firms that were engaged in the manufacture of electrical equipment had experienced repeated failures to produce reliable magnetos but with the help of Magneto Section the sequence of manufacturing operations was overhauled. It was then possible to produce a fairly reliable magneto at a rate of 20–30 per week, which improved over time.

4. **Engine Installation Section** This section administered all the Engine Examiners and Mechanics stationed at the AID aerodromes where the engines were installed in aircraft. They supervised tuning and performance. Additionally, the section kept the Construction Department informed of any deficiencies and failures in inspection by the Works inspection staff as discovered in flight tests. It was not always the case that the availability of engines matched the number of aircraft for which the engine was designed so that a different engine had to be installed. The installation of engines in these circumstances was important given the efficiency and reliability of the engines and the structure of the airframe.

5. **Personnel Section** This section's responsibilities were to maintain records of Engine Branch staff, transference, promotions etc., and to effect documentary engagement of new staff after their technical acceptance by examination by the Head of the Branch or officers i/c sections.

THE ORGANIZATION OF ENGINE BRANCH DISTRICTS

Engine Branch districts were formed in the latter part of 1916 on a purely geographical basis so that inspectors could readily visit contractors. There were three districts formed based on London, Birmingham and Coventry. There was, however, one problem with this arrangement and that was, for example, the same type of aircraft engines being in two adjacent districts such as Birmingham and Coventry. The standard of workmanship and test requirement could vary and it was necessary for there to

be the closest co-operation between the respective district offices with frequent visits being made by members of the Headquarters Construction Section. The London district included Lincoln and Bedford and inspection covered all rotary engines with one exception. At the end of the year a Scottish District Headquarters was set up in Glasgow and this included Newcastle and Manchester following the increase in engine manufacture and that for spare parts. With regard to the production of bright drawn steel used in engine construction as well as the production of wire rope, the materials work in Manchester, which had previously been under the direction of the inspection staff at Sheffield, was administered by the new Glasgow branch.

The district organizations had become well established before March 1917, which is just as well considering the huge expansion of work created by the absorption of the Admiralty inspection duties. Additional contracts were also being signed with new firms producing engines but the branch organization provided the flexibility needed to cope with the increased demands made on the districts. Within each district gauge sections were established and microphotography apparatus for the ready determination of the suitability of steel submitted after treatment by the engine manufacturers, and the facilities for the chemical analysis of steel were brought into play. The standard test bench test for engines was reduced from three to two hours but this involved more stringent examination of the engine after stripping.

A new system for the calibration of the jets in engine carburettors was then introduced. Previously the jets had been classified purely on the dimensions of the jet orifice but this permitted an error of between 30 and 40 per cent, which often delayed engine tuning. Up to that point there had been much wastage of time, labour and petrol and amongst the RAF 1A and 4A engines. For example, it had been found necessary to test them up to four or five times before being declared fit for use. Once the size of jet for a particular engine had been found that gave the best results, tests showed that carburetion was improved, which speeded up the process of tuning engines. After that only minor adjustments were found to be necessary, occupying hours instead of days.

An example of the development of a particular engine, from drawing board to production, is the BHP six-cylinder engine. This water-cooled engine was designed by Captain F.S. Halford in the Design Section and produced by the Galloway Engineering Co., an offshoot of Beardmore. Captain Halford was then seconded for special duties in further developing this engine. Additionally, he was involved in investigating the possibilities of supercharging aero-engines.

The Engine Branch Committee, modelled on the Progress and Allocation Committee, was established to maintain close contact between the section officers and the

Chief Inspector. This was intended to prevent overlapping and to ensure that section officers maintained a clear perspective of their own responsibilities and relationship one with the other. The minutes of committee meetings acted as instructions to district officers to act without additional confirmation. In April 1918 the Chief Inspector of Engines was appointed by the Director General of Aircraft Production to combine in one representative the functions of technical, supply and inspection departments to expedite the efficient production of the Sunbeam Arab engine. The Engine Branch of the AID may therefore claim to have maintained its fundamental organization and its methods, from its inception up to the Armistice, to have maintained them elastically in order to cope with the increased volume of inspection and to have adhered to the widest interpretation of its terms of reference to assist the production of the most efficient and reliable engines.

AERO ENGINES

Introduction

From the engine that powered the Wright Flyer a study of the history of aviation shows the enormous strides that mankind has made to develop internal combustion engines as well as jet engines with the enormous power that can propel several hundred passengers in a wide-bodied jet at 35,000ft many thousands of miles. The engine that propelled the Wright Flyer provided enough power to lift one man for a short distance across the sand. Considerable advances were made in aircraft and engine design even before the outbreak of the Great War in August 1914 and aerial operations only accelerated the process.

Le Rhône rotary engine,

Aero engines used in the Great War were of three types, rotary, radial and in-line engines. Rotary engines had cylinders which projected into the airflow which provided the air cooling. The rotary engine was an early type of internal combustion engine and was usually constructed with an odd number of cylinders such as the Le Rhône engine pictured here. The crankshaft actually remained stationary and the cylinders rotated taking the propeller with them. Alternatively, there were in-line engines, which could comprise cylinders in line, fore to aft or two banks of in-line cylinders in a Vee configuration.

The engine which powered the Wright Flyer the first ever powered flight in the history of aviation.

Rolls-Royce Kestrel 1b Aero engine.

An example of an in-line engine in use during the Great War is shown opposite, the Kestrel 1B.

The rotary engines were believed, at the outbreak of the Great War, to combine reliability with a good power-to-weight ratio but by the end of the war too much of the power output of the engine was being used to overcome the air resistance of the spinning engine and this type became obsolete. The rotation of the entire engine could also make aircraft fitted with them difficult to control. Inexperienced pilots in particular were faced with what was described as gyroscopic precession. A further problem leading to this engine type's obsolescence was the inefficient use of fuel and lubricating oil. The fuel/air mixture was aspirated through the hollow crankshaft and crankcase.

Comparative rotary engines

A series of early rotary engines were designed by Pierre Clerget. These were built in France at the Clerget-Blin plant and in Great Britain by Gwynne Limited and were installed in such aircraft as the Vickers Gunbus and the very successful British fighter, the Sopwith Camel. The distinguishing feature of the Clerget rotary engines was the normal intake and exhaust valves, unlike the Gnome, and the arrangement of the engine connecting rod was much simpler than in the Le Rhône. On the other hand, a major defect in the Clerget engine lay in the special-purpose piston rings, called obturator rings, located below the wrist pin to block heat transfer from the combustion area to the lower part of the cylinder and overcome their subsequent distortion. Since these rings were often made of brass they only had a lifespan of

hours, sometimes resulting in engine failure. Be that as it may, the Clerget engines were considered reliable even if they cost more per unit than rival engines. Another feature that distinguished the Clerget engines was a throttle. The ignition system with the rivals comprised switching engines on or off to provide a rudimentary form of engine speed control. The Bentley BR1 and BR2 engines were designed as improvements to the Clerget variety. Finally, the Clerget engines were air cooled with seven, nine or eleven cylinders, and had a double thrust ball race, which meant that they could be fitted to either tractor or pusher aircraft types. The chief points of difference from other rotary engines included pistons of aluminium alloy, connecting rods of tubular section and inlet/exhaust valves actuated mechanically by separate cams, tappets and rocker arms. The direction of rotation was counter clockwise as seen from the propeller-end of the engine and between any two consecutive firing strokes the engine turned through 80 degrees. For strength and lightness the rotary engines were constructed chiefly of steel.

RADIAL ENGINES

Rotary engines were enormously popular during WWI due to their dispensation for the need of water cooling and because the cylinders were exposed to the air they were readily accessible to mechanics during servicing. They were light and strong but there were drawbacks. They used castor oil for lubrication, which did not dissolve in gasoline, but they tended to spray this in all directions leaving a smelly mess and the engine power was limited, the best reaching between

Gnome rotary engine.

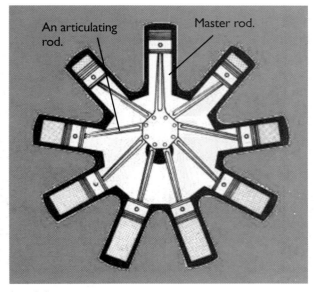

A radial engine.

260 and 280hp. The radial engine was a better design and grew in popularity particularly after the war ended. The cylinders extended outwards from the engine's hub and typically comprised between three to nine cylinders like the one shown here. The radial engine has the same sort of cylinders, spark plugs, pistons and valves as any water-cooled in-line four stroke engine, the difference is in the crankshaft. Instead of a long crankshaft as may be found in any motor car, there is a single hub and all the connecting rods connect to this hub. One of these rods is fixed and is generally known as the master rod. The articulating rods are mounted on pins that allow them to rotate as the crankshaft and pistons move. Pictured below is the ABC Wasp radial engine. Others examples included the Anzani 10 radial and the Salmon Z-9 radial.

ACQUISITION OF AERO-ENGINES BY THE OPPOSING POWERS

The Central Powers, Germany, Austria Hungary, Bulgaria and Turkey, all relied on Germany for the supply of aero-motors. Mercedes-Benz provided most of the aero-engines in the power range 100 to 150hp with Argus supplying 150hp engines. At the outbreak of war, the engines available to the RFC and RNAS did not exceed 80hp and it was not until the Canton-Unne (Salmson) 140hp engines became available that matters improved. In the first few months of the war the RFC obtained the 90hp RAF engines followed by the 120hp Beardmores then by the 100hp Monosoupape and 110hp Le Rhône engines. To sum up, the RFC had to manage with 90hp engines and a very few of the efficient 100 to 120hp variety at the outset of hostilities. To understand

Clerget rotary engine.

this situation more fully it is necessary to go back to the spring of 1914.

Naval and military engine competition

General Henderson, Director General of Military Aviation, was one of the judges and it was his opinion that high-powered engines would be required by the new service. The competition was for engines ranging from 90 to 200hp. with a prize of £5,000 for the best one. Of the sixty-seven entries twenty-three were in the range 125 to 200hp. Although there was a 200hp engine in the competition it was an engine of 100hp that won from nine that passed the test. This was a 100hp water-cooled Green engine. But could such an engine compete with the much higher-powered German engines? The Factory had been experimenting with a water-cooled 200hp engine but Henderson handed over the Factory drawings to private firms, including Rolls-Royce and Napier. Rolls-Royce wanted to develop their own 250hp engine but Napiers were prepared to co-operate with the Factory. Rolls-Royce continued to produce very good engines to power a variety of aircraft but at this time other worthwhile engines were coming off the production lines and have been considered in preceding paragraphs, the Le Rhône, Clerget and Hispano-Suiza for example. The question remains, 'Did the delay in ordering these engines much sooner cause the RFC to suffer as a result'? Did the Directorate purposely delay, hoping that the

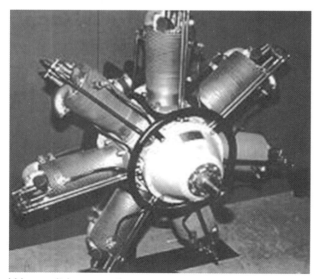

Wasp radial aero engine.

Factory could produce engines of equivalent of better performance? At this time the Factory was working on a 140hp engine that could not have taken the place of either the 110hp Le Rhône or the 200hp Hispano-Suiza. Contractual negotiations for the Hispano-Suiza engine were entered into promptly and a draft agreement was sent to the company on 3 November 1915. When an answer was not received the matter was reopened on 22 February 1916. The four months' delay should not have occurred but in the meantime the company was working on a 200hp engine rather than the 150hp one so no real harm seemed to have been caused since the former was purchased for the RFC. With regard to the 110 Le Rhône engine, it had originally been procured in 1915 but the French Government wanted this engine for the French air force. Could another firm be found to build it under licence? But it was a difficult one to build. At the time the British did not want both the Clerget and the Le Rhône engines and twelve months were spent comparing the two engines. Only then was the latter purchased. When it came to the 200hp Napier engine, this was ordered in large quantities before its worth had been proved. General Henderson defended the production of an engine designed in co-operation with the Factory on the grounds that in wartime gambles do sometimes have to be taken and that the RFC had to trust to luck. This was, as explained earlier, being developed alongside the 250hp Rolls-Royce engine, which proved not to be a gamble. The following section on supply will disclose which engines were ordered, when and for which aircraft.

SUPPLY MATTERS

Supply of spares for the Sopwith biplane 1913
Source: National Archive document AIR 1/363/231/3

This first example of supply illustrates the cost of acquiring aircraft spares at the beginning of the war. It concerns the Sopwith biplane in 1913

A letter from Captain Ellington to the Officer Commanding the Military Wing of the Flying Corps is on the subject of spares for the Sopwith Biplanes on order. They had been ordered in sets for spares considered necessary for a group of four aeroplanes for three months in peacetime. The quantities had been advised by the OC Flying Corps Farnborough. The sums are, of course, at 1913 prices. Some examples appear below:

1 top left plane with ailerons	£40
1 complete rudder	£4- 10/-
1 undercarriage complete with wheels and tyres	£48
4 propellers	£68
The total cost per aeroplane	£424.5s.6d

REPORTS ON VISITS TO THE WESTERN FRONT 3 MARCH 1917
Source: National Archive Document AIR 1/943/201/11

Notes were made on Colonel Courtney's visit to RFC Headquarters on 13 March on the matter of supply. It began with the supply of French aircraft and engines. The supply of complete units would be a matter for the French Quartermaster General but the supply of engines, aeroplanes and parts from the makers was arranged by the Paris Commission. The French had been asked for 200hp geared Hispano Suiza engines and Courtney was to try to get two of the improved non-geared 150hp engines. The special type required by the Expeditionary Force was one then being used on the French front and it was not desired to wait for any further modifications. The Sopwith 1½ Strutters were being delivered to the French and if the deliveries were slow this was entirely the due to conveyance by the French railways, which was a matter for the French. The report moved on to the Aries contract for 150 Hispano Suiza engines, of which 55 were believed to have already gone to England with 68 more to follow but these engines did not have the special interrupter gear required for the SPAD aircraft. Approximately 180 of the 150hp engines were being held in the Brassier Works and Colonel Courtney was attempting to see if he could get any of these engines for the RFC. In all, 150 of these engines were required by the RFC in the field for the second quarter of 1917.

Finally, the report dealt with the question of the role of the artillery machine. It must be regarded as a general utility machine suitable for several purposes, which did not possess the speed and climb of a fighter but should have good defensive armament. It should not be required to carry out extended reconnaissance missions but be capable of carrying out patrols of the front line. It should not be required to carry out special bombing missions but be capable of moderate bombing operations at short range if required. It should not be difficult to fly

Sopwith Tractor biplane.

and it should be capable of working from small hastily improvised aerodromes.

Supply problems in October 1916

Some snippets from letters written between the supply depots and HQ RFC France give an insight into problems that arose at that time. One concerns a letter sent from No.2 Aircraft Depot to HQ RFC on 9 October 1916. The Depot Commander was complaining about the failure of RFC wings to inform the Depot when they have been instructed to draw stores from the RFC railway siding at Candas Exchange station. At that time the Railway Operating Division was laying down a new siding and it had not been possible to unload all the stores that had arrived. The Depot staffs were therefore confronted with the situation of having to unload twenty-seven complete aeroplane cases, all of which were holding up trucks. This was on top of the ordinary daily consignment of stores and the clearing of a large quantity of ashes, although the letter does not explain the reason for the ashes. The unloading work for the day had suddenly to stop at about 16.00hrs when seven or eight lorries suddenly arrived from the wings. The wing personnel stated that their instructions were to load up with some wooden huts that had arrived during the night and had been unloaded on to the open field beyond the RFC siding by German POWs. Since the Depot Commander was unprepared for this situation confusion arose and he found that his men could not get as many aeroplane cases away as he would have liked. Thus the congestion on the siding did not benefit the railway authorities. He therefore asked if, in future, he could be informed of any future distribution intended so that he could arrange for stores to be unloaded at the ordinary station.

No.2 Aircraft Depot was again in need of the unskilled labour provided by German POWs. In a letter dated 22 December 1916 the Fifth Army was requested to make fifty POWs + escort available to work at the Depot, which would release skilled labour working on aircraft repairs. The period would be for two months or as long as may be required.

The supply of guns and ammunition was the subject of much of a letter dated 7 November 1916. It stated that Lewis, Maxim and Vickers guns were to be issued by depots on demand without reference to Advanced HQ RFC. Tracer ammunition and specially selected ammunition were to be issued on demand but care had to be taken by squadrons that they did not hold tracer ammunition above their establishment. It was of the utmost importance that the correct establishment of weapons be maintained and that guns that were surplus to requirements were returned to Aircraft Depots. On the other hand, signalling panels and armour piercing ammunition were not to be issued without reference to Advanced HQ RFC. Ground flares, double drums and

Klaxon horns were not to be issued from Aircraft Depots without due reference to higher authority.

The last of the stores letters of this period warns units not to hold stores above establishment. Squadrons arriving from England often had quantities of stores well in excess of establishment. Units were therefore to undertake stocktaking and return stores to the Aircraft Depots that were in surplus. For example, units were holding spares relating to Crossley and Leyland vehicles in excess of establishment. The Equipment Officer who signed the letter was of the opinion that all squadrons in the 12th Wing held only the established quantities as a result of stocktaking.

ARMY AND NAVY SUPPLY TO THE RAF
Source: CAB/21/21

With the impending formation of an Air Ministry supply to the new service was considered by a Cabinet Committee. It was not simply a matter of transferring all the aircraft and airfields to the RAF. Army and Royal Naval supply depots were already established that provided a great diversity of materials and equipment to the RFC and RNAS. To disrupt those sources of supply to air units in the middle of a war could be potentially disastrous. For example, daily supplies of fuel, bombs, aircraft spares and rations had to be maintained and the RAF had yet to establish its own maintenance units for supply and repairs. Consequently, the supply of various classes of equipment, materials and liquids to the RAF from 1 April 1918 was considered.

Fuels and lubricants should continue to be supplied from Army sources but in certain circumstances the Royal Navy would be approached for supply from seaplane bases. With regard to personal arms and equipment the quantities involved were so small that it would have been a waste of effort to create a RAF source in competition with the Army and the Navy. It was felt that there was no need to change the supply arrangements for camp and field equipment, at least until the end of the war. As opposed to personal arms, the supply and maintenance of machine guns and aircraft armament should be a matter for the Controller or Aeronautical Supplies through the Ministry of Munitions but it was felt that the testing of armament should remain with the Master General of Ordnance who was also responsible for ammunition and explosives.

Domestic stores, including barrack equipment, clothing, rations, forage, fuel and light and barrack services did not, in the Committee's view, merit fundamental change in the supply and maintenance arrangements, at least until the end of hostilities. The supply of barrack and hospital stores should remain with the Army for RAF land-based units and the Royal Navy for the RAF at sea. RAF personnel in 1918 remained in khaki and retained their equivalent Army ranks. Similarly those on board HM vessels at sea with RAF flying units who had previously been in the RNAS retained their naval uniforms. It was therefore decided that until new uniforms were designed supply arrangements should remain unchanged. New ranks and uniforms were to be introduced in 1919 when supply arrangements changed, although personnel serving in the Fleet Air Arm did retain naval uniforms. Rations, forage, fuel and light, it was felt, should continue to be supplied on the basis of there being land based or afloat, i.e. no change. Finally came the consideration of barrack services such as accommodation occupied by RAF personnel in isolated stations. In these cases it would be impractical to transfer Army accommodation to the RAF and so the Army should continue to administer and maintain it regarding it as being temporarily lent to the RAF.

SUPPLY OF AIRCRAFT AND ENGINES – POSITION IN DECEMBER 1917

Source: National Archive document: AIR1/6A/4/41 & 38, AIR1/6A/4/42, CAB/21/21

Aircraft requirements in peace and war

Since the Great War was the first in which combat aircraft had been used in large numbers the business of forecasting the needs of the air services was new. What the air services, the RFC and RNAS did know as the war progressed was the figures for combat losses. So aircraft and engine production had to account for what is known as 'wastage' due to combat losses and accidents and for the growth in the number of operational squadrons and flying training units. There was also the need to indicate to the aircraft industry which types were required. Add to this improvements as new designs came off the drawing

Sir William Weir.

board, which affected the contracts made with the aircraft industry. The meeting chaired by Sir William Weir, the Director General of Aircraft Production, in December 1917 addressed these matters and projections were made into the summer of 1919, well beyond the war's actual end. It is ironic that by this time aircraft coming off the production line were being taken directly to the breaker's yard following the massive run down from 185 service squadrons to just 25. There would not be a massive rearmament until 1935 when the threat posed by Adolf Hitler's Nazi regime could no longer be ignored. These matters were considered in a memo written by Sir William in September 1917.

Aeronautical supply position in relation to the general industrial situation

In anticipation of the importance of meeting the services' needs for aircraft and engines Sir William Weir wrote a memo to the War Cabinet on 11 September 1917. It was important, he said, to be able to supply with certainty the maximum supply of aircraft and engines of suitable character for the spring and early summer of 1918. The general industrial situation would be a critical element in determining the possibility/probability of meeting these needs. This might, he suggested, mean a readjustment of the manufacturing facilities in carrying out the programme and he further considered the actions that the German government might make with regard to their supply of aircraft and engines in the spring of 1918. Germany might, for example, cut back on the production of artillery and ammunition programmes to concentrate on aircraft production. It was therefore necessary to base Britain's requirements on a programme that envisaged some definite aerial campaign of an offensive character and to establish officially whether or not our industrial resources should be adjusted to ensure overwhelming air superiority. He continued by saying that unless this official authorization was obtained the completion of programmes in the proper time could not be guaranteed since production relied on both skilled and unskilled labour, raw materials, plant and facilities and transport facilities both at home and abroad. The supply of skilled labour was a critical element and already it was being found that the quality of recruits into the armed services was falling, particularly in aircrew applicants. As it was, there was an increasing reliance on female labour both in industry and the armed forces. The total supply of skilled engineering labour was already entirely devoted to war work. And so Sir William classified war work as follows:

Category A Requirements for offensive purposes or contributory thereto:

1. Artillery, rifles, machine guns, ammunition and other items used by armies in the field.

2. Aircraft, aero-engines and general aeronautical supplies.
3. Mechanical transport, including tanks.

Category B Requirements, the provision of which has been imposed on us by German submarine and aerial policies and which are of a defensive character:

1. Anti-aircraft guns for Home Defence, anti-submarine guns for merchant ships, mines, depth charges, paravanes, anti-submarine naval shipping, patrol boats, mine sweepers etc.
2. Seaplanes, ship borne aircraft, rigid and non rigid airships, naval kite balloons.

Category C Purely naval requirements:

1. Submarines, torpedo boat destroyers, light cruisers, battleships with their guns, machinery, torpedoes and equipment.

Category D Requirements ancillary to the above three categories:

1. Merchant service shipping.
2. Machine tools, small tools, factory buildings and equipment for manufacturing facilities in connection with the above.

Sir William drew the conclusion that the greatest claims on Britain's skilled labour supply was for the provision of requirements of a more or less defensive character. Aeronautical supply had been the last large service to impose its claims on industry during the Great War and had had to be content with a comparatively small ratio of skilled labour. And so the rate of acceleration in supply could only have been slow because of the nature of aeronautical supply work, particularly with aero-engines which required a high ratio of skilled labour.

He went on to demonstrate the relative importance and dimensions of aeronautical supply in relation to other war supplies and tabled the appropriate figures for expenditure by way of comparison.

Annual expenditure of Category A – £400 million of which £50 million represented the prevailing rate of aeronautical expenditure.

Annual expenditure of Category B – £60 million

Annual expenditure of Category C – £100 million

Annual expenditure of Category D – £80 million

Total annual expenditure at the prevailing rates = £680 million of which £50 million was attributable to aeronautical supply.

On the basis of the 1918 programme Sir William expected the expenditure for aeronautical supply to be £150 million and this figure did not include personnel. Accordingly the aeronautical programme could only be achieved by diverting resources from other programmes. He then questioned whether the sums committed to the aeronautical programme were large enough but this would depend upon the true war policy. This, in turn, involved a consideration of the influence on aerial strategy and a definite aerial plan of campaign. He believed that the achievement of the aeronautical programme was suffering through an indefinite knowledge of actual aerial policy for 1918. He stressed that it was important to know as soon as possible what that policy was to be since the longer its determination was left the more difficult it would be to make adjustments to manufacturing arrangements. There was also the supply of the requisite pilots, personnel, the provision of aerodromes and associated accommodation. Diversion of resources would then affect such programmes as the provision of submarines, lighter-than-air-craft, seaplanes etc.

Response to Sir William Weir's memo by Commodore Paine (Appendix II to the above)

Commodore Paine was in general agreement with Sir William on the need to make a decision on the aeronautical programme and echoed the view that an increase in aircraft meant the pilots to fly them and the airfields to house them. He singled out the lack of the suitable recruits from a dwindling supply of untapped labour, and provision of the appropriate training machines, as well as instructors. He then went on to list all the other needs that would arise, which were only too obvious, and even went so far as to suggest that Britain may need to put American pilots into the aircraft being produced in the existing programme

Commodore Godrey Paine.

With regard to the plan for an aerial campaign he said that no time should be lost in putting in place all that was necessary for an aerial offensive, It was useless to put off these arrangements until the requisite aircraft were ready for delivery. He considered that aircraft should be sent to units in batches between ten and twenty machines as they became available so that the offensive could be started at the earliest possible moment. On the matter of the availability of trained pilots he could not speak for the RFC but expected that, with existing training facilities, the RNAS could train, on average, 120 to 130 pilots a month and that three-quarters of these would be needed to man seaplanes. Again, he echoed Sir William's view that resources from other works all over the country would need to lose labour for the war effort and this would be the responsibility of the Master General of Ordnance.

More than the availability of training resources, he touched on the shortage of 5,000 men needed for the flying services and the solution to employ more women was almost at a standstill blaming the War Office in arriving at unsatisfactory solutions to female recruiting problems, which he did not mention. Nearly all the men who joined the Flying Corps, said Commodore Paine, were unskilled so must be trained, ab initio, if they were to become fitters riggers and other trades associated with aircraft.

He summed up by expressing his opinion that the Cabinet must take the view that aviation is more important than any other branch of the services and must be ruthless in cutting down the demands of other services. Like Sir William, he feared that Germany could put the greatest emphasis on aircraft and submarine production. Only by adopting the measures advocated by both men could Britain hope at least to be on a level with Germany by the spring of 1918. He believed that the exercise of both land power and sea power would have to come second to military aviation. He described powers of the old forms of warfare as waning compared to air power. These views may be 'over the top' and would certainly not receive a sympathetic reception on the part of their Lordships at the Admiralty nor those at the War Office but it was a sign of the times. Trenchard would make the same claims for air power and would have to be taken to task by Sir William Hankey, the Secretary to the Cabinet in the 1920s. The enthusiasts of the air were not hard to find and were, by the very nature of the fast-moving development of military aviation, people who were looking forward.

AIRCRAFT/ENGINE REQUIREMENTS IN 1918

The Director General of Aircraft Production wrote to the Secretary of the Air Board on 15 December 1917 referring to Sir Douglas Haig's letter of 20 November since the latter wished to know what the aircraft supply situation would be in August 1918. Sir William Weir reported that production would reach 3,500 a month of which 100 per month would be of the multiple engine type. There should therefore be no difficulty in reaching the establishment asked for by General Trenchard of 179 squadrons plus 20 for the Middle East and 20 for home defence. Chapter 5 contains reports from the Middle Eastern theatre that the air was almost absent of German aircraft. But it had to be decided right away what types of aeroplanes and engines were required. If this was done then Weir saw no reason why the previously stated establishment of squadrons should not be achieved by the beginning of 1919. As things stood the establishment of 180 by August together with necessary training establishments. This figure assumed a wastage of ten aircraft per squadron per month and there would also have to be an output of 800 training aeroplanes per month. In other words wastage and training requirements would account for 2,600 aeroplanes per month. This would leave 900 machines per month to build up the establishment plus additional wastage.

Technical advances had also to be considered. Again Chapter 5 refers to the minutes of the Air Policy Committee, when the designers had done all they could to design aeroplanes to match or exceed the performance of German machines, but they were waiting for better engines. One solution would be an adequate supply of the American Liberty engines. What were later known as Air Ministry specifications, which designers and aircraft producers had to meet, were in the Great War known as Expeditionary Force (EF) requirements since the air staff at HQ RFC in France had first-hand operational experience of the capabilities of enemy machines as compared with those of Allied machines. As an example the next paragraph deals with the EF requirements for a single-seat fighter discussed on 31 December 1917.

Sir William Weir met Generals Trenchard and Salmond and they discussed progress on a single-seat fighter. Trenchard remarked that the Martinsyde machine had a bad view and poor manoeuvrability. He suggested that a single-seat fighter using the Falcon engine with a better view than the Martinsyde would need to be ready by March. Trenchard asked if a special single-seat fighter might be designed to take the 300 Hispano-Suiza engine, meeting the EF performance requirements for speed, armament, climb, view etc. He further expressed his desire to meet all the designers of single-seat fighters where development was in hand to question them on certain characteristics. He considered that the 170 ABC SS fighters would be of no use to the EF unless they could carry the full armament and petrol specified. It was desirous that the big wings fitted to the DH9 machines go to the EF to be tried out on a Rolls-Royce-powered DH4 with outside fuel tanks. It was known that the wings of a DH9 could be fitted to a DH4

DH4.

without alteration. An endurance table for all DH9s, including those fitted with the Liberty engines, was requested. General Salmond asked for confirmation that arrangements were in hand for the fitting of bombsights

and bomb release gear for the standard DH9 to be operated by either pilot or passenger. The interchange ability of the BR2 engines and the Clerget was discussed. The back plate of the Clerget engines differed in some respects there being a difference of 2mm in some measurements. Since the French would not modify the Clerget engine the possibility of altering the BR2 engine was to be investigated. The discussion moved on to the bombing machines in general. The first twenty Handley Page machines would be fitted with Sunbeam Maori engines and the following 100 with Rolls-Royce Eagles. The question of which engines should be fitted to the thirty machines constructed by the Metropolitan Carriage & Wagon cmopany was left in abeyance but it was desirous that all of the Handley Page machines should be fitted with Rolls-Royce engines.

The requirement and forecast output of squadrons by type was as follows:

Aircraft by type	Number of squadrons required	Output forecast
1. Single-seat fighter	36	40 should be completed by April 1919
2. Single-seat fighter for ground work	15	5 squadrons of modified Camel should be completed by summer of 1918 as a temporary measure
3. Two-seater fighter reconnaissance	15	Output not later than summer of 1919
4. Short distance night bomber	10	Output not later than summer of 1919
5. Short distance day bomber	10	Output not later than summer of 1919
6. Long distance photo machine	1	Output not later than summer of 1919
7. Gun machine	1	Output not later than summer of 1919
8. Long distance day bomber	25	Output not later than summer of 1919
9. Long distance night bomber	20	Output not later than summer of 1919
10. Long distance fighter reconnaissance	20	Output not later than summer of 1919
11. Long distance gun machine	1	Output not later than summer of 1919
12. Artillery	30	Output not later than summer of 1919
13. Night flyer for Home Defence	10	Output not later than summer of 1919
14. Two-seater fighter	–	Not specified
15. Armoured machine	–	To be investigated

Bristol Fighter F2B.

The types of aircraft to equip these squadrons were:

Single-seater fighter	New machine to take the BR2 engine
Single-seater fighter for ground work	New machine to take the BR2 engine
Two-seater fighter reconnaissance	De Havilland 4 or 9
Short-distance night bomber	Handley Page
Short-distance day bomber	De Havilland 10

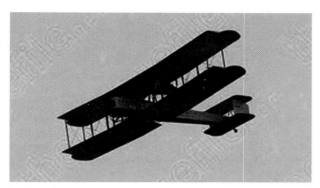

Vickers Bomber.

DH10 Amiens.

Handley Page Bomber.

Sopwith Dolphin.

Photo machine	De Havilland 10
Gun machine	De Havilland 10
Long-distance day bomber	De Havilland 10
Long-distance night bomber	Vickers bomber
Long-distance fighter reconnaissance	De Havilland 10
Long-distance gun machine	De Havilland 10
Artillery	Fighter
Night fighter Home Defence	Modified Dolphin

The total requirement of each aircraft type was:

De Havilland 4 or 9	15 squadrons
De Havilland 10	58 squadrons
New type single seater fighter	71 squadrons
Handley Page	10 squadrons
Vickers bomber	20 squadrons
Bristol Fighter	30 squadrons
Modified Camel	5 squadrons
Modified Dolphin	10 squadrons

NOTES ON AIRCRAFT REQUIREMENTS TO SUMMER 1919
Source: AIR 1/6A/4/42

Operational aircraft

With regard to single-seater fighters sufficient aircraft had to be produced to maintain existing squadrons as well as equipping the proposed new squadrons. It was decided that the resources allocated to the production of Sopwith Camels, SE5as and Dolphins would result in a surplus of approximately 150 aircraft per month. It was agreed that only ten squadrons of Handley Page bombers would suffice and provision had already been made to equip these squadrons and an output of forty machines per month would be required to cover wastage. The contractors at that time would have the capacity to produce slightly over 100 machines a month and Handley Page should only continue on the type for existing contracts. Future contracts would be transferred to the Vickers bomber. For artillery work the Bristol Fighter was earmarked and the requirement for these machines would gradually increase to 400 machines a month by November 1918. But the existing production capacity could not produce sufficient aircraft and it was decided that once the contract for producing RE8 aircraft was complete this would free up the capacity to produce between forty to fifty aircraft a month. The DH4 and DH9 were intended to meet the requirement for two-seat fighter reconnaissance aircraft. For this purpose the RFC had five squadrons of Bristol Fighters with Rolls-Royce 190 engines and three squadrons of DH4 with Rolls-Royce Eagle engines and the plan provided for nineteen additional squadrons in the bombing role. The additional squadrons would be equipped with DH9 machines until a newer type, the DH10, was forthcoming. To meet the requirement for DH10 machines (58 squadrons) the monthly output would need to increase from 84 in August 1918 to 800 a month in June 1919 and, after that, to 650 per month to cover wastage. To meet these requirements the DH9 contractors and all but one of the RE 8 contractors would transfer to the DH10 programme on completion of existing contracts. In spite of this there would still be a shortfall and from February 1919 additional capacity would be required to produce approximately 200 aircraft per month.

Training aircraft
After fulfilling the above requirements productive capacity would be available from Avro, AW 160 Beardmore, DH6 and Sopwith Scout contractors to the tune of 800 a month in April 1918, rising to 935 a month by August. This would approximately cover the requirements stated by the RFC, namely 800 per month and RNAS for 140 per month.

NOTES ON ENGINE REQUIREMENTS
Source: as above

As with the supply of aircraft, engine output estimates had not only to cover increases or decreases in the number of squadrons and aircraft, wastage and training. For details of these engines see the section on engines in the preceding technical part of this chapter.

Rotary engines
Requirements of these were expected to increase from 200 per month in April 1918 to 1,200 per month in April 1919 and from July 1919 onwards, approximately 540 per month were expected to be required. It was anticipated that deliveries of the BR1 and BR2, 130hp Clerget, 200hp Clerget and the 110hp Le Rhône would be 600 a month in April 1918, rising to 1,160 engines per month in November. From March 1919 onwards the output of BR2 engines was expected to be 960 per month on the assumption that Messrs Vickers also transfer to the construction of the BR2 engine on completion of their existing contract for the BR1. It was expected that a surplus of approximately 300 engines per month from April to November 1918 would be allocated for training purposes.

Hispano Suiza
The estimate for output of this engine ranged from 800 per month in May 1918 decreasing to 300 in April 1919. This would suffice to maintain existing squadrons and the equipment and maintenance of new types. It was anticipated that Messrs Wolsey would continue in production and that Messrs Austin, on completion of the existing contract, would transfer to another type. On this assumption output would be 900 in April 1918, rising to 1,125 in July and decreasing to 670 per month in October. On this basis it was expected that the proposed new squadrons could be maintained to the end of March 1919. Additionally, it was expected that a large quantity of this type of engine would be returning from single-seater fighter squadrons in France where engines were being replaced.

260hp Sunbeam
An assumption was made that the requirement for these engines, which equipped the medium flying boats, would die out in September of 1919. In the meantime the requirement would be 100 a month in April 1918, increasing to 250 in April 1919 with only 90 per month from June to cover wastage. Messrs Sunbeam's deliveries were thought to be 112 engines per month from November 1918, which would have been insufficient to meet requirements. To make up the shortfall there was a recommendation that two firms, Messrs Beardmore and Arrol Johnston, be transferred to the production of a Sunbeam engine of this type or another suitable for powering long-distance night bombing machines, once their contracts to build Beardmore engines were completed.

BHP
Requirements were for this engine amounted to 550 in April 1918 increasing to 740 in the December but gradually decreasing to 220 per month in July 1919. It was anticipated that deliveries of this engine would be 420 in April increasing to 650 in June 1918. An assumption was made that Messrs Beardmore might not continue on this type and that numbers would decrease to 600 engines per month by November, thus creating a shortage for the period April to August. The shortage would be quickly wiped out owing to the large quantity of BHP engines, which would become available from replaced squadrons. Messrs Siddely Deasy would be available to produce a new type of engine from 1 January 1919.

Rolls-Royce Eagle
These engines were definitely required for large flying boats, de Havilland 9 machines, two-seater reconnaissance work and Handley Page aircraft. The anticipated deliveries would, with the exception of a shortage during the month of May to September 1918,

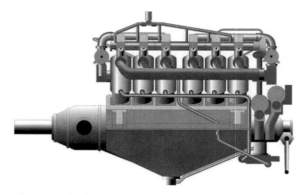

Rolls-Royce Eagle VIII.

cover the requirements and it was expected that there would be a slight surplus available from the beginning of 1919, which could be utilized in other types of aircraft.

Napier and Liberty engines

These engines, together with the Rolls-Royce Eagle, were required commencing in July and gradually working up to 1,300 per month in May 1919, and from August 1919 the figure was approximately 500 per month. It was hoped that Messrs Austin, on completion of their contract to build Sunbeam 'Arab' engines, and Messrs Siddeley Deasy would, towards the end of 1918, transfer production to the Eagle, Napier and Liberty engines. It was expected that 3,000 Liberty engines would arrive from the USA and if Messrs Napier continued with a production of thirty per month together with the surplus of Rolls-Royce Eagle engines then a surplus of 1,000 engines over requirements by the end of June 1919 was expected. This was believed to be a sensible quantity as a margin. The arrival of the Liberty engines was important and if deliveries over the period of May to October 1918 continued on the existing arrangements there would be a large quantity of engines during the period for which aircraft would not be available.

US Liberty engine.

Engines for training aircraft

The requirements were assessed as approximately 1,000 per month during the period May to August 1918 and afterwards 550 per month for wastage. It was advised that 230 of these engines were destined for aircraft of the RNAS.

AEROPLANES AND ENGINES IN USE WITH THE RNAS IN 1917

Introduction

It should be noted that the lists that follow are arranged in alphabetical order and do not include experimental types. The letters RAF stand for Royal Aircraft Factory.

Aircraft and engine	Remarks
Avro 80hp Gnome	Both two-seat and single-seat used exclusively for training work
BE2 C, D & E 75 and 80hp Renault, 90hp RAF engine	Two-seater tractor. Used as training machine. Also a night flyer for home defence against Zeppelins. A few also used for reconnaissance patrols in the Eastern Mediterranean.
Bristol Scout 80 & 100hp Gnome	Originally used as fast single-seat fighter, Now becoming out of date and used only for advanced training purposes.
Caudron 100hp Anzani & 80hp Gnome	Two-seater tractor used only as a school's machine.
Sopwith 1½ Strutter 110 & 130 Clerget	Both single-seater and two-seater. The single-seater was used as a bomber and the two-seater in the fighter reconnaissance role. This was one of the best machines in 1916 but was by 1917 obsolescent.
Sopwith Pup 80hp Le Rhône	Single-seater fighter. Very fast with an excellent rate of climb. Very considerable during 1916 in France but this machine was now outclassed by the latest Sopwith, Nieuport and SPAD fighters and was becoming obsolete. Would be used for higher training and also could be used on board for flying off the deck.

Sopwith F1 Camel 130hp Clerget	The latest Sopwith single-seater fighter. Only just produced and not available in quantities.	**4 August 1915**	Heavy vehicles..........1,189 Light vehicles..............348 Motor cycles................932 Total 2,469
Sopwith Triplane 130hp Clerget	A single-seater fighter of great speed and climbing power. The last machine produced by Sopwith before the Camel	**4 August 1916**	Heavy vehicles...........2,613 Light vehicles...........1,112 Motor cycles.............1,537 Total 5,262
SPAD 150 and 200hp Hispano Suiza	A French machine and single-seater fighter. Only lately produced and not yet available in quantities. The 200hp machine had a better performance in way of speed and climb than any machine yet produced.	**4 August 1917**	Heavy vehicles..........3,395 Light vehicles...........2,568 Motor cycles.............2,621 Total 8,584
Short 250hp Rolls-Royce and 240hp Sunbeam	A large two-seater land bomber that could carry a great weight of bombs but it had poor speed and climb and is therefore vulnerable and was becoming obsolete. A few were still used in France.	**4 August 1918**	Heavy vehicles..........5,927 Light vehicles...........5,500 Motor cycles.............4,066 Total 15,493*
		31 October 1918	Heavy vehicles..........6,819 Light vehicles...........6,293 Motor cycles.............4,592 Side cars...................2,668 Trailers.....................2,790 Misc. ....98 Total 23,260

THE GROWTH IN THE NUMBER OF MECHANICAL VEHICLES SUPPLIED TO THE RFC
* (The figures include RNAS vehicles from 4 August 1918)

4 August 1914

Heavy vehicles.........139
Light vehicles...........49
Motor cycles............132
Total 320

Epilogue

Some Thoughts on the Career of Air Marshal Sir Hugh Trenchard

An encyclopaedia on the birth of the Royal Air Force would not be complete without a close inspection of the career of Air Marshal Sir Hugh Trenchard. Chapter 5 was devoted to the last year of the Great War, a year in which Trenchard went from Commander of the RAF Force in the Field to become the first Chief of the Air Staff of the RAF followed by a resignation from that post only to be placed in command of the Independent Bombing Force and ultimately back to the post of Chief of the Air Staff. He was to hold this post for the following ten years; the RAF's most formative years. All holders of the post of Chief of the Air Staff would hold that post for two or three years but Trenchard wanted to make sure that the RAF was firmly established in a way that he wanted before he stood down.

Early career

From his days at school Trenchard was destined for a military career but, since in those early years there were

The young Trenchard.

no aeroplanes and thus no air arm, he was commissioned into the Army. Academically he was weak and it took several attempts to reach the standard required to be awarded a commission. When it came to the written word he was almost inarticulate. One has only to read the correspondence in the early 1920s between Trenchard and T.E. Lawrence (of Arabia) to realize how awkward was his phraseology. Not only was his correspondence with Lawrence remarkable, coming as it did from the Chief of the Air Staff to a 'ranker' at Uxbridge who was trying to escape his notorious past and disappear from the public eye, but Trenchard relied absolutely on Lawrence's discretion. In speaking about the tribal quarrels in the Middle East at a time when the RAF was using aeroplanes to keep the peace between feuding tribes, Trenchard had this to say:

> I do not want to kill either side and I am not doing much in it, but people who live by raiding almost all their lives do not understand our feelings on the subject and they dislike when we try to stop them and think that our methods are more brutal then theirs. Equally the poor unfortunate officers and men who are in the desert trying to stop the raiding do not like it – it is unpleasant and they always, I expect, feel the faults are half on each side as I do. However I hope for the best through patience and the Air, if I can only get the Ibn Saud fanatics to believe in it and go up in it.

By this he means that he would like them to go up flying and see for themselves the effectiveness of air power.

Shown overleaf is a photograph of the staff of the Central Flying School. A friend of Trenchard had got him to try flying and so he paid £75 to get his Royal Aero Club's pilot certificate, but it had not been easy for he was partially blind in one eye (but so was the Air Ace Mannock) and had a damaged lung from his injury sustained in the Boer War. He joined the staff of the Central Flying School and had to spend weeks to improve his flying skills but he remained an indifferent pilot so that when he was appointed an instructor he did not do any instructing but instead immersed himself in administrative duties. As the school examiner he wrote the paper to be sat by trainees, marked it and awarded himself his 'Wings'.

It is difficult in these circumstances to conjure up a picture of a future air marshal but he obviously saw the big picture about the future of the RFC and later in his career his subordinates likened him to a 'Pole Star' who could clearly see the way ahead. Initially he was appointed as

Trenchard is in the front row, third from the right.

Commander of the Military Wing Royal Flying Corps in Britain, replacing Lieutenant Colonel Sykes. He and the paths of Sykes would cross on a number of occasions in the years that lay ahead. He was disappointed at not going to war in France and asked to rejoin his regiment on active duty. General Sir David Henderson refused to release him and his new task was to raise the squadrons necessary to constitute the air component of the British Expeditionary Force (BEF). Trenchard was then to take up his first command post in the RFC in France only to find that his immediate superior was to be Sykes. One

Field Marshal Haig.

of Trenchard's reactions to disappointment was to threaten resignation for he did not like working under Sykes so Henderson himself assumed command of the RFC in France. Trenchard was appointed to command the First Wing comprising Nos.2 and 3 Squadrons. He would use the threat of resignation again when he did not get what he wanted.

As commander of the First Wing he was then on active service. Field Marshal Haig commanded the First Army and early in 1915 the Field Marshal asked for Trenchard's advice on the use of his aircraft in the planned offensive in the Merville/Neuve Chappelle region. It is well documented that every major Allied offensive during the protracted struggle in the trenches failed and although Trenchard's aircraft went into action with bombs strapped to the wings and fuselage, little was achieved and the artillery disregarded the information brought back by his reconnaissance aircrews. In spite of this Trenchard was offered the post of Chief of Staff at RAF HQ, a post that he declined since he wanted the post of Commander of the RFC in France. He was promoted to the rank of full colonel in June 1915 and when Henderson returned to the War Office in the summer of 1915 he got what he wanted. Haig was appointed commander of the BEF and Trenchard as a brigadier-general became commander of the RFC in the Field.

In his new post he had three priorities. Firstly he placed the greatest emphasis on co-operation with the ground forces, including reconnaissance and artillery co-operation and later tactical low-level bombing of enemy ground forces. As the man who would go on to command the IBF, at this time, he was opposed to strategic bombing that might divert air units from the Western Front. He did not oppose strategic bombing of targets in Germany in principle but felt it to be less important than the tactical use of aircraft given the limited resources at his disposal. Secondly there was the morale effect, not of his own airmen but on the effect that his aircraft might have on the enemy. Finally there was Trenchard's unswerving belief in the importance of offensive action.

On the passing of the RAF Act he was summoned back to London, travelling on a destroyer on 16 December, and met Lord Rothermere who was to be the RAF's first Air Minister. It was not long, however, before differences of opinion surfaced between the two men. Rothermere intended to use Trenchard's support in a press campaign against Haig and the CIGS General Sir William Robertson but the latter refused to take part since he had respect for both men and disliked political intrigue. Rothermere's brother, Lord Northcliffe, joined in the campaign and, after a twelve-hour confrontation wore Trenchard down accepting only that the latter consult with Haig to inform him that he was not behind the campaign. He was then appointed to the post of Chief of the Air Staff but it was not a good beginning and later disagreements followed.

Two of Rothemere's actions particularly irritated Trenchard. The Air Minister would adopt the habit of using outside advisers rather than officers on the Air Staff. He also insisted that the RAF recruit as many men as possible in competition for men in a tight labour market, Trenchard was more interested in quality not quantity. By March 1918 his relations with the Air Minister had deteorated to the point of resignation. This was Trenchard's reaction when he did not get what he wanted. His resignation was accepted and this meant that with a war still to be won, a senior air force officer was kicking his heels in London. This was an embarrassment for the government and he was offered several posts, which he turned down. These offers were made by Sir William Weir who had replaced Rothermere as Air Minister. He did not want to be the Grand Co-ordinator of British and American air policy, nor did he want to command all the RAF's units in the Middle East, the post of Inspector General of the RAF nor the new post of a London-based Command of bombing operations conducted from Ochey. Only one other post was on offer and that was command of the Independent Bombing Force being instituted in the Nancy area of France. He did not immediately accept this post but the story goes that whilst he was seated on a park bench in Central London he overheard two gentlemen who were highly critical of his behaviour in war time when his experience was being wasted. True or not Trenchard accepted the command of the IBF, the bombing campaign of targets in Germany and German-occupied France. This campaign is the subject of Chapter 6.

Meanwhile, Frederick Sykes, his rival, had been appointed Chief of the Air Staff and when the war ended he would again be unhappy to remain in any position subordinate to Sykes. Winston Churchill had become Minister of War and the Air and he liked Trenchard's offensive spirit, but how to move Sykes to make way for Trenchard? The government was in a period of austerity and Sykes' plan for the expansion of the air force to become a Commonwealth force did not fit with the government's plans. And so Churchill persuaded the Cabinet to move Sykes to the post of Minister for Civil Aviation and return Trenchard to the post of Chief of the Air Staff with the famous quote – 'he will make do with a little and will not have to be carried'. And so with an annual budget of £15 million he would have to run an air force. The RAF units on the North West Frontier, however, were funded by the India Office.

He remained in command until the end of the decade since he was anxious to ensure that the RAF was there to stay. He had to fight off attempts by the War Office and

MRAF, Sir Hugh Trenchard.

the Admiralty to have their aeroplanes returned to them, which would have left what remained of the RAF as unviable. Again, Churchill came to his rescue and when he moved to become Colonial Secretary he instituted a policy of air policing, that is maintaining internal security using aeroplanes. The speed with which aircraft could respond to tribal disputes far surpassed a response by troops. After warnings by the local Political Officer, that they were to comply with government demands or risk bombing, aircraft would respond using bombs and machine gun fire on the villages of local tribesmen until compliance was obtained.

What was the abiding legacy that Trenchard left his successors? He firmly believed that in a future war victory would go to a country that used its air force offensively from the start to lower the enemy's morale and reduce its industrial capacity to continue to wage war. This was a policy that was criticizsed by Sir Maurice Hankey when as Secretary to the Chiefs of Staff Sub-Committee, he responded to Trenchard's submission 'The War Object of an Air Force'. He said that Trenchard's claims for the morale effect of bombing were an abuse of language and that to suggest that air power alone could bring about the successful outcome in a war was going to be unacceptable to the War Office and the Admiralty. Trenchard had gone too far, but in his defence he was acutely aware that unless he could show that there were some military operations that could only be carried out efficiently by aircraft he always risked the demise of the RAF. This had the unfortunate effect of his organizing inter-war air exercises that were skewed in favour of the bomber. It was overlooked that if the bomber could always get through to their targets so, too, could enemy bombers. And so the RAF entered World War II with bombs that were of Great War vintage and until 1937, Great War biplane bombers were still on the strength of an RAF squadron. The RAF bombers that did go into action in 1939 and 1940 were badly mauled and the first decisive battle of the war would be fought by fighters in the Battle of Britain. Trenchard was a controversial man, obstinate and quite determined to get what he wanted but still a man who loved the RAF and was proud of his part in its creation.

Appendix A
Aircraft Technical Specification Sheets

AIRCRAFT IN OPERATIONAL SQUADRON SERVICE AND IN TRAINING UNITS BETWEEN 1 JANUARY 1912 AND 11 NOVEMBER 1918

Notes:
1. The information shown will relate to a representative mark/version of the type.
2. Details of test flying and development are to be found in Chapter 7.
3. Aircraft by squadrons are shown in Appendix B.

SQUADRON AND TRAINING AIRCRAFT
1. AFWK 8
2. Avro 504J
3. BAT Bantam
4. Blackburn Baby
5. Blackburn Kangaroo
6. Blériot XI and XXI
7. Breguet 4/5
8. Bristol Boxkite
9. Bristol Coanda Monoplane
10. Bristol Fighter
11. Bristol M1 C
12. Bristol Scout
13. Caproni Ca 42
14. Caudron G3
15. Cody V
16. Curtiss H12
17. Curtiss JN4
18. Deperdussin Monoplane
19. DH1A
20. DH2
21. DH4
22. DH6
23. DH9
24. DH9A
25. Fairey III
26. Fairey Campania
27. Felixstowe 2A
28. Felixstowe F3
29. Handley Page O/100
30. Handley Page O/400
31. Handley Page V1500
32. Henry Farman III
33. Henry Farman F20
34. Martinsyde Buzzard
35. Martinsyde G102
36. Martinsyde S1
37. Maurice Farman Longhorn
38. Maurice Farman Shorthorn
39. Morane I & II
40. Morane BB
41. Morane L & LA
42. Morane P
43. Nieuport 12
44. Nieuport 16
45. Nieuport 17
46. Nieuport 20
47. Nieuport 23
48. Nieuport 24
49. Nieuport 27
50. Nieuport 28
51. RA Factory BE2b
52. RA Factory BE2c
53. RA Factory BE2e
54. RA Factory BE8 & 8a
55. RA Factory BE9
56. RA Factory BE12
57. RA Factory FE2a
58. RA Factory FE2b
59. RA Factory RE1
60. RA Factory FE5
61. RA Factory FE7
62. RA Factory RE8
63. RA Factory SE2 & 2a
64. RA Factory SE5a
65. Short Bomber
66. Short 184
67. Short 320
68. Sopwith Camel
69. Sopwith Cuckoo
70. Sopwith 3 Seater
71. Sopwith Dolphin
72. Sopwith Pup
73. Sopwith Salamander
74. Sopwith Snipe
75. Sopwith 1½ Strutter
76. Sopwith Tabloid
77. Sopwith Triplane
78. Spad VII
79. Vickers FB5 (Gunbus) & 9
80. Vickers Vimy
81. Voisin LA
82. Wight Converted

ARMSTRONG WHITWORTH FK8

AIRCRAFT SPECIFICATION SHEET
Span: 43ft 6in
Length: 31ft 5in
Wing area: 540.0 sqft
Take-off weight: 2,811lb
Power plant: One 120hp Beardmore water-cooled in-line
Armament/bomb load: See text below
Performance
  Max. speed: 95mph at sea level
  Endurance: 3hrs 0min
  Service ceiling: 13,000ft

HISTORY
In the late summer of 1915 the FK3 was accepted by the War Office for substantial production to be used in the bombing and reconnaissance roles. The prototype had the pilot in the rear cockpit but the production aircraft had the observer with a spigot-mounted machine gun in that position. It was roughly equivalent in performance to the BE2c but had a smaller bomb load and rate of climb than the latter. But like all the RA Factory aircraft performance was sacrificed for stability and ease of handling and the flying qualities of the FK3 were superior

In the event, only one operational squadron would be equipped with the FK3, namely No.47 Squadron in Macedonia from September 1916 until early in 1918, primarily on reconnaissance and sometimes bombing duties. When flown on bombing missions the aircraft had to be flown as a single-seater, given the weight of the war load of 112lb. The ideal employment of the FK3 was in the training role and this aircraft could be seen at training establishments in the United Kingdom and Egypt. The FK8 was a scaled-up version of the FK3 and made its maiden flight in May 1916. First operational with No.55 Squadron in France and four other squadrons on the Western Front the FK8 also equipped units in Macedonia and Palestine. At home it was used on Home Defence squadrons and for training. It was a well-built

aircraft and well defended. Throughout 1917 and 1918 it was widely used on reconnaissance, patrol, day and night bombing and ground attack. A notable mission was flown on 27 March 1918 when an FK8 was set upon by eight Fokker DR1s. The aircraft was still loaded with bombs and ammunition when the fuel tank and rear cockpit were set ablaze. Although both crew members were seriously wounded they still accounted for four of the enemy aircraft before the pilot. 2nd Lieutenant McLeod successfully brought his aircraft down in no-man's land, for which he was awarded the Victoria Cross.

AVRO 504J

AIRCRAFT SPECIFICATION SHEET
Span: 36ft 0in
Length: 29ft 5in
Wing area: 330.0 sqft
Take-off weight: 1,800lb
Power plant: One 100hp Gnome Monosoupape rotary
Armament/bomb load: See text below
Performance
  Max. speed: 82mph at 6,500ft
  Endurance: 3hrs 0min
  Service ceiling: 13,000ft

HISTORY
The Avro 504J was used principally as a trainer. This aircraft was built in a number of variants going up to 504S. The Avro 504 was a development of the earlier 500 and was originally used for training and private flying. A small number of these aircraft were purchased by the RFC and the RNAS prior to the commencement of hostilities in 1914 and were soon part of the tactical air force with the British Expeditionary Force, indeed it was a 504 of the RFC that was the first British aircraft to be shot down, which happened on 22 August 1914. The pilot was 2nd Lieutenant Waterfall and his navigator was Lieutenant Bayly, both of No.5 Squadron. The RNAS used

these aircraft on a bombing mission to Lake Constance to attack the Zeppelin works at Friedrichshafen. Three set out from Belfort in north-eastern France on 21 November 1914, each carrying four 20lb bombs. One of these aircraft was shot down but the raid was successful. Several direct hits were recorded on the airship sheds and the hydrogen plant. It was soon obsolete as a training aircraft and those which were used as fighters were kept well away from London.

The 504J and K were used as trainers with thousands being made during the war. The 504K had modified engine bearers to accommodate a range of engines to cope with engine shortages (see Chapter 11, the section on Supply). By the end of the war 8,340 Avro 504s had been produced. Those 504s used to equip Home Defence squadrons were converted 504Js and Ks, which replaced the ageing BE2c aircraft, in turn, which lacked the altitude to make successful interceptions. They were modified to become single-seaters and a Lewis gun was fitted above the top wing on a Foster mounting (see Chapter 7). Following the end of the Great War the type continued in RAF service as trainers.

BRITISH AERIAL TRANSPORT BANTAM

AIRCRAFT SPECIFICATION SHEET
Span: 25ft 0in
Length: 18ft 5in
Wing area: 185 sqft
Take-off weight: 1,321lb
Power plant: One 170hp ABC Wasp 1 air-cooled radial
Armament/bomb load:
    Two fixed forward firing .303in Vickers machine guns

Performance
Max. speed: 128mph at 6,500ft
Endurance: 2hrs 15min
Service ceiling: 20,000ft

HISTORY
The Bantam was designed by Frederick Koolhoven, who previously worked for Armstrong. Designated the FK22, it was first powered by a 120hp ABC Mosquito radial engine but this was a failure and alternatives were chosen for the six prototypes on order. Of the three that were completed by the end of 1917, B9944 and B9946 were powered by the 170hp ABC Wasp I radial whilst B9945 received the 100hp Gnome Monosoupape rotary changed in early 1918 for a 110hp Le Rhône. The FK23 was named the Bantam MkI while the rotary-engined FK22 became the Bantam MkII. The four FK23s were completed to a variety of different configurations, all smaller than the original FK22, and it is not clear which of these was closest to the final form of the MkI. The synchronized Vickers guns were mounted at cockpit floor level firing between the lower pair of engine cylinders on either side. Experienced pilots found the aircraft highly manoeuvrable and it was fast but prone to dangerous spinning. In mid 1918 a Bantam went to Villacoublay in France for test flying and another went to the USA for evaluation. One of these aircraft was powered by the 200hp Wasp II radial and achieved a speed of 146mph. The Wasp II was, however, a very noisy engine and since it continued to give trouble its development was abandoned. When the war ended there was no need for the Bantam and, in any event, the British Aerial Transport Co. was taken over. Koolhoven returned to Holland and worked on a Lynx-powered Bantam 1, F1161 (G-EAYA). With this 200hp engine it achieved a speed of 152.8mph.

BLACKBURN BABY

AIRCRAFT SPECIFICATION SHEET

Span: 25ft 8in
Length: 23ft 0in
Wing area: 240 sqft
Take-off weight: 1,715lb
Power plant: One 130hp Clerget 9B rotary
Armament/bomb load: Synchonized Lewis gun, Le Prieur rockets and Rankindarts, two 65lb bombs
Performance
    Max. speed: 100mph at sea level
    Endurance: 2hrs 25min
    Service ceiling: 10,000ft

HISTORY

The Baby floatplanes were built by Blackburn, Sopwith, Fairey and Parnall to bring the total of the Baby produced to 457 machines. The power plants used were the 100hp Gnome Monosoupape and the 100hp Clerget. The Sopwith aircraft were armed with a single Lewis machine gun firing forward and upward through a cut-out in the top wing. In the other Babies a synchonized Lewis gun was mounted in the front cockpit. Forty of the Blackburn Babies were armed Rankin darts or Le Prieur rockets for anti-Zeppelin duties in lieu of a gun. The Sopwith Baby served widely with the RNAS during the last two years of the war at shore bases around the British coastline and aboard eleven seaplane carriers operating in the North Sea and the Mediterranean. On the Western Front they flew fighter patrols whilst in Italy, Egypt, Palestine and the Aegean they operated mainly as bombers. For bombing or anti-submarine work the Babies normally carried two 65lb bombs under the centre of the fuselage. Withdrawal from front-line service began well before the Armistice and many ended the war in training units.

BLACKBURN KANGAROO

AIRCRAFT SPECIFICATION SHEET

Span: 74ft 10.25in
Length: 44ft 2in
Wing area: 868 sqft
Take-off weight: 8,017lb
Power plant: Two 255hp Rolls-Royce Falcon II water-cooled Vee-type
Armament/bomb load: Two Lewis guns, up to 920lb of bombs
Performance
    Max. speed: 100mph at sea level
    Endurance: 8hrs 0min
    Service ceiling: 13,000ft

HISTORY

This was one of the lesser-known aircraft of the Great War and had its origins in the Blackburn Type GP, twin-engined floatplane whose prototype, No.1415, first appeared in July 1916. There were twenty Kangaroos in the original order for service as patrol bombers with the RTNAS but it was decided that these aircraft could more flexibly operated as landplanes and they were renumbered and rebuilt with wheeled undercarriages for the RFC. Each aircraft was crewed by four men and single Lewis guns could be fired from a front and rear Scarff ring. Four 230lb bombs or an equivalent weight of smaller bombs could be carried internally. Additional bombs could be carried under the centre of the fuselage. The long slender fuselage was liable to twist under stress but it was light on the controls and all crew members had an excellent view from their respective cockpits. No.246 Squadron was credited with the sinking of a U-boat in August 1918 and the probable damage of four others.

BLÉRIOT XI AND XXI

AIRCRAFT SPECIFICATION SHEET
Span: 29 ft 2.5in
Length: 25ft 7in
Wing area: 161.3sqft

Take-off weight: 882lb
Power plant: One 70hp Blériot Gnome
Armament/bomb load: Nil save personal arms of the pilot
Performance
    Max. speed: 55.9mph at sea level
    Endurance: 3½hrs
    Service ceiling: 6,562ft

HISTORY

This aircraft was developed from that with which Louis Blériot crossed the English Channel in 1909. This mark had the more powerful Gnome rotary engine in place of the 25hp Anzoni engine. Before the outbreak of war in 1914 the Blériot XIs established various speed, height and endurance records and the type possessed aerobatic qualities. The French and Italians possessed military versions from 1910, the Italians using theirs in a campaign in North Africa in 1911. The RFC military and naval wings received their first Blériot XI aircraft in 1912, eventually equipping Nos.1, 3, 6, 7, 9 and 16 Squadrons. These aircraft were used by the Allies for observation during the first year of the war. Of the five basic variants, one had a 140hp engine and they differed in undercarriage, elevators, rudders and control pylons. Some Blériot XI Militaire and Genie aircraft equipped units of the Belgian Aviation Militaire; rifles and revolvers were the only armament carried by pilots. A parasol-wing version equipped the French escadrilles and both British Air Services. The serial number allocations indicate that there were twenty-one parasol and up to forty-eight Blériot XI aircraft of other version in service with the RFC. The Blériot XXI was a derivative of the XI.

BREGUET 4 AND 5

AIRCRAFT SPECIFICATION SHEET
Span: 57ft 8½in
Length: 26ft 0¾ in

Wing area: 621.1sqft
Take-off weight: 4,740lb
Power plant: One 250hp Rolls-Royce Eagle – water-cooled V Type
Armament/bomb load: One Hotchkiss or Lewis machine gun and up to 7.25kg bombs
Performance
    Max speed: 85.7mph at sea level
    Cruising speed: 92mph
    Range: 435 miles
    Service ceiling: 14.108ft

HISTORY

Louis Breguet had designed tractor aircraft but the French Government insisted that the 4 and 5 be powered by a pusher engine so that the observer sitting in the front cockpit, would have an uninterrupted field of vision and machine gun fire. The original engine was the 200hp Canton Unné but this was replaced by the 220hp Renault engine. One hundred of these aircraft were built at the factory at Clermont Ferrand and saw service with the French Aviation Militaire. In the summer of 1915 the French Government issued a specification for a bomber to carry a 300kg bomb over a range of 370 miles. To meet this specification Breguet developed the BU3 version into the SN3 or Type 4B2 and and 5Ca2. (Ca refers to its cannon armament.) Production took place in both the Michelin and Breguet factories. The 4B2 was armed with a single Hotchkiss or Lewis gun in the cockpit and could carry up to 7.25kg bombs in Michelin automatic bomb racks. It was intended that the Ca2 should act as escort to the 4b2. In practice the cannon was found to be too heavy and was usually replaced by a standard machine gun. The Breguet 'pushers' had a good range with a satisfactory load but they were difficult to land, required a long take-off run and were too slow for a day bomber so were relegated to night operations in October 1916. The RNAS purchased some forty-six of the various models of this aircraft. British Breguet aircraft served with No.3 Wing in France.

BRISTOL BOXKITE

AIRCRAFT SPECIFICATION SHEET
Span: 46ft 6in
Length: 38ft 6in
Wing area: 517.0sqft
Take-off weight: 1150lb

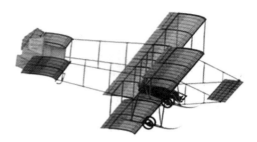

Power plant: One 70hp Le Rhône rotary
Armament/bomb load: See text below
Performance
   Max. speed: 40mph

HISTORY

The Boxkite was developed in 1910 at Britain's first private aircraft factory in Bristol, home of the British and Colonial Aircraft Company. The aircraft was built in quantity and was used for training at their flying schools at Larkhill and Brooklands and four of their aircraft were purchased by the War Office in 1911. It was intended, initially, to build copies of the Zodiac biplane designed by Gabriel Voisin under licence but this aircraft had a shallow wing camber and was unsatisfactory, added to which the Zodiac was underpowered for its weight but when these matters were addressed the aircraft was still found to be unsatisfactory so it was decided to design an aircraft modelled on the successful aircraft of Henry Farman. The first of these was flown at Larkhill on 30 July 1910. Farman sued Bristol for infringement of patents but Bristol's lawyers claimed that there had been substantial design improvements. The company was well known for the quality of its workmanship and the law suit was dropped. The first Boxkites constructed were equal span two-bay biplanes with a single elevator carried on booms in front of the wings. Lateral control was effected by ailerons on both upper and lower rings. A pair of rudders were mounted between the trailing edges of the tailplanes. Most of the aircraft eventually produced had an extended upper wing and were known as the *military version*. But by 1910 this aircraft had been overtaken by other designs and this Farman version was obsolescent. No serious attempt to develop the Boxkite was attempted

BRISTOL COANDA

AIRCRAFT SPECIFICATION SHEET
Span: 37ft 8in
Length: 29ft 3in
Wing area: 450 sqft
Take-off weight: 1,665lb
Power plant: One Gnome rotary 100hp

Armament/bomb load: Some equipped with 7.92mm machine gun, twelve 10lb light bombs
Performance
   Max. speed: 65–70mph
   Endurance: 5hrs
   Climb to: 3,000ft in 11 min

HISTORY

The first school and side-by-side monoplanes entered service with flying schools operated by Bristol at Larkhill and Brooklands. One tandem and two side-by-side machines were sold to Italy, with four tandem and three side-by-side aircraft being sold to Romania. The two Competition Monoplanes were purchased by the War Office after the Military Aircraft Competition, being used as trainers for the RFC. However, on 10 September 1912, one of the Competition Monoplanes crashed, killing Lieutenants E. Hotchkiss and C.A. Bettington. While this was traced to one of the bracing wires becoming detached, it resulted in a five-month ban of flying of all monoplanes by the military wing of the RFC.

Despite this ban, military monoplanes were purchased by Romani and Italy, with a production licence being granted to Caproni (although this licence was later cancelled, with only two being built by Caproni).

BRISTOL FIGHTER

AIRCRAFT SPECIFICATION SHEET
Span: 39ft 3in
Length: 25ft 10in
Wing area: 405.6 sqft

Take-off weight: 2,848lb
Power plant: One 275hp Rolls-Royce Falcon III water-
cooled, vee-type
Armament/bomb load: See text below
Performance
    Max. speed: 123mph at 5,000ft
    Endurance: 3hrs 0min
    Service ceiling: 18,000ft

HISTORY

Of all F.S. Barnwell's designs the Bristol Fighter was the most successful. The aircraft originated as the R2A, which had a centrally mounted forward-firing Vickers machine gun and a single Lewis gun mounted on a Scarff ring in the rear cockpit. Deliveries began in December 1916 with No.48 Squadron in France. They were operated as two-seaters with the observer's Lewis gun being the primary weapon, but losses were heavy. Once the aircraft was flown as a front-gun fighter, the Bristol fighter was an immediate success. With many hundreds more Bristol fighters on order the F2B version had wider-span tail planes, modified lower centre-sections and an even better view from the front cockpit. It was this version that went on to serve with such distinction, not only during the Great War but afterwards in air policing in the outposts of Empire remaining in service until 1932. By the spring of 1918, nicknamed the 'Brisfit', the aircraft had established a formidable reputation and enemy fighter pilots could be relied upon not to attack more than two Brisfits at a time. Under wartime contracts more than 5,250 were ordered for RFC service and the United States also purchased them. But the latter were fitted with the 400hp Liberty 12 engines, which rendered them a failure. The British version was powered by the Falcon engine but such was the demand for this power unit that Sunbeam Arabs were also used. In addition to the Western Front the Brisfits also saw service in Palestine and Italy and No.111 Squadron used them to transport Colonel T.E. Lawrence between General Headquarters and the Arab Guerrilla forces.

BRISTOL M1C

AIRCRAFT SPECIFICATION SHEET

Span: 30ft 9in
Length: 20ft 5½in
Wing area: 145.0 sqft
Take-off weight: 1,348lb
Power plant: One 110hp Le Rhône 9J rotary
Armament/bomb load: See text below
Performance
    Max. speed: 130mph at sea level
    Endurance: 1hr 45min
    Service ceiling: 10,000ft

HISTORY

The Bristol M1C might well have been the victim of prejudice against monoplanes at the commencement of the Great War. It was understood that the stress shared by four wings was less than that shared by two. Even as the Spitfire and the Hurricane were going into production Henry Folland of Glosters was insisting that his SS19 biplane would make a better fighter. Set up in October 1912 to investigate crashes by RFC monoplanes a committee did not officially condemn them but prejudice against them persisted throughout the war and during most of the inter-war years. But F.S. Barnwell, Bristol's designer, insisted that the prototype M1A (A5138), which reached 132 mph, proved that a monoplane could achieve a higher performance than a biplane. The M1A was powered by a 110hp Clerget 9Z rotary engine. The M1Bs were used for service trials, one of them going to the Middle East on operations in June 1917 but on the Western Front the hard-pressed fighter squadrons waited in vain. A flimsy excuse was that the landing speed of 49mph was too high for the small French airfields. In the event the M1C attracted a service contract for only 125 machines of which only a few saw operational service. This was in Mesopotamia and Macedonia. The need in the latter theatre was for a good escort fighter but the short range of the M1C limited its usefulness. Remaining

M1Cs, not issued to operational units, were allocated to training units in Egypt and the United Kingdom.

BRISTOL SCOUT

AIRCRAFT SPECIFICATION SHEET
Span: 24ft 7in
Length: 20ft 8in
Wing area: 198.0 sqft
Take-off weight: 1,200lb
Power plant: One 80hp Gnome rotary Vee type
Armament/bomb load: See below
Performance
   Max. speed: 92.7mph at sea level
   Endurance: 2hrs 30min
   Service ceiling: 15,500ft

HISTORY
The Bristol Scout could have been a very good fighting machine with more effective armament. Bristol could have waited until that was available but seemed to be more interested in producing the F2A and F2B. The Scout was designed by F.S. Barnwell and in February 1914 his design achieved an excellent speed for the day of 95mph. In addition to the prototype two more machines had been produced by the outbreak of war. These were requisitioned by the War Office and given the serial numbers 633 and 648, being allocated to Nos.3 and 5 Squadrons RFC in France. More orders followed. The prototype was classified as a Scout A and the second and third aircraft the Scout B. All subsequent aircraft in the initial order were classified as Scout Cs. Scout Cs began to be issued to squadrons in the spring of 1915. The RFC was to receive eighty-seven Scout Cs, with seventy-four machines going to the RNAS. Power was supplied by 80hp Gnomes and Le Rhônes. On entering squadron service the Scouts were mostly unarmed and it was left to units in the field to try a variety of small arms and later to fit machine guns. (It was the pilot of a Scout C, Captain

L.G. Hawker of No.6 Squadron, who won the VC by shooting down two German two-seaters.) The RNAS Scouts carried Ranken darts on anti-Zeppelin missions. Alternatively, four small bombs could be carried beneath the fuselage. In late 1915 Barnwell had come up with the Scout D, which had C type wings and enlarged rudders. This aircraft could be armed with synchronized Vickers guns but the RNAS preferred non-synchronized Lewis guns firing over the wing. No squadron was equipped entirely with Scouts and most units received one or two of these machines. Apart from operating over the Western Front, Scouts equipped units on Home Defence, in Palestine, Mesopotamia and Macedonia. The Scouts were officially removed from front-line service by mid 1916 but some were still in use as fighters in the spring of 1917.

CAPRONI CA42

© W.I. Boucher

AIRCRAFT SPECIFICATION SHEET
Span: 98ft 1⅛ in
Length: 49ft 6½ in
Wing area: 2152.8sqft
Take-off weight: 16,535lb
Power plant: Three 270hp Isota-Fraschini water-cooled Vee type
Armament/bomb load: See text below
Performance
   Max. speed: 87mph at sea level.
   Endurance: 7hrs 0min
   Service ceiling: 9,843ft

HISTORY
No.227 Squadron RAF was formed at Pizzone, Italy, the same day the RAF was formed, 1 April 1918, by the formation of the squadron from RNAS Flights (pictured

above). With the DH4 and the DH9 the Caproni Ca42 equipped the squadron but the latter did not survive in RAF service beyond the month. Well before the outbreak of the Great War, Italian bombers had been on long-range bombing missions raiding targets in Austria Hungary. The giant Caproni bombers began life in 1913 having a central nacelle with a pusher propeller and two slender booms with tractor propellers. All were 80hp Gnomes but the transmission gear on the tractor engines proved rather clumsy in operation. The military designation Ca4 was applied to a series of much larger triplanes, the first of which appeared in late 1917. There was side-by-side seating for the two pilots, which was necessary for an aircraft with an endurance of seven hours and a front gunner's position. Separated positions for rear gunners were installed in each of the two fuselage booms but the overall weight proved too much for the three engines resulting in low top speeds. Thus the original three aircraft were powered by 200hp engines, followed by twelve with 270hp Isotta-Fraschini engines. A coffin-shaped container was suspended between the main undercarriage wheels that could hold 3,179lb of bombs. Since the Ca4 was too slow for daylight operations it was not used for combat purposes by the RNAS and examples were returned to Italy after the war. No.227 Squadron was disbanded in December 1918 without ever becoming fully established. The Ca4s were withdrawn from RAF service the same month in which they entered service.

CAUDRON G3

AIRCRAFT SPECIFICATION SHEET
Span: 44ft 0in
Length: 21ft 0in
Wing area: 290.0sqft
Take-off weight: 1,577lb
Power plant: One 80hp Le Rhône rotary

Armament/bomb load: One small calibre machine gun and some hand-released bombs (optional)
Performance
    Max. speed: 68mph
    Service ceiling: 10,110ft

HISTORY
The G3 equipped Escadrille C11 of the French *Aéronautique Militaire* at the outbreak of war, and was well-suited for reconnaissance use, proving tough and reliable. As the war went on however, its low performance and the fact that it was unarmed made it vulnerable in front-line service, and so the French withdrew it from front-line operations in mid-1916. The Australian Flying Corps (AFC) operated the G3 during the Mesopotamian campaign of 1915–16.

The Italians also used the G3 for reconnaissance on a wide scale until 1917, as did the British RFC (continuing operations until October 1917), who also fitted some with light bombs and machine guns for ground attack.

It continued in use as a trainer after ceasing combat operations until after the end of the war. Caudron G3s in Chinese hands, namely the air force of Fengtian clique warlords, remained in service in training roles until the Mukden Incident, when most of them were captured by the Japanese, and their eventual fate is unknown. There were variants. Most G3s were the A2 model, used by various air forces for fire spotting on the west front, in Russia and in the Middle East. The G3 D2 was a two-seated trainer aircraft, equipped with dual controls and the E2 was a basic trainer. The R1 version, which had been developed from the basic version, was used by France and by the USA for taxi training, with fabric removed from large areas of the wing to prevent its becoming airborne. The last version, the G312, was equipped with a more powerful 100hp Anzani 10 engine. In Germany, Gotha built copies of the G3 as the LD3 and LD4 (*Land Doppeldecker* – 'Land Biplane').

CODY V

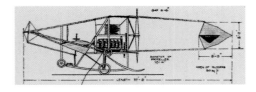

AIRCRAFT SPECIFICATION SHEET
Span: 43ft 0in
Length: 37ft 9in
Wing area: 430.0sqft
Take-off weight: 5,512lb
Power plant: Austro Daimler, water-cooled 6 Cyl. 120hp

Performance
  Max. speed: 72.4mph at sea level
  Range: 336 miles
  Time to altitude: 1,200ft in 3min 30sec

HISTORY

Cody took the new aircraft for its maiden flight on 23 July 1912, flying it to Salisbury on 27 July to take place in the trials. While Cody's biplane was, even in 1912, outdated, it was declared the winner, Cody being awarded the £4,000 first prize and a further £1,000 for the best British-built aircraft. (Although the vastly superior BE2 took part in the trials, as a product of the Royal Aircraft Factory, it was ineligible for the prizes.)

The War Office purchased the prototype Cody V, together with a second aircraft to be built to the same design. In October, Cody re-engined the biplane with a British-built 100hp (75kW) Green engine in order to enter the British Empire Michelin Cup competitions, winning the £600 prize for the fastest time over a 186-mile (299km) circuit.

After re-fitting with the Austro-Daimler engine it was delivered to the Royal Flying Corps on 30 November 1912, being issued to No. 4 Squadron in December that year. The second Cody V flew in January 1913, and was delivered in February. On 28 April 1913, the first prototype broke up in mid-air and the aircraft crashed, killing the pilot. The resulting investigation discovered that the aircraft's structure, which incorporated many parts from the 1911 Circuit of Britain aircraft, had deteriorated badly and was in 'precarious' condition by the time of the crash. The second aircraft, which was awaiting repair of damage that had been received in an accident in March, was never flown again, and in November that year it was given to the Science Museum, London, where it is displayed today.

CURTISS H12

AIRCRAFT SPECIFICATION SHEET

Span: 46ft 5in
Length: 92ft 71in
Wing area: 1216.0 sqft
Take-off weight: 10,650lb

Power plant: Two 275hp Rolls-Royce Eagles
Armament/bomb load:
  4 ×.303in Lewis guns on flexible mounts
  4 × 100lb bombs or 2 × 230lb
Performance
  Max. speed: 85mph at sea level
  Endurance: 6hrs
  Service ceiling: 10,650ft

HISTORY

Up until the entry of the United States into the war the sole domestic aircraft designer and manufacturer who had a routine business with the Allied powers was the Curtiss Company. The H12 design of late 1916 was a significantly scaled-up version of earlier H-boat designs. Initially intended to be powered by two 160hp Curtiss V-X-X engines, these were deemed unsatisfactory by the British, who substituted 275hp Rolls-Royce Eagle engines in the aircraft that they purchased.

As US participation in the war became imminent the US Navy was finally able to purchase these twin-engined flying boats. The first of twenty H12s were delivered in March 1917. Engines were the 200 Curtiss V-2-3 type, which were later replaced by Liberty engines. The serial numbers of these aircraft were A152 and A765 to A783.

While the H12 served in the RNAS in England, the US Navy opted not to assign the machine to foreign duty. Therefore, active service by the Navy was limited to anti-submarine patrol duty at domestic naval air stations.

CURTISS JN-3

AIRCRAFT SPECIFICATION SHEET

Span: 43ft 7.5in
Length: 27ft 4in
Wing area: 352.0 sqft
Take-off weight: 2,130lb
Power plant: One 90hp Curtiss OX-5 water-cooled, Vee-type
Armament/bomb load: See text below

DEPERDUSSIN MONOPLANE

Performance
   Max. speed: 75mph at sea level
   Endurance: 2hrs 15 min
   Service ceiling: 11,000ft

HISTORY

The Curtiss JN-4 is possibly North America's most famous World War I aircraft. It was widely used during World War I to train pilots, with an estimated 95 per cent of all trainees having flown a JN-4. The US version was called 'Jenny', a derivation from its official designation. It was a twin-seat (student in front of instructor) dual control biplane. Its tractor prop and manoeuvrability made it ideal for initial pilot training with a 90hp (67kW) Curtiss OX-5 V8 engine giving a top speed of 75mph (121km/h) and a service ceiling of 6,500ft. The British used the JN-4 (along with the Avro 504) for their primary World War I trainer using the Canadian Aeroplanes Ltd indigenous variant. Many Royal Flying Corps pilots earned their wings on the JN-4, both in Ontario and later in winter facilities at Camp Taliaferro, Texas.

  Although ostensibly a training aircraft, the Jenny was extensively modified while in service to undertake additional roles. Due to its robust but easily adapted structure able to be modified with ski undercarriage, the Canadian Jenny was flown year-round, even in inclement weather. The removable turtle-deck behind the cockpits allowed for conversion to stretcher or additional supplies and equipment storage, with the modified JN-4s becoming the first aerial ambulances, carrying out this role both during wartime and in later years. Most of the 6,813 Jennys built were unarmed, although some had machine guns and bomb racks for advanced training. With deployment limited to North American bases, none of these aircraft saw combat service in World War I.

AIRCRAFT SPECIFICATION SHEET
Span: 36ft 0in
Length: 26ft 0in
Take-off weight: 1664lb
Power plant: One 80hp Gnome rotary
Armament/bomb load: See text below
Performance
   Max. speed: 71mph at sea level
   Endurance: 2hrs 20min

HISTORY

This popular model of Deperdussin was produced in quantity and was a great improvement over the earlier Blériot-type machines. The Deperdussin had enough power and reliability to be able to make sustained cross-country flights and was also ideal for training. As such, Deperdussins equipped several flying schools. The Deperdussin had a distinguished career in the pre-war era as a training machine and also as a successful cross-country racer. One example came third in the 1911 Daily Mail Circuit of Britain contest. The Deperdussin type was available throughout the course of its life with several different engines, and seating arrangements. Versions of the Deperdussin were used by the military during 1912 and up to World War I. This is believed to have been the forty-third example of the Deperdussin collection and was used at Hendon as a training machine until it was damaged. It was then put up for sale and was acquired by Mr A.E. Grimmer who repaired the aircraft and flew it from the polo ground near Bedford. Richard Shuttleworth acquired the aircraft in 1935 and restored it to pristine condition at Old Warden. It flew again in 1937 and with only a period of storage during World War II has flown regularly since that time.

  Aside from training its military use was short lived. The Deperdussin TT was a French monoplane built in small numbers by Société Pour les Appareils Deperdussin or SPAD. The type's use by the French Air Force (then *Aviation Militaire*) was very brief, due to its frailty and lack of weapons. In February 1914, an experiment was made to install a machine gun in the nose of the craft, but it was not followed up. A number were used by the Naval Wing of the British Royal Flying Corps, one being fitted with floats and flown from Lake Windermere.

DE HAVILLAND 1A

AIRCRAFT SPECIFICATION SHEET
Span: 41ft 0in
Length: 28ft 11 ¼ in
Wing area: 362.25 sqft
Take-off weight: 2,340lb
Power plant: One 120hp Beardmore water-cooled in-line
Armament/bomb load: See text below
Performance
　　Max. speed: 88mph at 4,000ft
　　Endurance: 2hrs 30min
　　Service ceiling: 13,500ft

HISTORY
The DH1 was the third of Geoffrey de Havilland's designs to be built. The first two biplanes are basically the same and were followed by the FE1 for the Royal Aircraft Factory who went on to develop the FE2, FE2b and FE2d etc. The DH1 was flown in early 1915 at Hendon by de Havilland himself. It was put into production by Savages of King's Lynn and a total of 100 were built. An unusual feature was that the gun could be locked in a forward position and fired by the pilot should the observer be unable to do so. The DH1 was intended to have 120hp Beardmore engine but the engine was in comparatively short supply, so a 70hp Renault engine was substituted on the DH1 while eventually the Beardmore engined model was designated DH1A. The production machines were a mixture of DH1 and DH1A versions. Only seventy-seven were issued to the Royal Flying Corps, mostly used for Home Defence. However, No.14 Squadron received six for use in Palestine from the summer of 1916.

DE HAVILLAND 2

AIRCRAFT SPECIFICATION SHEET
Span: 28ft 3in
Length: 25ft 2½in
Wing area: 249.0sqft
Take-off weight: 1,441lb
Power plant: One 100hp Gnome Monosoupape rotary
Armament/bomb load: See text below
Performance
　　Max. speed: 93mph at sea level
　　Endurance: 2hrs 45min
　　Service ceiling: 14,500ft

HISTORY
The Airco DH2 was a single-seat fighter and the second project of designer Sir Geoffrey de Havilland, leveraging development of the 'pusher' propeller concept, where the propeller is situated behind the pilot. This design allowed the aircraft to be built without the need to synchronize the machine gun, which was implemented only at the end of 1916. The prototype of the DH2 made its first flight in July 1915. It entered service shortly afterwards and was delivered to No.24 Squadron RFC. In February 1916 it began active service on French territory. The Lewis machine gun was mounted in a nacelle and was difficult to implement to begin with. The movable gun mount forced the pilot not only to control the aircraft but also to aim the machine gun, which made combat even more difficult. Later on, pilots began to lock the gun down in a fixed position pointing forward. They managed to aim the weapon with the whole aircraft, and this was found to be more effective than attempting to move the machine gun around during engagements. The DH2 was often criticized for the complex procedures needed to master the technique of piloting and for the sharp reactions pilots needed for the controls. But all of this made the DH2 an outstanding fighter for experienced pilots. With the production of the DH2 the RFC gained

air superiority over the formerly feared but now rapidly outdating Fokker monoplanes, especially during the first battle on the Somme. The Allied air forces' domination lasted until the autumn of 1916, and this dominance was only ended with the introduction of the German Albatros DI/DII fighters. By the end of 1916 the Airco DH2 was being retired from the front, and until the middle of 1917 almost all remaining aircraft were transferred to training squadrons, where they remained in service until the beginning of 1918. Several units remained in service until the end of 1917, in Palestine on the Macedonian front. Not a single unit survived by the end of World War I.

DE HAVILLAND 4

AIRCRAFT SPECIFICATION SHEET
Span: 42ft 4 5/8in
Length: 30ft 8in
Wing area: 434.0sqft
Take-off weight: 3,313lb
Power plant: One 250hp Rolls-Royce III (Eagle III) water cooled Vee-type
Armament/bomb load: See text below
Performance
   Max. speed: 117mph at 6,500ft
   Endurance: 3hrs 30min
   Service ceiling: 16,000ft

HISTORY
The DH4 was designed by Geoffrey de Havilland around the 160 hp BHP engine. It was intended to be a high-speed day bomber but in the event was employed on a variety of duties. Even before the first prototype flew in August 1916 fifty had already been ordered with 250hp Rolls-Royce III or IV engines. It was light on the controls and easy to fly but one drawback was the siting of the fuel tank between the pilot and observer, which inhibited communication between the two crew members and rendered the aircraft vulnerable to enemy fire. The production aircraft were delivered from early 1917 armed with a forward-firing

Vickers gun synchronized with the Constantinesco gear. The RNAS DH4s mounted twin Vickers with a Lewis gun mounted on an elevated Scarff ring to improve the field of fire. The maximum bomb load was one 230lb bomb or two of 112lb. Alternatively, the aircraft could carry an equivalent weight of smaller bombs. The RFC DH4 aircraft first saw service with No.55 Squadron in France in March 1917 and became operational a month later. No.2 Squadron of the RNAS became operational at about the same time and eleven squadrons of both services went on to serve on the Western Front. The RNAS on the whole made more of the DH4's ability to out fly and climb above enemy fighters. In addition to bombing they were used for anti-submarine patrols, photographic reconnaissance and artillery spotting. Apart from the Western Front, DH4s also saw service at home, Russia, Mesopotamia, the Aegean and the Adriatic. The DH4 was withdrawn from service soon after the armistice.

DE HAVILLAND 6

AIRCRAFT SPECIFICATION SHEET
Span: 35ft 11in
Length: 27ft 3–5in
Wing area: 436 sqft
Take-off weight: 2,050lb
Power plant: One 90hp RAF 1a air-cooled Vee type
Armament/bomb load: Training aircraft
Performance
   Max. speed: 70mph
   Endurance: 2hrs 25min
   Stall speed: 40mph

HISTORY
The DH6 was specifically designed as a military trainer, at a time when it was usual for obsolete service types to be used in this role. Geoffrey de Havilland seems to have had two design criteria in mind. The first was that it should be cheap and easy to build, and above all, simple to repair after the mishaps common in ab-initio training. The top and bottom wings were 'brutally'

square cut, and were interchangeable. (Hence the roundels in unconventional positions on many wartime photographs of the type.) They were heavily cambered, and braced with cables rather than streamlined wires. On the original version of the type there was no stagger. Even the rudder, on the prototype of the usual curved de Havilland outline, was on production machines cut square. The fuselage structure was a straight box with no attempt at refinement of outline – the instructor and pupil sat in tandem on basketwork seats in a single cockpit that was Spartan even by the standards of the time. The standard engine was the ubiquitous and readily available 90hp (67kW) RAF 1a. Because of its use in the BE2 the engine had the advantage of being very familiar indeed to RFC mechanics. It was stuck onto the front of the DH6 in the most straightforward way possible, without any type of cowling, and the usual crudely upswept exhaust pipes of this type of engine were fitted. Eventually, even stocks of the RAF 1a ran short, and various other engines were fitted to DH6s, including the 90hp (67kW) Curtiss OX-5 and the 80hp (60kW) Renault. The DH6 has been frequently described as 'too safe' to make a good trainer; this referred to its gentle reaction to inexpert piloting rather than to excessive stability however, as it was designed with a degree of inherent instability about all three axes.

DE HAVILLAND 9

AIRCRAFT SPECIFICATION SHEET
Span: 42ft 4 5/8in
Length: 30ft 5in
Wing area: 434 sqft
Take-off weight: 3,790lb
Power plant: One 230hp Armstrong Siddeley Puma (but see notes below)
Armament/bomb load: One forward-firing Vickers plus one or two rear-mounted Lewis guns on a Scarff ring

Performance
Max. speed: 113mph
Endurance: 4hrs 30min
Service ceiling: 15,500ft

HISTORY
The DH9 was designed by de Havilland in 1916 as a successor to the DH4. It used the wings and tail unit of the DH4 but had a new fuselage. This enabled the pilot to sit closer to the gunner/observer and away from the engine and fuel tank. The other major change from the DH4 was the choice of the promising new BHP/Galloway Adriatic engine, which was predicted to produce 300hp (224kW) and so give the new aircraft an adequate performance to match enemy fighters. Based on the performance estimates for the DH9 (which were expected to surpass those of the DH4), and the similarity to the DH4, which meant that it would be easy to convert production over to the new aircraft, massive orders (4,630 aircraft) were placed. The prototype (a converted DH4) first flew at Hendon in July 1917. Unfortunately, the BHP engine proved unable to reliably deliver its expected power, with the engine being de-rated to 230hp (186kW) in order to improve reliability. This had a drastic effect on the aircraft's performance, especially at high altitude, with it being inferior to that of the DH4 it was supposed to replace. This meant that the DH9 would have to fight its way through enemy fighters, which could easily catch the DH9 where the DH4 could avoid many of these attacks and attempts were made to provide the DH9 with an adequate engine. The DH9's performance in action over the Western Front was a disaster, with heavy losses incurred, both due to its low performance, and engine failures (despite the prior de-rating of its engine). For example, between May and November 1918, two squadrons on the Western Front (Nos.99 and 104) lost fifty-four shot down, and another ninety-four written off in accidents. The DH9 was, however, more successful against the Turkish forces in the Middle East, where it faced less opposition, and it was used extensively for coastal patrols, to try to deter the operations of U-boats.

DE HAVILLAND 9A

AIRCRAFT SPECIFICATION SHEET

Span: 45ft 11½in
Length: 30ft 3in

Wing area: 486.75 sqft
Take-off weight: 4,645lb
Power plant: One 400hp Liberty 12A V12 piston
Armament/bomb load: One forward-firing Vickers machine gun and one or two rear-mounted Lewis guns on a Scarff ring. Up to 740lb of bombs on under wing fuselage racks
Performance
  Max. speed: 123mph at sea level
  Endurance: 5hrs 15min
  Service ceiling: 16,750ft

HISTORY

The Airco DH9A was a British single-engined two-seat biplane light bomber designed and first used shortly before the end of the First World War. It was a development of the unsuccessful Airco DH9 bomber, with a strengthened structure, and crucially, replacing the underpowered and unreliable Siddeley Puma engine of the DH9 with the American Liberty engine. Colloquially known as the 'Ninak' (from the designation *nine-A*), it served on in large numbers for the Royal Air Force (with almost 2,000 being built in the United Kingdom) following the end of the war, both at home and overseas, where it was used for colonial policing in the Middle East, finally being retired in 1931.The DH9A was planned as an improved version of the existing Airco DH9. The DH9 was a disappointment owing to its underpowered and unreliable engines, and the DH9A was planned to use much more powerful engines to resolve this. As the Rolls-Royce Eagle engine used in the successful DH4 was unavailable in sufficient quantities, the new 400hp (298kW) American Liberty engine was chosen instead. As Airco was busy developing the Airco DH10 twin-engined bomber, detailed design was carried out by Westland Aircraft. The DH9A was fitted with new, longer span wings, and a strengthened fuselage structure. The first prototype flew in March 1918, powered by a Rolls-Royce Eagle as no Liberty engines were yet available. The prototype proved successful, with the first Liberty-engined DH9A flying on 19 April 1918, and deliveries to the Royal Air Force starting in June. By the end of the war, a total of 2,250 DH9As had been ordered, with 885 having built by the end of the year. As it was decided that the DH9A would be a standard type in the post-war RAF, the majority of outstanding orders were fulfilled, with 1,730 being built under the wartime contracts before production ceased in 1919.

FAIREY III

AIRCRAFT SPECIFICATION SHEET
Span: 46ft 9in
Length: 36ft 6in
Wing area: 443.47sqft
Take-off weight: 6.301lb
Power plant: One Napier Lion X1A
Armament/bomb load: Two 7.7mm machine guns and and 220kg of bombs
Performance
  Max. speed: 130mph
  Service ceiling: 20,000ft

HISTORY

Fairey's IIID, first flown in prototype form in August 1920, was derived from the company's F128 experimental floatplane of 1917. This introduced the Fairey Patent Camber Gear evolved for the Hamble Baby, which was then described as a trailing-edge flap and used to increase the lift of the wings. Today we would regard these aerofoil control surfaces as drooped ailerons, for they were used as ailerons in flight, but could be drooped symmetrically to enhance the lift developed by the normal wing surface. Tested as a two-seat sea-plane, the F128 was known as the Fairey III. With a single frontal radiator behind the propeller and the floats replaced by a wheel landing gear, the designation became Fairey IIIA. In modified form the designation became Fairey IIIB. These had float landing gear, increased wing area, and ailerons on the upper wing in addition to the Patent Camber Gear on the lower. The IIIC that followed had a performance increase of some 14 per cent, almost entirely due to the installation of a Rolls-Royce Eagle VIII engine. It was regarded as one of the best seaplanes of its day, but it entered service too late to be involved in World War I. The Fairey IIID benefited from considerable experience with Fairey Ills in both RFC and RNAS use. The prototype retained the Eagle VIII engine, but of the 207 built for service with the RAF and Fleet Air Arm, 152 were powered by Napier Lion IIB, V or VA engines. In fact, on 30 October 1925 a IIID became the first standard FAA seaplane to be catapulted from a ship at sea. In landplane form, the IIID was one of the first service aircraft to have oleo-pneumatic (oil/air) shock absorbers. It was used to record the RAF's first flight from England to South Africa and its first official long-distance formation flight. Led by Wg Cdr C. W. H. Pulford, between 1 March and 21 June 1926 IIIDs completed a flight of almost 22,530km – Cairo–Cape Town–Cairo and thence to Lee-on-Solent. At no time throughout the period of almost four months was any delay caused by mechanical failure of any of the aircraft, speaking volumes for the soundness of the basic design of both airframe and engine.

FAIREY CAMPANIA

AIRCRAFT SPECIFICATION SHEET
Span: 61ft 7in
Length: 43ft 1in
Wing area: 674.6sqft
Take-off weight: 5,329lb
Power plant: One 260hp Sunbeam Maori II Water-cooled, Vee-twelve
Armament/bomb load: One Lewis.303in Lewis gun in rear cockpit and up to 6 × 116lb bombs
Performance
    Max. speed: 85mph at sea level.
    Endurance: 4hrs 30min
    Service ceiling: 6,000ft

HISTORY
The Fairey Campania was a British ship-borne, patrol and reconnaissance aircraft of World War I. It was a single-engine, two-seat biplane with twin main floats and backward-folding wings. The Campania was the first aeroplane ever designed specifically for carrier operations. The Royal Navy was an early leader in carrier aviation and, in the autumn of 1914, purchased the liner *Campania*

for conversion into a seaplane carrier. Operating seaplanes required the carrier to stop to hoist the aircraft out and in-board by crane, leaving the ship exceedingly vulnerable to U-boat attacks and the technique fell into disfavour with the Admiralty, and alternatives had to be sought. By the middle of 1916, *Campania* had been fitted with a 200ft (61m) flight deck forward and experiments were being carried out into launching aircraft from this. Against this background, the Admiralty issued a specification for a purpose-built, two-seat patrol and reconnaissance aircraft. The aircraft that Fairey designed in response first flew on 16 February 1917. It was a single-engined tractor biplane of fabric-covered wooden construction. The two-bay wings folded rearwards for storage. The crew of two sat in separate cockpits, with the observer's cockpit provided with a single Lewis gun on a Scarff ring. This was the first of two prototypes, designated F16 and powered by a 250hp (190kW) Rolls-Royce Eagle IV. The second, powered by an Eagle V of 275hp (205kW), was designated F17. Both prototypes would later see active service operating from Scapa Flow. Trials proving satisfactory, the type went into production and service. Most of the F17s shipped aboard the carriers *Campania*, *Nairana* and *Pegasus*; the first aircraft joined *Campania* and the type took its name from her. Only *Campania* possessed a flight-deck; Campanias operated from this using jettisonable, wheeled bogies fitted to the floats. The aircraft in the other ships took off from the water in the normal way. The Campania was declared obsolete in August 1919.

FELIXSTOWE 2A

AIRCRAFT SPECIFICATION SHEET

Span: 95ft 7½ in
Length: 46ft 3in
Wing area: 1,133.0sqft

Take-off weight: 10,978lb
Power plant: Two 345hp Eagle VIII V12 piston engines
Armament/bomb load: Four Lewis guns, one in the nose and three amidships. Up to 460lb of bombs under wings amidships.
Performance
   Max. speed: 95.5mph at 2,000ft
   Endurance: 6hrs
   Service ceiling: 9,600ft

HISTORY

The Felixstowe F2 was a 1917 British flying boat class designed and developed by Lieutenant Commander Porte at the Seaplane Experimental Station, Felixstowe, during World War I adapting a larger version of his superior Felixstowe F1 hull design married with the larger Curtiss H12 flying boat. The Felixstowe hull had superior water contacting attributes and became a key base technology in most seaplane designs thereafter. Before the war Porte had worked with American aircraft designer Glenn Curtiss on a flying boat, the America and when he returned to England he recommended the purchase from Curtiss of an improved version of the America flying boat on which he had worked, the Curtiss H-4 type, resulting in the RNAS receiving two prototype Americas and sixty-two H-4s. The Curtiss H-4s was found to have a number of problems, being underpowered with its hull too weak for sustained operations and having poor handling characteristics when afloat or taking off. To try to resolve the H-4's hydrodynamic issues, in 1915 Porte carried out a series of experiments on four H-4s fitted with a variety of modified hulls, using the results of these tests to design a new 36ft long (11m) hull, which was fitted to the wings and tail of a H-4, serial number 3580, with a pair of 150hp (112kW) Hispano-Suiza 8 engines as the Felixstowe F1. The combination of the new Porte-designed hull, this time fitted with two steps, with the wings of the H-12 and a new tail, and powered by two Rolls-Royce Eagle engines, was named the Felixstowe F2 and first flew in July 1916, proving greatly superior to the Curtiss on which it was based. It entered production as the Felixstowe F2A, being used as a patrol aircraft, with about 100 being completed by the end of World War I. The dazzle camouflage of the F2A was adopted as aid to identification during air combat and on the water in the event of being forced down. The Felixstowe F2A was widely used as a patrol aircraft over the North Sea until the end of the war. Its excellent performance and manoeuvrability made it an effective and popular type, often fighting enemy patrol and fighter aircraft, as well as hunting U-boats and Zeppelins.

FELIXSTOWE 3

AIRCRAFT SPECIFICATION SHEET

Span: 102ft 0 in
Length: 49ft 2in
Wing area: 1,432.0sqft
Take-off weight: 12,235lb
Power plant: Two 345hp Eagle VIII V12 engines (but see notes below)
Armament/bomb load: 4 × Lewis guns, one in the nose and three amidships. Up to 920lb of bombs under the wings.
Performance
   Max. speed: 91mph
   Endurance: 6hrs
   Service ceiling: 8,000ft

HISTORY

The Felixstowe F3 was a British World War I flying boat designed by Lieutenant Commander John Cyril Porte RN of the Seaplane Experimental Station, Felixstowe, the successor to the Felixstowe F2. The Felixstowe F2a entered production and service as a patrol aircraft, with about 100 being completed by the end of World War I. In February 1917, the first prototype of the Felixstowe F3 was flown. This was a larger and heavier development of the F2a, powered by two 320hp (239kW) Sunbeam Cossack engines. Large orders followed, with the production aircraft powered by Rolls-Royce Eagles. The F3's larger size gave it greater range and heavier bomb load than the F2, but poorer speed and agility. Approximately 100 Felixstowe F3s were produced before the end of the war, including eighteen built in the dockyards at Malta. The Felixstowe F.5 was intended to combine the good qualities of the F2 and F3, with the prototype first flying in May 1918. The prototype showed superior qualities to its predecessors but the production version was modified to make extensive use of components from the F3, in order to ease production, giving lower performance than either the F2a or F3. The Felixstowe was re-exported to America, and a re-jigged Felixstowe/Curtiss with the Curtiss Company provided the basis for the NC-4. The larger F3, which was less popular with its crews than the more manoeuvrable F2a, served in the Mediterranean as well as the North Sea.

HANDLEY PAGE O/100

AIRCRAFT SPECIFICATION SHEET
Span: 100ft 0in
Length: 62ft 10¼in
Wing area: 1,648sqft
Take-off weight: 13,360lb
Power plant: Two 260hp Rolls-Royce Eagle II water-cooled Vee type
Armament/bomb load: See text below
Performance
   Max. speed: 97.5mph at sea level
   Endurance: 8hrs 0min
   Service ceiling: 8,500ft

HISTORY
It was the Royal Navy and not the War Office that, in the first few months of the Great War, called for a bombing aircraft that could bomb Germany. Things have not changed since it is the Royal Navy and not the RAF that deploys the nuclear deterrent in the Trident submarines. In December 1914 the Air Department of the Admiralty laid down the specifications for a bomber that was to be a two-seat aircraft with a speed not less than 75mph and capable of carrying a load of six 112lb bombs. This aircraft, even in its inception, was nicknamed the 'Bloody Paralyser'. Following an order for forty of these aircraft the prototype flew on 18 December 1915 powered by two 250hp Rolls-Royce Eagle II engines. The last six of forty-six O/100s built by Handley Page had 320hp Sunbeam Cossack engines. The prototype had an enclosed crew cabin and 1,200lb of armour plating encasing the engines and front part of the fuselage but this made the aircraft unacceptably heavy and the armour did not feature on

the production models. The wings folded alongside the fuselage so that they could be housed in the standard British field hangar. In the event the O/100 was able to carry sixteen 112lb bombs internally with a crew of four. There were Lewis guns in the nose and dorsal position. A fifth gun could be fired through a trapdoor in the floor. This bomber went into service with No.3 Wing RNAS in November 1916 on the Western Front. These aircraft were employed on daylight sea patrols off the Flanders coast but in the spring of 1916 they concentrated in night bombing of railway stations, industrial targets and U-boat bases. Abroad these aircraft were used in campaigns against the Turks assisting General Allenby and T.E. Lawrence and in the Aegean in bombing raids on Constantinople.

HANDLEY PAGE O/400

AIRCRAFT SPECIFICATION SHEET
Span: 100ft 0in
Length: 62ft 10¼ in
Wing area: 1,648sqft
Take-off weight: 13,360lb
Power plant: Two 360hp Rolls-Royce Eagle VIII water-cooled Vee type. See text below
Armament/bomb load: See text below
Performance
   Max. speed: 97.5mph at sea level
   Endurance: 8hrs 0min
   Service ceiling: 8,500ft

HISTORY
Built from a O/100 airframe the prototype O/400 was numbered 3138. The difference lay in the fuel tanks, which were transferred from the engine nacelles to the fuselage, meaning, of course, that the engine nacelles were smaller as a result. Approximately 550 O/400s were built in the UK and a further 107 were assembled from components built in the USA powered with 350hp Liberty engines. At the same time as the O/100 was being transferred to night operations the O/400 became

operational as a day bomber in France. Then in October it too became a night bomber. Units equipped with O/400s were Nos.58, 97 and 115 Squadrons, the last two serving with the Independent Bombing Force. Nos.214, 215 and 216 Squadrons of the RNAS were also equipped with the type. On 31 October 1918 258 O/400 bombers were on charge to the RAF. Two of these were converted into troop transports to ferry pilots back from France to England. These aircraft remained in RAF service until 1920.

The O/400 also had progressively larger engines fitted. Indeed, the design of a bomber that could reach Berlin from airfields in East Anglia (the HPV1500) was already in the planning stage. Acting as a test bed for the HPV 1500 a O/400 was powered by two tandem pairs of 200hp Hispano-Suiza engines so that this aircraft's performance could be evaluated.

HP 1500

AIRCRAFT SPECIFICATION SHEET

Span: 126ft 0in
Length: 62ft 0in
Wing area: 3,000.0 sqft
Take-off weight: 30,000lb
Power PLANT: Four 375hp Rolls-Royce Eagle VIII water-cooled Vee type
Armament/bomb load: See text below
Performance
    Max. speed: 90.5mph at 6,000ft
    Endurance: 6hrs 0min
    Service ceiling: 11,000ft

HISTORY

The Handley Page V/1500 was a British night-flying heavy bomber built by Handley Page towards the end of World War I. It was a large four-engined biplane, which resembled a larger version of Handley Page's earlier O/100 and O/400 bombers. It was intended to bomb Berlin from East Anglian airfields but the end of the war stopped the

V/1500 being used against Germany. It was produced to meet a British Air Board 1917 requirement for a large night bomber capable of reaching deeper into Germany than the Handley Page O/100, which had recently entered service, carrying a 3,000lb (1,400 kg) bomb load. While the V/1500 had a similar fuselage to that of the O/100, it had longer-span, four-bay biplane wings and was powered by four 375hp (280kW) Rolls-Royce Eagle VIII engines mounted in two nacelles, so two engines were pulling in the conventional manner and two pushing, rather than the two Eagles of the smaller bomber. A relatively novel design feature was the gunner's position at the extreme rear of the fuselage, between the four fins. Owing to the pressure of work at Handley Page's Cricklewood factory, and to ensure security, the first prototype was constructed by Harland and Wolff at Belfast, Northern Ireland, being assembled at Cricklewood and first flying on 22 May 1918. Orders were placed for a total of 210 V/1500s, although only forty aircraft were completed, with a further twenty-two produced as spares. Three aircraft were delivered to No.166 Squadron at RAF Bircham Newton (Norfolk) during October 1918. The squadron commander did not get clear orders for his mission until November 8, due to debate at high level. A mission was scheduled for that night (to bomb Berlin, fly on to Prague as the Austro-Hungarian forces had surrendered by then, refuel, re-arm, and bomb Düsseldorf on the way back). No mission was flown – a technical expert insisted that all the engines on one aircraft be changed. The same happened the following day (but with a different aircraft). The three aircraft were about to taxi out after the second set of engine changes when an excited ground crew member ran out to stop them – the Armistice had just been declared.

HENRY FARMAN III

AIRCRAFT SPECIFICATION SHEET

Span: 33ft 9.75in
Length: 39ft 4.5in
Wing area: 430.56sqft

Take-off weight: 1,213lb
Power plant: One 50hp 7-cylinder Rotary Gnome engine
Performance
  Max. speed: 37mph

HISTORY

The Farman III, also known as the Henry Farman 1909 biplane, was an early French aircraft, designed and built in that year. Its design was widely imitated, so much so that aircraft of a similar layout were generally referred to as being of the Farman type. Henry Farman's first aircraft had been bought from the Voisin brothers in 1907. Soon after his first flights Farman begun to modify and improve the design of the aircraft, which was known as either the Farman I or Voisin-Farman I. During 1908 Farman re-covered the aircraft with 'Continental' rubberized fabric and added the side-curtains and it was re-designated the Farman I-bis. During 1908 the Voisin brothers built him another aircraft, to be called the Farman II, incorporating refinements of the design to Farman's specification. However, Voisin sold this aircraft to J.T.C. Moore-Brabazon. Brabazon subsequently exported the aircraft to England, where it became known as the *Bird of Passage*. This episode naturally angered Farman, and caused him to break his association with Voisin in early 1909 and start aircraft construction for himself, and he designed and built the Farman III. The Farman III was also a pusher biplane with a single forward elevator and originally had a cellular tailplane and ailerons on all four wings. It first flew in April 1909 powered by a 50hp (37kW) Vivinus four-cylinder inline engine. Farman soon introduced an open tailplane with trailing rudders and an extended-span upper wing and a lightweight four-wheel landing gear. Farman also replaced the engine with the new and more reliable 50hp (37kW) Gnome rotary engine. In late 1909, Henry Farman established two world distance records with flights of 180km (110 miles) in just under 3 hours 5 minutes at Rheims on 27 August and 232km (144 miles) in 4 hours 17 minutes and 53 seconds at Mourmelon on 3 November. The Farman III had enormous influence on European aircraft design, especially in England. Drawings and details of the aircraft were published in England by *Flight* magazine and it was so widely imitated that its layout became referred to as the 'Farman Type', e.g., the Bristol Boxkite.

HENRY FARMAN F20

AIRCRAFT SPECIFICATION SHEET
Span: 45ft 11in
Length: 27ft 3in
Wing area: 377sqft
Take-off weight: 1,460lb
Power plant: One 80hp Gnome Rotary

Armament/bomb load: One machine gun on flexible mount for observer and a small load of bombs
Performance
  Max. speed: 70mph
  Range: 160 miles
  Service ceiling: 1,050ft

HISTORY

Brothers Henry and Maurice Farman each established their own aviation businesses in France around 1908–09. In 1912, they combined their operations, although subsequent models were still often identified as Maurice or Henry Farmans. The Farman factory at Billacourt near Paris produced a range of similar wide-span biplanes, which were widely used in training and reconnaissance roles. The Central Flying School at Point Cook in Victoria used five examples of the Maurice Farman Shorthorn for pilot training between 1916 and 1919. The Shorthorn name refers to the length of the skids extending in front of the undercarriage, which were designed to prevent students from overturning the aircraft on landing. The Farman F20 was a military reconnaissance and trainer aircraft powered by an 80hp rotary engine. It was used by the French Air Service during World War I. The Farman HF20 and its derivatives were a family of reconnaissance aircraft produced in France shortly before and during World War I. It was a refined version of the Farman MF11 'Shorthorn' that did away with the type's distinctive landing skids and incorporated design features from Henry Farman's designs. It entered service with the French Belgian and Serbian armies in 1913 (two aircraft conducting reconnaissance during the Siege of Shkoder in the First Balkan War with one crashing), and with the British RFC and RNAS shortly after the outbreak of war. The type was also licence-built in the UK by Airco and Grahame-White. The HF20 was seriously underpowered, hence the very low service ceiling, and a variety of engines were trialled in the hope of correcting this, none with much success. The problem was eventually solved only when an engine of twice the power of the original power plant was fitted to the HF27 variant, by which time the aircraft was already obsolete. Nevertheless, the performance of this machine made it adequate for use on secondary fronts.

MARTINSYDE BUZZARD

AIRCRAFT SPECIFICATION SHEET
Span: 32ft 9 3/8in
Length: 25ft 5 ⅜in
Wing area: 320.0sqft
Take-off weight: 2,398lb
Power plant: One 300hp Hispano-Suiza 8 Fb water-cooled Vee type
Armament/bomb load: See text below
Performance
   Max. speed: 132–5mph at 15,000ft
   Endurance: 2hrs 30min
   Service ceiling: 24,000ft

HISTORY
In 1917, George Handasyde of Martinsyde designed a single seat biplane fighter powered by a Rolls-Royce Falcon V-12 engine, the Martinsyde F3, with a single prototype being built as a private venture without an official order, and it had flown at Brooklands aerodrome by October 1917. Six were ordered in 1917, with the first flying in November that year. Its performance during testing was impressive, demonstrating a maximum speed of 142mph (229km/h), and it was described in an official report as 'a great advance on all existing fighting scouts', resulting in an order for six pre-production aircraft and 150 production fighters being placed late in 1917. Martinsyde designed a new fighter based on the F3, and powered by a 300hp (224kW) Hispano-Suiza engine, the F4 Buzzard. The Buzzard, like the F3, was a single-

bay tractor biplane powered by a water-cooled engine. It had new lower wings compared with the F3 and the pilot's cockpit was positioned further aft, but otherwise the two aircraft were similar. The prototype F4 was tested in June 1918, and again demonstrated excellent performance, being easy to fly and manoeuvrable as well as very fast for the time. Deliveries to the RAF had just started when the Armistice between the Allies and Germany was signed. Martinsyde was instructed to complete only those aircraft which were part built, while all other orders were cancelled. The Buzzard was not adopted as a fighter by the post-war RAF, the cheaper Sopwith Snipe being preferred in spite of its lower performance. Despite the very limited production, four of the six Martinsyde F3s ordered were issued to Home Defence squadrons of the RAF in 1918, with two being operated by No.39 Squadron RAF on 8 July 1918 and one used by 141 Squadron. The RAF received fifty-seven F4 Buzzards before the end of World War I, but these did not reach operational squadrons. A few other Buzzards were used at the Central Flying School.

MARTINSYDE G102

AIRCRAFT SPECIFICATION SHEET
Span: 38ft 0in
Length: 27ft 6in
Wing area: 410sqft
Take-off weight: 2,458lb
Power plant: One 120hp Beardmore water-cooled in line
Armament/bomb load: One 230lb or two 112lb bombs. A Lewis gun firing over the top wing or attached to a bracket behind the pilot's left shoulder
Performance
   Max. speed: 103mph
   Endurance: 5hrs 30min
   Service ceiling: 15,000ft

HISTORY

An unusually large aircraft by contemporary standards for a single-seater, the Elephant two-bay equi-span staggered biplane was designed by A. A. Fletcher of the Martinsyde Company, a prototype powered by a 120hp Austro-Daimler engine entering test in the autumn of 1915. The initial production version, the G100, was powered by a 120hp six-cylinder Beardmore engine and was armed with a single 7.7mm Lewis gun mounted above the centre section (this later being augmented by a similar weapon bracket-mounted to port behind the cockpit), deliveries to the RFC commencing in 1916. The G100 was succeeded by the G102 version, which differed in having a 160hp Beardmore engine and replaced the lower-powered model progressively. The G100 and G102 Elephants were used in France and the Middle East, although only one RFC squadron was completely equipped with this type, a total of 270 being manufactured. While not particularly successful as a fighter owing to its poor agility in comparison with its smaller contemporaries, the Elephant performed a useful service as a bomber, carrying up to 104kg. The Martinsyde G100/102 served with Nos.18, 20, 21, 23, 27 Squadrons in France and with Nos.14 and 67 in Palestine and Nos. 30, 63 and 72 Squadrons in Mesopotamia. No. 27 Squadron was the only squadron fully equipped with Martinsydes. Lieutenant Stuart Campbell who joined 27 Squadron in 1917 described the Martinsyde as 'a delightful machine for leisurely pleasure but totally unsuitable for daylight bombing or indeed any kind of war mission'. He described it as very slow and sluggish on the controls when loaded with bombs. On bombing missions the aircraft could take two hours to reach the typical operational height of 15,000ft. Campbell commented that the only defence when attacked was to go into a dive and zig-zag for home.

MARTINSYDE S1

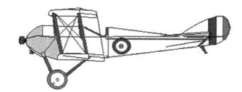

AIRCRAFT SPECIFICATION SHEET
Span: 27ft 8in
Length: 21ft 0in

Wing area: 280sqft
Take-off weight: 2,100lb
Power plant: One 80hp Gnome Rotary
Armament/bomb load: Forward-firing one .303in Lewis gun
Performance
  Max. speed: 87mph
  Service ceiling: 10,000ft

HISTORY

The Martinsyde Scout 1 was a British biplane aircraft of the early part of World War I built by Martinsyde Limited. It was a single-seat biplane with a Gnome engine in tractor configuration.

Sixty of the S1 were built and these were used for about six months on the Western Front by the RFC before it was relegated to training. Although initially intended for use in Home Defence operating from the UK, it was found to be inadequate for that too. An account of the S1 in action in Mesopotamia emphasized the poor record of the S1 in action over Kut in the Mesopotamian campaign. On 4 November 1915 the Turks claimed to have shot down two S1s and on 21 November they captured a third English aircraft, which, they claimed, 'was shot down by us'. The leader, a major, was wounded and imprisoned. This was the Martinsyde S1 (Martinsyde No.6) of Major Reilly of the Indian Flying Corps who was shot down by gunfire and taken prisoner. Reilly had spotted the large numbers of reinforcements at Ctesiphon digging in for the oncoming British attack. His report would fail to reach headquarters and Major General Townshend ordered the failed attack on Ctesiphon. Finally, on 26 November 1915 the Turks said that they had captured a fourth hostile aircraft, possibly the S1 flown by Lieutenant Fulton of No.30 Squadron RFC, which was shot down during the retreat to Kut on 22 November.

MAURICE FARMAN LONGHORN

AIRCRAFT SPECIFICATION SHEET
Span: 50ft 6in
Length: 37ft 2.8in
Wing area: 645.8sqft

Take-off weight: 1,885lb
Power plant: One 70hp Renault air-cooled 8C V8
Armament/bomb load: See text below
Performance
   Max. speed: 59mph at sea level
   Endurance: 3hrs 30min
   Service ceiling: 13,123ft

HISTORY

The Maurice Farman MF7 Longhorn is a French reconnaissance biplane developed before World War I, which served in both the French and British air services in the early stages of the war before being used as a trainer aircraft. It had a single Renault 'pusher' engine. Its name is derived from the distinctive front-mounted elevator and elongated skids. From 1912 the Maurice Farman-designed MF7 served with the French military as well as with many civil and military flying schools in France, Britain and elsewhere in Europe. It was an unequal-span biplane usually fitted with a 52kW Renault engine driving a pusher propeller. Characteristic of the design was the prominent frontal elevator, which led to the nickname 'Longhorn'. Next to the French – who used it initially for reconnaissance duties with seven escadrilles and later for training – the best customers were the RFC and RNAS who received a large number from France and others licence-built in the UK for training duties. There is an instance, however, of a Longhorn being used in action in Mesopotamia. On 12 November 1915, whilst at Azizieh, the, divisional Commander, Major General Townshend, ordered that the telegraph lines in rear of the Turkish positions before Baghdad be destroyed by an aeroplane, which was to land behind the enemy's lines. Volunteers were asked for by the Flight Commander, and Captain White with Captain F. Yeats-Brown, 17 Indian Cavalry, as his observer, volunteered for this task. He was flying a Longhorn and owing to the distance to be covered he had to carry tins of petrol and oil to fill up the tanks after landing for the return journey. The aircraft was damaged on landing but the mission was successful in that the telegraph wires were destroyed using guncotton. Although repairs to the aircraft were attempted both men were captured before they could take off.

MAURICE FARMAN SHORTHORN

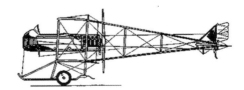

AIRCRAFT SPECIFICATION SHEET
Span: 53ft 0in
Length: 31ft 0in

Wing area: 613sqft
Take-off weight: 2,045lb
Power plant: One 100hp Renault 8-cylinder air-cooled in-line engine
Armament/bomb load:
   One 7.5mm machine gun
   18 × 16lb bombs
Performance
   Max. speed: 66mph at sea level
   Endurance: 3hrs 45min
   Service ceiling: 12,467ft

HISTORY

The Maurice Farman MF11 Shorthorn was a French reconnaissance and light bomber biplane developed during World War I by the Farman Aviation Works. It was essentially a Farman MF7 with a more powerful engine, and a more robust and aerodynamic fuselage, which was raised above the lower wing on struts. The aircraft was also fitted with a machine gun for the observer, whose position was changed from the rear seat to the front in order to give a clear field of fire. Its name derived from that of the MF7 Longhorn, as it lacked the characteristic front-mounted elevator and elongated skids of its predecessor. The MF11 served in both the British and French air services on the Western Front in the early stages of the war. As a light bomber it flew the first bombing raid of the war when on 21 December 1914 an MF11 of the Royal Naval Air Service attacked German artillery positions around Ostend, Belgium. The MF11 was withdrawn from front-line service on the Western Front in 1915, but continued to be used by the French in Macedonia and the Middle East, while the British also used it in the Dardanelles, and Africa. The Australian Flying Corps (AFC), provided with the MF11 by the British Indian Army, operated it during the Mesopotamian campaign of 1915–16. Italy's Società Italiana Aviazione, a Fiat company, licence-built a number of MF11s under the designation SIA 5 from early 1915, fitted with a fixed forward machine gun and a 74.5kW (100hp) Fiat A10 engine. In 1916, the AFC also bought some MF11s for training purposes.

MORANE – I AND II

AIRCRAFT SPECIFICATION SHEET
Span: 27ft 10in
Length: 18ft 6in
Wing area: 360sqft
Take-off weight: 1,433lb
Power plant: One 160hp Gnome rotary
Armament/bomb load: See text below
Performance
    Max. speed: 129mph
    Endurance: 4hrs 0min
    Service ceiling: 23,000ft

HISTORY
During the first half of 1917, Robert and Leon Morane, and Raymond Saulnier presented their newest fighter aircraft, the Morane Saulnier A-1, to the French military for review. It was favourably accepted and was produced in large numbers. Despite the fact that the Morane's flight characteristics were well liked by many pilots, the duration of its active service was limited to a mere three months. It was withdrawn from combat as a result of alleged structural failures and reliability problems with the 160hp Gnome engine. Many remaining aircraft of this type were refitted with smaller, more reliable power plants and used as advanced trainers for the duration of the war, and afterwards as well. Famed aviator Charles Nungesser was known to demonstrate his aerobatic skills to the public with his own personal MS A-1 after the war. In 1919, Lieutenant Temple Joyce became the world's champion 'looper', completing 300 consecutive loops with his A-1. One year later the record was raised to 1,111 consecutive loops performed by Alfred Fronval in his A-1. Successful exhibition flying of this type seems to contradict the question of the aircraft's lack of structural integrity. For World War I, the Morane-Saulnier A-1 had very modern lines and was very streamlined; it resembles small aircraft that you can see today at any general aviation airport. Some 1,210 were produced, but the type never made a big impact at the front. Not

long after its introduction it was withdrawn to serve as a trainer, as it was suspected of structural weakness. Some contemporary sources refer to this aircraft as the Type 27 and Type 29. The Type 27C1 carried one machine gun; the Type 29C1 carried two. Generally, high-wing monoplanes were called 'parasol types', so it may also be referred to that way.

MORANE – BB

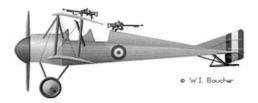

AIRCRAFT SPECIFICATION SHEET
Span: 28ft 5in
Length: 23ft 0in
Wing area: 247.57sqft
Take-off weight: 1,653lb
Power plant: One 110hp Le Rhône
Armament/bomb load: One 7.7 mm machine gun (Lewis guns pictured above)
Performance
    Max. speed: 91mph
    Service ceiling: 13,100ft

HISTORY
The Morane-Saulnier BB was a military observation aircraft produced in France during World War I for use by Britain's RFC. It was a conventional single-bay biplane design with seating for the pilot and observer in tandem, in open cockpits. The original order called for 150 aircraft powered by 110-hp Le Rhône engines, but shortages meant that most of the 94 aircraft eventually built were delivered with the 80hp Le Rhônes instead. A water-cooled Hispano-Suiza engine was trialled as an alternative in the Type BH, but this remained experimental only.

The type equipped a number of RFC and RNAS squadrons both in its original observation role and, equipped with a forward-firing Lewis gun mounted on the top wing, as a fighter.

Because the type 'BB' when pronounced in French sounds like Bébé (or baby), this became the type's nickname. Most of these Morane types had no fixed fin, or horizontal stabilizer with the result that they were not only very sensitive on the controls, but could not even be flown hands off. One early pilot noted that if one left the aircraft to its own devices it would end up going upside down in the opposite direction. Despite this, many were used as trainers, including a great many that had their wings stripped so they couldn't fly, creating what was known as a Penguin.

MORANE – L AND LA

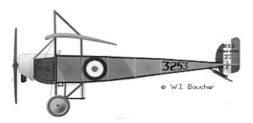

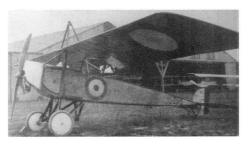

AIRCRAFT SPECIFICATION SHEET
Span: 36ft 9in
Length: 22ft 6 ¾ in
Wing area: 197sqft
Take-off weight: 1,441lb
Power plant: One 80hp RAF Gnome rotary
Armament/bomb load: 6 × 25lb bombs, small arms, then one machine gun
Performance
   Max. speed: 71.5mph at 6,560ft
   Endurance: 2hrs 30 min
   Service ceiling: 13,123ft

HISTORY
Over a period of two decades Morane Saulnier produced a string of parasol monoplanes. The first, which appeared in 1913, was the Type L (military designation MoS.3). This was a simple and rather frail-looking machine with a box-like fuselage and a 80hp Gnome or Le Rhône 9 C rotary engine in a horseshoe cowling. Lateral control was by wing warping. Upon the outbreak of war the Type L was ordered in large numbers, the intention being to use

it for reconnaissance but it was appreciably faster than the German two-seaters then in service, and crews were encouraged to take small arms with them in the cockpit. The most common weapon was the cavalry carbine, with which considerable success was achieved. France's Georges Guynemer scored his first aerial victory in a MoS3 in July 1915. It was a Morane L (and not a Type N as was believed for many years), which unwittingly brought about the so called 'Fokker Scourge' of 1915–16. The Type L has the distinction of being the first fighter aircraft during the early days of World War I when one was fitted with a machine gun firing through the propeller. Although initially fitted with a synchronizer, the irregular rate of fire afforded by the gas-operated Hotchkiss machine gun meant it didn't work half the time, and metal deflector plates had to be fitted to armour the propeller. The Type L gave excellent service in its intended reconnaissance role, and was also used for light bombing and agent dropping. Nearly 600 were built and examples could be found on No.3 Squadron RFC and No.1 Wing RNAS in France. Sub Lieutenant Warneford was flying a Morane L when he won a VC for destroying Zeppelin LZ 37. The six 25lb bombs carried by his aircraft was a typical bomb load for this aircraft. The LA (MoS4) was a developed version of the Type L having a rounded fuselage, ailerons and small fins above and below the rear fuselage. Examples served with Nos.1 and 3 Squadrons RFC during 1916/7.

MORANE – P

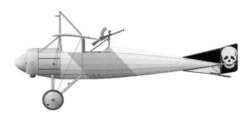

AIRCRAFT SPECIFICATION SHEET
Span: 36ft 8in
Length: 23ft 7in
Wing area: 194sqft
Take-off weight: 1,613lb
Power plant: One 110hp Le Rhône 9J rotary
Armament/bomb load: 1 Vickers machine gun and 1 or 2 Lewis guns, light load of bombs

Performance
    Max. speed: 97mph at 2,000ft
    Endurance: 2 hrs 30 min
    Service ceiling: 15,740ft

HISTORY

Morane-Saulnier's first commercially successful design was the Morane-Saulnier G, a boxy-looking wire-braced shoulder wing monoplane with wing warping, which led to the development of a whole series of aircraft and was very successful in racing, and setting records in its own right. The Type G was a single-seater, and was enlarged slightly to make the Morane-Saulnier H, a two-seater, and in parallel was given a faired fuselage to make the Morane-Saulnier N single-seat fighter. The AI lost out in the competition with the SPAD XIII but was built in limited numbers in case there was a problem with the SPAD though as it turned out, it was the AI that suffered structural problems. In parallel to the L the Morane-Saulnier BB was developed for the RFC, which was a Type P built as a biplane.

The Morane-Saulnier H was modified so that its wings were mounted parasol fashion, above the fuselage to afford the observer a better view, creating the Morane-Saulnier L. The Morane-Saulnier Type P was a World War I French parasol wing two-seat reconnaissance aeroplane. Morane-Saulnier built 595 for the French air force, and it was also used by the British until 1916–17. The Type P was larger, more powerful, and better armed than its predecessor, the Type L. It was also more popular than its sister plane, the Type LA.

The L was then fitted with a faired fuselage as on the N and ailerons to make the Morane-Saulnier LA, which was then completely redesigned (though looking very similar) to make the Morane-Saulnier P, which would be the basis for a whole family of aircraft developed in the 1920s.

NIEUPORT 12

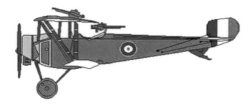

AIRCRAFT SPECIFICATION SHEET

Span: 29ft 6 in
Length: 22ft 11½ in
Wing area: 237sqft
Take-off weight: 1,874lb
Power plant: One 110hp Clerget rotary
Armament/bomb load: See text below
Performance
    Max. speed: 91mph
    Endurance: 3hrs approx
    Service ceiling: 13,000ft

HISTORY

The Nieuport 12 was a slightly enlarged version of the Nieuport 10 and had a 110hp or 130hp Clerget 9B rotary engine. The orders for the RFC and RNAS did not always specify an exact variant i.e., 10 or 12, contracts simply specifying Nieuport or Nieuport Scout. So it cannot be certain which of the Nieuport variants were held on service inventories. The Nieuport 10 from which the '12' was a derivative, was the first of a family of aircraft that would be the most attractive and successful of the Great War. The designer, Gustave Delage, joined the Nieuport company in January 1914 and his first design was the '10', a tractor biplane with a fuselage similar to the pre-war monoplanes. This two-seater appeared in two forms, the 10AV (AV = *avant*) and the 10AR (AR = *arrière*), meaning the position of the observer's cockpit in front of or behind the pilot. It is probable that the AR served as a prototype for the larger Nieuport 12. The Nieuport 10C was designed to act as a fighter with the front cockpit covered and the pilot would man a Lewis gun mounted to fire over the top wing upwards and outside the propeller arc. In the reconnaissance version the observer had to stand up in his cockpit to fire the Lewis gun with his head and shoulders occupying a small cut-out in the top wing. And so a basic reconnaissance machine could become, temporarily, a fighter.

NIEUPORT 16

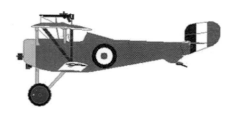

AIRCRAFT SPECIFICATION SHEET

Span: 24ft 9¼in
Length: 19ft ⅓ in
Wing area: 139.9sqft
Take-off weight: 1,213lb

Power plant: One 110hp Le Rhône rotary
Armament/bomb load: One synchronized Vickers gun, some carried Le Prieur rockets
Performance
  Max. speed: 96.8 mph at sea level
  Range: 205 miles
  Service ceiling: 15,092ft

HISTORY

The Nieuport 16 was a more powerful variant of the Nieuport 11. On the outbreak of the Great War the 11 was accepted as a fighter for the Aviation Militaire. Due to its diminutive size it was nicknamed the Bébé when it entered service in the summer of 1915. Six were purchased for No.3 Wing of the RNAS and they went into service with the RFC in France from March 1916 and helped to counter the 'Fokker Scourge'. There are no known serial numbers for the 11. Perhaps the RFC referred to their 11s and 13s by reference to their wing area. It is apparent that the RFC allocated serial numbers to a number of Nieuport Scouts. The 11 was used by the RNAS in the Dardanelles campaign. In 1916 the 16 appeared, powered by a 110hp Le Rhône engine in place of the 80hp Le Rhône rotary in the 11. The 16 mounted a synchronized Vickers gun instead of the overwing Lewis gun. Some 16s carried Le Prieur rockets (see photograph above) on the interplane struts. With these some achieved success in shooting down enemy observation balloons. The 16 did not equip RNAS units but was employed with Nos.1, 3, 11 and 29 Squadrons of the RFC. During the period of the Fokker Scourge both the 11 and 16 performed valuable service. Some 11s were converted to two-seat trainers powered by Clerget 7Z engines.

NIEUPORT 17

AIRCRAFT SPECIFICATION SHEET
Span: 26ft 9in
Length: 19ft 0in
Wing area: 158.8sqft
Take-off weight: 1,232lb
Power plant: One 110hp Le Rhône 9 J rotary

Armament/bomb load: One Lewis gun on Foster mounting on upper wing or 8 × Le Prieur rockets
Performance
  Max. speed: 110mph at 2,000ft
  Endurance: 1hrs 45min
  Service ceiling: 17,390ft

HISTORY

The type was a slightly larger development of the earlier Nieuport 11, and had a more powerful engine, larger wings, and a more refined structure in general. At first, it was equipped with a 110 hp Le Rhône 9J engine, though later versions were upgraded to a 130hp engine. It had outstanding manoeuvrability, and an excellent rate of climb. Unfortunately, the narrow lower wing, marking it as a 'sesquiplane' design with literally 'one-and-a-half wings', was weak due to its single spar construction, and had a disconcerting tendency to disintegrate in sustained dives at high speed. Initially, the Nieuport 17 retained the above wing-mounted Lewis gun on a Foster mounting, a curved metal rail that allowed the pilot to bring the gun down in order to change drums or clear jams. A few individual aircraft were fitted with two guns – but in practice this reduced performance unacceptably, and a single machine gun remained standard. It was ordered by the RFC and the RNAS, as it was superior to any British fighter at that time. The Germans supplied captured examples to several of their aircraft manufacturers for them to copy. This resulted in the Siemens-Schuckert DI which, apart from the engine installation, was a close copy and actually went into production, although in the event it was not used operationally on the Western Front. By early 1917, the Nieuport was outclassed in most respects by the latest German fighters. However, the SPAD SVII had already replaced the Nieuport fighters in many French squadrons by mid-1917. The British persisted with Nieuports a little longer, not replacing their last Nieuport 24bis until early 1918. Many Allied air aces flew Nieuport fighters, including Canadian ace W. A. Bishop, who received a VC while flying it, and most famously of all, Albert Ball, VC. Like the other Nieuport types, the 17 was used as an advanced trainer for prospective fighter pilots after its operational days were over

NIEUPORT 20

AIRCRAFT SPECIFICATION SHEET
Span: 29ft 6in
Length: 22ft 11½in
Wing area: 237sqft
Take-off weight: 1,874lb
Power plant: 110hp Le Rhône 9J
Armament/bomb load: See text below
Performance
  Max. speed: 91mph
  Endurance: 3hrs 0min
  Service ceiling: 13,000ft

HISTORY
The Nieuport 20 was developed from the Nieuport 12. To improve the performance of the Nieuport 10 a larger and re-engined version was developed as the Nieuport 12. A Lewis gun was fitted to the rear cockpit for use of the observer and the pilot sometimes had a Lewis gun fixed to the upper wing firing over the propeller. Late examples of the type, used by the RFC were sometimes fitted with a Nieuport or Scarff ring mounting for the observer's gun, and a synchronized Vickers gun for the pilot.

Indeed, as one can see from the above the whole series of Nieuport fighters were simply based on the early design with, in some cases, a larger more powerful engine and a variety of arrangements for the machine guns.

NIEUPORT 23

AIRCRAFT SPECIFICATION SHEET
Span: 26ft 11in
Length: 21ft 0in
Wing area: 14.8m²
Take-off weight: 1,263lb
Power plant: One 120hp Le Rhône 9Jb
Armament/bomb load:
  One forward-firing .303in Vickers machine gun
Performance
  Max. speed: 105mph
  Endurance: 1hrs 7min
  Service ceiling: 21,000ft

HISTORY
The Nieuport 23 was a fighter aircraft produced in France during World War I. It was a development of the Nieuport 17 intended to address structural weakness of the earlier type, and most were produced with a lighter version of the Le Rhône 9J engine that powered the Nieuport 17, offering a better power-to-weight ratio. Internally, the main difference between the Types 17 and 23 was a redesigned wing spar in the upper wing. This, however, did not prove satisfactory, and when the fighter displayed an unacceptably high accident rate due to shedding its wings in flight, the *Général chef du service aéronautique* ordered that either additional reinforcement be added to the wings or that the type be withdrawn from service. Some 150 new sets of wings were ordered to keep the type flying. External differences included better streamlining of the forward fuselage and a synchronized machine gun mounted on the upper fuselage and firing through the propeller disc. Nieuport 23s ordered for Britain's RFC nevertheless were fitted with machine guns that fired over the top of the upper wing, in the way that the Nieuport 17 had been armed. A trainer version was

produced as the Nieuport 23 École (or Nieuport 21/23) with an 80hp Le Rhône engine.

NIEUPORT 24

AIRCRAFT SPECIFICATION SHEET
Span: 26ft 10⅜in
Length: 19ft 3½in
Wing area: 161.5sqft
Take-off weight: 1,200lb
Power plant: One 130hp Le Rhône 9 Jb rotary
Armament/bomb load: One Lewis gun on Foster mounting
Performance
    Max. speed: 115.6mph
    Endurance: 1hr 30min approx
    Service ceiling: 18,208ft

HISTORY
The Nieuport 24 was a French biplane fighter aircraft during World War I designed as a replacement for the successful Nieuport 17. In the event its performance was little better than the type it was meant to replace, which was largely superseded by the SPAD S7 instead. Operational Nieuport 24s served with French, British and Russian units, and the type also served widely as an advanced trainer. The Nieuport 24 introduced a new fuselage of improved aerodynamic form, rounded wingtips, and a tail unit incorporating a small fixed fin and a curved rudder. The tailskid was sprung internally and had a neater appearance than that on earlier Nieuports. A 130hp Le Rhône rotary engine was fitted. There were initial structural problems with the new tail, and most production aircraft of the type were of the Nieuport 24bis model, which retained the fuselage and wings of the 24, but reverted to the Nieuport 17 type tailplane, tailskid and rectangular balanced rudder. The new tail was finally standardized on the Nieuport 27.

A batch of Nieuport 24bis were built in England for the RNAS.

In the summer of 1917, when the Nieuport 24 and 24bis were coming off the production line, most French fighter squadrons were replacing their Nieuport 17s with SPAD SVIIs – and many of the new fighters went to fighter training schools, and to France's allies, including the Russians, and the British, who used theirs well into 1918, due to a shortage of SE5as. A few French units retained the Nieuport through to late 1917 – the type was actually preferred by some pilots, especially the famous Charles Nungesser.

Some of the large number of Nieuport advanced trainers bought by the Americans for their flying schools in France in November 1917 were the 24s or 24bis.

NIEUPORT 27

AIRCRAFT SPECIFICATION SHEET
Span: 26ft 10⅜in
Length: 19ft 3½in
Wing area: 161.5sqft
Take-off weight: 1,200lb
Power plant: One 120hp Le Rhône 9 Jb rotary
Armament/bomb load: One Lewis gun on Foster mounting
Performance
    Max. speed: 115.6mph
    Endurance: 1hr 30min approx.
    Service ceiling: 18,208ft

HISTORY
The Nieuport 27 model was the last of the line of 'V-strut' single-seat fighters stemming from the Bébé of early 1916. A few operational examples supplemented the very similar Nieuport 24bis in opeational squadrons in late 1917 but most examples of the type served as

advanced trainers. The Nieuport 27's design closely followed the early form of the 24, including its semi-ronded rear fuselage and rounded wingtips and ailerons. The structural problems with the redesigned, rounded tail surfaces of the 24, which had resulted in the use of a Nieuport 17 type tail in the 24 bis, were by now overcome, so that the new version was able to standardize on the new tail. By now most Nieuport fighters were actually used as advanced trainers, and the 130hp Le Rhône Rotary engine of the 24bis was often replaced by a 110 or 129hp version. The handful of operational Nieuport 27s were armed either with a synchronized, fuselage-mounted Vikers machine gun (in French service) or a Lewis Gun mounted on a Foster mounting on the top wing (in British service). Two guns were occasionally fitted, but this has a severe effect on performance, which was at best little better than that of earlier models. The type served in small numbers wit hth French *Aéronautique Militaire* and also with the RFC during 1917 and early 1918, supplementing or replacing the Nieuport 24bis. However, by spring 1928 most Nieuport 'V-strut' fighters had been withdrawn from front-line service and replaced – with SPAD SXIIIs in French service, and with Royal Aircraft Factory SE5as in the RFC/RAF. The type was supplied to Italy, and built there by the Nieuport-Macchie Company at Varese, although the Iatlians ultimately preferred the Hanriot HS1. Some 120 Nieuport 27 aircraft were bought for the United States Army Air Service for use as trainers in 1918. French ace Charles Nungesser was the most famous pilot to use the 27. In 1919 Poland bought one Nieuport 27.

NIEUPORT 28

AIRCRAFT SPECIFICATION SHEET
Span: 26ft 9in
Length: 21ft 4in
Wing area: 169sqft
Take-off weight: 1,635lb
Power plant: One 160hp Gnome
 Monosoupape 9N rotary
Armament/bomb load: 2 × Vickers .303 rotary
Performance
  Max. speed: 122mph at sea level
  Range: 180 miles
  Service ceiling: 17,390ft

HISTORY
The Nieuport 28's principal claim to fame is that it was the first aircraft to see service with an American fighter squadron (the photograph is of Rickenbacker, the American ace, standing beside his machine). By the middle of 1917 it was obvious that the Nieuport 17 was unable to cope with the latest German fighters, and that direct developments of the 17, such as the Nieuport 24bis were unable to offer a substantially improved performance. In fact, the Nieuport was already being rapidly replaced in French service with the SPAD SVII. The Nieuport 28 design was an attempt to adapt the concept of the lightly built, highly manoeuvrable rotary-engined fighter typified by the Nieuport 17 to the more demanding condition of the times. It had a more powerful engine, and a new wing structure – for the first time a Nieuport biplane was fitted with conventional two-spar wings, top and bottom, in place of the sesquiplane 'V-strut' layout of earlier Nieuport types. Ailerons were fitted to the lower wings only. The tail unit's design closely followed that of the Nieuport 27, but the fuselage was much slimmer; in fact it was so narrow that the machine guns had to be offset to the left. The prototype (and, perhaps a handful of early production aircraft) had marked dihedral in the top wing only and a tightly spaced cabane structure. Production macines had only a slight dihedral in the upper wing, taller cabane struts, and two Vickers machine guns. By early 1918, when the first production Nieuport 28s became available, the type was already 'surplus' from the French point of view. The SPAD SXVIII was a superior aircraft in most respects, and was in any case firmly established as thestandard French fighter. On the other hand, the Americans were desperately short of fighters to equip the projected 'pursuit' (fighter) squadrons and since the SPAD was initially unavailabe the American Expeditionary Force (AEF) was obliged to acept the Nieuport 28 as an interim alternative and a total of 297 Nieuport 28s were purchased by the Americans. They were used to quip the very first American fighter squadrons.

ROYAL AIRCRAFT FACTORY BE2B

AIRCRAFT SPECIFICATION SHEET
Span: 35ft 0½in
Length: 29ft 6½in
Wing area: 352.0sqft
Take-off weight: 1,600lb
Power plant: One 70hp Renault air-cooled Vee-type
Armament/bomb load: Single 100lb bomb or three smaller ones. Rifles or revolvers were the only defensive armament carried by the observer in the early BEs
Performance
Max. speed: 70mph at sea level
   Endurance: 3hrs
   Service ceiling: 10,000ft

HISTORY
The BE variants were built, initially by the Royal Aircraft Factory, the letters BE standing for Blériot Experimental. This implied no connection with the Blériot factory but simply that, as a type, they were general purpose aircraft and this designation was adopted by the Royal Aircraft Factory in November 1911. The BE2 variants were designed by Geoffrey de Havilland and F. M. Green in the second half of 1911. The BE1 made its first flight on 1 January 1912 followed by the BE2 a month later. The latter had a 70hp Renault engine and was a two-seater with the pilot in the rear cockpit. On 12 August the aircraft achieved a British altitude record of 10,560ft and went on to win the Military Trials at Larkhill. Before the outbreak of war the BE2/2a equipped three RFC squadrons and at least one aircraft was in service with the RNAS in September 1913. On the Western Front BEs equipped Nos.2, 4, 6, 8, 9 (Wireless) and 16 Squadrons of the RFC. They were joined by the BE2b, which had a modified elevator and rudder controls and to give better protection to the crew the top decking and cockpit contours were redesigned. The BEs of the RNAS were quite often used for bombing and in the Home Defence role incendiary bullets were used against Zeppelins. Virtually all the early BEs saw service in France but a few operated in Egypt and RNAS BEs were used in the Dardanelles campaign. Some 164 known machines of the BE2, 2a and 2b version were constructed by nine British manufacturers. At the end of their operational life they were relegated to the training role.

ROYAL AIRCRAFT FACTORY BE2C

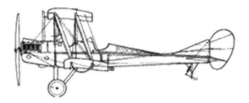

AIRCRAFT SPECIFICATION SHEET
Span: 37ft 0in
Length: 27ft 3in
Wing area: 371sqft
Take-off weight: 2,142lb
Power plant: One 90hp RAF 1a air-cooled Vee type
Armament/bomb load: Single 100lb bomb or three smaller ones. Riles or revolvers were the only defensive armament carried by the observer in the early BEs
Performance
   Max. speed: 72mph at 6,500ft
   Endurance: 3hrs 15min
   Service ceiling: 10,000ft

HISTORY
Since the War Office had decided that the role of an aircraft in war would predominantly be that of reconnaissance the Royal Aircraft Factory designed and built aeroplanes of inherent stability that were thus easier and safer to fly. Unfortunately, this proved to be the downfall of the BE type for air fighting became a fact of life on the Western Front. The front-gunned Fokker fighter aircraft could make short work of a BE, which could not outmanoeuvre it. The BE was too slow to make an escape if 'jumped' by an agile German fighter and it took forty-five minutes to reach its service ceiling of 10,000ft so it could not

outclimb the enemy. Edward Busk was one of the leading experimental test pilots at the Royal Aircraft Factory and his work resulted in the BE2c first flown in the summer of 1914. This version had equal wing spans with marked forward stagger and double ailerons in place of wing warp control. The BE2c reached France late in 1914 but it was not until April 1915 that a fully equipped squadron of BE2cs arrived in France. This was No.8 Squadron. The BE2c also served with No.1 Wing RNAS and with more than a dozen RFC squadrons. In Macedonia and the Middle East it was used in both the bomber and reconnaissance roles and as an anti-submarine aircraft in the Dardanelles and the Aegean. By 1916 the BE2d came into service with a large gravity fuel tank below the top wing. Whilst the BE2c may have often fallen prey to the Fokker, like the Hurricane of World War II, it was a stable gun platform and proved useful in the Home Defence role. In spite of the losses in France the BE2c continued in production, the last of this version being delivered in July 1917. A total production run of over 1,200 of these aircraft would continue in service until the Armistice, although latterly in the training role.

ROYAL AIRCRAFT FACTORY BE2E

AIRCRAFT SPECIFICATION SHEET

Span: 40ft 9in
Length: 27ft 3in
Wing area: 360sqft
Take-off weight: 2,100lb
Power plant: One 90hp RAF 1a air-cooled Vee type
Armament/bomb load: Normally one Lewis gun for the observer, 224lb of bombs
Performance
    Max. speed: 82mph at 6,500ft
    Endurance: 4hrs 0min
    Service ceiling: 10,000ft

HISTORY

An incident illustrating both the poor level of piloting skills with which new RFC pilots were sent to France in 1917 and the level of popularity of the BE2e on the Western Front at that time is recorded by Arthur Gould Lee, then a young RFC novice, in his book *No Parachute*. On 19 May 1917 six pilots newly arrived in France and, still to be allocated to a squadron, were each given a new BE2e to ferry between RFC depots at St Omer and Candas. One crashed in transit, three crashed on landing and one went missing (the pilot was killed). Lee, the pilot of the only aircraft to arrive safely, wrote in a letter to his wife: 'I felt rather a cad not crashing too because everyone is glad to see death-traps like Quirks written off, especially new ones.'

Fortunately, the BE2e was by this time already being rapidly replaced on the Western Front by later types, but for far too many young airmen this was more than a year too late.

ROYAL AIRCRAFT FACTORY BE8 AND 8A

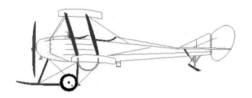

AIRCRAFT SPECIFICATION SHEET

Span: 39ft 6in
Length: 27ft 3in
Wing area: 368.0sqft
Take-off weight: 1,850lb
Power plant: One 80hp Gnome rotary
Armament/bomb load:
    Small arms operated by crew, one 100lb bomb
Performance
    Max. speed: 70mph at sea level
    Endurance: 1hr 30min
    Service ceiling: 10,000ft

HISTORY

The rotary-engined BE8 broadly followed the layout of previous designs, the BE3 and BE4, but its lower wings were attached directly to the fuselage, without the gap of the earlier designs, and the tail surfaces were modelled upon those of the original BE2. In common with most of its contemporary stable mates, the BE8 had wing-warping for lateral control and undercarriage skids to protect the propeller tips during landing. The prototype, which was powered by a 70hp Gnome and had no division between the cockpits, made its first flight on 20 August 1913. Production examples differed from the prototypes in having a decking between the cockpits and a triangular fin identical to that later adopted for the BE2c. They were powered by 80hp Gnome rotary engines driving four-bladed propellers. The two prototypes were later converted to production standard and transferred to the RFC, in whose service they bore the serials 423 and 424. Nicknamed 'The Bloater', the BE8 served in small numbers with Nos.1, 3, 5, 6 and 7 Squadrons of the RFC and at the Central Flying School, and two examples found their way to India. The type saw service on the Western Front in the early days of the war, but was regarded as being somewhat underpowered. Unfortunately, it proved to be rather prone to spinning, and as that manoeuvre and the recovery from it were far from universally understood, several machines were lost in crashes. The BE8's fuel system appears to have been a source of annoyance and the subject of criticism since, if the need arose to repressurize the tank manually, the hand pump was in the observer's cockpit and the pressure gauge was in the pilot's. Difficulty in communication could result in fuel overflowing, with the obvious fire risk. Although there is no evidence of such a fire actually occurring, the problem clearly reduced the crews' confidence in their mounts.

In January 1915 an attempt was made to improve the BE8's performance by the substitution of a 100hp Monosoupape for the 80hp engine. The conversion was made to 658 aircraft but, while it had the desired effect, the 'Mono' was relatively scarce, those available being needed for more potent aeroplanes, so no service BE8s were ever thus powered. So, underpowered, yet denied the proven remedy, the remaining BE8s were all withdrawn from front-line service by mid 1915, and finished their careers with training units.

ROYAL AIRCRAFT FACTORY BE9

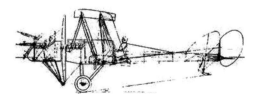

AIRCRAFT SPECIFICATION SHEET
Span: 40ft 10½in
Length: 29ft 0in

Wing area: 360sqft
Take-off weight: 2,100lb
Power plant: One 90hp RAF 1a air-cooled Vee type
Armament/bomb load: One Lewis gun
Performance
   Max. speed: 82mph at 6,500ft
   Endurance: 4hrs 0min
   Service ceiling: 10,000ft

HISTORY
The Royal Aircraft Factory BE9 (**Bl**ériot **E**xperimental) was a British prototype reconnaissance aircraft of World War I. The intention of the designers was to combine the high performance of tractor configuration aircraft with a good field of fire for the observer's machine gun, as provided by pushers. It was therefore decided to modify an example of the BE2c by adding a small wooden box (which soon gained the nickname 'pulpit') in front of the aircraft's propeller, which would accommodate a gunner armed with a Lewis gun on a trainable mount. The normal observer's cockpit of the BE2c was removed, allowing the engine (the standard air-cooled RAF 1a of the BE2) to be moved rearwards, while the wingspan was increased, and a larger fin was fitted. A general layout of this kind had various drawbacks – the most obvious being the perilous situation of the gunner – who was liable to injury by the propeller, or to be crushed by the engine in the mildest of crashes. The type was soon rendered superfluous by the availability of interrupter gears. Early testing indicated that performance was little different to the BE2c upon which it was based, although the 'difficulty' (surely an understatement) in communicating between the pilot and observer, separated by both engine and propeller, was reported and in September that year Serial No. 1700 was sent for testing in the field in France by a number of RFC units. While the BE9 carried out a few operational patrols in France, including one encounter with a German Fokker Eindecker, the opinion of those testing it was generally negative, with Major Hugh Dowding, the commander of 16 Squadron, stating that the BE9 was '...an extremely dangerous machine from the passenger's point of view', while Hugh Trenchard, head of the RFC in France said that 'this type of machine cannot be recommended'. It was sent back to the United

Kingdom early in 1916. Combat experience with the type proved inconclusive and it was not therefore ordered into mass production.

ROYAL AIRCRAFT FACTORY BE12

AIRCRAFT SPECIFICATION SHEET
Span: 37ft 0in
Length: 27ft 3in
Wing area: 371sqft
Take-off weight: 2,352lb
Power plant: One 150hp RAF 4a air-cooled V12
Armament/bomb load: 1 Vickers forward-firing machine gun, some aircraft had arrangement for a rearward-firing Lewis gun, bombs up to 336lb
Performance
  Max. speed: 82mph at 6,500ft
  Endurance: 4hrs 0min
  Service ceiling: 10,000ft

HISTORY
The Royal Aircraft Factory was known for the stability of its designs but this was achieved at the expense of manoeuvrability. By the summer of 1915 the BE2c aircraft were suffering heavy losses when in contact with the more nimble German fighters. The Factory's answer was to produce the BE12 but it was based on the same airframe. By covering in the front cockpit the BE12 was turned into a single-seat machine with a 150hp Factory 4 engine. This, it was hoped, would keep it out of trouble when confronting the enemy and production began in the spring of 1916 and by the end of August three RFC squadrons in France had been equipped with the BE12. It did not live up to expectations and Trenchard ordered its withdrawal only weeks after it had come into service.

It was changed to the light bomber role but it was even less manoeuvrable than the BE2c. BE12s saw service in Palestine and Macedonia as well as equipping six Home Defence squadrons. At least one noteworthy mission was achieved by a BE12 when an aircraft of No.37 Squadron shot down Zeppelin L48 in June 1917. Only a few BE12s remained in service at the time of the Armistice. They featured a variety of armament arrangements. One was to mount a Lewis gun on both sides of the fuselage to fire outside the arc of the propeller. Another was to mount a synchronized Vickers gun on the port side and on some of these aircraft a rearward-firing Lewis gun on the starboard side was added. Finally in the anti-Zeppelin role twin Lewis guns were mounted to fire forwards and upwards over the top wing.

ROYAL AIRCRAFT FACTORY FE.2A

AIRCRAFT SPECIFICATION SHEET
Span: 48ft 9in
Length: 32ft 3in
Wing area: 494.0sqft
Take-off weight: 1,378lb
Power plant: One 160hp Beardmore water-cooled inline
Armament/bomb load: See text below
Performance
  Max. speed: 91mph at sea level
  Endurance: 2hrs 30min
  Service ceiling: 11,000ft

HISTORY
Sharing little more than its configuration with the FE2 flown at Farnborough in 1913, the FE2a appeared early in 1915 and was designed to provide the RFC with an armed reconnaissance aircraft. It was a large three-bay biplane, using a flat centre section and outer panels that were identical with those of the BE2c, and incorporating dihedral. A short nacelle carried the observer/gunner in the nose ahead of the pilot, and the pusher engine. The tail unit was carried by four booms extending aft from

the wings and comprised a large tailplane with elevators, a kidney-shaped rudder and small triangular fin above the tailplane. A small nosewheel was provided ahead of the oleo-strutted main wheels to help prevent nosing over, and the whole of the upper wing centre section trailing-edge aft of the rear spar was hinged for use as a flap-cum-airbrake. Armament normally comprised a 7.7mm Lewis machine gun in the front cockpit on one of several alternative mounts. The first FE2a flew on 26 January 1915 with a 100hp Green six-cylinder inline water-cooled engine but proved underpowered and the 120hp Austro-Daimler built under licence by Beardmore became the standard for eleven more FE2as and early production examples of the FE2b. The latter was the 'productionized' version with the Beardmore engine, trailing-edge flap deleted, simplified fuel system and other changes to facilitate large-scale production by inexperienced companies. These comprised, apart from the RAF itself (which built only 47 FE2bs): Boulton & Paul (250); Barclay Curie (100); Garrett & Sons (60); Ransome, Sims & Jefferies (350); Alex Stephen and Sons (150) and G & J Weir (600). A 160hp Beardmore engine was adopted later, and the oleo undercarriage with nosewheel gave way to a simplified form without the nosewheel or, later, a non-oleo V-strut arrangement. All twelve FE2as and almost a thousand FE2bs went to RFC squadrons in France, where they engaged in offensive patrols over the enemy lines in the role of fighter escort for unarmed reconnaissance aircraft.

ROYAL AIRCRAFT FACTORY FE2B

AIRCRAFT SPECIFICATION SHEET
Span: 47ft 9in
Length: 32ft 3in
Wing area: 494.0sqft
Take-off weight: 3,037lb
Power plant: One 160hp Beardmore water-cooled inline

Armament/bomb load: One or two Lewis guns for the observer, one mounted in the front and one firing back over the top wing
Performance
    Max. speed: 80.5mph at sea level
    Endurance: 2hrs 30min
    Service ceiling: 11,000ft

HISTORY
The FE2a was quickly followed by the main production model, the FE2b, again powered by a Beardmore, initially the 120hp version while later FE2bs received the 160hp (119kW) Beardmore. The airbrake of the 'a' having proved unsatisfactory, it was simply omitted. A total of 1,939 FE2b/cs were built. The Royal Aircraft Factory itself built only a few; most construction was by private British manufacturers. The FE2b and FE2d variants remained in day operations well into 1917 while the 'b' continued as a standard night bomber until August 1918. At its peak, the FE2b equipped sixteen RFC squadrons in France and six Home Defence squadrons in England. On 18 June 1916, German ace Max Immelmann was killed in combat with FE2bs of No. 25 Squadron RFC. The squadron claimed the kill, but the German version of the encounter is either that Immelmann's Fokker Eindecker broke up after his synchronizer gear failed and he shot off his own propeller, or that he was hit by friendly fire from German anti-aircraft guns.

    In combat with single-seater fighters, the pilots of FE2b and FE2d fighters would form what is probably the first use of what later became known as a Lufbery circle (defensive circle). In the case of the FE2 the intention was that the gunner of each aircraft could cover the blind spot under the tail of his neighbour, and several gunners could fire on any enemy attacking the group. On occasion formations of FE2s fought their way back from far over the lines, while under heavy attack from German fighters, using this tactic.

ROYAL AIRCRAFT FACTORY RE1

AIRCRAFT SPECIFICATION SHEET
Span: 34ft 0in
Length: 27ft 3in
Wing area: 316sqft
Take-off weight: 1,580lb
Power plant: One 70hp Renault air-cooled upright V8 engine

Performance
Max. speed: 82mph at 6,500ft
Endurance: 4hrs 0min
Service ceiling: 10,000ft

HISTORY

At that time reconnaissance or scouting was seen as the only military purpose of aircraft. The RE1, completed in July 1913, was described in contemporary reports as intended for the same purposes as the BE2, using the same engine but being an aircraft of more modern refinement. It was a single-bay biplane with equal span, constant chord wings, unswept but with stagger. Wing warping was used for lateral control. The rudder was similar to that of the BE2, curved and extending below the fuselage, but a triangular fin was fitted that reached forward to the strongly swept leading edge of the BE2 style tailplane. The fuselage was flat sided with deep, rounded decking and slender overall to the rear. The cockpits were in tandem, the pilot's at the rear with sides cut to the bottom of the decking. He sat behind the trailing edge, with a cut-out in the upper wing to improve visibility. The observer's cockpit was between the wings and less deep. The air-cooled 70hp (52kW) Renault engine was uncowled and drove a four-bladed propeller. By September 1913 the only two RE1s built, serials 607 and 608, were with the Flying Department of the Royal Aircraft Factory, intended as experimental machines and were much modified. One desire was to make automatically stable aircraft, so they could be flown hands-off to give the pilot observation time. Within a month or so of completion, 607 had a wing extension of about 2ft (610mm) and 608 was probably built with the extension. In November 607 had four fins attached to the upper wing top surface, positioned above each pair of interplane struts and above each of the centre-section struts; soon after 608 had them too, plus a reduction of stagger and a finless, enlarged rudder. In the quest for stability 607, now with ailerons replacing wing warping, had a series of increases in dihedral, By March 1914 it could be flown hands off in 'squally conditions'. Later its stagger was also reduced and a rectangular tailplane fitted. In May 1914 the second RE1, no. 608, was transferred to the RFC and for a short while wore the number 362, though it went to war in August as 608. 607 stayed at Farnborough and was still at work in February 1915 doing photographic and wireless testing.

ROYAL AIRCRAFT FACTORY RE5

AIRCRAFT SPECIFICATION SHEET

Span: 44ft 6in
Length: 26ft 2in
Wing area: 498sqft
Take-off weight: 2,300lb
Power plant: One 120hp Beardmore built Austro-Daimler water-cooled in line
Armament/bomb load: Three 20lb bombs, Lewis gun in forward cockpit
Performance
Max. speed: 78mph at sea level
Endurance: 4hrs 30min
Service ceiling: 15,000ft

HISTORY

The RE5 was designed as a reconnaissance biplane using the experience of earlier RE series aircraft. It was a two-bay equal-span biplane with a fixed tailskid landing gear, with the wheels supported on skids and powered by a nose-mounted 120hp (89kW) Austro-Daimler engine driving a four-bladed propeller. The aircraft had two open cockpits with the observer/gunner in the forward cockpit under the upper wing and the pilot aft. The larger more capable Royal Aircraft Factory RE7 was a further development of the design. Some modified single-seat high-altitude aircraft were built with extended-span (57ft 2⅓in or 17.43m) upper wings supported by a pair of outward-leaning struts. Other RE5s were used for experimentation with airbrakes and for test flying the Royal Aircraft Factory 4 engine. Twenty-four RE5s were built at the Royal Aircraft Factory for the RFC, paid for by money given to the British Army to compensate for the transfer of the Army's airships to the Royal Navy. Six RE5s deployed to France in September 1914, partly equipping No.2 Squadron RFC, with examples being delivered to other squadrons, with no unit being completely equipped with the RE5. In total, eleven RE5s were sent to France, with a further nine being used by training units. The RE5s were used for reconnaissance and bombing missions over France, although at first they were not fitted with bomb-sights or bomb racks, bombs being carried in the observer's cockpit and dropped by hand when the aircraft was over the target.

Captain John Aidan Liddell was awarded the Victoria Cross for an action on 31 July 1915, being badly wounded when flying an RE5 but successfully recovering the aircraft and saving his observer. The RE5 was gradually phased out from front-line service during that year, only two remaining at the front on 25 September 1915.

ROYAL AIRCRAFT FACTORY RE7

AIRCRAFT SPECIFICATION SHEET
Span: 57ft 0in
Length: 31ft 10½in
Wing area: 548.0 sqft
Take-off weight: 3,449lb
Power plant: One 150hp RAF 4a air-cooled Vee type (in later models)
Armament/bomb load: 336lb, see text below
Performance
    Max. speed: 84.9mph at sea level
    Endurance: 6hrs 0min
    Service ceiling: 6,500ft

HISTORY
The RE7 was a British two-seat light bomber and reconnaissance biplane designed by the Royal Aircraft Factory and built under contracts by the Coventry Ordnance Works, Austin, Napier and Siddeley-Deasy for the RFC. Developed from the RE5, the RE7 was designed to carry heavier loads and also suitable for escort and reconnaissance duties. It was an-unequal span biplane with a fixed tailskid landing gear and powered by a nose-mounted 120hp (89kW) Beardmore engine driving a

four-bladed propeller. The aircraft was built by a number of different contractors with the first aircraft operational with the RFC in France in early 1916. The aircraft had two open cockpits with the observer/gunner in the forward cockpit under the upper wing and the pilot aft. It was soon found that the aircraft could not be used as an escort due to the limited field of fire for the single Lewis gun but the RE7 had a useful payload and was soon used as a light bomber with a more powerful engine (either a 150hp (112kW) RAF 4a or 160hp (119kW) Beardmore). Over a quarter of the aircraft built were used in France in the middle of 1916 but their slow speed and low ceiling with a bomb load made them vulnerable to attack. The RE7s were withdrawn and used for training and a number were used as engine test beds. Use was made of them as target tugs trailing a sleeve drogue for air-to-air firing practice; it was probably one of the first aircraft to do this. At least two RE7s were converted to three seaters.

ROYAL AIRCRAFT FACTORY RE8

AIRCRAFT SPECIFICATION SHEET
Span: 42ft 7in
Length: 27ft 10½in
Wing area: 377.5sqft
Take-off weight: 2,678lb
Power plant: One 150hp RAF 4a air-cooled Vee- type
Armament/bomb load: See text below
Performance
    Max. speed: 102mph at 6,500ft
    Endurance: 4hrs 15min
    Service ceiling: 13,500ft

HISTORY
The RE8 was a two-seat biplane reconnaissance and bomber aircraft intended as a replacement for the vulnerable BE2. The RE8 was more difficult to fly, and was

regarded with great suspicion at first in the RFC. Although eventually it gave reasonably satisfactory service, it was never an outstanding combat aircraft. In spite of this, the RE8 served as the standard British reconnaissance and artillery-spotting aircraft from mid-1917 to the end of the war, serving alongside the rather more popular Armstrong Whitworth FK8. Over 4,000 RE8s were eventually produced and they served in most theatres, including Italy, Russia, Palestine and Mesopotamia, as well as the Western Front. The first of two prototype RE8s flew on 17 June 1916. The new type was designed to overcome the failings of the BE2 – it had a more powerful motor giving an improved performance, in particular a heavier payload. It was also much better armed, with a synchronized forward-firing .303in Vickers machine gun and one or two Lewis guns on a Scarff ring in the observer's cockpit, which was finally moved to a position behind the pilot. It was (intentionally) less stable than the BE2, although modifications had to be made to *improve* stability before it could gain acceptance by pilots used to the BE2e – making the production version ideal for artillery spotting but giving it little chance of outmanoeuvring enemy fighters. Most RE8s were powered by the 150hp Royal Aircraft Factory 4a air-cooled twelve-cylinder engine installed so that the propeller inclined upwards to improve the take-off and landing run. This produced a 'broken back' appearance to the fuselage and an illusion that the tail sloped upwards. Like most RAF engine installations, the twin exhausts protruded over the upper wing to carry the fumes clear of the crew. As with the BE2e, the long extensions on the upper wing were reputed to be liable to collapse if the aircraft was dived too sharply. By November 1918, the RE8 was regarded as completely obsolete and surviving examples were quickly retired after the Armistice.

ROYAL AIRCRAFT FACTORY SE2 AND 2A

AIRCRAFT SPECIFICATION SHEET
Span: 27ft 6¼in
Length: 20ft 6in

Wing area: 190.0sqft
Take-off weight: 1,200lb
Power plant: One 80hp Gnome
Armament/bomb load: See text below
Performance
    Max. speed: 96mph at sea level
    Endurance: 2hrs 30min
    Service ceiling: 15,000ft

HISTORY

The forerunner of all single-seat scouting aircraft was the BS1 designed by Geoffrey de Havilland in 1912. When this prototype crashed it was rebuilt in a modified form and named the SE2 (Scout Experimental No.2). In mid 1914 the SE2's original monocoque rear fuselage was replaced with a wood-and-fabric structure and the tail unit, landing gear skids and engine cowling were revised. In this form it was designated the SE2A. After further test flying it went to France to join No.3 Squadron based at Moyenneville. The flying ace, Major McCudden VC, observed that the SE2A was a little faster than the Bristols with the same engine, but did not climb as well. The SE2A remained at the front until March 1915 but, in spite of its fighter-like qualities, it lacked the necessary armament, the pilot having only service revolver. Then two rifles were fixed on each side of the fuselage to fire at an angle outside the arc of the propeller arc. The question of armed development was taking a back seat to the Bristol Scout for which production orders had already been placed. The basic conception of the SE2A was, however, taken forward to the SE4, an aircraft with excellent flying qualities and a top speed of 135mph achieved in level flight.

ROYAL AIRCRAFT FACTORY SE5A

AIRCRAFT SPECIFICATION SHEET
Span: 26ft 7in
Length: 20ft 11in

Wing area: 244sqft
Take-off weight: 1,935lb
Power plant: One 200hp Wolsey Viper V 8 water-cooled
   engine
Armament/bomb load: One forward-firing Vickers
   .303in, one Lewis gun on a Foster mount, 4 × 25lb
   Cooper bombs
Performance
   Max. speed: 138mph
   Range: 300 miles
   Service ceiling: 17,000ft

HISTORY

The Royal Aircraft Factory SE5 was a British biplane
fighter aircraft of World War I. The first examples
reached the Western Front before the Sopwith Camel
and they had a much better overall performance, but
they had problems with their Hispano-Suiza engine,
particularly the geared-output H-S 8B-powered versions,
which meant that there was a chronic shortage of SE5s
until well into 1918 and fewer squadrons were equipped
with the type than with the Sopwith fighter. Together
with the Camel, the SE5 was instrumental in regaining
Allied air superiority in mid-1917 and maintaining this
for the rest of the war, ensuring there was no repetition
of the 'Bloody April' in 1917 when losses in the RFC were
much heavier than in the *Luftstreitkräfte*. Only seventy-
seven original SE5 aircraft were built before production
settled on the improved SE5a. The SE5a differed from
late production examples of the SE5 only in the type
of engine installed – a geared 200hp Hispano-Suiza 8b,
often turning a large clockwise-rotation four-bladed
propeller, replacing the 150hp model. A few were
converted as two-seat trainers and there were plans
for Curtiss to build 1,000 SE5s in the United States but
only one was completed before the end of the war. At
first, airframe construction outstripped the very limited
supply of French-built Hispano-Suiza engines and
squadrons earmarked to receive the new fighter had to
soldier on with Airco DH5s and Nieuport 24s until early
1918. The troublesome geared '8b' model was prone to
have serious gear reduction system problems, sometimes
with the propeller (and even the entire gearbox on a very
few occasions) separating from the engine and airframe
in flight, a problem shared with the similarly powered
Sopwith Dolphin. The introduction of the 200hp (149kW)
Wolseley Viper, a high-compression, direct-drive version
of the Hispano-Suiza 8a made under licence by Wolseley
Motors Limited, solved the SE5a's engine problems and
was adopted as the standard power plant.

SHORT BOMBER

AIRCRAFT SPECIFICATION SHEET

Span: 84ft 0in
Length: 45ft 0in
Wing area: 870sqft
Take-off weight: 6,800lb
Power plant: One 250hp Rolls-Royce Eagle III water-
   cooled V 12
Armament/bomb load: See text below
Performance
   Max. speed: 67mph at 6,500ft
   Endurance: 6hrs 0min
   Service ceiling: 10,600ft

HISTORY

The Short Bomber was a British two-seat long-range
reconnaissance, bombing and torpedo-carrying aircraft
designed by Short Brothers as a land-based development
of the very successful Short Type 184. The Bomber was
a three-bay biplane of wooden structure with fabric
covering. The fuselage was of box section with curved
upper decking mounted on the lower wing. The tailplane
included a split elevator with a single fin and rudder.
The undercarriage consisted of a four-wheeled assembly
under the nose and a skid under the tail. The crew of two
sat in tandem open cockpits behind the wing; initially
the observer/gunner sat in the forward cockpit so that he
could stand up to operate the machine-gun mounted on
the upper wing. This somewhat precarious activity was
rendered unnecessary by the invention of the gun-ring
mounting; in production aircraft the pilot occupied the
forward cockpit with the gunner behind him in the rear
cockpit, which was fitted with dual controls. Armament
comprised a rear-facing Lewis gun as well as provision
for one 14-inch Whitehead torpedo or various bombs of
up to 920lb. Initial testing with the prototype by Short
test pilot, Ronald Kemp, revealed that it was unable
to carry the required bomb load of six 112lb bombs, so
the wingspan was increased by 12ft. This provided the

required lift but at the same time rendered the aircraft unstable in both pitch and yaw. The fuselage length was increased by 4ft 5in, which solved the problem. The Short Bomber was intended for long-range missions; the maximum flight duration was approximately six hours. The first Bomber flew in 1915 and more than eighty aircraft were built. The Short Bomber entered service in late 1916 with No. 7 Squadron RNAS, flying its first bombing raid on the night of 15 November 1916, with four Shorts, each carrying eight 65lb (30 kg) bombs, attacking targets at Ostend along with eighteen Caudron G4s. No.7 Squadron RNAS continued bombing operations through the winter of 1916–17, but the Short Bomber was underpowered and was taken out of service in April 1917, when more powerful aircraft entered service. One of its last combat operations involved attacking the Zeebrugge Mole on four successive nights in April 1917, in preparation for the naval raid on St George's Day (23 April).

SHORT 184

AIRCRAFT SPECIFICATION SHEET
Span: 63ft 6½ in
Length: 40ft 7½in
Wing area: 688sqft
Take-off weight: 5,363lb
Power plant: One 260hp Sunbeam
Armament/bomb load: One Lewis gun in rear cockpit, one 14in torpedo or up to 520lb of bombs
Performance
   Max. speed: 88.5mph at 2,000ft
   Endurance: 2hrs 45min
   Service ceiling: 9,000ft

HISTORY
The Short Admiralty Type 184, often called the Short 225 after the power rating of the engine first fitted, was a British two-seat reconnaissance, bombing and torpedo-carrying folding-wing seaplane. It was first flown in 1915 and remained in service until after the Armistice in 1918. A Short 184 was the first aircraft to sink a ship using a torpedo, and another was the only British aircraft to take

part in the Battle of Jutland. Torpedo-dropping trials had been undertaken using a 160hp Gnome-powered Short Admiralty Type 166 but this had proved insufficiently powerful, and so in September 1914 a new specification was formulated for an aircraft to be powered by the 225hp Sunbeam Mohawk engine currently being developed. Similar in basic design to earlier Short floatplanes built for the Navy, the Type 184 was an equal-span three-bay tractor configuration biplane. The aircraft was fitted with a radio transmitter and receiver, which was powered by a wind-driven generator mounted on a hinged arm so that it could be folded back when not being used, and other equipment carried included a basket of carrier pigeons, intended to be used as a back-up for the radio in the event of forced landings. On 12 August 1915 a Short 184 was the first aircraft in the world to attack an enemy ship with an air-launched torpedo. However, the ship had already been crippled by a torpedo fired by a British submarine. On 17 August 1915, another Turkish ship was sunk by a torpedo of whose origin there was no doubt. On this occasion Flight Commander Edmonds torpedoed a Turkish transport ship a few miles north of the Dardanelles. The performance of the Type 184 in the climatic conditions of the Mediterranean was marginal, it being necessary to fly without an observer and carry a limited amount of fuel. The aircraft served in most theatres of the war and the principal use of the 184 was in anti-submarine patrol work. Although a substantial number of submarines were spotted and attacked, no confirmed sinkings were made.

SHORT 320

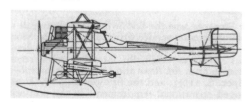

AIRCRAFT SPECIFICATION SHEET
Span: 75ft 0in
Length: 45ft 9in
Wing area: 810sqft
Take-off weight: 7,014lb

Power plant: One 320hp Sunbeam Cossack 12 cylinder, inline water-cooled engine
Armament/bomb load: One machine gun, one 1,000lb torpedo or two 230lb bombs
Performance
   Max. speed: 72.5mph
   Endurance: 6hrs 0min
   Service ceiling: 3,000ft

HISTORY

The Short Type 320, also known as the Short Admiralty Type 320, was a British two-seat reconnaissance, bombing and torpedo-carrying 'folder' seaplane. The Short Type 320 was designed to meet an official requirement for a seaplane to carry a Mark IX torpedo. It was larger than the earlier Short 184, and was a typical Short folder design of the time, with two-bay uneven span wings and a (238kW) Cossack engine. Two prototypes were built; the first being ready in July 1916, and the second in August that year. The prototypes were rushed to the Adriatic. In September 1916, the first prototype patrol aircraft was finished, but it proved to be little better than the Short 184 already in service, and was not ordered into production. The second prototype Type B was completed as a type A torpedo bomber. When the torpedo bomber went into production, it was powered by a 320hp engine, which was the origin of the name the Type 320. As with conventional biplane floatplanes, the torpedo was carried between the bottom of the fuselage and the floats. Unusually, the aircraft was flown from the rear cockpit, although this did cause a problem for an observer in the front seat since the latter had to stand to use the machine-gun, which was level with the top wing. When a torpedo was carried, the aircraft could not fly with an observer at the same time. The first operational use was on 2 September 1917, when six aircraft (five with torpedoes and one with bombs) were towed on rafts fifty miles south of Traste Bay to enable them to attack enemy submarines lying off Cattaro. They had to be towed into position as they could not carry enough fuel and a torpedo for the mission. The operation did not go well; with a gale force wind and heavy seas, two of the aircraft failed to take off, so the operation was abandoned. On the return journey, one aircraft was lost and the others were damaged. It appears that the Type 320 never launched a torpedo in action but continued to be used as a reconnaissance seaplane until the end of the war.

SOPWITH CAMEL

AIRCRAFT SPECIFICATION SHEET

Span: 28ft 0in
Length: 18ft 9in
Wing area: 231.0sqft
Take-off weight: 1,482lb

Power plant: One 130hp Clerget 9B rotary
Armament/bomb load: See text below
Performance
   Max. speed: 104.5mph at 10,000ft
   Endurance: 2hrs 30min
   Service ceiling: 18,000ft

HISTORY

The Camel was intended to replace the Pup and Triplane but Herbert Smith produced an aircraft that did not have the docile handling qualities of its predecessors. However in the hands of experienced pilots the Camel was to be credited with destroying more enemy aircraft than any other Allied type. The torque from its heavy rotary engine meant that it could out-turn any German fighter. The name of this aircraft was derived from its humpbacked appearance. The prototype was powered by a 110hp Clerget 9Z engine. From the succeeding batch the Admiralty had one with a 130hp Clerget; indeed, production aircraft were based on the Admiralty type with either the Clerget or Bentley engine. The Camel first became operational with No.4 Squadron RNAS in July 1917. RFC orders specified either the Clerget 9B, BR1 or 110hp Le Rhône 9J engine. Armament consisted of synchronized Vickers machine guns, the gear depending upon the engine fitted. Thus the Le Rhône Camels had the superior Constantinescu gear and were faster in the climb. No.70 Squadron RFC was the first to take delivery of Camels in July 1917 and by the end of the year 1,325 of these fighters had been delivered. The first operational use, however, was in the ground attack role. Armed with four 20lb Cooper bombs under the fuselage, they flew in the Battle of Ypres and Cambrai. Following heavy losses in this role the armour plated TF1 (Trench Fighter) was developed but it did not go into production. It did, however, yield valuable information for the design of the Salamander. In the Home Defence role the Le Rhône Camels were armed with twin Lewis guns on a Foster mounting over the centre section. The shipboard version of the Camel, the 2F1 underwent official trials in March 1917. It had a shorter span than the land version and had an upward angled Lewis gun, becoming operational in the spring of 1918. By the end of the war 2F1 Camels had served aboard five aircraft carriers, two battleships and twenty-six cruisers of the Royal Navy.

SOPWITH CUCKOO

AIRCRAFT SPECIFICATION SHEET
Span: 46ft 9in
Length: 28ft 6in
Wing area: 566.0sqft
Take-off weight: 3,883lb
Power plant: One 200hp Sunbeam, Arab V8 engine
Armament/bomb load: See text below
Performance
  Max. speed: 105.5mph at 6,500ft
  Range: 291 nautical miles
  Service ceiling: 12,100ft

HISTORY
Both the Admiralty and Captain Murray F. Seuter of the Royal Navy realized the value of a torpedo bomber in war. Previously torpedoes had been carried by seaplanes that depended on calm water to operate, so Seuter went to Sopwith to see if they could design and produce a land-based torpedo bomber carrying one or two 1000lb torpedoes with a four-hour endurance. The prototype made its maiden flight in June 1917 and was designated T1 with a cockpit aft of the trailing edge of the wing. The

torpedo was slung under the fuselage between the short-legged undercarriage. An order for one hundred of the T1 followed the official trials held in July 1917 and it was given the serial number N74. The original power plant, a 200hp Hispano-Suiza, was in such demand for the SE5a fighters that the production Cuckoos had to be powered with the 200hp Sunbeam Arabs. The two original contractors, Pegler and Fairfield, had no previous experience of aircraft manufacture and thus delivery was late so that it became necessary to place an additional order with Blackburn early in 1918. But only sixty Cuckoos were on charge to the RAF on 31 October 1918. By the time the first squadron of Cuckoos had embarked in HMS *Argus* they were too late to see combat service.

SOPWITH 3-SEATER

AIRCRAFT SPECIFICATION SHEET
Span: 40ft 9in
Length: 29ft 6in
Wing area: 397sqft
Take-off weight: 1,810lb
Power plant: One 80hp Gnome rotary
Armament/bomb load: One Lewis gun and small bombs
Performance
  Max. speed: 82mph at 6,500ft
  Endurance: 4hrs 0min
  Service ceiling: 10,000ft

HISTORY
The Sopwith 3-seater was a British aircraft designed and built prior to the start of World War I. One of the first aircraft built by the Sopwith Aviation Company, it was operated by both the RNAS and RFC being used briefly over Belgium by the RNAS following the start of the war. The three-seat tractor was flown on 7 February 1913

before being displayed at the International Aero Show at Olympia, London, opening on 14 February. It had two-bay wings, with lateral control by wing warping, and was powered by an 80hp (60kW) Gnome Lambda rotary engine. It had two cockpits, with the pilot sitting in the aft one and two passengers sat side-by-side in the forward one. Three transparent celluloid windows were placed in each side of the fuselage to give a good downwards view. The RFC received its 3-seaters between November 1913 and March 1914, with the first example being tested to destruction in the Royal Aircraft Factory at Farnborough, it being found that structural strength was inadequate. Despite this, the remaining eight aircraft were issued to No. 5 Squadron as two-seaters. Two were destroyed in a fatal mid-air collision on 12 May 1914, while several more were wrecked in accidents before the outbreak of World War I. No.5 Squadron left its remaining Tractor biplanes in England when it deployed to France in August 1914, these being briefly used as trainers at the Central Flying School. The RNAS aircraft were issued to seaplane stations to allow flying to continue when sea conditions were unsuitable for seaplane operation. On the outbreak of war, the RNAS acquired Sopwith's demonstrator. Three Sopwith Tractor biplanes went with the Eastchurch wing of the RNAS when it deployed to Belgium under the command of Wing Commander Charles Rumney Samson. These were used for reconnaissance and bombing missions, attempting to bomb Zeppelin sheds at Düsseldorf on 23 September and railway lines on 24 September, being withdrawn in October. The RNAS also used Sopwith Tractor biplanes for patrol duties from Great Yarmouth, one remaining in use until November 1915.

SOPWITH DOLPHIN

AIRCRAFT SPECIFICATION SHEET
Span: 32ft 6in
Length: 22ft 3in

Wing area: 263.25sqft
Take-off weight: 2,003lb
Power plant: One 200/220hp Hispano-Suiza 8E water cooled Vee type
Armament/bomb load: See text below
Performance
    Max. speed: 128mph at 10,000ft
    Endurance: 1hrs 45min
    Service ceiling: 21,000ft

HISTORY
The first prototype was completed in May 1917 and delivered to Martlesham Heath for official trials. Designed by Herbert Smith it had a 200hp Hispano-Suiza geared stationary engine, It was armed with twin forward-firing Vickers guns enclosed under the engine decking. The second prototype had improved control with a smaller fin but a bigger horn-balanced rudder. However, it still had a poor downward view. This problem was not addressed with the third prototype when the lower wing cut-outs were discontinued. Two Lewis guns replaced the Vickers and were placed on a top-wing attachment frame to fire forwards and upwards. The Dolphin then went into production. The Hispano-Suiza engines were in demand in 1917 for the SE5s, which makes the order for five hundred Dolphin surprising, the more so when two hundred more were ordered. The first operational Dolphins went to No.19 Squadron, the unit that would be honoured with the very first issue of the Spitfire twenty years later. Nos.23, 79 and 87 Squadrons were also equipped with Dolphins. They were not popular with pilots who were sandwiched between the engine immediately to their front and the fuel tank immediately behind. Behind the pilot's neck was steel frame tubing and the gun butts were in front of his face. The Lewis guns were found to be a hindrance and one or both were removed by squadrons. No.87 Squadron, for example, placed them on the lower wing to fire outside the arc of the propeller. In the ground attack role four 25lb Cooper bombs were carried. These aircraft also saw service on No.141 Home Defence squadron but they were unsuccessful in the night role. A few Dolphins that survived the war went to Polish squadrons in their war against Russia in 1920.

SOPWITH PUP

AIRCRAFT SPECIFICATION SHEET
Span: 26ft 6in
Length: 19ft 3¾in
Wing area: 254sqft
Take-off weight: 1,225lb
Power plant: One 80hp Le Rhône 9C rotary
Armament/bomb load: See text below

Performance
Max. speed: 115mph at sea level
Endurance: 3hrs 0min
Service ceiling: 17,000ft

HISTORY

The Pup was developed by Herbert Smith. It was a scaled-down version of the 1½ Strutter. Simple in construction and appearance, this rugged aircraft was powered by a 80hp engine and possessed excellent manoeuvrability. The Royal Navy was particularly interested in the Pup and the first of six prototypes, flown in February 1916, underwent Admiralty service trials. Initial orders were placed with Sopwith and Beardmore. Officially known as Admiralty Type 9901 it was powered by a Le Rhône 9C engine. The Navy Pups were first armed with one .303in Vickers gun mounted centrally in front of the pilot. Eight Le Prier rockets could also be carried. Commencing in the autumn of 1916, deliveries were firstly to No.1 Wing RNAS. Some 170 Pups were built for the Navy by Sopwith and Beardmore whilst Whitehead Aviation and the Standard Motor Company completed a further 1,670 for the RFC. In late 1916 and early 1917 Pups began operating on the Western Front. The famous naval No.8 Squadron assisted the RFC and its Pups accounted for twenty-one enemy aircraft in November and December 1917. But despite these successes Pups began to be withdrawn from front-line service units and large numbers were transferred to training units. At sea the Pups were modified for shipboard anti-Zeppelin duties when tripod-mounted Lewis guns replaced the Vickers and could be fired upwards through a centre-section. Pups were also used in pioneering take-offs from special

platforms fitted to cruisers and in take-offs and landings with aircraft carriers involving deck arrester gear. From July 1917 Pups served with three RFC squadrons and five RNAS Home Defence squadrons powered by 100hp Gnome Monosoupape and 80hp Gnomes but they had neither the range nor the altitude to deal satisfactorily with attacking Gotha bombers. Pups were carried by five aircraft carriers and seven cruisers. After the war Pups quickly disappeared, only eight finding their way on to the civil register.

SOPWITH SALAMANDER

AIRCRAFT SPECIFICATION SHEET
Span: 30ft 1.5in
Length: 19ft 6in
Wing area: 266.5sqft
Take-off weight: 2,510lb
Power plant: One 230hp Bentley BR2 rotary
Armament/bomb load: Two .303 in Vickers guns
Performance
Max. speed: 125mph at 500ft
Endurance: 1hr 45min approx.
Service ceiling: 14,000ft

HISTORY

The Sopwith TF2 (Trench Fighter) first flew on 27 April 1918. Known as the Salamander, the first prototype was sent to France for evaluation as a ground attack aircraft. It was very similar in design to the Sopwith Snipe having the same cowled two-row rotary engine. The cowling was cut away underneath the engine to improve cooling. Two .303in Vickers guns, with Constantinescu synchronized gear, fired between the propeller blades and each gun had 1,000 rounds of ammunition. Armour plating protected the pilot and the fuel tanks adding 650lb to the gross weight. Four 25lb Cooper bombs could be carried beneath the fuselage. During the last year of the war the ground-attack role had assumed greater importance and 500 of these aircraft were ordered from Sopwith with 600 more from five other manufacturers. But the Armistice intervened when only 102 Sopwith machines had been completed and only 37 of these were on charge to the RAF by 31 October 1918. Only two Salamanders had arrived in France by the end of the war; nevertheless Sopwiths continued in production until late 1919 bringing the total to over 160 machines. One Salamander was taken to the USA for further study.

SOPWITH SNIPE

AIRCRAFT SPECIFICATION SHEET
Span: 30ft 0in
Length: 19ft 2in
Wing area: 256.0sqft
Take-off weight: 2,020lb
Power plant: One 230hp Bentley BR2 rotary
Armament/bomb load: Two .303 Vickers guns
Performance
  Max. speed: 121mph at 10,000ft
  Endurance: 3hrs 0min
  Service ceiling: 19,500ft

HISTORY
The Snipe was a replacement for the Sopwith Camel. It would have improved performance and outlook from the cockpit. It was in the late summer of 1917 that six prototypes were ordered. The first of these was powered by a 150hp Bentley BR1 engine. Several modifications were then made when the more powerful BR2 engine was installed and in the spring of 1918 the Snipe went into production. Two synchronized Vickers machine guns mounted in front of the pilot constituted the standard

armament. Experiments were conducted with a third gun; a Lewis mounted on the top wing. It proved difficult to operate and its weight had an adverse effect on the aircraft's performance. Contracts were issued in March 1918. A total of 1,700 machines were to be produced by Sopwiths and six other manufacturers and deliveries began in mid 1918. By the end of September 161 Snipe MkIs had been delivered so that the Snipe could become operational with No.43 Squadron in October followed by No.208 Squadron and No.4 Squadron Australian Flying Corps. Two long-range MkIAs were allocated to No.45 Squadron to act as escorts to bombers of the Independent Bombing Force. In the bombing role the Snipes could carry four 20lb Cooper bombs beneath the fuselage. By the end of the year Snipes were serving with the Royal Navy and RAF squadrons, including a Home Defence unit. In 1919 the aircraft was selected to become the standard night fighter.

SOPWITH 1½ STRUTTER

AIRCRAFT SPECIFICATION SHEET
Span: 33ft 6in
Length: 25ft 3in
Wing area: 346.0sqft
Take-off weight: 2,342lb
Power plant: One 130hp Clerget 9B rotary
Armament/bomb load: One .303 forward-firing Vickers, one Lewis gun in observer's cockpit
Performance
  Max. speed: 102mph at 6,500ft
  Endurance: 3hrs 45min
  Service ceiling: 15,500ft

HISTORY
This very versatile aircraft was used by the British, French and other Allied services. Its roles included photographic reconnaissance, fighter reconnaissance, anti-submarine,

bomber, ground strafing and coastal patrol work. It was the first British service aircraft to be equipped with efficient synchronized forward-firing guns. The prototype No.3686 was completed in December 1915. Powered with a 110hp Clerget 9Z engine this two-seat biplane was produced, initially, for the RNAS and was designated the Admiralty Type 9400. The pilot could fire the Vickers gun with a Lewis gun in the rear cockpit. In later versions the observer had a Scarff ring in the rear cockpit in place of the original Nieuport mounting. The 1½ Strutter became operational with No.5 Wing RNAS in France with the task of escorting French bombers, then as a bomber in its own right with No.3 Wing RNAS later in 1916. These single-seat aircraft were the Admiralty Type 9700 and carried four 65lb bombs internally with an excellent combat radius but at this time the RFC was making demands on Sopwith's output, which delayed No.3 Wing operations. No.70 Squadron was the first RFC unit to be equipped with the 1½ Stutter and they took part in the Battle of the Somme in the summer of 1916. Between 1,400 and 1,500 1½ Strutters were built by eight British manufacturers including fifty-eight 'Ship Strutters' aboard carriers *Argus*, *Furious*, *Vindex* and other major naval vessels. The Navy was able to carry out useful experimental work in ditching trials, trials with deck arrester gear and in taking off from platforms on naval vessels. When the French Government took receipt of fifty aircraft this was the prelude to a French building programme, which resulted in some 4,500 1½ Strutters being constructed by four French manufacturers. They served extensively with the Aviation Militaire, mostly as single-seat bombers, and French 1½ Strutters were sold to other countries, including Belgium and Russia. In mid 1917 the RFC Strutters were replaced by the Camel and many were brought back to the UK to serve as night fighters.

SOPWITH TABLOID

AIRCRAFT SPECIFICATION SHEET
Span: 25ft 6in
Length: 20ft 4in
Wing area: 241.3sqft
Take-off weight: 1,120lb
Power plant: One 80hp Gnome rotary
Armament/bomb load: See below
Performance
    Max. speed: 92mph at sea level
    Endurance: 3hrs 30min
    Service ceiling: 15,000ft approx

HISTORY
The Tabloid was designed in 1913 as a racing aircraft. It had a square fuselage that housed side-by-side seats and a cowled 80hp Gnome rotary engine. The wings did not have ailerons for lateral control. When Harry Hawker flew the Tabloid at Farnborough on 29 November 1913 a level speed of 92mph was achieved. Then Howard Pixton won the Schneider Trophy race on 20 April 1914 flying a single-seat version of the aircraft (see left) and achieving an average speed of 86.78mph. This also marked an almost doubling of the speed of the 1913 winning aircraft. The Tabloid went into military production retaining its 80hp engine and wheel and skid landing gear. The first pair of RFC Tabloids arrived in France on 27 August 1914. They were of little value as fighting machines but they were good scouts. When they were armed it was either with a rifle or Lewis gun mounted on the fuselage or top wing firing outside the arc of the propeller. One Tabloid had steel deflector plates when a Lewis gun was strapped to the starboard side of the aircraft. The RNAS armed their Tabloids with a small load of 20lb bombs, which enabled them successfully to attack the railway station at Cologne and the Zeppelin works at Dusseldorf on 7 October 1914. Some RNAS Tabloids served in the Dardanelles and the Aegean, which included two carried by HMS *Ark Royal*. When production ceased in June 1915 only about forty of these aircraft had been built.

SOPWITH TRIPLANE

AIRCRAFT SPECIFICATION SHEET
Span: 26ft 6in
Length: 19ft 6in
Wing area: 231sqft
Take-off weight: 1,415lb
Power plant: One 130hp Clerget 9 B rotary
Armament/bomb load: One .303 in Vickers machine gun
Performance
    Max. speed: 116mph at 6,000ft
    Endurance: 2hrs 45min
    Service ceiling: 20,000ft

SPAD VII

AIRCRAFT SPECIFICATION SHEET

Span: 25ft 7¾in
Length: 19ft 11in
Wing area: 193.8sqft
Take-off weight: 1,632lb
Power plant: One 150hp Hispano-Suiza 8Aa water-cooled Vee type
Armament/bomb load: See text below
Performance
    Max. speed: 119mph at 6,562ft
    Endurance: 2hrs 15min
    Service ceiling: 17,500ft

HISTORY

The SPAD SVII was the first of a series of highly successful biplane fighter aircraft produced by Société Pour L'Aviation et ses Dérivés (SPAD) during World War I. Like its successors, the SVII was renowned as a sturdy and rugged aircraft with good climbing and diving characteristics. It was also a stable gun platform, although pilots used to the more manoeuvrable Nieuport fighters found it heavy on the controls. It was, however, flown by a number of the famous aces. Early production aircraft suffered from a number of defects, which took some time to solve and limited the delivery rate to units. While a few SPADs arrived at front-line units as early as August 1916, large numbers would only begin to appear in the first months of 1917. The combination of high speed and good diving ability promised to give Allied pilots the initiative to engage or leave combat. If the new fighter was a rugged and stable shooting platform, some pilots regretted its lack of manoeuvrability, especially when compared to lighter types such as the Nieuport 11 or 17. In the face of such performance, an initial production contract was made on 10 May 1916, calling for 268 machines, to be designated SPAD VII C1 (C1, from *avion de chasse*, indicating the aircraft was a single-seat

HISTORY

The Sopwith Triplane was a British single-seat fighter aircraft designed and manufactured by the Sopwith Aviation Company during World War I. Pilots nicknamed it the 'Tripehound' or simply the 'Tripe'. The Triplane became operational with the Royal Naval Air Service in early 1917 and was immediately successful. The Triplane was, nevertheless, built in comparatively small numbers and was withdrawn from active service as Sopwith Camels arrived in the latter half of 1917. Surviving aircraft continued to serve as operational trainers until the end of the war. The Triplane began as a private venture by the Sopwith Aviation Company. The fuselage and empennage closely mirrored those of the earlier Pup, but chief engineer Herbert Smith gave the new aircraft three narrow-chord wings to provide the pilot with an improved field of view. Ailerons were fitted to all three wings. By using the variable incidence tailplane, the aircraft could be trimmed to fly hands-off. The introduction of a smaller 8 ft span tailplane in February 1917 improved elevator response. The Triplane was initially powered by the 110hp Clerget 9Z nine-cylinder rotary engine, but most production examples were fitted with the 130hp Clerget 9B rotary. At least one Triplane was tested with a 110hp Le Rhône rotary engine, but this did not provide a significant improvement in performance. The Triplane's combat debut was highly successful. The new fighter's exceptional rate of climb and high service ceiling gave it a marked advantage over the Albatros DIII, though the Triplane was slower in a dive. The Germans were so impressed by the performance of the Triplane that it spawned a brief triplane craze among German aircraft manufacturers, resulting in no fewer than thirty-four different prototypes. For a variety of reasons, the Triplane's combat career was comparatively brief. In service, the Triplane proved difficult to repair. The fuel and oil tanks were inaccessible without substantial disassembly of the wings and fuselage. Even relatively minor repairs had to be made at rear echelon repair depots.

fighter). In early 1917, an improved version of the engine developing 180hp, the Hispano-Suiza 8Ab, was made available. This new power plant provided the SPAD VII with even better performance, the top speed increasing from 119mph to 129mph. The new engine gradually became the standard power plant for the SPAD VII and by April 1917, all newly produced aircraft were equipped with it. It became apparent that the British production lines of the SVII had lower quality standards than their French counterparts, resulting in aircraft with lower performances and handling. After some 220 aircraft had been produced, British production of the SVII was halted in favour of better types that were becoming available.

VICKERS FB5 AND 9

AIRCRAFT SPECIFICATION SHEET
Span: 36ft 6in
Length: 27ft 2in
Wing area: 382sqft
Take-off weight: 2,050lb
Power plant: One 100hp Gnome 9-cylinder Monosoupape rotary
Armament/bomb load: One Lewis gun in observer's cockpit
Performance
    Max. speed: 70mph at 5,000ft
    Endurance: 4hrs 30min
    Service ceiling: 9,000ft

HISTORY
The Vickers FB5, later called the 'Gunbus', was originally armed with a Maxim gun but the drum-fed more manoeuvrable Lewis gun replaced it. The production FB5s were powered by a Monosoupape engine and had a smaller nacelle, rectangular horizontal fin surface and modified rudder. The first specialized fighter squadron was No.11 and this unit was fully equipped with the

FB5 during the early months of 1915. They were not particularly fast machines but were useful in the aerial fighting and ground strafing with a light bomb load. The service ceiling was 9,000ft and it took nearly half an hour to reach that height. The onset of the 'Fokker Scourge' saw No.11 Squadron experimenting with twin Lewis guns. In December 1915 the FB9 appeared with a fully rotating Lewis gun on a ball and socket mounting in the prow of a more streamlined nacelle leading to a new nickname, the 'Streamlined Gunbus'. Only a few FB9s had the 110hp Le Rhône engine to replace the Monosoupape. At the Vickers Crayford works 115 FBf5s and 49 FB9s were built and a further 50 FB 9s were completed at the Weybridge factory. Little operational use of the FB5s was made by the RNAS and some of their aircraft were taken over by the RFC. FB9s made a brief appearance at the Battle of the Somme but from the autumn of 1916 both the FB5 and 9 were relegated to training duties.

VICKERS VIMY

AIRCRAFT SPECIFICATION SHEET
Span: 68ft 1in
Length: 43ft 6½in
Wing area: 1330.0sqft
Take-off weight: 10,884lb
Power plant: Two 360hp Rolls-Royce Eagle VIII water-cooled Vee type
Armament/bomb load: One Lewis gun on Scarff ring in nose and one amidships, 2,476lb of bombs
Performance
    Max. speed: 103mph at sea level
    Range: 900 miles approx.
    Service ceiling: 7,000ft

HISTORY
The Vickers Vimy was a British heavy bomber aircraft of World War I and postwar. It achieved success as both a

military and civil aircraft, setting several notable records in long-distance flights in the interwar period, the most celebrated of which was the first non-stop crossing of the Atlantic Ocean by Alcock and Brown in June 1919. Reginald Kirshaw 'Rex' Pierson, chief designer of Vickers Limited (Aviation Department) in Leighton Buzzard, designed a twin-engine biplane bomber, the Vickers FB27, to meet a requirement for a night bomber capable of attacking targets in Germany, a contract being placed for three prototypes on 14 August 1917. Design and production of the prototypes was extremely rapid, with the first flying on 30 November 1917, powered by two 200hp Hispano-Suiza engines. It was named after the Battle of Vimy Ridge. Owing to engine supply difficulties, the prototype Vimys were tested with a number of different engine types, including Sunbeam Maoris, Salmson 9Zm water-cooled radials, and Fiat A.12bis engines, before production orders were placed for aircraft powered by the 230hp BHP Puma, 400hp Fiat, 400hp Liberty L-12 and the 360hp Rolls-Royce Eagle VIII engines, with a total of 776 ordered before the end of World War I. Of these, only aircraft powered by the Eagle engine, known as the Vimy IV, were delivered to the RAF. By October 1918, only three aircraft had been delivered to the RAF, one of which had been deployed to France for use by the Independent Air Force. The war ended, however, before it could be used on operations. The Vimy only reached full service status in July 1919 when it entered service with No.58 Squadron in Egypt. The aircraft formed the main heavy bomber force of the RAF for much of the 1920s.

VOISIN LA

AIRCRAFT SPECIFICATION SHEET
Span: 48ft 4¼in
Length: 31ft 2in
Wing area: 534sqft
Take-off weight: 1,350lb

Power plant: One 150hp Salmson P9 water-cooled radial
Armament/bomb load: See text below
Performance
   Max. speed: 69.6mph at sea level
   Endurance: 4hrs 30min
   Service ceiling: 11,485ft

HISTORY
The British Voisin LA was an improved version of the Voisin III, a French two-seat bomber and ground attack aircraft of World War I, one of the first of its kind. It is also notable for being the first Allied aircraft in the war to win an aerial fight and shoot down an enemy aircraft, on 5 October 1914. It was a pusher biplane, developed by Voisin in 1914 as a more powerful version of the 1912 Voisin I design. It also incorporated a light steel frame, which made it more durable when operating out of the temporary wartime military aviation airfields. Early in the war, the Voisin III became the most common Allied bomber. Significant numbers were purchased by the French Air Force and the Imperial Russian Air Force. Russia ordered over 800 from France and built a further 400 under licence in Moscow. Around 100 were built in Italy, and 50 in the United Kingdom, while smaller numbers were purchased by Belgium and Romania. Like many other aircraft of its era, the Voisin III was a multipurpose aircraft. Its missions included reconnaissance, artillery spotting, training, day and night bombing as well as ground attack. The first Voisin III was powered by a single 120hp Salmson M9 engine, later the 150hp P9 and R9. It had a range of 125 miles, top speed of 70mph and ceiling 11,485ft. The Voisin III is also notable in being one of the first dedicated bombers. The steel frame construction of the aircraft enabled a bomb load of approximately 330lb to be carried. With development, the final variants of the type were able to carry twice this load. By 1916, advances in aircraft design made the Voisin III increasingly obsolete, as it became vulnerable to better performing German fighter aircraft. With mounting losses and better designs being introduced, a decision was made to withdraw Voisin III from day operations. Among other types, it was replaced by the Voisin V.

WIGHT CONVERTED

AIRCRAFT SPECIFICATION SHEET
Span: 65ft 6in
Length: 44ft 8½in
Wing area: 715.05sqft
Take-off weight: 5,560lb
Power plant: One 322hp Rolls-Royce Eagle IV V12
Armament/bomb load: 1 × 7.7mm machine gun, 4 × 50kg bombs
Performance
   Max. speed: 84mph

Endurance: 3hrs 30min
Service ceiling: 9,600ft

HISTORY

The Wight Seaplane was a British twin-float seaplane produced by J. Samuel White & Company Limited (Wight Aircraft). It was also known as the Admiralty Type 840. Designed by Howard T. Wright and built by the aircraft department of the shipbuilding company J. Samuel White & Company Limited, the Wight Seaplane was a slightly smaller version (61ft–18.59m – span) of the Wight Pusher Seaplane. The aircraft was a conventional two-float seaplane with tandem open cockpits and a nose-mounted 322hp Rolls-Royce Eagle IV V12 engine. Fifty-two aircraft were built and delivered and an extra twenty were produced as spares production being undertaken by Portholme Aviation and William Beardmore & Co., Ltd. The Wight Seaplane served with the RNAS at Dundee Felixstowe, Scapa Flow and Gibraltar, being used for anti-submarine patrols between 1915 and 1917. One of the most important tasks was to meet the U-boat threat in the English Channel and some Wight Converted floatplanes equipped No.241 Squadron based at Portland and No.243 Squadron based at Cherbourg in 1917. On 18 August 1917, a Wight Converted Seaplane flying from Cherbourg sank the German U-boat *UB-32* with a single 100lb bomb, the first submarine to be sunk in the English Channel by direct air action. Seven remained in service with the RAF at the end of World War I.

Appendix B

RAF Squadron Histories – Aircraft and Locations 1912 to 1918

NO.1 SQUADRON TO NO.274 SQUADRON

NOTE: ONLY SQUADRONS THAT WERE IN EXISTENCE AND IN SERVICE ON OR BEFORE 11/11/18 ARE LISTED. THIS APPENDIX LISTS:

SQUADRON LOCATIONS
SQUADRON AIRCRAFT

Notes:
F   = Formed
RF   = Reformed
DB   = Disbanded
Det/dets   = Detachment/s
(1/23)   = Indicates month and year when aircraft ceased to be operational with that unit.

SQUADRON HISTORIES – MAY 1912 TO 11 NOVEMBER 1918

No. 1 SQUADRON   MOTTO: In omnibus princeps (First in all things)

Month/Yr	Location	Aircraft type	Remarks
13/5/12	F @ Farnborough		From No.1 (Airship) Coy Air Batt, Royal Engineers
5/12		Beta (1/14))	
5/12		Gamma (1/14))	
5/12		Delta (1/14)) Airships	
5/12		Zeta (1/14))	
5/12		Eta (1/14))	
1/1/14			All airships transferred to the control of the Royal Navy
1/5/14			Unit restyled Airship Detachment RFC
1/5/14			Re-established at Brooklands as a cadre
14/8/14			Unit embodied
8/14		Longhorn (2/15)	
8/14		Vickers Boxkite (11/14)	
10/14		Martinsyde S1 (11/14)	
13/11/14	to Netheravon		
2/15		Avro 504 (10/15)	
3/15		BE8 (6/15)	
3/15		Caudron GIII (10/15)	
7/3/15	St Omer		
29/3/15	Bailleul (Asylum Ground)		
4/15		Bristol Scout (8/15)	
4/15		Morane I (12/15)	
4/15		Martinsyde S1 (8/15)	
8/15		Morane N (3/16)	
11/15		Morane LA (1/17)	
1/16		Morane BB (1/17)	

Month/Yr	Location	Aircraft type	Remarks
3/16		Nieuport 16 (8/16)	
6/16		Nieuport 20 (1/17)	
7/16		Morane P (1/17)	
7/16		Nieuport 17 (12/17)	
5/17		Nieuport 23 (12/17)	
8/17		Nieuport 24 (12/17)	
9/17		Nieuport 27 (12/17)	
1/18		SE5a (2/19)	
29/3/18	Ste-Marie-Cappel		
13/4/18	Clairmarais South		
5/8/18	Fienvillers		
6/10/18	Senlis-le-Sec		
26/10/18	Bouvincourt	SE5a (2/19)	from 26 Oct 18

No. 2 SQUADRON   MOTTO: Hereward

Month/Yr	Location	Aircraft type	Remarks
13/5/12	F @ Farnborough		From No.2 (Aeroplane Coy, Air Batt. RE
5/12		Bristol Boxkite (12/12)	
5/12		Breguet Biplane (12/12)	
5/12		BE1 (unknown)	
5/12		Longhorn (8/14)	
7/12		BE2 (8/12)	
7/12		Henry Farman biplane (12/12}	
2/13		BE2a (8/15)	
26/2/14	Montrose		Det Limerick
4/13		BE2 (9/14)	
4/14		Shorthorn (5/15)	
30/6/14	Netheravon		
5/8/14	Farnborough		
8/14		RE1 (8/14)	
12/8/14	Swingate Down		
13/8/14	Amiens		
16/8/14	Maubeuge		
24/8/14	Berlaimont		
25/8/14	Le Cateau		
25/8/14	St Quentin		
26/8/14	La Fère		
28/8/14	Compiègne		
30/8/14	Senlis		
31/8/14	Juilly		
2/9/14	Serris		
9/14		BE2c (12/14)	
3/9/14	Touquin		
4/9/14	Melun		
7/9/14	Touquin		
9/9/14	Coulommiers		
12/9/14	Fère-en Tardenois		
9/14		RE5 (2/15)	
17/10/14	St Omer		
27/11/14	Merville		Det St Omer
2/15		Vickers FB 5 (2/15)	
2/15		BE2b (8/15)	
2/15		BE2c (6/17)	

Month/Yr	Location	Aircraft type	Remarks
30/6/15	Hesdigneul		
7/15		Bristol Scout (12/15)	
7/16		BE2d (6/17)	
1/17		BE2e (6/17)	
4/17		AW FK (2/19)	
9/6/18	Floringham		
20/1018	Mazingarbe		
26/10/18	Genech		

No. 3 SQUADRON   MOTTO: Tertius primus erit (The third shall be first)

Month/Yr	Location	Aircraft type	Remarks
13/5/12	F @ Larkhilll		From detachment of No.2 Aeroplane Coy. Air Batt. RE
5/12		Henry Farman III (6/12)	
5/12		Avro Type E (8/12)	
5/12		Bristol Boxkite (8/12)	
5/12		Deperdussin Monoplane (9/12)	
5/12		Nieuport Monoplane (9/12)	
5/12		Bristol Prier Monoplane (9/12)	
5/12		BE3 (10/13)	
8/12		BE4 (3/14)	
9/12		Bristol Coanda Monoplane (9/12)	
9/12		Longhorn (8/13)	
10/12		Blériot XXI (4/13)	
3/13		BE2a (4/13)	
3/13		Henry Farman F.20	
4/13		Blériot XI (6/15)	
5/13		Avro Type Es (8/13)	
16/6/13	Netheravon		
3/14		SE2 (5/14)	
8/14		BE2c (8/14)	
8/14		Blériot XI Parasol (3/15)	
12/8/14	Swingate Down		
13/8/14	Amiens		
8/14		BE8 (8/14)	
16/8/14	Maubeuge		
24/8/14	Le Cateau		
8/14		Tabloid (9/14)	
25/8/14	St Quentin		
26/8/14	La Fère		
28/8/14	Compiègne		
30/8/14	Senlis		
31/8/14	Juilly		
9/14		BE8 (9/14)	
2/9/14	Serris		
3/9/14	Touquin		
4/9/14	Melun		
7/9/14	Touquin		
9/9/14	Coulommiers		
12/9/14	Fère-en Tardenois		
9/14		Bristol Scout (?)	
5/10/14	Amiens		
8/10/14	Abbeville		
9/10/14	Moyenneville		

Month/Yr	Location	Aircraft type	Remarks
12/10/14	St Omer		Det Hinges
8/14		SE2 (3/15)	
24/11/14	Gonneham		
12/14		Morane L (9/15)	
1/6/15	Lozinghem		
9/15		Morane LA (1/17)	
10/15		Morane N (7/16)	
12/15		Morane BB (12/16)	
16/3/16	Bruay		
1/4/16	Bertangles		
10/4/16	Lahoussoye		
5/16		Nieuport 16 (1916)	8/16
		Morane P (10/17)	
23/1/17	Laviéville		
15/7/17	Longavesnes		
26/8/17	Lechelles		
10/10/17	Warloy		
8/17		Camel (2/19)	
25/3/18	Vert Galand		
26/3/18	Valheureux		
15/10/18	Léchelle		
4/11/18	Inchy		

No. 4 SQUADRON   MOTTO: In futurum videre (To see into the future)

Month/Yr	Location	Aircraft type	Remarks
16/9/12	F & Farnborough		Nucleus from No.2 Squadron
12/12		Cody V (3/13)	
12/12		Breguet Biplane (1/14)	
1/13		BE4 (2/13)	
1/13		Longhorn (8/14)	
4/13		BE1 (?)	
4/13		Caudron G H (7/14)	
14/6/13	Netheravon		
11/13		BE2 (9/14)	
1/14		BE2a (10/15)	
7/14		BE2c (8/14)	
21/7/14	Eastchurch		(A & B Flights) det Netheravon
8/14		Shorthorn (8/14)	
13/8/14	Amiens		Det Swingate Down
16/8/14	Maubeuge		
24/8/14	Le Cateau		
25/8/14	St Quentin		
26/8/14	La Fère		
28/8/14	Compiègne		
30/8/14	Senlis		
31/8/14	Juilly		
2/9/14	Serris		
3/9/14	Touquin		
4/9/14	Melun		
7/9/14	Touquin		
9/9/14	Coulommiers		
12/9/14	Fère-en-Tardenois		
9/14		Shorthorn (1915)	
6/10/14	Amiens		

Month/Yr	Location	Aircraft type	Remarks
8/10/14	Abbeville		
9/10/14	Moyenneville		
12/10/14	St Omer		Det Poperinghe, Dunkirk Bailleul (town ground)
12/14		Tabloid (1/15)	
1/15		BE2b (10/15)	
2/15		Martinsyde S1 (4/15)	
2/15		Voisin LA (7/15)	
3/15		Bristol Scout (3/16)	
21/4/15	Bailleul (town ground)		
4/15		BE2c (5/17)	
5/15		Caudron GIII (6/15)	
6/15		Morane II (9/15)	
20/7/15	Vert Galand		
5/8/15	Baizieux		
7/11/15	Allonville		
2/16	Baizieux		
2/16	Marieux		
27/3/16	Baizieux		
7/16		BE2d (5/17)	
7/16		BE2e (5/17)	
1/17		BE2g (5/17)	
28/2/17	Warloy		
30/5/17	Abeele		
6/17		RE8 (2/19)	
18/11/17	Chocques		
8/4/18	Treizennes		
16/4/18	St Omer		
18/9/18	Ste-Marie-Cappel		
21/10/18	Linselles	RE8 (2/19)	

No. 5 SQUADRON   MOTTO: Frangus non flectas (Thou mayst break but shall not bend me)

Month/Yr	Location	Aircraft type	Remarks
26/7/13	F @ South Farnborough		Nucleus from No.3 Squadron
7/13		Avro Type E (7/14)	
7/13		Longhorn (8/14)	
7/13		Henry Farman F20 (3/15)	
1/14		SE2a (3/14)	
2/14		Sopwith 3-Seater (8/14	
1914		BE1 (8/14)	
6/14		Tabloid (8/14)	
28/5/14	Netheravon		
6/7/14	Gosport (Fort Grange)		
7/14		Avro 504 (8/15)	
14/8/14	Swingate Down		
15/8/14	Amiens		
8/14		BE8 (9/14)	
18/8/14	Maubeuge		
24/8/14	Le Cateau		
25/8/14	St Quentin		
26/8/14	La Fère		
28/8/14	Compiègne		
30/8/14	Senlis		
31/8/14	Juilly		

Month/Yr	Location	Aircraft type	Remarks
9/14		Henry Farman F27 (9/14)	
2/9/14	Serris		
3/9/14	Pezarche		
4/9/14	Melun		
6/9/14	La Boiserotte		
7/9/14	Touquin		
8/9/14	Rebais		
9/9/14	Coulommiers		
12/9/14	Fère-en Tardenois		
9/14		Bristol Scout (10/14)	
30/9/14	Amiens		
8/10/14	Abbeville		
9/10/14	Moyenneville		
12/10/14	St Omer		Dets.Eblinghem, Wallon-Cappel, Meteren Bailleul (town ground)
23/10/14	Bailleul (town ground)		
11/1/15	Bailleul (asylum ground)		Dets St Omer, Poperinghe Morbecque
1/15		Martinsyde S1 (8/15)	
2/15		Voisin LA (3/15)	
3/15		Blériot Parasol (5/15)	
3/15		Vickers FB5 (1/16)	
3/15		Bristol Scout (3/15)	
4/15		Caudron GIII (5/15)	
27/4/15	Abeele		
7/15		DH2 (8/15)	
8/15		BE2c (4/17)	
12/15		FE8 (5/16)	
1/16		DH2 (5/16)	
11/3/16	Droglandt		
6/16		BE2d (1917)	
2/10/16	Marieux		
1/17		BE2e (6/17)	
1/17		BE2f (6/17)	
1/17		BE2g (6/17)	
24/3/17	La Gorgue		
7/4/17	Savy		
6/17		RE8 (9/19)	
2/6/17	Ascq		Dets Les Moères
25/5/18	Le Hameau		
4/8/18	Bovelles		
24/8/18	Le Hameau		
14/10/18	Pronville		
24/10/18	Emerchicourt		
8/11/18	Aulnoy		

No. 6 SQUADRON   MOTTO: Oculi exercitus (The eyes of the army)

Month/Yr	Location	Aircraft type	Remarks
31/1/14	F@ Farnborough		
1/14		Longhorn (9/14)	
2/14		BE2 (8/14)	
3/14		Shorthorn (8/14)	
5/14		RE1 (8/14)	

Month/Yr	Location	Aircraft type	Remarks
6/14		RE5 (9/14)	
8/14		BE9 (1/15)	
9/14		Vickers FB 'Gun Carrier'(9/14)	
9/14		Henry Farman F20 (12/14)	
9/14		BE2a (9/15)	
21/9/14	Netheravon		
4/10/14	Farnborough		
7/10/14	Bruges		
8/10/14	Ostende		
13/10/14	St Pol		Dets Ypres, Boulogne
20/10/14	Poperinghe		
21/10/14	St Omer		
18/11/14	Bailleul		Det St Omer
11/14		Blériot XI (1/15)	
1/15		Martinsyde S1 (8/15)	
1/15		BE2c (2/17)	
8/3/15	Poperinghe		
24/4/15	Abeele		Det Droglandt
5/15		FE2a (3/16)	
6/15		Bristol Scout (6/16)	
11/15		Martinsyde G100 (2/16)	
12/15		FE2b (2/16)	
6/16		BE2d (5/17)	
10/16		BE2e (11/16)	
12/16		BE2f (2/17)	
12/16		BE2g (5/17)	
4/17		RE8 (7/20)	
16/11/17	Bertangles		
23/3/18	St-André-aux-Bois		
26/3/18	Le Crotoy		Dets Treizennnes, Rely, Auxi-le-Chateau
18/7/18	Fienvillers		
5/8/18	Bovelles		
17/8/18	Auxi-le-Chateau		
27/8/18	Ascq		
2/9/18	Moislains		
6/10/18	Longavesnes		
19/10/18	Bertry West		
20/10/18	Maretz		
9/11/18	Gondecourt	RE8 (7/20)	

No. 7 SQUADRON   MOTTO: Per diem, per noctem (By day and by night)

Month/Yr	Location	Aircraft type	Remarks
1/5/14	F @ Farnborough		
5/14		Longhorn (8/14)	
5/14		BE8 (8/14)	
5/14		Tabloid (8/14)	
8/8/14	DB – personnel transferred to other units		
29/9/14	RF @ Farnborough		
9/14		Henry Farman F20 (10/14)	
9/14		Morane H (10/14)	
9/14		Blériot I (10/14)	

Month/Yr	Location	Aircraft type	Remarks
9/14		Avro Type E (4/15)	
9/14		Vickers FB 'Gun Carrier' (4/15)	Dets Swingate Down, Netheravon
24/10/14	Netheravon		
10/14		RE5 (9/15)	
8/14	St Omer		Dets Boulogne
4/15		Voisin LA (9/15)	
6/15		Bristol Scout (6/16)	
7/15		BE2c (2/17)	
11/9/15	Droglandt		
12/12/15	Bailleul		
12/15		Morane LA (12/15)	
5/16		BE2d (10/16)	
30/7/16	Warloy		
10/16		BE2e (6/17)	
12/16		BE2f (5/17)	
12/16		BE2g (6/17)	
6/2/17	Moreuil		
15/4/17	Matigny		Det Nesle
23/5/17	Proven		
5/17		RE8 (10/19)	
13/4/18	Droglandt		
3/9/18	Proven		
22/10/18	Bisseghem		
1/11/18	Staceghem		
5/11/18	Menin		

No. 8 SQUADRON   MOTTO: Upsiam et passim (Everywhere unbounded)

Month/Yr	Location	Aircraft type	Remarks
1/1/15	F @ Brooklands		
1/15		BE2c (8/17)	
6/1/15	Gosport (Fort Grange)		
2/15		BE2a (10/15)	
2/15		BE2b (10/15)	
15/4/15	St Omer		
1/5/15	Abeele		
5/15	Oxeraere		
6/15		Bristol Scout (5/16)	
6/15		BE8 (7/15)	
24/7/15	Vert Galand		
8/15	Marieux		
20/2/16	La Bellevue		
6/16		BE2d (1917)	
3/2/17	Soncamp		
2/17		BE2e (8/17)	
9/5/17	Boiry-St-Martin		
8/17		AW FK 8 (12/18)	
18/10/17	Longsvesnes		
29/10/17	Mons-en-Chaussée		
11/3/18	Nurlu		
22//3/18	Chipilly		
24/3/18	Poulainville		
28/3/18	Vert Galand		
12/4/19	Auxi-le-Chateau		Dets Bruay, Poulainville, Avesnes-le-Comte & Vignacourt

Month/Yr	Location	Aircraft type	Remarks
5/8/18	Vignacourt		
18/8/18	La Bellevue		Det Foucaucourt
22/9/18	Estrées-en-Chaussée		
8/10/18	Hervilly		
18/10/18	Malincourt		

No. 9 SQUADRON   MOTTO: **Per noctum volamus (Through the night we fly)**

Month/Yr	Location	Aircraft type	Remarks
8/12/14	F @ St Omer		Wireless Flt redesignated
12/14		BE2a (2/15)	
12/14		Longhorn (2/15)	
12/14		Blériot XI (3/15)	
12/14		Shorthorn (3/15)	
1/15		BE2b (2/15)	
1/15		BE2c (2/15)	
1/15		Blériot Parasol (3/15)	
			Dets Bailleul, Chocques,
22/3/15	DB – elements incorporated into Nos.2, 5, 6 & 15 Sqns		
1/4/15	RF & Brooklands		
4/15		BE2 (7/15)	
4/15		Blériot XI (8/15)	
4/15		Longhorn (11/15)	
23/7/15	Swingate Down		
7/15		BE8A (11/15)	
7/15		Avro 504 (11/15)	
7/15		Martinsyde S.1 (11/15)	
8/15		BE2c (10/16)	
11/15		RE7 (11/15)	
12/12/15	St Omer		
12/15		Bristol Scout (6/16)	
24/12/15	Bertangles		
26/3/16	Allonville		
6/16		BE2d (9/16)	
15/7/16	Chipilly		
8/16		BE2e (6/17)	
3/9/16	Morlancourt		Dets Mons-en-Chaussée
27/4/17	Nurlu		
5/17		RE8 (5/19)	
16/5/17	Estrées-en-Chaussée		
10/6/17	Proven		
11/4/18	Calais		
6/6/18	Agenvillers		
7/18		Bristol F2B Fighter (10/18)	
17/7/18	Quevauvillers		
15/8/18	Amiens		
7/9/18	Proyart		
15/9/18	Athies		
6/10/18	Montigny Farm		
18/10/18	Prémont Farm		
29/10/18	Tarcienne	RE8 (5/19)	

No. 10 SQUADRON   MOTTO: Rem acu tangere (To hit the mark)

Month/Yr	Location	Aircraft type	Remarks
1/1/15	F @ Farnborough		Nucleus from No.1 RAS
1/15		Longhorn (4/15)	
1/15		Shorthorn (4/15)	
1/15		Blériot XI (4/15)	
1/15		Martinsyde S.1 (4/15)	
1/15		BE2c (4/17)	
8/1/15	Brooklands		
1/4/15	Hounslow		
7/4/15	Neheravon		
27/7/15	St Omer		
30/7/15	Aire		
7/8/15	Chocques		
6/16		BE12 (7/16)	
7/16		BE2d (2/17)	
12/16		BE2e (7/17)	
7/17		BE2f (7/17)	
1/17		BE2g (7/17)	
7/17		AWFK 8 (2/19)	
18/11/17	Abeele		
12/4/18	Droglandt		
6/18		Bristol F2b Fighter (10/18)	
22/9/18	Abeele		
21/10/18	Menin		
5/11/18	Stacegham	AWFK 8 (2/19)	

No. 11 SQUADRON   MOTTO: Ociores acrierosque (Swifter and keener than eagles)

Month/Yr	Location	Aircraft type	Remarks
14/2/15	F @ Netheravon		Nucleus from No.7 Sqn
2/15		Henry Farman F20 (6/15)	
2/15		Vickers FB 'Gun Carrier'	
6/15		Vickers FB5 (7/16)	
25/7/15	St Omer		
29/7/15	Vert Galland		
20/9/15	Villers- Bretonneux		Det Vert Galand
27/10/15	Bertangles		
12/15		Bristol Scout (2/16)	
1/16	Savy		
2/16		DH2 (3/16)	
4/16		Nieuport 16 (8/16)	
5/16		Vickers ES1 (6/16)	
5/16		Bristol Scout (8/16)	
5/16		Vickers FB9 (7/16)	
6/16		FE2b (6/17)	
7/16		Nieuport 17 (8/16)	
31/8/16	Izel-le-Hameau		
5/17		Bristol F2b Fighter (10/19)	
1/6/17	La Bellevue		
27/3/18	Fienville		
16/4/18	Remaisnil		
7/7/18	Le Quesnoy		
19/9/18	Vert Galand		
15/10/18	Mory		
1/11/18	Béthencourt		

No. 12 SQUADRON   MOTTO: (Leads the field)

Month/Yr	Location	Aircraft type	Remarks
14/2/15	F @ Netheravon		Nucleus from No.1 Sqn
5/15		Avro 504 (9/15)	
6/15		BE2c (2/17)	
6/9/15	St Omer		
9/15		Martinsyde S1 (10/15)	
9/15		BE2b (11/15)	
9/15		Voisin LA (11/15)	
9/15		RE7 (1/16)	
9/15		RE5 (2/16)	
10/15		Morane H (11/15)	
11/15		Bristol Scout (5/16)	
11/15		Morane LA (2/16)	
28/2/16	Vert Galand		
2/16		FE2b (2/16)	
3/3/16	Avesnes-le-Comte		
2/16		Morane BB (2/16)	
7/16		BE2d (8/17)	
12/16		BE2e (8/17)	
9/5/17	Wagnonlieu		
7/7/17	Ablainzevelle		
8/17		RE8 (7/19)	
8/17	Courcelles-le-Comte		
16/12/17	Boiry-St-Martin		
22/3/18	Soncamp		
3/18		Bristol F2b Fighter (7/22)	
17/9/18	Mory		
14/10/18	Estourmel		

No. 13 SQUADRON   MOTTO: Ajuvamus tuendo (We assist by watching)

Month/Yr	Location	Aircraft type	Remarks
10/1/15	F @ Gosport (Fort Grange)		Nucleus from No.8 Sqn
1/15		BE2c (4/17)	
1/15		Bristol Scout (5/16)	
19/10/15	St Omer		
21/10/15	Vert Galand		
12/3/16	Le Hameau		
18/3/16	Savy		
7/16		BE2d (7/17)	
9/16		BE2e (1/17	
4/17		BE2e (7/17)	
9/5/17	Etrun		
6/17		RE8 (3/19)	
2/3/18	Le Hameau		
22/9/18	Mory		
19/10/18	Carnières	RE8 (3/19)	

No. 14 SQUADRON   MOTTO: (I spread my wings and keep my promise)

Month/Yr	Location	Aircraft type	Remarks
3/2/15	F @ Shoreham		Nucleus from No.3 RAS
2/15		Longhorn (8/15)	
11/5/15	Hounslow		
5/15		BE2c (11/17)	
5/15		Caudron GIII (8/15)	

Month/Yr	Location	Aircraft type	Remarks
5/8/15	Gosport (Fort Grange)		
7/11/15	En route Egypt		
19/11/15	Alexandria		
23/11/15	Ismailia		Dets Mersah Matruh, Fayoum, Heliopolis
11/15		Shorthorn (1916)	
11/15		BE2e (9/18)	
11/15		Martinsyde S1 (?)	
6/12/15		Heliopolis	Dets Ismailia, Abu Gandir, Qantara
29/1/16		Ismailia	Dets El Hammam, Sidi Barrani, Sollum, Mersah Matruh, Suez, Heliopolis, Port Said, Salmana, Rabigh and Mustabig
1915		Martinsyde G100 (1917)	
6/16		DH1A (3/17)	
20/1/17	Kilo 143/Ujret et Zol		Dets Yenbo, El Weigh
25/3/17	Rafah		Dets Deir el Ballah, El Weigh
27/4/17	Deir el Ballah		Dets Suez, Kilo 143 El Weigh, Aqaba
7/17		Vickers FB 19 Mk II (8/17)	
10/17		RE8 (11/18)	
20/11/17	Julis		
30/11/17	Junction Station		Dets Jericho, Jerusalem
2/18		Nieuport 17 (10/18)	
24/10/18	Qantara		
6/11/18	Mikra Bay	RE8 (11/18)	

No. 15 SQUADRON   MOTTO: Aim Sure

Month/Yr	Location	Aircraft type	Remarks
1/3/15	F @ South Farnborough		Nucleus from No.1 RAS
13/4/15	Hounslow		
4/15		Henry Farman F20 (10/15)	
4/15		Longhorn (10/15)	
4/15		Shorthorn (10/15)	
4/15		Avro 504 (10/15)	
4/15		Blériot XI (9/15)	
4/15		BE2c (7/17)	
11/5/15	Swingate Down		
10/15		Morane H (12/15)	
11/15		Morane L (12/15)	
23/12/15	St Omer		
5/1/16	Droglandt		
8/3/16	Vert Galand		
27/3/16	Marieux		
8/16		BE2d (8/17)	
2/10/16	Léalvillers (Clairfaye Farm)		
8/16		BE2e (5/17)	
1/17		BE2f (5/17)	
1/17		BE2g (5/17)	
5/17		RE8 (2/19)	
6/7/17	Courcelles-le-Comte		
7/7/17	La Gorgue		Dets Claimarais
18/8/17	Savy		

Month/Yr	Location	Aircraft type	Remarks
30/8/17	Longavesnes		
8/10/17	Léchelle		
30/11/17	Bapaume		
5/12/17	Léchelle		
22/3/18	Laviéville		
25/3/18	Lahoussoye		
26/3/18	Fienvillers		
10/4/18	Vert Galand		
14/9/18	Senlis-le-Sec		
2/10/18	Léchelle (Quatre Vents Farm		
15/10/18	Selvigny (Ferme Guillemin)	RE8 (2/19)	

No. 16 SQUADRON   MOTTO: Operta aperta (Hidden things are revealed)

Month/Yr	Location	Aircraft type	Remarks
10/2/15	F @ St Omer		From flts of Nos.2 & 6 Sqns
2/15		RE5 (2/15)	
2/15		Vickers FB5 (3/15)	
2/15		Blériot XI (3/15)	
26/2/15	Flight added from No.5 Sqn		
2/15		Martinsyde S1 (5/15)	
6/3/15	La Gorgue		Det Aire
3/15		Voisin LA (5/15)	
3/15		BE2c (4/17)	
5/15		BE2a (6/15)	
5/15		Shorthorn (11/15)	
1/6/15	Chocques		
6/15		BE2b (6/15)	
18/7/15	Merville		
8/15		Bristol Scout (6/16)	
10/15		FE2a (1/16)	
10/15		FE2b (2/16)	
12/12/15	La Gorgue		
6/16		BE2d (11/16)	
7/16		BE2e (5/17)	
31/8/16	Bruay		
4/17		BE2f (5/17)	
4/17		BE2g (8/17)	
25/5/17	Camblain-l'Abbé		
5/17		RE8 (2/19)	
21/10/18	La Brayelle		
25/10/18	Auchy	RE8 (219)	

No. 17 SQUADRON   MOTTO: Excellere contende (Strive to excel)

Month/Yr	Location	Aircraft type	Remarks
1/2/15	F @ Gosport (Fort Grange)		
2/15		BE2c (11/15)	
5/8/15	Hounslow		
15/11/15	En route Egypt		
11/12/15	Alexandria		
18/12/15	Heliopolis		
12/15		BE2c (6/18)	Flts @ Hammam, Suez, Port Sudan, dets Fayoum, Minya, Assiyut, Rahad, Nahud, Jebel el Hillah

Month/Yr	Location	Aircraft type	Remarks
2/7/16	En route to Salonika		
21/7/16	Mikra Bay		
7/16		Bristol Scout (9/16)	
7/16		DH2 (?)	Flts @ Lahana, Avret, Hisar Orlyak, Marian, Amberkoj
11/16		BE12a (9/18)	
7/17		SPAD SVII (12/17)	Det Florina (used loaned French Nieuport 17) (12/17)
12/17		SE5a (4/18)	
8/12/17	Lahana		Flt @ Amberkoj det Mudros
3/18		AWFK 8 (12/18)	
8/18		DH9 (11/19)	
22/9/18	Amberkoj		
26/9/18	Stojakovo		Flt @ Amberkoj
2/10/18	Radovo		Flt @ Amberkoj
13/10/18	Amberkoj		Flts at Philipopolis, Mustapha Pasha, Mikra Bay & Batum

No. 18 SQUADRON   MOTTO: Animo et Fide (With courage and faith)

Month/Yr	Location	Aircraft type	Remarks
11/5/18	F @ Northolt		Nucleus from No.4 RAS
5/15		Martinsyde S1 (10/15)	
5/15		Shorthorn (11/15)	
1916		Bristol Scout (1915)	
16/8/15	Mousehold Heath		
9/15		Vickers FB5 (4/16)	
18/11/15	St Omer		
25/11/15	Treizennes		
12/2/16	Auchel		
1/16		DH2 (4/16)	
3/16		Martinsyde G100 (6/16)	
1//4/16	Bruay		
4/16		FE2b (6/17)	
22/7/16	Treizennes		
2/8/16	Bruay		
6/9/16	Laviéville		
10/12/16	St-Leger-les-Authie		
27/1/17	Bertangles		
25/5/17	Baizieux		
6/17		DH4 (8/19)	
10/7/17	La Bellevue		
11/10/17	Auchel		
2/2/18	Treizennes		
9/4/18	Serny		
17/8/18	Maisoncelle		
9/18		DH9A (8/19)	
13/10/18	Le Hameau		
27/10/18	La Brayelle		

No. 19 SQUADRON   MOTTO: Possunt quia posse videntur (They can because they think they can)

Month/Yr	Location	Aircraft type	Remarks
1//9/15	F @ Castle Bromwich		Nucleus from No.5 RAS
9/15		Shorthorn (10/15)	
9/15		Avro 504 (10/15)	

Month/Yr	Location	Aircraft type	Remarks
9/15		Caudron GIII (10/15)	
10/15		BE2c (12/15)	
12/15		RE7 (12/15)	
31/1/16	Netheravon		
2/16		Avro 504 (6/16)	
2/16		Caudron GIII (7/16)	
2/16		Bristol Scout (7/16)	
2/16		BE2c (7/16)	
2/16		RE7 (7/16)	
2/16		FE2b (7/16)	
2/16		BE12 (2/17)	
2/16		Martinsyde S1 (7/16)	
2/16		RE5 (7/16)	
29/3/16	Filton		
30/7/16	St Omer		
1/8/16	Fienvillers		
10/16		SPAD SVII (1/18)	
2//4/17	Vert Galand		
31/5/17	Liettres		
14/8/17	Poperinghe		
5/9/17	Bailleul (Asylum Ground)		
11/17		Dolphin (2/19)	
25/12/17	Ste-Marie-Cappel		
13/2 18	Bailleul		
23/3/18	Ste-Marie-Cappel		
31/3/18	Savy		
17/8/18	Cappelle		
23/9/18	Savy		
24/10/18	Abscon		

No. 20 SQUADRON   MOTTO: Facta non verba (Deeds not words)

Month/Yr	Location	Aircraft type	Remarks
1/9/15	F @ Netheravon		Nucleus from No.7 RAS
9/15		Curtiss JN 3 (1/16)	
9/15		BE2c (1/16)	
10/16		Martinsyde S1 (11/15)	
15/12/15	Filton		
12/15		FE2b (6/16)	
16/1/16	St Omer		
23/1/16	Clairmarais		
2/16		FE2a (3/16)	
2/16		Martinsyde G100 (6/16)	
6/16		FE2d (9/17)	
9/16		RE7 (1/17)	
19/1/17	Boisdinghem		
15/4/17	Ste-Marie-Cappel		
8/17		Bristol F2b Fighter (5/19)	
13/4/18	Boisdinghem		
26/8/18	Vignacourt		
16/9/18	Suzanne		
24/9/18	Proyart		
7/10/18	Moislains		
25/10/18	Iris Farm		

No.21 SQUADRON   MOTTO: Viribus vincimus (By strength we conquer)

Month/Yr	Location	Aircraft type	Remarks
23/7/15	F @ Netheravon		Nucleus from No.8 RAS
7/15		RE7 (8/16)	
23/1/16	Boisdinghem		
2/16		Bristol Scout (3/16)	
4/16		BE2c (8/16)	
2/4/16	Ste-André-aux-Bois		
4/16		BE2e (8/16)	
6/16		Martinsyde G100 (6/16)	
19/6/16	Fienvillers		
28/7/16	Boisdinghem		
8/16		BE12 (2/17)	
25/8/16	Bertangles		
2/17		RE8 (2/19)	
16/2/17	Boisdinghem		
24/3/17	Droglandt		
19/5/17	La Lovie		
13/4/18	St-Inglevert		
22/4/18	Floringhem		
19/10/18	Hesdigneul		
25/10/18	Seclin		
11/11/18	Froidmont		

No. 22 SQUADRON   MOTTO: Preux et audacieux (Valiant and brave)

Month/Yr	Location	Aircraft type	Remarks
1/9/15	F @ Gosport (Fort Grange)		Nucleus from No.13 Sqn
9/15		Longhorn (10/15)	
9/15			BE2c (3/16)
9/15			Blériot XI (3/16)
24/9/15	Gosport (Fort Rowner)		
10/15			Caudron GIII (10/15)
10/15			BE8A (11/15)
10/15			Curtiss JN 3 (1/16)
10/15			Martinsyde S1A (6/16)
10/15			Bristol Scout (3/16)
1/16			Avro 504 (3/16)
3/16			FE2b (8/17)
1/4/16	St Omer		
1/4/16	Vert Galand		
16/4/16	Bertangles		
27/4/16	Chipilly		
1/5/17	Flez		
3/7/17	Warloy		
5/7/17	Izel-le-Hameau		
7/17		Bristol F2b Fighter (8/19)	
14/8/17	Boisdinghem		
10/9/17	Estrée-Blanche		
22/1/18	Auchel		
2/2/18	Treizennes		
21/3/18	Serny		
23/3/18	Vert Galand		
9/4/18	Serny		
30/7/18		Maisoncelle	
22/10/18		Izel-le-Hameau	
26/10/18		Aniche	

No. 23 SQUADRON   MOTTO: Semper aggressus (Always having attacked)

Month/Yr	Location	Aircraft type	Remarks
1/9/15	F @ Gosport (Fort Grange)		Nucleus from No.14 Sqn
9/15		Blériot XI (9/15)	
9/15		Caudron GIII (12/15)	
9/15		Shorthorn (1/16)	
9/15		Avro 504A (3/16)	
10/15		Martinsyde S1 (3/16)	
10/15		BE2c (3/16)	Det Suttons Farm
1/16		FE2b (4/17)	
15/3/16	St Omer		
16/3/16	Fienvillers		
18/3/16	Le Hameau		
3/16		Martinsyde G100 (5/16)	
1/9/16	Fienvillers		
5/9/16	Vert Galand		
2/17		SPAD SVII (4/18)	
5/3/17	Baizieux		
23/5/17	Auchel		
29/5/17	Bruay		Dets Erquinghem
13/6/17	La Lovie		
12/17		SPAD SXIII (5/18)	
16/2/18	Matigny		
22/3/18	Moreuil		
28/3/18	Bertangles		
29/4/18	St Omer		
4/18		Dolphin (3/19)	
16/5/18	Bertangles		
13/9/18	Cappy		
11/10/18	Hancourt		
25/10/18	Bertry East		

No. 24 SQUADRON   MOTTO: In omnia parati (Ready in all things)

Month/Yr	Location	Aircraft type	Remarks
1/9/15	F @ Hounslow		Nucleus from No.17 Sqn
10/15		Curtiss JN 4 (11/15)	
10/15		Caudron GIII (11/15)	
10/15		Avro 504 (11/15)	
10/15		BE2c (11/15)	
10/15		Blériot XI (11/15)	
10/15		Bristol Scout (11/15)	
10/15		Longhorn (11/15)	
10/15		Shorthorn (11/15)	
11/15		Vickers FB5 (2/16)	
1/16		DH2 (6/17)	
7/2/16	St Omer		
10/2/16	Bertangles		
17/12/16	Chipilly		
17/4/17	Flez		
5/17		DH5 (1/18)	
10/7/17	Baizieux		
23/9/17	Teteghem		
24/11/17	Marieux		
12/17		SE5a (1/19)	
30/12/17	Villers-Bretonneux		

Month/Yr	Location	Aircraft type	Remarks
26/1/18	Matigny		
22/3/18	Moreuil		
26/3/18	Bertangles		
28/3/18	Conteville		
14/8/18	Bertangles		
8/9/18	Cappy		
6/10/18	Athies		
27/10/18	Busigny		
11/11/18	to Bisseghem		

No. 25 SQUADRON   MOTTO: Feriens tego (Striking I defend)

Month/Yr	Location	Aircraft type	Remarks
25/9/15	F @ Montrose		Nucleus from No.6 RAS
9/15		Shorthorn (11/15)	
9/15		Caudron GIII (11/15)	
9/15		Curtiss JN4 (12/15)	
9/15		Martinsyde SI (12/15)	
9/15		Avro 504 (12/15)	
11/15		BE2c (12/15)	
31/12/15	Thetford		
1/16		Vickers FB5 (2/16)	
2/16		FE2b (5/17)	
2/16		Morane L (216)	
19/2/16	Folkestone		
20/2	St Omer		
1/4/16	Lozinghem		
7/16		FE2c (7/16)	
3/17		FE2d (8/17)	
6/17		DH4 (8/19)	
11/10/17	Boisdinghem		
3/2/18	Serny		
6/3/18	Villers-Bretonneux		
24/3/18	Beauvois		
27/10/18	La Brayelle	DH9A (10/19)	

No. 26 SQUADRON   MOTTO: N wagter in die Lug (A guard in the sky)

Month/Yr	Location	Aircraft type	Remarks
8/10/15	F @ Netheravon		From personnel of the South African Flying Unit
23/12/15	En route to East Africa		
31/1/16	Mombasa		
1/16		BE2c (1/18)	
1/2/16	Mbuyuni		
23/3/16	Taveta		
28/3/16	Mbuyuni		
5/16		Henry Farman F27 (1/18)	Flts @ Kahe, Marago-Opuni, Lassiti, Kwa-Lokua,Palms Mbagui, Dakawa, Morogoro, Dar-es-Salaam, Tulo, Kilwa, Dodoma, Iringa, Ubena, Itigi, Shinyanga, Songea, Narungombe, Dets @ Fort Johnson, Mtonia, Mwembe, Songea, Likuju, Itigi, Tabora, Maranda, Mbarangandu and Tunduru

Month/Yr	Location	Aircraft type	Remarks
1/18	Dar-es-Salaam		
8/2/18	en route to South Africa		
4/3/18	Capetown		
6/6/18	en route to United Kingdom		
8/7/18	Blandford		
8/7/18	DB		

No. 27 SQUADRON   MOTTO: Quam celerrime ad astra (With all speed to the stars)

Month/Yr	Location	Aircraft type	Remarks
5/11/15	F @ Hounslow		Nucleus from No.24 Sqn used various aircraft
10/12/15	Swingate Down		
2/16		Martinsyde G100/102 (11/17)	
1/3/16	St Omer		
2/3/16	Treizennes		
7/6/16	St-Andre-aux-Bois		
19/6/16	Fienvillers		
31/5/17	Claimarais North		
12/10/17	Serny		
10/17		DH4 (10/18)	
7/3/18	Villers-Bretonneux		
24/3/18	Beauvois		
29/3/18	Ruisseauville		
3/6/18	Fourneuil		
21/6/18	Ruisseauville		
15/11/18	Chailly		
7/8/18	Beauvois		
9/18		DH9 (3/19)	
29/10/18	Villers-les-Cagnicourt		

No. 28 SQUADRON   MOTTO: Quicquid agas age (Whatsoever you may do, do)

Month/Yr	Location	Aircraft type	Remarks
7/11/15	F @ Gosport (Fort Grange)		Nucleus from No.22 Sqn
11/15		BE2a (?)	
11/15		Avro 504 (4/17)	
11/15	Gosport (Fort Rowner)		
12/15		BE2c (4/17)	
4/17		Henry Farman F20 (7/17)	
4/17		FE2b (7/17)	
4/17		DH2 (7/17)	
12/5/17	Gosport (Fort Grange)		
23/7/17	Yatesbury		
7/17		Pup (9/17)	
7/17		DH5 (9/17)	
7/17		Avro 504 (9/17)	
7/17		Bristol Scout (9/17)	
8/17		Camel (2/19)	
8/10/17	St Omer		
10/10/17	Droglandt		
29/10/17	Candas		
12/11/17	Milan		
17/11/17	Ghedi		
22/11/17	Verona		
28/11/17	Frossa		

Month/Yr	Location	Aircraft type	Remarks
20/8/18	Sarcedo		
22/10/18	Treviso		
6/11/18	Sarcedo		

No. 29 SQUADRON   MOTTO: Impiger at acer (Energetic and keen)

Month/Yr	Location	Aircraft type	Remarks
7/11/15	F @ Gosport (Fort Grange)		Nucleus from No.23 Sqn
11/15		Longhorn (3/16)	
11/15		Avro 504A (3/16)	
11/15		Caudron GIII (3/16)	
12/15		BE2c (3/16)	
2/16		BE2b (3/16)	
3/16		DH2 (3/17)	
25/3/16	St Omer		
15/4/16	Abeele		
6/16		FE8 (8/16)	
23/10/16	Le Hameau		
3/17		Nieuport 16 (4/17)	
4/17		Nieuport 17 (11/17)	
5/17		Nieuport 23 (11/17)	
5/7/17	Poperinghe		
8/17		Nieuport 24 (12/17)	
10/17		Nieuport 27 (4/18)	
16/2/18	La Lovie		
11/4/18	Tetegham		
4/18		SE5a (8/19)	
22/4/18	St Omer		
11/6/18	Vignacourt		
22.7/18	St Omer		
1/8/18	Hoog Huis		
25/9/18	La Lovie		
5/10/18	Hoog Huis		
23/10/18	Marcke	SE5a (8/19)	

No. 30 SQUADRON   MOTTO: Ventre a terre (All out)

Month/Yr	Location	Aircraft type	Remarks
24/3/15			RFC Detached Flt at Moascar designated as No. 30 Sqn, although this date was not notified to the unit until 31/7/15
3/15		Longhorn (11/15)	
3/15		Shorthorn (10/16)	
3/15		BE2c (2/18)	
5/8/15			Air unit personnel in Mesopotamia gazetted to the RFC. This unit was using types above, plus see below
8/15		Caudron GIII (11/15)	
8/15		Martinsyde S1 (11/15)	
7/11/15			No.30 Sqn organized with HQ and B Flt (a reinforcement draft which had arrived 4/11)

Month/Yr	Location	Aircraft type	Remarks
			at Basra, and A Flt (the original air unit personnel) deployed forward at Aziziya where it was joined by by B Flt on 9/11 and detached a section to Lajj
26/11/15			Flt in Egypt relieved by A Flt, No.14 Sqn and began to move to Basra
28/11/15	Kut al Imara		
7/12/15	Ali Gharbi		
27/12/15			Element from Egypt arrived to become C Flt remaining at Basra until 30/4/16
6/1/16	Musandeg		
10/1/16	Sheikh Saad		
16/1/16	Ora		
28/2/16	RNAS unit joined No.30 Sqn and remained until 29/6/16 flying	BE2c Short 827 Voisin LA.S and Henry Farman F27	
1/4/16	Camp Wadi		
6/5/16	Sheikh Saad		
	Flts @ Basra, Arab Village		Dets Zobeir, Barjisayah
6/16		Voisin LAS (11/16)	
7/16		Henri Farman F27 (5/17)	
9/16		Martinsyde G100 (11/17)	
9/10/16	Arab Village		
			Flt @ Sinn Abtar Det Nasiryah
26/2/17	Shumran		Det Nasiryah
2/3/17	Sheikh Jaad		Det Nasiryah
3/3/17	Azizya		Det Nasiryah
5/3/17	Zeur		Det Nasiryah
8/3/17	Bustan		Flt @ Bawi det Nasiryah
11/3/17	Baghdad		Flts @ Bawi, Kazirin Baquba, Fort Kermea Det Nasiryah
7/4/17	Fort Kermea		Flts @ Sindiya,
20/4/17	Barura		Flt @ Baghdad
4/17		Bristol Scout (10/17)	
4/5/17	Baghdad		Dets Sindiya, Jadida, Baquba
5/17		BE2e (4/19)	
9/17		SPAD SVII (5/18)	
13/9/17	Baquba		Flts @ Falluja, Madhij,
18/10/17	Shahraban		Flts @ Baquba, Falluja
25/10/17	Baquba		Flt @ Falluja
10/17		RE8 (4/19)	
11/17		Vickers FB19 Mk II (11/17)	
2/12/17	Qalat Mufti		Flt @ Falluja
8/12/17	Baquba		Flts @ Falluja,Ramadi,

Month/Yr	Location	Aircraft type	Remarks
12/17		DH4 (1/18)	
1/18		Martinsyde G100 (4/18)	
1/3/18	Qubba		Flts @ Ramadi, Hit
5/4/18	Baquba		Flts @ Ramadi, Kifri, Hit dets Hamadan, Tuz Khurmatli
18/9/18	Kifri	Martinsyde G100 (2/19)	Flt at Baquba dets Hamadan and Zinjan

No. 31 SQUADRON   MOTTO: In caelum indicum primus (First into Indian skies)

Month/Yr	Location	Aircraft type	Remarks
11/10/15	A Flt F @ South Farnborough	from No.1 RAS	
11/15		BE2c (2/20)	
27/11/15	En route to India		
29/12/15	Nowshera		
18/1/16	'B' Flight F @ Gosport from No.22 Sqn		
1/3/16	'A' and 'B' Flights to Risalpur		
4/16	'A' Flt to Murree		
10/5/16	'C' Flight F @ Gosport from Home Defence Brigade		
4/7/16	'C' Flt to Murree		
29/7/16	'B' Flt to Murree		
5/10/16	Risalpur		
3/17		Henry Farman F27 (1918)	
10/17		BE2e (2/20)	Dets Bannu, Tank, Khanpur Dera,Ghazi Khan, Lahore
6/19		Bristol F2b Fighter (4/31)	Dets Bannu, Tank,Kohat

No. 32 SQUADRON   MOTTO: Adeste comites (Rally round comrades)

Month/Yr	Location	Aircraft type	Remarks
12/1/16	F @ Netheravon		Nucleus from No.21 Sqn
1/16		Henry Farman F20 (5/16)	
1/16		Vickers FB5 (5/16)	
5/16		Vickers ES1 (7/16)	
2/16		DH2 (7/17)	
28/5/16	St Omer		
4/6/16	Auchel		
7/6/16	Treizennes		
21/7/16	Vert Galand		
25/10/16	Léalvillers		
5/17		DH5 (3/18)	
3/7/17	Abeele		
8/7/17	Droglandt		
12/17		SE5a (3/19)	
5/3/18	Bailleul		
27/3/18	Belleville Farm		
29/3/18	Beauvois		
3/6/18	Fouquerolles		
21/6/18	Ruisseauville		
18/7/18	Touquin		

Month/Yr	Location	Aircraft type	Remarks
3/8/18	La Bellevue		
27/10/18	Pronville		
1/11/18	La Brayelle	SE5a (3/19)	

No. 33 SQUADRON   MOTTO: Loyalty

Month/Yr	Location	Aircraft type	Remarks
12/1/16	F @ Filton		Nucleus from No.20 Sqn
1/16		BE2c (6/17)	
29/3/16	Tadcaster		Dets York (Kavesmire), Bramham Moor, Coal Ashton, Beverley
6/16		BE12 (6/17)	
7/16		Bristol Scout (11/16)	
310/16	Gainsborough		Dets Scampton, Kirton-in-Lindsey, Elsham
1/17		BE2e (9/17)	
6/17		BE12a (9/17)	
6/17		FE2b (8/18)	
6/17		FE2d (8/18)	
12/6/17	Kirton-in-Lindsey		Dets Scampton, Elsham
6/18		Bristol F2b Fighter (8/18)	
8/18		Avro 504K (6/19)	

No. 34 SQUADRON   MOTTO: Lupus vult, lupus volat (Wolf wishes, wolf flies)

Month/Yr	Location	Aircraft type	Remarks
12/1/16	F @ Castle Bromwich	Nucleus from No.19 Sqn.	
2/16		Caudron GIII (1916)	
2/16		BE2c (1/17)	
2/16		BE2e (1/17)	
15/6/16	Lilbourne		
10/7/16	Allonville		
12/16		BE2f (2/17)	
12/16		BE2g (2/17)	
1/17		RE8 (5/19)	
1/2/17	Villers-Bretonneux		
18/4/17	Estrées-en-Chaussée		
16/5/17	Nurlu		
26/5/17	Villers-Bretonneux		
10/6/17	Estrées-en-Chaussée		
29/6/17	Bray-Dunes		
1/11/17	Candas		
13/11/17	Milan		
18/11/17	Ghedi		
22/11/17	Verona		
28/11/17	Grossa		
3/12/17	Istrana		Det Marcon
30/3/18	Villaverla		
4/18		Bristol F2b Fighter (7/18)	
23/10/18	San Luca		

No. 35 SQUADRON   MOTTO: Uno animo agimus (We act with one accord)

Month/Yr	Location	Aircraft type	Remarks
1/2/16	F @ Thetford		Nucleus from No.9 RS
2/16		BE2c (4/16)	
2/16		FE2b (12/16)	

Month/Yr	Location	Aircraft type	Remarks
2/16		Vickers FB5 (12/16)	
4/16		DH2 (6/16)	
4/16		Henry Farman F20 (6/16)	
16/6/16	Narborough		
10/16		AW FK8 (1/19)	
26/1/17	St Omer		
4/2/17	St-André-aux Bois		
5/4/17	Savy		
13/5/17	Villers-Bretonneux		
23/5/17	Mons-en-Chaussée		
13/7/17	Savy		
19/8/17	La Gorgue		
5/10/17	La Lovie		
17/10/17	Bruay		
7/11/17	Estrées-en-Chaussée		
2/18		Bristol F2b Fighter (7/18)	
22/3/18	Chipilly		
24/3/18	Poulainville		
28/3/18	Abbeville		
5/4/18	Poulainville		
2/5/18	Flesselles		
7/9/18	Suzanne		
15/9/18	Moislains		
9/18		Bristol F2b Fighter (1/19)	
6/10/18	Longavesnes		
17/10/18	Elincourt		
10/11/18	Flaumont		
11/11/18	to Grand Fayt		

No. 36 SQUADRON   MOTTO: Rajawali raja langit (Eagle king of the sky)

Month/Yr	Location	Aircraft type	Remarks
1/2/16	F @ Cramlington		From HD Flt
2/16		BE2c (6/17)	
2/16		Bristol Scout (7/16)	
5/16		BE12 (8/17)	Dets Seaton Carew & Ashington, Hylton
12/10/16	Newcastle		Dets Seaton Carew & Ashington, Hylton
12/16		BE2e (8/17)	
6/17		FE2b (8/18)	
9/17		FE2d (8/18)	
4/18		Pup (11/18)	
4/18		Bristol F2b Fighter (6/19)	
1/7/18	Hylton/Usworth	Bristol F2b	Dets Seaton Carew & Ashington

No. 37 SQUADRON   MOTTO: Wise without eyes

Month/Yr	Location	Aircraft type	Remarks
15/4/16	F @ Norwich		Nucleus from No.9 RS
16/4/16	Orfordness		
20/5/16	DB – absorbed by Experimental Establishment		
15/9/16	RF @ Woodford Green		Nucleus from No.39 Sqn
29/9/16	Woodham Mortimer		Dets Goldhanger, Stow Maries, Rochford

Month/Yr	Location	Aircraft type	Remarks
9/16		BE2d (2/18)	
9/16		BE12 (5/18)	
12/16		BE2e (4/18)	
12/16		BE12a (5/18)	
5/17		1½ Strutter (8/17)	
6/17		Pup (7/17)	
6/17		RE7 (10/17)	
12/17		BE12b (5/18)	
5/18		SE5a (7/18)	
22/6/18	Stow Maries		Det Goldhanger
7/18		Camel (7/19)	

No. 38 SQUADRON   MOTTO: Anter lucem (Before the dawn)

Month/Yr	Location	Aircraft type	Remarks
1/4/16	F @ Thetford		Nucleus from No.12 RS
22/5/16	DB – redesignated as No.25 RS		
14/7/16	RF @ Castle Bromwich		Nucleus from No.54 Sqn
7/16		BE12 (7/17)	
1/10/16	Melton Mowbray		Dets Stamford, Leadenham & Buckminster
11/16		BE2e (9/17)	
11/16		FE2b (1/19)	
7/17		FE2d (4/18)	
25/5/18	Buckminster		Dets Leadenham & Stamford
31/5/18		Capelle – depot remained at Buckminster until 14/8/18 became No.90 Sqn	
24/8/18	Beauregard		
29/9/18	St-Pol		
26/10/18	Harlebeck	FE2b (1/19)	

No. 39 SQUADRON   MOTTO: Die Noctuque (By day and night)

Month/Yr	Location	Aircraft type	Remarks
15/4/16	F @ Hounslow		From elements of No.19 RS
4/16	BE2c (11/17)		dets Suttons Farm, Hainault Farm
4/16		Bristol Scout (6/16)	
30/6/16	Woodford Green		Dets Suttons Farm, Hainault, Weald Basset, Gosport & Biggin Hill
6/16		BE12 (12/17)	
12/16		BE12a (12/17)	
12/16		BE2e (1/18)	
4/17		Nieuport 20 (6/17)	
5/17		AW FK 8 (7/17)	
6/17		SE 5 (8/17)	
7/17		Camel (8/17)	
12/17		Bristol F2b Fighter (11/18)	
9/12/17	North Weald		

No. 40 SQUADRON   MOTTO: Hostem coelo expellere (To drive the enemy from the sky)

Month/Yr	Location	Aircraft type	Remarks
26/2/16	F @ Gosport		Nucleus from No.23 Sqn
2/16		BE2c (8/16)	
2/16		Avro 504 (8/16)	
8/16		FE8 (3/17)	

Month/Yr	Location	Aircraft type	Remarks
19/8/16	St Omer		
25/8/16	Treizennes		
3/17		Nieuport 17 (10/17)	
25/4/17	Auchel		
29/4/17	Bruay		
5/17		Nieuport 23 (10/17)	
8/17		Nieuport 24 (8/17)	
10/17		SE5 (1918)	
10/17		SE5a (2/19)	
4/6/18	Bryas		
24/10/18	Aniche		

No. 41 SQUADRON   MOTTO: Seek and Destroy

Month/Yr	Location	Aircraft type	Remarks
15/4/16	F @ Gosport (Fort Rowner)		Nucleus from No.28Sqn
22/5/16	DB – renumbered as No.27 RS		
14/7/16	RF @ Gosport (Fort Rowner)	Nucleus from No.27 RS	
7/16		Vickers FB5 (10/16)	
7/16		DH2 (10/16)	
9/16		FE8 (7/17)	
15/10/16	St Omer		
21/10/16	Abeele		
24/5/17	Hondschoote		
15/6/17	Abeele		
3/7/17	Léalvillers		
7/17		DH5 (11/17)	
11/17		SE5a (2/19)	
22/3/18	Marieux		
27/3/18	Fienvillers		
29/3/18	Alquines		
9/4/18	Savy		
11/4/18	Serny		
19/5/18	Estrée – Blanche		
1/6/18	Conteville		
14/8/18	St Omer		
20/9/18	Droglandt		
23/10/18	Halluin		

No. 42 SQUADRON   MOTTO: Fortiter in re (Bravely in action)

Month/Yr	Location	Aircraft type	Remarks
26/2/16	F @ Netheravon		Nucleus from No.19 Sqn
1/4/16	Filton		
4/16		BE2d (8/16)	
4/16		BE2e (4/17)	
8/8/16	St Omer		
15/8/16	Bailleul (Town Ground)		
1/9/16	La Gorgue		
8/11/16	Bailleul (Town Ground)		
4/17		RE8 (2/19)	Det Abeele
16/11/17	Fienvillers		
16/11/17	Candas		
1/12/17	Padua		
2/12/17	San Pelagio		
7/12/17	Istrana		

Month/Yr	Location	Aircraft type	Remarks
17/12/17	Grossa		Dets Limbraga, San Luca
19/2/18	San Luca		
10/3/18	Poggio Renatico		
18/3/18	Fienvillers		
22/3/18	Chocques		
9/4/18	Treizennes		
25/4/18	Rely		
13/10/18	Chocques		
22/10/18	Ascq		

No. 43 SQUADRON   MOTTO: Gloria finis (Glory in the end)

Month/Yr	Location	Aircraft type	Remarks
15/4/16	F @ Montrose		Nucleus from No.18 RS
19/4/16	Stirling		
5/16		AW FK 3 (8/16)	
6/16		BE2c (8/16)	
6/16		Avro 504 (8/16)	
30/8/16	Netheravon		
8/16		Bristol Scout (12/16)	
11/16		BE2c (11/16)	
12/16		1½ Strutter (9/17)	
9/12/16	Northolt		
17/1/17	St Omer		
25/1/17	Treizennes		
30/5/17	Lozinghem		
9/17		Camel (10/18)	
15/1/18	La Gorgue		
22/3/18	Avesnes-le-Comte		
3/6/18	Fouquerolles		
21/6/18	Estrée-Blanche		
14/7/18	Touquin		
2/8/18	Fienvillers		
8/18		Snipe (9/19)	
6/10/18	Senlis-le-Sec		
31/10/18	Bouvincourt		

No. 44 SQUADRON   MOTTO: Fulmina regis justa (The King's thunderbolts are righteous)

Month/Yr	Location	Aircraft type	Remarks
15/4/16	F @ Catterick		Nucleus from No.6 RS
18/4/16	Turnhouse		
22/5/16		DB – redesignated as No.26 RS	
24/7/17	RF @ Hainault Farm		Nucleus from No.39 Sqn
7/17		1½ Strutter (9/17)	
		Camel (6/19)	

No. 45 SQUADRON   MOTTO: Per Ardue surge (Through difficulties I arise

Month/Yr	Location	Aircraft type	Remarks
1/3/16	F @ Gosport (Fort Grange)		Nucleus from No.22 Sqn
3/16		Avro 504 (4/16)	
3/16		Martinsyde S1 (9/16)	
3/16		BE2c (9/16)	
3/16		Bristol Scout (9/16)	
4/16		FE2b (9/16)	

Month/Yr	Location	Aircraft type	Remarks
3/5/16	Thetford		
21/5/16	Sedgeford		
5/16		Henry Farman F20 (9/16)	
9/16		1½ Strutter (8/17)	
12/10/16	St Omer		
15/10/16	Fienvillers		
4/12/16	Ste-Marie-Cappel		
4/17		Nieuport 12 (5/17)	
4/17		Nieuport 10 (5/17)	
7/17		Camel (1/19)	
16/11/17	Fienvillers		
16/12/17	Candas		
18/12/17	Padua		
18/12/17	San Pelagio		
26/12/17	Istrana		
17/3/18	Grossa		
22/9/18	Bettoncourt		
10/18		Snipe (1/19)	

No. 46 SQUADRON   MOTTO: We rise to conquer

Month/Yr	Location	Aircraft type	Remarks
19/4/16	F @ Brooklands		Nucleus from No.2 RS
20/4/16	Wyton		
4/16		BE2c (9/16)	
1917		BE2e (9/16)	
9/16		Nieuport 12 (4/17)	
20/10/16	St Omer		
26/10/16	Droglandt		
1/17		Nieuport 20 (4/17)	
25/4/17	Boisdinghem		
4/17		Pup (11/17)	
12/5/17	La Gorgue		
6/7/17	Bruay		
10/7/17	Suttons Farm		
30/8/17	Ste-Marie-Cappel		
7/9/17	Filescamp Farm		
11/17		Camel (2/19)	
16/5/18	Liettres		
17/6/18	Serny		
14/8/18	Poulainville		
8/9/18	Cappy		
6/10/18	Athies		
27/10/18	Busigny		

No. 47 SQUADRON   MOTTO: Nili nomen roboris omen (The name of the Nile is an omen of our strength)

Month/Yr	Location	Aircraft type	Remarks
1/3/16	F @ Beverley		
3/16		BE2c (8/16)	
3/16		AW FK3 (9/16)	
6/16		Bristol Scout (7/16)	
5/9/16	En route Salonika		
20/9/16	Mikra Bay		
10/16		BE12 (4/18)	Flt @ Yanesh

Month/Yr	Location	Aircraft type	Remarks
2/17		DH2 (1/18)	
2/17		AW FK3 (7/18)	
6/17		Vickers FB19 MkII (4/18)	
9/17		BE12a (2/18)	
10/17		BE2e (4/18)	
27/10/17	Yanesh		Flts @ Mikra Bay, Kukush, Snevche, Hadzi, Junas, Kirec, Kalabac, Hajdarli, Amberkoj Dets Thasos, Florina, Mudros, Gmuldjina, Dedeagatch
11/17		SE5a (4/18)	
2/18		Bristol MIC (5/18)	
3/18		AW FK8 (1/19)	
8/18		DH9 (10/19)	

No. 48 SQUADRON   MOTTO: Forte et Fidele

Month/Yr	Location	Aircraft type	Remarks
15/4/16	F @ Netheravon		Nucleus from No.7 RS used various aircraft
8/6/16	Rendcomb		
3/17		Bristol F2a Fighter (7/17)	
8/3/17	La Bellevue		
5/17		Bristol F2a Fighter (5/19)	
10/7/17	Bray-Dunes		
15/9/17	Leffrinckhoucke		
22/12/17	Flez		
22/3/18	Champien		
24/3/18	Bertangles		
28/3/18	Conteville		
3/4/18	Bertangles		
26/8/18	Boisdinghem		
30/9/18	Ste-Marie-Cappel		
29/10/18	Reckem		

No. 49 SQUADRON   MOTTO: Cave Canem (Beware of the dog)

Month/Yr	Location	Aircraft type	Remarks
15/4/16	F @ Swingate Down		Nucleus from No.13 RS
4/16		BE2c (11/17)	
4/16		Avro 504 (11/17)	
12/16		RE7 (11/17)	
4/17		Martinsyde G100 (11/17)	
4/17		DH4 (4/18)	
12/11/17	La Bellevue		
26/3/18	Les Eauvis		
29/3/18	Boisdinghem		
30/3/18	Petite Synthe		
4/18		DH9 (7/19)	
3/5/18	Conteville		
2/6/18	Fourneuil		
21/6/18	Beauvois		
15/7/18	Rozay-en-Brie		
4/8/18	Beauvois		
29/10/18	Villers-lès-Cagnicourt		

No. 50 SQUADRON   MOTTO: From defence to attack

Month/Yr	Location	Aircraft type	Remarks
15/5/16	F @ Swingate Down		Nucleus from No.20 RS
5/16		BE2c (9/17)	
5/16		BE12 (5/18)	
6/16		Vickers ES 1 (7/17)	
23/10/16	Harrietsham		Dets Detling, Bekesbourne Throwley
12/16		BE12a (8/17)	
12/16		BE2e (2/18)	
3/17		Bristol M.1B (3/17)	
5/17		RE8 (6/17)	
5/17		AW FK8 (1/18)	
6/17		Pup (7/17)	
1/18		BE12b (6/18)	
5/3/18	Bekesbourne		
5/18		SE5a (7/18)	
7/18		Camel (6/19)	

No. 51 SQUADRON   MOTTO: Swift and sure

Month/Yr	Location	Aircraft type	Remarks
15/5/16	F @ Norwich		Nucleus from No.9 RS
5/16		BE2c (1/17)	
5/16		BE12 (1/17)	
1/6/16	Thetford		
23/9/16	Hingham		Dets Harling Road, Mattishal Narborough
10/16		FE2b (11/18)	
12/16		BE2e (3/17)	
7/8/17	Marham		Dets Mattishal, Tydd St Mary
1918		Martinsyde G100 (1917)	
1/18		BE12b (1918)	
10/18		Camel (6/19)	

No. 52 SQUADRON   MOTTO: Sudore quam sanguine (By sweat other than through blood)

Month/Yr	Location	Aircraft type	Remarks
15/5/16	F @ Hounslow		Nucleus from No.39 Sqn
5/16			BE2c (11/16)
5/16			BE12 (11/16)
11/16			RE8 (2/17)
17/11/16	St Omer		
18/11/16	Bertangles		
15/12/16	Chipilly		
25/1/17	Méaulte		
2/17		BE2f (5/17)	
2/17		BE2g (5/17)	
29/3/17	Longavesnes		
5/17		RE8 (2/19)	
15/6/17	Bray-Dunes		
6/12/17	Izel-le-Hameau		
4/1/18	Lahoussoye		
12/1/18	Matigny		
23/1/18	Golancourt		
22/3/18	Catigny		
24/1/18	Lahoussoye		

Month/Yr	Location	Aircraft type	Remarks
25/1/18	Poulainville		
28/3/18	Abbeville		
3/5/18	Mont-de-Soissons		
5/5/18	Fismes		
27/5/18	Cramaille		
28/5/18	La Ferté		
29/5/19	Trécon		
30/6/18	Auxi-le-Chateau		
4/8/18	Izel-le-Hameau		
24/8/18	Savy		
19/10/18	Bourlon		
21/10/18	Escadoeuvres		
25/10/18	Avesnes-le-Sec		
10/11/18	Aulnoy		

No.53 SQUADRON   MOTTO: United in effort

Month/Yr	Location	Aircraft type	Remarks
15/5/16	F @ Catterick		Nucleus from No.14 RS
5/16		AW FK3 (12/16)	
5/16		Avro 504 (12/16)	
11/12/16	Farnborough		
12/16		BE2e (4/17)	
26/12/16	St Omer		
12/16		BE2g (4/17)	
4/1/17	Bailleul (Town Ground)		
2/17		RE8 (4/19)	
1/2/18	Abeele		
21/2/18	Villeselve		
23/3/18	Allonville		
24/3/18	Fienvillers		
26/3/18	Boisdinghem		
6/4/18	Abeele		
12/4/18	Ste-Marie-Cappel		
12/4/18	Clairmarais South		
21/4/18	Abeele		
21/10/18	Coucou		
6/11/18	Sweveghem	RE8 (4/19)	

No. 54 SQUADRON   MOTTO: Audax omnia perpeti (Boldness to endure anything)

Month/Yr	Location	Aircraft type	Remarks
15/5/16	F @ Castle Bromwich		Nucleus from No.5 RS
5/16		BE2c (12/16)	
6/16		BE12 (6/16)	
7/16		Avro 504 (?)	
22/12/16	London Colney		
12/16		Pup (12/17)	
24/12/16	St Omer		
26/12/16	Bertangles		
11/1/17	Chipilly		
18/4/17	Flez		
18/6/17	Bray-Dunes		
16/7/17	Leffrinckhoucke		
8/9/17	Teteghem		
6/12/17	Bruay		
12/17		Camel (2/19)	

Month/Yr	Location	Aircraft type	Remarks
18/12/17	Lahoussoye		
1/1/18	Flez		
22/3/18	Champien		
24/3/18	Bertangles		
28/3/18	Conteville		
7/4/18	Clairmarais South		
29/4/18	Caffiers		
1/6/18	St Omer		
11/6/18	Vignacourt		
16/11/18	Boisdinghem		
30/6/18	Liettres		
14/7/18	Touquin		
4/8/18	Fienvillers		
25/8/18	Avesnes-le-Comte		
17/10/18	Rely		
24/10/18	Merchin	Camel (2/19)	

No. 55 SQUADRON   MOTTO: Nil nos tremefacit (Nothing shakes us)

Month/Yr	Location	Aircraft type	Remarks
8/6/16	F @ Castle Bromwich		Nucleus from No.34 Sqn No.5 RS
6/16		BE2c (2/17)	
10/6/16	Lilbourne		
6/16		AW FK3 (2/17)	
6/16		Avro 504K (2/17)	
1/17		DH4 (1/19)	
5/3/17	Fienvillers		
31/5/17	Boisdinghem		
11/10/17	Ochey		
7/11/17	Tantonville		
5/6/18	Azelot		

No. 56 SQUADRON   MOTTO: Quid si coelum ruat (What if heaven falls)

Month/Yr	Location	Aircraft type	Remarks
8/6/16	F @ Gosport (Fort Rowner)		Nucleus from No.28 Sqn used various aircraft
14 Jul 16	London Colney		
3/17		SE5 (8/17)	
5/4/17	St Omer		
7/4/17	Vert Galand		
31/5/17	Liettres		
6/17		SE5a (2/19)	
21/6/17	Bekesbourne		Dets Rochford
5/7/17	Estrée-Blanche		
20/11/17	Laviéville		
21/1/18	Baizieux		
25/3/18	Valhereux		
16/1018	Léchelle		
227/10/18	Esnes		
29/10/18	La Targette	SE5a (2/19)	

No. 57 SQUADRON   MOTTO: Corpus non animum muto (I change my body not my spirit)

Month/Yr	Location	Aircraft type	Remarks
8/6/16	F (HQ and A Flt) @ Copmanthorpe		Nucleus from No.33 Sqn B & C Flts @ Tadcaster

Month/Yr	Location	Aircraft type	Remarks
6/16		BE2c (10/16)	
6/17		Avro 504K (10/16)	
20/8/16	Tadcaster		
10/16		FE2d (6/17)	
16/12/16	St-André-aux-Bois		
22/1/17	Fienvillers		
5/17		DH4 (5/19)	
11/6/17	Droglandt		
27/6/17	Boisdinghem		
23/11/17	Ste-Marie-Cappel		
24/3/18	Le Quesnoy		
19/9/18	Vert Galand		
22/10/18	Mory		
9/11/18	Beauvois		

No. 58 SQUADRON   MOTTO: Alis nocturnis (On the wings of the night)

Month/Yr	Location	Aircraft type	Remarks
8/6/16	F @ Cramlington		Nucleus from No.36 Sqn used various aircraft
12/16		BE2b (10/18)	
22/12/17	Dover		
10/1/18	St Omer		
13/1/18	Treizennes		
1/2/18	Claimarais		
25/3/18	Auchel		Det Le Hameau
23/4/18	Fauquembergues		
31/8/18	Alquines		
9/18		HPO/400 (1/20)	
27/10/18	Provin		

No. 59 SQUADRON   MOTTO: Ab uno disce omnes (From one learn all)

Month/Yr	Location	Aircraft type	Remarks
21/6/18	F @ Narborough		Nucleus from No.35 Sqn used various aircraft
2/17		RE8 (8/19)	
13/2/17	St Omer		
23/2/17	La Bellevue		
1/6/17	Le Hameau		
15/6/17	Longavesnes		
15/7/17	Mons-en-Chaussée		
29/10/17	Longavesnes		
30/11/17	Estrée-en- Chaussée		
16/12/17	Courcelles-le-Comte		
22/3/18	Léalvillers		
26/3/18	Fienvillers		
12/4/18	Vert Galand		
4/18		Bristol F2b Fighter(8/19)	
17/9/18	Beugnâtre		
14/8/18	Caudry		

No. 60 SQUADRON   MOTTO: Per ardua ad aethera tendo (I strive through difficulties to the sky)

Month/Yr	Location	Aircraft type	Remarks
15/5/16	F @ Gosport		Nucleus from No.1 RS
5/16		Morane H (5/16)	

Month/Yr	Location	Aircraft type	Remarks
28/5/16	St Omer		
31/5/16	Boisdinghem		
5/16		Morane LA (6/16)	
5/16		Morane BB (8/16)	
5/16		Morane N (9/16)	
16/6/16	Vert Galand		
7/16		Morane I (10/16)	
7/16		Morane V (10/16)	
3/8/16	St André-aux Bois		
8/16		Nieuport 16 (4/17)	
8/16		Nieuport 17 (8/17)	
23/8/16	Le Hameau		
1/9/16	Savy		
18/1/17	Filescamp Farm		
3/17		Nieuport 23 (8/17)	
7/17		SE5 (8/17)	
8/17		SE5a (1/19)	
7/9/17	Ste-Marie-Capelle		
8/3/18	Bailleul		
23/3/18	La Bellevue		
27/3/18	Fienvillers		
12/4/18	Boifles		
17/9/18	Baizieux		
14/10/18	Beugnâtre		
31/10/18	Quiévy		

No. 61 SQUADRON   MOTTO: Per purum tonantes (Thundering through the clear sky)

Month/Yr	Location	Aircraft type	Remarks
5/7/16	F @ Wye		Nucleus from No.20 RS
24/8/16	DB aborbed into No.63 Sqn		
24/7/17	RF @ Rochford		Nucleus from No.37 Sqn
7/17		Pup (1/18)	
12/17		SE5a (7/18)	
6/18		Camel (6/19)	

No. 62 SQUADRON   MOTTO: Inseperato (Unexpectedly)

Month/Yr	Location	Aircraft type	Remarks
28/7/16	F @ Netheravon		Nucleus from No.42 Sqn & No.7 RS
8/8/16	Filton		used various aircraft
5/17		Bristol F2b Fighter (7/19)	
17/7/17	Rendcomb		
23/1/18	St Omer		
30//1/18	Serny		
8/3/18	Cachy		
24/3/18	Remaisnil		
29/3/18	Planques		
7/8/18	Croisette		
26/9/18	La Bellevue		
29/10/18	Villers-lès-Cagnicourt		

No. 63 SQUADRON   MOTTO: Pone nos ad hostem (Follow us to find the enemy)

Month/Yr	Location	Aircraft type	Remarks
5/7/16	F @ Stirling		Nucleus from Nos.43 & 61 Sqns
7/16		DH4 (6/17)	

Month/Yr	Location	Aircraft type	Remarks
10/16		BE12 (5/17)	
10/16		BE2e (12/19)	
10/16		Avro 504K (5/17)	
10/16		AW FK3 (5/17)	
31/10/16	Cramlington		
5/17		RE8 (6/17)	
23/6/17	En route Middle East		
13/8/17	Basra		
8/17		DH4 (4/19)	
8/17		Bristol Scout (2/18)	
9/17		RE8 (2/20)	Det Baghdad
3/9/17	Samarra		
10/17		SPAD SVII (4/18)	
10/17		Martinsyde G100 (4/18)	Dets Akab, Ramadi, Hit, Baquba, Tuz Khurmatli
17/10/18	Tikrit		
10/18		Martinsyde G102 (8/19)	

No. 64 SQUADRON   MOTTO: Tenax propositi (Firmness of purpose)

Month/Yr	Location	Aircraft type	Remarks
1/8/16	F @ Sedgeford		Nucleus from No.45 Squadron
8/16		Henry Farman F20 (6/17)	
8/16		BE2c (12/16)	
8/16		FE2b (6/17)	
6/17		Pup (8/17)	
6/17		Avro 504 (10/17)	
6/17		DH5 (3/18)	
14/10/17	St Omer		
15/10/17	Le Hameau		
1/18		SE5a (2/19)	
24/10/18	Aniche		

No. 65 SQUADRON   MOTTO: Vi et armis (By force of arms)

Month/Yr	Location	Aircraft type	Remarks
1/8/16	F @ Wyton		Nucleus from No.46 Sqn used various aircraft
29/5/17	Wye		
7/17		Camel (2/19)	
24/10/17	La Lovie		
4/1117	La Bailluel (Asylum Ground)		
17/2/18	Poperinghe		
21/3/18	Droglandt		
24/3/18	Clairmarais		
28/3/18	Conteville		
6/4/18	Bertangles		
12/8/18	Cappelle		
16/8/18	Bray-Dunes		
19/9/18	Petite Synthe		
25/10/18	Bisseghem		

No. 66 SQUADRON   MOTTO: Cavete praemonui (Beware, I have given a warning)

Month/Yr	Location	Aircraft type	Remarks
24/6/16	F @ Filton		Nucleus from No.19 Sqn
2/7/16	Netheravon		
7/16		BE2b, 2c & 2d (2/17)	
7/16		BE12 (2/17)	
7/16		Avro 504K (2/17)	
27/7/16	Filton		
2/17		Pup (10/17)	
3/3/17	St Omer		
18/5/17	Vert Galand		
31/5/17	Liettres		
20/6/17	Calais		
6/7/17	Estrée-Blanche		
10/17		Camel (3/19)	
11/11/17	Candas		
22/11/17	Milan		
29/11/17	Verona		
4/12/17	Grossa		
18/2/18	Treviso		
10/3/18	San Pietro-in-Gu		
1/11/18	Arcade		
6/11/18	San Pietro-in-Gu		

No. 67 SQUADRON   MOTTO: No odds too great

Month/Yr	Location	Aircraft type	Remarks
12/9/16	F @ Heliopolis		No.1 Sqn AFC renumbered
9/16		BE2c (11/17)	
9/16		Avro 504K (12/16)	
9/16		BE2e (2/18)	
9/16		Martinsyde G100/102 (2/18)	Dets Suez, Sherika, Qantara
17/12/16	Mustabig		
12/16		Bristol Scout (1917)	
12/1/17	Kilo 143/Ujret et Zol		
26/3/17	Rafah		
15/6/17	Deir el Ballah		
7/17		BE12a (2/18)	
17/9/17	Weli Sheikh Nuran		
10/17		RE8 (2/18)	
13/12/17	Julis		
1/18		Bristol F2b Fighter (2/18)	
6/2/18	DB renumbered No.1 Sqn AFC		

No. 68 SQUADRON   MOTTO: Vzdy Pripraven (Always Ready)

Month/Yr	Location	Aircraft type	Remarks
30/1/17	F @ Harlaxton		
1/17		DH5 (1/18)	
21/9/17	Baizieux		
1/18		SE5a (1/18)	
19/1/18	DB renumbered No.2 Sqn AFC		

No. 69 SQUADRON   MOTTO: With vigilance we serve

Month/Yr	Location	Aircraft type	Remarks
28/12/16	F @ South Carlton		No.2 Sqn AFC renumbered used various aircraft
8/17		RE8 (1/18)	
24/8/17	Lympne		
9/9/17	St Omer		
10/9/17	Savy		
9/11/17	Bailleul (Town Ground)		
19/1/18	DB renumbered as No.3 Sqn AFC		

No. 70 SQUADRON   MOTTO: Usquam (Anywhere)

Month/Yr	Location	Aircraft type	Remarks
22/4/16	F @ South Farnborough		
4/16		1½ Strutter (7/17)	
31//5/16	A Flt to Fienvillers		
3/7/16	B Flt to Fienvillers		
1/8/16	C Flt to Fienvillers		
16/12/16	Auchel		
2/3/17	Vert Galand		
2/4/17	Fienvillers		
14/5/17	Boisdinghem		
6/17		Camel (3/19)	
27/6/17	Liettres		
8/9/17	Poperinghe		
15/3/18	Marieux		
28/3/18	Fienvillers		
16/4/18	Remaisnil		
8/7/18	Boisdinghem		
1/8/18	Esquerdes		
22/9/18	Droglandt		
23/10/18	Menin		

No. 71 SQUADRON   MOTTO: First from the Eyrie

Month/Yr	Location	Aircraft type	Remarks
27/3/17	F Castle Bromwich	Used various A/C	
12//17		Camel (1/18)	
18/12/17	to St Omer		
22/12/17	to Bruay		
19/1/18	DB renumbered as No.4 Sqn AFC		

No. 72 SQUADRON   MOTTO: Swift

Month/Yr	Location	Aircraft type	Remarks
28/6/17	F @ Upavon		Nucleus from A Flt CFS
8/7/17	Netheravon		
7/17		Avro 504 (12/17)	
7/17		Pup (12/17)	
1/11/17	Sedgeford		
25/12/17	En route to persian Gulf		
2/3/18	Basra		
3/18		DH4 (6/18)	
3/18		Bristol M1.C (2/19)	
3/18		SE5a (2/19)	

Month/Yr	Location	Aircraft type	Remarks
3/18	Baghdad		
4/18		SPAD SVII (1/19)	
4/18		Martinsyde G100 (11/18)	Flts @ Mirjana, Samarra Dets Hamadan, Tikrit, Baku, Kazvin, Zinjan

No. 73 SQUADRON   MOTTO: Tutor et Ultor (Protector and avenger)

Month/Yr	Location	Aircraft type	Remarks
2/7/17	F @ Upavon		Nucleus from B Flt CFS used various aircraft
10/7/17	Lilbourne		
11/17		Camel (2/19)	
9/1/18	St Omer		
12/1/18	Liettres		
5/3/18	Champien		
23/3/18	Cachy		
24/3/18	Remaisnil		
30/3/18	Beauvois		
3/6/18	Fouquerolles		
21/6/18	Planques		
14/7/18	Touquin		
4//8/18	La Bellevue		
16/9/18	Foucaucourt		
23/9/18	Estrées-en-Chaussée		
8/10/18	Hervilly		
17/10/18	Malincourt		

No. 74 SQUADRON   MOTTO: I fear no man

Month/Yr	Location	Aircraft type	Remarks
1/7/17	F @ Northolt		Nucleus from No.2 TS used various aircraft
10/7/17	London Colney		
25/3/18	Goldhanger		
3/18		SE5a (2/19)	
30/3/18	St Omer		
2/4/18	Teteghem		
9/4/18	La Lovie		
11/4/18	Clairmarais North		
7/8/18	Clairmarais South		
28/9/18	La Lovie		
3/10/18	Clairmaarais South		
23/10/18	Marcke		
1/11/18	Cuerne		

No. 75 SQUADRON   MOTTO: Ake ake kia kaka (Maori – Forever and ever be strong)

Month/Yr	Location	Aircraft type	Remarks
1/10/16	F @ Tadcaster		Nucleus from No.33 Sqn
10/16		BE2c (9/17)	
12/10/16	Goldhanger		Dets Yelling, Old Weston, Therfield
10/16		BE12 (7/18)	
1/17		BE2e (7/18)	
8/9/18	Elmswell		Dets Harling Road & Hadleigh
9/17		FE2b (10/17)	
1/18		BE12b (7/18)	
7/18		Avro 504K (NF) (1/19)	

No. 76 SQUADRON   MOTTO: Resolute

Month/Yr	Location	Aircraft type	Remarks
15/9/16	F @ Cramlington		Nucleus from No.36 Sqn
9/16		BE2c (1917)	
9/16		BE12 (8/18)	
9/16		DH6 (1917)	
10/10/16	Ripon and Catterick		Dets Copmanthorpe,Helperby
12/16		BE2e (8/18)	
12/16		BE12a (8/18)	
5/17		RE8 (7/18)	
3/18		BE12b (8/18)	
7/18		Bristol F2b Fighter (8/18)	
8/18		Avro 504K (NF) (5/19)	

No. 77 SQUADRON   MOTTO: Esse potius quam videri (To be rather than seen)

Month/Yr	Location	Aircraft type	Remarks
1/10/16	F @ Thetford		Nucleus from No.51 Sqn
16/10/16	Edinburgh		Dets Turnhouse, New Haggerston, Whiteburn Penston
10/16		BE2c (11/18)	
10/16		BE12 (11/18)	
10/16		DH6 (12/16)	
10/16		BE2d (12/16)	
1/17		BE2e (11/18)	
5/17		RE8 (7/18)	
12/17		BE12b (9/18)	
5/18	Penston		Det Whiteburn
9/18		Avro 504K (NF) (6/19)	

No. 78 SQUADRON   MOTTO: Nemo non paratus (Nobody unprepared}

Month/Yr	Location	Aircraft type	Remarks
1/11/16	F @ Newhaven		Dets Telscombe Cliffs
11/16		BE2c (9/17)	
11/16		BE12 (1/18)	
25/12/16	Hove		Dets Talscombe Cliffs Gosport, Chiddingstone Causeway
12/16		BE2e (12/17)	
12/16		BE12a (1/18)	
7/17		SE5 (7/17)	
8/17		1½ Strutter (2/18)	
20/9/17	Suttons Farm		Det Biggin Hill
9/17		FE2d (10/17)	
12/17		BE12b (1/18)	
1/18		Camel (7/19)	
10/18		Snipe (7/19)	

No. 79 SQUADRON   MOTTO: Nil nobis obstare potest (Nothing can stop us)

Month/Yr	Location	Aircraft type	Remarks
1/8/17	F @ Gosport		Nucleus from No.27 TS used various aircraft
8/8/17	Beaulieu		
12/17		Dolphin (7/19)	
20/2/18	St Omer		
22/2/18	Estrée-Blanche		

Month/Yr	Location	Aircraft type	Remarks
5/3/18	Champien		
22/3/18	Cachy		
24/3/18	Beauvois		
16/5/18	Ste-Marie-Cappel		
22/10/18	Reckem		

No. 80 SQUADRON   MOTTO: Strike true

Month/Yr	Location	Aircraft type	Remarks
1/8/17	F @ Thetford		Nucleus from No.36 TS used various aircraft
10/8/17	Montrose		
27/11/17	Beverley		
12/17		Camel (12/18)	
27/1/18	Boisdinghem		
27/2/18	Serny		
5/3/18	Champien		
22/3/18	Cachy		
24/3/18	Remaisnil		
29/3/18	Wamin		
30/3/18	Belleville Farm		
4/4/18	La Bellevue		
3/6/18	Fouquerolles		
21/6/18	Liettres		
14/7/18	Touquin		
4/8/18	Vignacourt		
31/8/18	Allonville		
8/9/18	Assevillers		
8/10/18	Bouvincourt		
27/10/18	Bertry West		
10/11/18	Flaumont		

No. 81 SQUADRON   MOTTO: Non solum nobis (Not for us alone)

Month/Yr	Location	Aircraft type	Remarks
7/1/17	F @ Gosport	Used various aircraft	Nucleus from No.1 RS
15/1/17	Scampton		
4/7/18	DB – merged into No.34 TDS		

No. 82 SQUADRON   MOTTO: Super omnia ubique (Over all things everywhere)

Month/Yr	Location	Aircraft type	Remarks
7/1/17	F @ Doncaster	Used various aircraft	Nucleus from No.15 RS
6/2/17	Beverley		
30/3/17	Waddington		
7/17		AW FK8 (2/19)	
17/11/17	St Omer		
20/11/17	Savy		
22/1/18	Golancourt		
22/3/18	Catigny		
24/3/18	Allonville		
27/3/18	Agenvillers		
7/6/18	Quevauvillers		
15/7/18	Haussimont		
2/8/18	Quelmes		
3/9/18	Droglandt		
20/9/18	Proven		

Month/Yr	Location	Aircraft type	Remarks
22/10/18	Bisseghem		
6/11/18	Menin		

No. 83 SQUADRON   MOTTO: Strike to defend

Month/Yr	Location	Aircraft type	Remarks
7/1/17	F @ Montrose	Used various aircraft	Nucleus from No.18 RS
15/1/17	Spittlegate		
15/9/17	Wyton		
12/12/17	Narborough		
12/17		FE2b (2/19)	
6/3/18	St Omer		
7/3/18	Auchel		
2/5/18	Franqueville		
9/10/18	Lahoussoye		
26/10/18	Estrées-en-Chausée		

No. 84 SQUADRON   MOTTO: Scipiones pungunt (Scorpions sting)

Month/Yr	Location	Aircraft type	Remarks
7/1/17	F @ Beaulieu		Nucleus from No.16 RS
1/17		BE12a (3/17)	
1/17		BE12 (3/17)	
1/17		BE2c (3/17)	
22/3/17	Lilbourne		
3/17		Nieuport 12 (8/17)	
3/17		Curtiss JN 4 (8/17)	
3/17		Avro 504 (8/17)	
3/17		1½ Strutter (8/17)	
8/17		SE5a (8/19)	
23/9/18	Liettres		
12/11/17	Le Hameau		
29/12/17	Flez		
22/3/18	Champien		
23/3/18	Vert Galand		
28/3//18	Conteville		
4/4/18	Bertangles		
8/9/18	As013villers		
8/10/18	Bouvincourt		
25/10/18	Bertry West		

No. 85 SQUADRON   MOTTO: Noctu diuque venamur (We hunt by day and night)

Month/Yr	Location	Aircraft type	Remarks
1/8/17	F @ Upavon	used various aircraft	Nucleus from C Flt CFS
10/8/17	Norwich		
27/11/17	Hounslow		
5/18		SE5a (2/19)	
22/5/18	Marquise		
25/5/18	Petite Synthe		
11/6/18	St Omer		
13/8/18	Bertangles		
5/9/18	Savy		
23/9/18	Foucaucourt		
9/10/18	Estrées-en-Chaussée		
27/10/18	Escaufourt		
9/11/18	Phallempin		

No. 86 SQUADRON   MOTTO: Ad Libertatum volamus (We fly to freedom)

Month/Yr	Location	Aircraft type	Remarks
1/9/17	F @ Shoreham		Nucleus from No.3 TS used various aircraft
17/9/17	Wye		
16/12/17	Northolt		
4/7/18	DB – absorbed by No.30 TDS		

No. 87 SQUADRON   MOTTO: Maxcimus me metuit (The most powerful fear me)

Month/Yr	Location	Aircraft type	Remarks
1/9/17	F @ Upavon	Used various aircraft	Nucleus from D Flt CFS
15/9/17	Sedgeford		
19/12/17	Hounslow		
12/17		Dolphin (2/19)	
24/4/18	St Omer		
27/4/18	Petite Synthe		
27/5/18	Estrées-lès-Crécy		
29/6/18	Rougefay		
19/9/18	Soncamp		
4/11/18	Boussières		

No. 88 SQUADRON   MOTTO: En garde (Be on your guard)

Month/Yr	Location	Aircraft type	Remarks
24/7/17	F @ Gosport	Used various aircraft	Nucleus from No.1 TS
2/8/17	Harling Road		
3/18		Bristol F2b Fighter (8/19)	
2/4/18	Kenley		
16/4/18	Cappelle		
19/7/18	Drionville		
2/8/18	Serny		
21/10/18	Floringhem		
23/10/18	Ascq		
26/10/18	Gondecourt		
28/10/18	Bersée		

No. 89 SQUADRON   MOTTO: Del auxilio Telis meis (By the help of God with my own weapons)

Month/Yr	Location	Aircraft type	Remarks
24/7/17	F @ Catterick	Used various aircraft	Nucleus from No.6 TS
7/8/17	Harling Road		
17/7/18	Upper Heyford		
7/18		SE5a (7/18)	
29/7/18	DB		

No. 90 SQUADRON   MOTTO: Celer (Swift)

Month/Yr	Location	Aircraft type	Remarks
8/10/17	F @ Shawbury	Used various aircraft	Nucleus from No.10 TS
18/10/17	Shotwick		
15/7/18	Brockworth		
7/18		Dolphin (7/18)	
29/7/18	DB		

No. 91 SQUADRON   MOTTO: We seek alone

Month/Yr	Location	Aircraft type	Remarks
1/9/17	F @ Spittlegate		Nucleus from No.11 TS
14/9/17	Chattis Hill		

Month/Yr	Location	Aircraft type	Remarks
15/3/18	Tangmere		
28/8/18	Kenley		
8/18		Dolphin (7/19)	

No. 92 SQUADRON   MOTTO: Aut pugna aut morere (Either fight or die)

Month/Yr	Location	Aircraft type	Remarks
1/9/17	F @ London Colney	Nucleus from No.56 TS	
9/17		Pup (4/18)	
14/9/17	Chattis Hill		
17/3/18	Tangmere		
5/18		SE5a (8/19)	
2/7/18	Bray-Dunes		
19/7/18	Drionville		
2/8/18	Serny		
27/9/18	Proyart		
9/10/18	Estrées-en-Chaussées		
25/10/18	Bertry East		

No. 93 SQUADRON   MOTTO: Ad arma parati (Ready for Battle)

Month/Yr	Location	Aircraft type	Remarks
23/9/17	F @ Croydon	Used various aircraft	Nucleus from No.40 TS
3/10/17	Chattis Hill		
19/3/18	Tangmere		
17/8/18	DB		

No. 94 SQUADRON   MOTTO: Avenge

Month/Yr	Location	Aircraft type	Remarks
30/7/17	F @ Gosport	Used various aircraft	Nucleus from No.55 TS
2/8/17	Harling Road		
27/7/18	Shoreham		
19/8/18	Upper Heyford		
9/18		SE5a (1/19)	
31/10/18	Senlis-le- Sec		

No. 95 SQUADRON   MOTTO: Trans mare exivi (I went out over the sea)

Month/Yr	Location	Aircraft type	Remarks
8/10/17	F @ Ternhill	Used various aircraft	Nucleus from No.43 TS
30/10/17	Shotwick		
4/7/18	DB		
1/10/18	RF @ Kenley	For Buzzard	Nucleus from Nos. 21, 28, 30 and 51 TDSs

No. 96 SQUADRON   MOTTO: Nocturni obambulamus (We prowl by night)

Month/Yr	Location	Aircraft type	Remarks
8/10/17	F @ South Carlton	Used various aircraft	Nucleus from No.45 TS
30/10/17	Shotwick		
4/7/18	DB absorbed by No.51 TDS		
28/9/18	RF @ Wyton		Nucleus from Nos.2,32,38 & 46 TDS
11/18		Salamander (12/18)	

No. 97 SQUADRON   MOTTO: Achieve your aim

Month/Yr	Location	Aircraft type	Remarks
1/12/17	F @ Waddington	Used various aircraft	Nucleus from No.51 TS
21/1/18	Stonehenge		

Month/Yr	Location	Aircraft type	Remarks
31/3/18	Netheravon		
6/18		HPO/400 (3/19)	
3/8/18	Xaffévillers		

No. 98 SQUADRON   MOTTO: Never failing

Month/Yr	Location	Aircraft type	Remarks
15/8/18	F @ Harlaxton	Used various aircraft	Nucleus from No.44 TS
30/8/17	Old Sarum		
2/18		DH9 (3/19)	
1/3/18	Lympne		
1/4/18	St Omer		
3/4/18	Clairmarais		
12/4/18	Alquines		
25/5/18	Coudekerque		
6/6/18	Ruisseauville		
21/6/18	Drionville		
13/7/18	Chailly		
3/8/18	Blangermont		
27/10/18	Abscon		

No. 99 SQUADRON   MOTTO: Quisque tenax (Each tenacious)

Month/Yr	Location	Aircraft type	Remarks
15/8/17	F @ Yatesbury	Used various aircraft	Nucleus from No.13 TS
30/8/17	Ford Farm		
3/18		DH9 (11/18)	
23/4/18	St Omer		
4/5/18	Tantonville		
5/6/18	Azelot		
9/18		DH9A (3/20)	

No. 100 SQUADRON   MOTTO: Sarang tebuan jangan dijolok (Malay – Never stir up a hornet's nest)

Month/Yr	Location	Aircraft type	Remarks
11/2/17	F @ Hingham	Used various aircraft	Nucleus from No.51 Sqn
23/2/17	Farnborough		
2/17		BE2c (1/18)	
21/3/17	St André-aux-Bois		
3/17		FE2b (8/18)	
1/4/17	Izel-le-Hameau		
4/17		BE2e (8/17)	
16/5/17	Treizennes		
5/10/17	Ochey		
1/18		FE2c (8/18)	
3/4/18	Villesneux		
9/5/18	Ochey		
10/8/18	Xaffévillers		
8/18		HPO/400 (9/19)	

No. 101 SQUADRON   MOTTO: Mens agitat (Mind over matter)

Month/Yr	Location	Aircraft type	Remarks
12/7/17	F @ Farnborough		
25/7/17	St-André-aux-Bois		
7/17		FE2b (3/19)	
7/17		BE12 (3/18)	

Month/Yr	Location	Aircraft type	Remarks
7/17		BE12a (3/18)	
7/8/17	Le Hameau		
31/8/17	Clairmarais South		
2/2/18	Auchel		
16/2/18	Catigny		
24/3/18	Fienvillers		
25/3/18	Haute Vissée		
7/4/18	Famechon		
8/9/18	Lahoussoye		
8/10/18	Proyart East		
25/10/18	Hancourt		

No. 102 SQUADRON   MOTTO: Tentate et perficite (Attempt and Achieve)

Month/Yr	Location	Aircraft type	Remarks
9/8/17	F @ Hingham		
24/9/17	St-André-aux-Bois		
9/17		FE2b (3/19)	
28/9/17	Le Hameau		
3/10/17	Treizennes		
5/3/18	Le Hameau		
10/4/18	Surcamps		
19/9/18	Famechon		
19/10/18	Hurtebise Farm		
23/10/18	La Targette		
27/10/18	Bévillers		

No. 103 SQUADRON   MOTTO: Nili me tangere (Touch me not)

Month/Yr	Location	Aircraft type	Remarks
1/9/17	F @ Beaulieu	Used various aircraft	Nucleus from No.16 TS
8/9/17	Old Sarum		
3/18		DH9 (3/19)	
12/5/18	Serny		
3/6/18	Fourneuil		
21/6/18	Serny		
21/10/18	Floringhem		
26/10/18	Ronchin		

No. 104 SQUADRON   MOTTO: Strike hard

Month/Yr	Location	Aircraft type	Remarks
1/9/17	F @ Wyton	Used various aircraft	Nucleus from No.20 TS
16/9/17	Andover		
4/18		DH9 (2/19)	
19/5/18	St Omer		
20/5/18	Azelot		

No. 105 SQUADRON   MOTTO: Fortis in proeliis (Valiant in battles)

Month/Yr	Location	Aircraft type	Remarks
23/9/17	F @ Waddington	Used various aircraft	Nucleus from No.51 TS
3/10/17	Andover		
4/18		RE8 (12/18)	
16/5/18	Ayr		
19/5/18	Omagh		Dets Oranmore & Castlebar

No. 106 SQUADRON   MOTTO: Pro libertate (For freedom)

Month/Yr	Location	Aircraft type	Remarks
23/9/17	F @ Spittlegate		Nucleus from No. 49 TS
3/10/17	Andover		
5/18		RE8 (1/19)	
21/5/18	Ayr		
30/5/18	Fermoy		

No. 107 SQUADRON   MOTTO: Nous y serons (We shall be there)

Month/Yr	Location	Aircraft type	Remarks
8/10/17	F @ Catterick	Used various aircraft	Nucleus from No.46 TS
18/10/17	Stonehenge		
2/12/17	Lake Down		
5/18		DH9 (3/19)	
5/6/18	Le Quesnoy		
25/6/18	Drionville		
15/7/18	Chailly		
3/8/18	Ecoivres		
26/10/18	Moislains		

No. 108 SQUADRON   MOTTO: Viribus contractis (With gathering strength)

Month/Yr	Location	Aircraft type	Remarks
1/11/17	F @ Montrose	Used various aircraft	Nucleus from No.52 TS
12/11/17	Stonehenge		
2/12/17	Lake Down		
16/6/18	Kenley		
6/18		DH9 (2/19)	
22/7/18	Cappelle		
27/10/18	Bisseghem		

No. 109 SQUADRON   MOTTO: Primi histati (The first of the legion)

Month/Yr	Location	Aircraft type	Remarks
1/11/17	F @ South Carlton	Used various aircraft	Nucleus from No.61 TS
12/11/17	Stonehenge		
2/12/17	Lake Down		
7/18		DH9 (8/18)	
19/8/18	DB		

No. 110 SQUADRON   MOTTO: Nec timeo nec sperno (I neither fear nor despise)

Month/Yr	Location	Aircraft type	Remarks
1/11/17	Rendcomb	Used various aircraft	Nucleus from No.38 TS
12/11/17	Dover (Swingate Down)		
26/11/17	Sedgeford		
15/6/18	Kenley		
8/18		DH9A (8/19)	
1/9/18	Bettoncourt		

No. 111 SQUADRON   MOTTO: Adstantes (Standing by)

Month/Yr	Location	Aircraft type	Remarks
1/8/17	F @ Deir-el-Ballah		Nucleus from No.14 Sqn
8/17		Bristol Scout (10/17)	
8//17		Bristol M.1B (1/18)	
8/17		DH2 (12/17)	
8/17		Vickers FB19 MkII (1/18)	
1/12/17	Julis		

Month/Yr	Location	Aircraft type	Remarks
1/18		Nieuport 17, 23 & 24 (7/18)	Det Sarona
30/3/18	Ramleh		Det Sarona
18/10/18	Qantara		

No. 112 SQUADRON   MOTTO: Swift in destruction

Month/Yr	Location	Aircraft type	Remarks
25/7/17	F @ Detling		From 'B' Flight No.50 Sqn
30/7/17	Throwley		
7/17		Pup (3/18)	
3/18		Camel (6/19)	

No. 113 SQUADRON   MOTTO: Velox et vindex (Swift to vengeance)

Month/Yr	Location	Aircraft type	Remarks
1/8/17	F @ Ismailia		
8/17		BE2e (4/18)	
9/17		RE8 (2/20)	
10/10/17	Sheikh Nuran		
23/11/17	Julis		Det Khirbet Deiren
17/1/18	Sarona		
2/18		Nieuport 17,23 & 24 (10/18)	
			Dets El Affule & Haifa

No. 114 SQUADRON   MOTTO: With speed I strike

Month/Yr	Location	Aircraft type	Remarks
22/9/17	F @ Lahore		From two flights of No.31 Sqn
9/17		BE2c (10/19)	
9/17		Henry Farman F27 (1918)	
9/17		BE2e (4/20)	Dets Quetta, Aden
22/7/18	Quetta		
5/11/18	Lahore		det Jubbulpore

No. 115 SQUADRON   MOTTO: Despite the elements

Month/Yr	Location	Aircraft type	Remarks
1/12/17	F @ Catterick	Used various aircraft	
15/4/18	Netheravon		
7/18		HPO/400 (3/19)	
17/7/18	Castle Bromwich		
29/8/18	Roville-aux-Chênes		
11/11/18	St-Inglevert		

No. 116 SQUADRON   MOTTO: Precision in defence

Month/Yr	Location	Aircraft type	Remarks
1/12/17	F @ Andover	used various aircraft	
31/3/18	Netheravon		
27/7/18	Kenley		
8/18		HPO/400 (11/18)	
28/9/18	Feltham		

No. 117 SQUADRON   MOTTO: It shall be done

Month/Yr	Location	Aircraft type	Remarks
1/1/18	F @ Waddington	Used various aircraft	
3/4/18	Hucknall		
15/7/18	Norwich		
10/18		DH9 (10/19)	

No. 118 SQUADRON   MOTTO: Occido redeoque (kill and return)

Month/Yr	Location	Aircraft type	Remarks
1/18	F @ Catterick	(for HPO/400)	
		Used various aircraft	
15/4/18	Netheravon		
7/8/18	Bicester		
7/9/18	DB		

No. 119 SQUADRON   MOTTO: By night by day

Month/Yr	Location	Aircraft type	Remarks
1/1/18	F @ Andover	Used various aircraft	
1/3/18	Duxford		
19/8/18	Thetford		
26/9/18	Wyton		
9/18		DH9 (12/18)	

No. 120 SQUADRON   MOTTO: Endurance

Month/Yr	Location	Aircraft type	Remarks
1/1/18	F @ Cramlington	Used various aircraft	
3/8/18	Bracebridge Heath		

No.121 SQUADRON   MOTTO: For liberty

Month/Yr	Location	Aircraft type	Remarks
1/1/18	F @ Narborough	(for DH9) used various aircraft	
10/8/18	Filton		
17/8/18	DB		

No. 122 SQUADRON   MOTTO: Victuri volamus (We fly to conquer)

Month/Yr	Location	Aircraft type	Remarks
1/1/18	F @ Sedgford	(for DH9) used various aircraft	
17/8/18	DB		
29/10/18	RF @ Upper Heyford	(for DH10)	Nucleus from Nos.9, 10, 11 and 15 TDSs

No. 123 SQUADRON   MOTTO: Swift to strike

Month/Yr	Location	Aircraft type	Remarks
1/2/18	F @ Waddington	(for DH9) used various aircraft	
1/3/18	Duxford		
17/8/18	DB		

No. 124 SQUADRON   MOTTO: Danger is our opportunity

Month/Yr	Location	Aircraft type	Remarks
1/2/18	F @ Old Sarum	(for DH9) used various aircraft	
1/3/18	Fowlmere		
17/8/18	DB		

No. 125 SQUADRON   MOTTO: Nunquam demandi (Never to be tamed)

Month/Yr	Location	Aircraft type	Remarks
1/2/18	F @ Old Sarum	(for DH9) used various aircraft	
1/3/18	Fowlmere		
17/8/18	DB		

No. 126 SQUADRON   MOTTO: Foremost in attack

Month/Yr	Location	Aircraft type	Remarks
1/2/18	F @ Old Sarum	(for DH9) used various aircraft	
1/3/18	Fowlmere		
17/8/18	DB		

No. 127 SQUADRON   MOTTO: Eothen (Out of the East)

Month/Yr	Location	Aircraft type	Remarks
1/2/18	F @ Catterick	(for DH9) used various aircraft	
4/7/18	DB		absorbed by No.49 TDS

No. 128 SQUADRON   MOTTO: Fulminus Instar (Like a thunderbolt)

Month/Yr	Location	Aircraft type	Remarks
1/2/18	F @ Thetford	(for DH9) used various aircraft	
4/7/18	DB		

No. 129 SQUADRON   MOTTO: I will defend the Right

Month/Yr	Location	Aircraft type	Remarks
1/3/18	F @ Duxford	(for DH9) used various aircraft	
4/7/18	DB		

No. 130 SQUADRON   MOTTO: Strong to Serve

Month/Yr	Location	Aircraft type	Remarks
1/3/18	F @ Wyton	(for DH9) used various aircraft	
1/4/18	Hucknall		
4/7/18	DB		

No. 131 SQUADRON   MOTTO: Invicta (Unconquered)

Month/Yr	Location	Aircraft type	Remarks
15/3/18	F @ Shawbury	(for DH9) used various aircaft	
17/8/18	DB		

No. 132 SQUADRON   MOTTO: Cave leopardum (Beware the leopard)

Month/Yr	Location	Aircraft type	Remarks
1/3/18	F @ Ternhill	(for HPO/400) used various aircraft	
19/8/18	Castle Bromwich		

No. 133 SQUADRON   MOTTO: Let us to the battle

Month/Yr	Location	Aircraft type	Remarks
1/3/18	F @ Ternhill	(for HPO/400) used various aircraft	
4/7/18	DB		

No. 134 SQUADRON   MOTTO: Per ardua volabimus (We shall fly through hardships)

Month/Yr	Location	Aircraft type	Remarks
1/3/18	F @ Ternhill	(for HPO/400) used various aircraft	
4/7/18	DB		

No. 135 SQUADRON   MOTTO: Pennas ubique monstramus (We show our wings everywhere)

Month/Yr	Location	Aircraft type	Remarks
1/4/18	F @ Hucknall	(for DH9) used various aircraft	
4/7//18	DB		

No. 136 SQUADRON   MOTTO: Nihil Fortius (Nothing is stronger)

Month/Yr	Location	Aircraft type	Remarks
1/4/18	F @ Lakedown	(for DH9) used various aircraft	
4/7/18	DB		

No. 137 SQUADRON   MOTTO: Do right, fear nought

Month/Yr	Location	Aircraft type	Remarks
1/4/18	F @ Shawbury	(for DH9) used various aircraft	
4/7/18	DB		

No. 138 SQUADRON   MOTTO: For freedom

Month/Yr	Location	Aircraft type	Remarks
30/9/18	F @ Chingford		Nucleus from Nos.1, 5, 36 & 45 TDSs
10/18		Bristol F2b (2/19)	

No. 139 SQUADRON   MOTTO: Si placer necamus (We destroy at will)

Month/Yr	Location	Aircraft type	Remarks
3/7/18	F @ Villaverla		from 'Z' Flt of No.34 Sqn
7/18		Bristol F2b (2/19)	
10/10/18	Grossa		
2/11/18	Arcade		

No. 141 SQUADRON   MOTTO: Caedimus noctu (We slay by night)

Month/Yr	Location	Aircraft type	Remarks
1/1/18	F @ Rochford		From 'A'Flt No.61 Sqn
1/18		Dolphin (4/18)	
1/18		BE12 (3/18)	
9/2/18	Biggin Hill		
2/18		BE12b (3/18)	
2/18		Pup (3/18)	
3/18		Bristol F2b Fighter	

No. 142 SQUADRON   MOTTO: Determination

Month/Yr	Location	Aircraft type	Remarks
2/2/18	F @ Ismailia		
2/18		BE12a (6/18)	
13/2/18	Julis		
3/18		Martinsyde G102 (6/18)	
4/18		RE8 (4/19)	
18/4/18	Ramleh		Det Jerusalem
5/18		AW FK8 (4/19)	
6/18		BE2e (3/19)	
18/9/18	Sarona		Dets Jerusalem & El Affule
4/10/18	Ramleh		Dets Damascus & Haifa

No. 143 SQUADRON   MOTTO: Vincere et vivere (To conquer is to live)

Month/Yr	Location	Aircraft type	Remarks
1/2/18	F @ Throwley		Nucleus from No.112 Sqn
2/18		AW FK8 (3/18	
14/2/18	Detling		
3/18		SE5a (8/18)	
8/18		Camel (10/19)	

No. 144 SQUADRON   MOTTO: Who shall stop us

Month/Yr	Location	Aircraft type	Remarks
20/3/18	F @ Port Said		
4/18		BE2e (7/18)	
5/18		BE12a (8/18)	
6/18		Martinsyde S1 (8/18)	
7/18		RE8 (7/18)	
14/8/18	Junction Station		
8/18		DH9 (12/18)	Dets Haifa, Mudros
6/11/18	Mikra Bay	DH9 (12/18)	Dets Mudros & Amberkoj

No. 145 SQUADRON   MOTTO: Diu noctuque pugnamus (We fight by day and night)

Month/Yr	Location	Aircraft type	Remarks
15/5/18	F @ Aboukir		
1/6/18	Abu Sueir		
8/18		SE5a (2/19	det Junction Station
25/8/18	Qantara		
13/9/18	Ramleh		
20/10/18	Qantara		

No. 148 SQUADRON   MOTTO: Trusty

Month/Yr	Location	Aircraft type	Remarks
10/2/18	F @ Andover		
1/3/18	Ford Junction		
3/18		FE2b (2/19)	
25/4/18	Auchel		
3/5/18	Sains-lès-Pernes		
22/10/18	Camblain-l'Abbé		
31/10/18	Erre	FE2b (2/19)	

No. 149 SQUADRON   MOTTO: Fortis nocte

Month/Yr	Location	Aircraft type	Remarks
1/3/18	F @ Ford Junction		
3/18		FE2b (8/19)	
2/6/18	Marquise		
4/6/18	Quilen		
16/6/18	Alquines		Dets Abeele, Clairmarais
16/9/18	Clairmarais North		
25/10/18	Ste-Marguerite		

No. 150 SQUADRON   MOTTO: Always ahead (Greek script)

Month/Yr	Location	Aircraft type	Remarks
1/4/18	F @ Kirec		From elements of Nos.17 and 47 Sqns
4/18		Bristol M1C (1/19)	
4/18		SE5a (2/19)	Det Marian
5/18		Camel (2/19)	
7/18		BE12a (12/18)	
8/18		BE2e (1/19)	Det Amberkoj
20/10/18		Mikra Bay	Dets Kirec, Gumuljina & Dedeagatch

No. 151 SQUADRON   MOTTO: Foy pour devoir (Fidelity unto duty)

Month/Yr	Location	Aircraft type	Remarks
12/6/18	F @ Hainault Farm		From Flts of Nos.44, 78 & 112 Sqns
6/18			Camel (2/19)

Month/Yr	Location	Aircraft type	Remarks
19/6/18	Marquise		
23/6/18	Fontaine-sur-Maye		Det Famechon
8/9/18	Vignacourt		
8/10/18	Bancourt		

No. 152 SQUADRON   MOTTO: Faithful ally

Month/Yr	Location	Aircraft type	Remarks
1/10/18	F @ Rochford		
10/18		Camel (2/19)	
18/10/18	Carvin		

No. 153 SQUADRON   MOTTO: Noctividus (Seeing by night)

Month/Yr	Location	Aircraft type	Remarks
4/11/18	F @ Hainault Farm		Nucleus from 6th Bde units
11/18		Camel (6/19)	

No. 154 SQUADRON   MOTTO: His modis ad vactoriam (By this means to victory)

Month/Yr	Location	Aircraft type	Remarks
7/8/18	F @ Chingford	for Bristol F2b Fighter	Nucleus from Nos.33, 37, 39 & 44 TDSs
11/9/18	DB		

No. 155 SQUADRON   MOTTO: Eternal vigilance

Month/Yr	Location	Aircraft type	Remarks
14/9/18	F @ Chingford		Nucleus from Nos.1, 26, 55 & 57 TDSs
9/18		DH9A (12/18)	

No. 156 SQUADRON   MOTTO: We light the way

Month/Yr	Location	Aircraft type	Remarks
12/10/18	F @ Wyton		Nucleus from Nos. 27, 35, 52 & 53 TDSs
11/18		DH9A (11/18)	

No. 157 SQUADRON   MOTTO: Our cannon speak our thoughts

Month/Yr	Location	Aircraft type	Remarks
14/7/18	F @ Upper Heyford		Nucleus from CFS and Nos.3, 43 & 56 TDSs
		Used various aircraft	
11/18		Salamander (2/19)	

No. 158 SQUADRON   MOTTO: Strength in unity

Month/Yr	Location	Aircraft type	Remarks
4/9/18	F @ Upper Heyford	(for Salamander)	Nucleus from CFS and Nos. 42, 50 and 53 TDSs

No. 166 SQUADRON   MOTTO: Tenacity

Month/Yr	Location	Aircraft type	Remarks
13/6/18	F @ Bircham Newton		
6/18		FE2b (10/18)	
10/18		HP V/1500 (5/19)	

No. 185 SQUADRON   MOTTO: Ara fejn hu (Maltese – Look where it is)

Month/Yr	Location	Aircraft type	Remarks
21/10/18	F @ East Fortune		Nucleus from Nos. 31, 33, 39 & 49 TDSs
11/18		Cuckoo (4/19)	

No. 201 SQUADRON   MOTTO: Hic et Ubique (Here and everywhere)

Month/Yr	Location	Aircraft type	Remarks
			The original No.1 Sqn RNAS Formed at Fort Grange, Gosport on 17/10/14. It moved to France on 28/2/15 and in 6/15 was restyled as No.1 Wing. RNAS. On 1/3/16 'A' Sqn of No.1 Wg was detached and from 3/7/16 it was referred to as the 'Detached Squadron RNAS'. The unit was again redesignated as No.1 (Naval) Sqn on 3/12/16
3/12/16	F @ Furnes as No.1 (Naval) Sqn 'Detached Sqn RNAS' renamed		
12/16		Nieuport 17 (2/17)	
12/16		Sopwith Triplane (12/17)	
15/2/17	Chipilly		
11/4/17	La Bellevue		
1/6/17	Bailleul (Asylum Ground)		
2/11/17	Middle Aerodrome		
10/12/17	Dover (Guston Road)		
12/17		Camel (1/19)	
16/2/18	Teteghem		
27/3/18	Ste-Marie-Cappel		
28/3/18	Fienvillers		
1/4/18	redesignated as No.201 Sqn RAF		
12/4/18	Nouex-les- Auxi		
20/7/18	Ste-Marie-Cappel		
6/8/18	Poulainville		
14/8/18	Nouex-les-Auxi		
19/9/18	Baizieux		
14/10/18	Beugnâtre		
27/10/18	La Targette		
10/18		Snipe (10/18)	

No. 202 SQUADRON   MOTTO: Semper vigilate (Be always vigilant)

Month/Yr	Location	Aircraft type	Remarks
			No.2 Sqn RNAS was formed at Eastchurch on 17/10/14. In June 1915 it was redesignated No.2 Wing and on 2/8/15 it moved to France. On 12/8/15 the unit was withdrawn to Dover for redeployment to Imbros for operations in the Aegean. A new No.2 Sqn was formed from 'B' Sqn of No.1 Wing, RNAS on 5/11/16

Month/Yr	Location	Aircraft type	Remarks
5/11/16	F @ St Pol as No.2 Naval Sqn		Ex 'B' Sqn No.1 Wing RNAS
11/16		Pup (1917)	
11/16		Farman F40 (1917)	
11/16		1½ Strutter (11/17)	
3/17		DH4 (3/19)	
26/1/18	Bergues		
1/4/18			Redesignated as No.202 Sqn RAF
5/18		DH9 (9/18)	

No. 203 SQUADRON   MOTTO: Occidens orienque (West and East)

Month/Yr	Location	Aircraft type	Remarks
			The Eastchurch Squadron of the RNAS formed in 5/14. This unit deployed to Ostend on 27/8/14, moving to St Pol on 1/9/14. The Sqn withdrew to Dover on 26/2/15 where it was redesignated No.3 Sqn RNAS before moving to the Aegean in the following month. In June 1915 it was restyled No.3 Wing and disbanded at the end of the year. A new No.3 Wing RNAS was formed by redesignating an element of No.1 Wing RNAS on 5/11/16
5/11/16	F @ St Pol as No.3 (Naval) Sqn RNAS		Ex 'C' Sqn No.1 Wing RNAS
11/16		Nieuport II (2/17)	
11/16		Bristol Scout (2/17)	
2/17		Pup (7/17)	
1/2/17	Vert Galand		
28/2/17	Bertangles		
26/3/17	Marieux		
15/6/17	Furnes		
7/17		Camel (3/19)	
6/9/17	Bray-Dunes		
1/11/17	Walmer		
11/3/18	St Eloi		
28/3/18	Treizennes		
1/4/18	redesignated as No.203 Sqn RAF		
9/4/18	Liettres		
16/5/18	Filescamp Farm		
14/8/18	Allonville		
6/9/18	Filescamp Farm		
23/9/18	Le Hameau		
24/10/18	Bruille		

No. 204 SQUADRON   MOTTO: Praedam mari quaero (I seek my prey in the sea)

Month/Yr	Location	Aircraft type	Remarks
			The RNAS Defence Flight at Dover became No.4 Sqn RNAS on 29/3/15. On 3/8/15 the unit moved to Eastchurch and was redesignated as

Month/Yr	Location	Aircraft type	Remarks
			No.4 Wing. A new No.4 Squadron was formed from an element of No.5 Wing on 31/12/16
31/12/16	F @ Coudekerque as No. 4 (Naval) Squadron		Ex ' A' Sqn No.5 Wing RNAS
12/16		1½ Strutter (3/ 17)	
3//17		Pup (6/17)	
1/4/17	Bray-Dunes		
6/17		Camel (2/19)	
2/1/18	Walmer		
6/3/18	Bray-Dunes		
1/4/18			Redesignated as No.204 squadron RAF
13/4/18	Teteghem		
30/4/18	Cappelle		
9/5/18	Teteghem		
24/10/18	Heule		

No. 205 SQUADRON   MOTTO: Pertama di - Malaya (First in Malaya)

Month/Yr	Location	Aircraft type	Remarks
31/12/16	F @ Coudekerque		As No.5 (Naval) Squadron ex 'B' Sqn, No.5 Wg. RNAS
12/16		1½ Strutter (7/17)	
1/4/17	Petite Synthe		
4/17		DH4 (9/18)	
6/3/18	Villers-Brettoneux		
11/3/18	Mons-en-Chausée		
22/3/18	Champien		
24/3/18	Bertangles		
28/3/18	Bois-de-Roche		
1/4/18	redesignated No.205 Sqn. RAF		
25/8/18	Bovelles		
16/9/18	Proyart East		
9/18		DH9A (3/19)	
7/10/18	Moislains		

No. 206 SQUADRON   MOTTO: Nihil nos effugit (Naught escapes us)

Month/Yr	Location	Aircraft type	Remarks
			The first No.6 Sqn RNAS was formed on 1 Nov 16 by redesignating 'A' Sqn of No.4 Wing This unit was disbanded in Aug 17. A new No.6 (Naval) Sqn was formed on 1 Nov 17
1/11/17	F @ Dover (Guston Road)		As No.6 (Naval) Sqn – from the Walmer Defence Flight
11/17		DH4 (3/18)	
14/1/18	Petite Synthe		
2/18		DH9 (1/20)	
31/3/18	Ste-Marie-Cappel		
1/4/18			Redesignated No.206 Sqn RAF
11/4/18	Boisdinghem		
15/4/18	Alquines		
29/5/18	Boisdinghem		
5/6/18	Alquines		
5/10/18	Ste-Marie-Cappel		
24/10/18	Linselles		

No. 207 SQUADRON   MOTTO: Semper paratus (Always prepared)

Month/Yr	Location	Aircraft type	Remarks
1/11/16	F @ Petite-Synthe		As No.7 (Naval) Sqn ex 'B' Sqn No.4 Wing RNAS
11/16		Caudron GIV (12/16)	
11/16		1½ Strutter (4/17)	
11/16		Short Bomber (6/17)	
2/4/17	Coudekerque		
4/17		HPO/100 (4/18)	
28/7/17			Split into Nos.7 & 7A Sqns RNAS Dets
			Redcar, later Manston – Detachment became 'A' Sqn RNAS
1/4/18			Redesignated as No.207 Sqn RAF
22/4/18	Netheravon		
4/18		HP 0/400 (8/19)	
13/5/18	Andover		
7/6/18	Ligescourt		
25/10/18	Estrées-en-Chaussée		

No. 208 SQUADRON   MOTTO: Vigilant

Month/Yr	Location	Aircraft type	Remarks
25/10/16	F @ St Pol		As No.8 (Naval) Sqn – one Flt from each of Nos.1, 4 & 5 Wings
26/10/16	Vert Galand		
10/16		1½ Strutter (11/16)	
10/16		Nieuport 17 (12/16)	
10/16		Pup (2/17)	
2/17		Sopwith Triplane (9/17)	
7/2/17	Furnes		
28/3/17	Auchel		
16/5/17	St-Eloi		
9/17		Camel (11/18)	
28/2/18	Bray-Dunes		
1/3/18	Walmer		
29/3/18	Tetegham		
1/4/18			Redesignated as No.208 Sqn. RAF
2/4/18	La Gorgue		
9/4/18	Serny		
30/7/18	Tramecourt		
22/9/18	Foucaucourt		
9/10/18	Estrées-en-Chaussés		
26/10/18	Maretz		
11/18		Snipe (11/19)	

No. 209 SQUADRON   MOTTO: Might and Main

Month/Yr	Location	Aircraft type	Remarks
1/2/17	F @ St Pol		As No.9 (Naval) Sqn
			Nucleus from No.8 (Naval) Sqn
2/17		Nieuport 17 (6/17)	
2/17		Pup (7/17)	
2/17		Sopwith Triplane (7/17)	
15/5/17	Furnes		
15/6/17	Flez		

Month/Yr	Location	Aircraft type	Remarks
7/17		Camel (2/19)	
5/7/17	Le Hameau		
10/7/17	Frontier Aerodrome		
25/7/17	Leffrinckhoucke		
1/10/17	Frontier Aerodrome		
10/10/17	Middle Aerodrome		
16/2/18	Dover (Guston Road)		
20/3/18	Middle Aerodrome		
21/3/18	Teteghem		
21/3/18	Bray-Dunes		
23/3/18	Cappelle		
27/3/18	Bailleul		
29/3/18	Clairmarais		
1/4/18			Redesignated No.209 Sqn. RAF
7/4/18	Bertangles		
20/7/18	Quelmes		
6/8/18	Bertangles		
14/8/18	Le Hameau		
24/10/18	Bruille		

No. 210 SQUADRON   MOTTO: Yn y nwyfre yn hedfan (Hovering in the heavens)

Month/Yr	Location	Aircraft type	Remarks
12/2/17	F @ St-Pol		As No.10 (Naval) Sqn. RNAS
2/17		Nieuport 12 (5/17)	
2/17		Nieuport 17 (5/17)	
2/17		Sopwith Triplane (7/17)	
27/3/17	Furnes		
15/5/17	Droglandt		
7/17		Camel (2/19)	
4/10/17	Leffrinckhoucke		
27/11/17	Tetegham		
1/4/18	redesignated No.210 Sqn RAF		
1/4/18	Treizennes		
9/4/18	Liettres		
27/4/18	St Omer		
30/5/18	Ste-Marie-Cappel		
9/7/18	Teteghem		
22/7/18	Eringhem		
23/10/18	Boussieres		

No. 211 SQUADRON   MOTTO: Toujours a propos (Always at the right moment)

Month/Yr	Location	Aircraft type	Remarks
			The first No.11 Sqn RNAS formed at Dunkerque on 8/3/17 but, after moving to Hondschoote on 11/7/17 it disbanded on 27/8/17
10/3/18	F @ Petite Synthe		As No.11 (Naval) Squadron RNAS
3/18		DH4 (4/18)	
3/18		DH9 (3/19)	
1/4/8			Redesiganated No.211 Sqn. RAF
24/10/18	Iris Farm		

No. 212 SQUADRON   MOTTO: Amari ad astra (From the sea to the stars)

Month/Yr	Location	Aircraft type	Remarks
			No.12 (Naval) Sqn was a training unit formed at St-Pol in Apr 17, moving to Petite Synthe on 1/7/17
			Unlike other RNAS squadrons it disbanded on 1/4/18 rather than being absorbed into the RAF as No.212 Sqn
20/8/18	F @ Great Yarmouth		Nos.490, 557 \7 558 Flts
8/18		DH4 (1/19)	
8/18		DH9A (2/20)	
8/18		DH9 (1919)	
10/18		Camel (1/19)	

No. 213 SQUADRON   MOTTO: Irritatus lacessit crabro (The hornet attacks when roused)

Month/Yr	Location	Aircraft type	Remarks
15/1/18	F @ St-Pol		as No.13 (Naval) Sqn ex St-Pol Defence Sqn
1/18		Camel (3/19	
25/1/18	Bergues		
1/4/18			Redesignated No.213 Sqn RAF

No. 214 SQUADRON   MOTTO: Ultra in Umbris (Avenging in the shadows)

Month/Yr	Location	Aircraft type	Remarks
9/12/17	F @ Coudekerque		As No.14 (Naval) Sqn – from No.7A Sqn, RNAS
12/17		HPO/100 (1918)	
10/3/18	Alquines		
26/3/18	Coudekerque		
1/4/18			Redesignated as No.214 Sqn RAF
29/6/18	St-Inglevert		
6/18		HPO/400 (2/20)	
24/10/18	Quilen		
30/10/18	Chemy		

No. 215 SQUADRON   MOTTO: Surgite nox adeste (Arise, night is at hand)

Month/Yr	Location	Aircraft type	Remarks
10/3/18	F @ Coudekerque		as No.15 (Naval) Sqn – Nucleus from Nos.7 and 14 Sqns RNAS
3/18		HPO/100 (5/18)	
1/4/18			Redesignated as No.215 Sqn. RAF
23/4/18	Netheravon		
5/18		HPO/400 (2/19)	
13/5/18	Andover		
4/7/18	Alquines		
19/8/18	Xaffévillers		

No. 216 SQUADRON   MOTTO: CCXVI dona ferens (216 bearing wings)

Month/Yr	Location	Aircraft type	Remarks
8/1/18	F @ Ochey		As No.16 (Naval) Sqn ex 'A' Sqn RNAS
1/18		HPO/100 (1918)	
3/18		HPO/400 (10/21)	
30/3/18	Villesneux		

Month/Yr	Location	Aircraft type	Remarks
1/4/18			Redesignated No.216 Sqn. RAF Det Cramaille
9/5/18	Ochey		
26/8/18	Autrevillle		
28/9/18	Rovilles-aux-Chenes		

No. 217 SQUADRON   MOTTO: Woe to the enemy

Month/Yr	Location	Aircraft type	Remarks
23/1/18	F @ Bierne		As No.17 (Naval) Sqn ex-RN Seaplane Base
1/18		DH4 3/19)	
1/2/18	Bergues		
1/4/18			Redesignated No.217 Sqn. RAF
10/7/18	Crochte		

No. 218 SQUADRON   MOTTO: In Time

Month/Yr	Location	Aircraft type	Remarks
24/4/18	F @ Dover (Guston Road)		
4/18		DH9 (2/19)	
23/5/18	Petite Synthe		
7/7/19	Fréthun		
25/10/18	Reumont		

No. 219 SQUADRON   MOTTO: From Dusk till Dawn

Month/Yr	Location	Aircraft type	Remarks
22/7/18	F @ Westgate and Manston		(seaplanes – Nos.406 & 442 Flts.) (landplanes – Nos. 470, 555 & 556 Flts.) Dets Bacton, Burgh Castle
7/18		Hamble Baby (10/18)	
7/18		Sopwith Baby (11/18)	
7/18		DH9 (6/19)	
7/18		Camel (6/19)	
7/18		Short 184 (2/20)	
10/18		Fairey IIIB (2/20)	

No. 220 SQUADRON   MOTTO: We observe unseen (Greek script)

Month/Yr	Location	Aircraft type	Remarks
1/4/18	F @ Imbros		From 'C' Sqn (later Nos. 475, 476 & 477 Flts)
4/18		DH4 (1/19)	
6/18		DH9 (1/19)	
7/18		Camel (1/19)	
9/18			Adopted No.220 Sqn numberplate Det San Stephano

No. 221 SQUADRON   MOTTO: From sea to sea

Month/Yr	Location	Aircraft type	Remarks
1/4/18	F @ Stavros		From 'D' Sqn (later Nos. 552, 553 & 554 Flts)
4/18		DH4 (10/18)	
4/18		Camel (9/18)	
7/18		DH9 (10/18	
9/18			Adopted No.221 Sqn numberplate Assets absorbed by No.222 Sqn
15/10/18	Mudros	DH9 (9/19)	

No. 222 SQUADRON   MOTTO: Pambili Bo (Zulu)

Month/Yr	Location	Aircraft type	Remarks
1/4/18		F @ Thasos	From 'A' Sqn (later Nos. 478, 479 & 480 Flts
4/18		DH4 (2/19)	
4/18		Camel (2/19)	Det Stavros
11/11/18	Mudros	DH9 (2/19)	Dets Amberkoj & Dedeagatch
		DH4 (2/19)	
		Camel (2/19)	

No. 223 SQUADRON   MOTTO: Alae defendunt Africam (Wings defend Africa)

Month/Yr	Location	Aircraft type	Remarks
1/4/18	F @ Mitylebe		ex 'B' Sqn, (later Nos. 559, 560 and 561 Flts
4/18		Camel (5/19)	
21/4/18	Stavros		
5/18		DH4 (5/19)	
7/18		DH9 (5/19)	
11/18	Mudros		

No. 224 SQUADRON   MOTTO: Fedele All'Amico (Italian – Faithful to a friend)

Month/Yr	Location	Aircraft type	Remarks
1/4/18	F @ Alimini		Nos. 496,197 & 498 Flts
4/18		DH4 (4/19)	
6/18		DH9 (4/19)	
14/6	Andrano		
9/11/18	Pizzone		

No. 225 SQUADRON   MOTTO: We guide the sword

Month/Yr	Location	Aircraft type	Remarks
1/4/18	F @ Alimini		Nos. 481, 482 & 483 Flts
4/18		1½ Strutter (6/18)	
4/18		Hamble Baby Convert (6/18)	
4/18		Camel (12/18)	det Pizzone
14/6/18	Andrano		
9/11/18	Pizzone		

No. 226 SQUADRON   MOTTO: Non sibi sed patriae (For country not for self)

Month/Yr	Location	Aircraft type	Remarks
1/4/18	F @ Pizzone		Nos. 472, 473 & 474 Flts
4/18		DH4 (11/18)	
6/18		DH9 (11/18)	
6/18		Camel (11/18)	
1/10/18	Andrano		
3/10/18	Pizzone		
8/10/18	Mudros		
11/11/18	Taranto		

No. 227 SQUADRON

Month/Yr	Location	Aircraft type	Remarks
1/4/18	F @ Pizzone		Nos. 499, 500 & 551 Flts
4/18		Caproni Ca 42 (4/18)	
4/18		DH4 (12/18)	
6/18		DH9 (12/18)	
12/18	Disbanded without ever becoming fully established		

No. 228 SQUADRON   MOTTO: Auxilium a caelo (Help from the sky)

Month/Yr	Location	Aircraft type	Remarks
20/8/18	F & Great Yarmouth		Nos. 324, 325 & 326 Flts
8/18		Felixstowe F2a (3/19)	
8/18		Curtiss H12/16 (1919)	

No. 229 SQUADRON   MOTTO: Be bold

Month/Yr	Location	Aircraft type	Remarks
20/8/18	F @ Great Yarmouth		Nos. 428, 429, 454 & 455 Flts
8/18		Sopwith Baby (10/18)	
8/18		Hamble Baby (10/18)	
8/18		Short 184 (3/19)	
8/18		Short 320 (3/19)	
8/18		Fairey IIIC (3/19)	

No. 230 SQUADRON   MOTTO: Kita chari jauh (Malay - We seek far)

Month/Yr	Location	Aircraft type	Remarks
20/8/18	F @ Felixstowe		Nos. 327, 328 & 487 Flts
8/18		Curtiss H16 (3/19)	
8/18		Felixstowe F2a (3/19)	
9/18		Camel (12/18)	Det Butley
9/18		Felixstowe F3 (3/19)	
9/18		Short 184 (3/19)	
10/18		Fairey IIIB/C (3/19)	

No. 231 SQUADRON   MOTTO: Prepared to Attack

Month/Yr	Location	Aircraft type	Remarks
20/8/18	F @ Felixstowe		Nos. 329 & 330 Flts
8/18		Felixstowe F2a (3/19)	
8/18		Felixstowe F3 (3/19)	
11/18		Felixstowe F5 (3/19)	

No. 232 SQUADRON   MOTTO: Strike

Month/Yr	Location	Aircraft type	Remarks
20/8/18	F @ Felixstowe		Nos. 333, 334 & 335 Flts
8/18		Felixstowe F2a (1/19)	
8/18		Felixstowe F3 (1/19)	

No. 233 Squadron   Motto: Fortis et fidelis (Strong and faithful)

Month/Yr	Location	Aircraft type	Remarks
31/8/18	F @ Dover Harbour & Guston Road		Nos. 407,471 & 491 Flts
8/18		Camel (11/18)	Det Walmer
8/18		DH9 (3/19)	
8/18		Short 184 (5/19)	

No. 234 Squadron   Motto: Ignem mortemque despuimu (We spit fire and death)

Month/Yr	Location	Aircraft type	Remarks
8/18	F & Trescoe		Nos. 350, 351, 352 & 353 Flts
8/18	Trescoe	Curtiss H12 (5/19)	
8/18		Short 184 (5/19)	
8/18		Felixstowe F3 (5/19)	

No. 235 SQUADRON   MOTTO: Jaculamur humi (We strike them to the ground)

Month/Yr	Location	Aircraft type	Remarks
8/18	F @ Newlyn		Nos. 424 & 425 Flts
		Short 184 (2/19)	

No. 236 SQUADRON   MOTTO: Speculati nuntiate (Having watched, bring word)

Month/Yr	Location	Aircraft type	Remarks
8/18	F @ Mullion		Nos. 493, 515 & 516 Flts
8/18		DH6 (3/19)	
8/18		DH9 (5/19)	

No. 237 SQUADRON   MOTTO: Primum agmen in caelo (The vanguard is in the sky)

Month/Yr	Location	Aircraft type	Remarks
8/18	F @ Cattewater		Nos. 420, 421, 422 & 423 Flts
8/18		Short 184 (5/19)	

No. 238 SQUADRON   MOTTO: Ad finem (To the end)

Month/Yr	Location	Aircraft type	Remarks
20/8/18	F @ Cattewater		Nos. 347, 348 & 349 Flts
8/18		Curtiss H.16 (1919)	
8/18		Short 184 (5/19)	
8/18		Felixstowe F2a (5/19)	
8/18		Felixstowe F3 (5/19)	Dets Holy Island, Killinghome & Calshot

No. 239 SQUADRON   MOTTO: Exploramus (We seek out)

Month/Yr	Location	Aircraft type	Remarks
8/18	F @ Torquay		No. 418 Flt
8/18		Short 184 (5/19)	

No.240 SQUADRON   MOTTO: Sjo-Vordur Lopt-Vordur (Guardian of the sea, guardian of the sky)

Month/Yr	Location	Aircraft type	Remarks
20/8/09	F @ Calshot		
8/18		Short 320 (5/19)	
8/18		Felixstowe F2a (5/19)	
8/18		Campania (5/19)	
8/18		Short 184 (5/19)	
8/18		Curtiss H.12 (1919)	

No. 241 SQUADRON   MOTTO: Find and forewarn

Month/Yr	Location	Aircraft type	Remarks
8/18	F @ Portland		Nos. 416, 417 & 513 Flts det Chickerall
8/18		DH6 (1/19)	
8/18		Short 184 (6/19)	
8/18		Campania (6/19)	
8/18		Wight Converted (6/19)	

No. 242 SQUADRON   MOTTO: Toujours pret (Always ready)

Month/Yr	Location	Aircraft type	Remarks
8/18	F @ Newhaven		Nos. 408, 409 & 514 Flts det Telscombe Cliffs
8/18		Short 184 (5/19)	
8/18		DH6 (1/19)	
10/18		Campania (11/18)	

No. 243 SQUADRON   MOTTO: Swift in pursuit

Month/Yr	Location	Aircraft type	Remarks
8/18	F @ Cherbourg		Nos. 411 & 415 Flts
8/18		Short 184 (3/19)	
8/18		Wight Converted (3/19)	

No. 244 SQUADRON

Month/Yr	Location	Aircraft type	Remarks
25/7/18	F @ Bangor		Nos. 521, 522 & 530 Flts
			Dets Tallaght, Llangefni & Luce Bay
7/18		DH6 (1/19)	

No. 245 SQUADRON   MOTTO: Fugo no Fugio (I put to flight, I do not flee)

Month/Yr	Location	Aircraft type	Remarks
8/18	F @ Fishguard		Nos. 426 & 427 Flts
8/18		Short 184 (5/19)	

No. 246 SQUADRON

Month/Yr	Location	Aircraft type	Remarks
8/18	F @ Seaton Carew		Nos. 402, 403, 451, 452 & 495 Flts
8/18		FE2b 910/18)	
8/18		Kangaroo (11/18)	
8/18		Short 184 (3/19)	
8/18		Sopwith Baby (10/18)	

No. 247 SQUADRON   MOTTO: Rise from the East

Month/Yr	Location	Aircraft type	Remarks
20/8/18	F @ Felixstowe		Nos. 336, 337 & 338 Flts
8/18		Felixstowe F2A (1/19)	
8/18		Felixstowe F3 (1/19)	

No. 248 SQUADRON   MOTTO: Il fauten finir (It is necessary to make an end of it)

Month/Yr	Location	Aircraft type	Remarks
8/18	F @ Hornsea		Nos. 404, 405 & 453 Flts
			det North Coates
8/18		Sopwith Baby (11/18)	
		Short 184 (3/19)	
		Short 320 (3/19)	

No. 249 SQUADRON   MOTTO: Pugnis et cacibus (With fists and heels)

Month/Yr	Location	Aircraft type	Remarks
18/8/18	F @ Dundee		Nos. 400, 401, 419 & 450 Flts
8/18		Sopwith Baby (11/18)	
8/18		Hamble Baby (11/18)	
8/18		Short 184 (3/19)	

No. 250 SQUADRON   MOTTO: Close to the sun

Month/Yr	Location	Aircraft type	Remarks
10/5/18	F @ Padstow		Nos. 494, 500, 501, 502 & 503 Flts
5/18		DH6 (5/19)	
5/18		DH9 (5/19)	Det Westward Ho

No. 251 SQUADRON   MOTTO: However wind blows

Month/Yr	Location	Aircraft type	Remarks
5/18	F @ Hornsea		Nos. 504, 505, 506 & 510 Flts
5/18		DH6 (1/19)	Dets Atwick, Greenland Top, West Ayton
			Owthorpe, Seaton Carew & Redcar
11/18		DH9 (1/19)	

No. 252 SQUADRON   MOTTO: With or on

Month/Yr	Location	Aircraft type	Remarks
5/18	F @ Tynemouth		Nos. 495, 507, 508, 509 & 510 Flts
5/18		DH6 (1/19)	
5/18		Kangaroo (8/18)	Dets Cramlington, Seaton Carew & Redcar

No. 253 SQUADRON   MOTTO: Come one, come all

Month/Yr	Location	Aircraft type	Remarks
7/6/18	Bembridge		Nos. 412, 413, 511, 512 & 513 Flts
6/18		Hamble Baby (1918)	Dets Brading & Chickerall
6/18		Short 184 (5/19)	
6/18		Campania (5/19)	
8/18		DH6 (1/19)	

No. 254 SQUADRON   MOTTO: Fljuga vakta ok ljosta (Norse – To fly, to watch and to strike)

Month/Yr	Location	Aircraft type	Remarks
5/18	F @ Prawle Point		Nos. 492, 515, 516, 517 & 518 Flts
5/18		DH6 (2/19)	Det Mullion
5/18		DH9 (2/19)	

No. 255 SQUADRON   MOTTO: Ad auroram (To the break of dawn)

Month/Yr	Location	Aircraft type	Remarks
25/7/8	F @ Pembroke		Nos. 519, 520, 521, 522, 523 & 524 Flts
7/18		DH6 (1/19)	Dets Llangefni & Luce Bay

No. 256 SQUADRON   MOTTO: Addimus vim viribus (Strength to strength)

Month/Yr	Location	Aircraft type	Remarks
6/18	F @ Seahouses		Nos. 495, 525, 526, 527 & 528 Flts
6/18		DH6 (1/19)	Dets New Haggerston, Rennington Cairncross & Ashington
11/18		Kangaroo (1/19	

No. 257 SQUADRON   MOTTO: Thay myay gvee shin shwe hti (Burmese – Death or glory)

Month/Yr	Location	Aircraft type	Remarks
18/8/18	Dundee		Nos. 318 & 319 Flts
8/18		Felixstowe F2A (4/19)	
8/18		Curtiss H.16 (1918)	

No. 258 SQUADRON   MOTTO: In medias re (Into the middle of things)

Month/Yr	Location	Aircraft type	Remarks
25/7/18	F @ Luce Bay		Nos. 523, 524 @ 529 Flts
7/18		DH6 (3/19)	
		Fairey IIIA (3/19)	

No. 259 SQUADRON

Month/Yr	Location	Aircraft type	Remarks
			No.259 Sqn was officially authorized to form at Felixstowe on 20/8/18 and was to have comprised Nos. 342, 343 and 344 Flts operating Felixstowe F2As. Although usually annotated as having been formally disbanded on 13/9/19 it is unlikely that the squadron ever had more than a notional existence.

No. 260 SQUADRON   MOTTO: Celer et fortis (Swift and strong)

Month/Yr	Location	Aircraft type	Remarks
8/18	F @ Westward Ho	Nos.502 & 503 Flts	
8/18		DH6 (2/19)	
8/18		DH9 (2/19)	

No. 261 SQUADRON

Month/Yr	Location	Aircraft type	Remarks
			No.261 Sqn was officially authorized to form at Felixstowe on 20/8/18 and was to have comprised Nos. 339, 340 and 341 Flts operating Felixstowe F2As. Although usually annotated as having been formally disbanded on 13/9/19 it is unlikely that the Squadron ever had more than a notional existence.

No. 263 SQUADRON   MOTTO: Ex ungue leonem (From his claws one knows the lion)

Month/Yr	Location	Aircraft type	Remarks
27/9/18	F @ Otranto		Nos. 359, 435, 436 & 441 Flts
9/18		Sopwith Baby (5/19)	Det Santa Maria di Leucca
		Hamble Baby (1919)	
		Short 184 (5/19)	
		Short 320 (5/19)	
		Felixstowe F3 (5/19)	
11/18	Taranto		

No. 264 SQUADRON   MOTTO: We defy

Month/Yr	Location	Aircraft type	Remarks
27/9/18	F @ Suda Bay		Nos.439 & 440 Flts
9/18		Short 184 (12/18)	det Siros

No. 265 SQUADRON

Month/Yr	Location	Aircraft type	Remarks
			Intended to form at Gibraltar with Nos. 364, 365 & 366 Flts to operate Short 184s and Felixstowe F3s. However, the squadron does not appear to have ever been formally embodied.

No. 266 SQUADRON MOTTO: Hlabezulu (The stabber of the sky)

Month/Yr	Location	Aircraft type	Remarks
27/9/18	F @ Mudros		Nos. 437 & 438 Flts
9/18		Short 184 (3/19)	det Skyros
		Short 320 (3/19)	

No. 267 SQUADRON MOTTO: Sine mora (Without delay)

Month/Yr	Location	Aircraft type	Remarks
27/9/18	F @ Kalafrana		Nos. 360, 361, 362 & 363 Flts
9/18		Short 184 (10/21)	det Alexandria
9/18		Felixstowe F2A (2/23)	
9/18		Felixstowe F3 (6/21)	

No. 268 SQUADRON MOTTO: Adjidaumo (Chippeway Indian – Tail in the air)

Month/Yr	Location	Aircraft type	Remarks
8/18	F @ Kalafrana		Nos. 433 & 434 Flts
8/18		Short 184 (10/19)	
8/18		Short 320 (10/19)	

No. 269 SQUADRON MOTTO: Omnia videmus (We see all things)

Month/Yr	Location	Aircraft type	Remarks
6/10/18	F @ Port Said		Nos. 431 & 432 Flts
10/18		BE2e (3/19)	
10/18		Short 184 (11/19)	

No. 271 SQUADRON MOTTO: Death and Life

Month/Yr	Location	Aircraft type	Remarks
27/9/18	F @ Taranto		Nos. 357, 358, 359 & 367 Flts
9/18		Short 184 (12/18)	det Otranto
9/18		Felixstowe F3 (12/18)	

No. 272 SQUADRON MOTTO: On, On!

Month/Yr	Location	Aircraft type	Remarks
25/7/18	F @ Macrihanish		Nos. 531, 532 & 533 Flts
7/18		DH6 (3/19)	
11/18		Fairey IIIA (3/19)	

No. 273 SQUADRON

Month/Yr	Location	Aircraft type	Remarks
8/18	F @ Burgh Castle		Nos. 470, 485, 486 & 534 Flts
8/18		DH4 (3/19)	Dets Covehithe, Westgate &
8/18		DH9 (3/19)	Manston
8/18		Camel (3/19)	

No. 274 SQUADRON MOTTO: Supero (I overcome)

Month/Yr	Location	Aircraft type	Remarks
			No. 274 Sqn was first authorized to form at Seaton Carew in 11/18 and was to have flown Vimys in the anti-submarine role. This plan was never fulfilled 15/6/19

Appendix C

Duties Assigned to Officers of the Air Department, March 1914 – Naval Wing

Assistant Director of the Air Department	f and general
Lieutenant Malone	Semi-official Board minutes, Parliamentary questions, purchase of new aircraft and supervision of personal records
Lieutenant Maude	Works, Coast Guard and distribution of Intelligence
Lieutenant Robertson	Gunnery, torpedo, wireless telegraphy, Aerial Navigation Act, meteorology, CID papers, signalling, GPO, kites and M. Branch papers.
Engineering Lieutenant Briggs	Motor transport, boats, lighting, heating hydrogen, stores, inspection, reports and general engineering
Assistant Paymaster Jackson	Officers' records, application for service, handbooks and conferences
Mr Booth	Inventions, designs of aircraft, advisory committee papers and distribution of their contents
Mr Griffin	Finance and general supervision of clerical work

The above was virtually the composition of the department on the outbreak of war. Several officers were added to the Staff during the first few months of the war but the organization remained the same until the beginning of February 1915 when the Central Air Office and the post of Inspecting Captain of aircraft was abolished.

Appendix D
War Establishments of an Aeroplane Squadron (Provisional)

PERSONNEL

Detail	Officers	Warrant Officers & Sergeants	Air Mechanics	Total
Headquarters (excluding attached)	7	2	15	24
Headquarters (attached)	–	–	3	3
Three flights	12	18	120	150
Total squadron (excluding attached)	19	20	135	174
(including attached)	19	20	138	177
Headquarters:				
Commanding Officer	1	–	–	1
Officer flyers	6	–	–	6
Sergeants	–	2	–	2
Air mechanics, incl drivers mechanical transport and batmen	–	–	15	15
	7	2	15	24
Attached RAMC (Royal Army Medical Corps)	–	–	3	3
Total headquarters including attached	7	2	18	27
Three flights, each:				
Officer fliers	4	–	–	4
Sergeants	–	6	–	6
Air mechanics	–	–	40	40
Total flights	4	6	40	50
Total three flights	12	18	120	120

TRANSPORT

Detail	Headquarters Vehicles	Headquarters Drivers	Flight Vehicles	Flight Drivers	Total Vehicles	Total Drivers
Headquarters						
Motor car	1	1	–	–	1	1
Motor lorry, 30cwt	1	2	–	–	1	2
Spare driver MT		1	–	–	–	1
A Flight (totals × 3)						
Motor cars	–	–	2	2	6	6
Motor lorries 30cwt	–	–	3	6	9	18
Motor repair lorry	–	–	1	2	3	6
Shed lorry	–	–	2	4	6	12
Trailer trucks to hangar lorries	–	–	2	–	6	–
Motor cycles	–	–	2	–	6	–
	2	4	12	14	38	46

DISTRIBUTION BY TRADES: RANK AND FILE

Detail	Headquarters	Three flights each	Total
Riggers	–	5	15
Sailmakers	1	4	13
Carpenters and joiners	–	2	6
Clerks	–	–	–
Fitters and turners	–	10	30
Painters	1	–	1
Photographers	1	–	1
Blacksmiths	1	1	4
Drivers, Mechanical Transport	4	14	46
Total	8	36	116

Appendix E
Raids by German Naval Airships during 1915 – Bomb Damage and Casualties

THE NIGHT OF 19/20 JANUARY
AIRSHIP L3 NORFOLK

Only one town was subjected to bombing by this airship and that was Yarmouth. Nine HE bombs in all were thrown in the ten minutes between 20.25 and 20.35hrs. Aim appears to have been taken on prominent buildings. These included St Peter's church, the drill hall and the gasworks. All were missed but glass in the church was broken. Another fell in Norfolk Square, two in Crown Road, one in St Peter's Place, one in Garden Lane, one on Trinity House Wharf, one in the fish market and one on the racecourse. The fourth bomb did the most damage when several houses were wrecked and houses within a radius of forty yards lost their windows. The seventh bomb damaged some windows and roofs by concussion. The eighth fell in the river and slightly damaged a steam drifter. The fifth and ninth bombs did not explode. One person was killed.

AIRSHIP L4 NORFOLK

Four locations, in all, were attacked. A flare and two incendiary bombs were dropped. The incendiary dropped on Wyndham Street, Sheringham, did considerable damage but caused no casualties. The second incendiary landed on a building plot. The second group of targets lay in the path of the airship as it crossed the coast between Brancaster and Hunstanton at 21.50hrs. An incendiary bomb was dropped in a field. Returning to Brancaster a further incendiary was dropped and another close to a cottage did practically no damage. Over Snettisham a HE bomb landed near a church doing much damage to windows. Eight HE bombs and one incendiary were dropped over King's Lynn. Casualties amounted to a man and a woman being killed and a further two persons being injured. Damage included the demolition of two houses in Bentinck Street and the damaging of several others there. In East Street and Albert Street there was considerable damage but no one was seriously injured. The incendiary bomb that fell on a house in Cresswell Street caused a small fire, which was quickly extinguished. Even though three people were in the house at the time no one was hurt. The bombs that were dropped on an allotment at the end of Great Lewis Street and in a garden of a house near the docks caused no damage. The final bomb dropped by *L3* that night did, however, cause considerable damage to the power station of the King's Lynn Docks and Railway Co.

THE NIGHT OF 14/15 APRIL
AIRSHIP L9 TYNESIDE

Incendiaries were dropped on West Sleekburn and Barrington. At Choppington three HE bombs and one incendiary resulted in broken windows. The same number were dropped at Bedlington and a warehouse was damaged at Cramlington following the dropping of one HE and five incendiaries. Two incendiaries were dropped at Seaton Barn, one HE bomb at Dinnington and one incendiary at Benton. Following the dropping of six incendiaries at Benton one woman and a child were slightly injured when a cottage was hit. There was also light damage to the railway. Finally one HE bomb fell in the River Tyne and one HE was dropped on Hebburn. All HE bombs were probably 50kg in weight. The monetary damage caused by the raid was estimated at £55.

THE NIGHT OF 15/16 APRIL
AIRSHIP L37 (ASSUMED) ESSEX

Two HE bombs were dropped both at Maldon and Heybridge whereas thirty incendiaries were dropped between the two locations, although one failed to ignite. At Heybridge one woman was slightly injured when a house was damaged and a fowl house destroyed.

AIRSHIP L9 SUFFOLK

At Henham Hall, one HE bomb and twenty-three incendiaries were dropped with no result whereas only two HE bombs and four incendiaries were dropped at Reydon causing damage by concussion to windows and the roof of a cottage Two incendiaries dropped at Southwold caused slight damage to a shed and truck at the railway station. At Easton Bavents two incendiaries caused no damage but at Lowestoft and Oulton Broad three HE bombs and seven incendiaries caused damage to two houses, stables and a timberyard and six horses were either killed or injured. There is no doubt that some of the supposed incendiaries dropped were in reality acetylene flares, but the correct number of these could not be ascertained. The monetary value of the damage caused by the raid was estimated to be £6,498.

THE NIGHT OF 29/30 APRIL
AIRSHIP LZ37 (PROBABLY) OVER SOUTHEND

Four HE bombs were dropped, two of which did not explode and the questionable number of ninety incendiaries. Casualties amounted to one woman killed and two men injured one of whom was a soldier. A house and timber yard were burned out and several houses were damaged by fire and concussion. The monetary damage was estimated to be £5,301.

THE NIGHT OF 16/17 MAY
AIRSHIP LZ38 OVER EAST KENT

On Ramsgate four HE and sixteen incendiaries were dropped, resulting in the death of a man and a woman, with one woman injured. A hotel was badly damaged and two other buildings and fishing smacks were slightly damaged. At Oxney thirty-three incendiaries were dropped, one of which failed to ignite but without result. The monetary damage was put at £1,600.

THE NIGHT OF 26/27 MAY
AIRSHIP LZ38 OVER SOUTHEND

Twenty-three HE grenades and forty-seven incendiaries were dropped killing one woman and injuring a child. The monetary value of the damage was estimated to be £947.

THE NIGHT OF 31 MAY/1 JUNE
AIRSHIP LZ38 OVER LONDON

The first action was over Stoke Newington when nine HE grenades (four did not explode) and twenty-four incendiaries were dropped. Two children were killed and injuries were sustained by three men, two women and four children. Damage to property included one house gutted by fire and several more or less damaged. Dalston was hit by two HE grenades and twenty-nine incendiaries, killing a man and a woman with injuries sustained by a man and a woman. The damage was to a house, which was burned out. At Hoxton and Shoreditch two HE grenades and twenty-three incendiaries were dropped. Injuries were sustained by two civilian men and two soldiers, two women and two children. On this occasion three houses were gutted and several business premises more or less badly damaged. A station on the Great Eastern Railway was lightly damaged. At Whitechapel ten HE grenades were dropped; only one did not explode. Nine incendiaries were also dropped resulting in the deaths of two children and the injuring of four men, five women and a child. Damage to property amounted to a store slightly damaged. Stepney was next where four HE grenades were dropped but two failed to explode. Two incendiaries were also dropped but there were no casualties and damage to property was limited to broken glass and light fires. At West Ham only two incendiaries were dropped and there were no casualties or damage. Finally, at Leytonstone there were five HE grenades resulting only in minor damage and slight injuries to two men and a woman. The monetary value of the damage was estimated to be £18,596.

THE NIGHT OF 4/5 JUNE
AIRSHIP L9 OVER EAST RIDING OF YORKSHIRE

Over Kilham one incendiary was dropped and two HE bombs were dropped over Driffield, both attacks without result.

AIRSHIP L10 OVER KENT

Over Sittingbourne three HE bombs and eight incendiaries were dropped resulting in injury to a man and a woman. There were several fires and a house was burned out. Only one HE bomb was dropped at Rainham with no result whereas at Gravesend five HE bombs and three incendiaries resulted in injury to two men, three women and one child. The damage at this location included the demolition of two houses, one badly and other slightly damaged. A yacht club hostel was burned and a stable destroyed killing two horses. Total damage at this location amounted to £4,050 and the total for the raid estimated to be £8,740

THE NIGHT OF 6/7 JUNE
AIRSHIP L9 OVER YORKSHIRE AND LINCOLNSHIRE

At Wyton Bar only two incendiaries were dropped and there was no damage nor casualties. In Hull things were very different when thirteen HE bombs and thirty-nine incendiaries (three or four did not explode) were dropped killing five men, thirteen women and six children together with the injuring of twenty men, thirteen women and seven children.

The damage was considerable when about forty houses and shops were demolished or wrecked and many damaged. A school was damaged and a sawmill burned out. Over Grimsby seven incendiaries were dropped, one of which failed to ignite. There were no casualties but damage to three railway trucks. The value of the monetary damage was estimated to be £44,795.

THE NIGHT OF 15/16 JUNE
AIRSHIP L10 (PROBABLY) OVER NORTHUMBERLAND AND DURHAM

The attack upon Wallsend in Northumberland included the dropping of ten HE bombs and six incendiaries. There were no casualties but serious damage was inflicted on the NE Marine Engineering Works and there was also slight damage to the colliery and several houses. Over Willington Quay and East Howdon two HE bombs and eight incendiaries were dropped and one police constable was killed. The Antimony Works were damaged and several houses more or less seriously damaged. The attack upon Hebburn was made by just one HE bomb and one incendiary, which caused no casualties and only slight damage to colliery property. It was far more serious at Jarrow where nine HE bombs and twelve incendiaries were used resulting in the death of seventeen men and injury to seventy-two when the plant at Palmer's Works was seriously damaged together with the glass and roofs of a large number of houses. At Blyth three HE bombs were dropped together with one incendiary. Whilst there were no casualties a fairground and a large number of houses were damaged. The value of the monetary damage was estimated to be £44,760.

Appendix F

Contact Air Patrol Instructions Issued by GHQ (France) on 26 May 1916

A certain number of aeroplanes, bearing distinctive markings should be detailed to carry out tactical observation of the battlefield having no other duties and reporting to the headquarters of the formation by which they were detailed, usually the Army Corps. The machines are ordered to fly low above and in the rear of our own lines, to receive signals:

1. From assaulting infantry by means of a. flares, b. the flashing of mirrors (vigilant periscope) with both of which officers and NCOs and a proportion of other ranks of the infantry would be provided. These signals might be given by the infantry.

    a. On the initiative of company, platoon and section commanders when it was desired to make their positions known
    b. On the signal from their aeroplane 'where are you'?
    c. At certain definite hours previously arranged in orders
    d. On reaching a previously arranged position.

2. From Battalion and Brigade Headquarters by means of ground signals or lamps. Battalion and Brigade Headquarters which are to be marked by a ground signal, and units are to be provided with a ground signalling sheet or panel and a lamp.

EXPERIENCE IN BATTLE

The aeroplane is to answer by lamp and in both cases the Morse code is to be used. In addition to transmitting information or requests received from the infantry, the aeroplane detailed for tactical reconnaissance is to carry out continuous observation of the front of the formation and to keep the Command informed as regards:

a. During preliminary bombardment – any movement of the enemy.
b. During the attack – Progress of the attack and positions reached and the movements of reserves and impending counter attack.

The information received by the aeroplane from the infantry is to be transmitted at the outset by wireless and dropping messages. Messages dropped, however, will allow of fuller information being given than could be sent by wireless and this method is to be adopted whenever possible. As in the case of the French, the position reached by the infantry including Battalion and Brigade HQs is to be indicated by the observer on tracings prepared beforehand and dropped with the message.

A signal code was laid down for communication between infantry, Headquarters and the aircraft observer and various ground signals were devised. e.g., the aerial observer might show a white very light which asked, 'Where are you?' There were also ground signalling panels that consisted of large louvre shutters painted white on one side and a neutral tint on the other. These were connected by tapes and arranged horizontally on the ground in such a manner that of the shutter being activated by the tapes the white side was exposed uppermost for periods according to the Morse code, which could easily be observed from an aircraft between 5 and 6,000ft.

Appendix G

Deployment of RFC Squadrons on the Western Front – January 1917

Unit	Aircraft	Based at (during the period January to August 1917)
No.1 Squadron	Nieuport 17, 23, 24 & 27	Bailleul (Asylum Ground)
No.2 Squadron	BE2c, d& e, AW FK	Hesdigneul
No.4 Squadron	BE2c	Baizieux and Warloy-Baillon
No.5 Squadron	BE2d	Marieux and La Gorgue
No.6 Squadron	BE2c,d & f, RE8	Abeele (det Droglandt)
No.7 Squadron	BE2c	Warloy-Baillon, Moreuil, Matigny det Nesle and Proven
No.8 Squadron	BE2d & e	La Bellevue, Soncamp and Boiry St Martin
No.9 Squadron	BE2e, RE 8	Morlancourt dets. Mons-en-Chaussée, Nurlu, Estrées-en-Chausée and Proven
No.10 Squadron	BE2c	Choques
No.12 Squadron	BE2d & e, RE8	Avesnes-le-Comte, Wagnonlieu, Ablainzevelle, and Courcelles-le-Comte
No.13 Squadron	BE2c, d & e, RE8	Savy and Etrun
No.15 Squadron	BE2c, d, e, f & g RE8	Léalvillers (Claifaye Farm), Courcelles-le-Comte, La Gorgue (det Clairmarais), Savy
No.16 Squadron	BE2e, f & g, RE8	Bruay and Camblain-l'Abbé
No.18 Squadron	FE2b, DH4	St-Leger-les-Authie, Bertangles, Baizieux and La Bellevue
No.19 Squadron	BE12, SPAD SVII	Fienvillers, Vert Galand and Liettres
No.20 Squadron	FE2d, RE7, Bristol F2b	Clairmarais, Boisdinghem and Ste-Marie-Cappel
No.21 Squadron	BE12, RE8	Bertangles, Boisdinghem, Droglandt and La Lovie
No.22 Squadron	FE2b	Bertangles, Chipilly, Flez, Warloy-Baillon, Izel-le-Hameau and Boisdinghem
No.23 Squadron	FE2b, SPAD SVII	Vert Galand, Baizieux, Auchel, Bruay (Dets Erquibghem) and La Lovie
No.24 Squadron	DH2 & 5	Chipilly, Lez and Baizieux
No.25 Squadron	FE2d, DH4	Lozinghem
No.27 Squadron	Martinsyde G100/102	Fienvillers and Claimarais North
No.29 Squadron	DH2, Nieuport 16,17, 23, 24	Le Hameau and Poperinghe
No.32 Squadron	DH2 & 5	Léalvillers, Abeele and Droglandt
No.34 Squadron	BE2c, e, f, g, RE8	Allonville, Villers-Bretonneux, Estrées-en-Chausée, Nurlu, Villers-Bretonneux, and Bray Dunes
No.35 Squadron	AW FK8	St Omer, St André-aux-Bois, Savy, Villers, Bretonneux, Mons-en-Chausée, Savy and La Gorgue
No.40 Squadron	FE8, Nieuport 17, 23, 24	Treizennes, Auchel and Bruay
No.41 Squadron	FE8, DH5	Abeele, Hondschoote, Abeele and Léalvillers
No.42 Squadron	BE2e, RE8	Bailleul (Town Ground)
No.43 Squadron	1½ Strutter	Northolt, St Omer, Treizennes, Lozinghem
No.45 Squadron	1½ Strutter	Ste-Marie-Cappel
No.46 Squadron	Nieuport 12 & 20, Sopwith Pup	Droglandt, Boisdinghem, La Gorgue, Bruay and Suttons Farm
No.52 Squadron	BE2f & g, RE 8	Chipilly, Méaulte, Longavesnes & Bray-Dunes
No.53 Squadron	BE2e, g, RE8	St Omer, Bailleul (Town Ground)
No.54 Squadron	Avro 504?, Sopwith Pup	Bertangles, Chipilly, Flez, Bray-Dunes and Leffrinckhoucke
No.55 Squadron	BE2c AWFK3, Avro 504K, DH4	Lilbourne, Fienvillers and Boisdinghem

Unit	Aircraft	Based at (during the period January to August 1917)
No.56 Squadron	SE5 & 5a	St Omer, Vert Galand, Liettres (return to UK)
No.60 Squadron	Nieuport 16,17 & 23, SE5 & 5a	Savy and Filescamp Farm
No.66 Squadron	Sopwith Pup	St Omer, Vert Galand, Liettres,Calais and Estrèe-Blanche
No.70 Squadron	1½ Strutter, Camel	Auchel, Vert Galand, Fienvillers, Boisdinghem, and Liettres
No.210 Squadron	Nieuport 12 & 17	Fumes and Droglandt
	Sopwith Triplane, Camel	

Appendix H

Deployment of RFC Wings/Squadrons on the Western Front – 2 March 1918 (AH 228/6)

Northern Area Fourth and First Army Fronts

To First Army	1 scout squadron
To Fourth Army	2 scout squadrons and 1 fighter reconnaissance squadron

Centre Area

First Army	3 scout squadrons
To Third Army	1 fighter squadron
	1 fighter reconnaissance squadron

Southern Area

To Third Army	2 scout squadrons
	1 fighter reconnaissance squadron
To Fifth Army	3 scout squadrons
	1 fighter reconnaissance squadron

9th (GHQ) Wing

Units	Base	Area
Nos.25 and 27 fighter recce sqns	Villers Brettoneux	Fifth Army
No.82 fighter recc sqn	Cachy	Fifth Army
Nos.73, 79 and 80 scout sqns	Champien	Fifth Army
No.101 night flying sqn	Catigny	Fifth Army
No.83 night flying sqn	Auchel	First Army
No.102 night flying sqn	Le Hameau	Third Army
No.58 night flying sqn	Clairmarais	Second Army

Appendix J
Draft Air Force Act 1917

Air Force

ARRANGEMENT OF CLAUSES

* * *

Part I

ESTABLISHMENT OF AIR FORCE

Clause

1. Raising and number of Air Force
2. Government, discipline and pay of Air Force
3. Transfer and attaching to Air Force of members of Naval and Military forces
4. Rights of officers
5. Application of Military Service Acts
6. Air Force Reserve and Auxiliary Air Force
7. Consequential amendments of Naval Discipline Act and Army Act

Part II

ESTABLISHMENT OF AIR COUNCIL

8. Establishment of Air Council
9. Staff remuneration and expenses
10. Style, seal and proceedings to Air Council
11. Provisions as to sitting in Parliament

Part III

DISCIPLINE &c

12. Application of Army Act to Air Force
13. Application of other Acts

Part IV

GENERAL

14. Short Title

* * *

SCHEDULE

197-5

Air Force

DRAFT OF A

BILL TO

Make provision for the establishment, administration and discipline of an Air Force, and for purposes connected therewith.

Be it enacted by the King's most Excellent Majesty, by and with the advice and consent of the Lords Spiritual and Temporal, and Commons in this present Parliament assembled and by the authority of the same, as follows:-

PART I

ESTABLISHMENT OF AIR FORCE

1. It shall be lawful for His Majesty to raise and maintain a force, to be called the Air Force consisting of such number of officers and men as may from time to time be provided by Parliament.

2. (1) Subject to the provisions of this Act it shall be lawful for His Majesty by order signified under the hand of the Secretary of State to make orders with respect to the government, discipline, pay and allowances and pensions of the Air Force and with respect to all other matters and things relating to the Air Force including any matter by this Act authorised to be prescribed or expressed to be subject to orders or regulations.

   (2) The said orders may provide for the formation of men of the Air Force into separate units and for the formation of such units into corps and for appointing, transferring or attaching men of the air force to corps and for posting, attaching and otherwise dealing with such men within the corps and may regulate the appointment, rank, duties and numbers of the officers and non commissioned officers of the Air Force

   (3) Subject to the provision of any such order, the Air Council hereinafter may make general or special regulations with respect to any matter with respect to which His Majesty may make orders under this section: provided that the administration of pensions other than service pensions within the meaning of Ministry of Pensions Act 1916 shall vest in the Minister of Pensions.

   (4) Where a man entered the Air Force before the date of any order or regulation made under this Part of the Act, nothing in such order or regulation shall render him liable without his consent to be appointed, transferred or attached to any portion of the Air Force to which he could not, without his consent have been appointed, transferred or attached, if the said order or regulation had not been made.

   (5) All orders and regulations made under this section shall be laid before Parliament as soon as may be after they are made.

3. Subject to the provisions of this section any officer, petty officer, non commissioned officer, or man, belonging to any of His Majesty's Naval or Military Forces may be attached to the Air Force for any period not exceeding four years, or may be transferred to the Air Force from the force to which he so belongs, and if so transferred shall cease to be a member of the force from which he was transferred. Provided that:-

   (a) No such person shall otherwise than as hereinafter provided, be so attached without his consent, nor be so transferred except on an application made by him in the prescribed manner; and

   (b) Every person who at the date when the Air Force is established belongs to the Royal Naval Air Service, the Royal Flying Corps or to any unit of the Navy or Army engaged in the defence against aircraft which is designated by the Admiralty or Army Council for the purpose, shall be deemed to have applied to be transferred to the Air Force, but if within three months after the passing of this Act he gives notice in writing to his commanding office that he does not desire to be so transferred, he shall not be so transferred, or if he has already been so transferred, shall forthwith be re-transferred to the Navy or the Army as the case may be; and

   (c) Every person who holds a commission (other than a temporary commission) in any of His Majesty's Naval or Military Forces, and who is at the date when the Air Force is established attached to the Royal Naval Air Service, or the Royal Flying Corps, or to any such unit as aforesaid, shall be deemed to have been as from that date attached to the Air Force for the duration of the present war; and

(d) Such provisions with respect to rank in the Air Force and pay and allowances as His Majesty may by Royal Warrant direct shall apply in the case of persons so attached or transferred; and

(e) When any person is transferred to the Air Force under this section, then for the purposes of any provisions relating to pensions, gratuity , retired or half-pay, if he had not been so transferred, shall be deemed to be service towards pension, gratuity, retired or half-pay with the Air Force; and

(f) When a person is attached to the Air Force under this section, the fact that he is so attached shall not affect any right to any pension, gratuity, retired or half-pay already earned by him in that branch of His Majesty's Naval or Military forces to which be belonged at the date on which he was so attached, and the period during which he is so attached shall for the purpose of any provisions relating to pensions' gratuity, retired or half-pay, be deemed service with that branch of His Majesty's Naval or Military forces to which he belonged at the date on which he is so attached; and

(g) Regulations made by the Air Council may provide that in the case of a person so transferred, the time during which he had held a commission or served in the force from which he is transferred shall, for such purposes as may be prescribed, be aggregated with the time he held a commission or served in the Air Force, and that his entry or enlistment in the force from which he is transferred shall, for such purposes as may be prescribed, be treated as enlistment into the Air Force; and

(h) During the continuance or the present war the period during which a person is to be attached to the Air Force may be the duration or the war instead of a period not exceeding four years.

4. Officers in the Air Force shall enjoy all such powers, rights, immunities and privileges as are enjoyed by commissioned officers of His Majesty's Navy or Army as such, whether conferred by statute or otherwise, and nothing in the succession to the Crown Act 1707 shall extend to any member of the House of Commons who, being an officer in His Majesty's Navy or Army, receives a commission in the Air Force.

5. (1) The Army Council and the Air Council may jointly direct that that any of the men who, by virtue of the Military Services Act 1916 and 1917, are deemed to have enlisted by His Majesty's regular forces and to have transferred to the reserve shall, on being called up for service be liable to be transferred to the Air Force and the man to whom such directions relate shall be transferred accordingly.

(2) There shall be included amongst the exceptions mentioned in the First Schedule tothe Military Service Act, 1916, the following paragraph:-

(3) Men serving in the Air Force [or who, though not serving in the Air Force, are recommended for exception by the Air Council].

6. (1) It shall be lawful for His Majesty to raise and maintain an Air Force Reserve and an Auxiliary Air Force consisting in each case of such numbers of officers, non commissioned officers, and men as may from time to time be provided by Parliament.

(2) His Majesty may, by Order in Council, apply with the necessary adaptations to the Air Force Reserve or to the Auxiliary Air Force or to the officers and men of any such force any enactment relating to the Army Reserve or to the Territorial Force or to the officers or men of these forces, and such Order in Council shall be laid before both Houses of Parliament.

7. The amendments set out in the second column of the tables in Part I and Part II of the First Schedule to the Act (being amendments consequential on the establishment of an air force) shall be made in the provisions of the Naval Discipline Act and the Army Act respectively mentioned in the first column of these tables, and section two of the Naval Discipline Act 1917 (which relates to the printing and construction of the Naval Discipline Act made by the Act in like manner as it applies to the amendments thereof made by that Act.

PART II

ESTABLISHMENT OF AIR COUNCIL

8. (1) For the purpose of the administration of matters relating to the Air Force and to the defence of the realm by air there shall be established an Air Council consisting of members appointed by His Majesty, who shall hold office during His Majesty's pleasure and on other members who shall be appointed in such manner and subject to such provisions as His Majesty may by Order in Council direct.

(2) His Majesty may by Order in Council fix the date on which the Air Council is to be established and make provision with respect to the proceedings of the Air Council and the manner in which the business of the Council is to be distributed among the members thereof.

(3)   On the establishment of the Air Council the Air Board constituted under the New Ministries and Secretaries Act, 1916 shall cease to exist, and all the powers and duties of that Board shall be transferred to the Council.

9. (1)   The Air Council may appoint such secretaries, officers, and servants as the Council may, with the sanction of the Treasury, determine.

(2)   There shall be paid, out of the monies provided by Parliament, to the members of the Air Council, and to the secretaries, officers and servants of the Council, such salaries or remuneration as the Treasury may determine.

10. (1)   The Air Council may sue and be sued and may for all purposes be described by that name.

(2)   The Air Council shall have an official seal, which shall be officially and judicially noticed, and that seal shall be authenticated by the signature of the President, or of a secretary, or of some person authorised by the Council to act on behalf of a secretary.

(3)   Every document purporting to be an instrument issued by the Air Council, authenticated in manner provided by this Act, or to be signed by a secretary or any person authorised by the Council to act on behalf of a secretary, shall be received in evidence , and be deemed to be such an instrument without further proof, unless the contrary is shown.

(4)   A certificate signed by the President of the Air Council that any instrument purporting to be made or issued by the Council is so made or issued shall be conclusive evidence of the fact.

(5)   The Documentary Evidence Act, 1868, as amended by the Documentary Evidence Act, 1892, shall apply to the Air Council as if that Council were mentioned in the first column of the schedule to the first-mentioned Act, and as if the President, or a secretary of the Council, or any person authorised by the President to act on behalf of the Council, was mentioned in the second column of the schedule.

11. (1)   The office of the President of the Air Council shall not render the person holding it incapable of being elected to, or of voting in the Commons House of Parliament, and shall be deemed to be an office included in Schedule H of the Representation of the People Act, 1867; in Schedule H of the Representation of the People (Scotland) Act, 1868, in Schedule E of the Representation of the People (Ireland) Act 1868; and in Part I of the Schedule of the Promissory Oaths Act, 1868.

(2)   One member of the Air Council, in addition to the President, and one of the Secretaries to the Air Council, shall not by virtue of his office be incapable of being elected to or of voting in the Commons House of Parliament.

PART III

DISCIPLINE, &c.

12. (1)   The Army Act shall, subject to the modifications set out in the Second Schedule to this Act (being amendments required to adapt this Act to the circumstances of the Air Force) apply with respect to the Air Force, and shall, as so modified, take effect as a separate Act of Parliament , and may be printed as a separate Act by the printers to His Majesty and entitled 'An Act to provide for the Discipline and Regulation of the Air Force' and that Act may, subject to any modifications which may from time to time be made therein, be cited as the Air Force Act:

Provided for the purposes of Section 88 of the Air Force Act (relating to the continuance of men in the Air Force Service in case of imminent material danger) the proclamation issued under section 88 of the Army Act on the outbreak of the present war shall have effect as if it had been issued under the first-mentioned, as well as the last-mentioned section, and had been applied to the Air Force as well as to the Army.

(2)   The Air Force Act shall continue in force only as long as the Army Act continues in force.

(3)   Whereby enactment passed after the passing of this Act and for the time being in force for any enactments or words , or to be added to or omitted from the Army Act or the Air Force Act, then all copies of the Air Force Act printed after such direction takes effect shall be printed with the said enactments or words added to the said Act or omitted there from, or printed therein in lieu of any enactments or words for which the same are to be substituted, according as such direction requires, and with the sections and subsections numbered in accordance with such direction, and the said Act shall be construed as if it had at the time at which such direction takes effect been enacted with such addition, omission, or substitution:
Provided that any addition to, omission from and substitution in the Army Act shall, in its application to the Air Force Act, have effect, subject to such modifications and exceptions as His Majesty in Council may declare to be necessary for adapting the same to the air force.

(4) A reference in any enactment passed after the passing of this Act to the Air Force shall, unless the context otherwise requires, be construed to refer to the Air Force Act as amended by any enactment for the time being in force.

13. His Majesty may by Order in Council apply with the necessary modifications and adaptations to the Air Council, in relation to the President of the Air Council, and the Air Force, and the officers and men thereof, and air force property of institutions, any of the enactments [specified in the Third Schedule to this Act and any other enactment not specially applied by this Act], relating to the Air Council, the Secretary of State for the War Department, the Army, or the officers and soldiers thereof (including enactments conferring any powers, rights or immunities, or imposing any duties or disabilities on such officers or soldiers), or to military property or institutions, and every such Order in Council shall be laid before both Houses of Parliament.

PART IV

GENERAL

14. This Act may be cited as the Air Force Act, 1917.

Appendix K
Testing of Military Aircraft at the Experimental Aircraft Flight – Martlesham Heath 1917 and 1918

Maker and name of aircraft	Serial No.	Remarks
1917		
January		
Martinsyde G102 Elephant	None	Trials aircraft
February		
Martinsyde RG	None	Handling trials
Nieuport Scout	5173	French aircraft trials
Wight Quadraplane	N.546	Handling trials
March		
Armstrong Whitworth FK10	B.4000	Airframe trials
Bristol MIB	----	Developed in MIC
De Havilland (Airco) 4	A.2129	Engine trials
		A.2128 Engine trials
Nieuport Triplane	A.6686	French aircraft trials
Parnall Panther	N.91	Shipboard aircraft tests
SE5	A.4845	Prototype trials
Sopwith Pup	----	Production aircraft trials
Sopwith Camel F1/3	----	Production aircraft trials
Sopwith Camel F1/3	----	Experimental motor tests
Sopwith Camel F2FI	----	Performance trials
Vickers FB14D	None	Handling trials
Vickers FB14D	C.4547	General handling trials
April		
Armstrong Whitworth FK8	N513	Engine trials
Armstrong Whitworth FK8	A.2696	Performance trials
FE2b	----	Production aircraft tests
Sopwith B1	B.1496	Handling and bombing trials
May		
Armstrong Whitworth FK8	B.215	Engine trials
Martinsyde F2	None	Handling trials
SE5a	A.4563	Developed SE5 aircraft
Sopwith Pup	A.653	Experimental motor trials
Sopwith Camel F1/3	N.6336	Motor trials
Sopwith Camel F1/1	----	Tapered wing trials
Sopwith Camel FIARI	N.518	Bentley ARI motor tests
Vickers FB12C	A.7351	Engine trials aircraft
Vickers FB19F MkII Bullet	A.5225	Handling trials
Vickers FB16A	A.8963	Handling and engine trials
Vickers FB25	----	Crashed at Martlesham Heath

Maker and name of aircraft	Serial No.	Remarks
June		
Avro 529	3694	Crashed at Martlesham Heath
BE2d	---	Development aircraft
De Havilland (Airco) 6	---	Production aircraft tests
Sopwith Camel FIFI	B.3751	First production motor trials
SE5	----	Engine trials (British)
Sopwith Camel 2FI	----	RNAS performance tests
Sopwith Dolphin 5F1	----	Prototype fighter aircraft tests
Vickers FB12C	A.7352	Anzani engine trials aircraft
July		
Austin Ball ARB 1	None	Handling trials
Austin Ball AFT 1	None	Rebuilt aircraft
Bristol F2B	A7183	Engine trials
De Havilland (Airco) 4	A.7532	Armament trials
De Havilland (Airco) 5	A.9186	Production aircraft tests
Martinsyde F1	A.3933	Handling trials
Martinsyde G	None	Revised airframe
SE5a	B.4862	First Viper-engined aircraft
Sopwith Camel F1/3	----	Experimental motor tests
Sopwith Camel F1/1	----	Motor and handling trials
Sopwith Camel FIFI	----	Motor trials aircraft
Sopwith Camel 2FI	N.5	First RNAS aircraft tests
Sopwith 1½ Strutter	A.8194	Trials aircraft
Vickers FB26 Vampire 1	B.1484	Extended handling trials
August		
De Havilland (Airco) 4	A.7446	Engine trials
De Havilland (Airco) 4	A.2148	Engine trials
De Havilland (Airco) 4	A.8083	Engine trials
Handley Page O/400	C.9681	Handling trials
Sopwith Camel 2FI	----	Bentley BRI motor tests
Sopwith Camel 1FI	B.3851	Motor trials
Sopwith Camel 1FI	B.3888	Motor trials
Sopwith Camel 1FI	B.3835	Motor trials
Sopwith 1.F.I.	---	Gnome Monosoupape trials
Sopwith 1½ Strutter	B.762	Single seat fighter trials
Sopwith Dolphin 5FI	----	Second prototype fighter aircraft tests
SPAD S7	A.8965	French aircraft trials
September		
RE8	B.2251	Handling trials
SE5	----	High-compression motor tests
Sopwith Dolphin 5FI	----	Third prototype fighter aircraft tests
Sopwith Dolphin 5FI	----	Fourth prototype fighter aircraft trials
October		
Halberstadt DH	G/5BDE	Captured German aircraft
Port Victoria PV8	N.540	Light Fighter tests

Maker and name of aircraft	Serial No.	Remarks
The Eastchurch Kitten	----	Light Fighter tests
Sopwith Camel 1FI	----	Aircraft for the USAS
November		
Albatros DV	D.2129/17 G56	Captured German aircraft
Avro 529A	3695	Crashed at Martlesham
Avro 530	1811	Motor trials
De Havilland (Airco) 4	A.7673	Armament trials
De Havilland (Airco) 9	A.7559	Prototype trials
Martinsyde F3	B.1490	Handling trials
NEI	B.3971	Night fighter trials
Pfalz DIII A	4184/17 G.141	Captured German aircraft
Rumpler C.V.	C,8500/16	Captured German aircraft
SE5	A.8916	Wolsey Viper motor tests
Sopwith Dolphin 5FI	C.3777	First production aircraft tests
December		
Beardmore WBH	None	Cleaned up BE2c
Bristol MIC	C.4902	Production aircraft
Bristol MIC	C.4908	Production aircraft
Bristol F.2B	B.1181	Engine trials
De Havilland (Airco) 4	N.5960	First RNAS aircraft
De Havilland (Airco) 9	C.6051	First production aircraft
SE 5A	B.4899	Second Viper-engined aircraft
SE 5A	B.4875	Triple gun mounting tests
Siddeley RTI	B.6625	Prototype aircraft trials
Siddeley RTI	B.6626	Modified airframe trials
Sopwith 1FI	----	Gnome Monosoupape trials
Sopwith Snipe	B9963	First prototype aircraft trials
Sopwith Snipe	B.9964	Third prototype aircraft trials

1918

January		
British Air Transport FK.22/2		
Later Bantam	B.9945	Fighter prototype trials
Blackburn Kangaroo	B.9970	Comparison trials with Avro 529
Bristol F2B	----	Falcon-engined trials
Bristol F2B	B.1202	Hispano-Suiza motor trials
De Havilland (Airco) 9	C.6052	Trials with Fiat A12 motor
De Havilland (Airco) 9	C.6051	Siddeley Puma motor trials
February		
Bristol F2B	B.1206	Siddeley Puma motor trials
March		
Austin AFT Osprey	X.15	Experimental triplane tests
Boulton and Paul Bobolink P3	C.8665	Evaluation trials
Boulton and Paul Bourges P7		
MkII later K.129/G-EACE	F.2903	Bomber trials

Maker and name of aircraft	Serial No.	Remarks
Bristol F2B	B.1204	Sunbeam Arab motor trials
Bristol Scout F	B.3989	Fighter tests, motor trials
De Havilland (Airco) 9A	B.7664	Handling trials

April

De Havilland (Airco) 10 Amiens I	C.8658	Handling and bomber trials

May

De Havilland (Airco) 9	C.2207	Siddeley Puma motor trials

June

Blackburn Blackbird	N.113	Crashed at Martlesham Heath

July

Austin Ball AFB1	----	SPAD Type wings trial
BE2c	----	Production aircraft trials
BE12a	C.3188	Experimental fighter trials
Beardmore WBIV	N.38	Shipboard fighter trials
De Havilland (Airco) 10 Amiens II	C.8659	Bombing and Rolls Royce Eagle motor tests
De Havilland (Airco) 10 Amiens III	C.8860	Liberty motor and bombing tests

August

De Havilland (Airco) 10 Amiens III	C.4283	Re-designed motor nacelle tests

September

Bristol F2B	B.1201	RAF4D motor trials
Bristol F2B	C.4654	HC Siddeley motor tests
Bristol Braemar MkI	C.4296	Triplane bomber trials
Bristol Scout FI	B.3991	Developed fighter handling trials
De Havilland (Airco) 10A Amiens IIIA	F.1869	Revised airframe handling tests

October

British Air Transport FK23 Bantam MkI	None	Developed prototype tests
Blackburn Blackbird	N.114	Re-designed aircraft evaluated
Bristol F2B	B.1200	Wolsey Viper motor trials

November

British Air Transport FK23	F.1654	Revised airframe trials

December

BE12A	A.591	Modified aircraft trials
Caudron GIV Twin	B.8892	Tests with Orfordness

Appendix L

Admiralty Air Board Specification for Aeroplanes Type A3b

Source: National Archive document AIR1/642/17/122/250

TYPE: Night Bomber. To carry the maximum load with a definite performance. To have folding wings with two or three engines.

LOAD TO BE CARRIED	lbs
Crew of three	540
Fuel for 300 miles at full speed at 6,000ft	
Three Lewis guns and ammunition	180
Holt's flares and parachute lights	20
Bombs and gear, at least	3000

PERFORMANCE FULLY LOADED
Speed 80–85 mph at 6,000ft
Climb to 10,000ft in one hour

LANDING SPEED WITHOUT BOMBS to be not greater than 45 mph. Machine to be able to pull up in 200 yards in a calm.

MISCELLANEOUS
The weight per wheel to be not greater than 11 times the product of the wheel and tyre dimensions in inches. Engines to be silenced so as to be practically inaudible with full load at 6,000ft. Gun layer must be able to lie or crouch down when sighting or releasing bombs and easy communication for steering purposes is to be provided between pilot and gun layer. If possible gun racks to be arranged to be quickly detachable, Machine to fold within the following dimensions:

80ft long, by 40ft wide, by 25ft high.
Strength factors with full load to be not less than 5 throughout.

Appendix M

List of Military Officers Selected to Attend the Course of Instruction at the Central Flying School, Commencing 17 September 1913

Rank & Name	Unit	Address
Lt Col N.J.G. Cameron	Cameron Highlanders (General Staff)	War Office, Whitehall
Major G.C. Merrick DSO	Royal Artillery (General Staff)	War Office, Whitehall
Captain T.C.R. Higgins	Royal Lancaster Regiment	1st Battalion, Dover
Captain H.H. Shott DSO	Royal Berkshire Regiment	Attached 1st Battalion, Dover
Captain G.M. Griffith	Royal Garr. Artillery	No.67 Coy. Portsmouth
Lieutenant R.V. Pollok	15th Hussars	Longmoor, East Liss
Lieutenant D.S. Lewis * Woolwich	Royal Engineers	4th Signal Coy.
Lieutenant J. Empson	Royal Fusiliers	4th Battalion, Parkhurst
Lieutenant H le M Brock	Royal Warwickshire Regiment	The Rectory, St Peter-in-the-Wood, Guernsey
Lieutenant B.C.M. Western	East Lancashire, Regiment	Edgewood, Rotherfield, Sussex
Lieutenant W.G.S Mitchell	Highland Light Infantry	c/o of Vickers Flying School, Brooklands
Lieutenant R.E. Lewis	West India Regiment	The Aviary, Byfleet, Hants Oyster Lane
2nd Lieutenant C.G. Hosking	Royal Field Artillery	102nd Battalion, Woolwich
2nd Lieutenant D Corbbet-Wilson	Royal Flying Corps Special Reserve	Darver, Kilkenny, Ireland
2nd Lieutenant H.C. Biard	Royal Flying Corps Special Reserve	Pentriff, St Matthew's Gardens, St Leonards-on-Sea
2nd Lieutenant G.N. Humphreys	Royal Flying Corps Special Reserve	7 St George's Road, Worthing
2nd Lieutenant D.E. Stodart	Royal Flying Corps Special Reserve	Constitutional Club, Northumberland Avenue

* To join on 29 September 1913

Bibliography

My thanks go to members of the Research Department of the RAF Museum, Hendon, to the Head Librarian Royal Engineers Library, Chatham and the staff of the National Archive Kew. This is also an acknowledgement of the help I received in referring to the publications listed. (The remarks below are those of the author, who wishes to explain the value of the source books in compiling this encyclopaedia.)

RAF Museum, Research Dept, The National Archive at Kew and the Library of the Royal Engineers in Chatham all provide the facility to photograph documents including photographs and maps. Over 2,000 images were photographed during my visits to these locations and constitute the source material quoted throughout the work.

Publication	Value
Action Stations a series of publications that detail the RAF airfields both at home and abroad. Variously dated for the series of publications under this heading	Invaluable in compiling Chapter 9
Aircraft of the RAF 1918 by Owen Thetford, Putnam Press First published 1957	Useful data and photographs
The *Central Blue* by MRAF Sir John Slessor, Cassell & Co. Ltd First published 1956	Good on the contribution made by senior members of the RAF in developing British air power
The First Great Air War by Richard Townshend Bickers, Coronet Books, Hodder and Stoughton First published 1988	Much valuable information about air combat and the air aces.
Martlesham Heath by Gordon Kinsey, Terence Dalton, Lavenham, Suffolk First published 1975	Invaluable in compiling Appendix K on the testing of military aircraft in 1917/8
The *Paladins* by John James, Macdonald and Company Ltd First published 1990	The social history of the RAF and was the inspiration for embarking on three encyclopaedias of the RAF
RAF Squadrons by Wing Commander C.G. Jefford, Airlife Publishing Company First published 1988	Invaluable in compiling Appendices A and B
Thesis on the *War in Mesopotamia* presented to the US Army Command and General Staff College by Major Peter J Lambert USAF First published 1999	Very useful in writing Chapter 5 on the Mesopotamian campaign during the Great War

Index

Airfields, seaplane bases and landing grounds

RFC and RNAS Stations/Seaplane bases and landing Grounds (Home and Overseas) in alphabetical order. Airfields on the Western Front are on page 275.